Craig Claiborne's
The New
New York Times
COOKBOOK

By Craig Claiborne with Pierre Franey

Times
BOOKS

Third printing, December 1979

Published by TIMES BOOKS, a division
of Quadrangle/The New York Times Book Co., Inc.
Three Park Avenue, New York, N.Y. 10016

Published simultaneously in Canada by
Fitzhenry & Whiteside, Ltd., Toronto

Library of Congress Cataloging in Publication Data
Main entry under title:

Craig Claiborne's *The New New York Times* cookbook.

Includes index.
  1. Cookery, International.   2. Cookery, American.
I. Claiborne, Craig.   II. Franey, Pierre.   III. New
York Times.
TX725.A1C63 1979   641.5   79-51428
ISBN 0-8129-0835-X

Manufactured in the United States of America

For Joan Whitman, without whose diligence and editorial eye the quality and scope of this volume would have been diminished beyond measure. With affection and thanks.

Craig Claiborne
Pierre Franey

Contents

VI. Poultry 250

Chicken, turkey, duck, capon and goose: roasted, baked, stuffed, sautéed, simmered, fried, shredded, grilled and jellied with herbs and spices, in delicate and pungent sauces.

VII. Fish and Shellfish 317

Striped bass, trout, cod, eel, salmon, flounder, shad, sole and squid: baked, poached, grilled, marinated, sautéed, stuffed, fried and creamed. Crab, lobster, scallops, shrimp and mussels: steamed fried, broiled, sautéed, steamed and baked.

VIII. Stews and Casseroles 398

Versatile and elegant mixtures using beef, lamb, pork, veal, chicken, seafood and fresh vegetables, pasta, beans and rice for savory stews, casseroles, ragouts, gumbo and paella.

IX. Pasta 431

Fettucelle, tagliarini, spaghetti, linguine, rigatoni, ravioli, lasagne and gnocchi dishes, with sauces of fresh vegetables, meats, seafoods and cheeses.

X. Rice, Potatoes and Beans 454

How to make a perfect batch of rice and ways to vary it; recipes for potatoes puréed, sautéed, roasted and souffléed as well as flageolets, frijoles, lentils and other beans.

XI. Vegetables 469

How to prepare and cook artichokes, whole leeks, corn and squash; recipes that sauté, bake, braise, fry, steam, purée, stuff and cream vegetables for mixtures, casseroles, gratinées, and puddings, with delicious and varied sauces.

Preface

If one of the major attributes of this book is a considerable diversity in flavor and taste—and it is most assuredly international in scope—it is due to an incalculable extent to a peculiar fact of geography. It could not have happened anywhere in the world other than New York. It is not chauvinistic to say that where food is concerned, New York is and has been for more than a century the focal point of the globe. That is not to say that Paris does not have a greater wealth in the world's restaurants, for that it does.

But New York offers the broadest possible ethnic diversity, and it is pre-eminent as a gastronomic crossroad. A few years ago the great chefs of France and the world discovered that an occasional visit to New York would enhance their reputations. Some of them came for a day or a week en route to cooking demonstrations or other engagements in California, China and Japan.

It has been my great good fortune that many of them were generous enough to drive out to Long Island where they shared with readers of *The New York Times* their "secrets," the dishes for which they were much praised in the confines of their own kitchens and restaurants—Paul Bocuse of Lyons, Alain Chapel of Mionnay, Jean Troisgros of Roanne, Gaston Lenotre of Paris and many others. During their stays in my home, they produced such dishes as an elaborately good mousse of chicken livers, an extraordinary salad with greens and herbs and quickly sautéed chicken breasts, delectable desserts, pâtés, terrines, main courses by the hundreds.

At other times, the finest chefs of New York have come into my home to pass a few hours, a day or an evening confecting their most desirable creations that have titillated the public palate over the years. One of the most agreeable reminiscences of my life, in fact was an interview that occurred one February day. Seppi Renggli, the celebrated chef of New York's Four Seasons restaurant, was scheduled to come to prepare a several course dinner for the vicarious delectation and delight of those who read *The New York Times* food columns.

Seppi, handsome, soft-spoken and dedicated, had arisen in his New Jersey home at 5 A.M. to reach my home at an appointed hour. He had stopped by his restaurant to obtain a few supplies and by the time his car turned into my driveway, snowflakes were coming down with a vengeance. A veritable tempest had been building and an hour or so after his arrival, the radio announced that the expressway back to New York was closed. So were all other highways. The power in my home failed and Seppi proceeded to cook (the gas stove worked) by lamp and candlelight an unforgettable dinner for eight. Meanwhile, my roadway had become impassable because of the snowfall. Thus the two of us sat before a roaring fire, sipping a fine Bordeaux, raising a glass now and then to toast our absent friends.

In addition to the great chefs, there are included here the recipes of scores of great, lesser sung, amateur chefs, many of them from foreign shores: Thailand, Japan, China and so on. There are classic and traditional dishes that have been adapted in the most authentic manner possible to the resources of America.

Finally, and most important, are the immeasurable contributions of Pierre Franey. Pierre and I have worked together for more than twenty years. He was for many years chef of Le Pavillon when it was considered, almost without challenge, the greatest French restaurant in America. We have worked side by side day after day and often on weekends to provide the readers of *The Times* food columns with the greatest assortment, the most varied collection of recipes that it has been within our power to produce. It is certainly not all foie gras and truffles. There is an abundance of recipes that use leftovers, ground meats, stuffed vegetables and many of the less expensive viands.

Thus this volume is a compilation of the best recipes that have appeared in *The New York Times* food pages—Sunday and daily—during the past decade. They include the contributions from hundreds of interviews with fine cooks and chefs, plus the recipes that have been developed by Pierre Franey and myself.

Craig Claiborne's

The New
New York Times
COOKBOOK

I. De Gustibus

De gustibus, translated literally, means "about tastes." The full Latin expression is de gustibus non disputandum (est), which means "there is no disputing about tastes."

In a dialogue that has been going on for many years with readers of *The New York Times*, under the heading De Gustibus, the full Latin phrase has been proved grossly untrue. There are disputes and agreements; there are tentative queries and adamant statements; there is the excitement of discovery and sharing.

Throughout it all, of course, is one man's taste (call it quirks if you will), in both senses of the word: a sense of discernment in what is seemly and appropriate, and the mouth's reaction to what is put in it.

One of the happiest thoughts to cross my mind within recent years is that as food editor of *The New York Times*, I, along with Pierre Franey, have played some small role in what has often been referred to as the gastronomic revolution in America.

What Nostradamus could have divined twenty years ago that today such dishes as coq au vin and beef bourguignon—once the hallmark of fine French restaurants—would become such common coinage in the nation's home kitchens as to be embarrassingly old hat.

In truth, the genesis of that revolution began about a quarter century ago, shortly after the end of World War II. Those were the good old days when steamship companies resumed their trans-Atlantic crossings and food mavens with a certain amount of wherewithal started to flock back to the temples of gastronomy in France, places like Pyramide in Vienne, Père Bise in Talloires, and the Grand Vefour in Paris. The most fortunate and deserving chefs—Dumaine, Bise and so on— were elevated by their new-found American clientele to an almost godlike status.

The vineyards of Europe were replanted or otherwise revitalized and Americans in certain numbers (small at first) were discovering the delights of the harvest of the great châteaus of Bordeaux, the grand estates of Burgundy, the wines of the Rhine and Moselle, thanks to the writings of that learned and good man, the late Frank Schoonmaker.

America in those years was not very keenly tuned in to the "exotic" foods of Europe and elsewhere. Which is not to say that French cooking was totally unknown in the home kitchens of this country. In those days, one of the ubiquitous bibles of cooking was *The Boston Cooking School Cook Book* (a highly sophisticated manual in its original editions, before it was "modernized" by editors more than a decade ago). Fannie Farmer, the founder of the Boston Cooking School, incorporated in her work a sizable number of creditable recipes from the French repertory, particularly desserts like charlotte russe, Bavarian creams and mousses. She details a method for making puff pastry and includes various sauces such as hollandaise and champagne sauce.

Some of the admissions and omissions in the book are laughable in the light of today's taste. There is but one mention of mussels in the book. "Mussels," Mrs. Farmer stated, "eaten in England and other parts of Europe, are similar to oysters, though of inferior quality."

But if America's home cooks learned much from Mrs. Farmer, fine cooking was not the hallmark of a well-run household nor, as it is today, something of a status symbol.

Food in the homes across the nation was mostly regional—dishes like fried chicken, chili con carne, baked ham, a not-too-authentic Italian-style tomato sauce, roast turkey, clam chowder, Boston baked beans, salads with Russian dressing, broiled steaks and chops and the like. There was (and is) a great deal of backyard barbecuing.

One of the first "exotic" innovations in this country was the Caesar salad, which is said to have come to the United States from Mexico. Legends about its origins vary but the most often quoted is that a restaurant owner named Caesar (one source pinpoints him as Caesar Cardini and definitely situates the restaurant in Tia Juana) catered to a crowd of Hollywood stars who crossed the border to patronize his establishment. Early morning they were still there and his larder was almost empty. They demanded food and he brought forth all the things he could muster from the ice box—lettuce, eggs, grated cheese, anchovies, lemons and so on. He tossed them together and the salad was the result.

At approximately the same time that pizza became a national rage after World War II, Americans in vast numbers also learned about shish kebab and avidly added it to their repertory. No one knows precisely when or what route this dish took from Turkey or Greece, but arrive it did to give favorable competition to hamburgers, steak and chicken on the charcoal grill.

Two principal factors have been responsible in the past twenty years for the increased and notably sophisticated approach to food in this country. Chief among them is undoubtedly the increased affluence and mobility of the American public. And the precise date of their hegiras could surely be listed as June 17, 1947, the date of the inaugural commercial airline flight around the world. It was a Pan-American flight with a crew of ten. It cost the twenty-one passengers $1700 apiece. It was a flight that, within a few short years, put the waterfront in Barcelona, the Ginza of Tokyo and the Left Bank of Paris only a brief and winged hop away.

Suddenly Americans were sampling and enjoying fondues before a roaring fire in St. Moritz; sashimi and sushi in Osaka; spanakopetes and tyropeta in the plaka in Athens; paella in Valencia, and gazpacho in Seville.

If the average American had a problem in analyzing the ingredients and techniques used for making one dish or another, solution was shortly at hand in the form of cookbooks that specialized in international recipes, and cooking schools that did the same.

(It seems hard to believe that twenty years ago, when I first joined *The New York Times*, there was a "shelter" or "family" magazine, supposedly catering to adult minds, that would not print recipes that called for wine on the theory that it might offend readers in the so-called Bible Belt. The editors shortly learned the errors in their judgment.)

But in those early years, cooking schools were still rare. In fact, the single European-based institution of grand reputation was the Cordon Bleu, about which I have always had mixed feelings. It must have been estimable in its early years after the war, but when I visited the school in 1957 it was then in its old location and a grievous disappointment with its tedious, old-fashioned teaching methods and primitive equipment.

In this country there was James Beard, who as much as anyone else, through his books and cooking classes, had a profound effect on American taste. Jim was the first great pioneer in this country's world of gastronomy and his influence is to this day beyond measure. There were cooking classes at the

China Institute in New York but, in the beginning, instruction was exceedingly basic and very much for neophytes.

When Grace Chu, the first of America's great Chinese cooking instructors, came on the scene, she set in motion an intense and continuing interest in Chinese cooking methods. She was joined in this missionary work by the well-known Florence Lin, and eventually by Virginia Lee, who brought a new depth to instruction in Chinese cuisine. And there is Marcella Hazan with her cucina Italiana and Diana Kennedy with her classic Mexican.

In 1961 Julia Child came into the arena with *Mastering the Art of French Cooking,* a collaboration with Simone Beck and Louisette Bertholle. And, shortly thereafter, her enormously popular demonstrations on public television.

When my columns first began in 1957 there were not more than two or three cooking schools of any consequence in the New York area. In late 1978—nom de dieu—when a listing of cooking schools in Manhattan alone was published, there were nearly fifty schools, embracing such diverse cuisines as Chinese, Mexican, Japanese, Mediterranean and, of course, French and Italian.

To fully appreciate the magnitude of this revolution it must be viewed in the light of this nation's cultural heritage. I dote on and will defend mightily a good deal of American cooking—fried chicken, Philadelphia scrapple, chili con carne, Charleston she-crab soup, pecan pie, Cajun cookery.

But the fact is that America—unlike France, Italy, China and so on—does not have a national legacy of "great" cooking that has been handed down from generation to generation. Many of its "great" dishes are wholly regional—the gumbos and crawfish dishes of Louisiana, the Mexican-inspired foods of the Southwest, the chowders of New England. Most of American cooking is coarse, unpretentious and unsophisticated (grits, chili, clam chowder).

Thus, the gastronomic revolution here has started from scratch. And, curiously, there are conceivably more fine cooks in the nation today than you will find in France. They are better read about food and their options in books on great cooking are practically limitless.

Consider the vast number of international dishes with which the average American food enthusiast is conversant. He or she may not have sampled them all, but can discuss them without apology. Among the main course and side dishes—names chosen at random—vitello tonnato, salade niçoise, ratatouille, bouillabaisse, gazpacho, coulibiac of salmon, kung pao chicken, hot and sour soup, spring rolls, spaghetti carbonara, saltimbocca, seviche, duck à l'orange, gravlaks, guacamole, fettucine in numerous ways, couscous and sushi. Among breads, croissants and brioches; among desserts, croquembouches, tart Tatin and dacquoise.

The staples for making such foods of distinction are also widely available. Fresh herbs and greens such as tarragon, shallots, rosemary, thyme, arugula and celery root, to choose a few brief examples. Not bad for a nation that only two decades ago rarely offered fresh mushrooms and sour cream outside metropolitan centers.

Moules marinière are a commonplace wherever they are now available in this country. And escargots are getting to be a downright bore. You can find them stuffed in mushrooms with snail butter even in the provinces. Quiches with a multitude of flavors have become a national plague. And how about chicken Kiev or cordon bleu? Soufflés? Crêpes? Omelets? Naturally! Country pâtés and truffle-studded terrines? But of course.

And consider the bewildering proliferation of pot and pan shops from one coast to the other. And the cheese shops. One wonders how there are enough cows in Europe to provide such a bulk of imports to this country.

Almost any decent kitchen in the nation now uses wine vinegars and imported olive oils and mustards reflexively. And pepper freshly ground in a pepper mill.

One of the most trenchant observations about the American appetite "coming of age" was made by my friend and colleague Jim Villas, writing in *Town and Country* magazine. In the article he quoted the Count Ghislain de Voguë who said: "First you had to build a nation. Then you had to show your power. Now, at last, you are learning how to live."

Although Americans have become more sophisticated about food, they have also become a nation of culinary schizophrenics. They live in mortal dread of high-calorie foods and shun some of the greatest pleasures of the table while mindlessly gorging themselves on all sorts of plain and junk foods. Who would dare remonstrate when the palate is placated with two or three hamburgers or a whole pizza downed with a Coke? It's only the sign of a happy husband or boy or girl with a healthy all-American appetite.

But deep-seated feelings of guilt blossom in the Yankee breast at the sight of cream soups, hollandaise and béarnaise

...Le vase ou meurt cette Verveine....

3 July 1965

Claires – Sauce mignonnette
Gâteau de foies de volailles
Quenelles de Flounders
Sauce Orly
Salade panachée

Myrtilles au Kirsch

Crépy Goutte d'Or
(Grand vin de Savoie)

Elizabeth Franey

sauces, anchovy butter for broiled fish, pastry creams and whipped cream if it is to be spooned over a foreign dessert such as a gâteau St. Honoré.

They will drink two or three sugar-laden apéritifs at a cocktail party and consume those vacuous high-calorie cocktail companions—peanuts, cheese dips with their attendant scoops in the form of cheese-flavored crackers sculptured into the shape of fish—only to arise the next morning and piously drop a sugar-substitute in their coffee.

I have spent the bulk of my adult life in writing about dining well and great cooking, and by great cooking I do not mean the haute cuisine of France to the exclusion of all others. I love good hamburgers and chili con carne. And foie gras and sauternes and those small birds known as ortolans. There is at least one occasion on which I tend to eat butter with glorious disregard of consequences. And that is when the first crop of corn arrives. I become downright lustful and slather on the butter and attack the corn while the golden rich liquid fairly dribbles down my cheeks.

(I am always flabbergasted and amused in steak houses that the meat is served without melted butter, which enormously enhances its flavor, and yet limitless quantities of butter are served on the side that patrons spread on bread and consume in quantity with their baked potatoes.)

Given my profession and the fact that I dote on good food, I am often asked how I maintain a fairly constant weight. Such an inquiry is understandably if lamentably born of the panic in the kitchen that one eats haute cuisine at one's peril. Although I have sampled virtually every one of the dishes for which a recipe appears under my name, my weight remains generally at 158 pounds in the morning, 162 pounds before retiring, and my health is good.

Yet the sad assumption remains that those recipes that call for a cup or two of heavy cream and a couple of egg yolks and are designed, let us say, for six to eight people, are deadly. In the first place, those recipes are intended for special, festive occasions. In the second place, one cup of cream in a recipe designed for eight works out to two tablespoons per person.

As to my "diet," it involves only this precept: Eat in moderation and savor your food.

I take pleasure in breakfast and plot it according to whim. It always begins with freshly squeezed grapefruit juice, which I am convinced is one of the finest foods for preventing head colds. It might embrace fruits and melons in season, a hot thin soup with unbuttered toast, plus tea or black coffee. An excellent breakfast "soup," by the way, is a combination of equal parts clam broth and tomato juice with lemon juice and freshly ground pepper. Half a tomato cut into cubes and added at the last moment just to heat through is excellent.

If I am alone for the midday meal, I dine simply—perhaps on a small sandwich made with tuna fish or a tin of sardines. Or perhaps a salad lightly seasoned with a little vinegar and oil plus the tinned fish in modest quantities. If I dine alone in the evening, I will content myself with one grilled lamb chop, a baked potato with a small pat of butter, a mixed salad and fruit for dessert.

Meals taken with friends in restaurants are also taken in moderation. Although I insist on small portions, that goal is not easily achieved. Thus I eat as much of what is put before me as I consider discreet, and I have found that I eat in far smaller quantities than most of my acquaintances. I do find that Japanese food, properly chosen, is the one least likely to cause overweight, followed closely by Chinese food.

When it comes to excess, the fault lies not with the glories of our foods, but in ourselves. To the gluttons of the world I wish punishment in the form of signs worn around the neck, stating: "It is I who have gluttonized, who have eaten to excess and, therefore, given a bad name to butter and cream and the other good things of life."

We have often written about the neuroses induced in children who are browbeaten by their parents to "eat everything on your plate." It encouraged a note from a reader who told us: "An old friend, whose youth was spent during the Great Depression, was urged until the age of 13 to clean his plate because every morsel had a price on it. After the age of 13 or so, his family struck it rich and, Depression days behind, he was told that in his new affluence it was only proper to leave a few morsels on the plate." As a result the poor fellow has been suffering chronic indigestion for the past 44 years.

If I am asked, as I have been on numerous occasions, what are the ingredients of a successful party, my answer is several, beginning with a desire to please. Beyond a host or hostess who genuinely cares about the pleasure of the guests come food, interestingly and conscientiously prepared; a consistency of atmosphere (no Dom Perignon out of plastic cups at the beach, please, although a California Chablis served in the same way is fine), and guests characterized by any interest at all so long as each possesses a sense of humor.

The three sorts of foods that inevitably give me pleasure at gatherings are a grand assortment of appetizers, both hot and cold; picnics with hampers full of imported cheeses, salamis, crisp loaves of breads, fruits to be eaten out of hand and wines; covered dish or casserole suppers, cooked preferably by friends who know their onions. All of which says that I like variety and choice when dining. A well-laid smorgasbord is of divine inspiration. And chili is conceivably America's greatest contribution to the world's cuisine.

If I am not snobbish about foods, I am not without my aversions. I believe crusts should be neatly trimmed from the sides of the bread on sandwiches (perhaps England's greatest contribution to gastronomy). It is simply more elegant and they taste better in the same sense that Chinese food tastes better when eaten with chopsticks. And I abhor tepid soup.

One last thing that I find particularly loathsome. If you would have me dine in peace and pleasure, do not ask me to pose my dinner plate—be it Spode or paper—on my lap.

Speaking of parties, we are reminded of an anecdote about a black-tie dinner where the hostess was known more for her money than taste and the excellence of her kitchen.

At some point during the week prior to the dinner she had prepared a salmon mousse. The fact is she had made the mousse for another meal earlier in the week and for one reason or another had never served it. There was some question in her mind as to the salutary condition of that mousse, but in that it did not reek she decided to serve it anyway.

The evening arrived. The mousse was spooned onto chilled serving plates and the mold in which the mousse had set was placed on the floor for the kitten to lick.

The guests enjoyed the mousse and the plates were cleared from the table. The lady of the house walked into the kitchen and there on the back porch was that poor little kitten, paws upturned and out cold. The hostess ran to the phone and called her doctor. On hearing the facts, he urged her to rush all the guests to the hospital to have their stomachs pumped. Which she did, herself among them.

On her return home, there was a knock on the door and a neighbor entered.

"I just came to tell you," he said, "I ran over your cat in the driveway. I wanted to tell you then but I saw you had guests and I didn't want to interfere."

A while ago, a magazine reporter came into my kitchen to discuss the care and preservation of a food-writer's stomach. One of the questions was: "When you dine alone, do you eat standing up?" The answer was an immediate and reflexive, "Of course not."

The second question was whether I set the table when I am alone. The answer was, in no uncertain tone, "Indeed I do." What's more, I situate the place mat with precision and on it I place a knife and fork (silver by Christofle) and a clear wine goblet (crystal by Baccarat). To the left of the fork is a crisply starched linen napkin.

Food—good food—is a blessing, and as sound and valid a reason for celebration as almost anything I know. By good food I mean food that has been conscientiously cooked and thoughtfully made, be it a hamburger or a fish mousse. Thus I give it its due: a proper setting and, if you want to term it that, ceremony. To eat food without thought or reflection is a profanity.

Since my first encounter with cigars at a "smoker" when I was a freshman at college, I have held them in vilest esteem. How anyone with a pretension to a sensitive palate could follow, let us say, sole in champagne sauce, a royal dish of squab and an elegant dessert with the foul stench and taste of a cigar is impossible to fathom. But come to think of it, I don't think they would be any more appropriate after oatmeal.

There is a place for everything, including cigars, and some of the places that come to mind are the open road, a canoe for one, an unpopulated golf course and, naturally, the Augean stables.

Someday there will probably come into being an organization called "The Society of Iceberg Lettuce Fanciers," or "Friends of Iceberg Lettuce." Each time we mention iceberg lettuce it is, with rare exceptions (certain Chinese or Mexican dishes), spoken of with disparagement. It is simply the commonplace and tasteless nature of the green. Watercress, Belgian endive, escarole, Boston lettuce, romaine and others are more sophisticated and have more class. To put it another way, iceberg is to other lettuces as peanuts are to almonds, hazelnuts and walnuts.

This inevitably raises the hackles on the backs of some cooks. We believe in equal space.

"I feel I must come to a half-hearted defense of the iceberg," one reader wrote. "Botanically, iceberg *is* in a class. True, it may be nutritionally low on the scale of salad greens, but to say that it is not sophisticated is being very elitist.

"How can iceberg become classy, sophisticated? Is there any hope of raising its social status? Maybe at the Restaurant Troisgros a masterpiece could be created utilizing iceberg. Or, maybe some country gentleman of fading gentility might be coaxed into raising iceberg and lending his name. It is possible that iceberg might achieve elevation to position through a farmer. After all didn't peanuts soar above almonds, hazelnuts and walnuts right into the Washington Social Register?

"Iceberg lettuce has become the lares et penates of the traditional American household and even the warmth of that American hearth cannot warm the frostiness of your remarks."

If we are unkind to iceberg lettuce, you should hear us on maraschino cherries!

In that America is doubtlessly the most dedicated salad eating nation in the world (and has contrived the greatest number and some of the most imaginative salads on earth), it is small wonder that salads, with or without iceberg lettuce, seem much on the mind of native gastronomes.

"I've been wanting to ask your opinion about something that I've thought of intermittently for thirty years," a reader wrote. "Namely, salad served as a separate course before the main course.

"At home, we always had salad along with the main course as a vegetable, but usually we ate it after the main course. I think that must be something like the way the English serve a savory. Then when I was 'grown-up' I started eating in restaurants, and sometime along the way the salad came early. I think it was called 'California style' back in the thirties. My question is what do you think of it? My own preference is still for salad as we had it at home."

We have heard many theories over the years as to how salads jumped from third or fourth course to first course a few decades ago. Some say it came about with the craze for slimming practices during the so-called golden age of Hollywood. This theory has it that a large salad, substantial enough for a

"First let me introduce myself. I'm Craig Claiborne,
and this is Julia Child."

Drawing by Modell; Copyright © 1974 by The New Yorker Magazine, Inc.

complete meal, was served at the beginning of a meal in order to dull the appetite for anything that followed. Another theory holds that mothers started serving salads at the beginning of meals to encourage children to down their proper share of greenery.

To our mind there is no hide-bound, "classic" moment during which a salad should be served in the course of a meal. In my own home a simple salad made with such things as Boston lettuce, Romaine, watercress, endive and perhaps arugula (anything but iceberg lettuce) is served with cheese after the main course and followed by dessert.

A clergyman subsequently wrote as follows: Concerning "the delicate question of the position of salad on the menu, in the days of my pious and impressionable youth, some Roman maestro of the culinary art indicated his preference as after the soup and before the pasta and main course. The reasoning being that if the salad were served with the main course, its vinegar-based dressing would be hostile to the appreciation of the accompanying wine."

The argument, logic, or whatever you choose to call it is that anything with vinegar in it is anathema to wines because it will in turn convert the wine into vinegar once the two are joined in the stomach. Some of these epicures will concede—reluctantly—that a salad dressing made with a touch of lemon would be acceptable. We find the argument precious, and almost invariably serve salad with cheese, bread and wine at every serious dinner.

It sometimes seems to me that the kitchen customs of many Americans are even more fascinating than their food preferences. Over the years, I have written numerous times about whether greens for the salad bowl should be torn with the fingers or cut with a knife. I have delved into this matter not so much as a matter of personal interest, but because I am so often queried about it, as though the total success or failure of a meal lay perilously in the balance on this point.

To restate a position, I almost invariably cut salad greens with a knife. I find it more expeditious and tearing the leaves can cause bruising. In my opinion, the result is equally as appealing to the eye. I would find the whole thing grandly unimportant, caring far more about the seasoning in the bowl than whether the green morsels contained therein have more of an angularity (cut) or roundness (broken) to them. But the readers take pen in hand and will not let the argument lie. Basically, the counteroffensive has nothing to do with esthetics, which I had thought was the point, but rather it has to do with chemistry.

To quote from one of the missives: "I know that cutting lettuce with a metal blade, though quicker, starts an oxidation process that causes the cut edge to darken in a short time. As a gourmet cook, I know that for best results each salad leaf should be lightly coated with oil or dressing. This is virtually impossible to do when lettuce has been cut."

I hasten to add that in my own kitchen these days I rarely use anything but stainless steel knives that are impermeable to rust. And the cut edges of lettuce leaves, provided the cutting blade is of stainless steel, will not rust.

Call it sentiment or the approach of senility, but I find pleasure in whiling away an afternoon in my own reflection of things past. Just recently, browsing through a handwritten service manual from the Swiss hotel school I attended, I was amused at the following admonitions for would-be hotel keepers or members of a hotel staff.

It must be remembered that it was an age—nearly twenty-five years ago—when tea bags had been invented, but you would certainly not find them in use "in the front of the house." Not in the main dining room of a respectable first-class European hotel.

Cups, we were advised, into which either coffee or tea are to be poured, should be heated thoroughly before placing them before a customer. This was customarily done by filling the cups with boiling water, draining and drying immediately before service.

The rules, translated from the French, continue as follows:

1. Cleanliness in all things is the best publicity for an establishment.

2. For hot drinks, you must make certain that water is boiling and not simply taken from a tap no matter how hot it is.

3. A client must always receive a full measure of whatever, be it a bar drink or anything else. Do not forget that a good reputation is the first condition of success.

4. In serving wines, always take the wine glass by the base or the stem, never by the rim or bowl. A customer does not like to see fingerprints on the part of the glass from which he will drink.

5. Bread, fruit, ice and so forth must never be touched with the waiter's fingers.

6. Drinking straws are used for drinking, not for stirring.

7. For the preparation of punch bowls, always check the condition of each bottle of wine to be added. If you do not wish to sample the wine, at least smell the cork to make certain the wine is in good shape. One bottle of "corky" wine can spoil the punch.

8. As you work, keep your work area neat and orderly. Empty bottles, soiled dishes and so forth must be gotten rid of as soon as possible.

9. Before serving a wine such as port or sherry, check the bottle to make certain it is not cloudy.

10. To the greatest degree possible, present the customer with a legible and accurate bill. It is human to err, but an error is frequently considered deliberate when committed by a waiter. A proper, clearly written bill will be proof.

11. The customer is not always right, but you must never let him think otherwise. If you do, it can create difficulties.

Without question, the single most gratifying piece of mail to be anchored in my mail box within recent memory was from Arlington Confection Company of Arlington, Texas. The letter, which forwarded a do-it-yourself kit with contents and instructions for making chewing gum at home, is as follows:

"We are enclosing a sample of our product so that you too may enjoy the difference between freshly prepared and commercially available chewing gum.

"As you will note, our product will make about sixteen feet of chewing gum approximately one-half inch in diameter, and/or may be portioned for chewing in numerous ways. POW! can be prepared with no color added, cut with cookie cutters, and the figures then painted with food color and a small artist brush for an absolutely great eye appealing, unique, after dinner treat.

"Also, we would like to point out that never before has the opportunity been available for Mr. (or Mrs.) Person Who Loves To Cook to prepare their own chewing gum, in the kitchen, with minimum ease, in a manner that best suits their individual preference. Finally, many people will no doubt find ways to flavor their gum which are now unknown to ourselves and other manufacturers.

"Thank you for your time" etc.

I am frequently asked if guests in my home do anything in my dining area and kitchen that might be called an annoyance, and the answer is one.

I do not object to elbows on the table. Off-color jokes I dote on. And life is too brief to be irked by those individuals who hold a wine glass by the bowl instead of the stem.

What I really find bothersome and subcutaneous are those who try to help with the dishes between courses or at the end of a meal. It yields to nothing but chaos and disaster. If one unappointed individual stands to help remove the dishes, the other guests rise almost in unison. And those who don't are generally guilt-ridden. Thus, what would otherwise be a fairly civilized occasion takes on the air of Mulberry Street during the Feast of San Gennaro.

There are times when I have stood by helplessly while perfectly well-meaning guests stack my dishwasher. Over the years I could have paid a butler what it has cost to replace wine glasses that were broken, repairs to the machine caused by waywardly stacked salad forks, or by the refuse that went part way down the drain because the dishes were improperly rinsed.

Equally as debilitating to my spirits are those well-meaning souls who attempt to "put away" the dishes. Have you ever searched for the bottom of the drip coffeemaker in its accustomed storage place, only to discover after a frenzied search that it is tucked away in the oven, the very spot no doubt where it is invariably to be found in their own home.

So much for the dining and kitchen area. There is an even greater annoyance when guests are assembled before or after a meal and drinks such as cocktails or coffee and liqueurs are served. I feel a certain reverence for some books in this world, several of which are to be found at almost any time scattered around the living area—on the cocktail table, assorted end tables, storage chests that double as book rests and so on. I do not mind stains on the wood. I cringe, however, at the sight of a stain on the dust jackets of my favorite books.

This protest brought forth some interesting views on the matter, one of the most incisive of which came from a woman who is a doctor of philosophy.

"My sympathies are with you," she stated. "My own worst experience was with the person with a passion to scour who attacked one of my tin-lined copper pots.

"But one's chances of success are small if you simply say 'no.' Food is too emotional an experience for many people. Some, otherwise civilized, really need to participate in some way. It's easy to set up a few innocuous chores ahead of time for such a person. I've had luck with a quiet corner, a knife and instructions to cut up—anything—into the smallest possible pieces. Another may prefer sorting (beans, forks, recipes) according to some obscure principle. Other time-consuming possibilities will occur on specific occasions. As a last resort, send the guest out to prune (the herbs in the garden, perhaps) the poison ivy."

And a doctor wrote: "How about the guests who charge right into cleaning the dishes and glasses without clearing the work area and without cleaning the sink and counter tops. Without even washing their hands. These guests seemingly delight in putting away streaky, smoky dishes and glasses; it's as if they get some sadistic delight in knowing that you will have to do them over again once they leave. This holds also for putting bottles and jars away without wiping. Furthermore, I don't expect to work when I'm invited out to dinner, so why should my friends be expected to work when they dine with me?"

Novel uses for kitchen utensils, or something for the birds. "We're excited about our recently acquired food processor," a doctor wrote. "We thought you might be interested in yet another justification for spending the amount of money the machine costs. Trim the excess fat from steaks and then, rather than rendering the fat, process the fat fine. Add any combination of seeds, peanut butter, oatmeal and cornmeal . . . a service to woodpeckers, titmice and chickadees."

Over the years we have often been accused of underestimating the yield on recipes and, therefore, the appetites of the average reader. This may be due to several factors. In the first place, I am an advocate of the theory that one should eat sparingly. And secondly, when guests are entertained at my table the meal more often than not consists of four courses, a first course, generally a soup or a light fish dish, a main course of poultry or meat with vegetable, salad and cheese offered simultaneously, and dessert. Yields on recipes are sometimes based on the numbers served during the course of a meal.

On the other hand, we were recently taken to task because the yield on a sauce to go with poultry was, according to one reader, half as much as it should have been to serve her guests.

A fairly typical scene in my East Hampton kitchen when a chef is visiting—in this case Jean Troisgros of the justly famous Troisgros Restaurant in Roanne. I stand at my typewriter, watching the chef and talking to him, taking down each step in his preparation of a dish (he frequently has three or four going at once); Pierre Franey to my left, acts as "sous-chef," helping in the preparation but also questioning the visitor as to technique and ingredients. Guests frequently join us in the kitchen. On a later day, Pierre and I make the dishes again to assure ourselves that the recipes are clear.

When I first wrote an article about Le Pavillon, then considered the greatest restaurant in New York, I declared Pierre Franey the finest chef in the country. Shortly thereafter we became friends and started preparing weekly menus in my home. For the past twenty years we have worked closely together in my kitchens in New York and East Hampton, devising our own recipes, recreating dishes we have eaten in restaurants here and abroad, testing recipes sent to us by friends and readers and retesting those that have been made in our kitchen by visiting chefs.

A typical corner of my kitchen may look cluttered but it is extremely efficient with equipment close at hand.

It took time to persuade Pierre that it was vital to measure ingredients accurately. Now he does this reflexively when I show up with a notebook.

With meals in my home there is always an appropriate wine for cooking or dining.

The cooking equipment in my home includes professional ranges and a collection of heavy copperware accumulated over many years on numerous trips abroad.

When Claudia Franey got married there was a big striped tent near my swimming pool and 170 guests and a four-foot wedding cake that was made by Albert Kumin, one of the world's greatest pastry chefs. There were also six chefs in the kitchen—Jacques Pépin, Jean Vergnes, Raymond Bruballa, Jean-Jacques Paimblanc, Jean-Louis Todeschine, plus the father of the bride. Roger Fessaguet, chef of La Caravelle, was tied up in traffic, but he got there in time for the wedding march. The chefs spent a couple of days and nights preparing the cold buffet of striped bass with salade russe, mussels vinaigrette, terrines of sweetbreads, pâtés of venison, galantines of duck and garlic sausages with lentils. The hot buffet included ten fillets of beef with truffle sauce, and fifteen roasted racks of lamb.

My fiftieth birthday party was held on the S.S. *France,* which I had called the greatest floating restaurant in the world. That's Julia and Jim on the far left, Al McCann of WOR on my left and Pierre Franey the third from the right.

Some of the best meals I have ever eaten were on the S.S. *France* and, one time, I interviewed and spent two days in the kitchen with Master Chef Henri Le Huédé, who was responsible for the faultless classic French cuisine that was served in the first-class dining room.

Alfred Knopf has long been known as one of the great becs fins of New York. Two of the pleasantest meals in my life were spent in Alfred's home where he has one of the most impressive wine collections on the East Coast. We also dined at La Caravelle restaurant where Alfred talked of wine with Robert Meyzin, one of the proprietors.

We had a joyous visit when Jean Troisgros came to East Hampton. He went to our local fish market looking striped bass straight in the eye for clarity, inspecting the gills for redness, both of which indicate a fresh catch. There was a brief stop at the poultry farm to pat the plump flesh of freshly killed fowl, and a half hour admiring the produce at our local vegetable farm. All of which he deemed splendid. The meal he prepared included an inspired salad of greens, truffles and quickly sautéed medallions of chicken, the whole annointed with a sauce, the soul of which was oil of walnut. Then a fish course followed by scallops of veal lightly coated with mustard and whole mustard seed. That plus a fine wheel of Brie, crusty French bread and fresh local strawberries was shared with friends on my deck.

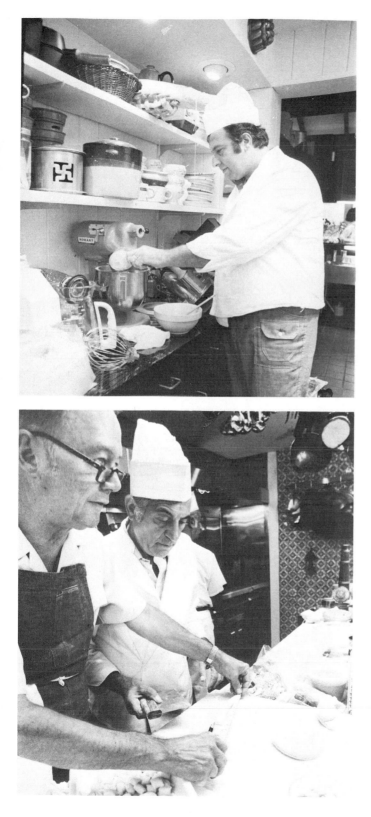

Not all the chefs who cook in my kitchen are from luxurious and celebrated restaurants of the world. We have great friends in the Migliucci family. The Migliuccis—Mario the father; Clemente the brother; and Joseph the son and nephew—are the principals in the kitchen at Mario's restaurant in the Bronx, which we had visited several times and found the Neapolitan cooking much to our liking. So they prepared an impressive array of dishes in my kitchen. As Mario kneaded the potato gnocchi, Clemente prepared the striped bass fillets, and Joe chopped and assembled the ingredients for octopus salad, I interrupted to measure and stir sauces to feel the consistency.

We dote on Chinese cooking, and particularly the hot dishes of Szechwan and Hunan. Therefore, it was a special treat when Wen Dah Tai came to our home and made some of the specialties of his Uncle Tai's Hunan Yuan restaurant in New York. He was accompanied by Norman Chi the maître d'hôtel and partner in the restaurant who acted as interpreter. Uncle Tai speaks very little English but he is eloquent with his hands. He is one of the greatest chefs of the world and has recently opened Uncle Tai's of Houston, Texas.

The ebullient Diana Kennedy, *the* expert in Mexican cooking.

Marcella Hazan, serious and elegant, is a great specialist in pasta and Italian dishes.

Ann Seranne, when she was managing editor of *Gourmet* Magazine, gave my first job writing for that publication. She is the beloved author of many cookbooks international in scope.

I am passionately devoted to Virginia Lee with whom I spent two years in my kitchen when we collaborated on a cookbook. A native of Shanghai, Virginia is a phenomenal expert in Chinese cuisine.

Paul Bocuse had two impressive "sous-chefs" when he spent the day in our kitchen: Pierre Franey and Jacques Pépin, two of the best-known French chefs in America. Before Paul arrived we had spent the morning shopping for les primeurs, the finest and freshest vegetables available at our local market, lobsters that would turn into an excellent navarin and freshly killed chickens. The chef was obviously impressed with the fare. "Impeccable," he stated, a word that he uses with enthusiasm and cunning abandon as he works. He sipped the lobster sauce from a wooden spoon, "Impeccable!" he exclaimed. But when he broke into the puff pastry that glorifies his truffle soup the host to his right beat him to the draw. "Impeccable," he said.

If you've ever wondered how long it takes for three professional chefs to turn out a veritable regale of ten dishes in a foreign and unaccustomed kitchen, the answer is approximately 4½ hours. That's with a lot of interruptions while I check the ingredients and take notes. Gino Innocenti, the distinguished owner of La Pace Hotel and Restaurant in Montecatini brought a few master chefs from his establishment along with hampers filled with half a calf's head, a calf's tongue, a large hen, mustard fruit and zampone for bollito misto; anchovies and capers and oil for the marvelous cold appetizer called carpaccio; chicken livers and bread for a delectable spread on rounds of toast; ham and pickles and chicken for a superior pasta dish; and endless quantities of cream and eggs and candied fruit for a wildly rich assortment of Italian desserts. One of them was a fantasy of spun sugar and we have a fond memory of one of the chefs standing on a step stool bandying about his forked whisk, after which our kitchen resembled the remains of a dismantled Christmas tree.

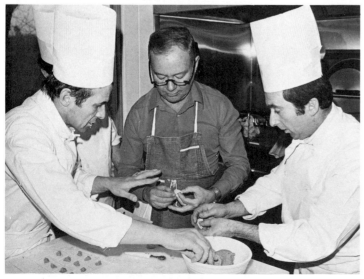

Gaston Lenotre, who is generally considered to be the greatest pastry chef in France and all of Europe, visited us when he was in New York promoting his book on desserts. He is a Merlin in all aspects of flavoring, baking and decorating. He is shown putting the finishing touches on a glorious specialty called Ambassadeur. He is, in fact, piping out the name of the cake in script using chocolate butter cream.

The one great holiday in my home is New Year's Eve. It has been a tradition for nearly twenty years for some of the greatest chefs and cooks in Manhattan and environs to come out and cook an elaborate buffet for more than 50 people. Cooking begins almost at dawn and proceeds throughout the day. The black tie dinner, invariably seated and with vintage wine, begins at 9:00 and ends around the stroke of midnight with champagne. The chefs involved in this particular evening were Roger Fessaguet, Ed Giobbi, Jean Vergnes and Pierre Franey.

When Pierre Franey and I devised a menu that we would command if we were allowed one last meal on this earth it included fine fat squab stuffed with truffles and foie gras. The meal would start with fresh caviar, proceed to striped bass with champagne sauce, the squab, braised endive, watercress and Boston lettuce salad, Brie and grapefruit sherbet. The wines would include a Romanee-Conti, 1959, and champagne, Dom Perignon, 1966.

That, too, is a matter of personal taste. My belief is in league with that of an old chef who stated years ago that "Les sauces les plus courtes sont les meilleurs," which is another way of saying that it is preferable to serve a modest amount of sauce than an excess. If the meat, fish, poultry and so on is of first quality and conscientiously cooked, a spoonful or so of sauce is sufficient.

The most appropriate way to answer the question of yields is to paraphrase a quote we read some years ago attributed to the late Alice B. Toklas. When she submitted the recipes for her cookbook she was queried by an editor for the yields of each recipe. "How can I foretell how hungry my guests will be when they sit down to dine?" Miss Toklas replied.

"Salt to taste" in recipes rather than a specific amount also seems to bother readers.

"You are often vague," a gentleman wrote, "unnecessarily vague I think, about the amount of salt to use. For instance, in your excellent recipe for roast chicken with rosemary, you say to sprinkle the chicken inside and out with salt and pepper 'to taste.'

"I know that I am being captious about the roast chicken recipe, since nothing fatal will happen if somebody uses more salt than you would use. But in your recipe for chicken liver pâté, it would be helpful to anyone who had never made a pâté if you told him that the only way to tell whether it is properly seasoned is to cook a bit of it and taste it. Some such advice is particularly important, since the seasoning is critical in a pâté.

"When I use one of your recipes that is vague on the salt question, I have learned to record the amount of salt I put in it and adjust that, if necessary, the next time around."

A good deal of thought has gone into this business of specifics where salt is concerned and somehow it has seemed saner to follow the track we have used over the years. In the first place, a tolerance for salt varies widely from individual to individual. One man's "lightly salted" can be another man's brine. I am also well aware that most medical authorities in this day and age advise a good deal of caution in the use of salt intake. A second point is that in my own kitchen we use kosher salt, if for no other reason than I like the feel of it.

Many people ask if we ever put a salt shaker on the table to permit guests to help themselves. The answer is yes. I feel no

16 Aout 1970

Menu

Tarte Pépin

Carrés d'agneau Persillés

Aubergines Farcies Niçoise

Fromage de Brie

Petits souffles des Peres

Chartreux

Jean Vergnes

Roland Pierre Castonguay

Claudine

J. Pepin

Gloria Pepin

Bordeaux Mission Haut Brion

1964

22

le 6 . 29 . 78

Jean Troisgros
(JEAN TROISGROS)

en vacances au
bord de la mer
chez mon ami Craig
avec un peu
de "nouvelle cuisine"

Audrey Levinson   Pierre Franey   Joseph J. Hyppis

Bill Aller Roberto Joann Donovan   [signature]
        Melissa Weston

slight if a guest wishes to add salt or pepper to the food off my stove.

There is one thing I cannot abide in that area, however. It is those people who, in Chinese restaurants, douse their food with soy sauce, frequently before they sample it.

And then there's the question of the proper time to add salt in cooking.

"A chemist friend," one reader wrote, "assures me that the taste of food that is salted during the cooking does not differ from that which is salted at the table. I have tested this and certainly cannot tell the difference. Thus, aside from pasta, I never salt anything but leave it to those at the table to do so to their own taste. I have been served over-salted food in many homes and even the finest restaurants. My question, therefore, is why do your recipes call for salt in the cooking, since each person's tolerance for salt is different?"

Quite honestly, we recommend the addition of salt to food as it cooks in the belief (empirical) that the salt flavor melds and blends better—gets to the heart of the matter—if the salt is added during the cooking process.

Another reader responded with the notion that "an equally important reason for adding salt when cooking is that it raises the boiling point of the cooking fluid, water or other. The higher temperature permits faster cooking, which preserves the flavor of fresh vegetables in particular."

It was the sort of column one writes when in the mood for trivia. It mentioned briefly that some people use their dishwashers for cooking fish that has been securely wrapped in aluminum foil.

It seems that numerous people take their trivia seriously. The mention of dishwasher cookery elicited a letter from a lawyer who informed us about how to defrost a turkey. The gentleman takes his frozen turkey, still encased in its tight plastic wrap, and runs it through the complete washer cycle. He then removes the wrapper and washes the turkey before roasting.

"I find," he observes, "that this method cuts one-third from the cooking time and the turkey is much more tender. In my estimation, quick defrosting helps perserve the taste of the food."

What many nonprofessional cooks do not seem to know is that most counter tops should not be used for cutting and slicing. After a period of a certain amount of use there are bound to be pockmarks. It is always preferable to have a smaller (but not too small) cutting slab placed on the counter tops for cutting and slicing. To our thinking, the slab should be portable so that it can be transferred from the counter top to the sink for easy washing.

We have experimented with a variety of cutting surfaces and heartily endorse the Joyce Chen plastic cutting slab, which has a wide distribution in the United States. The slab is a milk-white color and does not dull knives any more than wood does. It is made of solid polyethylene and, according to the package directions, it may be washed in either hot or cold water or in the dishwasher. Either a cleanser or bleach may be used to remove especially difficult stains. While the slab will withstand boiling water, it should be kept away from fire, hot pots and pans. We find the largest size the most practical.

Following this recommendation, we received this advice:

"Readers whose pocketbooks may not be able to withstand the $10- to $12.50-cost of the Joyce Chen models can obtain rectangular, or even circular, polyethylene slabs for only a dollar or two in plastic materials supply shops. Frequently, odd-shaped remnant pieces from custom cuttings are available for practically nothing if one is willing to give them a light sand-papering along the cut edges to eliminate roughness."

Chili, as we have long known, is dear to the hearts of our countrymen, north, south, east and west. The mail predictably swells when we write about chili, usually regarding whether it should be made with or without beans and/or tomatoes.

The following was a new one, however.

"I use chili in a marriage with tripe!" a gentleman wrote. "As you know, tripe needs another dominant food element to bring out the protein modesties of the tripe itself. Tripe marries well with many elements . . . and chili con carne, of sorts, is one of them. By that I mean: make bite-size streamers of tripe, cook (parboil a few minutes, wash in a weak vinegar solution or salted water), rinse, then slow-cook in beef or chicken broth and herbs, such as basil, oregano, dill, etc. Then add sautéed mushrooms, kidney beans, some sautéed chopped beef and a bit of thickening . . . and, voila!"

And another response: "You know what's sensational with chili? Cottage cheese!"

Over the years in writing recipes that call for cheese it has often been intimated that processed cheese may be good for setting traps for rodents but not for cooking. Not for adult cooks, anyway. Only a natural, aged cheese will do.

A reader recently sent us a copy of an amusing booklet prepared by Vrest Orton, president of the Vermont Country Store in Weston and Rockingham, Vermont. The booklet is titled "The Truth About Vermont Cheese" and the principal paragraph that catches the eye is as follows:

"Processed cheese is also made in Vermont. There are two things to be said about processed cheese, when compared to natural aged cheese. It is undoubtedly 100 percent clean. The other thing to be said is apocryphal, but nevertheless I can't resist telling the story: Processed cheese makers we are told hire little boys to run around to restaurants and hotels and grab the pieces of uneaten cheese from the plates and fetch them to the factory where they are ground up and *processed* into something that passes for cheese!

"Actually a third comment can be made: Processed cheese can be kept for months, even for years and it will never change. It won't ripen, age or get any better, and it can't get any worse."

We have only once, by choice, found an occasion to try "bacon" made of processed, textured vegetable protein foods, and let the moment slip by without recording our impressions. We were delighted to receive a communication from a highly lucid reader whose reaction so neatly dovetailed with our own that we offer it.

"As a chemist who has specialized in paints and plastics, I have a natural curiosity about what my fellow chemists are accomplishing in their own fields of specialization. Thus, I recently yielded to an impulse to try the textured vegetable protein product referred to as 'breakfast strips.' My first reaction was one of amusement as I observed how techniques which have long been used for 'marbleization' of plastics had, in this case, been cleverly applied to simulation of the familiar fat and lean structure of bacon strips. In this case, the 'fat' and 'lean' portions were the same material, differing only in color.

"I fried a few strips in cooking oil, as directed. The odor during cooking was somewhat reminiscent of the smoky aroma of frying bacon, but with an unmistakably synthetic musky undertone. Then came the tasting. The 'bacon' taste was not quite as realistic as the fruit flavor in a Life Saver; the texture suggested thin strips of compressed sawdust. Wholesome? The contents listed on the package label indicate the absence of any unwholesome ingredients. Nutritious? Undoubtedly. After all, soya protein is protein. But as an experience in eating, these strips are to bacon as Masonite is to solid walnut. Or as marbleized linoleum is to marble."

When I detailed what I consider the finest method for cooking fresh corn on the cob (drop the shucked corn into boiling water and cover; return the kettle to the boil and immediately remove from the heat; let stand for five to ten minutes), I added that if the corn stood longer it would toughen.

This prompted a letter from a reader that we print without further comment:

"I tried your method last evening, but after putting the lid back on the pot and letting it stand for ten minutes, I found that the lid had become sealed so tightly that it could not be removed. I tried in vain for more than two hours to remove the lid but to no avail. Today I put the pot back on the stove, reheated it until the lid was able to be removed. Much to my amazement, the corn appeared to be in very good condition and thoroughly edible. I, therefore, wish to take issue with your statement that the corn will toughen if left for more than ten minutes, since mine remained for over seventeen hours and still retained its freshness and flavor."

We have many times received suggestions from readers for their favorite method for preparing corn on the cob. Here are two variations on the same theme:

"Remove the exterior corn silk, lay the ears in their husks on the middle rack of the oven and turn on the oven to the highest temperature. When the smell of browned husks becomes noticeable, roll the ears over to the other side for the same amount of time, about five minutes each side. Remove ears from oven, hold each ear with a towel and shuck off the hot husk, which will be brittle and brown. The corn will have flavor from the husk and the texture of the kernels will be different from kernels cooked in water. The result is delectable."

"Roasting corn in its shuck really brings out its full flavor. The shuck gives the corn its own protection, and then becomes a handle for eating when peeled back. Then you roll the ear around in a stick of butter. It's the corniest corn taste— slightly toasted and so succulent the kernels seem to pop into your mouth. I usually eat at least four ears."

When instructions were published for making clarified butter, it was recommended that the butter be melted in a saucepan, measuring cup or whatever until a clear golden liquid appears on top with a milky substance on the bottom. The golden liquid, which is clarified butter, should be poured off and the milky substance discarded.

A reader recommended that it would be simpler to refrigerate the melted butter. In this fashion, he reasonably argues, the clarified butter solidifies and the milky substance can be poured off.

A long time ago we developed a theory that most people who truly care about what they eat fall into two groups, those who invariably save the tastiest tidbit for the very last bite; and those who gobble up the most flavorsome morsel of a dish at the moment of sitting down to dine.

Some time ago we read in a medical journal an amusing and enlightening explanation of such habits: "Guarding the most toothsome part of a meal for last could be an infantile expression of security; downing the best part first or eating excessively fast is a show of insecurity, the exhibition of a fear as to whether or not there will be a next meal."

We quite unequivocally belong to the group that saves the best to the end, working up slowly to that last exquisite swallow.

Pursuant to a column in which several ideas were offered for baking a moist meat loaf (the use of additional fat, a bit of additional liquid and so forth), numerous readers wrote to volunteer their favorite methods for producing a more juicy loaf. Among them:

—Knead some tomato sauce into the meat before baking. But care must be taken to avoid over-kneading or the texture of the meat will be lost.

—No matter what other ingredients I use, and these vary depending on what is on hand, I always add a generous helping of applesauce to the mixture.

—Into the beef chuck I grate a bit of onion and a small apple plus a potato, which keeps the meat fluffy. Instead of bread crumbs I prefer a mashed wet slice of white bread and I also add a tablespoon of salad oil.

And this suggestion on hamburgers:

"I would like to suggest to you that hamburgers are much better, even tastier, served on crisped English muffins. The crevasses of the muffins hold the juices and the texture matches the texture of the meat perfectly."

I have an absolute idée fixe when it comes to serving hot food on hot plates. Not just warm plates. Hot plates. That is why the following from a reader went far to warm my heart's cockles.

"Since moving to the United States a few years ago," she wrote, "I have become aware that my preoccupation with serving hot food on hot plates and serving dishes is not generally shared. I probably inherited this bias from my Canadian mother, who virtually baked the plates before putting them on the table. The quality of the cooking was another matter, which is best to overlook, but everything sizzled. Platters of meat and vegetables were whisked back to the 'warming oven' to await a second round. Maids (who still existed in the remotest recesses of my childhood memories) rushed back and forth, scarcely avoiding scotched fingers, with layers of napkins folded between their hands and the plates. Now I find that my dinner guests seem baffled or amused, or simply think I've made a blunder when I warn them that the plates are hot. One young guest, helping me serve, actually suggested that I run cold water over the plates in order to make them easier to handle!

"Have I stumbled onto a sort of gastronomic amnesia on the part of people of otherwise impeccable taste, unlikely to patronize any restaurant that served them as they serve themselves at home? Personally, I find that there is no extra work involved in putting plates and serving dishes into the bottom of my oven as I prepare a meal. Admittedly, it is a double oven and the space under the broiling tray is just the right temperature to heat, without cracking good china.

"But my dishwasher also has a 'dry' cycle, which is perfect for heating plates, and, in a pinch, hot water can always be poured over them in the sink at the last minute."

This view was heartily endorsed by readers, one of whom wrote:

"If I may be permitted to brag a little, I've gone one step further. When my various plates, bowls and platters are going into the oven, my salad plates are going into the fridge, and you should hear the pleased responses that elicits!"

Illusion in food is important in dining. Farcical though it may sound, I know of a man who is both excellent hunter and excellent cook. He has what they used to call a fine, upstanding character.

Otherwise honest, he told me that he resorts to one bit of trickery when, out of season, he buys domestic game from a butcher. He tosses a birdshot or two into each serving. Makes the birds taste better, he maintains.

Of course, you could carry this to endless limits. Add a fresh pea pod to your frozen peas, add a seed of a lemon to your store-bought mayonnaise. But for heaven's sake, add a touch of fresh lemon juice, too!

We are in receipt of a highly instructive and amusing criticism of our wayward use of English language.

"Your direction for chopping onions is written in a way that causes me to think you have inadvertently confused an adverb with an adjective.

"The instruction I refer to is: 'Slice onions thinly.' This brings to my mind the picture of a very thin housewife, standing sideways so as to be even thinner, slicing her onions in a thin manner."

"I am also disturbed," she continues, "when you instruct the cook to chop the onions finely, as it brings to mind a person in formal dress, chopping with white gloves on, so as to be fine enough for your recipe."

We intend to steer clear of the fray, but we are pleased to reprint the rebuttal of another reader.

"Your critic is herself confused. I write in your defense as to the correct grammatical structure of your 'Slice onions thinly.' In your sentence 'slice' is a transitive verb followed by the direct object 'onions,' and the adverb 'thinly' describes the manner of slicing the onions. The same applies to 'Chop onions finely.'

"Had you said, 'Add finely-chopped onions' or 'thinly-sliced onions,' both phrases have adjective functions in relation to the noun 'onions.' With hyphen omitted, 'finely' and 'thinly' become adverbs modifying the respective adjectives 'sliced' or 'chopped.' "

And this from a constant correspondent on matters of language:

"In the matter of 'slice thin' versus 'slice thinly' I find myself unable to remain silently and keep coolly. In my opinion, the

Under umbrellas on a driftwood bench
Beside a sea that wore Parisian ruffles
We drank champagne, ate food divinely French
Viz: hamburgers -- with truffles.

With love for Craig —
Phyllis McGinley

word 'thin' is needed as an adjective describing the condition resulting from the action of slicing.

"However, the overcorrect folk who always get things wrong because they don't know when to stop will probably continue not only to slice their onions thinly, but also lay them flatly, fry them brownly, keep them warmly and serve them hotly. The rest of us will try to steer clearly of such grammatical constructions."

Visitors to France frequently complain that their main problem in dining comes with unfamiliarity with the French language. We have a beguiling letter giving us the details of a bilingual menu used in the local hotel dining room in the town of Foix. We offer it herewith for would-be menu translators:

Pâté de Sanglier . . . . pie of wild board
Salade de coeurs de palmiers . . . . salad of palm tree
Consommé chaud . . . . consummate hot
Jambon du Pays . . . . smocked ham
Aile d'oie confite au sang . . . . wing of goose with blood
Assortment de légumes . . . . match of vegetables
Fonds d'artichauts . . . . funds of artichokes

---

Which puts me in mind of another example of translation from English into French. Some years ago I wrote a review of a recently published book that dealt with French cookery. I found the approach pretentious, ill-informed and woefully unworthy of the subject and stated as much, ending the diatribe by asking rhetorically, "How do you say 'Good grief, Charlie Brown!' in French?" Someone in Montreal took me seriously. A few days later we received the following in the morning mail:

"Good grief, Charlie Brown," the note explained, "can be translated in several ways, depending on where you stand in France. For example:

Alsace: Ça par example, Charlie Brown!
Anjou: Le diable m'emporte, Charlie Brown!
Auvergne: Jarnicoton, Charlie Brown!
Bourgogne: Coquin de sort, Charlie Brown!
Bretagne: Sacré tonnere, Charlie Brown!
Champagne: Par Bacchus, Charlie Brown!

Gascogne: Jarnique, Charlie Brown!
Ile de France (Région Parisienne, surtout): Merde alors, Charlie Brown!
Languedoc: Saperlipopette, Charlie Brown!
Limousin: Ma grande, jurée foue, Charlie Brown!
Lorraine: Bon sang de bon sang, Charlie Brown!
Normandie: Nom de Dieppe, Charlie Brown!
Orléans: Petard de sort, Charlie Brown!
Picardie: Sacré nom d'une pipe, Charlie Brown!
Provence: Ma fe de Dieou, Charlie Brown!''

So the next time you dine in France, you will know how to swear at the waiter no matter what province you're in.

There we were, economy class and soaring 40,000 feet above sea level, en route to Belgium, when the flight attendant came to ask, "May we serve you a cocktail?"

"Yes," we answered, "scotch and vodka."

"Scotch and vodka?"

"Yes," we said. "The scotch we drink before the meal, the vodka we drink with the caviar."

"We're not serving caviar this trip," she advised us, muttering something like "Buster" under her breath. "At least not back here in economy country."

"That we know," we told her. "We brought our own."

We are becoming fairly authoritative in this matter of provisioning ourselves against burnt peas, over-cooked meat, soggy macaroni and salads with dressings specified as "creamy French" and prepared with—as the label testifies—water, salad oil, tomato paste, vinegar, sugar, flavor and seasoning salt, xanthian gum, polysorbate 60 and potassium sorbate.

Our tote bag contained, in addition to a quarter-pound of caviar, about six ounces each of thinly sliced smoked sturgeon, smoked salmon and herring. These we had ordered on the afternoon of our departure from our favorite purveyor of such things, Murray's Sturgeon Shop. The proprietor had the foresight and good taste to pack alongside these provisions one sliced onion, capers, sour cream, cream cheese and fresh bagels. We had provided our own lemons.

For the uninitiated, we can offer a few commentaries about tote-bagging aboard airlines:

Flight attendants are generally not amused at such proceedings. Fellow passengers aren't either. You are either regarded with hostility because you are going against the swim, or with jealousy for the most transparent reasons. Thus you will feast with more comfort if you board with your package labeled: "Gift. Do not open before boarding." Then, when the moment of opening arrives, unveil the salmon and say something like "Wouldn't you just know Aunt Mary would do something extravagant like this."

The flight attendant, after taking the drink orders, will probably give you two glasses containing ice for each drink that is served. Use one for the apéritif, scotch or whatever. Put the miniature bottle of vodka in the other glass with ice so that it will chill a bit before sipping it with the caviar.

Be considerate and super tidy. Don't burden the flight attendants with your random leftovers. Gather the items as compactly as possible so they may be easily disposed of.

One more word about things we take aboard airlines, particularly for midday flights. We loathe those canned Bloody Mary mixes. Thus, we travel with a small insulated bag containing Tabasco sauce, Worcestershire and a fresh lime. We order plain tomato juice over ice, a miniature bottle of vodka and concoct our own.

These comments about outwitting airline chefs elicited interesting responses from readers who described their own techniques.

A gentleman from Boston told us that when he last traveled out of Scranton, Pennsylvania, he ordered a take-out package from a "fine Chinese restaurant" at the Scranton airport.

"I was greeted," he said, "with looks of disbelief and laughter. One stewardess actually told me it was against the law to bring food on board. I, of course, disputed this and she was unable to prove that such a law existed. I never enjoyed a flight more than with spareribs over Springfield and wor shu opp over Poughkeepsie."

Our friend and neighbor, Bobby Short, wrote to tell us that he flew with a friend from London to Kennedy with a delicious meal from Harrods—salted walnuts, prawn sandwiches, chicken sandwiches, fresh caviar, a few lemons and those shortbread wafers called Sweet Alice. The friend brought from his own "cellar" two bottles of Roederer's Cristal champagne, both of which had been nicely chilled.

And an inventive reader says she never buys the miniature bottles of alcohol sold on airplanes. "Over the years I have collected empty miniatures. I fill several of them with scotch for me and gin or sherry for my husband. When the cart comes around, I simply order empty glasses with ice."

Numerous inquiries were received from readers asking if

this were legal. A Federal Aviation Regulation, part 121.575, states as follows: "No person may drink any alcoholic beverage aboard an aircraft unless the certificate holder operating the aircraft has served that beverage to him." Or her, one presumes.

And yet another wrinkle:

"The regulation does not prohibit your drinking your own booze on board," wrote one reader. "It simply says that the airline personnel must serve it to you. The decision is usually up to the chief flight attendant, with final authority lodged in the captain. If you fancy a wine or spirit not stocked by the airline, you can hand your bottle over to the attendant and ask to be served from it. I have seen such requests honored and refused, depending on the good humor or good sense of the flight crew."

We have noted before that we have become absolutely enamored of French breadmaking and would only buy a commercially produced loaf in cases of emergency. Not so with rye bread. We think the best rye bread we've ever eaten anywhere, out of our oven or elsewhere, is a frozen—repeat frozen—loaf made by Kasanof's Baking Co., Inc., 219 Blue Hill Avenue, Roxbury, Massachusetts. It is called Kasanof's Jewish Caraway Rye. It is sold frozen in many supermarkets as well as in some specialty markets and delicatessens on the East Coast, and it is outstanding. When baked, the crumb or inside of the bread is well-textured and moist, the flavor is superior and the crust is a triumph of the commercial breadmaker's art. Let us underscore the fact that Kasanof's also sells a standard, nonfrozen supermarket loaf and it is routine in all respects.

We were taken to task recently by a reader who scolded us curtly but roundly concerning a recipe for lamb curry. The recipe contained lamb cubes, ginger, yogurt, coriander and other ingredients but not a speck of curry powder. "Look," the lady implored us, "which ingredient is missing? Curry! How much? Shame."

We will point out as briefly as possible that curry powder is not the offshoot of a curry plant, curry bush or curry tree. It is an all-embracing English word for almost any stewlike Indian dish, flavored with a combination of two and more often than not several spices. Curry powder is simply a commercial pack-

St Sylvestre 1976

31 décembre de l'année

du Bicentenaire des

Etats-Unis d'Amérique

Menue

La Brandade de Morue

Les Boudins Arlequin

Les deux Pâtés du Chef

La galantine du petit Cochon de lait

Le Coulibiac de Saumon à la Russe

Le Cochon de lait rôti et farci

La Purée St-Germain

L'Oie de la Suède en Aspic

La Jambe de Cochon farcie à la Piémontaise

Les Fromages de France

La Mousse au Chocolat sir Giobbi

Le "Fruit Cake" façon Craig

Les vins

Blanc de Blancs de Duc 1973

Château de Lachaise 1944

Liqueurs

aged convenience item, a blend of numerous spices traditionally used in Indian recipes.

Roasted sweet peppers are one of the joys of an Italian antipasto.

Cooks of our acquaintance generally use three methods for roasting: over the gas flame, on a baking dish in a very hot oven, or under the broiler. Frankly, we prefer the latter. We line the bottom of the broiler with heavy-duty foil and place the peppers about two inches below a high broiler flame. The peppers are turned with the fingers or tongs as they start to char on one side or another. As soon as the peppers are slightly charred all over we drop them into a paper bag, which is then tightly sealed. The peppers, which create their own steam, are left to stand until cool. The skin is then easily pulled off with the fingers. The peppers are then cored, seeded and cut into strips before dressing with lots of chopped parsley, salt, pepper, lemon juice or wine vinegar and lots of olive oil.

We learned how to make blender butter years ago in the good company of Ann Seranne, the cookbook author and genius in the kitchen. Her formula is to combine one cup of heavy cream (not that new dreadful pasteurized stuff with the long shelf life) with half a cup of ice water. The water must be as cold as ice can make it. Cover and blend on high speed for one or two minutes. The older the cream the faster it turns into butter. Pour the mass into a sieve lined with cheesecloth and let it drain.

At the beginning of the shad season we printed a recipe for stuffed shad and the directions required removing the fish from the oven after baking and then to make a cream sauce with the pan drippings. The total time for preparing the sauce was fifteen or twenty minutes.

We had an inquiry from a reader to ask how on earth such a dish could be kept warm with a twenty minute time lapse.

The answer would apply to almost any dish to be served with a sauce. Remove the fish to a warm but not overly hot place and cover it fairly loosely with a sheet of aluminum foil. If covered too closely, the food tends to steam through retained heat and this is not desirable.

As the dish stands, the plates on which it is to be served

should be heated thoroughly. When the sauce is finished, it should be boiling hot. When the dish is served on very hot plates and the piping hot sauce spooned over, you will give the impression of serving a very hot main course.

One of the saddest cooking experiences I've ever been witness to occurred on the sun deck of a beach house a few doors down from my own home.

I had been invited one splendid summer day to indulge in the provençale-style feast known as an aioli, an elaborate combination of foods including cooked salt cod, chick-peas, hard-cooked eggs and various vegetables. The cornerstone of the feast is a kind of mayonnaise heavily spiked with raw garlic.

The lady of the house, a marvelous cook whose family came from Provence, had spent the better part of that Sunday making mayonnaise. Almost the entire morning. Not that the quantity of mayonnaise she was to serve was all that vast. She simply decided to make mayonnaise "like grandma used to make," which is to say with a wooden spoon. No fancy modern devices, thank you. No wire whisk, no electric beater, nothing that smacks of a gadget.

Grandma made her mayonnaise with a wooden spoon and what's good enough for grandma in Provence is certainly good enough for the Eastern Shore of Long Island.

Well, when you make mayonnaise with a wooden spoon, you add an egg yolk or yolks to a wooden bowl along with seasonings like salt and pepper and mustard and a little vinegar and then you start stirring with that wooden spoon while gradually adding a good grade of olive oil, preferably from Provence. And you stir. And stir. And stir. And stir.

"And always stirring in the same direction," she cautioned. "Grandma said so."

With any kind of luck the mayonnaise starts to thicken and you're home safe.

Well, madame stirred and stirred and stirred and eventually the sauce started to thicken and come about before she got what might be called mayonnaise elbow.

But she had this enormous German shepherd, a huge animal that answered to the name of Graf. And Graf was, as German shepherds tend to be, hungry, so he jumped up on the rail and dived into that bowl and with two enthusiastic licks that vessel was so clean you'd think the party was over.

I knew of no logical reason for stirring a sauce, cake or whatever always in the same direction. But a reader informed us that the idea is solidly based on a long-held superstition.

"It was thought an insult to the sun (and thus unlucky) to do anything against the direction of the sun," she wrote. "To bring luck to any movement, including stirring cake batter, it had to be done with the sun—the direction we now call clockwise."

Another reader wrote to state that she always skimmed the surface of her soups as they simmered because she had always been taught to do so by her mother.

I am curious, she wrote, as to whether in this case some of the nutrients of the soup are now removed.

"I have been cooking for forty years and have only just begun to question my mother's directions."

We were intrigued by the letter for more reasons than one, for the inquiry brought to mind other voices, to borrow a phrase from Truman Capote.

Quite directly, my answer is as follows:

The scum or film that forms on the surface of soups as they cook are frequently referred to as "impurities" or "foreign matter," while the truth is that this scum is, except under what might be considered highly peculiar circumstances, not in the least injurious. The scum is removed purely and simply for cosmetic reasons. The soup simply looks more palatable and, therefore, more appetizing. Also, when skimming off the scum, you remove a good deal of unwanted fat.

This brought to mind the distinct memory of a lecture given by a professor of mine at a hotel school in Switzerland.

He observed that a perfectly conceived consommé would be crystal clear in body and surface. This clarity would be achieved, he noted, by taking your long simmered rich broth, skimming the surface with patience, then blending the broth with raw meat and egg white. This would be brought slowly to the boil and the whole would be strained through muslin.

"On the other hand," he advised, "many customers may look askance at this jewel of a consommé, for they will recall with affection mother's beef or chicken broth, which always had a little fat floating on top."

In that case, he said, if the customer sends back his consommé, add a small dash of any neutral-flavored oil (such as peanut, vegetable or corn oil) and send it back piping hot. He will be mollified."

More on doing as mother (or grandmother) did. One reader told me the story of a lady in her hometown who faced the dilemma of having a whole ham and not having a saw. She had never cooked a ham before, but she distinctly recalled that her mother always sawed off the end of a ham before cooking.

She got on the phone and asked her mother why she always sawed off the ends of her hams before baking. "I did that," her mother explained, "because my mother did it. I never wondered why."

The mother then telephoned her mother and asked her why she always sawed off the ends of her hams. "I simply never had a roasting pan large enough to hold a whole ham," the grandmother answered.

A fascinating letter arrived from a woman who is both a chemist and enjoys cooking. She explained how she goes about using fats in her own kitchen "with a hierarchical system.

"If fat has been used for french fries, it can be re-used for anything. If for fish, nothing but fish. If it is used for onion rings, it can be used again either for fish or fondue (bourguignonne).

"I always strain the hot used oil," she continued, "through filter paper to remove the brown particles because they burn on reheating. A good paper towel will serve if you have no lab supplies on hand. It's a boring job, but I can and do keep 'old' oil around for months (if it has only been used for french fries) by cleaning it up and keeping it in the refrigerator in a tightly closed jar."

The chemist added that when foods are cooked in oil, the oil extracts color from foods. Thus, when new batches of food are cooked in "old" oil, it is this color that is imparted to the new batch.

In early youth, the messages on the backs of cereal boxes are part of the culture and literature of childhood. Having outgrown that age a few years back, we can't recall giving serious thought to package drollery except to note what chemicals the manufacturer now uses to flavor and preserve.

Recently, however, our attention was arrested by the side panel on a package of Agnesi spaghetti, which is, along with De Cecco, one of the finest brands of imported pasta available in this country.

Jean-Claude
Lise Keller
(Canada)
9.18.66
Que ce "Pepin" au passé mémorable
Soit de votre Bonheur le protecteur durable,
Et nous vous souhaitons qu'un avenir prochain,
Soit pour vous synonymes de bien nombreux "Pepins"!

"Merci"

Mr. & Mrs. Petter Stone

Déjeuner de Mariage du Sieur
Jacques Pépin et de la Demoiselle
Gloria Aubira.
"Aux Sources" le 18 Septembre 1766

With all my love for
a happy life
Harry △

Salade de "bars" rayé mimosa
Fricassée de Volaille Vieille France
Côte de boeuf braisée au Chambertin
Le Riz Mandrake
Jambon de Campagne au porto
Sauce Belle-Aurore
Salade de courgettes et tomates
Jardinière de Légumes Porte-Maillot
Plateau de Fromages Français

Margo Plattner

Gâteau de Mariage "Venus-Armée"
Petits fours Glacé

A wonderful day
a wonderful party
a truly wonderful couple
Love Louis

Bolinger brut

Julie Augier
Eleanor Hempstead
Claudia Franey
Marjorie and Howard Johnson
Judge and Mrs William H Stafford
Jeannette E Rattray

Karl Plattner

The notation that caught our eye was instructions for "A New Method for Cooking Spaghetti." The instructions are as follows:

Bring five quarts of water to the boil in a large kettle and add salt to taste. This will be sufficient for one pound of spaghetti. Add the spaghetti and stir well until strands of spaghetti float free. When the water returns to the boil, cook the spaghetti two minutes and immediately remove the kettle from the heat. Cover with a clean cloth and then add the lid. Let the spaghetti stand approximately nine minutes. Do not uncover the kettle during this period. Drain the spaghetti and serve with a sauce.

Recently we tried this method while preparing spaghetti marinara, and the reactions of those who dined on the dish were generally favorable. The spaghetti was left to stand exactly nine minutes after the pot was covered. To one guest the spaghetti seemed a trifle overcooked, not al dente enough.

Of course, it is logical to ask what the advantages of using such a method would be. For a professional Italian chef or an experienced spaghetti cooker there are probably no advantages. To many home cooks, however, those who find the cooking of spaghetti tedious and tricky, it is a great simplification. By using the method it is not necessary to lift slippery strands of the pasta from the boiling water to test for doneness.

Should you consider using this method, you should adjust the standing time of the spaghetti according to your own taste. If left to stand eight minutes instead of nine, you will come out with firmer strands. Accordingly, the package notes that if cooking a pasta that is thicker than spaghetti, it should be boiled for three minutes instead of two.

A note with enclosure is now before us from a reader who sent along the label from a package of noodles from the California firm, the Reis Noodle Company. The "preparation directions" are as follows:

1. Bring six cups of water, one teaspoon of salt, one tablespoon of butter or margarine to a boil.

2. Add package of Clever Mrs. Reis noodles, stir, cover and remove from heat.

3. Let Kindly Mrs. Reis noodles stand three minutes, drain, butter and serve.

The instructions add: Use six ounces of Finicky Mrs. Reis noodles to eight ounces of old ordinary noodles.

II. Appetizers

Brie and Roquefort Cheese Loaf

1. Trim off and discard the "crust" of the Brie. Cut both the Brie and Roquefort into 1-inch cubes and put the pieces into the container of a food processor.

2. Blend until smooth. Remove the cheese and refrigerate until it is manageable. Shape it into a round or oval loaf.

3. Spread out a length of wax paper and sprinkle the nuts in the center. Roll the cheese loaf in them until the loaf is coated all over. Roll the loaf in plastic wrap and refrigerate. Let soften slightly before serving.

Yield: 20 or more servings.

½ pound Brie at room temperature
½ pound Roquefort cheese at room temperature
¾ cup coarsely ground walnuts or pecans

Fondue Bruxelloise *(A deep-fried cheese appetizer)*

1. Grate the cheese and set it aside. Butter a square or rectangular dish (a 12- x 7½- x 2-inch dish is suitable) and set it aside.

2. Melt the 4 tablespoons butter in a saucepan and add the flour, stirring with a wire whisk. When blended, add the milk, stirring rapidly with the whisk. When blended and smooth, add the cream, nutmeg, cayenne, salt and pepper.

3. Remove the sauce from the heat and add the egg yolks, stirring rapidly with the whisk. Return to the heat and stir vigorously with the whisk, letting the sauce just come to the boil. Remove from the heat and let cool for a minute or so. Add the cheese, stirring until it melts.

4. Spoon and scrape the mixture into the prepared dish and smooth it over with a plastic spatula. Cover closely with a buttered rectangle of wax paper. Refrigerate, preferably overnight.

5. When ready to cook, use a knife to cut the cheese mixture into triangles measuring 2½ to 3 inches to the side. Separate the triangles. Beat the egg with the water, salt and pepper. Dip the triangles, first in flour, then in the egg mixture, then in bread crumbs. Continue until all the triangles are breaded.

¼ pound cheese, preferably Gruyère, or Swiss cheese may be used
4 tablespoons butter, plus butter for greasing the pan
4 tablespoons flour
1½ cups milk
½ cup heavy cream
⅛ teaspoon grated nutmeg
Dash of cayenne pepper
Salt and freshly ground pepper to taste
3 egg yolks
1 egg
3 tablespoons water
Flour for dredging
1½ cups fine fresh bread crumbs
Peanut, vegetable or corn oil for deep frying
Fried parsley for garnish (see recipe below)

6. Heat the oil and add the triangles, a few at a time. Cook 2 or 3 minutes, or until golden and cooked throughout. Drain. Serve hot, garnished with fried parsley.

Yield: 6 to 8 servings.

Fried parsley

6 cups loosely packed parsley
Oil for deep frying
Salt

1. If the parsley has any trace of sand or soil, it should be washed. To do this, rinse in several changes of cold water and shake off the excess moisture, using a salad basket. Pat dry with a clean cloth or paper toweling.

2. Heat the oil and fry the parsley, a handful at a time, using a slotted spoon to see that the parsley cooks evenly in the oil. When done, it will be dark green, or greenish black, and crisp. Drain on absorbent toweling. Sprinkle with salt before serving.

Yield: 6 to 8 servings.

Cheese Crusts Fribourgeoise

2 teaspoons butter
1 tablespoon flour
½ cup milk
Salt and freshly ground pepper
1 egg, lightly beaten
½ pound grated Gruyère cheese, about 2½ cups
¼ teaspoon grated nutmeg
Pinch of cayenne pepper
2 tablespoons dry white wine
¾ teaspoon finely chopped garlic
12 slices French bread cut on the bias

1. Melt the butter in a small saucepan and stir in the flour, using a wire whisk. Add the milk, stirring rapidly with the whisk. Add salt and pepper to taste and let cool.

2. Preheat the oven to 400 degrees.

3. Spoon the white sauce into a mixing bowl and add the egg, cheese, nutmeg, cayenne, wine and garlic. Blend well with a fork.

4. Toast the bread lightly on both sides and spoon equal amounts of the cheese mixture on one side. Smooth it over. Place the toast on a baking sheet and bake for 10 minutes.

Yield: 4 to 6 servings.

Crostini La Pace

¼ cup olive oil
¼ cup finely chopped onion
¼ cup coarsely chopped celery
¼ cup coarsely chopped carrot
¼ pound round of beef, cut into ½-inch cubes
¼ pound lean pork, cut into ½-inch cubes
Salt and freshly ground pepper

1. Heat ¼ cup of oil in a saucepan and add the onion, celery and carrot. Cook, stirring frequently, for about 10 minutes until the onion is golden brown.

2. Add the beef, pork, salt and pepper to taste, and continue cooking for about 15 minutes, stirring frequently.

3. Sprinkle with white wine and nutmeg and cook until wine is reduced, about 10 minutes, stirring frequently.

4. Add the chicken livers and cook, stirring occasionally, for 15 minutes.

5. Add the capers and anchovies and cook for about 10 minutes longer. Stir and add the Cognac and sherry.

6. Remove the saucepan from the heat and add the butter. Stir over very low heat, gradually adding about ¼ cup of broth. Add salt and pepper to taste. Spoon the mixture into the container of a food processor or electric blender and blend until smooth.

7. Preheat the oven to 400 degrees.

8. Arrange the slices of bread on a baking sheet and sprinkle or brush each slice with a little olive oil. Bake for 10 to 15 minutes, or until crusty.

9. Brush each slice with a little of the remaining beef broth and spread each slice with the paste.

Yield: 8 to 12 servings.

¼ cup dry white wine
¼ teaspoon nutmeg
½ pound chicken livers, cut into ½-inch cubes
3 tablespoons drained capers
3 flat anchovies, drained
2 teaspoons Cognac
2 teaspoons dry sherry
2 tablespoons butter at room temperature
½ cup hot beef broth
1 loaf French bread cut into ½-inch thick slices
Olive oil

Bagna Caôda *(Anchovy and garlic sauce for cold vegetables)*

The Italian bagna caôda is one of the most savory, delectable and unlikely appetizers. It is a sort of fondue (in the original and proper sense of the word, meaning melted) containing anchovies that melt in a bath of olive oil and butter and in keen liaison with twenty thinly sliced garlic cloves. Twenty is, of course, an arbitrary number. Frequently there are more.

1. Combine the oil, butter, anchovies and garlic in a saucepan. Cook over very low heat for about 1 hour. The sauce must barely simmer as it cooks.

2. Slice the truffle thinly, if used, and add it to the saucepan. Add the cream and simmer about 5 minutes longer. Serve with assorted vegetables cut into bite-size cubes and lengths.

Yield: 4 servings.

1 cup olive oil
½ cup butter
2 2-ounce cans anchovy fillets
20 cloves garlic, peeled and thinly sliced (about ½ cup)
1 small white truffle, available in Italian specialty food stores, optional
¼ cup heavy cream
Assorted raw vegetables

Taramosalata *(A carp roe spread)*

1. Place the English muffin in a small bowl and add water to cover. Let stand until thoroughly saturated with water; then squeeze the muffin to extract most of the excess moisture. Put the squeezed muffin in the container of a food processor or electric blender.

2. Add the tarama, garlic, lemon juice, olive oil and water and blend to a mayonnaise-type consistency. Spoon the taramosalata into a bowl and fold in the scallion.

Yield: 20 or more servings.

1 English muffin, preferably onion-flavored
10 tablespoons tarama, available in specialty food shops
1 clove garlic, finely minced
5 tablespoons lemon juice, more or less to taste
⅔ cup olive oil
2 tablespoons water
½ cup chopped scallions

Melitzanosalata *(Eggplant and sesame spread)*

2 eggplant, about 1 pound each
½ cup sesame seed paste (not sesame oil), available in specialty food shops
6 tablespoons lemon juice
½ cup olive oil
⅓ cup water
3 cloves garlic, finely minced
Salt and freshly ground pepper to taste
¾ teaspoon crushed dried oregano
½ cup chopped scallions
1 cup peeled, seeded, cubed tomato
¼ cup finely chopped parsley

1. Place the unpeeled eggplant over a gas flame, turning them as they cook and adjusting the flame as necessary. Cook until the eggplant are somewhat charred. The skin will no doubt burst during the cooking. When ready, the eggplant should be cooked through the center. Or, prick the eggplant in several places and place on a baking dish in an oven preheated to about 375 degrees, for about 1 hour. Let the eggplant stand until they are cool enough to handle.

2. Peel the eggplant and put the inner pulp in a mixing bowl.

3. Put the sesame seed paste, lemon juice, olive oil, water and garlic in the container of a food processor or electric blender and blend until a white paste is obtained. Add the eggplant pulp, salt, pepper and oregano and blend until smooth. Spoon the mixture into a bowl and, just before serving, fold in the remaining ingredients. Serve with Middle Eastern bread.

Yield: 20 or more servings.

Hummus bi Tahini *(Chick-pea spread)*

½ cup sesame seed paste (not sesame oil), available in specialty food shops
⅓ cup water
¼ cup olive oil
6 tablespoons lemon juice
4 cloves garlic, peeled
3½ cups (two cans) well-drained chick-peas, or garbanzos
½ teaspoon ground cumin
1 teaspoon ground coriander seeds
5 scallions, trimmed and chopped
Salt and freshly ground pepper to taste

1. Combine the sesame seed paste, water, oil, lemon juice and garlic in the container of a food processor or electric blender. Blend until smooth and light colored.

2. Add the chick-peas, cumin and coriander. Blend to a purée. Fold in the scallions and add salt and pepper to taste. Serve with Middle Eastern bread.

Yield: 20 or more servings.

Tabbouleh *(A Lebanese appetizer)*

1. Cover the bulgur with cold water and allow to stand 1 hour. Drain and squeeze out the extra water.

2. Add the remaining ingredients except the tomatoes and mix well with the hands. Pile into a dish and garnish with the tomatoes.

Yield: 6 servings.

1	cup fine (No. 1) bulgur wheat
¾	cup finely chopped onion
½	cup finely chopped scallions, green part and all
1	teaspoon salt
¼	teaspoon freshly ground pepper
1½	cups finely chopped Italian parsley
½	cup finely chopped fresh mint leaves
½	cup lemon juice
¾	cup olive oil
2	tomatoes, skinned and cut into wedges, or chopped

Guacamole

1. Cut the avocado in half and peel it. Discard the pit. Scoop the pulp into a mixing bowl and add the lime juice.

2. Put the tomato cubes in a small bowl and add salt to taste. Toss and refrigerate until ready to use.

3. Put ½ the minced onion, the chilies and ½ the coriander into a mortar and grind to a paste. Or do this in a food processor.

4. Using a knife and fork, cut the avocado flesh back and forth until smooth but coarse. The texture must not be too smooth. Add the onion mixture and salt to taste. Blend.

5. When ready to serve, add the remaining chopped onion and coriander. Drain the tomato and add it. Mix well.

Yield: 4 to 6 servings.

1	large ripe avocado
	Juice of ½ lime
¾	cup red, ripe tomato, seeded and cut into small cubes
	Salt
½	cup finely minced onion
1 or	2 fresh or canned serrano chilies, trimmed at the ends
¼	cup finely chopped fresh coriander leaves

Tapenade

1 2-ounce can anchovies, undrained
3 tablespoons drained capers
  Juice of 1 lemon
1 tablespoon imported mustard, such as Dijon or Düsseldorf
3 dried figs, stems removed
¾ to 1 cup olive oil
2 tablespoons cold water
¼ cup finely chopped, stoned black olives, preferably Greek or Italian olives packed in brine

1. Empty the anchovies and the oil in which they were packed into the container of a food processor or electric blender.

2. Add the capers, lemon juice, mustard and figs and start blending. Gradually add the olive oil while blending. Add ¾ cup and, if desired, continue adding more oil. The tapenade should have the consistency of a thin mayonnaise. Add the cold water. Serve in a bowl, sprinkled with chopped olives, as a dip.

Yield: About 1½ cups.

Eggs in tapenade

1½ cups tapenade (see recipe above)
8 to 10 hard-cooked eggs
8 to 10 capers
  Parsley for garnish

Spoon the tapenade over the bottom of a serving dish. Cut the eggs in half and arrange them cut side down. Garnish with capers and parsley sprigs.

Yield: 8 or more servings.

Ham-stuffed Eggs

There is an argument to the effect that the most interesting dishes to work with in any cuisine are those whose character can be changed at will. One of the great foods for summer feasting—cold stuffed eggs—fits that definition precisely. The fillings are virtually without end. Cold cubed chicken, ham, turkey, veal and poached fish can be used, garnished with anchovies, olives, pimientos and other kindred edibles. The sweet herbs are virtuous: parsley, chives, tarragon, chervil, even rosemary. The egg yolks, sieved or blended, are generally bound with mayonnaise and/or butter. Add a bit of salt and pepper and your creativity can take it from there.

4 hard-cooked eggs (see instructions below)
1 ounce boiled ham
1 tablespoon imported mustard, such as Dijon or Düsseldorf

1. Split the eggs in half. Put the yolks in a sieve and press through with the fingers.

2. Cut the ham into very fine dice and chop it. Combine the sieved yolks and ham in a mixing bowl. Add the mustard and butter. Stir to blend.

3. Add the remaining ingredients except the cutouts and blend thoroughly. Equip a pastry bag with a star tube (No. 4). Fill the bag with the ham mixture and pipe it into the egg hollows. Garnish the top of each egg with a small slice of black or green olive or other cutout.

Yield: 8 stuffed egg halves.

2 tablespoons butter at room temperature
¼ teaspoon Worcestershire sauce
2 teaspoons mayonnaise
Salt and freshly ground pepper
1 tablespoon finely chopped chives
Cutouts of black or green olives, pimientos, pickles and so on

---

Place any given number of eggs in a saucepan and add warm water to cover. Add a little salt, if desired, to facilitate later peeling. Bring slowly to the boil and simmer for about 12 minutes. Cool immediately under cold running water. Drain and peel.

Hard-cooked eggs

Sardine-stuffed Eggs

1. Split the eggs in half. Put the yolks in a sieve and press through with the fingers.

2. Drain the sardines and put them in a bowl. Press with the back of a fork until smooth. Add the vinegar, mayonnaise, butter, parsley, salt and pepper to taste and sieved egg yolks and blend.

3. Equip a pastry bag with a star tube (No. 4). Fill the bag with the sardine mixture and pipe it into the egg hollows. Garnish the top of each stuffed egg half with a small slice of black or green olive or other cutout.

Yield: 8 stuffed egg halves.

4 hard-cooked eggs (see instructions above)
1 3¾-ounce can skinless and boneless sardines
2 teaspoons cider vinegar
1 tablespoon mayonnaise
2 tablespoons butter at room temperature
1 tablespoon finely chopped parsley or dill or a combination of both
Salt and freshly ground pepper
Cutouts of black or green olives, pimientos, pickles and so on

Curried Stuffed Eggs

4 hard-cooked eggs (see instructions above)
2 teaspoons butter
1 tablespoon finely chopped onion
1 teaspoon curry powder
¼ cup heavy cream
3 tablespoons butter at room temperature
Salt and freshly ground pepper
8 small cutouts of solid fruit from chutney

1. Split the eggs in half. Put the yolks in a sieve and press through with the fingers.
2. Heat the butter in a small skillet and add the onion. Cook until wilted. Add the curry powder and cook briefly, stirring. Add the cream, stirring, and bring just to the boil. Remove from the heat and let cool.
3. Add the butter and curry mixture to the egg yolks. Add salt and pepper to taste. Blend thoroughly.
4. Equip a pastry bag with a star tube (No. 4). Fill the bag with curried mixture and pipe it into the egg hollows. Garnish the top of each stuffed egg with a small cutout of chutney.
Yield: 8 stuffed egg halves.

Salmon and Dill Stuffed Eggs

4 hard-cooked eggs (see instructions above)
1 to 3 slices smoked salmon
1½ ounces (half a small package) cream cheese
1 tablespoon finely minced onion
1 tablespoon finely chopped dill
Salt and freshly ground pepper
Small dill sprigs for garnish

1. Split the eggs in half. Put the yolks in a sieve and press through with the fingers.
2. Chop the salmon not quite to a paste. There should be about 3 tablespoons. Add to the sieved egg yolks. Add the cream cheese, onion, chopped dill, salt and pepper to taste. Blend well.
3. Equip a pastry bag with a star tube (No. 4). Fill the bag with the salmon mixture and pipe it into the egg hollows. Garnish the top of each stuffed egg half with a small dill sprig.
Yield: 8 stuffed egg halves.

Spanakopetes *(Spinach in phyllo pastry triangles)*

1 pound fresh spinach in bulk, or 1 10-ounce package
1½ tablespoons olive oil
2 tablespoons butter
2 cups chopped onion
1 teaspoon finely chopped garlic

1. Preheat the oven to 350 degrees.
2. If spinach in bulk is used, pull off and discard any tough stems and blemished leaves. Wash and drain well. If packaged spinach is used, rinse once and drain. Chop the spinach coarsely. Heat the oil in a skillet and add the spinach. Cook until wilted. Drain well.

3. Add the butter to the skillet and cook the onion, garlic and scallions until wilted, stirring often. When the mixture starts to brown, transfer it to a mixing bowl. Add the spinach, feta cheese, Parmesan, dill and parsley to the onion mixture. Beat the egg and yolk together lightly and add to the spinach mixture. Add very little salt. Add pepper to taste. Stir in the pine nuts, if desired.

4. Use one sheet of phyllo pastry for each two spinach triangles. Brush a marble or Formica surface with butter. Spread out one square of phyllo and, using a sharp knife, cut it lengthwise in half. Set one rectangle aside and keep it covered with a damp cloth. Keep all the sheets of phyllo covered when not using them or they will dry rapidly.

5. Brush one rectangle generously with melted butter. Fold half of the rectangle over to make a smaller rectangle. Add 2 tablespoons of the spinach mixture to the bottom of the rectangle. Fold one corner of the rectangle over the spinach filling in a triangle. Fold this filled triangle over itself toward the top. Continue folding up until a complete, self-contained triangle is produced. Brush this all over with butter and set aside. Continue making triangles until all the spinach filling is used.

6. Arrange the triangles on a baking sheet and bake about 20 minutes, or until puffed and golden brown.

Yield: 16 spinach triangles.

1	cup chopped scallions
1	cup crumbled or chopped feta cheese, about ¼ pound
¼	cup grated Parmesan cheese
¼	cup finely chopped fresh dill
⅓	cup finely chopped parsley
1	egg
1	egg yolk
	Salt and freshly ground pepper to taste
¼	cup pine nuts, optional
8	sheets phyllo pastry
¼	cup butter, melted

Meat-filled Phyllo Rolls

1. Heat the butter in a small skillet and add the onion and water. Cook, stirring often, until the liquid evaporates.

2. Add the meat and stir to break up the lumps that may form. Cook until meat is light brown, stirring often. Add the wine and cook until it comes to the boil. Add the tomato paste, salt and pepper to taste. Cover and cook slowly for about 15 minutes. Uncover and remove from heat. Let cool slightly. Add the Parmesan and beaten egg and blend well. Let cool.

3. Roll the 6 pastry sheets over themselves into a long, neat sausage-shaped bundle. Cut the bundle crosswise into 4 pieces of equal width (approximately 4 inches wide). Remember as you work with one strip of dough to keep the others covered with a damp cloth so that they won't dry out. Unroll one piece and keep the remainder covered. Spread out this strip on a flat surface.

1	tablespoon butter
½	cup finely chopped onion
1	tablespoon water
½	pound ground round steak
2	tablespoons dry white wine
6	tablespoons tomato paste
	Salt and freshly ground pepper
1	tablespoon Parmesan cheese
1	small egg, beaten
6	sheets phyllo pastry
4 to 6	tablespoons melted butter

4. Brush the strip with butter. Spoon about 2 teaspoons of meat filling toward one end of the strip. Start rolling the strip from that end. Roll the strip over itself to enclose the meat filling. Fold the two outer edges partly toward the center. Continue to roll the strip until all of it is used. Continue until all the strips and filling are used. As the rolls are made, arrange them on a baking sheet.

5. Meanwhile, preheat the oven to 350 degrees.

6. Before baking, brush the tops of each roll with butter. Place the baking sheet in the oven and bake for 15 to 20 minutes, or until golden brown.

Yield: About 24 pieces.

Bourekakia *(Cheese puffs)*

½	pound feta cheese, crumbled
1	3-ounce package cream cheese
1	tablespoon cream or rich milk
2	egg yolks
	Dash of nutmeg
10	strips phyllo pastry
½	pound sweet butter, melted

1. Preheat the oven to 350 degrees.

2. Combine the feta cheese, cream cheese, cream and egg yolks in a blender or whip until smooth in a bowl. Add nutmeg.

3. Remove the phyllo pastry from its wrapping and place between heavy plastic wrap to prevent the pastry from drying out.

4. Place one sheet of phyllo pastry on a flat surface and brush with melted butter and fold in half crosswise.

5. Cut folded pastry into 5 strips approximately 2 by 8 inches. Put ½ teaspoon of cheese mixture at one corner of each strip and fold to opposite side to form a triangle. Continue to fold each strip, keeping the triangle shape. Continue until all pastry sheets and cheese mixture are used. Brush triangles with melted butter. Place on cooky sheet and bake for 15 minutes, or until golden brown.

Yield: About 50 puffs.

Note: These cheese puffs can be made in advance and frozen before baking. Place in 350-degree oven while still frozen and bake for about 25 minutes.

Celeri Rémoulade *(Celery root with mustard mayonnaise)*

Knob celery, which also goes by the names celeriac and celery root, is not simply the base or root of stalk celery, the common variety of celery used in almost all American kitchens. It is another, separate vegetable, a root vegetable like turnips. It looks like a brownish globe and ranges in size from a goose egg to a cantaloupe. To use it, the brown outside skin must be pared away. When combined with mustard and mayonnaise, it makes a marvelous first course. It's also delicious combined with potatoes in puréed potatoes.

1. Peel the knob celery, trimming off all the dark spots. Slice the celery as thinly as possible using a food processor, hand slicer, mandolin or even a sharp knife. There should be about 3 cups.

2. Stack the slices and cut them into the finest julienne strips. Place in a mixing bowl and add the remaining ingredients. Toss with the hands until thoroughly blended.

Yield: 6 servings.

2 medium celery knobs, also known as celery root
1 tablespoon imported mustard, such as Dijon or Düsseldorf
1 tablespoon red wine vinegar
Salt and freshly ground pepper to taste
¾ cup freshly made mayonnaise

Breaded Mushrooms with Herbs

1. Rinse and drain the mushrooms. Dredge them in flour.

2. Blend the eggs, olive oil, salt and pepper to taste and water. Beat well. Blend the crumbs, oregano, marjoram, pepper flakes and thyme. Dip the mushrooms in the egg mixture, then in the crumbs. Dip a second time in egg and in crumbs.

3. Heat the oil to 360 degrees. Add the mushrooms and cook, stirring and turning with a slotted spoon, for 4 to 6 minutes, or until nicely browned all over. Drain well. Serve with anchovy mayonnaise and lemon wedges.

Yield: 6 servings.

1 pound mushrooms, the larger the better
½ cup flour
2 eggs
1 tablespoon olive oil
Salt and freshly ground pepper
¼ cup water
2 cups fresh bread crumbs
¼ teaspoon crushed oregano
¼ teaspoon crushed dried marjoram
¼ teaspoon crushed red pepper flakes
¼ teaspoon dried thyme
Peanut, vegetable or corn oil for deep frying
Anchovy mayonnaise (see recipe page 642)
Lemon wedges

Peppers and Anchovies Italian-style

1 pound green or red sweet (bell) peppers
3 tablespoons olive oil
1 2-ounce can flat anchovies
2 tablespoons drained capers
1 teaspoon oregano
  Salt and freshly ground pepper to taste
1 teaspoon finely chopped garlic
1 tablespoon red wine vinegar
1 tablespoon finely chopped parsley
  Lemon wedges

1. Core and seed the peppers and cut them lengthwise into ½-inch strips. There should be about 4 cups.

2. Heat the oil in a heavy skillet and add the peppers. Cook, stirring and shaking the skillet, for about 2 minutes.

3. Drain and chop the anchovies and add them to the peppers. Add the capers, oregano, salt, pepper and garlic. Cook, stirring and shaking the skillet, about 2 minutes. Sprinkle with wine vinegar and remove from the heat. Serve hot or cold sprinkled with parsley. Serve with lemon.

Yield: 6 to 8 servings.

Mozzarella Fresca con Pomodoro e Acciughe   *(Fresh mozzarella cheese with tomatoes and anchovies)*

¾ to 1 pound fresh mozzarella cheese
12 slices red, ripe tomatoes
36 flat anchovy fillets
6 teaspoons dried oregano, more or less to taste
4 to 6 tablespoons olive oil
  Freshly ground black pepper

Cut the mozzarella into 12 more or less equal slices and arrange them on a serving dish. Place 1 slice of tomato atop each. Garnish each serving with 3 flat anchovy fillets. Sprinkle each serving with equal amounts of oregano and olive oil. Add a few turns of the peppermill and serve at room temperature.

Yield: 6 to 12 servings.

Cherry Tomatoes with Sardine Mayonnaise

24 cherry tomatoes
  Salt
1 egg yolk
1 tablespoon wine vinegar
1 tablespoon imported mustard, such as Dijon or Düsseldorf
  Freshly ground pepper
  Tabasco sauce
1 cup peanut, vegetable or corn oil

1. Cut off a small round from the top of each tomato. Using a very small spoon, scoop out some of the inside. Salt each tomato and set aside.

2. Put the yolk in a bowl and add the vinegar, mustard, salt, pepper and Tabasco sauce to taste.

3. Beat with a wire whisk or an electric beater. Gradually add the oil, beating constantly. Continue beating until the mixture is thickened.

4. Chop the sardines and stir them in. Stir in the horseradish, if desired.

5. Fill the tomatoes with the sardine mayonnaise and garnish each with a parsley leaf. Leftover mayonnaise will keep for several days in the refrigerator.

Yield: 24 stuffed tomatoes.

2 to	4 sardines
1	tablespoon grated horseradish, optional
	Parsley leaves for garnish

Caponata   *(An Italian vegetable appetizer)*

1. Preheat the oven to 350 degrees.

2. Trim the ends of the zucchini. Split the zucchini lengthwise in half. Cut each half into 1-inch lengths.

3. Arrange the zucchini, onions, peppers and eggplant in one layer in a baking pan and place in the oven. Bake for 15 minutes to let part of the moisture in each vegetable evaporate.

4. Heat the oil in a large casserole and add all the vegetables including the tomatoes and potatoes. Sprinkle with the garlic, oregano, salt and pepper. Cook briefly and stir. Transfer to the oven. Do not cover. Bake for 40 minutes. Remove and cook over high heat until most of the liquid evaporates. Let cool. Refrigerate.

Yield: 8 or more servings.

4 to	6 small or medium zucchini
4	cups onions, cut into 1-inch cubes
4	cups sweet peppers, preferably a combination of green and red peppers, cored, seeded and cut into 1-inch cubes
1	medium eggplant, about ¾ pound, cut into 1-inch cubes
½	cup olive oil
4	cups tomatoes cored and cut into 1-inch cubes
2	cups potatoes peeled and cut into 1-inch cubes
2	cloves garlic, finely minced
2	teaspoons oregano
	Salt and freshly ground pepper to taste

Vegetable Loaf in Aspic with Watercress Cream Sauce

1. Prepare the vegetables for cooking and have them ready. Keep them in separate batches.

2. Split the celery ribs lengthwise into ½-inch strips.

3. Trim off and discard the tough bottoms from the asparagus. Scrape the sides of the asparagus, starting about 2 inches from the tip.

4. Cut the carrots lengthwise into ½-inch or slightly smaller strips.

5. Cut the turnip into approximately 16 pieces resembling french fried potatoes.

6. In a deep skillet, bring a large quantity of water to the boil. Add salt to taste. This will be used to cook each batch of vegetables, except the green peas, one batch at a time.

7. Cook the green beans for about 10 minutes, or until tender. Remove the beans and chill. Let the water continue to boil.

4	trimmed ribs of celery
⅓	pound fresh asparagus, 8 to 12 stalks
2	carrots, trimmed and scraped
1	medium-size white turnip, trimmed and peeled
½	pound tender young green beans, ends trimmed
	Salt to taste
¾	cup fresh or frozen green peas
	Quick tarragon aspic (see recipe below)
	Watercress cream sauce (see recipe page 648)

8. Similarly, cook the celery for 7 minutes; drain and chill. Cook the asparagus for 5 minutes; drain and chill. Cook the turnip for 5 minutes; drain and chill.

9. Using another saucepan, cook the peas briefly in boiling salted water until tender. Drain and chill.

10. Prepare the aspic in advance and let it cool. When ready to use, it should be at room temperature or slightly cooler but still liquid. If the aspic starts to set, it can be melted slowly over gentle heat.

11. Place a 9- x 5- x 2¾-inch pan in the refrigerator or freezer. When it is chilled, add a ¼-inch-thick layer of liquid aspic. Chill until the aspic sets.

12. Arrange neat rows of the prepared vegetables over the aspic, close to but not touching the ends or sides of the mold. Add another layer of aspic, just enough to barely cover the layer of vegetables. Chill until set. Add another layer of vegetables, another coating of aspic and chill. Continue until all the vegetables are used, ending with a coating of aspic. Cover with plastic wrap and chill overnight. Serve sliced with watercress sauce.

Yield: 8 to 10 servings.

Quick tarragon aspic

3 cups fresh or canned chicken broth
1 cup tomato juice
4 envelopes unflavored gelatin
  Salt and freshly ground pepper to taste
1 teaspoon sugar
2 eggshells, crushed
2 egg whites, lightly beaten
2 tablespoons Cognac
1 tablespoon finely chopped fresh tarragon, or 1 teaspoon dried

1. In a saucepan combine the chicken broth with the tomato juice, gelatin, salt, pepper, sugar, eggshells and egg whites and heat slowly, stirring constantly, until the mixture boils up in the pan.

2. Remove the pan from the heat and stir in the Cognac.

3. Strain the mixture through a sieve lined with a flannel cloth that has been rinsed in cold water and wrung out. Add the tarragon. If the aspic starts to set or becomes too firm, it may be reheated, then brought to any desired temperature.

Yield: About 1 quart.

Mock Head Cheese (*"Head" cheese made with pork knuckles*)

2½ pounds pork knuckles, 4 pieces
1½ pounds pigs' feet
12 cups water

1. Put the knuckles and pigs' feet in a small kettle and add water to cover. Bring to the boil and simmer about 1 minute. Drain well.

2. Return the knuckles and pigs' feet to a clean kettle and

add the 12 cups of water, carrots, celery, onion, allspice, bay leaf, salt, peppercorns, garlic and thyme.

3. Bring to the boil and simmer for 3 hours, skimming the surface as necessary. Remove from the heat and let cool.

4. Remove the knuckles and pigs' feet. Remove and reserve all meat and skin. There should be about 4 cups. Discard the bones. Strain the liquid. There should be about 3½ cups.

5. Combine the meat, skin and liquid. Cut the ham into ½-inch cubes and add it. Add the red pepper, vinegar, nutmeg and salt and bring to the boil. Cook down about ½ hour and remove from the heat. Stir in the chopped parsley.

6. Pour the mixture into a 9½- x 5¼- x 2-inch loaf pan and let stand until cool. Refrigerate overnight. Unmold and slice.

Yield: 8 to 12 servings.

2	small carrots
1	rib celery, quartered
1	onion stuck with 2 cloves
2	whole allspice
1	bay leaf
	Salt to taste
6	crushed peppercorns
2	cloves garlic, unpeeled but lightly flattened
2	sprigs fresh thyme, or ½ teaspoon dried
1	pound cooked ham steak
1	hot red pepper
2	tablespoons white wine vinegar
⅛	teaspoon ground nutmeg
¼	cup chopped parsley

Jambon Persillé *(Parsleyed ham)*

If parsley were as scarce as sturgeon eggs and as costly as truffles, it would conceivably be one of the world's most sought-after herbs. Happily, it is almost as abundant as meadow grass, as taken for granted in most kitchens throughout the world as salt and pepper. And without parsley sprigs, what would airline chefs resort to as they garnish those plastic trays?

Actually there are numerous dishes in which parsley plays a dominant part. Chief among these is the famed jambon persillé, a great specialty of Burgundy. This is, of course, a jellied, molded creation that, when sliced, presents a red and green mosaic pattern of ham with masses of parsley entrenched between the slices.

Traditionally, this dish is made with ham freshly cured in brine, but it is possible to make an excellent jambon persillé using canned ham and a few fresh pigs' knuckles.

1. Combine the pigs' knuckles in a large kettle with 8 cups water, salt and saltpeter. Let stand overnight in a cool place.

2. Drain. Add the remaining water and remaining ingredients except ham, 3 bunches parsley and vinegar. Simmer for 2 hours.

3. Remove the knuckles and set them aside.

8	fresh (not smoked) pigs' knuckles, about 4 pounds
12	cups water
1¼	cups kosher salt
½	teaspoon saltpeter, available in drugstores
2	cups dry white wine
2	cups fresh or canned chicken broth
1	cup coarsely chopped onion
5	cloves garlic, peeled but left whole
1	cup coarsely chopped white turnips
1	cup coarsely chopped carrots
1	cup leeks
2	whole cloves
1	bay leaf
6	peppercorns
20	sprigs parsley tied with string
1	3-pound canned ham
3	large bunches fresh parsley
2	tablespoons red wine vinegar

4. Strain the cooking liquid through a fine sieve. Pour it into a casserole. Skim off some of the surface fat.

5. Remove the ham from the can and scrape off the gelatin. Add the gelatin to the cooking liquid. Cut the ham into 4 lengthwise pieces of approximately the same size. Add them to the liquid. Return the knuckles to the casserole and continue cooking for about 30 minutes.

6. Remove the ham and knuckles with all the meat and bones. Cook the remaining liquid down to about 3 cups.

7. When the meats are cool enough to handle, remove all the meat, including the gelatinous skin, from the knuckles. Chop the gelatinous material into small pieces. Cut or chop the knuckle meat into slightly larger pieces. Combine the two and set aside.

8. Cut each ham piece into 4 long strips of approximately the same size. This will yield 16 strips. Set aside.

9. Cut off the tough stems of 3 large bunches of fresh parsley. Rinse well to remove all traces of sand. Squeeze in toweling to remove excess moisture. Chop the parsley finely. There should be about 2 cups.

10. Rub the bottom and sides of a 10-cup round bowl with liquid from the knuckles.

11. Sprinkle the bottom and sides of the bowl with 4 tablespoons of parsley. Arrange strips of ham close together but not quite touching over the bottom in one layer, trimming the ends as necessary to make them fit. Spoon 4 tablespoons of the chopped skin and knuckle meat over that. Sprinkle with 2 tablespoons of parsley.

12. Arrange another layer of ham strips, placing them close together as before. It is important that all the ham strips in each layer be aligned in the same direction. That way, when the completed dish is chilled and sliced, the slices will show a mosaic pattern. You might add a thin string trailing out over the mold and going in the same direction as the ham strips so you will know how to slice. Remove and discard the string, of course, before slicing.

13. Add 6 tablespoons of chopped skin and knuckle meat. Sprinkle with 2 tablespoons parsley. Continue making layers in this fashion until all the ham strips and chopped knuckle skin and meat are used, ending with the chopped skin and meat and a final generous layer of chopped parsley.

14. Spoon about 1 cup of the reduced cooking liquid over all. Sprinkle the vinegar over. Continue adding the cooking liquid gradually, taking care that it does not overflow. This will take several minutes because the liquid will flow below as

the ham mixture sits. You may be left with ½ cup or so of the liquid. Set this aside in a warm place.

15. Chill the parsleyed ham until almost set. Add one more layer of the liquid until the bowl almost but not quite overflows. Chill. When ready to serve, unmold and slice.

Yield: 20 or more servings.

Carpaccio   *(Sliced raw beef with shallot mayonnaise)*

1. Place each slice of meat, one at a time, between 2 sheets of plastic wrap and pound with a flat mallet or the bottom of a clean, heavy skillet, until the slices are approximately ⅛-inch thick. As the slices are prepared, arrange 2 on each of 6 chilled appetizer plates. Chill until ready to serve.

2. Wrap the chopped shallots in cheesecloth and run under cold water. Squeeze to extract most of the moisture. Add the shallots to the mayonnaise.

3. To serve, spread a little more than 1 tablespoon of the shallot mayonnaise over each slice. Garnish with lemon wedges. Serve a peppermill on the side.

Yield: 6 servings.

1½ pounds boneless shell steak, cut into 12 ¼-inch-thick slices
1 cup freshly made mayonnaise
2 tablespoons finely chopped shallots
12 seedless lemon wedges or lemon halves
Freshly ground pepper

Steak Tartare

1. The fresher the beef, the redder it will remain. After the meat is ground, it is best to serve it as expeditiously as possible. If the butcher grinds it, have him grind it twice. Or grind it at home using a meat grinder or a food processor. Take care not to overgrind the meat and make it mushy if a food processor is used.

2. Place 4 mounds of meat of equal weight in the center of 4 chilled plates. Make an indentation in the center of each mound and add 1 yolk. Or embed half a clean eggshell in the center of each mound and add the yolk to that.

3. Surround the meat with equal portions of onion, parsley, anchovy halves, capers, chopped chives and lemon half. Serve the Cognac, Worcestershire sauce, mustard and Tabasco sauce in bottles or separate containers on the side. All the quantities to be added to the meat are, of course, arbitrary and optional.

4. Blend the ingredients together as desired. Serve with buttered toast.

Yield: 4 servings.

1 pound top sirloin, or top round
4 egg yolks
½ cup finely chopped onion
4 teaspoons chopped parsley
6 flat anchovies, split in half lengthwise
¼ cup capers
8 teaspoons finely chopped chives
4 lemon halves
4 teaspoons Cognac
2 teaspoons Worcestershire sauce
4 teaspoons imported mustard, such as Dijon or Düsseldorf
Tabasco sauce to taste

Sautéed Brains

1	pair calf's brains, about 1 pound
12	peppercorns
	Salt
2	tablespoons wine vinegar
1	bay leaf
2	sprigs fresh thyme, or ½ teaspoon dried
	Freshly ground pepper
	Flour for dredging
3	tablespoons butter
3	tablespoons olive oil
3	tablespoons lemon juice
3	tablespoons water
1½	tablespoons finely chopped dill
2	tablespoons finely chopped parsley
½	teaspoon oregano
1	tablespoon capers

1. The calf's brain consists of a pair of lobes. Place them in a mixing bowl and add cold water to cover. Let them stand several hours, changing the cold water frequently.

2. Drain and pick over the brains to remove the outer membranes, blood and other extraneous matter. Place the brains in a saucepan and add cold water to about ½ inch above the brains. Add the peppercorns, salt to taste, vinegar, bay leaf and thyme. Bring to the boil and simmer for 3 minutes, no longer. Remove from the heat and drain. Run brains under cold water until chilled. They are now ready to cook when patted dry. If the brains are not to be cooked until later, leave them covered with cold water.

3. Season enough flour to coat the brains lightly with salt and pepper. Cut the brains into slices about ¼-inch thick. Dredge in flour. Heat the butter in a skillet and brown the slices on both sides. Add more butter if necessary. Transfer the brains to a serving dish.

4. Combine the olive oil, lemon juice, water, dill, parsley, oregano and capers in a saucepan and bring to the boil. Pour the sauce over the brains and serve lukewarm.

Yield: 6 or more servings.

Boiled Smoked Tongue with Sauce Piquante

1	3½-pound smoked beef tongue
	Sauce piquante (see recipe page 647)

1. Place the tongue in a kettle and add water to cover. Bring to the boil and simmer 40 minutes to the pound, for about 2 hours and 20 minutes, or until the tongue is thoroughly tender.

2. Drain the tongue and, using a two-pronged fork to hold it, skin the tongue and neatly trim the base with a sharp slicing knife. Cut the tongue against the grain to produce thin, neat, rectangular slices.

3. Serve hot with the hot sauce piquante spooned over the sliced tongue.

Yield: 8 or more servings.

Flajitas   *(Tex-Mex beef and tortillas)*

1. Prepare a very hot charcoal fire.
2. There should be about 12 individual steaks. Cut each of these in half. Blend the oil, garlic, vinegar, salt and pepper in a flat dish and add the meat, turning the slices to coat well.
3. Put about 4 slices of steak at a time on the hot grill and cook for 1 minute or less to a side, depending on the desired degree of doneness. Simultaneously, add a similar number of tortillas and cook them for a few seconds to a side just to heat through. Do not heat for long or they will dry out.
4. Place one steak in the center of a warm tortilla, spoon a little salsa cruda over the meat and fold the sides of the tortilla over and the ends up to enclose the meat. Eat like a sandwich.

Yield: 2 dozen.

3	pounds boneless sirloin, rib or club steaks, each about ½-inch thick
½	cup peanut oil
2	teaspoons chopped garlic
3	tablespoons red wine vinegar
	Salt and freshly ground pepper to taste
24	flour tortillas (see recipe below)
5	cups salsa cruda (see recipe below)

1. The volume of flour varies so it is best to measure by weight rather than by cups. Put the flour in a mixing bowl. Cut the shortening into bits and add it. Rub the two mixtures between the fingers to blend.
2. Dissolve the salt in the water and add it to the flour mixture, stirring. Knead the dough well, for about 3 minutes.
3. Shape the dough into a ball and put it in a small bowl. Cover and let stand for 2 hours at room temperature.
4. Knead the dough once more, for about 2 minutes. Pull off pieces of dough, one at a time, and shape into a ball roughly 1½ inches in diameter. Press the ball with the palm of the hand onto a floured board or pastry cloth. Roll it out into a circle about ⅛ inch thick and about 7 inches in diameter. As each tortilla is made, put it on a hot griddle or skillet and cook for about 20 seconds on one side, or until bubbles appear on the surface and the underside is speckled and dark brown. Turn and cook quite briefly on the other side. Continue until all the flour mixture is used.

Yield: About 2 dozen 7-inch tortillas.

Flour tortillas

1	pound flour, about 3¼ cups
½	cup solid white vegetable shortening, or lard
2	teaspoons salt
1	cup warm water (slightly hotter than lukewarm but not unpleasantly hot to the touch)

Salsa cruda   *(A raw tomato sauce, Mexican-style)*

2	pounds red, ripe tomatoes
1	cup finely chopped onion
¼ to	½ cup finely chopped hot green or red chilies, or use half hot chilies and half sweet peppers according to taste
	Salt and freshly ground pepper to taste
2 to	3 teaspoons finely minced garlic
½	cup finely chopped fresh coriander
1 to	2 tablespoons red wine vinegar

Core the tomatoes, but do not peel them. Cut them into ¼-inch cubes. Put in a mixing bowl. Add the remaining ingredients and stir to blend. Do not prepare this sauce more than 1 hour in advance.

Yield: About 5 cups.

Green Chili Gordas

12 dried tortillas (see note)
3 peeled green peppers
   (Anaheim), fresh or canned
⅔ cup hot milk
1 tablespoon melted lard or oil
¾ teaspoon salt
   Lard or oil for frying
1 medium-size onion, peeled
   and finely chopped
1½ cups sour cream, thinned
   with a little milk and salted

1. If the tortillas are not completely dry, spread them out onto a baking sheet and put them into a slow oven for about ½ hour. Remove and cool. When they are cool, break them into small pieces and blend until fine but not pulverized. Transfer to a bowl.

2. Remove and discard some of the seeds from the peppers and blend peppers with the hot milk until smooth. Add, together with melted lard and salt, to the ground tortillas and knead the mixture well. Add more milk if dough is not pliable enough. Set dough aside for about 1 hour or longer, well covered.

3. Divide dough into 12 equal portions and roll into balls about 1½ inches in diameter. Flatten to form 2-inch cakes about ⅜ inch thick.

4. Heat ¼ inch oil or lard in a frying pan and fry the cakes gently about 3 to 5 minutes on both sides (take care that the fat is not too hot, or it will make a crust on the outside instantaneously and the inside of the dough will not be heated through properly).

5. Drain well on paper toweling. (They will hold in a 350-degree oven for about 20 minutes if necessary.) Garnish with the chopped onion and sour cream and serve immediately.

Yield: 12 gordas.

Note: Defrosted tortillas will do perfectly well for this recipe.

Mushroom Tacos

One of the anecdotes that has always amused us about Diana Kennedy, who sets a splendid and authentic Mexican table, is her search for epazote, a much-used herb in Mexican cooking. For a long time she shopped all the local markets where Spanish and Mexican herbs are sold, with no success. One day, while jogging in Riverside Park, she found epazote growing wild and in abundance at her feet. It is a tall, greenish plant with flat pointed leaves and gives a distinctive, pungent flavor to Diana's mushroom tacos.

3 tablespoons peanut oil
1 small onion, finely chopped
2 cloves garlic, peeled and
   chopped

1. Heat 3 tablespoons oil to smoking in a saucepan, lower flame and cook the onion and garlic gently until soft but not brown.

2. Add the remaining ingredients, except tortillas and oil for frying, and cook the mixture, uncovered, over a fairly high flame, stirring from time to time, until the mushrooms are soft, 15 to 20 minutes. The mixture should be fairly dry. Set aside to cool a little.

3. Put a little of the mixture across one side of the tortilla—not in the center—and roll it up fairly tightly. Fasten with a toothpick. (If you are using defrosted tortillas and they are cracking, put them briefly into a steamer or colander over boiling water, or immerse them in hot fat for a few seconds only. This will make them softer and more flexible.)

4. Heat the oil or lard—there should be no more than ¼ inch in the frying pan or it will seep into the tacos—and fry them, turning them over and removing the toothpicks. They should be just crisp, but not hard. Drain on paper toweling and serve immediately. They become leathery if left heating through in the oven after you have made them. This is pan-to-mouth food and should be eaten as soon as your fingers can hold them. They can be served just as they are or with a little sour cream.

Yield: 12 tacos.

2	medium-size fresh tomatoes, peeled and chopped, or 1½ cups canned peeled tomatoes, drained
3	fresh hot green peppers (serranos), finely chopped
1	pound fresh mushrooms, finely sliced
3	sprigs epazote or parsley
1	teaspoon salt
12	tortillas (defrosted tortillas can be used)
	Oil or melted lard for frying

Sesame Chicken Wing Appetizers

1. Cut off and discard the small wing tips. Cut between and reserve the main wing bones and the second wing joint.

2. Crush the beans and add 1 tablespoon of water. Let stand.

3. Heat the oil in a wok or skillet and add the garlic and ginger. Stir briefly and add the chicken wings. Cook, stirring, until lightly browned, for about 3 minutes. Add the soy sauce and wine and cook, stirring, about 30 seconds longer. Add the soaked black beans.

4. Cover closely and let simmer for 8 to 10 minutes. Uncover, turn the heat to high and continue cooking, stirring, until liquid is almost evaporated and chicken pieces are glazed with sauce.

5. Remove from the heat and add the monosodium glutamate, if desired, and pepper. Toss. Just before serving, toss in the sesame seeds and scallions. This dish can be made in advance and reheated.

Yield: 8 or more servings.

12	chicken wings
1	tablespoon salted black beans
1	tablespoon water
1	tablespoon peanut, vegetable or corn oil
2	cloves garlic, crushed
2	slices fresh ginger root, cut into very fine shreds
3	tablespoons dark soy sauce
1½	tablespoons shao hsing wine, or dry sherry
½	teaspoon monosodium glutamate, optional
¼	teaspoon ground black pepper
1	tablespoon toasted sesame seeds
2	tablespoons chopped scallions, green part and all

Macquereau au Vin Blanc *(Mackerel in white wine)*

16	mackerel fillets, about 3 pounds
1	large carrot, trimmed and scraped
½	pound small white onions, peeled
2	cloves garlic, peeled and finely chopped
4	bay leaves
4	sprigs fresh thyme, or ½ teaspoon dried
1½	cups dry white wine
¼	cup peanut, vegetable or corn oil
1	teaspoon freshly ground white or black pepper Salt to taste
¼	cup distilled or white wine vinegar
¼	cup lemon juice
1	lemon, thinly sliced with seeds removed

1. The small diagonal belly bones of the mackerel should be cut away. If it has not already been removed, cut away and discard the thin, flabby belly flesh, leaving only the firm full-textured fillet. Leave the bone line that runs lengthwise down the center of the fillet intact.

2. Cut the carrot into very thin rounds, each about ⅛ inch thick. There should be about 1¼ cups. Put the carrot into a large skillet.

3. Cut the onions into very thin rounds, about the same thickness as the carrot rounds. There should be about 2 cups. Add the onion rings, garlic, bay leaves, thyme, wine, oil, pepper, salt, vinegar and lemon juice to the skillet. Cover and cook for 5 minutes.

4. Arrange the fillets, edges slightly overlapping, in a large skillet. Arrange the lemon slices on top. Pour the white wine mixture, including the vegetables and seasonings, over the fillets. Cover and bring to the boil. Let simmer for 6 minutes and remove from the heat.

5. Carefully transfer the fish fillets to a serving dish, arranging them neatly in rows, side by side. The rows should overlap. Pour the liquid and vegetables over the fish and let cool.
   Yield: 12 servings.

Marinated Snappers

16	very small snappers (baby bluefish), cleaned but with head and tail left on, gills removed
2	cups tarragon vinegar
3	cups water
3	onions, finely chopped
4	shallots, finely chopped
4	bay leaves
10	peppercorns Salt
2	whole cloves
6	parsley sprigs
2	small carrots, trimmed and sliced

1. Rinse the snappers and pat dry.

2. Combine the remaining ingredients and simmer for 30 minutes. Let cool and strain. Reserve a few carrot slices for garnish. Save the liquid but discard the remaining solids.

3. Preheat the oven to 450 degrees.

4. Put the fish in one layer in an earthenware, enamelware or stainless steel baking dish. Pour the marinade on top. The snappers must be completely covered with the liquid. Do not cover. Place in the oven and watch closely. When the liquid starts to simmer, open the oven door. Keep the oven door slightly ajar. Let fish continue to cook for 5 minutes, no longer.

5. Remove from the oven and let cool. Garnish with reserved carrot slices. If desired, add a little coarsely chopped parsley. Cover and refrigerate for a minimum of 4 days.
   Yield: 8 or more servings.

Broiled Snappers with Herbs

1. Preheat the broiler.

2. Stuff each snapper with a small sprig of fresh oregano. Arrange the fish in one layer in a lightly oiled baking dish. Brush lightly with soy sauce and stuff a lime slice in each gill flap. Brush with oil.

3. Broil for 3 to 5 minutes. Serve with lime wedges.

Yield: 4 servings.

16	very small snappers (baby bluefish), cleaned but with head and tail left on, gills removed
16	small sprigs fresh oregano or mint leaves
1	tablespoon soy sauce
8	lime slices, cut in half
1	teaspoon peanut oil

Brandade de Morue *(Mousse of salt cod)*

Salt cod, one of the great preserved fish of all times, is highly prized in Europe, particularly by the inhabitants of the Mediterranean countries. It goes by the name of bacalao in Spain and baccalá in Italy. The French term is morue. This mousse of salt cod from the south of France is delectable and easily made in the food processor.

1. Place the cod in a basin and add cold water to cover. Let soak, changing the water occasionally, for about 12 hours.

2. When ready to cook, preheat the oven to 375 degrees.

3. Place the potatoes in the oven and bake for 45 minutes to 1 hour, or until tender.

4. Drain the soaked cod and place it in a deep skillet. Add cold water to cover, ½ cup of milk, bay leaf and the onion stuck with cloves. Bring to the boil and simmer for about 3 minutes. Drain. If the cod is not boneless, carefully remove any skin and bones.

5. Gently heat the remaining milk, oil and cream in separate saucepans.

6. Split the potatoes in half. Scoop the hot flesh into the container of a food processor. Start blending and add the cod. Gradually add the hot milk, cream and oil. Beat in the salt, pepper, nutmeg and cayenne, and stir in the truffle, if desired.

7. Serve with triangles of French bread fried in olive oil, or with sliced French bread.

Yield: 12 to 20 servings.

1½	pounds dried salt cod, preferably boneless
1	pound potatoes, about 2
2	cups milk
1	bay leaf
½	onion stuck with 2 cloves
1	cup olive oil
1	cup heavy cream
	Salt and freshly ground pepper to taste
¼	teaspoon nutmeg
⅛	teaspoon cayenne pepper
1	truffle cut into ¼-inch cubes, optional

Escabeche of Fish

1¾ pounds (cleaned weight)
fish, left whole but with
head removed
Salt and freshly ground
pepper to taste
½ cup flour
2 cups oil, preferably olive oil
10 small cloves garlic, unpeeled
but lightly crushed
1 cup thinly sliced carrot
rounds
1 small onion, thinly sliced
⅓ cup wine vinegar
3 tablespoons water
2 sprigs fresh thyme, or ½
teaspoon dried
2 hot dried red pepper pods
1 bay leaf
6 parsley sprigs

1. Any firm-fleshed fresh fish such as porgy or sea bass can be used in this recipe. Score both sides of the fish with a sharp knife, making parallel and fairly deep gashes on both sides. Sprinkle inside and out with salt and pepper.

2. Put the flour in a bag and add the fish. Shake the bag until the fish is well coated with flour.

3. Heat the oil and, when it is very hot, add the fish. Cook for about 5 minutes, or until golden on one side. Turn and cook until golden brown all over, for about 3 or 4 minutes. Transfer the fish to a deep dish.

4. Strain the oil and reserve 1 cup of it. Pour the cup of oil into a saucepan and add the garlic cloves and carrot. Cook for about 1 minute and add the onion rings. Cook over high heat for about 2 minutes and add the vinegar, water, thyme, pepper pods, bay leaf, parsley sprigs and salt and pepper to taste. Cover and simmer for about 10 minutes.

5. Pour the mixture over the fish and cover with wax paper. Cover with a lid and refrigerate for about 24 hours.

Yield: 4 to 6 servings.

Gravlax   *(Salt- and sugar-cured salmon)*

2 bunches fresh dill
1 3½- to 4-pound section of
fresh salmon, preferably cut
from the center of the fish
¼ cup kosher salt
¼ cup sugar
1 teaspoon coarsely ground
white peppercorns
Mustard-dill sauce (see recipe
below)

1. Cut off and discard any very tough stems from the dill. Rinse the dill and pat it dry.

2. Bone the salmon section or have it boned. There should be two fillets of equal size and weight. Do not rinse the fish but pat it dry with paper toweling.

3. Combine the salt, sugar and pepper. Rub this mixture into the pink flesh of the salmon.

4. Spread ⅓ of the dill over the bottom of a flat dish. Add one of the salmon pieces, skin side down. Cover this with another third of the dill. Add the remaining piece of salmon, placing it sandwich-fashion over the dill, skin side up. Cover with the remaining dill and place a plate on top. Add a sizable weight and let stand in a very cool place or in the refrigerator for 48 hours. Turn the "sandwich" every 12 hours, always covering with the plate and weighting it down. Serve thinly sliced on the bias, like smoked salmon, with mustard-dill sauce.

Yield: 12 to 20 servings.

Combine the prepared mustard, dry mustard and sugar in a mixing bowl. Using a wire whisk, stir in the vinegar. Gradually add the oil, stirring rapidly with the whisk. Add the dill and salt. Taste and correct the flavors by gradually adding more sugar, vinegar or salt.

Yield: About 1½ cups.

Mustard-dill sauce

½ cup Dijon, Düsseldorf, or dark prepared mustard
2 teaspoons dry mustard
6 tablespoons sugar
¼ cup white vinegar
⅔ cup vegetable oil
½ cup chopped fresh dill
Salt

Anguilles au Vert *(Eel in green sauce)*

1. Cut off and discard the tough bottoms of the watercress. Place the watercress leaves in the container of an electric blender or food processor. It may be necessary to blend the watercress and other greens in 1 or 2 stages. In any event, start blending to a purée and continue until all the watercress is blended. Spoon and scrape into a saucepan.

2. Rinse and dry the spinach. Blend the spinach with the parsley, scallion, sage, tarragon, savory and dill. Do this in one or two stages until all the greens are a fine purée. There should be about 2 cups. Add to the watercress in the saucepan.

3. Cut the eel into 3-inch lengths. Melt the butter in a large skillet and add the eel pieces. Add salt and pepper to taste. Cook, turning often. When the eel change color, add the wine. Cover closely and simmer for 8 to 10 minutes. Spoon the eel pieces into a serving dish or mixing bowl. Let cool.

4. Add the yolks to the puréed greens and bring just to the boil, stirring constantly and vigorously with a wire whisk. Add salt and pepper to taste. Add lemon juice. Do not boil or the eggs will curdle. Immediately pour the sauce over the eel pieces. Let cool. Serve cold or at room temperature.

Yield: 6 to 10 servings.

1 bunch watercress
1 pound fresh spinach in bulk, or 1 10-ounce package
1 cup loosely packed fresh parsley
½ cup coarsely chopped green part of scallions
2 fresh sage leaves, or ½ teaspoon dried sage
2 sprigs fresh tarragon, or ½ teaspoon dried
2 sprigs fresh savory, or ½ teaspoon dried
½ cup loosely packed fresh dill, optional
1½ to 2 pounds cleaned, skinned fresh eel, 1 or 2 eel, depending on size
4 tablespoons butter
Salt and freshly ground pepper to taste
1 cup dry white wine
6 egg yolks
2 tablespoons lemon juice

Seviche of Scallops with Avocado

1½ pounds fresh bay scallops
5 tablespoons lime juice
½ squeezed lime shell
Salt and freshly ground pepper to taste
1 tablespoon finely chopped fresh hot green or red pepper, or 1 or 2 canned serrano chilies added according to taste
¼ teaspoon dried crushed oregano
1½ cups cubed, fresh, ripe but firm, unblemished avocado
2 tablespoons finely chopped fresh coriander leaves

1. Even if the scallops are small, cut them in half against the grain. Place them in a bowl and add 4 tablespoons of lime juice. Stir.

2. Cut the lime shell into tiny pieces and add them. Add salt and pepper and stir. Cover and refrigerate for at least 12 hours.

3. Add the remaining ingredients. Stir well and serve with crisp leaves of romaine lettuce.

Yield: 6 or more servings.

Raw Scallops in Soy Marinade

6 tablespoons soy sauce
3 tablespoons fresh lime juice
1½ tablespoons grated horseradish, preferably fresh
¼ teaspoon hot red pepper flakes
2 teaspoons olive oil
1 tablespoon chopped fresh coriander leaves
1 teaspoon finely chopped garlic
1 pint (1 pound) fresh raw scallops

In a small mixing bowl combine the soy sauce, lime juice, horseradish, pepper flakes, oil, coriander and garlic. Blend well. Add the scallops and stir to blend. Chill or serve immediately.

Yield: 6 or more servings.

Raw Fish with Green Peppercorns

1½ pounds skinless, boneless fillet of very fresh fish such as tuna, striped bass, sea trout and so on

1. Place the fillet on a flat surface and cut it on the diagonal into very thin slices like smoked salmon. As the slices are cut, arrange them neatly in one layer and slightly overlapping on a chilled platter.

2. Sprinkle with salt and pepper. Sprinkle with lime juice. Crush the peppercorns and smear them over the fish. Garnish with lime slices and parsley sprigs.

Yield: 8 to 12 servings.

Salt and freshly ground pepper to taste

2 tablespoons fresh lime juice

1 tablespoon green peppercorns (if possible, use the peppercorns packed in brine rather than those packed in vinegar or dry)

Lime slices for garnish

Parsley sprigs for garnish

Herring Salad

1. Soak the herring overnight and fillet it according to instructions below. Cut the herring into ½-inch cubes and put it in a mixing bowl.

2. Rinse the potatoes well and put them in a kettle. Add cold water to cover and salt to taste. If available, put in a few stems from fresh dill. Bring to the boil and cook until tender. Drain. When cool enough to handle, peel the potatoes and cut them into ¼-inch cubes. There should be about 3 cups. Put them in the bowl. Add the pickled beets.

3. Cut the corned beef into small cubes. There should be about 1 cup. Add the meat to the bowl.

4. Cut the pickles into small cubes. There should be about 1¼ cups. Put them in the bowl.

5. Chop the onion finely. There should be about ¾ cup. Put it in the bowl.

6. Peel and core the apples. Cut them into small cubes. There should be about 1½ cups. Put them in the bowl.

7. Add the mustards to another bowl and add the sugar and vinegar. Stir to blend and gradually beat in the oil. Whip the cream and fold it in. Stir this sauce into the herring mixture.

8. Spoon the salad into a 7- or 8-cup mixing bowl or a mold of equal volume. Pack it in and refrigerate. When ready to serve, unmold the salad onto a serving dish. Garnish with hard-cooked egg whites and yolks, separately sieved. Serve, if desired, with sharp sauce (see recipe below).

Yield: 12 or more servings for a buffet.

1 small salt herring

3 potatoes, about 1 pound
Salt to taste

½ pound pickled beets, canned or prepared according to any standard recipe, cut into ¼-inch cubes

¼ pound corned beef, or a combination of corned beef and cooked veal

2 sour pickles

1 onion, about ¼ pound

2 firm apples

1 tablespoon imported Swedish or German mustard

1 teaspoon Dijon mustard

1 tablespoon sugar

2 tablespoons red wine vinegar

¼ cup peanut or corn oil

¼ cup heavy cream

2 hard-cooked eggs, peeled

Sharp sauce

1 raw egg yolk
1 hard-cooked egg yolk, put through a sieve
1 teaspoon imported Swedish, French or German mustard
2 teaspoons red wine vinegar
¼ teaspoon Worcestershire sauce
   Salt and freshly ground pepper to taste
1 cup peanut oil
¾ cup heavy cream
2 tablespoons chopped fresh dill

1. Put the raw and cooked yolks in a mixing bowl and stir in the mustard, vinegar, Worcestershire sauce, salt and pepper.

2. Start beating with a wire whisk while gradually adding the oil. Continue beating until a mayonnaise forms and all the oil is added.

3. Whip the cream until stiff and fold it into the mayonnaise. Stir in the dill. Serve with herring salad.

Yield: About 3 cups.

How to fillet salt (schmaltz) herring

Using a pair of scissors, cut off the fins from the herring. Using a sharp knife, slit open the stomach and remove the roe or milch.

Turn the herring and, using the knife, slit the fish down the back, cutting off first one fillet, then the other, inserting the knife at the tail end and slicing through as close to the bone as possible. When the fillets have been cut off, skin them by pulling with the fingers, starting with the tail ends. Discard the skins. Rinse the fillets and pat them dry on paper towels or proceed as indicated in individual recipes.

Herring Rolls

2 large salt herring, soaked overnight in cold water
4 whole anchovy sprats (do not use smoked Brisling sardines, also sold as sprats)
¼ cup chopped red onion
¼ cup finely chopped parsley
2 tablespoons chopped fresh dill
3 tablespoons fine fresh bread crumbs
1 tablespoon butter
⅓ cup heavy cream

1. Preheat the oven to 350 degrees.

2. Fillet the herring according to instructions above.

3. Split the sprats down the stomach and, using the fingers, open them up. Pull off and discard the skin. Pull away and discard the bone. Chop the sprats to a pulp and add the onion, parsley and dill.

4. Place the herring fillets, skin side down, on a flat surface and cut each fillet in half lengthwise. Spoon equal portions of the sprat mixture in the center of each herring half. Roll up each half to enclose the filling. Arrange the rolls, pleat side down and close together, on a small baking dish (a round dish about 6 inches in diameter is suitable for this).

5. Sprinkle with the bread crumbs and dot with the butter. Pour the cream over all and bake for 15 minutes.

Yield: 12 servings for a buffet.

Mustard Herring

1. Fillet the herring according to instructions above. Place the fillets in a mixing bowl and add the white vinegar, water and sugar. Stir to dissolve the sugar. Cover and refrigerate for 2 hours or longer. Drain and pat dry.

2. Add the 2 mustards to a mixing bowl and stir in the vinegar, using a wire whisk. Add the pepper and cream and gradually stir in the oil. Add the dill.

3. Cut the herring fillets into 1-inch crosswise slices and arrange in 1 layer in a dish. Pour the mustard sauce over and serve.

Yield: 12 servings for a buffet.

The herring:

2   salt herring, soaked overnight in cold water
2   tablespoons white vinegar, preferably imported Swedish vinegar
½   cup water
1½   tablespoons sugar

The mustard sauce:

1   tablespoon mustard, preferably imported Swedish mustard, or use a dark domestic mustard
1   tablespoon Dijon or Düsseldorf mustard
2   tablespoons red wine vinegar
¼   teaspoon ground white pepper
½   cup heavy cream
½   cup peanut oil
2   tablespoons finely chopped dill

Matjes Herring with Dill and Sour Cream

Drain the fillets and cut them into 1-inch pieces. Arrange them neatly on a dish and sprinkle with chopped dill and onion. Garnish with bay leaves. Serve with sour cream on the side.

Yield: 12 servings for a buffet.

8   matjes herring fillets, available in tins where fine Swedish foods are sold
¼   cup chopped fresh dill
½   cup finely chopped onion
2   bay leaves for garnish
    Sour cream

Herring Tidbits with Leeks and Onion

1. Drain the tidbits and arrange them on a dish in a neat pattern.

2. Blend the leeks and onion. Spoon the mixture to one side of the tidbits. Spoon the sour cream down the other side.

Yield: 12 servings for a buffet.

36   herring tidbits, available in jars
⅓   cup finely chopped leeks, green part and all
⅓   cup finely chopped onion
1   cup sour cream

Spicken Herring *(Simple pickled herring)*

2 large salt herring, filleted
1 quart plus 3 tablespoons milk
3 tablespoons sugar
   Boiled potatoes
1 cup sour cream
¼ cup chopped chives

1. Place the 4 herring fillets in a bowl and add 1 quart of milk and the sugar. Refrigerate overnight.

2. Drain the herring and cut into 1-inch pieces. Serve with boiled potatoes and sour cream diluted with the remaining 3 tablespoons of milk. Garnish with chives.

Yield: 12 servings for a buffet.

Marinated Sprats

12 whole anchovy sprats (do not use smoked Brisling sardines, also sold as sprats)
2 tablespoons finely chopped dill
⅓ cup finely chopped red onion
3 tablespoons wine vinegar
¼ teaspoon finely ground pepper
½ clove garlic, crushed to a purée
½ cup peanut oil

1. Split the sprats down the stomach and, using the fingers, open them up. Pull away and discard the bone, but do not split the sprats in half. Cut off and discard the tail.

2. Arrange the sprats, split side down, on a flat surface. Blend the dill and onion and spoon equal portions of the mixture onto the center of each sprat. Fold the sprats, head to tail, to enclose the filling. Arrange them neatly on a flat dish in 1 layer. Blend the remaining ingredients and pour over the sprats. Refrigerate for an hour or so.

Yield: 12 servings for a buffet.

Baked Stuffed Clams

For the nonexpert and would-be clam shucker, there are two things to remember that facilitate opening the bivalves. Clams are closed tightly because of the powerful (but delicious and tender) muscle that joins the two shells together. If the clams are well-chilled before they are to be opened, the muscle tends to relax. The clams can be chilled for several hours in the refrigerator or briefly in the freezer. It is also imperative that the clam knife be sharp. Avoid those guillotinelike clam-shucking gadgets. They mangle clams and are quite frankly an abomination.

1. Preheat the oven to 400 degrees.

2. Open the clams or have them opened, discarding the top shell and loosening the clam on the bottom half shell.

3. Combine the shallots, garlic, basil, parsley, tomato, mushrooms, ½ cup of grated cheese, bread crumbs, bacon, salt and pepper to taste. Do not add much salt because the clams are salty. Grind the ingredients or blend them coarsely in a food processor. Grind or blend to a medium fine purée. Fold in the red pepper flakes and chives, if used.

4. Spoon the mixture over the clams and smooth it over. Arrange the clams on a baking dish and sprinkle with the remaining cheese. Sprinkle with the oil and wine. Bake for 20 minutes, or until golden brown and piping hot. Run briefly under the broiler for a deeper glaze.

Yield: 6 to 8 servings.

36 to 48 littleneck clams
6 shallots, peeled
4 cloves garlic, finely minced
½ cup loosely packed fresh basil
½ cup loosely packed fresh parsley leaves
1 small tomato, about ⅓ pound, cored and quartered
4 fresh mushrooms, sliced
¾ cup freshly grated Parmesan cheese
½ cup fresh bread crumbs
2 slices lean bacon, cut into pieces
Salt and freshly ground pepper
½ teaspoon red pepper flakes, more or less to taste, optional
1 tablespoon finely chopped chives, optional
¼ cup olive oil
½ cup dry white wine

Les Palourdes aux Aromates (Baked clams in spicy butter sauce)

1. Open the clams and arrange them on half shells neatly on a baking sheet.

2. Preheat the oven to 450 degrees.

3. In a saucepan, combine the chopped shallots and wine and cook briefly, stirring. Cut the butter into 1-inch cubes and add it. Heat, stirring, until the butter melts. Add salt, pepper, Tabasco, Worcestershire sauce and mustard. Bring just to the boil, stirring. Cook, stirring, for about 5 minutes. Add the basil and let the sauce cool to lukewarm.

4. Spoon the sauce over the clams and bake for 10 minutes. Run the clams under the broiler for about 15 seconds, no longer. Sprinkle with parsley.

Yield: 4 to 8 servings.

4 dozen clams
¼ cup finely chopped shallots
¼ cup dry white wine
16 tablespoons (2 sticks) sweet butter
Salt and freshly ground pepper to taste
Tabasco sauce to taste
½ teaspoon Worcestershire sauce
2 teaspoons imported mustard, such as Dijon or Düsseldorf
2 tablespoons chopped fresh basil
¼ cup chopped parsley

Clams au Beurre Blanc

24 littleneck clams, the smaller
   the better
4 tablespoons butter
½ cup dry white wine
2 tablespoons finely chopped
   shallots
   Freshly ground pepper to
   taste

1. Rinse the clams well. Put them in a casserole and add 2 tablespoons of butter and the wine. Sprinkle with shallots and pepper to taste.

2. Cover closely. The clams should start to open after 4 or 5 minutes of cooking. Remove them with a slotted spoon. Quickly break off one half shell, leaving each clam on one half shell.

3. Cook down the wine and clam liquid until it is reduced by half. Tilt the pan so that the sauce is concentrated in one small area. Gradually add the remaining 2 tablespoons of butter, stirring rapidly with a wire whisk. The sauce should be creamy and slightly thickened. It must not be overheated or it will curdle. Spoon the sauce over the clams and serve.

Yield: 4 servings.

Clams on the Half Shell with Mexican Tomato Sauce

36 littleneck clams, the smaller
   the better
1 cup firm, red, ripe, unpeeled
   tomatoes, cut into ½-inch
   cubes
2 tablespoons finely chopped
   onion
1 clove garlic, finely minced
½ cup finely chopped scallions
1 green pepper, finely chopped
¼ cup fresh lime juice
¼ cup olive oil
   Salt and freshly ground
   pepper to taste
½ cup chopped fresh coriander

Open the clams and discard half the shells. Leave the remaining clams on the half shell. Arrange them on a serving platter. Combine the remaining ingredients and spoon equal portions of the tomato mixture on each clam. Serve on the half shell.

Yield: 6 servings.

Oysters Bienville

1. Preheat the oven to 500 degrees.
2. Pour rock salt into 4 or 6 (the number will depend on the size and number of oysters) rimmed, heat-proof dishes large enough to hold the oysters in one layer. Place the dishes in the oven for at least 5 minutes to heat the salt.
3. Melt 2 tablespoons of butter in a saucepan and add the flour, stirring with a wire whisk. When blended, add the milk and cream, stirring rapidly with the whisk. Add the salt and pepper to taste.
4. Heat the remaining 1 tablespoon of butter in a saucepan and add the shallots. Cook briefly and add the garlic and mushrooms. Cook briefly. Add the shrimp and cook, stirring, for about 40 seconds. Add salt and pepper. Add the sherry, egg yolk, nutmeg, cayenne and parsley. Add the mixture to the cream sauce and blend well.
5. Top each oyster with equal amounts of the sauce. Arrange the oysters on the rock salt and bake for 10 minutes.

Yield: 4 to 6 servings.

Rock salt
3 tablespoons butter
3 tablespoons flour
¾ cup milk
½ cup heavy cream
Salt and freshly ground pepper to taste
2 teaspoons finely chopped shallots
1 clove garlic, finely minced
¼ pound mushrooms, finely chopped, about 1½ cups
¼ pound raw shrimp, shelled and deveined and finely chopped
2 tablespoons dry sherry
1 egg yolk
¼ teaspoon nutmeg
Pinch of cayenne pepper
1 tablespoon finely chopped parsley
24 to 36 oysters on the half shell

Oysters Casino

1. Preheat the oven to 500 degrees.
2. Pour rock salt into 2 rimmed, heat-proof dishes large enough to hold 6 oysters on the half shell in one layer. Place the dishes in the oven for at least 5 minutes to heat the salt.
3. Blend the butter and green peppers, salt and pepper. Add the parsley, chives, lemon juice, lemon rind and blend well. Spoon equal parts of this mixture onto each of the 12 oysters.
4. Cut the bacon strips into rectangles, each large enough to cover 1 oyster. Cover the butter topping with bacon and sprinkle each serving with ½ teaspoon of bread crumbs.
5. Arrange the oysters on the rock salt and place in the oven. Bake for 10 minutes, or until bacon is crisp and oysters are heated through.

Yield: 2 servings.

Rock salt
8 tablespoons butter
½ cup chopped green or red sweet pepper
Salt and freshly ground pepper to taste
1 tablespoon finely chopped parsley
1 tablespoon finely chopped chives
Juice of ½ lemon
Grated rind of lemon
12 oysters on the half shell
4 strips bacon
6 teaspoons fresh bread crumbs

Oysters Rockefeller

36 oysters
2 pounds fresh spinach, or 2 10-ounce packages
1 cup finely chopped scallions
½ cup finely chopped celery
½ cup finely chopped parsley
1 clove garlic, finely minced
1 2-ounce can anchovies, drained
8 tablespoons butter
1 tablespoon flour
½ cup heavy cream
   Tabasco sauce to taste
1 or 2 tablespoons Pernod, Ricard or other anise-flavored liqueur
⅓ cup grated Parmesan cheese

1. Preheat the oven to 450 degrees.
2. Open the oysters, leaving them on the half shell and reserving the oyster liquor.
3. Pick over the spinach and remove any tough stems and blemished leaves. Rinse well and put in a saucepan. Cover and cook, stirring, until spinach is wilted. Cook briefly and drain well. Squeeze to remove excess moisture. Blend or put through a food grinder. There should be about 2 cups.
4. Put the scallions, celery and parsley into the container of a food processor or an electric blender and blend. There should be about 1 cup finely blended.
5. Chop the garlic and anchovies together finely.
6. Heat 4 tablespoons of butter in a skillet and add the scallion and celery mixture. Stir about 1 minute and add the anchovy mixture. Cook, stirring, for about 1 minute and add the spinach. Stir to blend.
7. Heat the remaining 4 tablespoons of butter in a saucepan and add the flour. Blend, stirring with a wire whisk, and add the oyster liquor, stirring vigorously with the whisk. Stir in the cream. Season with Tabasco. Do not add salt. Add the spinach mixture and Pernod. Let cool.
8. Spoon equal portions of the mixture on top of the oysters and smooth over the tops. Sprinkle with Parmesan cheese. Bake for about 25 minutes, or until piping hot.

Yield: 6 servings.

Note: The same spinach topping is equally good (some think it is better) with clams on the half shell.

Cozze en Bianca   *(Mussels in broth)*

24 large, meaty mussels
¼ cup olive oil
4 cloves garlic, thinly sliced
½ teaspoon hot red pepper flakes
⅓ cup finely chopped parsley
   Crisp Italian bread

1. Rinse the mussels and drain well. Place in a kettle and cover. Steam until the mussels open.
2. Meanwhile, heat the oil in a casserole and add the garlic. Cook until the garlic starts to brown. Pour in the mussels and their liquid and toss. Sprinkle with pepper flakes and parsley and serve over sliced, crusty bread in soup bowls.

Yield: 4 servings.

Mussels with Anchovy Mayonnaise

1. Place the mussels in a kettle and add the wine, parsley, bay leaf and thyme. Cover and bring to the boil, shaking the kettle to redistribute the mussels occasionally. Cook until mussels open, about 5 minutes or longer. Let cool.

2. Drain the mussels but save the cooking liquid for the mayonnaise. Open the mussels and discard the top shell of each. Leave the mussels on the half shell.

3. Combine the mayonnaise with remaining ingredients and spoon over each mussel.

Yield: 6 to 8 servings.

2 quarts well-scrubbed mussels
¼ cup dry white wine
3 sprigs fresh parsley
1 bay leaf
2 sprigs fresh thyme, or 1 teaspoon dried
1 cup freshly made mayonnaise
2 teaspoons liquid in which mussels cooked
1 tablespoon finely chopped shallots
1 tablespoon chopped anchovy fillets

Mussels with Caper Mayonnaise

1. Put the mussels in a kettle and add the wine, bay leaf and pepper. Do not add salt. Cover and cook for 5 minutes or longer, until the mussels open.

2. Let the mussels cool. Remove the mussels from the shells (the liquid may be used for a small portion of soup). Combine the mussels with as much mayonnaise as it takes to bind them together. Add the capers, garlic and chopped dill and toss to blend. Serve at room temperature. Garnish with fresh dill sprigs.

Yield: 6 to 8 servings.

2 quarts well-scrubbed mussels, about 3½ pounds
¼ cup dry white wine
1 bay leaf
Freshly ground pepper to taste
3 sprigs fresh parsley
½ cup freshly made mayonnaise
3 tablespoons drained capers
1 teaspoon finely chopped garlic
1 tablespoon finely chopped dill
Fresh dill sprigs for garnish

Shrimp Rémoulade

The shrimp:

2 pounds fresh shrimp in the shell
16 allspice
1 large clove garlic, peeled and crushed
12 peppercorns, crushed
Salt to taste

The rémoulade sauce:

2 tablespoons creole mustard, available in shops specializing in fine foods
1 tablespoon tarragon wine vinegar
Salt and freshly ground pepper
1 cup olive oil
1 tablespoon paprika
½ cup finely chopped celery
1 cup chopped scallions
1 teaspoon chopped garlic
½ cup chopped parsley
2 tablespoons horseradish, preferably fresh
2 tablespoons anchovy paste
⅛ teaspoon cayenne pepper
2 tablespoons lemon juice
Tabasco sauce to taste

The garnish:

Shredded romaine lettuce
Lemon wedges

1. Put the shrimp in a saucepan and add water to cover. Add the allspice, garlic, peppercorns and salt. Bring gradually to the boil. Simmer for about 1 minute and remove from the heat. Let stand until cool. Peel and devein the shrimp. There should be about 4 cups.

2. For the sauce, put the mustard and vinegar in a mixing bowl and add salt and pepper to taste. Beat with a wire whisk and gradually add the oil, stirring constantly. Stir in the remaining ingredients for the sauce.

3. Put about ½ cup of shredded romaine on each of 8 salad plates. Arrange an equal number of shrimp on the lettuce. Spoon the sauce over to completely cover the shrimp. Serve with lemon wedges.

Yield: 8 servings.

Shrimp Seviche

1¼ pounds fresh shrimp in the shell
Salt
¼ teaspoon red pepper flakes

1. Cover the shrimp with cold water. Add salt to taste, pepper flakes and allspice. Bring to the boil and simmer for 30 seconds. Remove from the heat and let cool. Shell and devein the shrimps.

2. Put the shrimp in a bowl and add salt to taste and the remaining ingredients. Cover and refrigerate for several hours. Serve at room temperature.

Yield: 6 servings.

4	allspice
½	cup finely chopped onion
⅓	cup olive oil
½	cup lime juice
¼	cup chopped fresh coriander
½	lime shell (squeezed), cut into tiny cubes
2	long hot green or red chilies, cored, seeded and chopped
1	teaspoon finely chopped garlic
1	teaspoon oregano, crushed

Cold Shrimp à la Grecque

1. Rinse the shrimp and drain. Pat dry.

2. Heat the oil in a large skillet and add the garlic. Cook briefly without browning. Add the bay leaf and wine. Bring to the simmer and add the shrimp. Add half the lemon juice, dill and red pepper. Add salt and pepper and bring to the simmer. Cover and simmer for 5 minutes. Remove from the heat and let cool. Refrigerate.

3. When ready to serve, sprinkle with the remaining lemon juice.

Yield: 8 or more servings.

2	pounds fresh shrimp, shelled and deveined
¼	cup olive oil
2	teaspoons finely chopped garlic
1	bay leaf
1	cup dry white wine
	Juice of 2 lemons
¼	cup finely chopped dill
1	small dried hot red pepper
	Salt and freshly ground pepper to taste

Shrimp with a Tarragon and Anchovy Mayonnaise

1. Place the shrimp in a saucepan and add cold water to cover. Add the allspice, hot red pepper and salt to taste. Bring to the boil and simmer for 1 minute. Remove the shrimp from the heat and let cool. Drain, shell and devein the shrimp.

2. Combine the mayonnaise with the lemon juice, chopped anchovies and tarragon. Cut the shrimp in half and add them. Chill and serve cold.

Yield: 6 or more servings.

1½	pounds fresh shrimp, about 36
12	whole allspice
1	dried hot red pepper
	Salt
1	cup freshly made mayonnaise
2	teaspoons fresh lemon juice, or more to taste
6	anchovies, finely chopped
1	tablespoon chopped fresh tarragon, or 1 teaspoon dried

Shrimp with Mustard and Dill Sauce

2 pounds shrimp in the shell
1 bay leaf
12 whole allspice
6 sprigs parsley
1 rib celery with leaves, quartered
Water to cover
Salt to taste
10 peppercorns, crushed
1 cup freshly made mayonnaise
1 tablespoon imported mustard, such as Dijon or Düsseldorf
¼ cup finely chopped fresh dill

1. Combine the shrimp, bay leaf, allspice, parsley, celery, water, salt and peppercorns in a saucepan.

2. Bring to the boil and turn off the heat. Let the shrimp cool in the cooking liquid. Chill.

3. Shell and devein the shrimp. Combine the mayonnaise, mustard and dill and spoon over the shrimp.

Yield: 6 or more servings.

Shrimp with Dill and Cognac Sauce

1½ pounds boiled shrimp
¾ cup freshly made mayonnaise
1 tablespoon tomato paste
1 tablespoon finely chopped dill
2 teaspoons Cognac
1 tablespoon finely chopped chives, optional
Tabasco sauce to taste
Dill sprigs for garnish

Peel and devein the shrimp. There should be about 2 cups. Blend the mayonnaise, tomato paste, dill, Cognac, chives and Tabasco. Stir to blend. Pour this over the shrimp and mix thoroughly. Garnish with dill sprigs.

Yield: 4 servings.

Dahi Shrimp   (Shrimp with yogurt and dill)

2 pounds fresh shrimp
1 cup yogurt
2 teaspoons cayenne pepper (use less if you wish the dish less spicy)
2 cloves finely chopped garlic
1 teaspoon caraway seeds
¼ teaspoon ground turmeric
Salt
4 tablespoons oil, preferably mustard oil
¾ cup finely chopped fresh dill

1. Peel and devein the shrimp. Rinse well and drain. Pat dry and set aside.

2. Combine the yogurt, cayenne, garlic, caraway, turmeric and salt to taste. Add the shrimp and blend well. Cover and refrigerate until ready to use.

3. Heat the oil in a deep skillet or casserole and add the shrimp. Cook, stirring gently, and cover. Cook until the shrimp change color. Sprinkle with dill and serve hot. The pan juices will be quite liquid.

Yield: 8 to 12 servings.

Sushi

The giddy proliferation of Japanese restaurants in America in the last decade has been very much a part of this nation's much-heralded gastronomic revolution. Americans have developed a strong affinity for foods of extraordinary variety and flavor. And it is not stretching a point to propose that Japanese cooking was the world's first cuisine minceur.

Sushi, that gastronomic wonder of raw fish served on rice, is a prime example. The kinds of fish and shellfish that can be eaten as sushi are virtually endless. Tuna, one of the favorite fish, is seasonal, but sea bass, striped bass, fresh mackerel and even bluefish are all excellent. Salmon roe, sometimes called red caviar and available in jars, is delicious as a topping for sushi rice. Thinly sliced raw clams, even the large chowder clams sliced razor-thin along the meaty section, are delectable. Sea urchins, that delicacy so prized in Mediterranean regions, offer an incredibly good roe best eaten raw. Although raw shrimp are a great delicacy in Japan, they are not recommended to be served as sushi in this country unless they are caught live and out of the freshest waters. The vast majority of shrimp sold in America have been frozen. The important thing is that each morsel for sushi be of the freshest quality.

How to shape plain sushi

Prepare the fish or seafood and the rice to be used in making sushi. Follow the recipe for sushi rice carefully. Have ready a small bowl of prepared wasabi (Japanese horseradish), and a small bowl of cold water to which has been added a teaspoon of rice vinegar.

Take a thin slice of fish fillet or a piece of seafood in one hand. Dip the index finger of the other hand into the wasabi and smear a little of it into the center of the fish. Wet the palm and fingers with the vinegar water and take up about 1½ tablespoons of sushi rice. Shape it into a ball, using one hand. Apply it to the wasabi-smeared fish and shape it into an oval so that it just fits the fish. Serve with sushi dip.

Fish fillets for making sushi

Although tuna is the most basic, traditional fish for making sushi, it is by no means the sum of it. Almost any fresh-caught, firm-fleshed, saltwater fish may be used, including sea bass, striped bass, mackerel and so on.

The fillets must be free of bones and skin. Place a slab of the fish on a cutting board and, using a very sharp slicing knife, cut the fillet, preferably on the bias, into ¼-inch-thick slices.

Large clams for sushi

Open the clams and remove the body. Cut away any digestive organs, leaving the firm, meaty muscle of the shellfish. Cut the muscle into thin slices and add salt. Massage well and rinse under cold running water. These slices may be butterflied to make them larger. Score the slices gently with a knife without cutting through the meat.

Seaweed-wrapped Sushi (Doté)

There are several ways of wrapping foods in seaweed to be served as sushi. One of the most common is to shape about 1½ tablespoons of sushi rice into an oval, apply a dab of wasabi to the top and encircle the rice with a rectangle of laver or nori (seaweed; see directions for preparing below), leaving an open space at the top for other small ingredients such as tiny scallops, slivers of raw fish, salmon roe, sea-urchin roe and so on. At times a sprinkle of lemon juice is added.

Another common technique is to place a rectangle of seaweed flat on a rectangular shaping mat made with thin bamboo reeds. This device is called a makisushi and is available where Japanese cooking utensils are sold. Put 2 or 3 tablespoons of sushi rice in the center and, using the fingers, spread it out neatly over the seaweed but leave a margin top and bottom. Add a dab of wasabi to the center, left to right, and add a thin strip of tuna or other fish or seafood across the center. Add a strip of cucumber if desired. Or use strips of broiled eel and Japanese pickles in place of the tuna and cucumber.

Fold the bamboo mat over in such a manner that the filling is enclosed in seaweed. Cut the sushi roll into sections of any desired length and serve with sushi dip on the side.

Dried seaweed (laver or nori) for sushi

To prepare the seaweed for sushi, pass it quickly on both sides over heat such as a gas flame or a hot grill. Cut it to any desired size, and shape around sushi rice plus other ingredients.

Sushi vinegar

1 cup rice vinegar
1¼ cups sugar
¼ cup salt
Pinch of monosodium glutamate, optional

Combine all the ingredients in a saucepan and heat, stirring, until the sugar is dissolved. Remove from the heat.
Yield: About 1½ cups.

Sushi is traditionally served with a small saucer or bowl of light soy sauce with wasabi (Japanese horseradish) on the side. The wasabi is added to the soy sauce as desired.

1. Place the rice in a kettle and add cold water to cover. Stir rapidly with the hands and drain. Return the rice to the kettle and wash again, stirring. Drain. Repeat once more. Drain finally in a sieve and let stand for 1 hour.

2. Measure the rice once more. It should measure 3½ to 4 cups. Put it in a saucepan. Add an equal quantity of cold water. Add the kelp and bring to the boil. As soon as the water boils, remove and discard the kelp. Cover the saucepan and cook the rice over high heat (the lid may rock from the steam) for about 6 minutes, or until the rice is tender. Sprinkle with the mirin and cover with a cloth, then with the lid. Let stand for 20 minutes.

3. Empty the piping hot rice into a bowl, preferably wide and made of wood, and gradually add the vinegar, turning the rice with a wooden spoon so that the vinegar is evenly distributed. Traditionally the rice should be fanned to cool it quickly as the vinegar is stirred in. Smooth the rice into a thin layer and let it stand until thoroughly cooled.

Yield: About 6 cups.

Sushi dip

Sushi rice

3 cups rice (about 1½ pounds), preferably Japanese or Italian (such as Avorio), available in Japanese and Italian markets
1 piece dried kelp (seaweed) about 3 inches square, available in Japanese markets
1½ teaspoons mirin (sweet sake), available in Japanese markets
½ cup sushi vinegar (see recipe above)

Escargots Bourguignonne

Someone has claimed that snails, those elegant, fine-textured delicacies that grow on vine leaves, are merely a good excuse for gastronomes to eat lots of garlic without apology. That may be stretching things a bit, but snails do belong to that category of foods more or less neutral—like macaroni and potatoes—whose character relies on the flavors and seasonings with which they are linked. Snails do go well, of course, with garlic, but also with spinach and cheese and walnuts.

1. Wash the shells in hot water and drain well. Cool.

2. Empty the snails and their liquid into a saucepan and add all the remaining ingredients except the snail butter. Bring to the boil, cover and simmer for 10 minutes. Let cool and drain.

3. Spoon about ½ teaspoon of the snail butter into each of the shells. Add one snail to each shell, pushing it in with the fingers. Spoon equal portions of the remaining snail butter into the hole, filling it and smoothing off the butter at the

24 snail shells
1 7½-ounce can imported snails (24 snails), undrained
2 tablespoons dry white wine
1 shallot, thinly sliced
1 clove garlic, thinly sliced
1 sprig parsley
6 thin carrot rounds
¼ teaspoon thyme
¼ bay leaf
Salt and freshly ground pepper
Snail butter (see recipe below)

opening. This may be done in advance and the snails refrigerated or frozen.

4. When ready to cook, preheat the oven to 500 degrees.

5. Arrange the snails on 4 traditional snail dishes. Bake for 5 minutes, or until sizzling hot. Serve piping hot with French bread.

Yield: 4 servings.

Snail butter

12 tablespoons butter at room temperature
2 tablespoons fine fresh bread crumbs
4 tablespoons finely chopped parsley
1 tablespoon finely chopped shallots
1 tablespoon finely chopped garlic
  Salt and freshly ground pepper

Cream together all the ingredients and use for stuffing snails.

Yield: Sufficient butter for 24 snails.

Escargots Languedocienne *(Snails with spinach and pine nuts)*

1 pound fresh spinach in bulk, or 1 10-ounce package
3 tablespoons butter
1 7½-ounce can imported snails (24 snails), drained
1 clove garlic, finely minced
1 tablespoon finely chopped anchovy
3 tablespoons finely chopped pine nuts
¼ teaspoon grated orange rind
½ cup heavy cream
⅛ teaspoon freshly grated nutmeg
  Salt and freshly ground pepper
¼ cup finely shredded Gruyère cheese

1. Preheat the broiler.

2. Pick over the spinach and pull off any tough stems. Drop the spinach into boiling water, stir down and cook for about 1 minute. Drain well. Let cool. Press between the hands to extract excess moisture. Chop finely and set aside.

3. Heat 2 tablespoons of butter in a small skillet and add the snails, garlic, anchovy, pine nuts and grated orange rind. Stir and cook for about 2 minutes. Add the cream. Cook for about 2 minutes and remove from the heat.

4. Heat the remaining 1 tablespoon butter in a small skillet and, when it is light brown (noisette), add the spinach, nutmeg, salt and pepper to taste. Arrange the spinach in a small oval platter and spoon the snail mixture over. Sprinkle with cheese and brown briefly under the broiler.

Yield: 4 servings.

Snails en Brochette

1. Preheat the broiler.
2. Empty the snails with their liquid into a saucepan and add salt and pepper to taste, bay leaf, thyme and parsley sprigs. Cover and simmer for 10 minutes. Drain and let cool.
3. Arrange equal numbers of snails on each of 6 or 8 skewers.
4. Melt the butter and add the chopped parsley, ½ tablespoon chopped walnuts, garlic, shallots, salt and pepper to taste. Dip the skewered snails first in the butter mixture, then coat liberally with a combination of bread crumbs and the remaining walnuts.
5. Arrange the snails on a baking sheet and spoon the remaining butter mixture over all. Broil about 4 inches from the heat. When golden brown, turn the snails and brown the other side. Serve immediately.

Yield: 6 to 8 servings.

2 7½-ounce cans snails, undrained
Salt and freshly ground pepper
1 bay leaf
3 sprigs fresh thyme, or ½ teaspoon dried
2 sprigs fresh parsley
6 tablespoons butter at room temperature
1½ tablespoons finely chopped parsley
4½ tablespoons chopped walnuts
1½ teaspoons chopped garlic
1½ teaspoons chopped shallots
¾ cup fine bread crumbs

Country Pâté

1. Preheat the oven to 375 degrees.
2. Put the pork liver, pork butt, onion and garlic through a meat grinder, using the fine blade of the grinder. Grind into a mixing bowl.
3. Add the thyme, flour, saltpeter, salt, pepper, wine, eggs and nutmeg. Mix well with the hands until thoroughly blended and no lumps remain.
4. Select a 10- or 12-cup rectangular pâté mold. (One that measures 14 x 3¾ x 3½ inches is suitable.) Line the bottom and sides of the mold with the fatback slices, letting them hang generously over the sides of the mold. Spoon the mixture into the mold and smooth it over. Fold the fatback overhanging over the filling to completely enclose it.
5. Set the mold in a large basin and pour boiling water around it. Bake for 2 hours. The pâté is done when the internal temperature registers 160 degrees on a meat thermometer. Remove from the water bath. Cover with foil and weight the pâté with one or two heavy objects. Let stand until cool and then refrigerate.
6. When ready to serve, unmold the pâté and slice.

Yield: 18 or more servings.

3 pounds pork liver
2 pounds boneless pork butt, both lean and fat
2 cups coarsely chopped onion
1 clove garlic, chopped
1 teaspoon chopped fresh thyme, or ½ teaspoon dried
1 cup flour
½ teaspoon saltpeter, available in drugstores
2 teaspoons salt
½ teaspoon freshly ground pepper
½ cup dry white wine
4 eggs, lightly beaten
¼ teaspoon grated nutmeg
12 or more slices very thinly sliced unsalted fatback

Liver Pâté with Hazelnuts

1 pound coarsely ground pork
1 pound coarsely ground veal
⅛ pound salt pork, cut into ¼-inch cubes
¼ cup thinly sliced shallots
¼ pound mushrooms, thinly sliced
1½ bay leaves
1 teaspoon dried thyme
1 pound chicken livers, picked over to remove veins and connecting tissues
Salt and freshly ground pepper to taste
½ teaspoon ground nutmeg
¼ teaspoon allspice
2 tablespoons Cognac
1 egg, lightly beaten
½ cup broken hazelnuts
3 to 4 very thin slices unsalted pork fat, or lean bacon
1 cup flour
3 tablespoons water
Quick aspic (see recipe below)

1. Preheat the oven to 375 degrees.

2. Place the pork and veal in a mixing bowl.

3. Put the salt pork in a saucepan and, when it is rendered of its fat, add the shallots, mushrooms, half a bay leaf and thyme. Cook, stirring occasionally, for about 5 minutes and add the chicken livers, salt, pepper, nutmeg and allspice. Cook, stirring, until livers lose their red color. Add the Cognac and remove from the heat.

4. Spoon and scrape the mixture into the container of a food processor or electric blender. Add the egg and blend. Spoon out and add to the meats in the mixing bowl. Add the hazelnuts, salt and pepper and blend well. You may fry a little of the mixture to test for seasonings and add more as desired.

5. Spoon the mixture into a 6-cup pâté mold and place the remaining bay leaf in the center. Cover the top with the salt pork. Cover with a round or oval of wax paper cut to fit.

6. Blend the flour and water well, kneading. Shape it into a round or oval, to fit over the wax paper. Cover with another oval of wax paper and cover with the mold's lid.

7. Place the mold in a basin of water and bring to the boil on top of the stove. Place in the oven and bake for 2 hours. Remove. Add a 3-pound weight to the top of the pâté and let cool at room temperature. Refrigerate.

8. Scoop out and discard the untidy natural gelatin and liquid around the pâté. Clean the mold with a sponge to make it neat.

9. Pour quick-aspic around the pâté and on top. Let cool and spoon more aspic on top and around. Chill and repeat as often as necessary to give a nice aspic coating to the pâté.

Yield: 20 or more servings.

Quick aspic

3 cups chicken broth
1 cup tomato juice
4 envelopes unflavored gelatin
Salt and freshly ground pepper
1 teaspoon sugar
2 eggshells, crushed
2 egg whites, lightly beaten
2 tablespoons Cognac

1. In a saucepan, combine the chicken broth with the tomato juice, gelatin, salt and pepper to taste, sugar, eggshells and egg whites. Heat slowly, stirring constantly, until the mixture boils up in the pan.

2. Remove the pan from the heat and stir in the Cognac.

3. Strain the mixture through a sieve lined with a flannel cloth that has been rinsed in cold water and wrung out. If the aspic starts to set or becomes too firm, it may be reheated, then brought to any desired temperature.

Yield: About 1 quart.

Quick Pâté

1. Put the salt pork in a saucepan and add cold water to cover. Bring to the boil and drain.

2. Put the salt pork pieces in a heavy skillet and cook until rendered of fat, stirring occasionally. When slightly browned, add the ground pork, stirring to break up lumps.

3. Heat the chicken fat separately in a skillet and add the chicken livers and cook, turning the livers occasionally, until they lose their raw look. Add the chicken livers and chicken fat to the pork. Cover and cook for about 2 minutes.

4. Add the shallots, garlic, bay leaf, thyme, nutmeg, clove, allspice, salt and pepper to taste. Use very little salt. The salt pork adds its own salt. Add the cayenne and white wine. Cover and cook for 10 minutes. Remove from the heat and let stand until warm.

5. Put half the mixture in the container of a food processor. Process for several minutes, or until as fine as the pâté can become. Repeat with the rest of the mixture.

6. If desired, spoon the pâté into a small crock. Serve with buttered toast.

Yield: 6 to 8 servings.

¼ pound salt pork, cut into small rectangles about ½ inch wide and ⅛ inch thick
1 pound ground pork
½ cup rendered chicken fat, preferably homemade, although bottled chicken fat can be used
¾ pound chicken livers
¼ cup thinly sliced shallots
1 small clove garlic, finely minced
½ bay leaf
¼ teaspoon dried thyme
⅛ teaspoon nutmeg
1 clove, crushed
Pinch of ground allspice
Salt and freshly ground pepper to taste
Pinch of cayenne pepper
¼ cup dry white wine

Salmon Pâté

1. Place the fish in the container of a food processor or blender. Add about ¼ cup of cream and blend. Gradually add more cream until desired consistency is reached, taking care the mixture does not become too liquid. Stop the blending at intervals and scrape down the sides of the container with a plastic spatula. When properly blended, the mass should be mousselike, holding its shape when picked up with the spatula.

2. Spoon and scrape the mixture into a bowl and add the lemon juice, capers, dill, salt and pepper. Spoon the pâté into a serving dish such as a small soufflé mold. Cover and chill well, preferably overnight. Garnish, if desired, with chopped dill. Serve with lightly buttered toast.

Yield: 4 to 6 servings.

Note: This pâté is particularly good if made with the leftover morsels of a poached whole salmon, the bits that cling around the main bones of the fish, near and in the head of the fish. These morsels are rich and gelatinous.

2 cups cooked, boneless, skinless salmon (see note)
¼ to ½ cup heavy cream
2 tablespoons lemon juice, more or less to taste
2 tablespoons capers
1 tablespoon chopped fresh dill
Salt and freshly ground pepper to taste

Mousseline of Chicken Livers

¾ cup rendered chicken fat (see note)
1 cup thinly sliced onion
½ pound lean veal, cut into ½-inch cubes
  Salt and freshly ground pepper
¼ teaspoon grated nutmeg
1 teaspoon chopped garlic
½ bay leaf
2 sprigs fresh thyme, or ½ teaspoon dried
1 pound picked-over raw chicken livers
3 tablespoons Cognac
¼ cup heavy cream
¼ cup chopped pistachio nuts

1. Melt chicken fat in a skillet and add the onion. Cook, stirring, until wilted. Add the veal, salt, pepper and nutmeg. Cook for about 2 minutes, stirring, and add the garlic, bay leaf, thyme and chicken livers. Cook, stirring occasionally, for about 5 minutes.

2. Remove the thyme sprigs, if used, and bay leaf and add the Cognac. Pour the mixture into the container of a food processor or blender and blend to a purée. Spoon the mixture into a mixing bowl.

3. Whip the cream until stiff and fold it into the chicken liver mixture with a rubber spatula. Spoon the mixture into a mold and smooth it over. Chill well.

4. Spoon portions onto plates and sprinkle each serving with pistachio nuts. Serve with buttered toast. Or sprinkle the top of the mold with pistachios and let guests serve themselves from the mold.

Yield: 10 to 16 servings.

Note: Rendered chicken fat may be purchased in some supermarkets, but it is easy to prepare. Simply cook scraps of chicken fat in a skillet over moderate heat until rendered. Drain.

Terrine de Volaille

1 3½-pound chicken
1 pound boneless pork butt, both lean and fat, cubed
1 pound pork fat, cubed
¾ pound lean veal, cubed
½ pound chicken livers
⅓ cup finely chopped shallots
½ teaspoon chopped thyme
½ cup dry white wine
¼ teaspoon ground nutmeg
½ teaspoon saltpeter, available in drugstores

1. Skin and bone the chicken, reserving the skin and bones for broth (see recipe for aspic). Keep the chicken meat in as large portions as possible, but trim away all silvery nerve tissues, cartilage and so on.

2. Cut the fleshier pieces of chicken, such as the breasts and thighs, into 1½-inch cubes. Set aside in a bowl. Add the scraps of meat to another bowl.

3. Fit a meat grinder with the coarse blade and grind the boneless pork butt, pork fat, veal, chicken livers and any reserved scraps of chicken. Set aside.

4. In a saucepan combine the shallots, thyme and ¼ cup wine. Cook over moderately high heat until the wine is almost

completely reduced. Spoon out the solids and let cool. Add to the ground meat.

5. Sprinkle with nutmeg, saltpeter, truffles, pistachios and remaining ¼ cup wine and blend with the hands. Add the cubed chunks of chicken and stir to blend evenly. Cover with wax paper and a lid and let stand overnight in the refrigerator.

6. Preheat the oven to 375 degrees.

7. Line the bottom and sides of a 10-cup terrine or pâté mold with fatback slices, letting the slices hang generously over the sides. Spoon the chicken mixture into the mold and smooth it over. Fold the overhanging fatback over the filling to completely enclose it. Set the mold in a large basin and pour boiling water around it. Bake for 2½ to 3 hours. The terrine is done when the internal temperature registers 160 degrees on a meat thermometer.

8. Cover the terrine with heavy-duty aluminum foil and place a weight on top of the baked mixture. Refrigerate overnight.

9. Scrape off and discard the fat that has accumulated around the meat. Pour clear aspic over the meat and chill until the aspic is firm. Serve sliced.

Yield: 18 or more servings.

2	tablespoons chopped black truffles
½	cup pistachios
12 to	16 very thin slices fatback Aspic de volaille (see recipe below)

1. Combine the chicken bones and pork rind in a kettle and add water to cover. Bring to the boil and drain immediately. Run under cold water until thoroughly chilled.

2. Return the bones and rind to a clean kettle and add 2 quarts of water. Add the celery, carrot, onion, garlic and bay leaf. Return to the boil and simmer for about 3 hours, or until there are 2½ to 3 cups of liquid. Strain.

3. To clarify the aspic, pour the liquid into a saucepan. Add the gelatin and stir to dissolve. Add the egg white and crushed shells. Gradually bring to the boil. Strain through a fine sieve lined with a double thickness of cheesecloth. Let cool to room temperature, then chill briefly. Use while still liquid.

Yield: About 2½ cups.

Aspic de volaille

2	pounds chicken bones
1¼	pounds fresh pork rind (unsmoked bacon rind, available in pork stores)
1	cup chopped celery
1	cup chopped carrot
1	onion stuck with 2 cloves
2	cloves garlic, peeled
1	bay leaf
1	envelope unflavored gelatin
2	egg whites, beaten to a froth
2	eggshells, crushed

Pâté de Canard

1 4- to 5-pound duck
⅓ cup plus 6 tablespoons dry white wine
1 large truffle, cut into ½-inch cubes
2 tablespoons liquid from canned truffles, optional, or substitute port or Marsala wine
⅓ cup shelled pistachio nuts
¼ pound ham, cut into ½-inch cubes
4 sprigs parsley
¼ pound lean salt pork, cut into ¼-inch cubes
½ pound duck and chicken livers (the liver of the duck plus enough chicken livers to make ½ pound), picked over and cut in half
  Salt and freshly ground pepper to taste
½ pound thinly sliced mushrooms, about 2 cups
⅓ cup coarsely chopped shallots
1½ bay leaves
½ teaspoon chopped fresh thyme, or ¼ teaspoon dried
3 tablespoons Cognac
2 pounds twice-ground pork
½ teaspoon saltpeter, available in drugstores
½ pound fatback, cut into large, wafer-thin slices
1½ cups flour
½ cup water
  Aspic de canard (see recipe below)

1. Using a sharp boning knife, make a bone-deep incision lengthwise down the back of the duck. Carefully remove the skin of the duck, neatly carving as necessary between the flesh and the skin and separating the fat skin from the flesh by pulling with the fingers. Continue skinning the duck entirely. If you puncture the skin, it isn't serious. Most of the duck skin and fat will be discarded, although you want to save a solid rectangle of skin from the breast covering.

2. Place the duck skin on a flat surface. Carve out a rectangle (about 11 x 7 inches) from the part that covered the breast. Discard the rest. Using a sharp knife, slice away and discard about half the solid, excess fat from beneath the duck skin. Set the rectangle of skin aside.

3. Carefully bone away the breast of meat from the duck. This should yield 2 large slabs of duck meat plus the 2 "fillets" of breast meat. Put the 2 fillets in a bowl. Cut each of the larger slabs of breast meat into 6 lengthwise sections. Add these to the 2 fillets. There should be a total of 14 pieces.

4. Add ⅓ cup of wine, truffle, truffle liquid, pistachios and ham to the bowl. Blend. Add the parsley sprigs. Cover with the reserved rectangle of skin. Sprinkle 3 more tablespoons of wine over all. Cover with plastic wrap and refrigerate overnight.

5. Cut the meat from the legs and thighs, taking care to cut and pull away all gristle, white membranes, nerves and so on. Discard these. Cut the meat into 1-inch cubes.

6. Heat the cubed salt pork in a large, heavy skillet and, when it is rendered of fat and the pork pieces are crisp and brown, add the cubed duck pieces (not the breast meat) to the skillet. Add the livers and salt and pepper to taste. Cook over high heat, shaking the skillet and stirring so that the meat and livers cook evenly, for about 1 minute. Do not overcook. The livers must remain pink inside.

7. Add the mushrooms and shallots, ½ bay leaf and thyme and cook, stirring and shaking the skillet, for about 2 minutes. Add the Cognac and cook for 30 seconds. Remove from the heat and let cool.

8. Put the pork in a mixing bowl. Add salt and pepper to taste and the saltpeter.

9. Place the cooled liver mixture into the container of a food processor or blender and blend until smooth. Add this to the pork. Blend thoroughly with the fingers. Cover evenly with 3 tablespoons of dry white wine. Cover and refrigerate.

10. When ready to bake the pâté, line an 8- to 10-cup pâté mold with the thin slices of fatback, the edges slightly overlapping. The slices should also overhang the rim of the mold so that they can be folded over to enclose the pâté when finished.

11. Add about half the ground pork and liver mixture to the mold. Cover the bottom and sides of the fatback-lined mold with this. Set aside about 1 cup of the ground pork mixture to cover the filled mold.

12. Remove and set aside the duck skin from the bowl containing the breast meat, ham and truffles. Remove the strips of breast and cut neatly into ½-inch cubes. Discard the parsley sprigs.

13. Add the cubed breast meat, ham, truffles, pistachios and so on to the unused ground pork mixture (keeping the reserved 1 cup aside). Blend well. Add this to the center of the mold and smooth it over. Cover with the reserved cup of ground pork mixture and smooth this over. Cover with the reserved rectangle of duck skin, skin side up, and tuck in the sides of the skin. Add the bay leaf to the center and fold the overhanging edges of the fatback toward the center, ends overlapping.

14. Preheat the oven to 350 degrees.

15. Blend the flour with the water, kneading well. Shape it into an oval to fit neatly inside the mold.

16. Cover the mold with an oval of wax paper. Cover with the dough, pressing down. Set the mold in a basin of hot water and bring to the boil on top of the stove. Place in the oven and bake for 2½ hours, or until the internal temperature of the pâté is 160 degrees.

17. Remove the mold from its water bath. Add a weight to the top of the pastry on top of the mold. Let stand at room temperature until cool.

18. Chill in the refrigerator. The pâté must be thoroughly cold. Remove pastry and wax paper from top of the mold. Pour cool but still liquid aspic over the pâté. It should barely cover the pâté. Cover closely. Chill to set. This pâté is best made at least 24 hours in advance. Serve sliced with small sour pickles (cornichons) and a crusty loaf of bread.

Yield: 16 or more servings.

1. Preheat the oven to 400 degrees.

2. Scatter the duck pieces over a baking pan and add salt and pepper. Bake for 30 minutes, or until pieces are nicely browned and crisp.

3. Put the pieces in a kettle and add the onion, garlic, celery, carrots, bay leaf, thyme, chicken broth, water and salt and

Aspic de canard

The raw duck carcass, cut into pieces
Salt and freshly ground pepper

½ cup chopped onion
2 cloves garlic, finely minced
⅓ cup coarsely chopped celery
⅓ cup coarsely chopped carrots
1 bay leaf
2 sprigs fresh thyme, or ½ teaspoon dried
1 cup fresh or canned chicken broth
4 cups water
¼ cup dry white wine
1 envelope unflavored gelatin
2 egg whites, beaten until frothy
2 crushed eggshells
4 sprigs parsley

pepper to taste. Bring to the boil and simmer slowly for about 3 hours.

4. Strain. There should be about 3 cups of broth. Let cool, but do not let the liquid set. If it does set, reheat briefly to melt and let cool to room temperature again. Skim off all traces of fat.

5. Blend the wine and gelatin and stir to soften. Add this to the liquid. Place on the stove and heat, stirring, until the gelatin is thoroughly dissolved. Add the beaten egg whites, crushed shells and parsley. Gently bring to the boil and let simmer for about 15 minutes.

6. Line a sieve with cheesecloth and strain. Let cool to room temperature.

Yield: About 2½ cups.

III. Eggs and Luncheon Dishes

Oeufs au Beurre Noir *(Eggs with black butter and capers)*

1. Melt 1 tablespoon of the butter in a skillet and add the eggs. Cook them sunny side up to the desired degree of doneness. Sprinkle with salt and pepper to taste.

2. Transfer the eggs to an individual serving dish. To the skillet add the remaining ½ tablespoon of butter. When it starts to brown and turn darker, add the capers. Cook for about 30 seconds and add the wine vinegar. Pour the sauce over the eggs. Sprinkle with parsley and serve with French bread or toast.

Yield: 1 serving.

1½ tablespoons butter
2 very fresh eggs
 Salt and freshly ground pepper
1 tablespoon drained capers
¼ teaspoon red wine vinegar
1 teaspoon chopped parsley

Mock Eggs Benedict *(Eggs and ham on toast with cheese sauce)*

1. Melt 2 tablespoons butter in a saucepan and add the flour, stirring with a wire whisk.

2. When blended, add the milk, stirring rapidly with the whisk. Season with salt, pepper, Tabasco sauce, Worcestershire and nutmeg. Remove from the heat and add the cheese, stirring until melted.

3. In a skillet bring enough water to the boil to cover the eggs when added. Add the vinegar and salt to taste. Carefully break the eggs into the water, one at a time, and cook gently until the white is set and the yolk remains runny. Carefully remove and drain on paper toweling.

4. Meanwhile, heat the ham in remaining 1 tablespoon of butter, turning once.

5. Arrange the toast on 4 hot plates. Cover each slice with a slice of ham and add a poached egg to each serving. Bring the sauce to the boil and spoon it over. Sprinkle each serving gingerly with paprika and serve hot.

Yield: 4 servings.

3 tablespoons butter
2 tablespoons flour
1 cup milk, or use half milk and half cream
 Salt and freshly ground pepper to taste
 Tabasco sauce to taste
½ teaspoon Worcestershire sauce
⅛ teaspoon nutmeg
¼ pound grated cheese, such as Cheddar, Swiss, or Gruyère
¼ cup white vinegar
4 eggs
4 slices cooked ham
4 slices hot buttered toast
 Paprika

Scotch Eggs

8 large eggs
1 pound ground lean pork
¾ cup fine, fresh bread crumbs, preferably made from untrimmed English muffins
Salt and freshly ground pepper
1½ teaspoons crushed dried marjoram
1 tablespoon chopped fresh parsley
2 tablespoons heavy cream
Flour for dredging
¾ cup fine, fresh bread crumbs made from trimmed, day-old sandwich bread
Fat for deep frying

1. Place 6 of the eggs in a saucepan and add lukewarm water to cover. Bring to the boil and simmer for 12 to 15 minutes. Drain the eggs and run them immediately under cold running water. Drain once more. Peel the eggs and set aside.

2. Combine the pork, bread crumbs made from the English muffins, 1 raw egg lightly beaten, salt and pepper to taste, marjoram, parsley and cream. Blend well with the hands.

3. Divide the pork mixture into 6 equal portions. Place one portion on a sheet of plastic wrap. Cover with another sheet of plastic wrap. Press down evenly and smooth the meat into a flat oval large enough to enclose 1 hard-cooked egg.

4. Dredge the eggs in flour, shaking off excess flour. Place one egg in the center of the meat. Bring up the bottom edges of the other sheet of plastic wrap to enclose the egg, pinching the seams together and pressing so that the egg is neatly and evenly enclosed in the meat. Continue until all the eggs are wrapped in the pork mixture. Dredge the wrapped eggs once more in flour.

5. Break the remaining raw egg into a rimmed dish. Dip the flour-coated eggs in this, turning to coat evenly, then in the bread crumbs made from sandwich bread.

6. Heat the fat for deep frying in a deep skillet. Add the eggs and cook for about 5 minutes, turning often until the meat is cooked and golden brown. Serve hot or lukewarm. Serve the eggs sliced in half.

Yield: Six servings.

Scotch Woodcock

4 slices buttered toast
16 egg yolks
1 cup heavy cream
Salt and freshly ground pepper
2 tablespoons cold butter
Tabasco sauce to taste
4 teaspoons anchovy paste
8 flat fillets of anchovy
Buttered asparagus spears, optional

1. Prepare the toast and keep it warm.

2. Bring water to the boil in a saucepan large enough to hold the saucepan in which the eggs will be cooked.

3. Combine the yolks and cream in a mixing bowl and beat lightly to blend. Add salt and pepper to taste.

4. Pour the mixture into a heavy saucepan and set the saucepan in the boiling water. Cook, stirring constantly, taking care to scrape around the bottom of the saucepan to make certain the egg mixture does not stick. Continue cooking until the egg mixture has the texture of soft scrambled eggs. Do not over-

cook. The moment the eggs are done, add the cold butter and stir. This should stop the cooking action. Add Tabasco sauce.

5. Smear one side of each piece of toast with 1 teaspoon of anchovy paste. Heap equal amounts of the hot egg mixture onto the toast and garnish each serving with 2 crossed anchovies. Serve, if desired, with buttered asparagus spears.

Yield: 4 servings.

Les Oeufs en Cocotte aux Tomates *(Eggs in ramekins with tomato sauce)*

1. Preheat the oven to 400 degrees.

2. Heat 2 tablespoons butter in a saucepan and add the onion. Cook, stirring, until the onion is wilted, about 2 minutes.

3. Add the tomatoes, rosemary, salt and pepper to taste. Simmer for about 8 minutes and add a dash of Tabasco. Swirl in 2 tablespoons of butter and season to taste with salt and pepper.

4. Lightly grease with remaining butter 12 ramekins, or "cocottes" (see note). These should be about 1½ inches deep and 2 inches in diameter. Sprinkle the bottoms lightly with salt and pepper.

5. Spoon about 2 tablespoons of the tomato sauce in the bottom of each ramekin, but reserve a small portion to use as a garnish.

6. Break 1 egg into each ramekin and sprinkle lightly with salt and pepper. Arrange the ramekins in a baking dish and pour boiling water around them. This will keep them from baking too rapidly. Bake for 10 to 12 minutes. When cooked, the whites should be firm and the yolks liquid or just starting to firm. Do not overcook.

7. Spoon a little of the remaining tomato sauce on top of each serving. Sprinkle each serving with chopped parsley. Serve 2 eggs to each guest along with French bread or buttered toast. The traditional method of serving dishes in ramekins is to cover a small plate with a napkin, then place the ramekin on the napkin. Provide each guest with a salad fork and a small spoon.

Yield: 6 servings.

Note: In a pinch, you could use small Pyrex glass cups.

5 tablespoons butter, approximately
⅔ cup finely chopped onion
1 cup drained canned tomatoes, preferably imported Italian plum tomatoes (it may take about 2 cups to yield 1 cup drained)
1 teaspoon finely chopped rosemary
Salt and freshly ground pepper
Tabasco sauce
12 eggs
Chopped parsley for garnish

Les Oeufs en Cocotte aux Foies de Volailles *(Eggs in ramekins with chicken livers)*

½ pound chicken livers (4 to 6)
  Salt and freshly ground
  pepper
3 tablespoons peanut,
  vegetable or corn oil
4 tablespoons butter
3 tablespoons finely chopped
  shallots
4 tablespoons Madeira or
  Marsala wine
⅔ cup brown sauce, or canned
  brown beef gravy
12 eggs

1. Preheat the oven to 400 degrees.

2. Cut the chicken livers in half, then cut the halves into ¾-inch cubes. Sprinkle with salt and pepper to taste.

3. Heat the oil in a small skillet and, when it is quite hot, add the chicken livers, stirring and tossing over high heat, for about 1 minute. They must not become dry. Drain in a sieve.

4. Heat 1 tablespoon of butter in a small saucepan. Add the shallots and cook for about 30 seconds, stirring. Add the wine and brown sauce. Simmer about 2 minutes and add the chicken livers. Swirl in 2 tablespoons of butter and add salt and pepper to taste.

5. Lightly grease with remaining butter 12 ramekins or "cocottes" (see note). These should be about 1½ inches deep and 2 inches in diameter. Sprinkle the bottoms with salt and pepper.

6. Spoon about 2 tablespoons of the chicken liver mixture in the bottom of each ramekin, but reserve a small portion to use as garnish. Keep it warm.

7. Break 1 egg into each ramekin and sprinkle lightly with salt and pepper. Arrange the ramekins in a baking dish and pour boiling water around them. This will keep them from baking too rapidly. Bake for 10 to 12 minutes. When cooked, the whites should be firm and the yolks liquid or just starting to firm. Do not overcook.

8. Spoon a little of the remaining chicken liver mixture on top of each serving. Serve 2 to each guest along with French bread or buttered toast. The traditional method of serving dishes in ramekins is to cover a small plate with a napkin, then place the ramekin on the napkin. Provide each guest with a salad fork and a small spoon.

Yield: 6 servings.

Note: In a pinch, you could use small Pyrex glass cups.

Eggs Masséna *(Poached eggs in artichoke bottoms with béarnaise sauce)*

This is an indecently rich and inspired concoction of poached eggs nestled in hot artichoke bottoms and garnished with two sauces, one béarnaise, one made with fresh tomatoes. The name of the dish is attributed to André Masséna, who fought under Napoleon and was called one of the great soldiers of France. The Encyclopedia Brittanica points out, however, that "in private life [Masséna was] indolent, greedy, rapacious, ill-educated and morose." Whatever his shortcomings, the dish that bears his name is one of the great egg dishes in the world.

1. Preheat the oven to 350 degrees.

2. Place the artichoke bottoms hollowed-out side down in a baking dish and dot with 1 tablespoon butter. Ten minutes before serving, place the bottoms in the oven and bake for 10 minutes.

3. Heat 1 tablespoon of butter in a small saucepan and add the tomatoes, salt and pepper. Bring to the boil and simmer 10 minutes, stirring often from the bottom. Put the mixture through a sieve to remove the seeds.

4. Prepare the béarnaise sauce and keep warm.

5. Remove the marrow from the bones and cut it into ¼-inch thick rounds. Place in a saucepan of warm water. The water must not be too hot or the marrow will disintegrate.

6. Add the 8 cups water, vinegar and salt to a deep skillet large enough to hold the 6 eggs. Bring to the boil and break the eggs into the liquid. Let simmer for about 2 minutes.

7. When ready to serve, place the artichoke bottoms, hollowed-out side up, on individual dishes. Fill each bottom with béarnaise sauce. Add a poached egg and spoon the tomato sauce over that. Cover with a round of warm, drained marrow and sprinkle with chopped parsley.

Yield: 6 servings.

6	cooked, hollowed-out artichoke bottoms (see instructions page 471)
2	tablespoons butter
1	pound red, ripe tomatoes, peeled, or imported canned tomatoes
	Salt and freshly ground pepper
¾	cup béarnaise sauce (see recipe page 644)
3	marrow bones, cracked
8	cups water
¼	cup white vinegar
6	eggs
	Finely chopped parsley

Scrambled Eggs

1. Beat the eggs with the cream until blended.

2. Heat the butter in a heavy saucepan placed over gentle heat or in a basin of boiling water. Cook the eggs, stirring all around the bottom and sides of the saucepan until they are at the desired degree of firmness. As the eggs start to firm up, add salt. Use a plastic spatula or wooden spoon to stir.

Yield: 1 serving.

2	eggs
2	tablespoons heavy cream
1	teaspoon butter
	Salt to taste

When the eggs and cream are beaten, add 1 tablespoon chopped herbs such as parsley, tarragon, chives or chervil, or 1 tablespoon of the herbs mixed together.

Scrambled eggs with herbs

Plain Omelet

3 eggs
  Salt and pepper to taste
2 teaspoons heavy cream
1 tablespoon butter

1. Break the eggs into a bowl. Beat lightly with the salt, pepper and cream.

2. Heat the omelet pan until quite hot. Immediately add the butter and swirl it around to coat the bottom and sides of the pan. Add the beaten eggs. Shake the skillet to and fro, holding it flat on the burner. Simultaneously, stir the eggs rapidly with a fork, holding the tines parallel to the bottom of the skillet. The preparation of the omelet will take only seconds.

3. When the eggs are at the desired degree of doneness, tilt the pan (you will have to adjust the hand and fingers on the handle, shifting the palm to an upward position while holding the handle and lifting). Quickly, hit the handle with a light blow to make the omelet "jump" to the bottom of the curve of the skillet. Use a fork to "roll" the omelet onto a waiting plate. A perfect omelet has pointed edges and the seam is on the plate unseen.

Yield: 1 serving.

Omelet aux fines herbs

Before making the omelet, blend 1 teaspoon of chopped parsley, 1 teaspoon of chopped chives and 1 teaspoon chopped fresh tarragon, or ½ teaspoon dried. Add these mixed herbs to the eggs along with the salt and pepper.

Cheese omelet

Grate enough cheese, preferably Gruyère, to make ¼ cup. One tablespoon of grated Parmesan cheese may also be added. Prepare the plain omelet. Before turning the omelet out, add the grated cheese to the center of the omelet. Fold it down and turn it out onto a plate.

Omelette Pavillon

7 tablespoons butter
3 tablespoons flour
1 cup fresh or canned chicken broth
½ cup heavy cream
3 tablespoons finely chopped onion
2 cups peeled, seeded, chopped tomatoes

1. Heat 2 tablespoons of butter in a saucepan and add the flour. Stir with a wire whisk until blended. Add the chicken broth and cook, stirring vigorously with the whisk. Add the cream and bring to the boil. Simmer for about 10 minutes.

2. Meanwhile, heat 1 tablespoon of butter in a saucepan and add the onion. Cook, stirring, until wilted and add the tomatoes, thyme, bay leaf, salt and pepper. Simmer, stirring occasionally, for about 10 minutes.

3. Heat another tablespoon of butter and add the chicken. Cook, stirring, for about 30 seconds. Add 3 tablespoons of the cream sauce. Bring to the boil and remove from the heat. Set aside.

4. To the remaining cream sauce add the egg yolk and stir to blend. Add salt and pepper to taste and the grated Swiss cheese. Heat, stirring, just until the cheese melts. Set aside.

5. Beat the eggs with salt and pepper. Add 6 tablespoons of the tomato sauce. Heat the remaining 3 tablespoons of butter in an omelet pan or a Teflon skillet and, when it is hot, add the eggs. Cook, stirring, until the omelet is set on the bottom but moist and runny in the center. Spoon creamed chicken down the center of the omelet and add the remaining tomato sauce. Quickly turn the omelet out into a baking dish.

6. Spoon the remaining cream sauce over the omelet and sprinkle with grated Parmesan cheese. Run the dish under the broiler until golden brown.

Yield: 4 to 6 servings.

2	sprigs fresh thyme, or ½ teaspoon dried
1	bay leaf
	Salt and freshly ground pepper to taste
1	cup finely cubed cooked breast of chicken
1	egg yolk
¼	cup grated Swiss, Gruyère or Fontina cheese
10	eggs
3	tablespoons grated Parmesan cheese

Spanish Omelet

1. Core and seed the peppers. Cut the peppers into very fine julienne strips. There should be about 2 cups.

2. Peel the onions and cut them in half. Thinly slice the onions. There should be about 2 cups.

3. Heat the oil in a saucepan and add the onion and green pepper. Add salt and pepper and cook briskly, stirring, about 5 minutes. Add the garlic and tomatoes and cook for 15 minutes.

4. Beat the eggs until frothy and add salt and pepper. Add 1¼ cups of the tomato sauce and beat lightly.

5. Heat the butter in an omelet pan or in a Teflon skillet and add the egg mixture. Cook, shaking the pan and stirring with a fork. Let the omelet set on the bottom, but it should remain moist and runny in the center. When cooked, place a large serving plate over the pan and quickly invert the omelet onto the plate. Spoon the remaining tomato sauce into the center of the omelet as a garnish. This omelet is normally served hot, but it is good cold. In Burgundy, this omelet is frequently eaten with a dash of vinegar on each serving.

Yield: 4 to 6 servings.

2 or	3 red or green sweet peppers
2 or	3 Bermuda onions
2	tablespoons olive oil
	Salt and freshly ground pepper to taste
1	tablespoon finely minced garlic
1	cup peeled, chopped tomatoes
10	eggs
3	tablespoons butter
	Vinegar, optional

Soufflé au Fromage   *(Cheese soufflé)*

¼ pound Gruyère or Swiss
    cheese, cut into ¼-inch slices
8 large eggs
6 tablespoons butter
5 tablespoons flour
2 cups milk
    Salt and freshly ground
    pepper
⅛ teaspoon grated nutmeg
    Pinch of cayenne pepper
2 tablespoons cornstarch
3 tablespoons water
¼ cup grated Parmesan cheese
2 tablespoon grated Gruyère or
    Swiss cheese

1. Preheat the oven to 400 degrees.
2. Stack the cheese slices on a flat surface. Using a sharp knife, cut into ¼-inch strips. Cut the strips into ¼-inch cubes. There should be about 1 cup. Set aside.
3. Separate the eggs, placing the yolks in one bowl and the whites in another.
4. Use 2 tablespoons of butter and butter all around the inside rim and bottom of a 2-quart soufflé dish. Place the dish in the freezer until ready to use.
5. Melt the remaining butter in a saucepan and add the flour, stirring with a wire whisk. When blended, add the milk, stirring rapidly with the whisk. Add salt and pepper to taste, nutmeg and cayenne. Cook for 30 seconds, stirring.
6. Blend the cornstarch and water and add this to the bubbling sauce, stirring. Cook for about 2 minutes. Add yolks, stirring vigorously. Cook, stirring, for about 1 minute.
7. Spoon and scrape the mixture into a large mixing bowl. Add the cubed Gruyère or Swiss cheese and the Parmesan cheese. Blend well.
8. Beat the egg whites until stiff. Add half the whites to the soufflé mixture and beat them thoroughly. Add the remaining whites and fold them in quickly but gently with a rubber spatula.
9. Spoon and scrape the mixture into the soufflé dish. Sprinkle with the grated Gruyère and place in the oven.
10. Bake for 15 minutes. Reduce the oven heat to 375 degrees and bake for 15 minutes longer.
Yield: 4 to 6 servings.

Soufflé aux Oeufs   *(Eggs baked in a soufflé)*

1 recipe for cheese soufflé (see
    recipe above)
4 small eggs
    Salt and freshly ground pepper

1. Preheat the oven to 400 degrees.
2. Prepare the soufflé dish as indicated in the recipe. Prepare the basic mixture for the soufflé up to and including folding in the egg whites.
3. Spoon half the soufflé mixture into the soufflé dish. Using a spoon, make 4 indentations spaced about halfway between the rim and the center of the soufflé.
4. Break 1 egg over each indentation. The yolks should fall into the indentations. The whites may run to the center or rim. Don't be unnerved.

5. Sprinkle the eggs with salt and pepper to taste.

6. Spoon and scrape in the remaining soufflé mixture.

7. Sprinkle the soufflé with grated Gruyère cheese and place in the oven. Bake for 15 minutes. Reduce the oven heat to 375 degrees and bake for 15 minutes longer.

Yield: 4 servings.

Corn and Salmon Soufflé

1. Preheat the oven to 375 degrees. Generously butter 2 1-quart soufflé dishes or 1 8-cup soufflé dish. Refrigerate or place briefly in the freezer.

2. Cut and scrape the kernels from the cob. There should be about 1 cup. Set aside.

3. Flake the salmon coarsely. Set aside.

4. Melt the 3 tablespoons butter in a saucepan and add the flour, stirring with a wire whisk. When blended, add the milk, stirring rapidly with the whisk. When blended and smooth, add salt and pepper. Add the corn and cook, stirring frequently, for about 3 minutes. Remove from heat and add ¾ cup cheese.

5. Blend the cornstarch and water and add it. Cook briefly, stirring with the whisk.

6. Add the egg yolks, stirring them in briskly with the whisk. Add salt, pepper, nutmeg and cayenne. Heat briefly but do not boil. Remove from the heat and let cool briefly.

7. Beat the whites until stiff and fold them in.

8. Fill the soufflé dishes half full with the mixture. Add a layer of the salmon. Cover with the remaining mixture. Sprinkle with remaining cheese and bake for 25 to 35 minutes, or until well risen and nicely browned on top.

Yield: 4 to 8 servings.

4	ears corn
1	cup cooked, skinless, boneless salmon, fresh or canned
3	tablespoons butter
3	tablespoons flour
1	cup milk
	Salt and freshly ground pepper to taste
1	cup grated Gruyère, Muenster, Swiss or Cheddar cheese
1	tablespoon cornstarch
2	tablespoons water
6	eggs, separated
¼	teaspoon grated nutmeg
⅛	teaspoon cayenne pepper

Tuna Soufflé with Cheese

Years ago, Pierre Franey and I read a newspaper account dealing with a Frenchman who had pleaded guilty to smuggling some $12 million worth of heroin into New York. The account added that he whiled away his time in jail and became famous for his tuna soufflés. The more we thought about it, the more we agreed that a tuna soufflé might not be a bad trifle. Thus, the following.

1 8-ounce can tuna in olive oil
5 tablespoons butter, approximately
4 tablespoons flour
2 cups milk
   Salt and freshly ground pepper to taste
¼ teaspoon freshly grated nutmeg
3 or 4 drops Tabasco sauce
¼ teaspoon Worcestershire sauce
1 tablespoon prepared mustard, such as Dijon or Düsseldorf
1 tablespoon cornstarch
2 tablespoons water
8 eggs, separated
½ cup grated Parmesan cheese
⅔ cup finely diced Gruyère or Swiss cheese

1. Preheat the oven to 400 degrees.

2. Put the tuna with the oil in the container of a food processor or electric blender and blend until smooth.

3. Use about 1 tablespoon of the butter and rub it all over the bottom and sides of a 6- or 7-cup soufflé dish. Put the dish in the freezer.

4. Melt the remaining 4 tablespoons of butter in a saucepan and add the flour. Stir with a wire whisk until blended and add the milk, stirring rapidly with the whisk. Add salt, pepper, nutmeg and Tabasco. Stir in the blended tuna mixture and add the Worcestershire and mustard. When the sauce is bubbling, blend the cornstarch with water and add it, stirring vigorously with the whisk.

5. Stir the egg yolks and add them to the sauce, stirring constantly. Bring just to the boil and cook, stirring, for about 10 seconds. Remove from the heat and stir in the Parmesan cheese. Let cool briefly, for about 10 minutes. Stir in the small cubes of Gruyère.

6. Beat the egg whites until stiff. Add about one-third of them to the soufflé mixture and beat in with a whisk. Fold in the remaining whites with a rubber spatula, turning it over and around and scraping from the bottom to incorporate the whites evenly. Pour the mixture into the cold soufflé dish.

7. Bake for 15 minutes and reduce the oven heat to 375 degrees. Bake for 15 minutes, or until soufflé is well puffed and golden brown on top.

Yield: 6 servings.

Crêpes

¾ cup flour
1 large egg
   Salt to taste
1 cup milk
2 tablespoons melted butter

1. Scoop the flour into a mixing bowl and add the egg and salt. Add the milk, stirring with a wire whisk. Add the melted butter.

2. Heat a well-seasoned crêpe pan and add a thin layer of batter to cover the bottom. Cook briefly and turn. Cook briefly and turn out. Continue until all the batter is used.

Yield: 8 7-inch crêpes.

Parmesan crêpes

Add ¼ cup grated Parmesan cheese to the basic crêpe recipe. Before each crêpe is made, brush the crêpe pan with butter to prevent sticking. This is not necessary in making plain crêpes, but the cheese tends to make the crêpes stick.

Manicotti with Ricotta Cheese

1. Prepare the crêpes and lay them on a flat surface.
2. Blend the ricotta, yolks, parsley, salt to taste, nutmeg, 1 cup of Parmesan cheese and pepper to taste. Blend well. Spoon equal portions of the filling down the center of each crêpe and roll it.
3. Spoon about 3 tablespoons of tomato sauce over the bottom of a baking dish (a rectangular dish measuring 8- x 14-inches would be appropriate).
4. Spoon the remaining sauce over the crêpes and sprinkle with remaining 2 tablespoons of cheese. Pour the melted butter over all.
5. When ready to bake, preheat the oven to 400 degrees. Bake for about 20 minutes.

Yield: 4 to 8 servings.

8 Parmesan cheese crêpes (see recipe above)
2 cups ricotta cheese (or one 15-ounce carton)
2 egg yolks
2 tablespoons finely chopped parsley
  Salt
1/8 teaspoon grated nutmeg
1 cup plus 2 tablespoons grated Parmesan cheese
  Freshly ground pepper
2 cups tomato sauce, preferably homemade
2 tablespoons melted butter

Manicotti with Creamed Chicken and Almonds

1. Prepare the pancakes and have them ready.
2. Preheat the oven to 350 degrees.
3. Place the chicken breasts in a bowl and squeeze the lemon over it, adding the rind. Let stand.
4. Melt 1½ tablespoons of butter in a saucepan and add the onion. Cook, stirring, until the onion is wilted. Sprinkle with flour and cook, stirring with a wire whisk. Add the broth, stirring rapidly with the whisk. When thickened and smooth, add half the cream. Simmer for about 10 minutes, stirring occasionally, and add the Gruyère cheese, salt and pepper to taste. Stir to blend and set aside.
5. Meanwhile, melt 1 teaspoon of butter in a small skillet and add the almonds in one layer. Place in the oven and bake, shaking the skillet and stirring the almonds until they are golden brown. Remove and let cool.
6. Drain the chicken pieces. Pat dry. Sprinkle with salt and pepper to taste. Melt 2 tablespoons of butter in a skillet and add the chicken. Brown on both sides quickly, 3 or 4 minutes. Remove and add the vermouth. Cook for about 30 seconds, stirring. Pour the drippings into a bowl.
7. Cut the chicken into ½-inch cubes and add it to the bowl. Add the almonds. Add the remaining heavy cream, egg (if the egg is large, use only half of it), ricotta cheese, 4 tablespoons

12 manicotti pancakes (see recipe below)
2 chicken breasts, skinned, boned and cut in half
½ lemon
3½ tablespoons plus 1 teaspoon butter
¼ cup finely chopped onion
2 tablespoons flour
1 cup fresh or canned chicken broth
½ cup heavy cream
½ cup grated Gruyère or Swiss cheese
  Salt and freshly ground pepper
3 tablespoons blanched almonds
1 tablespoon dry vermouth
1 small egg
1 cup ricotta cheese
6 tablespoons freshly grated Parmesan cheese
3 tablespoons chopped parsley
½ teaspoon grated lemon rind

Parmesan cheese and chopped parsley. Blend well with a fork or whisk.

8. To assemble, spoon equal amounts of the chicken mixture down the center of the manicotti pancakes and roll them to enclose the filling. Select a baking dish large enough to hold the rolled manicotti in one layer. Spoon enough sauce into the dish to cover the bottom. Arrange the filled manicotti over the sauce. Cover with a layer of sauce, reserving some sauce to be served separately.

9. Cover the dish with foil and bake for 15 to 20 minutes until piping hot and bubbling. Sprinkle with remaining 2 tablespoons of Parmesan cheese and run briefly under the broiler to glaze. Sprinkle with lemon peel and serve hot with the remaining sauce, brought to the boil, on the side.

Yield: 6 to 12 servings.

Manicotti pancakes

3 eggs
1 cup water
1 cup flour
  Salt to taste
  Melted butter

1. Break the eggs into a bowl and beat with a whisk. Stir in the water. Add the flour gradually, stirring with the whisk. Add the salt and let stand for ½ hour.

2. Heat a 7- or 8-inch crêpe pan or small Teflon skillet and brush lightly with butter. Add about 3 tablespoons of the batter and tilt the pan this way and that until the batter covers the bottom. The crêpes should be quite thin but substantial enough to handle. Cook for about 35 seconds on one side and turn, using a spatula or the hands. Cook on the other side briefly, 2 to 3 seconds. Slide out.

3. Continue making pancakes until all the batter is used, brushing the skillet lightly with butter if necessary before each pancake is made.

Yield: 12 manicotti pancakes.

Crêpes aux Fruits de Mer Nantua *(Seafood-filled crêpes with lobster sauce)*

16 crêpes (see recipe on page 104 and double it)
1 1¼-pound lobster
6 tablespoons butter
½ cup finely chopped shallots
¼ cup plus 1 tablespoon Cognac
1 clove garlic, finely minced
2½ tablespoons tomato paste
¾ cup dry white wine

1. Prepare the crêpes, stack them and keep covered.

2. Split the lobster in half. Break off the claws and crack them. Remove and discard the tough sac near the eyes of the lobster. Remove the coral and liver from the carcass and set aside.

3. Heat half the butter in a heavy skillet and add the lobster tail, the claws and the carcass pieces. Sprinkle with shallots and cook over high heat, stirring, until lobster shell turns bright red. Add the ¼ cup Cognac and flame it. Add the garlic

and tomato paste, stirring. Add the wine, fish stock, parsley, bay leaf, thyme, salt and pepper to taste. Cook for about 10 minutes, stirring occasionally.

4. Preheat the oven to 400 degrees.

5. Remove the lobster pieces and, when cool enough to handle, remove the meat from the tail and claws and set aside. Chop the lobster shell coarsely and put it in a food processor or put it through the coarse blade of a meat grinder. Blend or grind coarsely. Return this to the sauce and cook about 5 minutes longer.

6. Blend the coral and liver with 2 tablespoons of butter and the flour. Stir this, bit by bit, into the sauce. Add the cream and bring to the boil. Sprinkle with salt and pepper and put the mixture through a fine sieve.

7. Cut the lobster meat into small pieces.

8. Heat the remaining tablespoon butter and add the mushrooms. Cook briefly and add the scallops and squid. Cook for about 30 seconds, stirring, and add the shrimp. Cook until shrimp turn pink. Cover and cook for 5 minutes. Uncover and reduce briefly. Add the remaining tablespoon of Cognac. Stir in about ⅓ cup of the lobster sauce and heat. Add the lobster and stir.

9. Fill the crêpes, one at a time, with equal portions of the mixture and fold the crêpes over to enclose the filling. Arrange the crêpes symmetrically in an oven-proof baking dish large enough to hold them. Spoon the remaining sauce over. Cover with foil and bake for 10 or 15 minutes, or until piping hot. Serve on hot plates.

Yield: 8 or more servings.

3 cups fish stock, or use fresh or bottled clam juice
1 tablespoon finely chopped fresh parsley
1 bay leaf
½ teaspoon dried thyme
Salt and freshly ground pepper
¼ cup flour
1 cup heavy cream
1 cup finely chopped fresh mushrooms
¾ pound small scallops, cut into small pieces
¾ pound squid, cut into small pieces, optional
¾ pound shrimp, shelled, deveined and cut into piece

Sunday Omelet Crêpe

1. In the center of each crêpe, put a scant teaspoon of either jam or jelly. Roll up the crêpe.

2. Heat an omelet pan. Add ⅓ of the butter. While butter is melting, beat eggs and cream together lightly with a fork. Add salt and pepper. Pour ⅓ cup of egg mixture into the hot omelet pan. Stir quickly with a fork until edges begin to cook. When omelet is almost set, place the rolled crêpe in the center and with a spatula quickly roll the omelet around the crêpe and slide it onto a warm platter.

3. Follow same steps with the remaining egg mixture and crêpes. Allow 3 crêpes per person.

Yield: 2 servings.

6 crêpes (see recipe on page 104)
Raspberry jam or some kind of tart jelly
4 tablespoons butter
7 eggs
2 tablespoons heavy cream
Salt and freshly ground pepper

Mexican-style Chicken with Crêpes

The chicken:

1 or 2 skinned, boned, whole
 chicken breasts, about 1
 pound total weight
 Fresh or canned chicken
 broth to cover
 Salt

The sauce:

 2 12-ounce can tomatillo
 entero (Spanish green
 tomatoes), available in
 Mexican and Spanish
 grocery stores
 2 small green hot chilies, or
 use canned drained serrano
 or jalapeno peppers
 1 clove garlic, finely minced
 3 tablespoons peanut,
 vegetable or corn oil
 ½ cup finely chopped onion
 ½ teaspoon sugar
 Salt
 1 tablespoon finely chopped
 fresh coriander

The assembly:

 8 7-inch crêpes (see recipe on
 page 104)
 ¾ cup sour cream

1. Place the chicken in a saucepan and add chicken broth to cover and salt to taste. Bring to the boil and simmer for 10 to 15 minutes. Do not overcook. Let chicken cool in cooking liquid.

2. Drain the tomatoes and put them into the container of a food processor or electric blender.

3. Remove and discard the stems, seeds and veins from the chilies. Add them to the tomatoes. Add the garlic and blend until finely puréed.

4. Heat the oil in a skillet and cook the onion until wilted. Add the tomato mixture, sugar and salt to taste. Cook, stirring often, for 6 or 7 minutes. Add more sugar and salt to taste. Just before using, stir in the coriander.

5. Prepare the crêpes and have them ready.

6. When ready to serve, preheat the oven to 400 degrees.

7. Shred the chicken, discarding all cartilage.

8. To assemble, lightly oil a baking dish large enough to hold the stuffed, rolled crêpes compactly. Place the crêpes, one at a time, on a flat surface and spoon in a layer of green tomato sauce. Add a portion of chicken and more sauce. Roll. Arrange the filled crêpes close together in the dish. Spoon any remaining sauce over the crêpes.

9. Place in the oven and bake for 8 to 10 minutes, or until piping hot. Serve with the sour cream spooned over each serving.

Yield: 4 to 8 servings.

Blini

 ¾ cup flour
 1 egg, separated
 2 teaspoons granular yeast
 ¾ cup milk
 Salt
 2 tablespoons heavy cream
 2 tablespoons chopped dill

1. Scoop the flour into a mixing bowl and add the egg yolk. Dissolve the yeast in the milk and add it, stirring with a wire whisk. Add salt to taste. Set in a warm place and let stand for about 2 hours, covered with a towel.

2. When ready to cook, add the cream and chopped dill. Beat the egg white and fold it in. Cook in a crêpe pan as with ordinary crêpes.

Yield: 8 blini.

Blini with Smoked Salmon and Red Caviar

1. Place the blini on a flat surface and arrange slices of smoked salmon down the center. Roll the blini.

2. Blend the sour cream with salt to taste. Spoon a dollop of sour cream over the blini and top with spoonfuls of red caviar. Garnish with dill or parsley.

Yield: 4 servings.

8	blini (see recipe above)
½	pound thinly sliced smoked salmon
1½	cups sour cream
	Salt
4	to 8 ounces red caviar
	Sprigs of dill or parsley for garnish

Zucchini and Ham Quiche

1. Preheat the oven to 350 degrees.

2. Roll out the pastry and line the quiche tin with pastry and then with foil. Add dried beans to weight the bottom down. Place in the oven and bake for 20 minutes. Remove the foil and beans from the pastry.

3. Heat the butter in a skillet and add the onion and garlic. Cook, stirring, until wilted. Add the salt and pepper to taste and zucchini and cook, stirring gently and shaking the pan occasionally, for about 5 minutes. Add the ham, stirring gently to blend, and remove from the heat.

4. Break the eggs into a mixing bowl. Beat well and add the milk, cream, salt and pepper to taste. Scrape into the zucchini mixture.

5. Increase oven heat to 375 degrees.

6. Pour the zucchini and custard mixture into the pastry. Sprinkle with cheese. Place the quiche on a baking sheet and bake for 30 minutes.

7. Reduce the oven heat to 350 degrees. Bake for 15 minutes longer.

Yield: 6 to 8 servings.

	Pastry to line a 10-inch quiche tin (see recipe below)
2	tablespoons butter
¼	cup finely chopped onion
1	small clove garlic, finely minced
	Salt and freshly ground pepper
1¼	pounds zucchini, trimmed and thinly sliced, about 5 cups
¼	pound sliced boiled ham, finely diced, about ¾ cup
4	large eggs
¾	cup milk
½	cup heavy cream
¼	cup grated Parmesan cheese

1. Put the flour and salt into the container of a food processor or a mixing bowl.

2. Add the lard and butter and process while gradually adding the water. Add only enough water so that the dough comes clean from the sides of the container and can be handled. Shape into a flat rectangle and wrap in plastic wrap or wax paper. Chill for 1 hour or longer.

Yield: Pastry for a 10-inch quiche.

Pastry dough

2	cups flour
½	teaspoon salt
½	cup lard or solid white shortening
3	tablespoons butter
3 to	4 tablespoons ice water

Mexican Quiche with Chilies and Cheese

Pastry for a 10-inch quiche
(see recipe page 109)
2 tablespoons butter
1 tablespoon finely chopped
  shallots
1 4-ounce can chopped green
  chilies
2 cups grated Gruyère,
  Cheddar or Swiss cheese
4 large or 6 small egg yolks,
  about ⅓ cup
1½ cups heavy cream
  Salt to taste

1. Preheat the oven to 425 degrees.

2. Roll out the pastry and line a quiche or pie tin with the pastry. Line the shell with foil, and add enough dried beans to weight the bottom down. Place the shell in the oven and bake for 10 minutes.

3. Remove the foil and dried beans. Return the shell to the oven and bake for 2 minutes longer.

4. Remove the shell and reduce the oven heat to 350 degrees.

5. Heat the butter in a small skillet and add the shallots. Cook briefly and add the chilies. Stir and remove from the heat. Let cool.

6. Scrape the chili mixture into the prebaked pie shell. Sprinkle evenly with the cheese.

7. Blend the egg yolks lightly beaten with the cream. Add salt to taste and pour the custard over the cheese. Place the pie on a baking sheet and bake for 35 minutes, or until the custard is set.

Yield: 6 to 8 servings.

Quiche de Poireaux *(Leek quiche)*

Pastry for a 10-inch quiche (see
recipe page 109)
3 large leeks, finely cut
  crosswise, about 4 cups
2 tablespoons butter
  Salt and freshly ground
  pepper to taste
¼ pound thinly slice boiled
  ham, cut into small pieces
4 large eggs, about 1 cup or
  slightly less
⅛ teaspoon grated nutmeg
¾ cup heavy cream
½ cup milk
½ cup grated Gruyère or Swiss
  cheese

1. Prepare the pastry and have it ready. Roll it out and line the bottom and sides of a 10-inch quiche tin with removable bottom. Refrigerate.

2. Wash and chop the leeks and have them ready.

3. Melt the butter in a skillet and add the leeks, salt and pepper. Cook for about 5 minutes, stirring occasionally. Add the ham and stir. Scrape the mixture into a mixing bowl. Let cool.

4. Preheat the oven to 400 degrees.

5. Put the eggs in a mixing bowl. Add salt and pepper to taste and nutmeg. Beat well with a whisk. Add the cream and milk. Pour the mixture into the bowl containing the leeks and ham. Blend.

6. Line the bottom of the pastry with aluminim foil and fill the bottom with sufficient dried beans or peas to weight the bottom. Place in the oven and bake for 15 minutes. Remove and let cool briefly. Remove aluminum foil and beans.

7. Spoon and pour the cream mixture into the baked pastry and sprinkle with cheese. Place on a baking sheet and bake for

15 minutes. Reduce oven heat to 375 degrees and bake for 35 minutes longer.

Yield: 6 to 8 servings.

Quiche of Sweetbreads and Mushrooms

1	small pair sweetbreads, about ¾ pound
	Salt and freshly ground pepper
½	pound fresh mushrooms, sliced, about 2½ cups
½	pound fresh spinach, trimmed and rinsed well
6	tablespoons butter
4	eggs
1½	plus ⅓ cups heavy cream
⅛	teaspoon grated nutmeg
¼	cup dry white wine
	Enough pastry for 6 individual pies or 1 10-inch quiche

1. Soak the sweetbreads for several hours in cold water to cover. Drain.

2. Place the sweetbreads in a large saucepan and add cold water to cover. Bring to the boil and simmer for 5 minutes. Drain immediately, run under cold water and let cool. Chill well.

3. Place the sweetbreads in a dish large enough to hold them and cover with a weight. Refrigerate for at least 6 hours.

4. Preheat the oven to 450 degrees.

5. Trim off the outside membranes and veins from the sweetbreads. Cut the sweetbreads into 1-inch cubes. Sprinkle with salt and pepper and set aside.

6. Sprinkle the mushrooms with salt and pepper and set aside.

7. Drop the spinach into boiling salted water. Simmer for 1 minute. Drain and run under cold water. Squeeze to extract most of the moisture. Chop coarsely and sprinkle with salt and pepper and set aside.

8. Heat 2 tablespoons of butter in each of 3 skillets. Cook the sweetbreads in one skillet, stirring and tossing, for about 5 minutes. Set aside. Cook the spinach in another skillet, for about 2 minutes, stirring and tossing. Set aside.

9. Beat together the eggs and 1½ cups cream. Season with salt, pepper and nutmeg.

10. Cook the mushrooms in the third skillet, for about 3 minutes, stirring and tossing. Add the sweetbreads and any pan juices to the mushrooms. Cook together, stirring, for about 1 minute. Scoop out the sweetbread mixture and set aside. Add the wine to that skillet and cook until almost totally reduced. Add the remaining ⅓ cup of heavy cream and cook, stirring, for about 1 minute. Add this to the egg and cream mixture.

11. Line 6 individual, disposable, aluminum pie pans or one 10-inch quiche pan with the pastry.

12. Add equal amounts of the spinach to the bottoms of each of the individual pie shells or the larger pie shell. Cover the

shells with equal portions of the sweetbread mixture. Pour in the egg mixture.

13. Place the pies on a baking sheet and bake the individual pies for 20 minutes, the larger pie for 30 minutes. Reduce the heat to 350 degrees and bake for 10 to 15 minutes longer.

Yield: 6 individual pies or one 10-inch pie.

Spanakopitta *(Greek-style spinach pie)*

3	pounds fresh spinach
¾	cup olive oil, approximately
2	bunches scallions, trimmed and chopped
¼	cup chopped parsley
½	pound feta cheese, crumbled
6	eggs, lightly beaten
	Salt and freshly ground pepper
10	sheets phyllo pastry

1. Preheat the oven to 350 degrees.

2. Pick over the spinach to remove and discard all blemished leaves and tough stems. Rinse the spinach in several changes of cold water to remove all traces of sand. Steam the spinach briefly over boiling water just until the leaves are wilted. Let cool. Chop the spinach coarsely.

3. Heat 1 tablespoon of oil in a skillet and add the scallions. Cook, stirring, until the scallions are wilted.

4. In a mixing bowl, combine the spinach, scallions, parsley, cheese, eggs, salt and pepper to taste. Add 1 tablespoon of oil and blend thoroughly.

5. Select a baking pan measuring approximately 13- x 9-inches. Or use a round pan of similar size. Cover the pan with one layer of phyllo pastry, letting the edges of the pastry hang over the sides. Brush the pastry generously with oil. Continue adding 4 more layers, brushing each layer with oil as it is added. Spoon the spinach mixture into the center and smooth it over. Cover with another layer of phyllo, brush with oil and continue adding 4 more layers, brushing oil between each layer. Use a sharp knife or scissors to trim off the overhanging edges of pastry. Bake the pie for 40 to 50 minutes, or until it is piping hot throughout and golden brown on top.

Yield: 18 or more servings.

Alsatian Meat Pie

To many cooks, a quiche is a quiche lorraine, but quiche is really the generic name for a host of nonsweet pies. One of the finest we know is this Alsatian meat pie made with veal or pork. It is a tasty appetizer or luncheon dish and was a specialty of Pierre Franey's Uncle Louis, a native of Alsace.

1. Line a 10-inch quiche pan with a removable bottom with the pastry and chill it.

2. Preheat the oven to 375 degrees.

3. Sprinkle the veal and pork with salt and pepper to taste and the nutmeg.

4. Heat the butter in a skillet and add the shallots and onion. Cook, stirring, until wilted and add the mushrooms. Cook for 5 minutes, stirring frequently. Add the meat, stirring and breaking up lumps of meat with the side of a large metal spoon. Cook until most of the liquid is given up.

5. Beat the egg and yolk with a fork until well blended and add the cream and salt and pepper to taste. Blend well and add the mixture to the meat. Stir well.

6. Pour the mixture into the prepared pie shell and bake for 15 minutes. Reduce the oven heat to 350 degrees. Bake for 30 to 35 minutes longer or until the custard is set. Remove from the oven and let stand. Serve lukewarm or at room temperature.

Yield: 8 servings.

	Alsatian pastry for 1 10-inch pie (see recipe below)
1	pound lean leg or shoulder of veal, ground, or use an equal quantity of ground lean pork
1/8	pound ground lean pork (in addition to the above meat)
	Salt and freshly ground pepper to taste
1/8	teaspoon grated nutmeg
2	teaspoons butter
1½	tablespoons finely chopped shallots
1/3	cup finely chopped onion
3/4	cup finely chopped mushrooms
1	whole egg
1	egg yolk
1	cup heavy cream

1. Put the flour in a mixing bowl and place it in the freezer. Place the butter in the freezer and let both stand for ½ hour or longer.

2. Remove the flour and cut the butter into bits adding it to the flour. Add salt. Using the fingers or a pastry blender, cut the butter into the flour until the mixture is like coarse cornmeal. Gradually add the oil, stirring with a two-pronged fork. When blended, add the milk gradually, working the pastry with the hands until it forms a dough. Knead briefly and gather the dough into a ball. Wrap it in wax paper and chill for at least 30 minutes.

3. Remove the dough from the refrigerator and place it on a lightly floured surface. Roll it out into a rectangle measuring about 12 by 6 inches. Fold a third of the dough over toward the center. Fold the other side of the dough over toward the center, thus making a three-layer package of dough. Cover and refrigerate for about ½ hour.

4. Roll out the dough once more on a lightly floured surface, sprinkling the surface with additional flour as necessary. Roll it into another rectangle. Fold the dough into thirds as before, cover and chill. The dough is now ready to be rolled into a circle for fitting into a 10-inch metal quiche pan.

Yield: Pastry for a 10-inch quiche.

Alsatian pastry

2½	cups flour
1/4	pound butter
	Salt to taste
6	tablespoons well-chilled corn oil
6	tablespoons cold milk, approximately

Welsh Rabbit

We subscribe to the story that a Welshman went hunting and returned home empty-handed. His wife concocted a dish with melted cheese and dubbed it "rabbit." Thus, Welsh rabbit, not rarebit.

½ pound very sharp Cheddar
cheese
1 teaspoon dry mustard
1 teaspoon paprika
⅛ teaspoon cayenne pepper
Freshly grated nutmeg to taste
½ cup beer
1 tablespoon butter
1 egg, lightly beaten
Salt
1 teaspoon Worcestershire sauce
4 slices dry toast

1. Grate the cheese and set it aside.
2. Put the mustard, paprika, cayenne and nutmeg in a small mixing bowl. Add the beer, a few drops at a time, stirring with a fork to make a paste. Continue adding and stirring until all the ingredients are well blended.
3. Melt the butter in a saucepan and add the beer mixture. Set the saucepan in a skillet and pour boiling water around the saucepan to a depth of about ½ inch. Let the water simmer until the beer mixture becomes quite hot.
4. Add the cheese and stir with a wooden spoon until the cheese melts. Add the egg, stirring constantly over the bottom of the saucepan, making sure all areas are covered. Add salt to taste and Worcestershire sauce. Continue "cooking" and stirring until the rabbit is thickened and smooth. The cheese mixture must not boil at any time or the egg will "scramble" or curdle.
5. When the rabbit is piping hot, it will thicken. Serve over dry toast with a peppermill on the side.
   Yield: 2 servings.

Golden Buck

½ cup yellow Cheddar cheese
4 eggs, beaten
2 tablespoons butter
½ cup dark beer
¼ cup heavy cream
Dash of Tabasco sauce
2 teaspoons Worcestershire
sauce
¼ teaspoon freshly ground
pepper
Salt
Buttered toast points

1. Cut the cheese into ½-inch cubes and put it in a heavy, small casserole. Add the eggs, butter, beer, cream, Tabasco, Worcestershire, pepper and salt to taste.
2. Place the casserole over moderate heat and cook, stirring constantly, until cheese is melted and the mixture is piping hot. Do not boil or the eggs will curdle.
3. Serve over buttered toast points.
   Yield: 2 to 4 servings.

Cheese Fondue

1. Grate or shred the cheese or cut into small cubes.
2. Rub the inside of a fondue pot (see note) with the clove of garlic. Add the wine and heat without boiling. This is probably best done at the stove, using a Flame Tamer or other heatproof pad to prevent sticking on the bottom.
3. Add the cheese and stir with a wooden spoon without stopping until the mixture is runny. Blend the kirsch and cornstarch and add it to the mixture, stirring. The cornstarch should bind the mixture and make it smooth. If desired, add a touch of salt to the fondue. The saltiness of Gruyère varies. When the fondue is boiling and smooth, it may be transferred to a fondue cooker with a flame for serving at table.
4. Cut the French bread into 1-inch cubes. Serve with fondue forks, first spearing a cube of bread and dipping it into the hot fondue. Serve with a peppermill on the side. If desired, add more kirsch to taste.

Yield: 6 to 8 servings.

Note: Prior to using an earthenware fondue pot or casserole, rub the inside and outside unglazed surface with a clove of garlic. Preheat the oven to 400 degrees. Fill the pot with water and place in the oven. Let simmer for about 1 hour. Fondue pots can be used over direct flame but it is chancy. There is less danger of breakage if the pot is placed over a heat-proof pad to insure equal distribution of heat.

3	pounds Gruyère cheese
1	clove garlic
2½	cups dry white wine
¼	cup kirsch
4	teaspoons cornstarch
	Salt, optional
1	loaf French bread
	Freshly ground pepper

Chilies con Queso *(Chili and cheese fondue California-style)*

1. Grate the cheese on the coarse grater. There should be about 4 cups.
2. Heat the butter in a chafing dish or electric cooker and add the garlic. Cook briefly and add the tomato. Stir and add the cheese and milk.
3. Bring gradually to the boil, stirring. Blend the cornstarch and water and stir it in. Add the chilies and salt. Serve hot with tostadas, corn chips, fried tortillas or French bread.

Yield: 6 to 8 servings.

1	pound Monterey Jack, Cheddar or Muenster cheese
2	tablespoons butter
1	teaspoon finely chopped garlic
¾	cup cored, unpeeled tomato cut into small cubes
½	cup milk
2	teaspoons cornstarch
1	tablespoon water
1 to 4	tablespoons chopped canned chilies
	Salt to taste

Pizza with Anchovies and Cheese

We discovered on an outing in Nova Scotia that we had much in common with the children of Sirio Maccioni, the tall, dapper owner of Le Cirque restaurant in Manhattan, and his wife, Egi. And that is a passion for homemade pizza. We made this discovery one Sunday morning while most of the rest of the group, including several chefs, were out in the woods hunting wild boar. Because I quite honestly could not kill a squirrel or any other animal, I stayed home with Egi and watched the yeast dough rise. And the children are right—her pizza is super!

Pizza dough for 2 13-inch pizzas (see recipe below)
8   tablespoons olive oil
8   tinned anchovies, drained and cut in half crosswise (use more anchovies if you prefer a more pronounced flavor)
¼   cup drained capers
1   cup well-drained canned tomatoes cut into ½-inch pieces
1   teaspoon dried oregano
    Salt to taste
2   cups grated whole-milk mozzarella cheese
    Freshly ground pepper to taste

1. Prepare the dough and let it rise.
2. Pour 2 tablespoons of olive oil into the center of each of 2 13-inch pizza pans. Spread it around the bottom and inner rim of the pans.
3. Using lightly floured fingers, work the dough into a ball. Divide it in half and, with floured fingers, pat each half into a somewhat thick circle. Add 1 circle of dough to the center of each pizza pan. Using the fingers, pat and press the dough to cover the bottom of the pans, rim to rim. Cover and let stand in a warm place for about ½ hour.
4. Meanwhile, preheat the oven to 350 degrees.
5. Scatter equal amounts of anchovies over the 2 pizzas. Sprinkle with capers and cover with tomato pieces. Sprinkle with oregano and just a touch of salt. Sprinkle the grated cheese over all and sprinkle generously with black pepper. Sprinkle with the remaining oil.
6. Place the pizzas in the oven and bake for about 15 minutes, or until the cheese is bubbling. Place the pans on the floor of the oven and continue baking for about 5 minutes, or until dough is crisp on the bottom.
Yield: 8 to 12 servings.

Pizza dough

3   cups flour
2   tablespoons olive oil
1½   envelopes granulated yeast
1   cup lukewarm water

1. Place the flour in a mixing bowl and stir in the olive oil.
2. Dissolve the yeast in the water. Stir this into the flour mixture, using a wooden spoon and a plastic spatula to scrape around the edges so that all the flour is incorporated. This will be a somewhat sticky dough. Scrape the dough into a compact mass. Cover with a cloth and let stand in a warm place for 30 minutes or longer until it rises.
Yield: Enough dough for 2 13-inch pizzas.

Pizza with Mushrooms and Cheese

1. Prepare the dough and let it rise.

2. Place the dried mushrooms in a bowl and add warm water to cover. Let stand for ½ hour or longer, until mushrooms soften.

3. Pour 2 tablespoons of olive oil into the center of each of 2 13-inch pizza pans. Spread it around the bottom and inner rim of the pans.

4. Using lightly floured fingers, work the dough into a ball. Divide it in half and, with floured fingers, pat each half into a somewhat thick circle. Add 1 circle of dough to the center of each pizza pan. Using the fingers, pat and press the dough to cover the bottom of the pans, rim to rim. Cover and let stand in a warm place for about ½ hour.

5. Meanwhile, preheat the oven to 350 degrees.

6. Scatter a layer of fresh mushroom slices all over the dough in both pans. Drain the dried mushrooms and squeeze to extract most of the moisture. Shred them and scatter these over the fresh mushrooms. Sprinkle lightly with salt.

7. Scatter the grated cheese over all and sprinkle generously with pepper. Sprinkle the remaining olive oil over all.

8. Place the pans in the oven and bake for about 15 minutes, or until the cheese is bubbling. Place the pans on the floor of the oven and continue baking for about 5 minutes, or until dough is crisp on the bottom.

Yield: 8 to 12 servings.

Pizza dough for 2 13-inch pizzas (see recipe above)
12 or more dried black mushrooms, preferably imported Italian mushrooms
8 tablespoons olive oil
4 cups thinly sliced fresh mushrooms
Salt to taste
2 cups grated mozzarella cheese
Freshly ground pepper to taste

IV. Soups

Beef Consommé

The consommé:

2 pounds neck bones
3 pounds beef bones with meat, such as shin of beef or short ribs of beef
5 quarts water
2 cups coarsely chopped green part of leeks
1 parsnip, scraped and cut into ½-inch slices
6 sprigs parsley
Salt and freshly ground pepper to taste
¾ pound carrots, peeled, trimmed and cut into 2-inch lengths
¾ pound turnips, peeled and cut in half
1 bay leaf
4 sprigs fresh thyme, or ½ teaspoon dried
2 whole cloves
1 large onion, about ½ pound, cut in half

The clarification:

5 egg whites, about ¾ cup
5 eggshells, crushed
½ cup coarsely chopped carrots
½ cup coarsely chopped celery
½ cup coarsely chopped onion
1 cup coarsely chopped green part of leeks
½ cup coarsely chopped parsley
1 pound very lean ground beef
½ cup crushed fresh or canned tomatoes
Salt to taste

1. Place the neck bones and bones with meat in a deep kettle and add cold water to cover. Bring to the boil and simmer for 5 minutes. Drain and run the bones under cold running water. Drain.

2. Add the 5 quarts of water to the kettle. Add all the remaining ingredients except the onion. Do not add salt at this time.

3. Place the onion, cut side down, on a very hot griddle or skillet and let it cook until the cut side is blackened. This will give color to the consommé. Add the onion halves to the kettle and bring to the boil. Simmer for about 5 hours.

4. Strain the broth. There should be about 12 cups (3 quarts). The meat from the bones may be used for sandwiches, salads and so on.

5. Put the egg whites, crushed shells, carrots, celery, onion, leeks and parsley in a large clean kettle and beat until the eggs are frothy and all the ingredients are well blended. Add the meat and beat again to blend.

6. Add the strained broth to the mixture and stir well. Add the tomatoes and salt to taste. Put the kettle on the stove and bring to the boil slowly. It is imperative that you stir this mixture often from the bottom until it boils.

7. When it starts to boil do not stir further. At the boil, however, you should baste the top occasionally as follows: Use a small spoon and dip it into the points of boil, that is to say the small bubbling "holes" that expose the clear broth. Dip the spoon into these holes and sprinkle the clear liquid over the top of the surface of the mass. Cook in this manner for about 45 minutes. As the mixture cooks it should be at the simmer and not at a full rolling boil.

8. Line a colander with a triple layer of cheesecloth. Carefully strain the mixture.

Yield: About 10 cups.

Chicken Consommé

1. Place 4½ pounds chicken bones and the chicken in a large kettle and add water to cover. Bring to the boil. Let simmer for about 3 minutes and drain. Add cold water to the kettle and let it run until the chicken and the chicken pieces are chilled. Drain thoroughly. Wash out the kettle and return the chicken and chicken pieces to the kettle. Add 2 cups of chopped celery, 1 cup chopped carrots, the bay leaf, 1 cup of leeks, ½ cup of parsley, 1 cup of onions, the thyme, peppercorns, allspice, cloves, the 6 quarts of water and salt. Bring to the boil and simmer for 30 minutes.

2. Meanwhile, split the unpeeled onion in half. Place the onion halves, cut side down, in an iron skillet and cook over moderate heat until the bottoms are almost charred. Add the onion halves to the kettle. At the end of 30 minutes' cooking time, remove the chicken and set it aside for another use such as for a casserole, sandwiches and so on. Let the soup continue to simmer for 3 hours longer. Strain the cooking liquid into another kettle. Discard the solids.

3. Using a sharp cleaver, chop the remaining meaty chicken bones into small pieces and put them in a mixing bowl. Add about 2 cups of the strained broth. Add the remaining parsley, onion, celery, leeks and carrots. Beat the egg whites until frothy. Add the whites and crushed eggshells and stir to blend. This mixture is called clarification. Add this to the kettle and let simmer slowly without disturbing the top of the mixture, for about 2 hours. However, as the mixture cooks, use a ladle and scoop out a little of the simmering liquid from around the perimeter of the kettle. Ladle this onto the center of the solids that float on top. Do this often. Strain the broth through a fine sieve lined with a linen napkin.

Yield: About 2½ quarts.

6	pounds meaty chicken bones (necks, backs, wings and so on)
1	3-pound chicken
2½	cups coarsely chopped celery
1½	cups coarsely chopped carrots
1	bay leaf
1½	cups coarsely chopped leeks
1	cup coarsely chopped parsley stems
1½	cups coarsely chopped onions
1	sprig fresh thyme, or 1 teaspoon dried
14	peppercorns, crushed
2	whole allspice
2	whole cloves
6	quarts (24 cups) water Salt to taste
1	large unpeeled onion
6	egg whites
6	eggshells, crushed

Consommé Julienne

Simmer the vegetables in separate saucepans with boiling salted water to cover. Cook each vegetable briefly and drain. Add the vegetables to the simmering broth and serve piping hot.

Yield: 4 to 6 servings.

½	cup finely shredded celery
½	cup finely shredded carrots
½	cup finely shredded leeks
½	cup finely shredded turnip
4	cups simmering beef consommé (see recipe page 118)

Consommé Madrilène

Prepare the recipe for chicken consommé but add 3 cups of cored, quartered tomatoes to the kettle along with the vegetables and the 6 quarts of water. After the mixture has been strained and is ready to be clarified, blend 5½ cups of fresh or canned tomatoes (or a combination of both) along with the eggshells and other clarifying ingredients. Add this to the kettle for the final 2 hours of cooking.

For each 4 servings of consommé madrilène, cut half a sweet pepper into small cubes. There should be about ¼ cup. Simmer this in a little consommé for about 2 minutes until crisp-tender. Add this to the 4 cups of consommé. Add half a cup of cubed, seeded tomatoes. Serve hot or cold.

Yield: 4 servings.

Consommé Royale

Royal custard (see recipe below)
6 **cups rich beef consommé (see recipe page 118)**

Prepare the custard as much as a day or two in advance. Unmold it, slice it and cut the slices into small lozenges or diamond shapes. Arrange equal portions of the custard in each of 6 hot consommé cups or soup bowls. Pour the hot consommé over all and serve immediately.

Yield: 6 servings.

Royal custard

2 **large egg yolks**
1 **whole egg**
½ **cup heavy cream**
½ **cup beef consommé (see recipe page 118)**
   Salt and freshly ground pepper to taste
⅛ **teaspoon grated nutmeg**
   Dash of cayenne pepper or Tabasco sauce

Preheat the oven to 325 degrees. Combine the yolks and egg and beat until blended but not frothy. Add the remaining ingredients and blend well. Strain this into a well-buttered small baking dish. A 1½-cup soufflé dish is ideal. Place the dish in a pan of hot water and bring the water to the simmer on top of the stove. Place this in the oven and bake for 15 to 25 minutes, or until a straw inserted in the center of the custard comes out clean. Remove and let cool.

Yield: Garnish for 6 or more servings of consommé.

Chicken and Tomato Broth with Sour Cream and Herbs

3 **cups fresh or canned chicken broth**
3 **cups tomato juice**
   A touch of Tabasco sauce
   Salt and freshly ground pepper

1. Combine the chicken broth and tomato juice in a saucepan and bring to the boil. Add the Tabasco, salt, pepper and lemon juice. Bring to a simmer without boiling.

2. Spoon equal amounts of parsley, scallions, green chilies and other herbs, if desired, into the bottom of each of 6 to 8 soup bowls. Pour equal portions of the soup into each bowl.

Beat the sour cream with salt to taste and spoon equal portions of sour cream atop each serving. Serve immediately with Parmesan toast.

Yield: 6 to 8 servings.

Note: Chopped Chinese parsley, which is really fresh coriander, is excellent in this dish. Other herbs that might be added include dill and a touch of celery leaf.

Juice of ½ lemon, or more to taste
½ cup chopped parsley (see note)
½ cup chopped scallions
¼ cup chopped, canned (or fresh) mild green chilies, optional
Other chopped herbs if desired (see note)
1 cup sour cream
Parmesan toast (see recipe below)

Parmesan toast

Preheat the oven to 450 degrees. Place the butter in a mixing bowl and work it with a plastic spatula or wire whisk until it is smooth and spreadable. Add the cheese and Tabasco and beat until thoroughly blended. Spread equal portions of the butter on one side of each slice of bread. Arrange the slices, buttered side up, on a baking sheet. Bake for 10 minutes, or until the bread is golden. The bread should brown on both sides without turning. Watch carefully to guard against burning or overbrowning. Let cool and cut each slice into two rectangles or triangles.

Yield: 6 to 12 servings.

¼ pound butter at room temperature
¾ cup freshly grated Parmesan cheese
⅛ teaspoon Tabasco sauce, optional
12 very thin slices bread

Scotch Broth with Mushrooms

1. Place the bones in a kettle and add cold water to cover. Bring to the boil. Drain. Chill thoroughly and return to a clean kettle. Add the 10 cups of water, onion, carrots, celery, turnips, salt, pepper, bay leaf and garlic. Bring to the boil and simmer for 1 hour. Add the barley and cook for 45 minutes.

2. Meanwhile, heat the butter in a skillet and add the mushrooms. Cook to wilt and add this to the soup. Continue cooking the soup for 15 minutes, a total of 2 hours.

Yield: 6 to 8 servings.

2 pounds meaty lamb bones
10 cups cold water
½ cup finely chopped onion
¾ cup carrots cut into ¼-inch cubes
½ cup celery, cut into ¼-inch cubes
¾ cup white turnips, cut into ¼-inch cubes
Salt and freshly ground pepper to taste
1 bay leaf
1 clove garlic, finely minced
½ cup medium pearled barley
1½ tablespoons butter
¼ pound mushrooms cut into ¼-inch cubes

Vegetable Soup

3 pounds raw, meaty short ribs of beef, or an equal weight of shin bone with meat
3 quarts water
Salt
1¼ pounds raw green or Savoy cabbage, chopped into 1-inch pieces
2 cups peeled white turnips, cut into ½-inch cubes
2 cups carrots, scraped and cut into ½-inch cubes
2 cups chopped leeks, optional
1 cup chopped onion
2 cups finely chopped celery with leaves
Freshly ground pepper
4 potatoes, about 1 pound, peeled and cut into ½-inch cubes

1. Place the ribs of beef or shin bone in a kettle and add cold water to cover. Bring to the boil and simmer for about 3 minutes. Drain and run under cold water. Return the bones to a clean kettle and add the 3 quarts of water and salt to taste. Bring to the boil and simmer for 30 minutes, skimming the surface as necessary to remove the foam and scum.

2. Add the cabbage, turnips, carrots, leeks, onion and celery. Sprinkle with pepper to taste and return to the boil. Simmer for 1 hour and 30 minutes. Add the potatoes and cook for 1 hour longer, skimming the surface as necessary. Remove the short ribs of beef or shin. Carve off the meat and cut it into 1-inch cubes. Return meat to the kettle. Discard the bones. Serve the soup piping hot in hot bowls.

Yield: 8 to 12 servings.

Note: One cup of dried "no soaking necessary" pea beans may be added to the soup at the same time as the cabbage and turnips. Grated Parmesan cheese may be served on the side if desired.

Crème d'Avocats (Cream of avocado soup)

2 tablespoons corn oil
2 tablespoons finely chopped onion
2 ripe, unblemished avocados
1 teaspoon lemon juice
5 cups fresh or canned chicken broth
3 cups heavy cream
1 egg yolk
Salt and freshly ground pepper
2 tablespoons port wine

1. Heat the oil in a saucepan and add the onion. Cook, stirring, until the onion is wilted. Meanwhile, peel the avocados and remove the pits. Finely dice enough of the flesh to make ½ cup. Add the lemon juice to the diced avocado to prevent discoloration. Blend the remaining avocado flesh in a blender or food processor. There should be about 2 cups.

2. Add the puréed avocado to the saucepan along with the chicken broth and stir with a wire whisk. Add the cream and blend well. Let simmer over low heat for about 20 minutes. Beat the egg yolk and add a little of the hot soup. Return this to the saucepan and cook briefly. Add salt and pepper to taste. Put the mixture through a fine sieve and reheat in a saucepan. Add the port wine and the reserved diced avocado. Serve hot.

Yield: 12 servings.

Cold Avocado Soup

4 ripe, unblemished avocados
3 cups fresh or canned chicken broth

Peel and pit the avocados and cut each into pieces. Put the flesh into the container of a blender or food processor. Add a little chicken broth to aid the processing. When very smooth, pour and scrape the avocado into a bowl. Add the chicken broth, sour cream, salt and pepper and blend well. For an even smoother soup, strain the soup through a fine sieve. Chill thoroughly.

Yield: 8 or more servings.

1 cup sour cream
Salt and freshly ground pepper, preferably white pepper, to taste

Borscht

1. Heat the butter in a large, deep saucepan or a small kettle and add the finely chopped onion. Cook, stirring, until wilted and add the garlic and cabbage. Continue cooking, stirring the cabbage until it is wilted.

2. Grate or shred the beets and add them to the cabbage. Add the tomatoes, vinegar, sugar, salt, pepper and beef broth. Bring to the boil and simmer for about 1 hour. Serve with boiled potatoes and sour cream beaten lightly with salt to taste on the side.

Yield: 4 to 6 servings.

2 tablespoons butter
1 cup finely chopped onion
1 clove garlic, finely minced
1½ cups finely shredded cabbage
6 to 8 medium-size beets, about 1½ pounds, trimmed and peeled
2 cups cored, peeled and chopped tomatoes
¼ cup red wine vinegar
1 teaspoon sugar
Salt and freshly ground pepper
5 cups fresh or canned beef broth
Boiled potatoes
Sour cream

Beet and Yogurt Soup

1. Wash the beets well and put them in a saucepan. Add the orange juice. If necessary, add water to cover the beets. Simmer slowly until tender (this may take up to 2 hours if beets are old). Drain and reserve both beets and cooking liquid. Reserve the beets for another use, such as salad.

2. Put the gelatin in a small bowl and add ½ cup of beet liquid. Stir. Add this to the remaining beet liquid. Add the tomato liquid, onion, coriander, salt and pepper. Refrigerate until soup sets.

3. Pour and scrape the mixture into the container of a food processor or electric blender. Add the yogurt and blend thoroughly. Taste the soup. Add more salt if desired. Refrigerate until ready to serve. Serve in chilled soup bowls and garnish with a dab of sour cream and a tarragon sprig.

Yield: 6 servings.

Note: To make tomato liquid, put red, ripe, cored and peeled tomatoes through a food mill.

1 pound beets, unpeeled
2 cups orange juice
1 envelope gelatin
2 cups fresh tomato liquid (see note)
2 tablespoons freshly grated onion
1 teaspoon chopped fresh coriander leaves, or ground coriander seeds
Salt and freshly ground pepper to taste
1 cup yogurt
Sour cream for garnish
Tarragon sprigs for garnish

Cream of Broccoli Soup

1   bunch (about 1¼ pounds)
    fresh, green, unblemished
    broccoli
4   tablespoons butter
6   tablespoons flour
5   cups fresh or canned chicken
    broth
    Salt and freshly ground
    pepper to taste
½   cup heavy cream
½   cup milk
¼   teaspoon grated nutmeg
    Cayenne pepper

1. Trim off enough of the top clusters of the bunch of broccoli to fill a 1-cup measure. This will be used as a garnish for the soup. Cut the rest of the broccoli into 2-inch pieces. Cut the large stems in half or into quarters.

2. Place the larger broccoli pieces—not the garnish—in a deep skillet or saucepan and add water to cover and salt to taste. Cook for about 5 minutes, or until crisp-tender. Do not overcook. Similarly, cook the garnish in boiling salted water for about 2 minutes. Drain both batches and set aside.

3. Meanwhile, melt the butter in a saucepan and add the flour, stirring with a wire whisk. When blended, add chicken broth, stirring rapidly with the whisk. Cook, stirring, until thickened and smooth. Add the large broccoli pieces (not the garnish) and simmer, stirring occasionally, for about 10 minutes.

4. Ladle the soup, solids and all, into the container of a food processor or electric blender. This will have to be done in two or three steps. Blend until smooth. Return this mixture to a saucepan and bring to the boil. Add salt and pepper to taste. Add the cooked garnish, heavy cream, milk, nutmeg and a touch of cayenne pepper.

5. Ladle the soup into individual, heated soup bowls—preferably cream soup dishes—and serve hot.

Yield: 6 to 8 servings.

Cream of Brussels Sprouts Soup

5   cups young, tender brussels
    sprouts
3   cups fresh or canned chicken
    broth
6   tablespoons butter
4   tablespoons flour
3   cups milk
¼   teaspoon freshly grated
    nutmeg
½   cup heavy cream
    A few drops of Tabasco sauce
    Salt and freshly ground
    pepper to taste

1. Trim off the tough ends of the sprouts. Drop them into boiling chicken broth and simmer until tender, about 20 minutes. Remove the sprouts and leave the cooking liquid. Blend the sprouts in a food processor or electric blender.

2. Melt half the butter in a saucepan and stir in the flour, using a wire whisk. When blended, add the reserved cooking liquid, stirring rapidly with the whisk. When blended and smooth, simmer for 10 minutes. Add the milk and nutmeg. Add the blended sprouts, cream, Tabasco, salt and pepper to taste. Swirl in the remaining butter and serve piping hot.

Yield: 8 or more servings.

Cabbage Soup with Pork Meatballs

1. Place the bones in a kettle and add cold water to cover. Bring to the boil and drain. Run under cold running water. Drain again. Set aside.

2. Remove the core from the cabbage. Discard very large and blemished outer leaves. Shred and chop the cabbage finely. There should be about 8 cups. Set aside.

3. Meanwhile, heat the salt pork in a heavy soup kettle and, when rendered of fat and crisp, add the onion. Cook until wilted, for about 5 minutes, and add the garlic. Add the cabbage and pork bones and 12 cups of water. Add the bay leaf, salt and pepper to taste. Bring to the boil and simmer, partly covered, for about 1½ hours. Skim the surface often to remove excess fat.

4. As the soup cooks, prepare the pork balls. Place the pork in a mixing bowl and add the remaining ingredients. Blend well with the hands. Shape into 24 balls. Add the pork balls to the soup and continue to simmer, partly covered, for about 15 minutes.

Yield: 6 to 8 servings.

The soup:

2 pounds meaty pork bones
1 3-pound head firm, unblemished green cabbage
¼ pound lean salt pork, cut into ¼-inch cubes
1 cup finely chopped onion
2 cloves garlic, finely minced
12 cups water
1 bay leaf
  Salt and freshly ground pepper

The meatballs:

½ pound ground pork
6 tablespoons bread crumbs
1 egg, lightly beaten
2 tablespoons heavy cream
1 tablespoon finely grated onion
1 tablespoon finely chopped parsley
1 teaspoon caraway seeds, crushed
  Salt and freshly ground pepper to taste

Crème Crécy *(Cream of carrot soup)*

1. Trim off the ends of the carrots. Pare the carrots and potatoes with a swivel-bladed vegetable scraper. Cut the carrots into rounds. Cube the potatoes. Set aside. Heat the butter in a kettle and add the onion. Cook briefly, stirring. Add the carrots, potatoes and chicken broth and bring to the boil. Add thyme and bay leaf. Bring to the boil and simmer for 30 to 40 minutes, or until the carrots and potatoes are tender.

2. Put the mixture through a food mill and let it chill. Put it in the container of a food processor or electric blender and blend. This may have to be done in two stages. If the soup is to be served hot, put it in a saucepan, bring to the boil and add the remaining ingredients. When the soup returns to the boil, serve it piping hot. Or pour it into a bowl, add remaining ingredients and chill thoroughly. Serve very cold.

Yield: 6 to 8 servings.

1 pound (8 to 10) carrots
1 pound (3 to 5) potatoes
2 tablespoons butter
½ cup coarsely chopped onion
6 cups fresh or canned chicken broth
2 sprigs fresh thyme, or ½ teaspoon dried
1 bay leaf
1 cup heavy cream
⅛ teaspoon Tabasco sauce, or to taste
½ teaspoon Worcestershire sauce
½ teaspoon sugar
  Salt and freshly ground pepper
1 cup cold milk

Crème DuBarry *(Cream of cauliflower soup)*

No one knows at what point in history or under what French chef's auspices cauliflower and the Comtesse DuBarry, mistress to Louis XV, became eternally associated. But on any menu, a dish bearing the name DuBarry indicates the invariable presence of cauliflower.

1 large or 2 small cauliflowers, about 3 pounds untrimmed
3 cups fresh or canned chicken broth
½ cup raw rice
 Salt and freshly ground pepper
3 cups milk
¼ teaspoon freshly ground nutmeg, or to taste
⅛ teaspoon cayenne pepper, or to taste
½ cup heavy cream

1. Trim the cauliflower of leaves and carve out and discard the center core. Cut or break the cauliflower into large flowerets. Place them in a kettle and add cold water to cover. Do not add salt. Cover with a lid and bring to the boil. Simmer for about 2 minutes, no longer. Drain immediately. Set aside about 3 pieces of cauliflower for garnish when the soup is cooked. Break them into smaller pieces. Place the remaining cauliflower in a saucepan and add the chicken stock. Add the rice, salt and pepper to taste. Simmer for 30 minutes.

2. Pour the cauliflower with broth into the container of a food processor or electric blender. This will probably have to be done in two or three steps. Blend until smooth and, as the cauliflower is blended, return it to the saucepan. Add the milk, salt and pepper to taste, nutmeg and cayenne. Bring to the boil and add the cream.

3. Spoon the piping hot soup into hot cream soup dishes and sprinkle the top of each serving with a few pieces of garnish.

Yield: 6 to 8 servings.

Cream of Celery Soup

4 tablespoons butter
1 clove garlic, finely minced
1 cup coarsely chopped onion
¼ cup flour
4 cups cubed root or knob celery, about 1¼ pounds
8 cups rib celery, trimmed and cut into 1-inch lengths
4 cups fresh or canned chicken broth
4 cups water
 Salt
½ cup heavy cream
 Freshly ground pepper to taste

1. Heat half the butter in a kettle or large saucepan and add the garlic and onion. Cook until wilted. Sprinkle with flour and stir to blend. Add the knob celery, rib celery, chicken broth, water and salt. Bring to the boil and simmer for about 45 minutes.

2. Purée the mixture in a food processor or electric blender and return it to the kettle or saucepan. Add the cream, salt and pepper to taste. Swirl in remaining 2 tablespoons of butter and serve.

Yield: 9 to 10 cups.

Cock-a-Leekie

Truss the chicken and put it in a kettle with the neck and giblets. Add the water, salt, peppercorns, bay leaf, parsley and carrot. Bring to the boil and simmer, skimming the surface often to remove scum and foam, for about 20 minutes. Add the leeks, onion and rice and continue simmering for 20 minutes longer. Remove and discard the parsley and bay leaf. Remove the chicken and giblets. Serve the soup as a first course. Serve the chicken later, carved, as a main course. You can, of course, serve the cut-up chicken in bowls with the soup.

Yield: 4 to 6 servings.

1	3-pound chicken with giblets
8	cups water, or to cover
	Salt to taste
10	peppercorns, crushed
1	bay leaf
2	sprigs parsley
1	carrot, trimmed, scraped and quartered
4	cups finely shredded leeks (before shredding, cut the leeks into 3-inch lengths)
¼	cup chopped onion
3	tablespoons rice

Potage Bonne Femme   *(Leek soup)*

1. Trim off the root ends at the very base of the leeks. Cut off the tops of the leeks crosswise at the center. Remove the bruised outside leaves. Split lengthwise, inserting a knife about 1 inch from the base. Give it a ¼-inch turn and make another lengthwise cut. This allows the leaves to be opened up. Drop the leeks into a basin of cold water and let stand until ready to use.

2. Shake the leeks to make certain they are cleared of inner dirt or sand. Cut them into fine, crosswise slices, about 3 cups. Peel the potatoes. Cut them into thin slices. Cut the slices into small squares. There should be about 4 cups. Soak the potatoes in cold water as they stand.

3. Melt the butter in a small kettle or large saucepan and add the leeks. Cook for about 5 minutes, stirring often. Do not brown. Add the chicken broth, water, salt and pepper to taste. Drain the potatoes and add them to the soup. Bring to the boil and simmer for about 45 minutes. Add the milk and, if desired, more salt and pepper to taste. Swirl in the butter.

Yield: 8 to 10 servings.

4	leeks
1¼	pounds Idaho potatoes
3	tablespoons butter
4	cups fresh or canned chicken broth
4	cups water
	Salt and freshly ground pepper
½	cup milk or heavy cream
2	tablespoons butter

Vichyssoise

Prepare the potage bonne femme and purée it in a food processor or blender, or put through a food mill.

Mushroom Soup

2 ounces dried mushrooms
2 tablespoons butter
1 cup finely chopped onion
1 pound fresh mushrooms, sliced, about 5 cups
¼ cup flour
Salt and freshly ground pepper
2 cups fresh or canned beef broth
1 cup heavy cream or sour cream, optional

1. Place the dried mushrooms in a bowl and add boiling water to cover. Let stand until thoroughly softened. Melt the butter in a saucepan and add the onion. Cook until wilted and add the fresh mushrooms. Stir and cook until wilted. Sprinkle with flour, salt and pepper to taste. Stir to coat the mushrooms and add the broth.

2. Drain the dried mushrooms and measure the soaking liquid. Add enough water to make 2 cups. Add this and the dried mushrooms to the saucepan. Simmer all together for 15 minutes.

3. Purée the mushrooms, using a food processor or electric blender. Return to the heat and bring to the boil. Add the cream, if desired. Serve piping hot or chill and serve cold.

Yield: 8 to 12 servings.

Onion Soup Burgundy-style

3 pounds onions
4 tablespoons butter
1 clove garlic, finely minced
Salt and freshly ground pepper to taste
2 tablespoons flour
10 cups water
1 cup dry white wine
1 bay leaf
1 sprig fresh thyme, or ½ teaspoon dried
12 very thin (¼-inch) slices French bread
2 cups grated Gruyère or Swiss cheese
6 tablespoons grated Parmesan cheese

1. Preheat the oven to 400 degrees.

2. Peel the onions and cut them in half. Slice each half wafer-thin. There should be about 12 cups. In a large, heavy, ovenproof casserole or deep skillet, heat the butter and add the onions and garlic. Cook, stirring, until onions are wilted and start to brown, about 10 minutes. Sprinkle with salt and pepper. Put the casserole in the oven and bake for 15 minutes.

3. Remove the casserole from the oven and sprinkle the onion mixture with flour, stirring to coat onion pieces evenly. Add the water and wine and cook over high heat, scraping around the bottom and sides to dissolve the browned particles. Add the bay leaf and thyme and simmer for 30 minutes, stirring frequently.

4. Meanwhile, put the bread slices on a baking sheet and bake until brown and crisp.

5. Increase the oven heat to 450 degrees.

6. Fill 6 individual ovenproof soup tureens, or one large tureen, with the soup. If individual tureens are used, place 2 slices of toast atop the soup. If a large tureen is used, cover with the toast, overlapping. Sprinkle the toast with the Gruyère, then the Parmesan. Place the tureens on a baking

dish such as a jelly roll pan to catch any drippings. Bake for about 10 minutes, or until the soup is piping hot, bubbling and brown on top.

Yield: 6 servings.

Pumpkin Soup

1. Scrape away the seeds and inside fibers of the pumpkin. Cut or pare away the outside skin of the pumpkin. Cut the pumpkin into 1½-inch cubes. There should be about 6 cups.

2. Heat the butter in a kettle and add the onion. Cook briefly. Add the pumpkin. Add the water and chicken broth, salt and pepper. Bring to the boil and cook until tender, about 20 minutes. Using a food processor, food mill or electric blender, purée the pumpkin mixture, liquid and all. Return the mixture to a clean kettle.

3. Add the milk and cream, nutmeg and cayenne, salt and pepper to taste. Meanwhile, combine the rice and water in a saucepan. Bring to the boil and simmer for about 2 minutes. Drain well. Add the rice to the soup and continue to simmer until the rice is tender. Serve hot.

Yield: 8 or more servings.

2½	pounds new pumpkin with skin and seeds
3	tablespoons butter
1	cup finely chopped onion
1	cup water
1	cup fresh or canned chicken broth
	Salt and freshly ground pepper to taste
1	cup milk
1	cup heavy cream
¼	teaspoon freshly grated nutmeg
⅛	teaspoon cayenne pepper
½	cup rice
1	cup water

Potage Germiny *(Cream of sorrel soup)*

1. Pick over and remove the tougher parts of the sorrel stems. Rinse the leaves and drain well. Place the leaves on a flat surface and cut them into fine shreds (chiffonade). There should be about 5 cups. Set aside.

2. Heat the butter in a large saucepan and add the onion. Cook, stirring often, until wilted. Add the sorrel and cook until wilted. Add the broth and bring to the boil. Simmer briefly. Beat the yolks and add the cream, stirring to blend. Add the yolk and cream mixture to the soup, stirring rapidly with a wire whisk. Bring just to the boil but do not boil. Add the Tabasco sauce, salt and pepper to taste. Serve piping hot or chill and serve very cold.

Yield: 6 servings.

1	pound tender, fresh, unblemished sorrel leaves
¼	cup butter
½	cup chopped onion
3	cups fresh or canned chicken broth
2	large egg yolks
1	cup heavy cream
⅛	teaspoon Tabasco sauce
	Salt and freshly ground pepper

Crème Florentine (Cream of spinach soup)

1½ pounds spinach in bulk, or 2
    10-ounce packages
3 cups water
   Salt
3 tablespoons butter
4 tablespoons flour
6 cups fresh or canned chicken
   broth
½ cup heavy cream
4 egg yolks
⅛ teaspoon freshly grated
   nutmeg, or to taste
   Cayenne pepper
2 tablespoons fresh lime or
   lemon juice

1. Pick over the spinach to remove any tough stems. Rinse the spinach well in several changes of cold water to remove any traces of sand. Bring the water to the boil and add salt to taste. Add the spinach, stirring it down to wilt. Cook for about 3 minutes and drain in a colander. Run under cold water and drain. Squeeze between the hands to extract excess moisture. There should be slightly more than ½ cup. Chop the spinach fine or blend it, stirring down as necessary with a spatula. Do not add liquid.

2. Melt the butter and add the flour, stirring with a wire whisk. When blended, add the broth, stirring rapidly with the whisk. Simmer for about 30 minutes, stirring frequently.

3. Blend the cream and yolks. Remove the soup from the heat and stir in the yolk and cream mixture. Add the spinach and bring the soup almost but not quite to the boil, stirring vigorously. Add the remaining ingredients. Serve piping hot or let cool, then refrigerate and serve cold.

Yield: 6 to 8 servings.

Chilled Tomato Soup with Mint

2 pounds fresh, red, ripe
   tomatoes
3 tablespoons butter
½ cup finely chopped onion
1 clove garlic, finely minced
4 whole allspice, crushed
3 tablespoons flour
3 cups fresh or canned chicken
   broth
½ cup sour cream
1 tablespoon chopped fresh
   mint (see note)
   Sour cream for garnish,
   optional

1. Core the tomatoes and cut them into eighths. Melt the butter in a saucepan and add the onion, garlic and allspice. Cook briefly and add the flour, stirring. Add the tomatoes and broth and stir constantly. Bring to the boil and let simmer for about 20 minutes. Strain through a food mill. Let cool, then chill thoroughly.

2. Put the soup in a mixing bowl and add the sour cream, stirring with a wire whisk to blend. Add the mint and garnish, if desired, with sour cream.

Yield: 6 to 8 servings.

Note: Small cubes of seedless cucumber are also delicious in this soup. If added, the mint is optional.

Cream of Fresh Tomato Soup

5 medium-size fresh tomatoes
3 medium-size potatoes, peeled
   and thinly sliced
1 small onion, finely chopped

1. Plunge the tomatoes into boiling water. Remove pan from heat and let the tomatoes stand for about 30 seconds or more in the water. Remove the tomatoes and run cold water over them. Skins will slip off easily. Slice the peeled tomatoes.

2. Place the tomatoes, potatoes, onion, salt and pepper to taste, bay leaf and basil in a saucepan. Cook over medium heat until potatoes are soft. Remove bay leaf. Press the tomato-potato mixture through a sieve or pour into the container of a food processor and purée until smooth.

3. Meanwhile, melt the butter in a saucepan and add the flour, stirring. Slowly add half the milk, stirring. When smooth, add the puréed tomato-potato mixture. Cook, stirring over low heat until well blended. Add remaining milk. If soup is too thick, add more milk or a little chicken broth. Add sugar to taste. Correct seasoning. Serve very hot.

Yield: 4 servings.

	Salt and freshly ground pepper
1	bay leaf
1	teaspoon dried basil
2	tablespoons butter
2	tablespoons flour
1	cup milk, approximately
1	tablespoon sugar, or to taste

Chilled Tomato and Yogurt Soup

1. Melt the butter in a saucepan and add the onion. Cook, stirring frequently, for about 10 minutes. Do not brown. Add the cucumber, tomatoes, basil and chicken broth. Cook, stirring frequently, for about 30 minutes.

2. Put the mixture, including the vegetable solids, through a sieve, or blend in a food processor or electric blender. Empty the mixture into a bowl and add the yogurt and salt to taste. Chill thoroughly. Add the mint and serve.

Yield: About 6 servings.

2	tablespoons butter
2	cups chopped onion
2	cups peeled, seeded, cubed cucumbers
3	cups peeled, cored, cubed tomatoes
3	basil leaves, or 1 teaspoon dried
2	cups fresh or canned chicken broth
2	cups yogurt
	Salt
1	teaspoon chopped fresh mint, optional

Cucumber, Tomato and Avocado Soup

1. Melt the butter in a deep saucepan or kettle and add the onion. Cook, stirring, until wilted and sprinkle with flour. Add the tomatoes, stirring rapidly with a whisk. Add the cucumbers, salt and pepper to taste. When blended, stir in the broth. Simmer for 25 minutes.

2. Pour the mixture, a few ladlesful at a time, into the container of a food processor or electric blender. Blend well. Strain the soup into a bowl if it is to be served cold and chill. If it is to be served hot, return it to the stove and heat thoroughly.

3. Peel the avocado and remove the pulp. Chop the flesh finely and add it to the soup, stirring rapidly with a whisk. Stir in the cream. Serve very cold or piping hot.

Yield: 8 servings.

4	tablespoons butter
1	cup chopped onion
4	tablespoons flour
4	cups peeled, cubed tomatoes, preferably fresh although canned may be used
4	cups peeled, cubed cucumbers
	Salt and freshly ground pepper to taste
4	cups fresh or canned chicken broth
1	ripe, unblemished avocado
1	cup heavy cream

Gazpacho

2 large, red, ripe tomatoes,
   cored, peeled and quartered
1 green pepper, cored, seeded
   and quartered
1 medium-size onion, peeled
   and quartered
1 small clove garlic, optional
1 2-ounce jar pimientos
1 cucumber, peeled and cut into
   cubes
3 cups tomato juice
⅓ cup red wine vinegar
¼ cup olive oil
¾ cup fresh or canned chicken
   broth
   Tabasco sauce to taste
   Salt and freshly ground
   pepper to taste
   Garlic croutons (see
   recipe below)

Put the tomatoes, pepper, onion, garlic, pimiento and cucumber in the container of a food processor or electric blender. Blend. Add tomato juice and blend again. Pour the mixture into a bowl and add the vinegar, oil, broth, Tabasco, salt and pepper. Blend well and cover. Refrigerate for several hours before serving. Serve well-chilled, sprinkled with croutons.

Yield: 8 to 12 servings.

Gazpacho Mexican-style

2 pounds red, ripe tomatoes,
   cored and finely chopped
2 tablespoons red wine vinegar
2 tablespoons chopped red
   onion
2 tablespoons chopped scallions
2 tablespoons chopped long
   green hot or mild chilies
2 cloves garlic, finely minced
1 cup cucumber chopped into
   ¼-inch dice
2 tablespoons chopped
   coriander leaves
2 tablespoons chopped fresh
   basil leaves
¼ cup olive oil
   Salt and freshly ground
   pepper
   Garlic croutons (see
   recipe below)

Combine all the ingredients in a mixing bowl except the garlic croutons. Quantities of various ingredients may be increased according to taste. Serve sprinkled with garlic croutons.

Yield: 4 to 6 servings.

Peel the garlic and crush each clove slightly. Heat the butter in a heavy skillet and, when it is hot, add the garlic and bread cubes. Cook, stirring and shaking the skillet, until the cubes are golden brown all over. Drain the cubes and discard the garlic.

Yield: 1½ cups.

Garlic croutons

2 cloves garlic
4 tablespoons butter
1½ cups bread cut into ½-inch cubes

Gazpacho with Corn and Zucchini

1. Drop the shucked corn into boiling water. Cover and, when the water returns to the boil, remove it immediately from the heat. Let stand for 5 minutes. Drain. Let the corn cool. Cut off the kernels. There should be about 1 cup.

2. Put the tomatoes into the container of a food processor or electric blender. It may be necessary to do this in two or three steps. Add the onion, garlic, the coarsely chopped cucumber and tomato juice. Blend thoroughly. Add salt and pepper to taste. Pour the mixture into a bowl and add the olive oil and vinegar.

3. Cut the zucchini into fine dice and add it. Add the corn. Add the diced cucumber and basil. Add more salt and pepper to taste. Chill thoroughly.

Yield: 6 to 8 servings.

2 ears corn on the cob
2 pounds fresh, red, ripe tomatoes, peeled and coarsely chopped
1 onion, preferably a red onion, coarsely chopped
2 cloves garlic, finely minced
2 cups peeled, coarsely chopped cucumber
1½ cups tomato juice
Salt and freshly ground pepper to taste
¼ cup olive oil
¼ cup red wine vinegar
½ small zucchini, peeled
1 cup finely diced cucumber
3 tablespoons finely minced fresh basil, or 1 teaspoon dried

Watercress Soup

1. Cut the watercress bunches in half and rinse well under cold running water. Drain well. Bring a large quantity of water to the boil and add the watercress. Stir and bring to the boil. Simmer for about 3 minutes and drain in a colander. Run under cold water. Drain and squeeze between the hands to extract most of the moisture. Put the watercress in the container of a food processor or electric blender and add ½ cup of broth. Blend, stirring down as necessary.

2. Melt 4 tablespoons of butter in a saucepan and add the

2 firm, bright green bunches of watercress
6 cups fresh or canned chicken broth
12 tablespoons butter
6 tablespoons flour
3 cups freshly cubed white bread
3 egg yolks
⅛ teaspoon grated nutmeg

flour, stirring with a wire whisk. When blended, add the remaining broth and simmer for 30 minutes.

3. Heat 4 tablespoons of butter in a skillet and add the bread cubes. Toss the cubes until golden brown all over. Set aside.

4. In a mixing bowl, blend the puréed watercress with the egg yolks and nutmeg. Add about ¼ cup of the boiling soup to the mixture, stirring. Add this to the soup, stirring constantly. Bring to the boil. Do not cook or the soup will curdle. Beat in the remaining 4 tablespoons of butter. Serve the hot soup in bowls, garnishing each serving with the bread croutons.

Yield: 6 to 8 servings.

Cold Zucchini Soup

5 or	6 small-to-medium-size zucchini
1	large onion, peeled and thinly sliced, about 1 cup
1½	teaspoons curry powder
3	cups fresh or canned chicken broth
1	cup heavy cream
½	cup milk
	Salt and freshly ground pepper
	Finely chopped chives

1. Rinse the zucchini and pat dry. Trim off the ends. Cut one zucchini in two and thinly slice one half. Stack the slices and cut them into very thin matchlike strips. There should be about 1 cup. Place in a saucepan and add cold water to cover. Boil 3 to 4 minutes and drain. Set aside.

2. Cut the remaining zucchini half and the other zucchini into 1-inch lengths. Cut each length into quarters. Place the pieces of quartered zucchini in a kettle or saucepan and add the onion slices. Sprinkle with curry powder and stir to coat the pieces. Add the chicken broth and bring to the boil. Cover and simmer for about 45 minutes.

3. Spoon and scrape the mixture into the container of a blender or food processor and blend to a fine purée. There should be about 4 cups. Add the cream, milk and salt and pepper to taste. Add the reserved zucchini strips. Chill thoroughly. Serve sprinkled with chopped chives.

Yield: 6 to 8 servings.

Manhattan Clam Chowder

24	chowder clams or razor clams
4	cups water
4	slices bacon
2	cups carrots, cut into fine dice
1½	cups celery, cut into small cubes

1. Wash the clams well. If razor clams are used, they may be placed in a basin of cold water to which about ½ cup of cornmeal is added. Let stand about 1 hour to disgorge excess sand. Drain well and rinse thoroughly. Drain again. Place the clams in a kettle and add the water. Simmer until the shells open.

2. Meanwhile, chop the bacon and put it in a kettle. Cook until the bacon is rendered of its fat. Add the carrots, celery,

onion and green pepper. Cook for about 5 minutes, stirring often. Add the garlic, thyme and bay leaf.

3. When the clams open, strain them but reserve both the clams and their liquid. Add 10 cups of liquid to the bacon mixture. (If there are not 10 cups, add enough water to make 10 cups.) Add the tomatoes. Cook for 15 minutes. Remove the clams from the shells and discard the shells. Chop the clams finely on a flat surface or put them through a meat grinder, using the small blade. Add them to the kettle and add the potatoes. Add salt and pepper to taste and cook for about 1 hour.

Yield: 8 to 10 servings.

2 cups chopped onion
¾ cup chopped green pepper
1 clove garlic, finely chopped
1 teaspoon thyme
1 bay leaf
1 cup fresh or canned tomatoes
4 cups potatoes, cut into ½-inch or slightly smaller cubes
Salt and freshly ground pepper to taste

New England Clam Chowder

1. Wash the clams well to remove all trace of sand. Put them in a kettle and add the water. Cover and bring to the boil. Cook until the clams open. When clams are cool enough to handle, remove them, one at a time. Cut out the flesh and discard the shells. Reserve all the juices that flow from the clams plus the kettle liquid. There should be about 6 cups. Put the clams on a flat surface and chop the clam meat coarsely. Or use a food processor to chop them. Do not overblend. The clams must retain a coarse texture.

2. Cut the salt pork into thin slices. Place on a flat surface and cut into small cubes. Heat the salt pork in a kettle and add the onion. Cook, stirring, for about 5 minutes, or until onions wilt. Add the flour and stir briskly to blend. Add the 6 cups of liquid (if there is not enough to make 6 cups, add enough water to make this quantity), stirring. Add the chopped clams.

3. Cut the potatoes lengthwise into ½-inch slices. Stack the slices and cut them into ½-inch strips. Cut the strips into ½-inch cubes. There should be about 4 cups. Cover with cold water and let stand until ready to add.

4. When the clams have cooked for 30 minutes, drain the potatoes and add them. Continue cooking for 30 minutes longer. Add the milk and cream and bring just to the boil. Do not boil or it will curdle. Add salt and pepper to taste. When ready to serve, add the butter and swirl it in. Serve piping hot with buttered toast or, if you prefer, oyster crackers.

Yield: 12 servings.

24 large cherrystone clams
1 quart water
2 ounces lean salt pork
2½ cups finely chopped onion
¼ cup flour
4 large potatoes, about 1½ pounds, peeled
1 quart milk
1 cup heavy cream
Salt and freshly ground pepper to taste
4 tablespoons butter

Clam Soup

4 quarts soft-shell clams
Salt
½ cup olive oil
6 shallots, peeled and thinly sliced
4 cloves garlic, thinly sliced
3 dried hot red peppers, crushed
10 sprigs fresh basil
1 cup dry white wine
2¼ cups canned tomatoes, preferably Italian plum tomatoes
1 cup water
½ cup coarsely chopped parsley
1 teaspoon dried oregano
Freshly ground pepper

1. Soak the soft-shell clams for several hours in several changes of cold, salted water. Wash thoroughly.

2. Heat the oil in a kettle and add the shallots and garlic. Cook for about 30 seconds, stirring, and add the clams and crushed red peppers. Add the basil and wine and cover. Cook for 5 minutes and add the tomatoes, water, parsley and oregano. Stir. Add salt and pepper to taste and cook for 20 minutes.

Yield: 8 servings.

Cream of Clam and Leek Soup

36 littleneck clams, the smaller the better
2 tablespoons butter
3 cups leeks, trimmed, rinsed well and cut crosswise into fine shreds
¾ cup finely chopped onion
1 clove garlic, finely minced
2 cups dry white wine
Salt and freshly ground pepper to taste
2 cups heavy cream, or use half and half or part cream and part milk
1 cup milk
1 small hot, dried red pepper, optional
2 tablespoons Ricard, Pernod, or other anise-flavored liqueur

1. Rinse the clams in several changes of cold water. Drain well. Heat the butter in a heavy casserole or kettle and add the leeks. Cook for about 2 minutes, stirring often. Add the onion and garlic. Cook briefly, stirring. Add the wine, a little salt (the clams will give up their liquid, which is salty) and pepper. Cover and bring to the boil. Let simmer for about 5 minutes.

2. Add the clams, 2 cups of cream, 1 cup of milk and hot pepper and cover closely. Let cook for about 10 minutes or until the clams open. Add the Ricard and stir. Serve piping hot with a soup spoon and oyster fork.

Yield: 6 servings.

Fish Soup with Mussels and Clams

1. Cut the fish into 1-inch cubes and set aside. Place the bones in a kettle and add the water, wine and mussels. Bring to the boil and simmer until the mussels open. Drain, but reserve both the broth and the mussels. There should be about 8 cups of broth. Remove the mussels from the shells. Pull off and discard the stringlike band that is a part of each mussel. Set the prepared mussels aside.

2. Heat the oil in a kettle and add the leeks, onion, celery, garlic, thyme, bay leaf, salt, pepper and saffron. Cook, stirring, for about 5 minutes and add the tomatoes and tomato paste. Add the hot red pepper flakes and simmer for 30 minutes, stirring occasionally. Add the cubed fish and stir to blend. Add the broth to the fish mixture and bring to the boil. Add the clams and simmer until they open. Add the Ricard and mussels and serve piping hot.

Yield: 8 to 12 servings.

1¾	pounds boneless cod, sea bass or other white-flesh fish
¾	pound bones from a nonoily fish such as cod or sea bass
6	cups water
1	cup dry white wine
1	quart well-scrubbed mussels
4	tablespoons olive oil
1	cup finely minced leeks
1	cup finely chopped onion
1	cup finely minced celery
3	cloves garlic, finely chopped
2	sprigs fresh thyme, or 1 teaspoon dried
1	bay leaf
	Salt and freshly ground pepper to taste
1	tablespoon stem saffron
4	cups canned tomatoes, preferably Italian plum tomatoes
1	6-ounce can tomato paste
	Hot red pepper flakes
24	well-scrubbed littleneck clams, the smaller the better
2	tablespoons Ricard, Pernod, or other anise-flavored liqueur

Billi Bi

This cream of mussel soup is, to my mind, one of the greatest, and perhaps the greatest, soups ever created. It was served at Maxim's in Paris and was for many years the favorite dish of William B. Leeds, an American tin magnate. Mr. Leeds spent much time in Paris, dined more often than not at Maxim's, and invariably began his meal with the soup. He became so thoroughly associated with the dish it was renamed in his honor on the menu.

7 quarts cleaned mussels
4 tablespoons finely chopped shallots
8 tablespoons finely chopped onion
4 tablespoons finely chopped parsley
¼ teaspoon chopped fresh thyme, or ½ teaspoon dried
1 bay leaf
Salt and freshly ground pepper
1 cup dry white wine
4 tablespoons butter, cut into small cubes, plus 2 tablespoons
2 tablespoons flour
1½ cups heavy cream
2 egg yolks
Finely chopped parsley for garnish

1. The mussels must be well cleaned and tested to see if they are alive. To do this, take the top shell in one hand, the bottom in the other and pull the shells gently in opposite directions. If they remain firmly together, they are alive. If they open, they will probably be full of silt and should be discarded.

2. Place the mussels in a deep kettle and add the shallots, onion, 4 tablespoons chopped parsley, thyme, bay leaf, salt, pepper, wine and 4 tablespoons of butter cut into cubes. Cover and bring to the boil. Simmer for about 10 minutes, shaking and tossing the mussels in the kettle to redistribute them. Cook mussels only until they are opened.

3. Remove the mussles from the shells and discard the shells. Keep the mussels warm.

4. Strain the cooking liquid from the kettle into a saucepan and reduce it over high heat for about 5 minutes.

5. Make a beurre manié by blending the flour and remaining 2 tablespoons of butter. Add it bit by bit to the soup, stirring. Blend the cream and yolks and add it to the soup, stirring. Make certain the soup does not boil more than a second or two or it may curdle. Put the mussels in the soup just to heat through. Serve sprinkled with chopped parsley.

Yield: 6 to 8 servings.

Maryland Crab Soup

6 large live crabs
10 cups water
Salt and freshly ground pepper to taste
1 cup dry white wine
1 bay leaf
1 hot, dried red pepper, optional
3 ears corn, shucked
2 tablespoons butter
1¼ cups chopped onion
1 teaspoon garlic
1 cup chopped green peppers
1½ cups chopped celery
1 cup diced carrots
3 cups peeled, cored and chopped fresh or canned tomatoes

1. Rinse the crabs under cold running water. Place in a kettle and add the water, salt, pepper, wine, bay leaf and hot pepper and bring to the boil. Cover and cook for about 15 minutes. Drain and strain the broth. There should be about 10 cups. Set the crabs aside to cool. As the crabs cook, drop the ears of corn into boiling water. Cover and, when the water returns to the boil, turn off heat. Let stand 5 minutes. Drain and let cool.

2. Heat the butter in a kettle and add the onion and garlic. Cook briefly, stirring, until onion is wilted. Add the green pepper, celery and carrots. Cook for about 10 minutes and add the crab broth and tomatoes. Cook for 15 minutes and add the beans. Cook for 1 hour. Scrape the corn kernels from the cob. There should be about 1½ cups. Add this to the soup.

3. Remove the meat from the claws and body of the crabs. There should be about 2 cups. Add this to the soup. Add

Worcestershire sauce and Tabasco. Add the sherry and bring just to the boil. Serve hot in hot soup bowls.

Yield: 8 or more servings.

2 cups string beans, cut into 1-inch lengths
1 teaspoon Worcestershire sauce
Tabasco sauce to taste
½ cup sweet or dry sherry wine

Corn and Crabmeat Chowder

1. Scrape the corn off the cob. There should be about 1½ cups.

2. Melt 4 tablespoons of butter in a saucepan, stirring with a wire whisk. When melted, add the flour, stirring until blended.

3. Add the broth and milk, stirring rapidly with the whisk. Cook, stirring frequently, for about 10 minutes.

4. Meanwhile, melt the remaining butter in another saucepan and add the onion. Cook until wilted. Add the crabmeat, corn, salt, pepper and cayenne. Cook briefly and add to the sauce. Add the cream and bring to the boil. Simmer gently for about 5 minutes.

Yield: 4 to 6 servings.

3 ears cooked corn
5 tablespoons butter
5 tablespoons flour
2 cups fresh or canned chicken broth
2½ cups milk
¼ cup finely chopped onion
¾ cup picked over, fresh or frozen crabmeat (about 6 ounces)
Salt and freshly ground pepper to taste
⅛ teaspoon cayenne pepper
½ cup heavy cream

She-crab Soup

1. Melt the butter in a large saucepan and add the flour, stirring with a wire whisk. Add the milk, stirring rapidly with the whisk. Cook, stirring, until thickened and smooth.

2. Add the nutmeg, paprika, salt, pepper and cayenne and stir. Add the crabmeat, stirring gently, and bring just to the boil. Add the lemon slices and sherry and pour into a soup tureen or serve in individual bowls.

Yield: 6 to 8 servings.

Note: This is called she-crab soup because the soup traditionally is made with the meat and coral or roe that comes only from female crabs.

2 tablespoons butter
3 tablespoons flour
3 cups milk
¼ teaspoon freshly grated nutmeg, or more to taste
¼ teaspoon paprika
Salt and freshly ground black pepper
⅛ teaspoon cayenne pepper
2 cups picked-over crabmeat, preferably with a certain amount of coral or roe
10 lemon slices
¼ cup Amontillado sherry

Oyster Stew

3 cups milk
1 bay leaf
1 rib celery with leaves
1 small onion, peeled and quartered
2 sprigs fresh thyme, or ½ teaspoon dried
12 to 24 oysters, 1 to 2 cups, depending on size and whether you want several or few oysters in each serving
 Salt to taste
¾ cup heavy cream
1 egg yolk
 Tabasco sauce to taste
½ teaspoon celery salt
 Freshly ground pepper to taste
2 tablespoons butter
½ teaspoon Worcestershire sauce, optional

1. Combine the milk, bay leaf, celery, onion and thyme in a saucepan. Bring just to the boil but do not boil. Pour the oysters into a deep skillet large enough to hold the stew. Sprinkle with salt and bring to the boil. Cook just until the oysters curl. Strain the milk over the oysters and stir. Discard the solids. Do not boil.

2. Beat the cream with the egg yolk and add Tabasco, celery salt, salt and pepper to taste. Add this to the stew. Bring just to the boil and swirl in the butter. Add the Worcestershire and serve piping hot with buttered toast or oyster crackers.

Yield: 4 servings.

Fish Soup

For those who fancy fish and seafood (and pity those who don't), there is nothing more gratifying to the senses of taste and well-being than a piping hot fish soup. We are fortunate to live in a community where fresh fish and shellfish are found in abundance, and we are constantly improvising our own soups, as well as enjoying those of many other nationalities. We urge you, by the way, to make your own fish stock, a recipe for which appears on page 659. In a pinch, a combination of water and bottled clam juice, or plain water, can be substituted, but the soup will not have the flavor that the stock gives it.

3 tablespoons olive oil
1 cup chopped onion
1 teaspoon finely minced garlic

1. Heat the oil in a kettle and add the onion, garlic and saffron. Stir in the flour, using a wire whisk. Add the fish stock, tomatoes and wine, stirring rapidly with the whisk. When blended, cook, stirring frequently, for about ½ hour.

2. Cut the fish into 1½-inch cubes (there should be about 3 cups). Add the fish and cook for about 5 minutes, or until fish flakes easily. Add the remaining ingredients and simmer for about 5 minutes longer.

Yield: 8 servings.

½	tablespoon loosely packed saffron stems
¼	cup flour
2	cups fish stock or water
2	cups peeled, chopped, red, ripe tomatoes, fresh or canned
1	cup dry white wine
1¼	pounds fillet of white-fleshed, nonoily fish such as sea trout or sea bass
1	pint scrubbed, well-cleaned mussels or very small littleneck clams
½	teaspoon dried thyme
1	cup heavy cream
	Salt and freshly ground pepper
	Tabasco sauce

Fish Soup with Pasta and Cheese

1. Wash the fish heads well under cold running water. Place in a kettle and add the water. Bring to the boil and simmer for 45 minutes. Strain and press the solids with the back of a heavy spoon to extract as much juice as possible. Discard the solids.

2. Heat the oil in a skillet and add the garlic and onion and brown lightly. Add the celery, carrots and bay leaves. Cook for 10 minutes. Add this mixture to the fish broth and bring to the boil. Add the potatoes, parsley, Swiss chard and tomatoes and simmer for 45 minutes to 1 hour. Add the broken up pasta and simmer just until the pasta is tender, about 10 minutes. Stir in the cheese and serve.

Yield: 16 to 20 servings.

7½	pounds fish heads, gills removed
6	quarts water
¾	cup olive oil
6	cloves garlic, finely chopped
1½	cups coarsely chopped onion
1½	cups chopped celery
¾	cup chopped carrots
2	bay leaves
1	cup potatoes, peeled and cut into ½-inch cubes
¾	cup chopped parsley
4	cups shredded Swiss chard or lettuce
3½	cups imported Italian canned tomatoes, or an equal amount of red, ripe fresh tomatoes
¾	pound broken perciatelli, linguine or lingue di passeri
1	cup freshly grated Parmesan cheese

Fish Soup with Potatoes

2 tablespoons butter
1 cup finely chopped onion
½ cup finely chopped celery
2 tablespoons flour
1 cup finely diced carrots
1 cup dry white wine
1 tomato, about ½ pound, peeled, seeded and diced
6 cups water
Salt and freshly ground pepper
½ teaspoon saffron
½ teaspoon thyme
1 pound potatoes, peeled and cut into ½-inch cubes
1 pound fish fillets such as striped bass, sea bass, sole, flounder, and so on, cut into ½-inch cubes
⅓ cup heavy cream

Melt the butter in a kettle or deep saucepan and add the onion and celery. Cook 5 minutes. Sprinkle with flour and stir to coat the vegetable pieces. Add the carrots and wine, stirring. Add the tomato, water, salt and pepper to taste, saffron and thyme. Cook 20 minutes and add the cubed potatoes. Cook 20 minutes and add the cubed fish. Simmer 10 minutes and stir in the cream. Bring to the boil and serve hot.

Yield: 6 to 8 servings.

Cioppino

There is a fish soup indigenous to California that is as much a part of American culture as Boston clam chowder in the East or oyster gumbo in the South. At its best—and the best we've ever sampled was in Dinah Shore's kitchen—cioppino is delectable. When Dinah invited us to dine in her home, we accepted with unusual alacrity. In addition to being a well-known singer, she is justly celebrated as one of the finest cooks in Beverly Hills.

Dinah told us that she had first discovered cioppino at a small restaurant in Hawaii, and that the finest she had ever sampled was at a food festival at San Pedro, about eighteen miles from Los Angeles. While San Francisco claims to be the birthplace of the soup, the fishermen of San Pedro are equally adamant in their assertion that their ancestors are the true source. In any event, Dinah's recipe, printed here, came from a San Pedro source.

1. Heat the oil and butter in a kettle and add the onion, leek and garlic. Cook, stirring often, until the vegetables are lightly browned. Add the green peppers and continue cooking, stirring, until peppers wilt. Add the tomatoes and tomato sauce. Add salt and pepper to taste, bay leaf, oregano, thyme, basil and about ¼ teaspoon red pepper flakes. Add the fish stock and cook slowly for about 2 hours, stirring often to prevent burning. More fish stock may be added if desired. Add the clam juice and wine and continue cooking about 10 minutes. The soup may be made in advance to this point.

2. Twenty minutes or so before serving, return the soup to the boil and add the striped bass or other fish. Cook for about 5 minutes and add the scallops and shrimp. Simmer for about 8 minutes and add the clams, oysters, lobster tail and crab. Cook, stirring gently, for about 5 minutes, or until the clams open. Serve in very hot soup bowls with red pepper flakes on the side.

Yield: 10 servings.

2	tablespoons olive oil
2	tablespoons butter
3	cups chopped onion
1	leek, trimmed, washed well and finely chopped
2 to 4	cloves garlic, finely chopped
2	green peppers, cored, seeded and cut into thin strips
4	cups chopped imported peeled tomatoes
1	cup fresh or canned tomato sauce
	Salt and freshly ground pepper
1	bay leaf
1	teaspoon dried oregano
1	teaspoon dried thyme
1	tablespoon dried basil
	Red pepper flakes
2	cups fish stock or water
1	cup fresh or bottled clam juice
1	cup dry white wine
1	pound firm-fleshed fish such as striped bass, red snapper, rock cod or sea bass, cut into bite-size pieces
½	pound fresh scallops, preferably bay scallops
1	pound raw shrimp, shelled and deveined
1	dozen well-washed small clams in the shell
¼	cup shucked oysters with their liquor
½	pound lobster tail, cooked in the shell, optional
1	hard-shell crab, cooked in the shell and cracked, optional

Fish Soup with Aioli

¼ cup olive oil
1½ cups chopped onion
1½ cups cored, seeded, chopped green pepper
¾ cup thinly sliced pepperoni
4 thin slices lemon
1 teaspoon loosely packed stem saffron
2 quarts fresh fish broth
2 or more 1-pound lobsters
30 littleneck clams
2 quarts mussels
5 cups boneless, skinless fish fillets such as blackfish, cod or striped bass cut into 1½-inch cubes
1 cup aioli (see recipe below)

1. Heat the oil in a kettle and add the onion, green pepper, pepperoni, lemon and saffron. Cook until the onion and pepper are wilted. Add the broth and bring to the boil. Add the lobsters and cook for about 5 minutes, covered. Add the clams and cook for about 5 minutes, covered. Add the mussels and cook for about 3 minutes, covered.

2. When almost all the clams and mussels are opened, add the fish. Simmer briefly, just until all the clams and mussels are opened. Take care not to overcook or the fish will fall apart. Cut the lobster into serving pieces. Serve with aioli on the side.

Yield: 10 servings.

Aioli

Finely chop 6 or more large cloves of garlic. Add them to 1 cup of homemade mayonnaise (see recipe page 642). Spoon into fish soup.

Fish Chowder à la Caraja

5 tablespoons butter
¾ cup finely chopped onion
1 cup finely chopped celery
1 cup finely diced carrots
¾ cup white part of leek, cut into very fine julienne strips
2 cloves garlic, finely minced
4 cups fish broth
2 tablespoons flour
3½ cups potatoes (about 1½ pounds), peeled and cut into ¼-inch cubes
2 cups white-flesh, nonoily fish such as sea trout (weakfish), sole or striped bass, cut into 1-inch cubes
1½ cups heavy cream or milk
Salt and freshly ground pepper to taste

1. Melt 3 tablespoons of butter in a saucepan and add the onion, celery, carrots, leeks and garlic. Cook, stirring often, for about 10 minutes. Add the fish broth and bring to the boil. Blend remaining 2 tablespoons of butter with the flour and add it, bit by bit, to the soup, stirring constantly.

2. Add the potatoes and continue cooking until the potatoes are tender but firm. Do not overcook or the potatoes will become mushy. Add the fish and simmer just until fish is piping hot, about 2 minutes. Add the cream or milk, salt and pepper to taste, and bring to the boil. Do not boil but serve piping hot.

Yield: 6 or more servings.

Hot and Sour Fish Soup

There are some recipes for which fresh coriander is a *sine qua non,* and among them is this irresistible hot and sour fish soup served at Uncle Tai's Hunan Yuan Restaurant in New York.

1. Place the fish bones in a kettle and let cold running water flow over them to remove all traces of blood. When the water runs clear, drain and add enough cold water to barely cover the bones. Do not add salt. Bring to the boil and let simmer over very gentle heat for about 20 minutes. Strain. Reserve broth and discard bones. Add 6 to 7 cups of the broth to a saucepan and bring to the boil.

2. Meanwhile, scrape the ginger. Cut the ginger into the thinnest possible slices. Stack the slices and cut them into the finest possible shreds. Set aside. Add scrapings to the soup. Trim the scallions and cut into 2-inch lengths. Cut the lengths into very fine shreds. Set aside. Pluck or cut off the coriander leaves from the stems. Set leaves aside. Crush the stems and add to the soup.

3. Strain the soup into another saucepan and add the shredded ginger, scallions, coriander leaves, vinegar, white pepper, sesame oil and salt. Stir to blend the flavors, but do not cook. Cut the fish into ½-inch cubes and add it. Bring just to the boil and cook just until the fish loses its raw look. Spoon into individual soup bowls and serve piping hot.

Yield: 6 servings.

3 to	4 pounds very fresh fish bones, preferably with head but with gills removed
	Water
1	1½-inch length fresh ginger
4	scallions
20	sprigs of fresh coriander leaves
3 to	4 tablespoons white vinegar
⅛ to	¼ teaspoon ground white pepper
½	teaspoon sesame oil
	Salt
½	pound skinless, boneless nonoily fish, such as flounder, fluke, sole, striped bass, etc.

Japanese Fish and Mushroom Soup

Put the dashi in a saucepan and add the salt, monosodium glutamate and soy sauce. Add the mushrooms and bring to the boil. Arrange 1 shrimp in each of 3 soup bowls and add a few shreds of lemon peel. Pour equal quantities of boiling hot soup into the bowls and serve immediately.

Yield: 3 servings.

3	cups dashi or soup stock (see recipe page 659)
	Salt
⅛	teaspoon monosodium glutamate, optional
½	teaspoon light soy sauce
12	thin slices fresh mushroom
3	shrimp (see recipe below for shrimp to garnish Japanese soups)
	Grated lemon peel

Shrimp to garnish Japanese soups

If the shrimp are whole, tear off the head. In any event, peel the shrimp tail, leaving the last tail section intact. Butterfly the shrimp without cutting through. Score each shrimp on the underside at ½-inch intervals. Sprinkle with salt and dip lightly in cornstarch. Drop the shrimp into rapidly boiling water and cook for 30 to 40 seconds, just until heated through. Drain and drop immediately into ice water. Drain and pat dry. Use one shrimp in each serving of piping hot soup.

Tom Yam Kung (Thai shrimp and herb soup)

Two of the most interesting flavors in the course of a Thai meal served in the home of Karen and Wanchai Sriuttamayotin were the lemon grass (it smacks of lemon peel but is more astringent to the taste) and makrut leaves, which are the leaves of a special lime tree. Both of these ingredients, used in this consummately good shrimp soup, are available in Chinese markets.

1½ pounds neck bones of pork
6 cups water
2 teaspoons dried lemon grass (see note), or use 1 teaspoon grated lemon peel
2 dried makrut leaves, also called kaffirlime leaves (see note)
2 or more tablespoons fish sauce (see note)
1 pound small-to-medium-size shrimp in the shell
¾ cup thinly sliced fresh mushrooms
3 tablespoons or more lemon juice to taste
1 tablespoon chili paste with oil (see note)
¼ teaspoon or more powdered Thai red chili pepper to taste (see note)
8 sprigs fresh coriander leaves, coarsely chopped
Shredded hot, green, fresh chilies
¼ cup chopped scallions

1. Place the bones in a kettle and add the water. Bring to the boil without salt and simmer for about 1 hour, or until the liquid is reduced to 4 cups. Strain the liquid into a 2- or 3-quart saucepan and bring to the boil. Discard the bones. Add the lemon grass, makrut leaves and fish sauce. Do not add salt. The fish sauce is quite salty. Simmer for 15 minutes to abstract the flavor of the herbs. Strain.

2. Meanwhile, peel and devein the shrimp but leave the last tail segment intact. Bring the soup to the boil. Add the shrimp to the boiling soup. Simmer for about 10 minutes and add the mushrooms. Simmer about 2 minutes longer. Add the lemon juice, chili paste with oil and powdered red chili pepper. Serve piping hot in individual bowls with the chopped coriander, shredded green chilies and chopped scallion as garnishes.

Yield: 4 to 6 servings.

Note: All the unfamiliar ingredients listed here are available in Oriental markets.

Mulligatawny Soup

1. Combine the chicken, broth, salt, pepper, carrots, whole onion, celery, mushrooms and parsley in a saucepan. Bring to the boil and cook for 10 minutes. Skim to remove the surface foam, partly cover and continue to cook for 1 hour or longer, until the chicken is tender. Strain the broth. Reserve half a chicken breast, remove the bone and cut the chicken into very thin slices. The rest of the chicken may be refrigerated for another use.

2. Melt the butter and add the chopped onion. Cook, stirring, for about 5 minutes. Do not let the onion brown. Stir in the flour and curry powder. Gradually add the strained broth, while stirring, and bring to the boil, skimming as needed. Simmer for 10 minutes. Adjust the seasoning if necessary. Stir in the cream and rice and return to the boil. Serve in hot cups or soup bowls and garnish each serving with julienne strips of chicken.

Yield: 4 to 6 servings.

1   5-pound stewing chicken, cut into serving pieces
4   cups canned or fresh chicken broth
    Salt and freshly ground pepper to taste
1   carrot, scraped and sliced
1   whole onion
2   ribs celery with leaves
¼   pound mushrooms
3   sprigs parsley
3   tablespoons butter
½   cup finely chopped onion
1½ tablespoons flour
1   tablespoon curry powder, or more to taste
½   cup heavy cream
¼   cup cooked rice

Chicken Gumbo

1. Dredge the chicken pieces in the flour seasoned with salt, pepper and paprika. Shake the pieces to remove excess flour. Heat the bacon fat in a large skillet and brown the chicken on all sides. As it is browned, transfer the pieces to a deep saucepan or kettle. Add the chicken broth and cover. Cook for 20 to 30 minutes, or until chicken is tender.

2. Meanwhile, melt the butter in a saucepan and add the onion. Cook, stirring, until wilted and add the green pepper. Cook, stirring, for about 2 minutes. When the chicken has cooked for 20 minutes, or until tender, add the pepper and onion mixture. Continue cooking for about 10 minutes. Remove the chicken pieces and let cool.

3. Drop the shucked corn in the boiling water to cover. When the water returns to a boil, cover and remove from the heat. Let stand for 5 minutes. Drain and let cool. When cool enough to handle, cut the kernels from the cob. There should be about 1½ cups. Set it aside.

4. Add the tomatoes, rice and hot pepper flakes to the kettle. Simmer for about 5 minutes, stirring frequently. Add the okra and cook for 10 minutes longer, or until the rice is tender without being mushy. Meanwhile, skin and bone the chicken

1   3½-pound chicken, cut into serving pieces
½   cup flour
    Salt and freshly ground pepper
2   tablespoons sweet paprika
3   tablespoons bacon fat
4   cups boiling chicken broth
2   tablespoons butter
1   cup finely chopped onion
¾   cup chopped green pepper
3   ears sweet corn, or 1½ cups frozen corn kernels (do not use cream-style corn and do not defrost before using)
2   cups canned tomatoes, preferably Italian plum tomatoes
¼   cup uncooked rice
½   teaspoon hot red pepper flakes
1   10-ounce package frozen cut okra

pieces. Shred the chicken and add it to the kettle. Add the corn. Bring to the boil and serve very hot.

Yield: 6 to 8 servings.

Turkey Soup

1	turkey carcass
1	cup turkey meat, cut into ½-inch cubes, for garnish
16	cups water
	Leftover giblet gravy, if any, optional
1	cup coarsely chopped onion
1	bay leaf
	Salt and freshly ground pepper to taste
2	whole cloves
4	sprigs fresh parsley
2	sprigs fresh thyme, or ½ teaspoon dried
3	whole carrots, trimmed and scraped
3	whole ribs celery, trimmed and scraped
½	cup broken vermicelli, cappelini or spaghettini

1. Pick over the carcass and reserve any tender morsels of meat. Use this for the cup of meat indicated, adding more meat as necessary.

2. Place the carcass in a kettle and set the meat aside. Add any jellied gravy that may have accumulated on the turkey platter or dish. Add the water to the kettle. Add the leftover giblet gravy, if there is any. Add the onion, bay leaf, salt, pepper, cloves, parsley, thyme, carrots and celery. Bring to the boil and simmer for 1 hour, skimming the surface as necessary.

3. Strain the soup through a sieve lined with a clean kitchen towel or a double thickness of cheesecloth. Discard all the solids except the carrots and celery.

4. Pour about 2 cups of the soup into a saucepan and add the vermicelli. Cook until just tender. Add this to the soup. Cut the carrots and celery into ½-inch cubes and add them. Add the 1 cup of cubed turkey meat. Bring to the boil. Serve piping hot.

Yield: About 14 cups.

Quadretti con Fegatini en Brodo *(Small pasta and chicken livers in broth)*

½	pound chicken livers
	Salt to taste
1	cup egg noodle "flakes," or imported quadretti
4	cups fresh or canned chicken broth
2 or	3 fresh sage leaves, or ½ teaspoon rubbed sage
	Freshly grated Parmeasan cheese

1. Put the chicken livers in a saucepan and add cold water to cover. Add salt to taste. Bring to the boil and simmer for 5 minutes. Drain and let cool.

2. Drop the pasta into boiling salted water and simmer, stirring frequently, for about 6 minutes. Remember they will cook further in the chicken broth. Drain.

3. Slice the chicken livers thinly, then cut the liver slices into ¼-inch or smaller cubes.

4. Add the pasta and cubed chicken livers to the broth. Add the sage and simmer for 10 to 15 minutes. Serve piping hot with grated Parmesan on the side.

Yield: 4 to 6 servings.

Pho Ga *(Rice-noodle soup with chicken)*

One of the great dishes of summer is, curiously enough, a hot soup of Vietnamese origin—elegant, humble and eminently delicious. It is essentially a summer dish in that its goodness is based, as with so many Vietnamese dishes, on fresh herbs. The basic herbs for our version are the ones generally available in America—fresh basil, fresh mint and fresh coriander. Made with rice noodles, the soup is called pho. When served with chicken, it is called pho ga; with beef it is pho bo.

1. Place the chicken in a kettle and add the chicken broth to cover. Do not add salt. Bring to the boil and simmer for about 20 minutes. Turn off the heat and let the chicken stand for 30 minutes or so.

2. Meanwhile, rinse the mint, basil and coriander leaves separately. Pat dry and arrange in separate bowls. Put the scallions in a bowl. Pour boiling water over the bean sprouts. Drain immediately. Rinse under cold water and drain. Arrange in a bowl. Cut the cucumber into thin slices. Stack the slices and cut them into thin strips. Place in another bowl. Peel the onion and slice it thin, top to bottom rather than crosswise into rings. Arrange the onion slices in a bowl and toss in the vinegar. Cut the limes top to bottom and off center to avoid the seedy portion. Each lime should produce 4 seedless wedges. Arrange in a bowl or add them to the mint bowl. Cut the chilies into ⅛-inch slices crosswise. Arrange in another bowl. Add the nuoc mam to another bowl or to a pitcher.

3. Skin the chicken and remove the meat from the bones. Tear the meat into bite-size pieces. Strain the broth into a saucepan. Bring it to the boil and add the monosodium glutamate, if used. Do not add salt. The nuoc mam will add the salty flavor. Add a little of the broth to the chicken meat to keep it moist.

4. Place the noodles in a large bowl and add boiling water to cover. If the water from the tap is steaming, that is hot enough. Let the noodles stand briefly and drain. Add more very hot water; let stand briefly and drain. Continue adding hot water and draining about 7 times, or until noodles are thoroughly tender without being mushy. They overcook easily.

5. When ready to serve, arrange all the bowls of seasonings in the center of the dining table. Heat the chicken meat. Drain

1	3½-pound chicken
	Fresh or canned chicken broth to cover
16 to	20 fresh mint leaves
16 to	20 fresh basil leaves
16 to	20 fresh coriander leaves
1	cup chopped scallions
2	cups fresh bean sprouts
1	4-inch length of trimmed, peeled cucumber, optional
1	small red onion
1	tablespoon red wine vinegar
1 or	2 limes
1 or	2 long, hot, green or red chilies
1	cup nuoc mam sauce (see recipe page 654), or pure nuoc mam or Chinese fish sauce straight from the bottle (see note)
½	teaspoon monosodium glutamate, optional
1	pound rice noodles, preferably Vietnamese or Thai (see note)
⅓	pound very lean and tender beef, such as rib or shell steak, sliced as thin as possible, optional (if beef is used, the name of this dish would be pho bo)
4 to	6 raw eggs, optional
	Freshly ground pepper

the noodles and add equal portions to each of 4 to 6 hot soup bowls, the deeper the better to help retain the heat. Top with equal amounts of chicken. Ladle the boiling broth over all. If the beef is used, add equal amounts to each serving. If the eggs are used, put the meat on one side of the noodles and break an egg on the opposite side. Ladle the boiling broth over the meat and eggs. The eggs will remain almost raw. Serve immediately. This dish must be eaten piping hot.

6. Let each participant at the table add seasonings, including lime juice, cucumber, freshly ground pepper, nuoc mam and so on, according to individual taste.

Yield: 4 to 6 servings.

Note: Bottled fish sauce and rice noodles are available in Oriental groceries and supermarkets.

Mock Turtle Soup

This is a delectable soup made with a calf's head, which is available in well-supplied butcher shops. The reason for the name is that the meat of the cooked calf's head has much the same texture as that of turtle in real turtle soup.

After you have made a kettle of mock turtle soup, you can put it to a marvelous second use as the base of Lady Curzon's soup. This soup is otherwise almost impossible to make in certain areas of America, where the sale of canned turtle soup is forbidden by law because green turtles are among the endangered species of the world. Lady Curzon, by the way, was an American married to the British viceroy to India.

½ calf's head, boned, about ¾ pound
1 calf's tongue, cleaned
3 quarts veal broth (made with the reserved head bones if desired), or chicken broth
Salt and freshly ground pepper
2 tablespoons butter
3 tablespoons finely chopped shallots
1 cup finely chopped onion
¼ pound cooked diced ham, about 1 cup
1 cup thinly sliced mushrooms

1. Place the boned calf's head and calf's tongue in a kettle and add cold water to cover. Bring to the boil and simmer for 5 minutes. Drain well and run under cold water until thoroughly chilled. Drain well. Cut the meat into 1-inch cubes. Discard any fatty portions. Cut away and discard the white bristly portion around the mouth. Return the cubed meat and the whole tongue to a clean kettle. Add the veal broth and bring to the boil. If necessary, add a little salt and pepper. Simmer for 1½ hours, covered.

2. Meanwhile, melt the butter in a saucepan and add the shallots and onion. Cook until wilted and add the ham and mushrooms. Tie the allspice, cloves and sage together in a small cheesecloth bag. Add it. Add the marjoram, thyme, savory, bay leaf, parsley, basil and cayenne. Cook for 10 min-

utes, stirring often. Sprinkle the mixture with the flour, stirring. Spoon off 2 cups of the broth from the calf's head and add it to the mixture, stirring. Cover and cook for 1 hour. Remove the cheesecloth bag and bay leaf.

3. Pour the mixture into the container of a food processor or electric blender and blend thoroughly. Add this to the soup. Add the mace, 1 cup of Madeira, salt and pepper to taste. Remove the tongue from the soup. Cut it in half. Use one-half for other purposes such as sandwiches. Cut the remaining half into cubes and return it to the soup.

4. Serve the piping hot soup in bowls with more Madeira on the side. This soup keeps well when refrigerated. It can be also used to prepare Lady Curzon's soup (see following recipe).

Yield: 18 or more servings.

3	whole allspice
3	whole cloves
1	tablespoon dried sage
1	teaspoon dried marjoram
1	teaspoon chopped fresh thyme, or half the amount dried
1	teaspoon dried savory, optional
1	bay leaf
¼	cup chopped fresh parsley
2	teaspoons chopped fresh basil, or half the amount dried
⅛	teaspoon cayenne pepper
2	tablespoons flour
¼	teaspoon ground mace
1	cup Madeira plus additional wine to serve on the side

Lady Curzon's Soup

1. Heat the butter in a saucepan and add the mushrooms. Cook until wilted. Sprinkle with curry powder. Cook briefly, stirring with a wire whisk. Add the soup, stirring constantly with the whisk.

2. Blend the cream and egg yolk. Remove the soup from the heat and add the yolk mixture, stirring constantly with the whisk. Return the soup to the heat and cook briefly until piping hot but not quite boiling. If the soup boils, the yolk may curdle.

3. Pour the soup into cups (this soup is traditionally served in demitasse cups) and serve. Or—and this is traditional—float equal amounts of whipped cream on top of each serving and run briefly under a hot broiler until the whipped cream starts to brown.

Yield: 4 to 6 servings.

1	tablespoon butter
½	cup finely diced mushrooms
2	tablespoons curry powder
3	cups mock turtle soup with meat (see preceding recipe), or use canned turtle soup if available
½	cup heavy cream
1	egg yolk
1	cup whipped cream, optional

Philadelphia Pepper Pot

¼ cup sweet butter
1 cup finely chopped onion
1 whole onion stuck with 2 cloves
½ cup finely chopped celery
½ cup finely chopped carrot
½ cup chopped sweet green or red pepper (or use hot fresh pepper if desired)
3½ tablespoons flour
5 cups fresh or canned chicken broth
1½ pounds veal bones
2 pounds honeycomb tripe, cut into bite-size pieces
1 whole clove garlic
1 dried hot red pepper, or more to taste
1 bay leaf
1 teaspoon dried marjoram
1 teaspoon dried basil
½ teaspoon dried thyme
Salt and freshly ground pepper to taste
2 cups peeled potatoes cut into ½-inch cubes
1 cup heavy cream

1. Heat the butter in a deep kettle or casserole and, when it is hot but not brown, add the chopped onion, whole onion with cloves, celery, carrot and green or red pepper. Cook, stirring, for about 10 minutes. Do not brown. Sprinkle with flour and stir to coat the vegetables evenly. Add the chicken broth, stirring constantly to prevent lumping. Add the veal bones, tripe, garlic, dried hot red pepper, bay leaf, marjoram, basil, thyme, salt and pepper. Bring to the boil and simmer covered for 1½ to 2 hours, or until tripe is tender.

2. Remove the whole onion with cloves, the veal bones (pull off any meat, shred it and return it to the pot) and bay leaf. Add the potatoes and cook until potatoes are tender. Add the heavy cream and bring to the boil. Serve piping hot in hot soup bowls with crusty French or Italian bread. More ground pepper may be added before serving.

Yield: 6 to 8 servings.

Oxtail Soup with Paprika

3 pounds meaty oxtail, cut into 2-inch lengths
3 quarts water
Salt
1 pound green or red sweet peppers (see note)
4 tablespoons butter
4 cups thinly sliced onion
2 tablespoons sweet or hot paprika
2 cloves garlic, finely minced
5 tablespoons flour
Freshly ground pepper
2 cups sour cream

1. Trim excess fat from the pieces of oxtail. Place the pieces in a kettle and add water to cover. Bring to the boil and simmer for about 3 minutes. Drain and run under cold running water. Return the pieces to a clean kettle and add 3 quarts of water and salt to taste. Bring to the boil and simmer for 1 hour.

2. Core and seed the peppers. Cut them in half and cut the halves into thin strips. There should be about 5 cups. Heat the butter in a kettle and add the onions and peppers and cook briefly until wilted. Sprinkle with paprika, garlic and flour, stirring. Gradually add about half the oxtail broth, stirring rapidly to prevent lumping. Return this mixture to the remaining broth and oxtail in the kettle. Add salt and pepper to taste.

Bring to the boil and simmer for about 2½ hours. The total cooking time should be about 3½ hours, or until oxtail meat is tender and almost falling from the bone.

3. Beat the sour cream with a little salt to make it smooth and seasoned. Serve the hot soup in individual bowls with the sour cream on the side to be added according to taste.

Yield: 8 to 12 servings.

Note: If your taste runs to the piquant side, a few hot Hungarian or other peppers may be used to replace part of the sweet peppers in this recipe.

Soup des Bergers *(Shepherds' lamb soup)*

1. Put the bones and boneless lamb in a kettle and add water to cover. Bring to the boil and simmer for about 3 minutes, stirring briefly. Remove from the heat. Place the kettle under a faucet and let cold water run into it until meat and bones are chilled. Drain the meat and return it to a clean kettle. Add 16 cups of cold water and bring to the boil.

2. Heat the butter in a skillet and add the onion and garlic. Cook briefly and add the carrots, zucchini and celery. Cook for about 5 minutes, stirring occasionally. Add this to the soup. Add the tomatoes, salt and pepper. Stir. Add thyme and bay leaf. Cook the soup for 1 hour. Drain the potatoes and add them. Cook for 30 minutes longer. Remove the bones and meat from the kettle. Remove the meat from the bones. Cube all the meat and return it to the kettle. Serve piping hot.

Yield: 8 or more servings.

2	pounds lamb bones
1½	pounds boneless lamb from shoulder, cut into 2 or 3 pieces
16	cups water, plus water to cover for parboiling
2	tablespoons butter
1	cup finely chopped onion
1	clove garlic, finely minced
4	large carrots, about 1 pound, trimmed, scraped and cut into ½-inch cubes
2	zucchini, trimmed and cut into ½-inch cubes, about 2 cups
3	ribs celery, trimmed and cut into small cubes, about 1 cup
1	cup chopped peeled tomatoes, fresh or canned Salt and freshly ground pepper to taste
½	teaspoon thyme
½	bay leaf
4	large potatoes, peeled and cut into ½-inch cubes, about 2 cups, dropped into cold water

Mayeritsa Avgolemono

The first time I tasted this soup was on a memorable night in Athens with my friend Leon Lianides, the proprietor of New York's much esteemed Coach House restaurant, and his wife, Aphrodite. It was Holy Saturday and a night of brilliant stars and moonlight. After a midnight candle-lighting ceremony, we joined a Greek artist, Jannis Spyropolous, and his wife for a traditional Greek Easter feast. It consisted merely of soup and bread, but it was incredibly delicious. In years past, I had dined on avgolemono soup, that Hellenic specialty made of an abundantly rich broth thickened and flavored with lemon and eggs. But on this occasion I was told that the soup was named mayeritsa avgolemono and that in that moment in thousands and thousands of households throughout the island, celebrants would be dining on this particular soup made with the head of lamb and assorted other odd parts of the animal. Later, Leon explained that nothing is wasted in Greece. Roast baby lamb is the inevitable main dish for the principal feast of Easter day, thus the parts used in the soup the night before.

The liver, neck, knuckles and head from a 12- to 14-pound baby lamb
5 quarts water
3 to 4 pounds meaty veal bones
4 ribs celery, coarsely chopped
2 onions, sliced
2 sprigs parsley
Salt
3 bunches scallions, minced
1 cup minced leeks
¼ pound butter
1 cup minced fresh dill
½ cup raw rice
5 eggs
Juice of 2 lemons
Freshly ground pepper

1. Soak the lamb's head in cold water to cover for 3 hours. Drain. In an 8-quart kettle, combine the 5 quarts of water with the head, liver, knuckles and neck of lamb, the veal bones, celery, onions, parsley and salt to taste. Bring to the boil and simmer for 20 minutes. Remove the liver with a slotted spoon and reserve. Simmer the remaining mixture for 1 hour, or until meat is tender, skimming off the scum that rises to the surface. Strain the broth and reserve. Remove as much meat as possible from the lamb's head and bones. Discard the bones and chop the meat and liver very fine.

2. In a skillet, sauté the scallions and leeks in the butter until transparent. Add the dill and meat and sauté for about 10 minutes. Add the rice and sauté for another 5 minutes. Reserve 1 cup of the strained broth. Bring the remaining broth to a boil. Add the sautéed ingredients and then simmer until rice is tender. Remove from the fire.

3. Beat the eggs until they are light and frothy. Add the juice of 2 lemons in a stream, beating constantly until sauce is thickened. Whisk in the reserved cup of broth and stir the sauce into the soup. Add salt and pepper to taste and serve.

Yield: 12 or more servings.

Mutton or Lamb and Barley Soup

1. Place the bones in a kettle and add cold water to cover. Bring to the boil and simmer for about 1 minute. Drain well and run under cold running water until chilled. Drain. Return to a clean kettle. Add the 20 cups of water, salt to taste and peppercorns and bring to the boil. Simmer for 2 hours.

2. Add the barley and vegetables, including the ¾ cup parsley, and cook for 1 hour longer. Remove the neck bones. Pull off the meat and cut into bite-size morsels. Discard the bones. Return the meat to the kettle and add salt and pepper to taste. If desired, sprinkle with more chopped parsley before serving.

Yield: 8 to 12 servings.

4 pounds meaty neck bones of mutton or lamb, cut into 2-inch pieces
20 cups water
Salt
20 peppercorns, crushed
½ cup barley
2 cups finely diced carrots
2 cups diced leeks
1 cup finely diced rutabaga
2 cups finely diced celery
2 cups chopped onion
1 tablespoon finely minced garlic
¾ cup finely chopped parsley

Petite Marmite Henri IV

1. Place the beef in one saucepan, the chicken in another. Add cold water to cover and bring to the boil. Simmer for about 2 minutes. Drain. Pour the beef broth and water into a large saucepan or small kettle. Add salt and pepper. Add the beef and simmer for 1 hour.

2. Meanwhile, trim the leek and cut it into 1½-inch lengths. Cut each length of leek into eighths. There should be about 2 cups. Trim and scrape the carrots. Quarter them and cut each quarter into 1-inch lengths. There should be about 1½ cups. Peel the turnips. Cut the turnips into ½-inch thick slices. Cut the slices into pieces about the same size as the carrot pieces. There should be about 1½ cups. Cut the celery ribs into neat shapes about the size of the carrot pieces. There should be about 1 cup. Drop all the vegetables into a quantity of boiling water to cover. When the water returns to the boil, drain.

3. When the beef has simmered for 1 hour, add the chicken and vegetables to the kettle. Bring to the boil and simmer for 1 hour longer. At frequent intervals, skim off the fat from the top of the soup. Serve sprinkled with chopped parsley and with toasted buttered slices of French bread.

Yield: 4 to 6 servings.

1¼ pounds lean beef, cut into ½-inch cubes
½ chicken, including breast, leg, thigh, wing and gizzard, cut across the bone into 1½-inch pieces
6 cups fresh or canned beef broth
6 cups water
Salt and freshly ground pepper to taste
1 leek
4 carrots, about ½ pound
½ pound white turnips
3 ribs celery
2 small white onions, peeled
Finely chopped parsley for garnish
Buttered toast

Shchi   *(Sauerkraut and beef soup)*

This rich, hearty soup, pronounced shkee, was served to us by Maria Robbins, who was born in the Ukraine and maintains that it is a more common "everyday" dish in Russia than borscht. It is traditionally served with piroshki.

2   pounds sauerkraut
10   cups fresh or canned beef
   broth
1   tablespoon plus 1 teaspoon
   sugar
2   tablespoons tomato paste
4   tablespoons butter
2   cups chopped onion
⅓   cup chopped celery
1   cup chopped carrots
1   cup chopped parsnip,
   optional
½   bay leaf
   Salt
1   tablespoon lemon juice

1. Drain the sauerkraut. Rinse it in cold water and squeeze to extract most of the moisture. Put the sauerkraut in a Dutch oven or heavy casserole and add ½ cup of broth, the tablespoon of sugar and tomato paste. Stir and cover. Cook for about 45 minutes. Add a little more broth if the sauerkraut starts to become dry.

2. Heat the butter in a skillet and add the onion. Cook, stirring, until wilted. Add the celery, carrots and parsnip, if used. Add this to the sauerkraut. Cover and let cook for about 10 minutes. Add the remaining broth, the bay leaf, remaining teaspoon of sugar, salt and lemon juice. Cover and cook for 1 hour. Serve hot with piroshki.

Yield: 4 to 6 servings.

Beef broth

2   pounds chuck
4   marrow bones
2   carrots, scraped and quartered
1   onion, peeled and stuck with
   4 cloves
1   parsnip, trimmed and
   quartered
3   ribs celery, trimmed and
   quartered
5   quarts water
   Salt
12   peppercorns

Combine all the ingredients in a kettle and bring to the boil. Simmer 3 to 4 hours. Skim the surface frequently to remove foam and scum. Strain and reserve the broth for the soup and the beef for the piroshki. Discard the vegetables. Skim the surface to remove excess fat.

Yield: About 3 quarts.

Note: Leftover beef broth can be frozen.

Piroshki   *(Meat-filled dumplings)*

The dough:

1½   cups milk
4   tablespoons butter
1   envelope granular yeast
⅓   cup warm water
3   tablespoons sugar

1. To prepare the dough, put the milk in a saucepan and bring just to the boil. Remove from the heat and add the 4 tablespoons butter. Let stand until the butter melts and the mixture is just warm.

2. Combine the yeast with the water and ¼ teaspoon of sugar. Stir to dissolve the yeast.

3. Measure out 4 cups of flour into a large bowl and add the remaining sugar and the salt. Stir. Make a well in the center and add 2 eggs, warm milk and butter mixture and the yeast. Start combining the flour with the center liquid ingredients, working rapidly and beating with a wooden spoon until well blended. Scoop out onto a floured board and start kneading. Add more flour, up to 1 more cup, until the dough is smooth and no longer sticky. Add the flour about ¼ cup at a time. Gather the dough into a ball. Rub a warm bowl with butter and add the ball of dough.

4. Cover the dough with plastic wrap and let rise in a warm place until double in bulk, about 1½ hours. Punch down and let rise again, about 1 hour.

5. Meanwhile, to make the filling grind the beef, using the fine blade of a food grinder. There should be about 4 cups.

6. Heat the oil in a skillet and add the onion. Cook until golden brown and add the beef. Blend well, adding salt and pepper to taste.

7. Heat the butter in another skillet and add the mushrooms, salt and pepper to taste. A good deal of liquid will come from the mushrooms. Cook this down briefly. The mixture should not be very dry. Add this to the meat mixture. Blend well.

8. Preheat the oven to 350 degrees.

9. Turn the dough out onto a lightly floured board when it is ready. Knead it briefly and divide it into four pieces. Work one part at a time and keep the remainder covered. Roll out one piece at a time into a long, snakelike rope. Cut this off into 1½-inch lengths. Roll each piece into a ball and flatten with the fingers, turning it around and around into a 3-inch circle. Add to each circle 1 level teaspoon of filling. Fold the dough over to enclose the meat. Press around the edges to seal, tucking the pointed edges under. Place on a baking sheet. Continue making piroshki until all the dough and filling are used. Brush with remaining beaten egg and bake 25 minutes. Serve hot with the soup. These are also good cold and can be reheated.

Yield: About 45 piroshki.

4 to 5 cups unbleached flour
1 tablespoon salt, or to taste
3 eggs, slightly beaten

The filling:

2 pounds chuck, used for the beef broth (see preceding recipe)
⅓ cup oil
2 cups finely chopped onion
Salt and freshly ground pepper
4 tablespoons butter
1 pound fresh mushrooms, cut into very fine dice or chopped

Pozole

The soup:

2 ancho chilies
2 pasilla chilies
2 whole chicken breasts with bone and skin, about 2 pounds
1½ pounds boneless pork loin, cut into 1-inch cubes
2 quarts pork broth (see note), or water
1 whole onion, peeled
2 whole large garlic cloves, peeled
1 bay leaf
2 sprigs fresh thyme, or ½ teaspoon dried
Salt
1¾ cups water
1 tablespoon peanut, vegetable or corn oil
2 16-ounce cans whole hominy, available where Spanish and Puerto Rican foods are sold

The garnishes:

Toasted tortillas or corn chips
1 small head iceberg lettuce, shredded and coarsely chopped
8 radishes, thinly sliced
3 tablespoons crushed oregano leaves
Hot powdered pepper or cayenne pepper
12 lemon or lime wedges
Coarsely chopped fresh coriander leaves, optional
1 avocado, peeled and cubed, optional

We have a special enthusiasm for this Mexican soup and have made abbreviated versions of it in our own kitchen. This one, however, is superior. It is the recipe of Margarita de Rosenzweig-Diaz, who says it is best made with two kinds of dried chilies. It is one of those dishes where garnishes play an essential role and it is, of course, a meal in itself.

1. Place the ancho and pasilla chilies in a bowl and add water to cover. Soak several hours, turning occasionally, until slightly softened.

2. Put the chicken and pork in a kettle and add pork broth to cover. Add the whole onion, 1 clove of garlic, bay leaf, thyme and salt to taste. Bring to the boil and simmer, skimming the surface to remove the scum and foam. Cook for 30 minutes, or until pork is tender.

3. Meanwhile, drain the chilies. Remove and discard the stems. Split the chilies in half and remove and discard the seeds. Slice away and discard the inside veins. Put the chilies in a saucepan and add 1½ cups cold water. Bring to the boil and cook, stirring down occasionally, until the chilies are tender. Pour the chilies and their cooking liquid into the container of a food processor or electric blender. Add the remaining 1 clove of garlic. Blend to a fine purée. Heat the oil in a saucepan and add the purée, stirring. Add salt to taste. Rinse out the processor container with the remaining ¼ cup of water and add it to the saucepan. Cook briefly, stirring.

4. When the pork and chicken have cooked for 30 minutes, remove the chicken and let the remaining ingredients continue to simmer. When the chicken is cool enough to handle, pull away and discard the skin and bones. Cut the meat into 2-inch pieces.

5. Discard the thyme, bay leaf, garlic and onion from the soup. Add the chicken and the puréed chili mixture. Drain 1 can of hominy and add it. Do not drain the remaining can of hominy, but add the hominy and liquid to the soup. Continue cooking for 30 minutes, skimming the surface to remove the scum and fat.

6. Serve boiling hot in very hot bowls. Serve with corn chips on the side. Serve the remaining garnishes to be added to the soup according to each guest's whim and appetite.

Yield: 4 to 6 servings.

Note: Place neck bones of pork in a kettle of water to cover and add salt to taste. Simmer for 1 hour and strain.

Potage Tourangelle *(A white bean and flageolet soup from Touraine)*

1. Place the white beans and flageolets in separate bowls and add enough water to cover the beans to a depth of about 1 inch above the beans. Soak overnight. Drain.

2. Place the beans in separate kettles. To each kettle add 6 cups of water, salt, 1 onion stuck with a clove, 1 clove minced garlic, half a bay leaf and 1 sprig thyme. Bring to the boil. Simmer the white beans for 1¼ hours, or until tender. Simmer the flageolets for about 1½ hours, or until tender. Remove and reserve ½ cup of flageolets for garnish. Remove and discard the pieces of bay leaf and sprigs of thyme. Purée all the remaining ingredients including the liquid. Return to a kettle and bring to the boil. Add the cream and bring to the boil. Swirl in the butter.

3. Meanwhile, cook the string beans separately until tender. Drain and add them to the soup. Add the reserved flageolets. Bring to the boil and serve piping hot.

Yield: 10 or more servings.

½	pound dried white beans such as white kidney beans, Great Northern, California or Michigan pea beans
½	pound dried flageolets
12	cups water
	Salt to taste
2	onions, each stuck with 1 clove
2	cloves garlic, finely minced
1	bay leaf
2	sprigs fresh thyme, or ¼ teaspoon dried
½	cup heavy cream
¼	cup butter
½	cup fresh string beans cut into ½-inch lengths

Purée Mongole *(Purée of split pea soup)*

1. Core the tomatoes and cut them into 1-inch cubes. There should be about 2 cups. Heat 2 tablespoons of butter in a kettle and add the onion. Cook until wilted, stirring, and add the tomatoes. Cook for about 5 minutes and add the ham hock, split peas, chicken broth, water, salt and pepper. Cook for about 2 hours.

2. Meanwhile, peel the turnip, if used, and carrot. Slice each very thinly. Cut the slices into very thin strips to resemble match sticks about 1 inch long. There should be about ⅔ cup each. Drop the carrot sticks into boiling salted water and cook for about 5 minutes. Add the turnip and cook for 5 to 10 minutes until crisp-tender. Drain well.

3. Remove the ham hock from the soup and put the soup into the container of a food processor or electric blender. Blend the soup, one portion at a time, and return it to a kettle. Add the cream and bring to the boil. Add the strips of carrot and turnip and swirl in the remaining 3 tablespoons of butter.

Yield: 10 to 14 servings.

1½	pounds tomatoes
5	tablespoons butter
1	cup coarsely chopped onion
1	2-pound ham hock
1	pound yellow split peas
4	cups fresh or canned chicken broth
4	cups water
	Salt and freshly ground pepper to taste
1	white turnip, about ¼ pound, optional
1	carrot
1	cup heavy cream

Country-style Bean Soup

6 pigs' feet, about 4 pounds
¼ pound lean salt pork
   Salt and freshly ground
   pepper to taste
1 cup coarsely chopped onion
2 cloves garlic, finely minced
10 cups water
1 pound dried pinto, cranberry
   or black beans
1 bay leaf
2 sprigs parsley
1 cup chopped sweet green or
   red pepper
¼ teaspoon dried thyme

1. Rinse the pigs' feet and drain well. Pat dry. Cut the salt pork into ¼-inch slices. Cut the slices into ¼-inch strips. Cut the strips into ¼-inch cubes. Put the cubed salt pork into a kettle large enough to hold the pigs' feet in one layer. When the pork is rendered of most of its fat, add the pigs' feet in one layer. Sprinkle with salt and pepper. Brown lightly on one side and turn.

2. Sprinkle the onion and garlic around and between pigs' feet. Cook briefly, stirring occasionally, for about 5 minutes. Add the water, beans, bay leaf, parsley, pepper and thyme. Add salt and pepper to taste. Cover the kettle and cook for 3 hours.

Yield: 6 servings.

Lentil Soup

3 tablespoons butter
¼ pound slice of smoked ham,
   fat left on, cut into quarters
¼ cup coarsely chopped onion
½ pound dried lentils
5 cups fresh or canned chicken
   broth
2 cups water
½ bay leaf
1 sprig fresh thyme, or ¼
   teaspoon dried
   Salt and freshly ground
   pepper

1. Heat 1 tablespoon of butter in a small kettle or deep saucepan and add the ham and onion. Cook briefly until onion wilts. Add the lentils and 4 cups of the chicken broth. Add the remaining ingredients and simmer for 30 to 40 minutes. Remove ½ cup of the soup with lentils and set aside. Discard the bay leaf. Remove the ham pieces and set aside.

2. Put the soup through a food mill to eliminate the coarse lentil hulls. Return the soup to the stove and bring to the boil. Add the remaining cup of chicken broth and the reserved soup with lentils. Finely dice the ham and add it to the soup. Return the soup to the boil and swirl in the remaining butter.

Yield: 4 to 6 servings.

Soupe au Pistou *(Bean soup with basil sauce)*

The soup:

¾ cup dried pea beans
3 quarts water
2 potatoes, about 1¼ pounds
½ pound green beans
1½ pounds lima beans in the
   shell, or 1 10-ounce
   package frozen

1. Place the beans in a kettle and add the water. Bring to the boil and simmer for 30 minutes. Peel the potatoes and cut them into ½-inch cubes. There should be about 3½ cups. Add them to the kettle. Trim the green beans and cut them into ½-inch lengths. There should be about 2 cups. Add them to the kettle. Shell the fresh lima beans, if used. There should be about 1 cup of beans. Add them to the kettle. If frozen lima

beans are used, do not add them at this point. Add salt and pepper to taste. Cover and simmer for 50 minutes.

2. Peel and core the tomatoes and cut them into ½-inch cubes. Add them to the kettle. Trim and discard the ends of the zucchini and cut them into ½-inch cubes. Add them to the kettle. If frozen lima beans are used, add them. Cover and cook for 30 minutes longer.

3. Meanwhile, blend to a paste the basil and garlic. Stir in the oil gradually. This is the pistou. When ready to serve, add the pasta to the soup and simmer for about 1 minute. Stir in the pistou and serve piping hot in hot bowls.

Yield: 8 or more servings.

	Salt and freshly ground pepper
2	red, ripe tomatoes, about 1¼ pounds, or 2 cups chopped canned imported tomatoes
3 or	4 small zucchini, about 1 pound
¼	cup broken small pasta, preferably capellini or vermicelli

The pistou:

10 or	12 leaves fresh basil
2 to	4 cloves fresh garlic, peeled
3	tablespoons olive oil

Fabada Asturiana *(A hearty bean soup from the region of Asturia in Spain)*

1. Place the beans in a bowl and add cold water to cover to a depth of 1 inch above the top of the beans. Soak overnight. Drain.

2. Put the beans in a kettle and add the 12 cups of water, salt pork, onion, garlic, salt, ham hock, lean pork and tomatoes. Bring to the boil and simmer for about 1¼ hours, or until beans are tender. Add the morcilla sausages and potatoes and cook about 20 minutes longer.

3. Remove the lean pork and set it aside for another use or cut it into small cubes and return to the soup. Slice the sausages and return them to the soup. Remove the ham hock. Discard the bone and fat. Cut the meat into cubes and add it to the soup. Bring the soup to the boil and skim off the fat.

Yield: 10 or more servings.

Note: Morcilla blood sausages are available in Spanish and Mexican markets.

1	pound dried white beans such as white kidney beans, Great Northern, California or Michigan pea beans
12	cups water
½	cup streaky salt pork in one piece
2	cups finely chopped onion
1	tablespoon finely chopped garlic
	Salt to taste
1	ham hock
½	pound pork in one piece, preferably tenderloin, or use pork chops
1	cup tomatoes
3	morcilla sausages (Spanish blood sausages), see note
3	potatoes, peeled and cut into ½-inch cubes, about 2 cups

Cuban Black Bean Soup

1 pound black beans (see note)
12 cups water
Salt to taste
¼ pound lean salt pork cut/ into ¼-inch cubes
2 cups finely chopped onion
1 tablespoon finely chopped garlic
1 cup chopped green pepper
½ teaspoon oregano
½ cup finely chopped cooked, smoked ham, preferably a country ham
1 cup crushed fresh or canned tomatoes
2 tablespoons chopped fresh coriander leaves
1 to 2 cups fresh or canned beef broth
1 teaspoon cumin
Wine vinegar

1. Place the beans in a bowl and add cold water to cover to a depth of 1 inch above the top of the beans. Soak overnight. Drain.

2. Place the beans in a kettle and add the 12 cups of water. Add salt to taste. Bring to the boil. As the beans cook, heat the salt pork in a skillet and, when it is rendered of fat, add the onion, garlic and green pepper and cook until onion is wilted. Add the oregano, ham, tomatoes and coriander leaves. Cook briefly. This mixture is known as a sofrito.

3. Spoon and scrape the sofrito into the beans and continue cooking 1½ to 2 hours, or until beans are thoroughly tender. If they become too dry, add beef broth. When ready to serve, add the cumin and dilute with beef broth to the desired consistency. Serve piping hot with vinegar on the side to be added according to individual taste. Chopped hard-cooked egg white is sometimes served as a garnish. And, if the vinegar is omitted, lemon slices stuck with one clove each also may be used as a garnish.

Yield: 10 or more servings.

Note: Black beans (black turtle beans) are available at Spanish, Mexican and Puerto Rican markets.

Caldo Verde

⅓ pound dried white lima beans
6 tablespoons olive oil
3 cups onions cut into 8 to 16 thin wedges
8 cups boiling water
Salt to taste
¾ pound beef, cut into ¾-inch or smaller cubes
¾ pound bratwurst, kielbasa (Polish sausage) or krainer sausage cut into ½-inch rounds
2 cups chopped tomatoes
1 pound greens of the cabbage family such as collard greens, broccoli leaves, mustard greens or, as a last resort, green cabbage
Freshly ground pepper to taste

1. Place the beans in a bowl and add cold water to cover to a depth of about 2 inches above the beans. Let stand overnight.

2. Drain the beans. Remove and discard the tough skin on each bean. Heat the oil in a kettle and add the onions. Cook, stirring often, until the onions are golden brown. Add half the boiling water and salt to taste. At boil, add the beef, sausages, tomatoes and beans. Simmer for 1 hour, skimming the surface as necessary to remove the scum and foam.

3. Remove any tough stems from the greens. Shred the leaves finely (chiffonade). Add the remaining boiling water and the greens to the kettle and simmer 1½ hours longer. Add salt and pepper to taste.

Yield: 6 or more servings.

Misoshiru   *(Japanese bean soup)*

1. Pour the dashi into a saucepan and add the bean paste, stirring constantly. Taste the soup. If it is not strong enough, stir in a little more bean paste. If it is too strong, thin it with more dashi.

2. When ready to serve, strain the soup into another saucepan. Add the monosodium glutamate, if used, and mushrooms. Bring to the boil and pour equal quantities into 3 soup bowls. Garnish each serving with chopped scallions.

Yield: 3 servings.

Note: Many ingredients can be added to this soup including bean curd cut into cubes and shrimp or eel. Very small cherrystone clams, cooked just until they open, are also excellent served in the shell.

3	cups dashi or soup stock (see recipe page 659)
⅓	cup miso (bean paste), available in Japanese food outlets
⅛	teaspoon monosodium glutamate, optional
½	cup thinly sliced fresh mushrooms (see note)
2 or	3 tablespoons chopped scallion for garnish

Abgushteh Limon   *(Persian lemon soup)*

1. Put the water in a casserole large enough to hold the chicken comfortably. Add the chicken, parsley and onion. Scrape the carrots and trim off the ends. Quarter the carrots, then cut each quarter in half. Add them to the casserole. Add the beef broth, salt and pepper to taste. Cook for 1 hour and 45 minutes.

2. Prick 2 holes at opposite extremes of each lemon. Add them to the soup and cook for 1 hour longer. Remove the parsley. Remove the chicken and save it for a future meal. Press the lemons with the back of a spoon to extract inside juices. The lemons may be served with the soup although they are quite sour and not for all tastes. Normally they are removed. Serve the soup with the vegetables.

Yield: 6 to 8 servings.

5	cups water
1	3-pound chicken
12	sprigs parsley tied with a string
1	¾-pound onion, peeled and quartered
4	carrots, about ¾ pound
1½	cups fresh or canned beef broth
	Salt and freshly ground pepper to taste
5	dried lemons, available in stores that specialize in Middle Eastern foods

Cold Barley and Yogurt Soup

1. Heat the butter in a saucepan and add the onion. Cook until wilted and add the barley. Add the chicken broth and bring to the boil. Cover and simmer for about 1 hour.

2. Cool the soup, then refrigerate it. When thoroughly cold, stir in the yogurt and 2 tablespoons chopped mint. Add salt to taste and chill thoroughly. Serve sprinkled with chopped mint on top.

Yield: 6 servings.

2	tablespoons butter
1	cup finely chopped onion
⅓	cup medium pearl barley
3	cups fresh or canned chicken broth
3	cups yogurt
2	tablespoons finely chopped mint, plus chopped mint for garnish
	Salt

V. Meats

High-temperature Rib Roast of Beef

To judge from the correspondence we receive, this recipe for roasting beef marked some sort of record in popularity. The technique of roasting the beef at a high temperature and then turning off the oven was developed by Ann Seranne, a good friend and an innovative genius in the kitchen. One word of caution: This method should be attempted only with a well-insulated oven.

1 2- to 4-rib roast of beef, short ribs removed, 4½ to 12 pounds
Flour
Salt and freshly ground pepper to taste

1. Remove the roast from the refrigerator 2½ to 4 hours before cooking. Preheat the oven to 500 degrees.

2. Place the roast in an open shallow roasting pan, fat side up. Sprinkle with a little flour and rub the flour into the fat lightly. Season with salt and pepper. Put the roast in the preheated oven and roast according to the chart below, timing exactly. When cooking time is finished, turn off the oven. Do not open the door at any time.

3. Leave the roast in the oven until oven is lukewarm, or for about 2 hours. Roast will have a crunchy brown outside and an internal heat that will be suitable for serving for as long as 4 hours.

Yield: 2 servings per rib.

Note: To make thin pan gravy, remove excess fat from the meat drippings, leaving any meat pieces in the pan. Stir in ½ to 1 cup beef stock or broth. Bring to the boil, scraping the bottom of the pan to loosen the meat pieces. Simmer for 1 minute and season to taste.

Roasting chart

Ribs	Weight Without Short Ribs	Roast at 500 Degrees
2	4½ to 5 pounds	25 to 30 minutes
3	8 to 9 pounds	40 to 45 minutes
4	11 to 12 pounds	55 to 60 minutes

This works out to be about 15 minutes per rib, or approximately 5 minutes cooking time per pound of trimmed, ready-to-cook roast.

Roast Ribs of Beef

1. Preheat the oven to 500 degrees.

2. A very light layer of fat may be trimmed from the roast but leave a layer of fat at least ¼ inch thick. Arrange the roast fat side up in a shallow baking dish and sprinkle with salt. Pour the water around the meat. Place in the oven and bake for 15 minutes.

3. Reduce oven heat to 400 degrees and continue baking for 25 minutes. Reduce oven heat to 350 degrees and bake for 15 minutes for rare beef, 30 minutes for medium rare, longer for well done. Carefully transfer the roast to a serving dish, rib side down. Cover loosely with foil to keep warm.

4. Pour off all the fat from the roasting pan, but save about ½ cup for preparing Yorkshire pudding. To make a light "juice" for the beef, add about ½ cup of cold water to the pan and stir to dissolve the brown particles that cling to the bottom and sides of the pan. Serve the beef sliced with Yorkshire pudding and grated horseradish or horseradish cream on the side, if desired.

Yield: 6 to 8 servings.

1 6-pound standing rib roast with ribs (but with the ends of ribs and chine bone removed)
Salt to taste
¼ cup cold water

1. Preheat the oven to 425 degrees.

2. Combine the milk and nutmeg in a mixing bowl. Put the eggs in another bowl and beat until frothy. Add this to the milk and stir.

3. Pour the beef drippings into a heat-proof baking dish and place on the stove over moderate heat. When quite hot and almost smoking, add the batter. Smooth it over with a rubber spatula. Place the pudding in the oven and bake for about 15 minutes. Turn the baking dish as the cooking proceeds for even cooking.

Yield: 8 or more servings.

Yorkshire pudding

1 cup milk
⅛ teaspoon grated nutmeg
4 large eggs, about ¾ cup when measured
½ cup beef drippings

Blend all the ingredients and serve.
Yield: About 1 cup.

Horseradish cream

½ cup freshly grated horseradish
¾ cup sour cream
Salt to taste

Costata di Bue *(Boiled ribs of beef)*

Don't be put off by the idea of boiling a rib roast of beef. It is an absolutely triumphant dish that we were served at Savini's in Rome. The beef is rare and is served hot with an elegantly conceived salsa verde. Pure joy!

1   9½-pound ready-to-cook rib roast of beef (4-rib roast)
4   large carrots, trimmed and scraped
2   turnips, about 1½ pounds, trimmed and peeled
8 to   12 "new" red potatoes
1   pound zucchini
½   pound green beans
    Beef broth to cover
    Salt to taste
    Salsa verde (see recipe below)
    Coarse salt for garnish

1. Place the beef in a large kettle and add cold water to cover. Bring to the boil and simmer for about 2 minutes. Drain thoroughly and run briefly under cold water. Let stand at room temperature until ready to cook.

2. Meanwhile, quarter the carrots lengthwise and cut them into 2-inch lengths. Set aside. Cut the turnips into eighths. Set aside. Peel the potatoes and add cold water to cover. Set aside. Trim the ends of the zucchini. Cut them into convenient serving pieces. Trim the green beans and cut them into 2-inch lengths.

3. Place the ribs of beef in a kettle and add beef broth to cover. If necessary, add water to make certain the beef is covered. Add salt to taste. Bring to the boil and simmer for 1 hour.

4. Add the carrots and potatoes and cook for 15 minutes. Add the zucchini, turnips and green beans and cook for 15 minutes longer.

5. Remove the meat and cover with foil. Let it rest for 15 minutes. Stand the rib roast on one end and carve like roast beef. Serve with the cooked vegetables. Serve with salsa verde and coarse salt on the side.

Yield: 8 to 10 servings.

Salsa verde

3   tablespoons coarsely chopped chives
1   cup chopped parsley
¼   cup coarsely chopped onion
6   small cornichons
2   tablespoons drained capers
3   anchovy fillets
1   clove garlic, chopped
24   small cocktail onions, drained
¼   cup red wine vinegar
1¼   cups olive oil
    Salt and freshly ground pepper to taste

Combine all the ingredients in the container of a food processor or electric blender and blend. Do not overblend. This sauce must retain a coarse consistency. Serve with boiled meats, poultry, fish and so on.

Yield: About 2 cups.

Chorizo-stuffed Rump Roast

1. Preheat the oven to 375 degrees.

2. Make a hole lengthwise through the center of the meat. To do this, run a long, thin, sharp knife through the center. If a sharpening steel is available, this will assist in making the hole. Stuff the opening with lengths of chorizo or other partly cooked sausage. Sprinkle the meat on all sides with salt and pepper to taste.

3. Heat the oil in a heavy Dutch oven or casserole and brown the meat all over, turning it frequently, for about 10 minutes. Remove the meat and pour off the fat. Return the meat and scatter the onion, carrots, garlic and celery around it. Add the chili powder and oregano and pour the tomatoes over all. Add the beef broth, salt and pepper to taste and cover. Bring to the boil on top of the stove.

4. Place the meat in the oven and bake for 2½ to 3 hours, or until the roast is thoroughly cooked and tender. Remove the meat and skim the surface of the sauce to remove all fat. Serve the roast sliced with the sauce.

Yield: 8 or more servings.

1	3½-pound rump roast or eye round
½	pound chorizo sausage or kielbasa (Polish sausage)
	Salt and freshly ground pepper
2	tablespoons peanut, vegetable or corn oil
1	cup chopped onion
¾	cup chopped carrots
1	teaspoon finely minced garlic
½	cup chopped celery
2	tablespoons chili powder
1	tablespoon oregano, crumbled
1	17-ounce can peeled tomatoes with tomato paste, or 2 cups peeled tomatoes plus 2 tablespoons tomato paste
1	cup fresh or canned beef broth
	Salt and freshly ground pepper to taste

Steak au Poivre

1. Pound the meat lightly with a flat mallet.

2. Crush the dried peppercorns coarsely, using the bottom of a clean skillet or a spice mill. Add the red pepper flakes and mix well. Rub the steaks on both sides with the peppercorn mixture. Crush the green peppercorns and smear this and salt on both sides of the steaks. Rub with olive oil and let stand for 1 or 2 hours.

3. There are two usual methods for cooking the steaks, either over hot charcoal or in a skillet. If charcoal is used, simply grill over hot coals for 2 or 3 minutes to a side for rare meat, longer if you want well-done steaks. Alternatively, heat 2 heavy skillets and add 3 tablespoons butter to each. When the butter is almost brown, add the steaks and cook for 2 minutes

2	strip sirloin steaks, each about 1½ inches thick
1	teaspoon white peppercorns
1	teaspoon black peppercorns
1	teaspoon Szechwan peppercorns
¼	teaspoon crushed red pepper flakes
1	teaspoon drained green peppercorns packed in brine
	Salt to taste
2	tablespoons olive oil
6	tablespoons butter

to a side for rare meat, longer for medium or well-done steaks. If cooked over charcoal, pour the 6 tablespoons of hot melted butter over the steaks after they are cooked.

4. When the steaks are cooked, remove them to a hot platter and let rest for 5 to 10 minutes before slicing. Using a sharp knife, cut the steaks on the bias into thin slices. Serve with the pan juices.

Yield: 6 servings.

Steak Persillade

1¾ pounds boneless shell steak, trimmed of excess outside fat
Salt and freshly ground pepper to taste
4 tablespoons butter
2 tablespoons finely chopped shallots
5 tablespoons chopped parsley

1. Place the steak on a flat surface and cut it into thin strips that measure about 2 inches long and ½ inch wide. Sprinkle the pieces with salt and pepper. Have ready two warm skillets.

2. Heat one skillet and add 2 tablespoons butter. Add about half the meat (the pieces should not be crowded in the skillet or the inside juices will run). The meat should also cook over very high heat. Turn the pieces of meat so that they cook quickly and evenly for a total of 2 to 3 minutes. Transfer the cooked pieces to the second warmed skillet.

3. Add 2 more tablespoons of butter to the skillet in which the meat cooked. When very hot add the second batch of steak and cook quickly as before. When second batch is cooked, combine the two batches.

4. Add the shallots and, if necessary, more salt and pepper. Sprinkle with 4 tablespoons of parsley. Toss quickly in the very hot skillet and serve hot. Before serving, sprinkle with the remaining tablespoon of parsley.

Yield: 4 to 6 servings.

Entrecôtes Mirabeau   *(Shell steaks with anchovies)*

The steaks and garnish:

4 shell steaks, about ¾ pound each
Salt and freshly ground pepper
12 flat anchovy fillets
8 pimiento-stuffed green olives
16 leaves fresh tarragon, optional

1. Sprinkle the steaks on all sides with salt and pepper to taste. Preferably, grill them for about 4 minutes to a side for rare meat, 5 minutes to a side for medium rare, and so on up to 7 or 8 minutes to a side for well done. Or cook the steaks to the desired degree of doneness in a little butter in a hot skillet.

2. Place the anchovy fillets on a flat surface and split each in half lengthwise. Arrange 6 of the anchovy halves in a lattice pattern over the steaks. Split the stuffed olives down the

center crosswise. Arrange 4 olive pieces, sliced side up, in a symmetrical pattern inside the lattice. Garnish, if desired, with fresh tarragon leaves.

3. Melt the 3 tablespoons butter in a small saucepan and add the chopped anchovies and lemon juice. Spoon about 2 teaspoons of the anchovy butter on top of each steak and serve.

Yield: 4 servings.

The anchovy butter:

3 tablespoons butter at room temperature
1 tablespoon finely chopped anchovies, or anchovy paste
1 teaspoon lemon juice

Swiss Steak Jardinière

1. Dredge the steaks on both sides with flour seasoned with salt and pepper. If desired, pound the steak lightly, although this is not necessary.

2. Heat the oil in a heavy skillet and brown the steaks for about 5 minutes on each side. Pour off the fat from the skillet. Add the onion and garlic and cook briefly. Add the wine, water, thyme, bay leaf and celery. Stir in the tomato paste. Cover and cook for about 1 hour. Add the carrots and cook for 40 minutes longer, or until meat is fork-tender. Add the peas and cook for about 5 minutes.

Yield: 6 servings.

6 6-ounce chicken steaks (also labeled boneless beef blade and boneless top chuck steak)
¼ cup flour
Salt and freshly ground pepper to taste
3 tablespoons peanut, vegetable or corn oil
1 cup coarsely chopped onion
1 clove garlic, finely minced
½ cup dry white wine
2 cups water
2 sprigs fresh thyme, or ½ teaspoon dried
1 bay leaf
1 cup chopped celery
1 tablespoon tomato paste
12 small carrots, or 4 large carrots quartered, about ½ pound
1 cup frozen peas

Skirt Steak

1. Cut the skirt steak into 6 lengths. Sprinkle each piece with salt and pepper. Heat a skillet until very hot and add 1 tablespoon of butter. Add half the pieces of meat in one layer. Cook the pieces over very high heat for 2 to 4 minutes to a side. Remember that the thickness of steak varies and the thinner pieces should be cooked more quickly than the others. The steak should be served slightly rare in the center.

2. When the first pieces of steak are cooked, transfer them to a warm platter. Add the remaining pieces. Cook in the same

2 pounds skirt steak
Salt and freshly ground pepper to taste
4 tablespoons butter
2 tablespoons finely chopped shallots
1 small clove garlic, finely minced
3 tablespoons chopped parsley

manner. Remove to the platter. Pour off the fat from the skillet and add 3 tablespoons of butter. Cook quickly and add the shallots and garlic. Cook for about 30 seconds, stirring. Pour over the steak, sprinkle with parsley and serve.

Yield: 6 servings.

Beef Scaloppine Casalinga   *(Beef fillets with Marsala and mushroom sauce)*

8 slices fillet of beef, each about ½ inch thick
¾ cup salad oil
½ cup finely chopped onion
½ cup prosciutto or baked ham cut into very thin strips
⅓ pound fresh mushrooms, thinly sliced, about 2 cups, sprinkled with lemon juice
2 tablespoons butter
⅓ cup canned brown beef gravy
1 cup Marsala
2 tablespoons finely chopped parsley
Flour for dredging
Oil for shallow frying
8 rounds of mozzarella cheese, about ⅓ inch thick and 3 inches in diameter

1. Preheat the oven to 500 degrees.

2. Place the beef slices on a flat surface and pound lightly with a mallet. Set aside.

3. Heat the oil in a skillet and add the onion. Cook, stirring often, to brown lightly, for about 10 minutes. Add the prosciutto and mushrooms. Cook slowly, for about 10 minutes. Empty the mixture into a sieve and drain well, pressing down the the back of a wooden spoon to extract most of the oil.

4. Heat the butter in another skillet and add the mushroom mixture. Blend well and add the beef gravy and Marsala. Sprinkle with parsley and simmer for about 20 minutes.

5. Dredge the meat lightly in flour. Add oil to a depth of about ½ inch to a skillet and add the meat. Cook quickly, turning once, until golden on both sides, about 2 minutes. Transfer the meat to a colander and let drain.

6. Spoon half the mushroom sauce over a baking dish and arrange the beef slices on top. Spoon the remaining sauce over and top each slice with a slice of mozzarella cheese. Bake for 10 to 15 minutes, or until piping hot and the cheese melted.

Yield: 8 servings.

French Pot Roast with Red Wine Sauce

1 5- to 6-pound round roast of beef
½ cup red wine vinegar
2¼ cups chopped onion
2¼ cups chopped carrots
1½ cups chopped celery
2 cups chopped leeks, optional
2 cloves garlic, crushed
3 sprigs parsley
1 teaspoon each of leaf sage, dried rosemary, marjoram and coriander seeds
4 to 5 cups dry red wine

1. Place the beef in a mixing bowl. Combine the vinegar, 1½ cups each chopped onion and carrots, 1 cup of celery, the leeks, if used, garlic and parsley in a saucepan. Tie the sage, rosemary, marjoram and coriander seeds in a cheesecloth bag and add the bag. Bring to the boil, stirring. Pour the vinegar mixture over the meat and add enough wine to barely cover the meat. Sprinkle with salt and pepper to taste. Cover closely and refrigerate overnight or longer, for up to 3 days.

2. Remove the meat and pat it dry. Strain and reserve 3 cups of the liquid. Discard the remaining liquid and vegetables.

3. Heat the salt pork in a heavy Dutch oven or casserole and cook, stirring, until it is rendered of fat. Scoop out and discard the solids.

4. Sprinkle the beef with salt and pepper. Add it to the Dutch oven or casserole and brown well on all sides. Transfer the meat to a warm place.

5. Add remaining ¾ cup each of chopped onion and carrots and remaining ½ cup of celery. Cook, stirring, until onion is wilted. Sprinkle with the flour and stir to blend thoroughly. Add the reserved marinade and beef broth, stirring with a wire whisk. When the mixture is thickened, add the meat. Cover closely and cook over low heat for about 3 hours, or until the roast is thoroughly tender.

6. Remove the meat and keep it warm. Cook the sauce down to the desired consistency. Slice the meat and serve with the sauce.

Yield: 6 to 10 servings.

Salt and freshly ground pepper
¾ cup diced salt pork, or 2 tablespoons vegetable oil
¼ cup flour
2 cups fresh or canned beef broth

Boeuf Bouilli à la Jambe de Bois   *(Boiled beef)*

1. Place the beef, including the end bones of beef, if used, in a kettle with cold water to cover.

2. Pull off and discard any tough outer leaves of the cabbage. Cut the cabbage into quarters and add to the kettle. Bring to the boil and simmer for 5 minutes. Drain. Run both the beef and cabbage under cold water and drain again. Set the cabbage aside. Return the beef to a clean kettle and add the 8 quarts of water, bay leaves, salt, peppercorns, thyme, parsley, allspice, cloves, garlic and leek tops. Bring to the boil. Boil the meat partly covered for about 1½ hours.

3. Meanwhile, as the beef cooks, peel the turnips and cut them into quarters or eighths, depending on size. Set aside. Peel and quarter potatoes. Drop into cold water and set aside. Trim and scrape the carrots. Cut them into 2-inch lengths. Tie the pieces in cheesecloth. Set aside. Peel the onions and tie them in cheesecloth. Set aside. Split the leeks down to the base, but do not cut through. Rinse between the leaves thoroughly. Tie the leeks together in a bundle. Set aside. Tie each heart of celery with string and set aside.

4. After the beef has cooked 1½ hours, add the packages of carrots, onions, leeks and celery. Let simmer for 45 minutes. Add the cabbage, potatoes and turnips. Let simmer for 20 to 30 minutes, or until the the vegetables and the beef are tender. The total cooking time is from 2¾ to 3 hours. When the meat and vegetables are removed, continue to cook down the broth to concentrate it.

5. To serve, untie the various pieces of string and cheesecloth. Serve the vegetables with the beef slices. Serve with cor-

7 pounds center-section shin of beef (see note)
2½ pounds cabbage
8 quarts (32 cups) water
2 bay leaves
 Salt
1 teaspoon crushed peppercorns
2 sprigs fresh thyme, or 1 teaspoon dried
4 sprigs fresh parsley
4 allspice
2 whole cloves
4 cloves garlic, peeled and left whole
2 leek tops, green part only, tied in a bundle
1 pound white turnips
1 pound potatoes
¾ pound carrots, trimmed
20 small white onions, peeled
4 leeks, trimmed, split and rinsed thoroughly
2 hearts of celery, trimmed but ribs left intact at base
 Fresh tomato sauce (see recipe page 650)
 Sauce Raifort (see recipe page 646)

nichons, coarse salt, such as kosher salt, imported French mustard, fresh tomato sauce, horseradish sauce and so on.

6. Serve the broth now or on another occasion with croutons and freshly grated Parmesan cheese.

Yield: 12 or more servings.

Note: If the shin of beef is available with the entire bone, have the butcher saw off the bone ends. Add the ends to the kettle when cooking the shin. These bones are not essential, however.

New England Boiled Dinner

1	6½-pound corned beef
6	quarts water
5 or	6 carrots, about 1 pound
8 to	12 small white turnips or 1 rutabaga, about ¾ pound
8	small, whole white onions, about ¾ pound
1 or	2 young heads of cabbage, about 4 pounds
10	potatoes, about 1¾ pounds
10	young beets, about 1 pound
	Salt
¼	pound butter
	Horseradish, preferably freshly grated
	Mustard

1. Place the corned beef in a large kettle or Dutch oven and add the water. The water should cover the top of the beef by about 2 inches. Cover and cook for about 2 hours, or until the corned beef is almost tender. Do not add salt.

2. Meanwhile, trim the carrots and cut them in half widthwise. Cut each half into quarters. Set aside. Peel the turnips and set aside. Peel the onions and set aside. If 2 cabbages are used, quarter them. If 1 head is used, cut it into eighths. Pull away any tough outer leaves and cut away part of the core of each section. Set aside. Peel the potatoes and drop them into cold water to prevent discoloration. Set aside. Peel the beets and set aside.

3. After approximately 2 hours, when the meat is almost tender, add all the vegetables except the beets. Taste the cooking liquid. It should not need salt. If it does, add it to taste. Cook until vegetables are tender.

4. Put the beets in a saucepan and add water to cover and salt to taste and cook until tender.

5. Remove the meat and slice it thin. Arrange the drained vegetables symmetrically on a hot platter. Melt the butter and pour it over the vegetables. Serve with horseradish and mustard on the side.

Yield: About 10 servings.

Corned Beef and Cabbage

1	3-pound slab of corned beef
16	cups water
1	whole carrot, scraped
2	whole onions, peeled and stuck with 4 cloves

1. Place the corned beef in a kettle and add the water, carrot and onions.

2. If the leek is used, trim the end. Split the leek down the center almost but not through the root end. Insert the bay leaf, parsley and thyme in the center and tie with a string. Add it to

the kettle. Otherwise omit the leek and simply add the other ingredients to the kettle. Add the peppercorns.

3. Bring to the boil and simmer for 2 to 2½ hours. The cooking time of corned beef varies greatly because of the unpredictable quality of the meat. Cook until fork-tender. Approximately 15 minutes before the beef is tender, core the cabbage and peel the potatoes. Cut the cabbage into eighths. Add cabbage and potatoes to the kettle and cook for 15 minutes, or until the vegetables are tender. As the vegetables cook, prepare the parsley sauce, which is made with 1 cup of the corned beef cooking liquid.

4. Serve the corned beef sliced with the cabbage wedges and potatoes. Serve with parsley sauce and mustard.

Yield: 6 to 8 servings.

1. Melt the butter in a saucepan and add the flour, stirring with a wire whisk. When blended, add the broth, stirring rapidly with the whisk. When blended and smooth, add the milk, salt and pepper. Simmer for about 5 minutes.

2. Add the parsley and stir to blend. Add lemon juice and serve piping hot.

Yield: About 1¾ cups.

1	leek, optional
1	bay leaf
2	sprigs fresh parsley
2	sprigs fresh thyme, or ½ teaspoon dried
12	peppercorns, crushed
1	2½-pound cabbage
1½	pounds small potatoes, preferably the red-skinned variety
	Mustard
	Parsley sauce (see recipe below)

Parsley sauce

2	tablespoons butter
3	tablespoons flour
1	cup broth from the corned beef
½	cup milk
	Salt and freshly ground pepper to taste
1½	cups finely chopped parsley
	Juice of ½ lemon

Carne en Salsa Roja *(Beef in red chili sauce)*

1. Cut the meat or have the butcher cut it into 1½-inch cubes. Set aside.

2. Pull off and discard the tough stems of the chilies. Split the chilies open. Remove and discard the seeds and veins. Place the chilies in a saucepan and add the water. Bring to the boil and simmer for about 10 minutes, stirring occasionally to redistribute the chilies. Remove from the heat and let cool.

3. Put the chilies with all their cooking liquid in the container of a food processor or electric blender. This may have to be done in two or more steps. Add the onion and garlic and blend all the ingredients thoroughly. As they are blended, pour the mixture into a bowl. Set aside.

4. Heat the oil in a large, fairly deep, heavy skillet or casserole. Add the meat and cook until brown, stirring occasionally,

4	pounds chuck steak
¼	pound dried chilies, a combination of about 12 chilies pasilla and 6 chilies anchos, available in Spanish markets
5	cups water
1	onion, about ¼ pound, peeled and cut into eighths
6	whole cloves garlic, peeled
¼	cup peanut, vegetable or corn oil
	Salt to taste
3	cups potatoes cut into ¾-inch cubes

about 10 minutes. Add the chili mixture and salt to taste. Bring to the boil. Cover and simmer for 30 minutes.

5. Add the potatoes and cook for 40 to 45 minutes, or until meat is tender and potatoes are cooked. When ready to serve, the sauce for this dish should be ample but not too liquid.

Yield: 8 to 12 servings.

Carne en Salsa Verde *(Beef in green tomato sauce)*

4	pounds chuck steak
¼	cup oil
2	15¼-ounce cans whole green Spanish tomatoes
1	large bunch, about ¼ pound, fresh coriander leaves
1	onion, about ¼ pound, peeled and cut into eighths
6	whole cloves garlic, peeled
	Salt to taste
6 to	8 medium size zucchini, about 2 pounds

1. Cut the meat or have the butcher cut the meat into 1½-inch cubes.

2. Heat the oil in a large, heavy skillet or casserole. Add the meat and cook, stirring occasionally, until it gives up its liquid. Continue cooking until most of the liquid evaporates, about 20 minutes.

3. Meanwhile, put the canned tomatoes into the container of a food processor or electric blender. Because of the volume of the ingredients, it will be necessary to do this entire step in two stages. Rinse and drain the coriander. Chop coarsely, discarding only very tough stems. There should be about 3 cups loosely packed. Blend the tomatoes, coriander, onion and garlic to a fine purée. There should be about 8 cups.

4. Add the purée to the meat and add salt. Cover and cook for 30 minutes. Add 2 cups of water and bring to the boil. Simmer for 30 minutes.

5. Meanwhile, trim the zucchini. Cut each zucchini into thirds. Cut each section into 8 lengthwise pieces. Add the zucchini to the beef. Cook for 1 hour longer.

Yield: 8 to 12 servings.

Irish Spiced Beef

1	6½-pound brisket of beef
3	cups coarse salt, such as sea salt or kosher salt
½	cup diced white turnip
½	cup diced carrot
½	cup diced celery
½	cup finely chopped onion

1. Rub the meat with a damp cloth and set aside.

2. Combine the remaining ingredients and rub the mixture all over the meat. Put the meat and salt mixture into a plastic bag large enough to hold it. Unless the bag is thick, insert it into a second bag. Close tightly and place in a pan. Refrigerate for 7 days, turning the bag once each day so that the meat is evenly seasoned.

3. Remove the beef from the bag. Scrape off the surface seasonings and place in a kettle. Add cold water to cover and bring to the boil. Simmer for 2 to 3 hours or even longer, depending on the quality of the meat. Serve hot or cold with vegetables, in sandwiches and so on.

Yield: 12 to 24 servings.

2 tablespoons finely chopped shallots
3 bay leaves, coarsely chopped
1 clove garlic, finely minced
½ teaspoon coarsely ground black pepper
½ teaspoon dried thyme
½ teaspoon ground allspice
½ teaspoon ground cloves
½ teaspoon mace
1 teaspoon saltpeter, available in drugstores
2 tablespoons brown sugar

Deviled Beef Ribs

1. Preheat the oven to 450 degrees.

2. Sprinkle the ribs with salt and pepper to taste and place them in one layer in a large roasting pan. Place the ribs in the oven and bake for 1 hour. Turn the ribs in the pan and reduce the oven heat to 400 degrees. Bake for 30 minutes longer.

3. Blend the ½ cup of wine and the mustard and brush the ribs with approximately half the mixture. Sprinkle the ribs generously with half the bread crumbs. Dribble the remaining mustard mixture over the ribs, then sprinkle with the remaining bread crumbs. Bake for 1 hour longer.

4. For the sauce, combine the shallots and ¼ cup of wine. Cook until reduced by half and sprinkle with pepper to taste. Continue cooking until almost all the wine has evaporated. Add the brown sauce and simmer for 10 minutes. Add the cream and Escoffier sauce and bring to the boil. Remove from the heat and stir in the mustard and salt to taste. Serve the sauce over the ribs.

Yield: 5 to 10 servings.

The ribs:

10 chuck beef ribs, about 5 pounds
Salt and freshly ground pepper
½ cup dry white wine
4 tablespoons imported mustard, such as Dijon or Düsseldorf
1½ cups fine, fresh bread crumbs

The sauce:

2 tablespoons finely chopped shallots
¼ cup dry white wine
Freshly ground pepper
¼ cup brown sauce, or canned beef gravy
½ cup heavy cream
1 tablespoon Escoffier sauce, either sauce Robert or diable
1 tablespoon imported mustard, such as Dijon or Düsseldorf
Salt

Beef Ribs with Aquavit

5	pounds short ribs of beef
½	cup flour
½	teaspoon paprika
	Salt and freshly ground pepper to taste
1	cup finely chopped onion
1	cup diced carrots
¾	cup diced celery
1	clove garlic, finely minced
1	bay leaf
3	sprigs parsley
2	sprigs fresh thyme
⅓	cup aquavit or vodka
1	tablespoon caraway seeds
2	cups fresh or canned beef broth
2	cups water

1. Preheat the oven to 450 degrees.

2. Dredge the pieces of ribs on all sides with a blend of flour, paprika, salt and pepper. Arrange the pieces meaty side down in one layer in a roasting pan. Place in the oven and bake for 30 minutes. Turn the pieces. Continue baking for 30 minutes longer.

3. Remove the pan and pour off the fat. Scatter the onion, carrots, celery and garlic over the meat. Add the bay leaf, parsley and thyme. Return the pan to the oven and bake for about 5 minutes. Sprinkle the aquavit over the meat. Sprinkle with caraway seeds and add the broth and water. Bring to the boil on top of the stove. Cover closely with foil. Reduce the oven heat to 350 degrees. Return the beef to the oven and continue baking for 1 hour.

4. Uncover. Baste the ribs and continue baking, uncovered, for about 15 minutes.

Yield: 8 or more servings.

Chili con Carne with Cubed Meat

To our mind, no matter how Texans and assorted citizens of the West and Southwest may boast otherwise, there is no such thing as "the one real, authentic recipe" for chili con carne. Part of the fun is in composing your own version and we must admit to a keen fancy for almost all honestly conceived chilies.

Our personal favorite came to us from a friend, Margaret Field, who lives in San Antonio. "Meat for chili," Mrs. Field told us, "must always be cut in cubes. When you add cumin and oregano, you should always rub them between the palms of the hands, because that brings out the flavor. The chili should also be made at least twenty-four hours in advance." Mrs. Field's chili contains neither tomatoes nor beans, although pinto beans may be served on the side.

The second chili recipe is our own version with ground meat. To our taste, it is enhanced by the addition of chili paste with garlic, which is available in Oriental markets.

We happen to have a passion for a choice of things to be added to chili—among them a raw tomato sauce served cold, chopped lettuce, sour cream, grated Cheddar cheese, chopped fresh coriander leaves and hot pepper flakes.

1. Trim the meat and cut it into 1-inch cubes. Heat the oil in a deep kettle and add the cubed meat. Cook, stirring, just until the meat loses its red color.

2. Sift together the flour and chili powder and sprinkle the meat with it, stirring constantly so that the pieces are evenly coated.

3. Place the cumin and oregano in the palm of one hand. Rub the spices between the palms, sprinkling over the meat. Add the garlic and stir. Add the broth, stirring the meat constantly. Add salt and pepper and bring to the boil. Partly cover and simmer for 3 to 4 hours, or until the meat almost falls apart. If necessary, add more broth as the meat cooks. This chili should not be soupy, however. Serve with pinto beans (see recipe page 466), if desired

Yield: 8 to 12 servings.

- 5 pounds lean chuck roast
- ½ cup olive oil
- ½ cup flour
- ½ cup chili powder, more or less to taste
- 2 teaspoons cumin seeds
- 2 teaspoons dried oregano
- 6 to 10 cloves garlic, finely minced
- 4 cups fresh or canned beef broth
  Salt and freshly ground pepper

Chili con Carne with Ground Meat

1. Put the suet in a large deep casserole or Dutch oven. Cook until rendered of fat. Scrape out solids. Pour off all but 3 tablespoons of fat. Or use bacon fat.

2. Add the onion and green pepper. Cook until the onion is wilted.

3. Add the meat. Using a heavy metal spoon, cook, chopping down with the spoon to break up lumps in the meat.

4. Add the garlic and black pepper and stir to blend. Add the chili powder, oregano, cumin and celery salt. Stir and add the vinegar. Add the tomatoes with tomato paste, water, salt, pepper and, if desired, chili paste with garlic. Bring to the boil, stirring to break up tomatoes. Cook over low heat for about 30 minutes.

Yield: 8 servings.

- ¼ pound beef suet from the kidney, or use bacon fat
- 3 cups chopped onion
- 1½ cups finely chopped green pepper
- 3 pounds ground beef
- 3 tablespoons finely chopped garlic
- ¾ teaspoon ground black pepper
- 6 tablespoons chili powder
- 1 tablespoon crushed dried oregano
- 1 teaspoon ground cumin
- 1 teaspoon celery salt
- 1 tablespoon red wine vinegar
- 1 35-ounce can tomatoes with tomato paste and basil leaf
- 1 cup water
  Salt and freshly ground pepper to taste
- 1 tablespoon chili paste with garlic, optional

Chinese Beef Balls with Two Kinds of Mushrooms

40	small or 20 large dried black mushrooms
¾	pound not too lean ground beef
½	tablespoon finely chopped fresh ginger
3	tablespoons light soy sauce
½	tablespoon shao hsing wine, or dry sherry
½	tablespoon cornstarch
½	teaspoon sugar
⅛	teaspoon ground white pepper
	Salt to taste
1½	teaspoons sesame oil
24	fresh or frozen shelled green peas
1	tablespoon corn oil
1	14-ounce can straw mushrooms, available in Chinese markets

1. Place the dried mushrooms in a mixing bowl and add very hot water to cover. Let stand for 20 minutes or longer.

2. Combine the beef, ginger, 1 tablespoon soy sauce, wine, cornstarch, half the sugar, pepper, salt and 1 teaspoon sesame oil in a mixing bowl. Blend well. Using the fingers, shape the mixture into 24 small meatballs. Press 1 pea halfway into each ball as a garnish. As the meat is shaped, arrange the balls in pairs, pea-side up, down the center of a round baking dish.

3. Squeeze the black mushrooms to extract most of the liquid. Cut off and discard the stems. Combine with the remaining soy sauce, the remaining sesame oil, corn oil and the remaining sugar. Bring to the boil, stirring. Remove from the heat and spoon the mushrooms to one side of the row of meatballs.

4. Drain the straw mushrooms and squeeze them to extract most of the moisture. Add these to the small amount of sauce in the saucepan. Stir around and pour these to the other side of the meatballs.

5. Arrange the baking dish on a rack over, but not touching, boiling water. A steamer may be used. A pair of chopsticks placed separate but parallel in a wok partly filled with water is also convenient. Cover and steam for about 10 minutes.

Yield: 6 to 12 servings.

Bitokes à la Russe (*Russian hamburgers*)

2	pounds ground beef, preferably ground round
16	tablespoons butter
¼	teaspoon grated nutmeg
	Salt and freshly ground pepper
2	cups fresh bread crumbs, approximately
½	cup finely chopped onion
1	tablespoon flour
¼	cup dry white wine
1	cup sour cream
½	cup heavy cream

1. Put the meat in a bowl and add 12 tablespoons of butter. Add nutmeg, salt and pepper to taste. Mix well and shape the mixture into 16 balls of approximately the same size.

2. Roll the balls, one at a time, in bread crumbs to coat lightly. Flatten each ball into a neat hamburger shape, about 1 inch high and 2½ inches in diameter. Score the tops of each patty with the back of a knife, making a crisscross pattern.

3. Heat the remaining butter in a large skillet and add the patties. Cook for about 3 minutes until browned on one side, then turn and cook for 3 to 5 minutes or longer. Transfer the patties to a warm platter.

4. Add the chopped onion to the skillet and cook until wilted. Sprinkle with flour and stir to blend. Add the wine,

stirring, and when it boils, add the sour cream. When heated thoroughly, remove the skillet and stir the sauce off heat for about 1 minute. Add salt and pepper to taste and the heavy cream. Bring just to the boil. If desired, strain the sauce. Serve the sauce, piping hot, over the patties.

Yield: 8 servings.

Meatballs Stroganoff

1. Place the meat in a mixing bowl and add the egg. Soak the crumbs in milk and add this to the meat. Add the nutmeg, salt and pepper to taste and mix well with the hands. Shape the mixture into balls about 1½ inches in diameter. There should be 38 to 40 meatballs.

2. Sprinkle a pan with the paprika and roll the meatballs in it. Heat the butter in a heavy skillet and cook the meatballs, turning gently, until they are nicely browned, about 5 minutes. Sprinkle the mushrooms and onion between and around the meatballs and shake the skillet to distribute the ingredients evenly. Cook for about 1 minute and partly cover. Simmer for about 5 minutes and add the wine and brown sauce. Stir in the heavy cream. Partly cover and cook over low heat for about 15 minutes. Stir in the sour cream and bring just to the boil without cooking. Sprinkle with parsley and serve piping hot with fine buttered noodles as an accompaniment.

Yield: 4 to 6 servings.

1	pound ground round steak
1	egg, lightly beaten
⅓	cup fine, fresh bread crumbs
¼	cup milk
¼	teaspoon grated nutmeg
	Salt and freshly ground pepper to taste
3	tablespoons paprika
4	tablespoons butter
¼	pound mushrooms, thinly sliced
⅓	cup finely chopped onion
¼	cup dry sherry
2	tablespoons brown sauce, or canned beef gravy
¼	cup heavy cream
1	cup sour cream
¼	cup finely chopped parsley

How to Cook Hamburgers

We have long held a theory that the simplest dishes in the world are frequently the most difficult to cook. It is, we feel, more difficult to scramble an egg than make a good soufflé; it is far more difficult to make a succulent and splendid roast chicken than a platter of coq au vin. The same is true of hamburgers. It takes talent to turn out a hamburger with class. And, oh, how we dote on them!

Shape ground beef, preferably round steak or sirloin (the ground tail of porterhouse or T-bone makes excellent hamburgers) into round flat patties.

The preferred method for cooking hamburgers is on a grill fired with charcoal or gas-fired coals. The grill should be very hot when the hamburgers are added. Cook until nicely grilled on one side, turn and cook to the desired degree of doneness. Add a touch of butter, salt and pepper to taste.

There are two recommended methods for cooking hamburgers in a skillet. In the first, sprinkle a light layer of salt in the bottom of a heavy skillet such as a black iron skillet. Heat the skillet thoroughly and add the hamburgers. If the heat is hot enough under the skillet, they will not stick. When cooked on one side, use a pancake turner and, with a quick motion, scoop under the hamburgers, turning them in the skillet. Reduce the heat and continue cooking the hamburgers to the desired degree of doneness. Add a touch of butter, salt and pepper to taste.

The more conventional method of skillet cookery is to melt for each hamburger about half a teaspoon of butter in a heavy skillet and, when it is hot but not browning, add the hamburger. Cook until browned on one side, turn and continue cooking to the desired degree of doneness. Sprinkle with salt and pepper and serve with the pan juices.

Hamburger Deluxe

¼ pound ground round steak or sirloin
Salt
2 teaspoons butter
2 or 3 dashes Tabasco sauce
3 or 4 dashes Worcestershire sauce
½ teaspoon lemon juice
1 slice trimmed, buttered toast, or one split, toasted hamburger bun
Freshly ground pepper to taste
1 tablespoon finely chopped parsley

1. Shape the meat into a round patty, handling it as little as possible. Grill or cook in a skillet as indicated above.

2. As the meat cooks, melt the butter and add the Tabasco, Worcestershire and lemon juice. Transfer the hamburger to the toast or bun and sprinkle with salt and pepper to taste. Pour the butter sauce over it. Sprinkle with parsley and serve immediately.

Yield: 1 serving.

Pizza Burgers

1. Place the meat in a bowl and add 4 tablespoons Parmesan cheese, butter, salt and pepper to taste. Blend well and shape into 6 patties of equal size. Grill or cook in a skillet as indicated above.

2. Arrange the hamburgers on a baking sheet. Spoon 1 tablespoon or more of the marinara sauce on each hamburger patty. Sprinkle with remaining Parmesan cheese. Top with equal amounts of mozzarella and broil until cheese melts. Transfer the hamburgers onto toasted hamburger bun bottoms. Serve immediately with the toasted tops on the side.

Yield: 6 pizza burgers.

2 pounds ground round steak or sirloin
4 tablespoons plus 6 teaspoons freshly grated Parmesan cheese
2 tablespoons cold butter, cut into small pieces
Salt and freshly ground pepper
Marinara sauce (see recipe page 446)
6 ¼-inch thick slices mozzarella cheese, cut into small cubes
6 toasted hamburger buns

Mexican Burgers

1. Place the meat in a bowl and add the garlic, chili powder, salt and pepper to taste. Work with the hands to blend the ingredients. Shape the mixture into 4 ¼-pound patties and grill or cook in a skillet as indicated above.

2. Place 1 patty on each of 4 toasted bun bottoms. Spoon the chili sauce over the hamburgers and serve with the toasted tops on the side.

Yield: 4 Mexican burgers.

1 pound ground round steak or sirloin
1 teaspoon finely chopped garlic
1 tablespoon chili powder
Salt and freshly ground pepper
4 toasted hamburger buns
Brown chili sauce (see recipe page 652)

Hamburgers à la Holstein

1. Shape the meat into 4 patties and cook in a skillet or grill. Place 1 patty on each of 4 toasted bun bottoms.

2. Meanwhile, fry the eggs sunny-side-up in oil, taking care that the eggs do not touch each other and stick together as they fry. Remove with a pancake turner and place 1 fried egg on each hamburger. Garnish each egg with 3 flat anchovy fillets or rolled anchovies. Heat the butter in a skillet until it is hazelnut brown (beurre noisette) and pour equal amounts of it over the hamburgers topped with eggs and anchovies.

Yield: 4 servings.

1 pound ground round steak or sirloin
4 toasted hamburger bun bottoms, or rounds of toast
4 eggs
2 tablespoons peanut, corn or vegetable oil
12 flat fillets or rolled, caper-stuffed anchovies
4 tablespoons butter

Moussaka à la Grecque *(An eggplant and meat casserole)*

6 tablespoons olive oil
3 cups finely chopped onion
3 cups rich, concentrated but not too salty beef broth
3 pounds lean ground chuck
Salt and freshly ground pepper
2 cups tomato sauce, approximately (see recipe below)
3 large eggplant, about 4 pounds total weight
3 cups water
¾ cup dry red wine
2 quarts béchamel sauce, approximately (see recipe below)
¼ cup fine fresh bread crumbs
4 cups freshly grated cheese, preferably a combination of Parmesan and pecorino (use twice as much Parmesan as pecorino), or use all Parmesan
2 eggs, lightly beaten
Milk

1. Preheat the oven to 400 degrees.

2. Heat 4 tablespoons oil in a large kettle and add the onion. Cook, stirring, until wilted and add ½ cup beef broth. Cook, uncovered, until most of the liquid has evaporated. Add the ground meat and stir briefly. Add the remaining broth and cook, breaking up any lumps with the side of a wooden spoon. Add very little salt. Remember that the meat will become saltier as the broth cooks down. Add pepper to taste. Cover closely and let simmer for about 1½ hours.

3. As the meat cooks, prepare the tomato sauce and set aside.

4. Meanwhile, trim off the ends of the eggplant but do not peel the eggplant. Cut the eggplant lengthwise into slices about ⅛ inch thick. Save the outside, unpeeled slices of the eggplant along with the inside slices. Select a baking pan, preferably an enameled pan measuring about 17- x 11½- x 2-inches. Arrange the unpeeled outside slices of eggplant against the inside of the pan, resting them upright, slices slightly overlapping. Arrange more slices of eggplant, standing them upright and edges slightly overlapping. Arrange them in neat rows, one against the other, until all the slices are used. They probably won't fill the pan. Add 3 cups of water and cover closely with foil. Bake for 35 minutes and remove. Uncover and pour off most of the liquid from the pan. Let the eggplant slices stand until cool.

5. When the meat has cooked the specified time, select a small wire strainer and a small ladle. Dip the strainer into the meat, pressing down to allow the liquid to accumulate in the center of the strainer. Use the ladle to scoop out most of the liquid. Specifically, scoop out and discard all but about 1 cup of liquid.

6. Add the tomato sauce and red wine to the meat sauce and continue cooking for about 1 hour, or until the meat sauce is quite thick. Remove from the heat and let cool slightly while proceeding to the béchamel sauce.

7. Rub the pan in which the eggplant slices were baked with 2 tablespoons of oil. Sprinkle with bread crumbs and shake to coat the bottom and sides of the pan. Shake out the excess.

8. Discard the sliced, outside ends of the eggplant. Arrange about half the remaining slices of eggplant over the crumb-coated pan, edges slightly overlapping. Sprinkle with ¾ cup of cheese.

9. Beat the eggs with ¼ cup of grated cheese and stir it into the meat sauce. Bring to the boil, stirring.

10. Spoon the meat sauce over the layer of eggplant, smoothing the top with a rubber spatula. Sprinkle the meat with another ¾ cup of cheese. Arrange a second layer of eggplant over, edges slightly overlapping. There may be too many slices. Use for another purpose. Sprinkle the second layer of eggplant with ¾ cup of grated cheese. Spoon the béchamel sauce over the top and smooth it over with a spatula. Sprinkle with ¾ cup of cheese.

11. When ready to cook the moussaka, preheat the oven to 350 degrees. Place the pan in the oven and bake for 40 to 45 minutes, or until the topping is barely set in the center. Remove the moussaka from the oven and let cool for 30 minutes or longer.

12. Although the moussaka could be served directly from the oven, it is infinitely preferable to refrigerate it overnight before serving. This will allow the moussaka layers to become firm prior to cutting into serving pieces.

13. After refrigeration, remove the moussaka and cut it into 12 to 20 pieces of more or less equal size. When ready to serve, preheat the oven to 500 degrees. Pour a thin layer of milk into the bottom of 1 or more baking pans. Disposable aluminum foil baking pans are good for this. Arrange 2 or more squares of moussaka in each pan and bake until piping hot throughout, about 15 minutes. The pieces should be almost but not quite touching. Transfer the squares to individual dishes, sprinkle with more cheese and serve immediately.

Yield: 12 to 20 pieces.

Combine all the ingredients in a saucepan and cook, uncovered, for about 30 minutes.

Yield: About 2 cups.

Tomato sauce *(For moussaka only)*

2 cups tomato purée
  Salt and freshly ground pepper to taste
1 tablespoon nutmeg
½ teaspoon ground cinnamon
2 tablespoons sugar

1. Heat the butter in a 3-quart saucepan. When melted, add the flour, stirring with a wire whisk. Add the cornstarch and stir to blend.

2. Add about one third of the milk, stirring rapidly with the whisk. Quickly add another one third, stirring rapidly and constantly, covering all the bottom and sides of the saucepan. Add the last of the milk, stirring rapidly and constantly.

3. When thickened and smooth, remove from the heat. Beat

Béchamel sauce *(For moussaka only)*

½ pound butter
¾ cup flour
½ cup cornstarch
7 cups hot milk
3 eggs, lightly beaten
¼ teaspoon nutmeg

the eggs and nutmeg and add to the saucepan, stirring with the whisk. Cook briefly, stirring constantly.

Yield: About 2 quarts.

Meat and Spinach Loaf

1   **pound loose fresh spinach, or 1 10-ounce package**
1¼ **pounds ground beef, veal or pork, or a combination of all**
½   **cup fresh bread crumbs**
    Salt
1½ **teaspoons freshly ground pepper**
¼   **teaspoon grated nutmeg**
½   **cup coarsely chopped celery**
½   **cup loosely packed parsley**
¼   **cup milk**
1   **clove garlic, finely minced**
1   **tablespoon butter**
½   **cup finely chopped onion**
2   **eggs, lightly beaten**
3   **slices bacon**

1. Preheat the oven to 350 degrees.

2. If the spinach is in bulk, pick it over to remove any tough stems. Rinse the spinach well in cold water, drain, place in a saucepan and cover. It is not necessary to add liquid; the spinach will cook in the water clinging to the leaves. Cook for about 2 minutes, stirring once or twice. Transfer to a colander and douse with cold water to chill. Drain and press with the hands to extract most of the moisture. Chop the spinach.

3. Put the meat in a mixing bowl and add the chopped spinach, bread crumbs, salt to taste, pepper and nutmeg.

4. Put the celery, parsley and milk in the container of a food processor or electric blender. Blend well and add to the meat mixture. Add the garlic.

5. Heat the butter in a small skillet and cook the onion until wilted. Add it to the meat mixture. Add the eggs and blend well with the hands. Shape and fit into an oval or round baking dish, or place in a loaf pan. Cover with the bacon and bake for 1¼ to 1½ hours. Pour off the fat and let the loaf stand for 20 minutes before slicing. Serve, if desired, with tomato sauce.

Yield: 6 to 8 servings.

Beef and Kidney Pie

2   **pounds very tender prime beef, preferably fillet, or use top sirloin, in one piece**
2   **veal or beef kidneys, about 1½ pounds**
4   **tablespoons butter**
3   **tablespoons finely chopped shallots**
½   **cup chopped onion**
1   **clove garlic finely minced**
6   **cups thinly sliced mushrooms, about 1 pound**

1. Cut the beef into small rounds about ½ inch thick and 3 inches in diameter. If fillet is used, cut the fillet ends into 2- or 3-inch lengths. Set aside.

2. Cut the kidneys into rounds about ½ inch thick. Set aside.

3. Heat 2 tablespoons of the butter in a heavy casserole and add the shallots, onion and garlic. Cook, stirring, until the onion is wilted. Add the mushrooms, salt and pepper to taste. Cook for about 5 minutes. Sprinkle with flour and tarragon and stir to blend. Add the wine and stir rapidly until thickened and smooth. Add the tomatoes and broth and bring to

the boil, stirring. Continue cooking while browning the meat and kidneys.

4. Sprinkle the beef and kidneys with salt and pepper. Heat remaining 2 tablespoons of butter in a skillet large enough to hold the beef without crowding. Add the beef in one layer and cook over high heat for about 2 minutes. Turn and brown quickly on the other side. As the meat is browned on both sides, transfer the pieces temporarily to a side dish and keep warm. When all the beef is cooked, add the pieces and the accumulated juices to the tomato and mushroom stew. Continue cooking.

5. When the beef is cooked, start adding the kidney pieces to the skillet, cooking them in similar fashion until quickly browned on both sides. As the pieces cook, transfer them to the side dish. Add the water to the skillet and stir to dissolve the brown particles that cling to the bottom and sides of the skillet. Add this to the stew.

6. Drain the kidneys and discard the kidney juices. Add the kidneys to the stew. Add the bay leaf. Cover and cook for about 30 minutes longer. As the stew cooks, skim off and discard the fat and scum that accumulates on the surface. Let cool and add the Worcestershire sauce.

7. Preheat the oven to 375 degrees.

8. Spoon the stew into an oval, round or rectangular baking dish. It should almost but not quite fill the dish. Arrange the egg wedges, yolk side down, symmetrically over the stew. Brush around the outer rim and sides of the baking dish with the yolk beaten with a little water.

9. Roll out the dough to fit the baking dish, leaving a 1- or 2-inch margin. Neatly fit the pastry over the dish, letting the overlapping margin hang down. Press gently around the pastry to seal it against the yolk mixture. Trim off the bottom of the pastry. Cut small slits or one round on top of the dough to allow steam to escape. You may gather scraps of dough together and roll out to make a pattern on top of the pie. Brush spots where cutouts will be applied with the yolk mixture before adding. Brush the top and sides of the dough with the yolk mixture all around to aid browning.

10. Place the dish on a baking sheet, which will facilitate turning the dish in the oven for even browning. Place in the oven and bake until piping hot and the pastry is nicely browned. The cooking time on this dish is about 45 minutes if fillet of beef and veal kidney are used; about 1 hour or longer if a lesser cut of beef and beef kidney are used.

Yield: 8 or more servings.

Salt and freshly ground pepper
¼ cup flour
1 teaspoon dried tarragon
2 cups dry white wine
1 cup chopped fresh or canned imported tomatoes
1¾ cups fresh or canned beef broth
½ cup water
1 bay leaf
1 tablespoon Worcestershire sauce
4 hard-cooked eggs, peeled and quartered
1 egg yolk
Pie pastry (see recipe page 608)

Braciole *(Beef birds in brown sauce)*

6 thin slices of beef, each measuring about 6 to 7 inches and slightly less than ¼ inch thick
2 slices fresh orange peel
3 tablespoons butter
¾ cup finely chopped onion or scallions
½ cup chopped heart of celery, including leaves
½ teaspoon oregano
  Fresh ground pepper
½ cup fresh bread crumbs
4 tablespoons Marsala
¼ cup pine nuts
  Salt
6 thin slices prosciutto
2 tablespoons olive oil
4 cups brown sauce (see recipe below)
1 tablespoon Escoffier sauce Robert (available commercially in bottles), or ⅓ cup Madeira, optional

1. If the slices of beef are not thin enough, place them on a flat surface and pound them lightly with a flat mallet or the bottom of a clean skillet.

2. Cut the orange peel into very thin strips (julienne) and cut the strips into very thin dice.

3. Heat 1 tablespoon of butter and add the onion, celery, oregano and pepper and cook, stirring, until pale yellow.

4. Place the bread crumbs in a mixing bowl and add the onion mixture and orange peel. Add 2 tablespoons of Marsala, pine nuts and salt to taste. Blend well. Spoon equal amounts of the mixture onto the slices of beef, pressing down with the fingers to help it adhere. Spread a slice of prosciutto on top. Roll the meat jelly-roll fashion and skewer each serving or tie with string.

5. Melt 2 tablespoons each butter and olive oil in a skillet and brown the beef on all sides for 10 to 15 minutes. Remove the braccioli and pour off the fat from the skillet. Add remaining 2 tablespoons of Marsala and stir to dissolve the brown particles that cling to the bottom of the skillet.

6. Add the brown sauce to a casserole and add the braciole. Cover closely and simmer for 1 hour or longer until the beef is tender. Add the sauce Robert or Madeira, if desired, and serve piping hot with rice.

Yield: 6 servings.

Brown sauce

8 tablespoons butter
¾ pound ham, cut into small cubes
½ pound fresh mushrooms, finely chopped
2 carrots, scraped and cut into thin slices
2 onions, thinly sliced
⅓ cup flour
8 cups fresh beef broth
1 bay leaf
½ cup tomato purée
½ cup dry red wine
  Salt and freshly ground pepper to taste
1 tablespoon Escoffier sauce diable

1. Melt the butter and add the ham, mushrooms, carrots and onions. Cook, stirring frequently, until the ingredients are almost dry and starting to brown.

2. Sprinkle with flour and cook, stirring, until flour starts to darken. Add the broth, stirring rapidly with a wire whisk. When thickened and smooth, add the bay leaf. Cover and cook, stirring occasionally, for about 1 hour. Add the tomato purée, wine, salt, pepper and Escoffier sauce, if desired. Continue to cook for 45 minutes longer, stirring occasionally. Strain the sauce.

3. If the sauce is not thickened, you may blend 4 teaspoons butter with 4 teaspoons flour and add it bit by bit, stirring with the whisk.

Yield: About 8 cups.

Note: Leftover brown sauce freezes well.

Rouladen   *(German-style meat rolls)*

1. Place the meat on a flat surface and pat dry. Sprinkle meat on one side with salt and pepper. Sprinkle with equal amounts of marjoram and spread top to bottom and side to side with mustard.

2. Remove the rind from the bacon and cut the bacon into ¼-inch cubes. There should be about 2½ cups. Set ½ cup bacon aside for later use. Combine the 2 cups of bacon, 2 cups of chopped onion, parsley and chives. Sprinkle the meat with equal portions of this mixture, leaving a clear margin of about ½ inch around the edges of each slice. Place 1 pickle about 1 inch from the bottom of each slice and start rolling the meat from the bottom up, folding the sides toward the center as you roll. Use a skewer to keep the roll intact.

3. Heat 2 tablespoons of butter in a saucepan and add the carrots, remaining 1 cup onions and reserved ½ cup bacon. Cook, stirring, until vegetables are lightly browned, for about 10 minutes. Remove the vegetables and bacon with a slotted spoon. Set aside.

4. Heat the remaining 6 tablespoons of butter in one or two heavy skillets large enough to hold the meat rolls. Add the meat rolls to the skillet or skillets and cook, turning to brown on all sides. Scrape the bottom of the pan as necessary to loosen any brown particles that stick to it. When the rolls are well browned, remove them and keep warm. Add the wine and beef broth, stirring to dissolve the brown particles. Blend the flour and water and stir it in. Return the meat rolls and any liquid that has accumulated around them to the skillet. Add the reserved vegetables and bacon. Cover. Cook, turning the rolls occasionally, for 1 hour.

5. Remove the meat rolls and keep them warm. Pour and spoon the sauce into the container of an electric blender or food processor. It may be necessary to do this in two steps. Blend until smooth and return the sauce to the skillet. Add the cream, stir and bring to the boil. Add the meat rolls, cover and simmer for 15 minutes longer over low heat. Serve with freshly cooked spaetzle.

Yield: 12 servings.

Note: For the authentic German taste, the bacon used in this recipe should be double-smoked. Double-smoked bacon is available in German food shops.

12	slices top round, about 3 pounds, each slice measuring about 4 by 11 inches and each slice weighing about ¼ pound
	Salt and freshly ground pepper
1	tablespoon or more dried marjoram
¼	cup or more prepared mustard, preferably imported mustard, such as Dijon or Düsseldorf
½	pound bacon, preferably slab bacon, unsliced (see note)
3	cups finely chopped onion
½	cup finely chopped parsley
½	cup finely chopped chives, approximately
12	small imported cornichons, or use ½-inch strips of dill pickles
8	tablespoons butter, approximately
1½	cups thinly sliced carrots
1¼	cups dry red wine
1	cup fresh or canned beef broth
1	teaspoon flour
2	teaspoons water
1	cup heavy cream

Satay Bumbu (*Indonesian skewered beef*)

The marinated meat:

1 pound (trimmed weight) lean sirloin or top round of beef, trimmed of all fat, cut into 1-inch cubes
2 teaspoons ground coriander seeds
¼ teaspoon ground cumin
2 cloves garlic, mashed to a pulp
1 teaspoon sugar
Salt to taste
1 tablespoon fresh lemon juice

The grilling sauce:

3 tablespoons ketjap manis (see recipe page 655)
1 teaspoon lemon juice
1 tablespoon peanut, vegetable or corn oil
2 teaspoons water

1. Put the beef in a mixing bowl and add the coriander, cumin, garlic, sugar, salt and lemon juice. Mix and massage the beef cubes so that the flavors permeate the meat. Cover and let stand for 1 hour or longer.

2. Blend the ketjap manis, lemon juice, oil and water. Set aside.

3. When ready to cook, arrange 4 or 5 pieces of beef on each of 12 wooden skewers. Dip the skewered meat in the sauce until the pieces are well coated. Arrange on a hot grill and broil for 1 or 2 minutes on each side to the desired degree of doneness. Or you may broil the skewered meat in the home broiler, arranging them on aluminum foil. Take care to cover the exposed skewer ends with foil to prevent burning as the food broils.

Yield: 6 or more servings with other dishes.

Kushiyaki (*Japanese skewered beef and shrimp*)

¾ pound flank steak
½ cup soy sauce
½ cup sake
¼ cup mirin, or use sugared sherry (see note)
12 large shrimp, about ½ pound
½ teaspoon salt
24 pieces of scallion, green part only, each cut into 1½-inch lengths
18 pieces of scallion, white part only, each cut into 1½-inch lengths

1. The flank steak can be sliced more easily if it is first frozen. Remove from the freezer ½ hour before slicing. Cut the flank steak against the grain into ¼-inch thick slices.

2. Blend the soy sauce, half the sake and the mirin in a mixing bowl. Add the beef and let stand briefly.

3. Peel the shrimp but leave the last tail segment intact. Put them in a bowl and add the remaining sake and salt.

4. Use 6 skewers and arrange one shrimp, then two green pieces of scallion, another shrimp and two more green pieces of scallion. Spear the shrimp and scallion pieces down the center and push them close together.

5. Similarly, thread pieces of beef on each of 6 skewers, alternating them with three pieces of white scallion. Adjust the quantities of skewered beef so that all the meat is used.

6. Preheat the broiler to high. Arrange the skewered foods on a rack and place about 2 inches from the source of heat.

Broil for 3 or 4 minutes to a side until lightly browned. Brush with marinade as the skewered foods are cooked. The foods may also be grilled, basting often.

Yield: 6 servings.

Note: Mirin is a sweet sake, widely available in wine and spirit shops in metropolitan areas. As a substitute for mirin, blend 1 cup of dry sherry with ½ cup of sugar. Boil briefly until sugar dissolves. Let cool.

Nua Pad Kanha *(Thai beef with Chinese vegetables)*

1. Cut the meat into thin, bite-size pieces. This is facilitated if the meat is partly frozen.

2. Heat the oil in a wok or skillet and cook the garlic until it is nicely browned, a bit darker than golden. Add the beef and stir-fry quickly until the meat is cooked through. Add the oyster sauce, stirring. Add the Chinese vegetable and cook, stirring, for about 1 minute. Cover and cook for about 1 minute. Uncover, add the fish sauce and continue cooking for about 2 minutes.

Yield: 4 to 6 servings.

Note: Unfamiliar ingredients are available at Oriental stores.

1 pound lean round steak
2 tablespoons corn oil
2 tablespoons coarsely chopped garlic
3 or more tablespoons bottled oyster sauce (see note)
3 cups Chinese broccoli, Chinese cabbage or other Chinese vegetable, cut on the bias into large bite-size pieces
1 teaspoon fish sauce (see note)

Hunan Beef

Keen observers of Chinese food served in America have often noted that the dominant number of beef dishes specify flank steak. "What in the name of heavens happens to the rest of the beef?" We took the occasion of a visit to our kitchen by one of New York's finest Chinese chefs to find out.

The chef is Wen Dah Tai, better known as Uncle Tai, and he told us over a cup of tea that the remainder of a cow was in no sense wasted or ignored in the Chinese kitchen. The fillet is always cut into neat cubes and used in high-class banquet dishes; the shin of beef, the juiciest part, goes into a cold appetizer, five-flavored beef; and the rest of the animal goes into casserole dishes.

We also learned that hot Hunanese cooking is not only a professional outlet, it is a predilection for the chef. It is empirically true that hot food pleases the body and appetite in hot, humid, climates, and Hunan is such a place. East Hampton must be too, judging by our predilection.

1½ pounds flank steak
⅔ cup plus 3 tablespoons water
½ teaspoon bicarbonate of soda
¼ teaspoon salt
3 tablespoons shao hsing wine, or dry sherry
1 egg white
3½ tablespoons cornstarch
4 cups plus 2 tablespoons peanut, vegetable or corn oil
2 scallions, cut into ½-inch lengths, about ⅓ cup
3 tablespoons dried orange peel (see note)
3 thin slices fresh ginger, cut into ½-inch cubes
1 long, thin, fresh, hot red pepper, chopped, optional
3 tablespoons soy sauce
¼ teaspoon monosodium glutamate, optional
2 tablespoons sugar
1 teaspoon sesame oil
¼ cup chicken broth
10 dried small hot red pepper pods

1. Place the flank steak on a flat surface and, holding a sharp knife parallel to the beef, slice it in half widthwise. Cut each half into very thin strips, about ¼ inch each. There should be about 4 cups loosely packed.

2. Place the beef in a mixing bowl and add ⅔ cup water blended with the bicarbonate of soda. Refrigerate overnight or for at least 1 hour. When ready to cook, rinse the beef thoroughly under cold running water. Drain thoroughly and pat dry.

3. To the meat add the salt, 1 tablespoon wine and egg white. Stir in a circular motion until the white is bubbly. Add 1½ tablespoons of cornstarch and 2 tablespoons of oil. Stir to blend.

4. Combine the scallions, dried orange peel, fresh ginger and fresh red pepper, if used. Set aside.

5. Combine the remaining 2 tablespoons wine, soy sauce, monosodium glutamate, if used, sugar, remaining 2 tablespoons of cornstarch blended with remaining 3 tablespoons water, sesame oil and chicken broth. Stir to blend.

6. Heat the remaining 4 cups of oil in a wok or skillet and, when it is almost smoking, add the beef. Cook for about 45 seconds, stirring constantly, and scoop it out. Drain the meat well, but leave the oil in the wok, continuously heating. Return the meat to the wok and cook over high heat for about 15 seconds, stirring. Drain once more. Return the meat a third time to the hot oil and cook, stirring. Drain the meat. The purpose of this is to make the meat crisp on the outside but retain its juiciness within.

7. Drain the wok completely. Return 2 tablespoons of the oil to the wok and add the hot pepper pods, stirring over high heat until brown and almost blackened, about 30 seconds. Remove. Add the scallion mixture and stir. Add the beef and cook, stirring constantly, for about 10 seconds. Add the wine mixture, stirring, and cook for about 15 seconds until piping hot and the meat is well coated.

Yield: 4 to 8 servings.

Note: Dried orange peel is available in many Oriental grocery and spice stores. It may be made at home, however, by peeling an orange, eliminating as much of the white pulpy part as possible. The peel is cut into pieces, placed on a baking sheet and baked in a 200-degree oven until dried. It may be stored for months in a tight container.

Beef Hash Bonne Femme

1. Peel the potatoes and cut them into quarters. Put them in a casserole with boiling salted water to cover and simmer for 20 minutes, or until tender. Do not let them become mushy.

2. Preheat the oven to 400 degrees.

3. Meanwhile, grind the meat or chop it fine. There should be about 4 cups loosely packed.

4. When the potatoes are cooked, drain and put them through a food mill or ricer. Whip in 2 tablespoons of butter. Beat in the milk and add salt to taste.

5. Heat the remaining 2 tablespoons of butter and add the onion. Cook, stirring, for about 3 minutes and add the garlic, meat, salt, pepper and nutmeg. Cook, stirring, for about 5 minutes. Fold in the potatoes and parsley. Add the eggs and blend well.

6. Butter a 6-cup charlotte mold or another mold of equal capacity. Sprinkle with bread crumbs, shaking them around to coat the bottom and sides evenly. Shake the excess crumbs out and reserve them.

7. Spoon in the meat and potato mixture and smooth it on top. Sprinkle with reserved bread crumbs and cover with a buttered round of wax paper. Place the mold in a slightly larger utensil and pour boiling water around it. Set this in the oven and bake for 45 minutes. Remove from the oven and let the mold stand in the water bath for 10 minutes.

8. Remove the mold and wipe the bottom. Invert it onto a round plate. Serve with tomato sauce spooned over and around it.

Yield: 4 to 6 servings.

6 potatoes, about 1¼ pounds
Salt
1 pound leftover boiled beef brisket, shin of beef or leftover pork or veal
4 tablespoons butter
½ cup milk
1 cup finely chopped onion
1 clove garlic, finely minced
Freshly ground pepper
¼ teaspoon grated nutmeg
¼ cup finely chopped parsley
3 eggs, lightly beaten
½ cup bread crumbs, preferably made from golden brown toast

Langue de Boeuf Fumé *(Smoked tongue with Madeira sauce)*

1. Place the tongue in a bowl and add cold water to cover. Let stand overnight. Drain.

2. Place the tongue in a kettle and add cold water to cover. Add the onion, bay leaf and thyme. Bring to the boil and simmer for about 2½ hours, or until quite tender.

3. Drain the tongue and cut off the bulky throat section. Peel off and discard the tough outer skin.

4. Preheat the oven to 400 degrees.

5. Place the tongue in a baking dish and pour about 1 cup of

1 3½-pound smoked tongue
1 onion stuck with 3 cloves
1 bay leaf
3 sprigs fresh thyme, or ½ teaspoon dried
2 cups sauce madère (see recipe page 652)

Madeira sauce over it. Place in the oven for about 10 minutes to glaze it. Slice the tongue thinly and serve the remaining sauce on the side.

Yield: 8 servings.

Tripe Lyonnaise

1½ **pounds honeycomb tripe**
4 **cups water**
Salt
1 **bay leaf**
1 **small onion, stuck with 3 whole cloves**
10 **peppercorns**
1 **carrot, scraped and cut into 2-inch lengths**
3 **sprigs fresh parsley**
1 **rib celery, cut into quarters**
2 **sprigs fresh thyme, or ½ teaspoon dried**
1 **hot red pepper**
2 **tablespoons butter**
1 **large or 2 medium-size onions, peeled and sliced as thinly as possible, about 2 cups**
1 **small clove garlic, peeled but left whole**
2 **tablespoons red wine vinegar, or more to taste**
Chopped parsley for garnish
Assorted mustards

1. Put the tripe in a kettle and add the water, salt to taste, peppercorns, carrot, parsley, bay leaf, onion stuck with cloves, celery, thyme and red pepper. Cover and cook for about 5 hours. Let cool.

2. Drain the tripe and cut it into thin, bite-size strips (there should be about 2 cups).

3. Heat the butter in a skillet and add the tripe. Cook, stirring briefly, and add the sliced onions. Cook over moderately high heat until the onions start to brown, stirring gently and shaking the skillet. Add the garlic, turn the heat to low and cook, stirring frequently, for about 10 minutes longer. Remove garlic.

4. Add the vinegar and serve sprinkled with chopped parsley. Serve mustard on the side, letting guests help themselves.

Yield: 4 to 6 servings.

Trippa alla Romana *(Tripe with fresh mint)*

4 **pounds honeycomb tripe**
2 **ounces salt pork**
1 **cup finely chopped onion**
2 **cloves garlic, finely minced**
½ **cup finely chopped celery**
1 **cup finely chopped carrot**
1 **cup dry white wine**
1½ **cups fresh tomato sauce**
3 **cups fresh or canned chicken broth**

1. Wash the tripe well and put it in a kettle. Add boiling water to cover and bring to the boil. Simmer for about 5 minutes and drain. Let cool. Using a large knife, cut the tripe into ½-inch shreds, or cut it into 1-inch cubes. There should be about 8 cups.

2. Cut the salt pork into small rectangles and put the pieces in a saucepan. Add cold water to cover and bring to the boil. Drain. Add the pork to a heavy kettle large enough to hold the tripe.

3. When the pork starts to give up its fat, add the onion and garlic. Cook until the onion is wilted. Add the celery and carrot and cook briefly. Add the tripe, wine, tomato sauce, broth, salt and pepper. Bring to the boil. Cover closely and cook for about 5 hours, or until tripe is tender. Uncover the casserole for the last 15 minutes to let the sauce cook down somewhat. Stir in the mint and serve with grated Parmesan cheese on the side.

Yield: 10 to 12 servings.

Salt and freshly ground pepper to taste
1 or 2 tablespoons finely chopped fresh mint
Freshly grated Parmesan cheese

Côtes de Veau Pavillon   (Sautéed veal chops with vinegar glaze)

Sprinkle the chops on both sides with salt and pepper to taste. Heat 2 tablespoons butter in a skillet and add the chops. Brown on both sides, turning once. They should cook about 5 minutes to a side. Add the garlic, bay leaves and thyme and cook for about 3 minutes. Pour the vinegar around the chops and turn the heat to high. Add the broth, cover closely and cook for about 20 minutes.

Yield: 4 servings.

4 loin veal chops, about ½ pound each
Salt and freshly ground pepper
2 tablespoons butter
4 whole cloves garlic, peeled
2 bay leaves
4 sprigs fresh thyme, or ½ teaspoon dried
1 tablespoon red wine vinegar
½ cup fresh or canned chicken broth

Veal à la Oskar

1. Sprinkle the chops on both sides with salt and pepper. Skewer the tail of each chop to hold it neatly in place.

2. Scrape the sides of the asparagus spears but leave the tips intact. Put in a skillet with cold water to cover and salt to taste. Bring to the boil and simmer for about 3 minutes, or until crisp-tender. Drain.

3. Heat 2 tablespoons of butter in a heavy skillet large enough to hold the chops in one layer. Brown on one side, for about 10 minutes. Turn and brown on the other side, for about 10 minutes.

4. Melt a teaspoon of butter in a small skillet and add the shrimp. Cook briefly just to heat through.

5. Arrange the chops on a serving platter and garnish each with 2 asparagus spears. Spoon béarnaise sauce over the asparagus and garnish the top of each serving with 1 shrimp.

Yield: 4 servings.

4 loin veal chops, about 2½ pounds
Salt and freshly ground pepper
8 asparagus spears
2 tablespoons plus 1 teaspoon butter
4 cooked, peeled shrimp
¾ cup béarnaise sauce (see recipe page 644)

Veal Chops with Belgian Endive

4 loin veal chops, about ½
pound each
Salt and freshly ground
pepper to taste
¼ cup flour
4 tablespoons butter
4 firm, white, unblemished
heads of Belgian endive
2 tablespoons water
2 tablespoons finely chopped
shallots
3 tablespoons Cognac
1½ cups heavy cream
¼ cup freshly grated Parmesan
cheese

1. Sprinkle the chops on both sides with salt and pepper. Dredge lightly in flour. Heat 3 tablespoons butter in a heavy skillet large enough to hold the chops in one layer. Cook chops over moderately low heat for 8 to 10 minutes and turn. Cook, uncovered, for 15 minutes longer.

2. While the chops are cooking, place the endive in a heavy saucepan. Add the remaining tablespoon of butter, salt, pepper and the water. Cover closely and simmer for 25 minutes. Take care that they do not burn. If necessary, add a bit more water.

3. When the chops are done, transfer them to a warm platter and cover with foil.

4. Add the shallots to the skillet and cook, stirring with a wooden spoon, for 30 seconds. Add the Cognac and flame it. Stir with the spoon to dissolve the brown particles that cling to the bottom and sides of the skillet. Add the cream and cook, stirring, over high heat. Cook for about 5 minutes or until the cream is thick and smooth. Strain the sauce into a saucepan and add salt and pepper to taste.

5. Preheat the oven to 400 degrees. Arrange the chops in one layer in an oval gratin or baking dish. Press the endive gently to remove any excess liquid. Arrange them around the chops. Spoon the sauce over all and sprinkle with the cheese. Bake, uncovered, for 15 minutes.

Yield: 4 servings.

Escalopes de Veau à l'Anglaise *(Breaded veal scaloppine)*

One of the fundamental principles of any traditional cooking is that almost every dish is a variation on another dish. Perhaps the finest and most basic illustration of this can be found in a plain, unadorned, breaded veal cutlet or scaloppine. With a bit of hot butter and a garnish of lemon, it can be delectable as is. But over the years, chefs have dramatically altered this basic recipe by simply adding other foods—capers, chopped eggs, anchovies, cheese, mushrooms and so on. Veal, of course, is one of the most versatile of foods and adapts well to scores of flavors and seasonings.

1. Pound the meat with a flat mallet to make it thin. Sprinkle with salt and pepper. Dredge first in flour, then in the beaten egg mixed with water and finally in bread crumbs. As each piece is breaded, transfer to a flat surface and pound lightly with the flat side of a heavy kitchen knife to help crumbs adhere.

2. Heat the oil and butter in a heavy skillet and cook the meat until brown on one side. If the skillet is not large enough to hold them in one layer, this will have to be repeated two or more times. When the veal is brown on one side, turn and cook to brown on the other side. Cook until cooked through. Total cooking time for each slice should be from 3 to 5 minutes, depending on the thickness of meat and the degree of heat. If necessary, add a little more oil and butter to the skillet until all pieces are cooked.

3. Place one slice of veal on each of four serving dishes. Surround each serving with 1 tablespoon of hot brown sauce and pour over each serving 1 tablespoon of sizzling beurre noisette. Garnish each serving with a sprig of parsley.

Yield: 4 servings.

1½ pounds veal scaloppine, 4 thin slices
Salt and freshly ground pepper
2 tablespoons flour
1 large egg, beaten
2 tablespoons water
1½ cups bread crumbs
3 tablespoons oil, plus more as necessary
1 tablespoon butter, plus more as necessary
4 tablespoons brown sauce, or canned brown beef gravy, optional
4 tablespoons beurre noisette (see recipe below), optional
Parsley sprigs for garnish

Add any given amount of butter to a small skillet. Cook over moderate heat, shaking the skillet so that the butter browns evenly. At first the butter will foam. This will subside. When the butter becomes hazelnut brown, remove it immediately from the heat and spoon over the scaloppine.

Beurre noisette (*Hazelnut butter*)

Escalopes de Veau Milanese (*Breaded veal scaloppine with Parmesan cheese*)

Prepare the recipe for escalopes de veau à l'anglaise. Use ¼ cup of freshly grated Parmesan cheese and 1¼ cups of bread crumbs rather than the bread indicated in the original recipe. Cook precisely as for the scaloppine à l'anglaise.

Yield: 4 servings.

Escalopes de Veau Holstein (*Breaded veal scaloppine with fried eggs*)

Prepare the recipe for escalopes de veau à l'anglaise. Add 1 egg cooked sunny-side up atop each serving. Garnish around the yolk of each egg with 4 flat anchovies arranged in a tick-tack-toe pattern. If desired, spoon the brown sauce and beurre noisette around each serving.

Yield: 4 servings.

Escalopes de Veau Troisgros *(Veal scaloppine with mustard and tomato sauce)*

8 to 10 slices veal scaloppine,
 about 1 pound
 Salt and freshly ground
 pepper
 2 teaspoons imported
 mustard, such as Dijon or
 Düsseldorf
 1 tablespoon mustard seeds
 2 tablespoons butter
 1¾ cups fresh tomato sauce (see
 recipe page 650)

1. Pound the scaloppine lightly with a flat mallet. Sprinkle on both sides with salt and pepper. Spread about ¼ teaspoon of mustard on one side of the scaloppine. Sprinkle with half the mustard seeds. Turn the scaloppine and spread with mustard. Sprinkle with remaining mustard seeds.

2. Heat the butter in a skillet and, when very hot but not burning, add the veal pieces. You may have to double the butter and use two skillets. Cook the pieces over very high heat to brown lightly on one side, for about 30 seconds. The veal must cook quickly. Turn the pieces and cook for about 30 seconds on the other side.

3. Spoon equal portions of sauce on each of four hot plates. Arrange two or three pieces of veal neatly on the sauce and serve hot.

Yield: 4 servings.

Veal Scaloppine with Avocado and Tomato

6 slices veal scaloppine, about 6
 ounces each
 Salt and freshly ground
 pepper to taste
 2 firm but ripe avocados, about
 1 pound each
 Juice of 1 lemon
 2 firm but ripe tomatoes, about
 ¾ pound each
 7 tablespoons butter
 ¼ cup chopped onion
 2 cloves garlic, finely chopped
 2 teaspoons curry powder
 5 tablespoons flour
 ½ chicken bouillon cube
 1 cup milk
 ¼ cup heavy cream
 ¼ cup olive oil
 ¼ cup scotch whiskey
 6 thin slices Muenster cheese

1. Place the scaloppine on a flat surface and pound with a mallet. Sprinkle with salt and pepper.

2. Peel the avocados and discard the skin and seeds. Cut the avocados into ½-inch or slightly larger cubes and place in a mixing bowl. There should be about 4 cups. Add the lemon juice and toss to coat.

3. Core, peel and seed the tomatoes. Cut into ½-inch cubes. There should be about 2 cups. Add this to the avocados.

4. Heat 4 tablespoons of butter and add the onion. Cook briefly to wilt and add the garlic. Cook briefly and remove from the heat. Add the avocado mixture, sprinkle with half the curry powder and add salt to taste. Stir and cook briefly just to heat thoroughly. Set aside.

5. In a saucepan, heat the remaining 3 tablespoons of butter and add half the flour, stirring with a wire whisk. Sprinkle with remaining curry powder, stirring. Add the bouillon cube, milk and cream, stirring with the whisk. Cook for about 10 minutes, stirring often.

6. Dust the scaloppine lightly on both sides with the remaining flour.

7. Heat the oil in a skillet and, when it is quite hot, add the meat. Cook for about 45 seconds and turn. Cook for 5 seconds and transfer to a baking dish. This may have to be done in two

stages. Add the scotch to the pan, stirring. Reduce quickly by half and add the avocado mixture. Stir and turn off the heat.

8. Spoon equal amounts of avocado mixture over the veal and spoon half the cream sauce over this. Place 1 slice of Muenster cheese, folded in half, on top. Cover with remaining cream sauce and run briefly under the broiler. This may have to be done in two stages.

Yield: 6 servings.

Escalopes de Veau à la Moutarde   *(Veal scaloppine with mustard sauce)*

1. Place the scaloppine on a flat surface and pound with a flat metal meat pounder or the bottom of a clean skillet. Blend the flour with salt and pepper and dredge the scaloppine on all sides.

2. Heat the butter in a large heavy skillet until it is quite hot but not brown. Add the scaloppine (note that they shrink as they cook). Cook quickly until golden, for about 2 minutes, on one side and turn. Cook until golden on the other side. Remove the scaloppine to a warm dish and keep warm and covered with foil.

3. Add the shallots to the skillet and cook briefly, stirring. Add the wine and cook, stirring, until it is almost evaporated. Add the cream and let it boil up, stirring. Cook for about 30 seconds and turn off the heat. Stir in the mustard. Do not cook further. Pour sauce over veal and serve.

Yield: 2 or 3 servings.

- 8 veal scaloppine, about ¾ pound
- ⅓ cup flour
  Salt and freshly ground pepper to taste
- 4 tablespoons butter
- 2 tablespoons finely minced shallots
- ¼ cup dry white wine
- ½ cup heavy cream
- 1 tablespoon imported mustard, such as Dijon or Düsseldorf

Veal Piccata with Lemon

1. Unless the scaloppine are very small, cut them into pieces measuring about 3 inches by 3 inches. Place them between sheets of wax paper and pound lightly to flatten, using the bottom of a heavy skillet or a flat mallet.

2. Blend the flour with salt and pepper. Dip the meat into the flour to coat lightly. Using a large heavy skillet, heat the butter and oil and, when it is very hot but not brown, add the meat in one layer. Cook over relatively high heat until golden brown on one side. Turn and cook until golden brown on the other.

3. Carefully pour off the fat from the skillet, holding the

- ½ pound veal scaloppine, cut into ¼-inch thick slices
  Flour for dredging
  Salt and freshly ground pepper to taste
- 2 tablespoons butter
- 2 tablespoons olive oil
- 2 tablespoons dry white wine
- 2 tablespoons lemon juice
- 2 thin lemon slices
- 2 teaspoons finely chopped parsley

meat back with a spoon or lid. Return the skillet to the heat and add the wine. Cook briefly until it starts to evaporate stirring to dissolve any brown particles in the skillet. Add the lemon juice and turn the meat in the thin sauce thus created. Transfer the meat to two plates and garnish each with a lemon slice and parsley.

Yield: 2 servings

Veal Scaloppine with Marsala

½   **pound veal scaloppine, cut into ¼-inch thick slices**
    Flour for dredging
    Salt and freshly ground pepper to taste
2   **tablespoons butter**
2   **tablespoons olive oil**
¼   **cup Marsala**

1. Unless the scaloppine are very small, cut them into pieces measuring about 3 inches by 3 inches. Place them between sheets of wax paper and pound lightly to flatten, using the bottom of a heavy skillet or a flat mallet. Blend the flour with salt and pepper. Dip the meat into flour to coat lightly.

2. Using a large, heavy skillet, heat the butter and oil and, when it is very hot but not brown, add the meat in one layer. Cook over relatively high heat until golden brown on one side. Turn and cook until golden brown on the other.

3. Transfer the meat to two plates and keep warm. To the skillet add the wine and stir to dissolve the particles in the pan. Reduce wine slightly and pour equal amounts over each serving.

Yield: 2 servings

Rollatini di Vitello al Pomodoro *(Veal rolls with tomato sauce)*

¼   **pound prosciutto or other ham**
⅓   **cup fine, soft bread crumbs**
½   **cup freshly grated Parmesan cheese**
4   **tablespoons finely chopped parsley**
½   **teaspoon freshly grated nutmeg**
2   **eggs**
1   **teaspoon dried oregano**
2   **tablespoons chopped fresh basil, or ½ teaspoon dried**
¼   **cup heavy cream**
1½   **teaspoons chopped garlic**

1. Chop the prosciutto finely. Combine it in a mixing bowl with the bread crumbs, cheese, parsley, nutmeg, eggs, oregano, basil, heavy cream, 1 teaspoon garlic, salt and pepper to taste. Blend well.

2. Pound the pieces of veal lightly without breaking the meat. Spoon equal portions of the stuffing onto each slice and smooth it over the meat with a spatula. Roll and tie with string.

3. Heat the butter in a heavy skillet and brown the meat on all sides, for about 10 minutes. Remove the meat rolls and add the onion and remaining garlic to the skillet. Cook, stirring, for about 3 minutes and add the wine. Stir to dissolve the brown particles that cling to the bottom and sides of the skillet. Add the tomatoes, salt and pepper to taste and bring to the

boil. Return the meat rolls and cover. Cook for about 45 minutes. Serve with spaghetti or other pasta and more grated Parmesan cheese.

Yield: 6 servings.

Salt and freshly ground pepper
12 thin slices of veal scaloppine, preferably cut from the leg
1 tablespoon butter
3 tablespoons finely chopped onion
½ cup dry white wine
2 cups drained canned tomatoes, preferably Italian plum tomatoes

Ossobuco Milanese

It may be a cliché, the thought that the nearer the bone, the sweeter the meat, but it is the absolute reason why dishes made with shanks of meat are rich in flavor. One of the most admired dishes in the cooking of Italy is ossobuco, veal shanks perfumed with herbs and, classically, grated lemon and orange peel.

The stinco di vitello is a braised shank of veal creation that we adapted from a dish sampled not long ago at the fashionable El Toula restaurant in Rome. The recipe calls for a purée of white truffles, which is a nice conceit but not essential to the success of the dish.

3 veal shanks, each sawed into 3 pieces 2 inches thick
⅓ cup flour
2 teaspoons salt
½ teaspoon freshly ground pepper
3 tablespoons olive oil
3 tablespoons butter
½ teaspoon ground sage
1 teaspoon rosemary
1 medium-size onion, finely chopped
3 cloves garlic
2 small carrots, diced
1 rib celery, diced
1½ cups dry white wine
1¼ cups fresh or canned chicken broth
2 tablespoons tomato paste
1½ tablespoons chopped parsley
1 tablespoon grated lemon peel

1. Dredge the meat in the flour seasoned with 1 teaspoon of the salt and the pepper. Heat the oil and butter together in a large skillet. Using medium heat, cook the meat on all sides until golden brown. If necessary, add a little more oil or butter.

2. Arrange the meat in a Dutch oven, standing each piece on its side so the marrow in the bones does not fall out as the meat cooks. Sprinkle the veal with the sage and rosemary. Add the onion, 1 clove minced garlic, the carrots and celery. Sprinkle the vegetables with the remaining 1 teaspoon of salt. Cover the Dutch oven closely and cook for 10 minutes. Remove the cover and add the wine, chicken broth and tomato paste. Cover and simmer the dish on top of the stove for 2 hours.

3. Mince the remaining 2 cloves of garlic and combine with the parsley and lemon peel. Sprinkle the mixture, called gremolata, over the veal and serve immediately.

Yield: 6 to 8 servings.

Stinco di Vitello *(Braised veal shank)*

The veal:

1 3½- to 4-pound veal shank, taken from the leg
Salt and freshly ground pepper
2 tablespoons butter
½ cup carrot rounds
½ cup coarsely chopped onion
½ cup chopped celery
1 clove garlic, cut into quarters
1 cup dry white wine
1 cup fresh or canned chicken broth
½ cup chopped tomatoes
4 sprigs fresh parsley
1 bay leaf
2 sprigs fresh thyme
2 tablespoons white truffle purée, available in cans where fine Italian foods are sold, optional
1 teaspoon cornstarch
2 teaspoons dry white wine

The vegetable garnish:

8 small white onions, peeled, about ¾ pound
Salt
2 large carrots, trimmed, scraped and quartered
1 large potato, peeled and cut into 10 wedges
2 tablespoons butter
1 cup freshly shelled peas
Freshly ground pepper

1. Sprinkle the veal with salt and pepper to taste. Heat 2 tablespoons of butter in a casserole and brown the meat all over until golden, about 5 minutes. Scatter around it the carrot rounds, onion, celery and garlic and cook for about 5 minutes. Add the wine, chicken broth, tomatoes, parsley, bay leaf, thyme, salt and pepper to taste. Cover closely and cook for about 2 hours, or until fork tender.

2. Transfer the meat to a warm platter and cover with foil to keep warm.

3. Strain the sauce through a sieve, pushing through as much liquid from the solids as possible, using a heavy metal or wooden spoon. Discard the solids. Let the sauce simmer slowly for about 10 minutes and add the truffle purée, if desired. Simmer briefly. Blend the cornstarch with wine and stir it in. Simmer for about 30 seconds and remove from the heat.

4. Meanwhile, prepare the vegetables for garnish. Put the onions in a saucepan and add cold water to cover and salt to taste. Simmer for about 10 minutes and add the carrots. Simmer for 5 minutes longer. Drain.

5. As the onions cook, put the potatoes in another saucepan and add cold water to cover and salt to taste. Bring to the boil and simmer for 1 minute. Drain.

6. Heat the butter in a large casserole and add the onions, carrots, potatoes and peas. Sprinkle with salt and pepper to taste. Cover and cook for about 5 minutes. Add ½ cup of the sauce and cover. Cook for about 10 minutes longer or until tender. Serve the meat carved with the vegetables. Serve the sauce separately.

Yield: 8 to 12 servings.

Roast Veal Stuffed with Tarragon-flavored Scrambled Eggs

1 4-pound shoulder of veal, boned and with pocket
6 eggs
1 teaspoon dried tarragon

1. Preheat the oven to 450 degrees.

2. Open up the roast for stuffing.

3. In a mixing bowl, combine the eggs with the tarragon, salt, pepper and heavy cream. Beat well until blended. In a

saucepan heat 1 tablespoon of butter and add the eggs. Cook, stirring, to the soft stage. Remove from the heat and stir in 1 teaspoon of butter.

4. Sprinkle the veal with salt and pepper. Line it well with the thin slices of ham, covering the open surface. Spoon the eggs up and down the center. Arrange the pickles down the center of the eggs. Overlap the edges of the meat so that they enclose the egg mixture. Tie securely up and down with string so that the stuffing does not come out. Sprinkle the veal outside with salt and pepper.

5. Rub a flameproof baking dish with the remaining 3 tablespoons of butter. Scatter the onions, carrots, garlic and celery over the bottom of the dish. Add the veal. Heat the dish on top of the stove and put it in the oven. No liquid is necessary. Bake uncovered for 1½ hours. Cover with foil and bake for 30 minutes longer, basting occasionally. Then reduce oven heat to 400 degrees. Bake for 30 minutes longer.

6. Cut away the trussing string. Slice and serve with the natural juices and pan vegetables.

Yield: 6 to 8 servings.

Salt and freshly ground pepper to taste
⅓ cup heavy cream
4 tablespoons plus 1 teaspoon butter
¼ pound thinly sliced boiled or baked ham, or prosciutto
16 small pickles, preferably cornichons
2 onions, about ½ pound, peeled and cut into thin rounds
2 carrots, about ½ pound, scraped and cut into thin rounds
1 clove garlic, cut in half
1 rib celery, cut into 1-inch lengths

Sauté of Veal with Mushrooms and Crabmeat

1. Place the veal steaks, one at a time, in a clean towel. Pound lightly with a flat mallet. When ready they should be about ¾ inch thick. Sprinkle with salt and pepper.

2. Heat 2 tablespoons of the butter in a heavy skillet and add the steaks, cooking over high heat. Cook for about 2 minutes and turn. Reduce the heat and cook for about 4 minutes. Turn the steaks once more and cook for about 1 minute longer. Transfer the steaks to a warm platter. Add the water to the skillet and stir. Pour this sauce over the veal.

3. Separately heat 1 tablespoon of butter in a heavy skillet and add the mushroom slices. Cook, stirring and tossing, for about 2 minutes. Pour the mushrooms over the veal.

4. Add remaining 2 tablespoons of butter to another skillet and add the crabmeat. Cook, tossing and stirring gently, just until crab is heated through. Pour the crabmeat over the veal.

Yield: 6 servings.

6 boneless veal steaks taken from the loin or saddle
Salt and freshly ground pepper to taste
5 tablespoons salted butter
2 tablespoons water
6 large mushrooms, about ¼ pound, thinly sliced
⅓ pound fresh lump crabmeat

Veal Sauté in Tomato Sauce

4 pounds veal shoulder and/or breast, boned and cut into 2-inch cubes
Salt and freshly ground pepper to taste
4 tablespoons oil
2 cups finely chopped onion
1 tablespoon finely chopped garlic
1 teaspoon stem saffron, optional
¼ cup flour
¼ cup dry white wine
3½ cups peeled, chopped tomatoes or the contents of a 1-pound-12-ounce can whole peeled tomatoes
1 cup fresh or canned chicken broth
2 teaspoons dried rosemary

1. Preheat the oven to 375 degrees.
2. Sprinkle the veal with salt and pepper. Heat the oil in a heavy, large casserole or Dutch oven and add the meat. Cook, stirring frequently, for about 20 minutes. In the beginning the meat will give up liquid. This will evaporate as the meat cooks. Continue until the meat is browned all over.
3. Add the onion, garlic and saffron, if desired, and cook, stirring occasionally, for about 5 minutes. Sprinkle with flour and stir until the pieces of meat are evenly coated. Add the wine, tomatoes and chicken broth. Sprinkle with salt and pepper to taste.
4. Add the dried rosemary. Cover and bake for 1 hour.
Yield: 6 to 8 servings.

Curried Veal

4½ to 5 pounds boneless veal (neck or shoulder meat of veal is good for this), cut into 2-inch cubes
Salt and freshly ground pepper to taste
2 tablespoons butter
1½ cups chopped onion
2 cloves garlic, finely minced
½ cup finely chopped celery
¼ cup curry powder
1 banana, peeled and cut into small dice, about 1 cup
1 apple, peeled and cored and cut into small dice, about 1 cup
1½ cups fresh or canned chicken broth
½ cup canned tomatoes with tomato paste

1. Sprinkle the meat with salt and pepper.
2. Heat the butter in a large, heavy casserole and add the onion and garlic. Add the meat and stir well. Cook briefly until the meat loses its pink color. Sprinkle with celery and stir. Add the curry, stirring to blend. Add the banana, apple, chicken broth and tomatoes. Mix well. Cover. Cook the veal, stirring occasionally, until the meat is fork-tender, about 1½ hours. Skim off any excess fat from the sauce and serve.
Yield: 6 to 8 servings.

Bitokes de Veau Smitane   *(Veal patties with pepper and sour cream sauce)*

1. Place the veal in a mixing bowl and add 6 tablespoons sour cream, the bread crumbs, 3 teaspoons paprika, the finely chopped onion, salt and pepper to taste and the dill. Blend well with the fingers.

2. Divide the mixture into 12 portions of approximately the same weight. Using wet fingers, shape the portions into neat, round, flat patties. Arrange on a baking dish and refrigerate.

3. Meanwhile, prepare the sauce. Remove the cores and seeds from the peppers. Cut them in half lengthwise. Slice the halves lengthwise into ½-inch strips. Heat half the oil and half the butter in a skillet and add the pepper strips. Cook for about 4 minutes and add the coarsely chopped onion. Cook, stirring, until wilted and add the remaining teaspoon paprika. Add the wine and cook, stirring, for about 30 minutes. Add salt to taste.

4. Heat the remaining oil and butter in a skillet and brown the patties on one side, for about 3 minutes. Turn and brown on the other. Continue cooking to the desired degree of doneness.

5. Reheat the pepper strips and onions and stir in the remaining sour cream. Stir and remove from the heat. Add salt to taste. Heat thoroughly, but do not boil or the sauce will curdle. Serve the patties with the sauce spooned over.

Yield: 6 servings.

2	pounds ground veal
2	cups sour cream
1	cup fine, fresh bread crumbs
4	teaspoons paprika
2	tablespoons finely chopped onion
	Salt and freshly ground pepper
2	tablespoons chopped dill
2	sweet red or green peppers
6	tablespoons peanut oil
2	tablespoons butter
¼	cup coarsely chopped onion
1	cup dry white wine

Ground Veal Patties with Cognac and Cream Sauce

1. Put the veal in a mixing bowl. Cut prosciutto slices into very thin strips, then cut the strips into very fine dice. There should be about ¾ cup. Add the prosciutto to the veal. Add very little salt (the prosciutto is salty), pepper and the nutmeg. Stir the mixture to blend well and shape it into 4 patties. Dust the patties on all sides with flour.

2. Melt the butter in a skillet and, when it is quite hot, add the meat patties. Cook until golden brown and turn. Reduce the heat and cook the patties until done to the desired degree. Transfer the patties to hot plates and keep warm. Pour off most of the fat from the skillet.

3. Add the cream to the skillet and cook over high heat until it is reduced almost by half. Add the lemon, Cognac, salt and pepper to taste. Stir and serve piping hot on the patties.

Yield: 4 servings.

1	pound ground veal
¼	pound prosciutto or boiled ham, sliced as thin as possible
	Salt and freshly ground pepper to taste
¼	teaspoon freshly grated nutmeg
¼	cup flour
2	tablespoons butter
¾	cup heavy cream
	Juice of ½ lemon
1	tablespoon Cognac

Ris de Veau à l'Anglaise *(Breaded sweetbreads)*

There is no more reason why sweetbreads are the basis for some of the most elegant dishes in the world than there is in why people climb mountains or take to the air in ascension balloons. Sweetbread dishes are simply a natural thread in the fabric of fine dining, and have been for centuries. They, along with brains, are the choicest part of the calf to people of taste and discernment.

Sweetbreads should always be soaked, to rid them of residual blood, and weighted, which gives them a firmer, more appetizing texture.

1 pound sweetbreads
   Salt
½ cup flour
1 egg
2 tablespoons water
2 tablespoons plus 1 teaspoon
   peanut, vegetable or corn oil
   Freshly ground pepper
1¼ cups fresh bread crumbs
7 tablespoons butter
   Lemon slices for garnish

1. Soak the sweetbreads in cold water in the refrigerator for several hours, changing the water frequently. Drain.

2. Put the sweetbreads in a saucepan and add cold water to cover and salt to taste. Bring to the boil and simmer for 5 minutes, no longer. Drain and cover with cold water. When the sweetbreads are cool, drain them. Place them on a cake rack. Cover with another rack and weight them down. For this we have used everything from meat pounders to saucepans filled with stones. Weight the sweetbreads for about 2 hours.

3. Pick over the sweetbreads and remove any odd membranes, filaments or tendons. Cut the sweetbreads into 8 flat pieces. Dredge the pieces on all sides in flour.

4. Beat the egg and stir in the water, 1 teaspoon of oil, salt and pepper to taste. Dip the sweetbreads first in the egg mixture, then in the bread crumbs. When well coated, tap lightly to help the crumbs adhere. In a large skillet, heat 3 tablespoons of butter and remaining 2 tablespoons of oil. Add the sweetbreads. Cook until golden on one side. Turn and cook until golden on the other side.

5. Remove the sweetbreads to a warm platter. Wipe out the skillet and add the remaining butter. Cook until the foam subsides and the butter is hazelnut brown. Pour the butter over the sweetbreads. Garnish with lemon slices and serve immediately.

Yield: 4 servings.

Curried Sweetbreads with Mushrooms

3½ pounds sweetbreads
6 tablespoons butter
1 cup finely chopped onion

1. Put the sweetbreads in a bowl and add cold water to cover. Soak overnight or for several hours in the refrigerator, changing the water occasionally. Drain.

2. Put the sweetbreads in a large saucepan and add cold water to cover. Bring to the boil and simmer for 5 minutes. Drain immediately. Run under cold water and let stand in the water until thoroughly chilled. Drain. Put the sweetbreads on a rack in a flat pan and cover with another flat pan of the same size. Cover with a heavy weight and let stand for several hours. Cut the sweetbreads into 1-inch cubes, cutting, trimming or pulling off and discarding connecting tissues and so forth as necessary. Set aside.

3. Heat 2 tablespoons of butter in a saucepan or skillet and add the onion. Cook until wilted and sprinkle with curry powder. Cook briefly, stirring, and add the apple and banana. Add the tomato paste, stirring, and add the chicken broth. Continue stirring until well blended. Add salt to taste. Pour the sauce into the container of a food processor or electric blender and blend until smooth. Set aside.

4. Meanwhile, heat the remaining butter in a large, heavy skillet or casserole and add the sweetbreads. Cook, stirring and shaking the skillet, for about 5 minutes. Add the mushrooms and salt and pepper to taste. Cook, stirring often, for about 10 minutes and add the wine. Cook until most of the wine is evaporated. Add the sauce. Cook, stirring occasionally, for 15 or 20 minutes. Serve with rice, in puff pastry shells or on toast.

Yield: 6 to 8 servings.

3 tablespoons curry powder
1 cup finely chopped apple
½ cup finely chopped banana
2 tablespoons tomato paste
2 cups fresh or canned chicken broth
Salt
½ pound mushrooms, quartered if small, or cut into eighths if large (3½ to 4 cups)
Freshly ground pepper
½ cup dry white wine

Ris de Veau à la Crème *(Sweetbreads in cream sauce)*

1. Place the sweetbreads in a mixing bowl and add cold water to cover. Soak for several hours but change the water frequently. The soaking will make the sweetbreads white.

2. When the sweetbreads are ready, drain them. Use a paring knife and cut away the arteries and so on. Place the sweetbreads in a saucepan and add cold water to cover and salt to taste. Bring to the boil and simmer for 5 minutes. Drain immediately, then run under cold water until well chilled.

3. Place a cake rack in a dish and cover with a clean towel. Add the sweetbreads in one layer and cover with the towel. Add a heavy weight (we used a flour crock filled with flour) and let stand for several hours. Cut the sweetbreads into cubes.

4. If the mushrooms are very small, leave them whole. Otherwise, quarter or slice them. Melt 1 tablespoon of the butter in a small skillet and add the shallots and mushrooms. Cook,

2 pounds sweetbreads
Salt
¼ pound fresh mushrooms
2 tablespoons butter
1 tablespoon finely chopped shallots
Freshly ground pepper
1 tablespoon flour
½ cup milk
½ cup heavy cream
⅛ teaspoon grated nutmeg
Tabasco sauce to taste
4 to 6 slices buttered toast

stirring, for about 3 minutes and add the sweetbreads, salt and pepper to taste. Cook, stirring frequently, for about 10 minutes.

5. In a small saucepan, heat the remaining butter and add the flour, stirring with a wire whisk. When blended, add the milk and cream, stirring rapidly with the whisk. Add the nutmeg and Tabasco. Add the sweetbreads and mushroom mixture and blend. Simmer for 25 minutes. Serve on buttered toast.

Yield: 4 to 6 servings.

Foie de Veau à l'Anglaise *(Sautéed calf's liver with bacon)*

8 slices bacon
8 thin slices calf's liver, about
   1¼ pounds
   Salt and freshly ground
   pepper to taste
¼ cup flour
2 tablespoons vegetable, peanut
   or corn oil
6 tablespoons butter
1 tablespoon Worcestershire
   sauce

1. Arrange the bacon slices in one layer in a skillet. Cook, turning as often as necessary, until browned and crisp. Drain on paper toweling. Pour off all but about 1 teaspoon of the bacon fat.

2. Sprinkle the liver with salt and pepper on both sides. Dredge lightly in flour, shaking to remove excess.

3. Add the oil to the skillet and, when hot, add as many slices of liver as the skillet will hold in one layer. Cook over high heat for 1 minute or longer until nicely browned. The cooking time will vary, depending on the thickness of the slices. Turn and cook for 1 minute or longer to the desired degree of doneness. Continue until all the slices are cooked. Transfer the liver to a warm platter and keep warm.

4. Pour off any fat that is left in the pan. Wipe out the pan with a clean cloth or paper toweling. Add the butter to the skillet and cook over high heat until butter is hazelnut brown.

5. Garnish the liver with the bacon. Spoon the Worcestershire sauce over and around the liver. Pour the hazelnut butter over all and serve immediately.

Yield: 4 servings.

Sautéed Calf's Liver with Vinegar Glaze

1 pound calf's liver, sliced (see
   note)
½ cup flour
   Salt and freshly ground
   pepper

1. The liver may be cut into 4 to 8 slices according to taste. We prefer it sliced thin. Blend the flour with the salt and pepper and dredge the liver slices on all sides with the mixture.

2. Heat half the butter in a heavy skillet and add the liver. Cook on one side, for 2 minutes or according to taste. Turn the

liver and cook that side for 2 minutes more. Transfer the liver to a heated platter and sprinkle with the parsley.

3. Add the remaining butter to the skillet. Let it brown briefly. Pour this over the liver. Add the vinegar to the skillet and bring to the boil, swirling it around in the skillet. Pour this over the liver.

Yield: 4 servings.

Note: If you can persuade your butcher to remove the nerves or veins in each slice of liver, so much the better. Or this may be done at home with a small, sharp knife or scissors.

8	tablespoons butter
¼	cup finely chopped parsley
¼	cup sherry wine or red wine vinegar

Brains in Beer Batter

1. Prepare the batter.
2. Cut the brains into 24 cubes of equal size. Place in a bowl and add lemon juice, parsley, 2 tablespoons oil, salt and pepper to taste.
3. Heat the oil for deep frying. Dip the pieces of brains, one at a time, in the beer batter and then put in the hot fat. Cook, turning and submerging the pieces in the oil as necessary, until golden brown all over. Drain on absorbent paper toweling.

Yield: 4 to 6 servings.

	Beer batter (see recipe below)
2	sets precooked calf's brains, about 1 pound (see recipe below)
	Juice of ½ lemon
2	tablespoons chopped parsley
2	tablespoons peanut, vegetable or corn oil
	Salt and freshly ground pepper
	Oil for deep frying

1. Place the flour in a bowl and stir in the beer, salt and oil. Stir to blend roughly. There should be a few small lumps. Cover the bowl with plastic wrap and let stand in a warm place for about 3 hours.
2. Stir in the egg yolk.
3. When ready to cook, beat the white until stiff and fold it in.

Beer batter

¾	cup flour
½	cup beer at room temperature
	Salt to taste
1	teaspoon peanut, vegetable or corn oil
1	egg, separated

1. A calf's brain consists of a pair of lobes. Place in a mixing bowl and add cold water to cover. Let stand for several hours, changing the cold water frequently.
2. Drain and pick over the brains to remove the outer membranes, blood and other extraneous matter. Place the brains in a saucepan and add cold water to cover to a depth of about ½ inch above the brains. Add the peppercorns, salt to taste, vinegar, bay leaf and thyme. Bring to the boil and simmer for about 3 minutes. Let cool in the cooking liquid. They are now ready to be drained and given a final preparation as for brains in beer batter.

Precooked calf's brains

2	sets calf's brains (about 1 pound)
12	peppercorns
	Salt
2	tablespoons vinegar
1	bay leaf
2	sprigs fresh thyme, or ½ teaspoon dried

Veal Kidneys in Red Wine Sauce

3 tablespoons coarsely chopped shallots
1 cup dry red wine
½ bay leaf
2 sprigs fresh thyme, or ½ teaspoon dried
½ teaspoon crushed peppercorns
2 sprigs parsley
4 teaspoons red wine vinegar
1 10¾-ounce can brown beef gravy
Salt and freshly ground pepper
3 veal kidneys, about 1¾ pounds
5 tablespoons butter
½ pound fresh mushrooms, thinly sliced
½ cup heavy cream

1. Combine the shallots, wine, bay leaf, thyme, peppercorns, parsley and 1 teaspoon of wine vinegar in a saucepan. Bring to the boil and cook for about 5 minutes over high heat to reduce. Add the brown beef gravy and simmer for 15 minutes. Add salt and pepper to taste and the remaining vinegar.

2. Meanwhile, split the kidneys in half and cut away the white center core. Thinly slice the kidneys crosswise and sprinkle with salt and pepper to taste. Heat 2 tablespoons of butter in a skillet and, when it is very hot and starts to brown, add the kidneys. Cook, shaking the skillet and stirring, over high heat for 2 to 3 minutes, no longer. Turn the kidneys into a colander and let stand for 10 to 15 minutes to drain thoroughly. Do not wash the skillet.

3. To the skillet in which the kidneys cooked add 1 tablespoon of butter and the mushrooms. Cook over high heat until the mushrooms give up their juices and then until the liquid evaporates.

4. Add the drained kidneys to the mushrooms. Strain the sauce over all and bring to the boil. Add the heavy cream and, when it reaches the boil, swirl in the remaining butter. Add salt and pepper to taste and serve piping hot.

Yield: 4 to 6 servings.

Roast Leg of Lamb

1 6- to 7-pound leg of lamb
3 cloves garlic cut into slivers
Salt and freshly ground pepper

1. Preheat the oven to 450 degrees.

2. Place the meat fat side down. Cut off and discard the loose flap from the under side. Using a boning or large paring knife, follow the outlines of the top leg bone, known as the aitch bone. Bone it all around and sever it at the joint. Crack the bone and save it.

3. Turn the leg over and "French" the very end of the shank bone, cutting away about 1½ inches of meat surrounding the bone. Tie the boned section of the leg with string.

4. With the tip of a small knife, make 16 or so slits in the meat and insert slivers of garlic. Place the lamb, fat side down, in a baking dish. Sprinkle with salt and pepper and add the reserved aitch bone.

5. Bake the lamb for 30 minutes. Turn and cook for 15 minutes. Pour off all fat. Bake for 20 minutes longer and add 1 cup

of water. Cover with foil. Reduce heat to 400 degrees and bake for 25 minutes.

6. Pour pan juices into a saucepan and reheat. Let lamb rest for 20 minutes. Add juices that accumulate around the lamb to the saucepan. Serve the sauce with the sliced lamb.

Yield: 8 or more servings.

High-temperature Roast Leg of Lamb

Inspired by the immensely popular technique for roasting beef developed by Ann Seranne, Dorothy Moore attempted a similar "fool-proof" recipe for cooking a whole leg of lamb. The technique is simple—roasting at a high temperature and then turning off the oven—and the results are admirable. As with the beef, this should not be attempted unless the oven is well insulated.

1. It is recommended that you have the butcher remove and set aside the hip bone of the lamb. This is the upper bone that is attached to the main (straight) leg bone. This can also be done in the home kitchen. Using a sharp knife, cut away a very thin layer of top fat. Do not cut away all the fat, however. Leave a thin coating.

2. Place the lamb, fat-side up, in a shallow roasting pan. Make several gashes in the fat and near the bone of the lamb. Insert slivers of garlic in the gashes. Rub the lamb all over with salt, pepper, bay leaf, thyme and rosemary leaves. Add the vermouth and olive oil. The lamb may be covered closely and refrigerated at this point for several hours or overnight. Remember, however, it is best to let the lamb return to room temperature before putting it in the oven.

3. Preheat the oven to 500 degrees.

4. If you wish the lamb to be rare, place it in the oven and bake for 15 minutes. Turn off the oven. Do not open the door at any time until the lamb is ready to be carved and served. Let stand in the oven for 3 hours. If you wish the lamb to be medium well done, let it bake for 20 minutes. Turn off the oven and, without opening the door, let stand for 3½ hours. If you wish the lamb to be well done, let it bake for 25 minutes and let it stand in the oven for 3¾ hours.

5. Strain the pan liquid. Strain off most of the surface fat from the drippings. Reheat and serve the natural sauce with the lamb when carved.

Yield: 8 or more servings.

1 small leg of lamb, about 6 pounds
2 cloves garlic, cut into slivers
   Salt and freshly ground pepper
1 bay leaf, broken
3 sprigs fresh thyme, chopped, or ½ teaspoon dried
½ teaspoon rosemary leaves
2 tablespoons dry vermouth
2 tablespoons olive oil

Leg of Lamb with Flageolets

1 pound dried flageolets
2 pounds onions, thinly sliced
¼ cup butter
2 pounds potatoes, unpeeled and thinly sliced
2 tablespoons salt
¼ teaspoon pepper
1 cup fresh or canned beef broth
1 bay leaf
1 6- to 7-pound leg of lamb
1 teaspoon rosemary

1. Cover beans with cold water. Refrigerate, covered, overnight.
2. Drain the beans. Into a 6-quart saucepan pour 2 quarts water. Bring to a boil and add beans. Cover and simmer for 45 minutes or until tender. Drain.
3. Preheat the oven to 325 degrees.
4. Sauté the onions in hot butter until golden.
5. In a baking dish (one measuring 13- x 10- x 4-inches is ideal), layer half of the potatoes, onions, beans, salt and pepper. Repeat layering. Heat broth with bay leaf to boiling. Pour over the vegetables.
6. Rub the lamb with rosemary. Place on top of vegetables. Bake uncovered for 2 to 2½ hours, or until rare or medium well done.
   Yield: 8 servings.

Roast Baby Lamb with Artichokes

1 12- to 14-pound baby lamb
½ cup butter at room temperature
Juice of 6 lemons
2 cloves garlic, minced
2 tablespoons oregano
Salt and freshly ground pepper
Boiling water
8 large artichokes
¼ cup flour
Chopped fresh dill
Parsley sprigs for garnish

1. Preheat the oven to 500 degrees.
2. Wipe the lamb with a damp cloth. Rub all over with butter, juice of 2 lemons, garlic, oregano, salt and pepper. Place the lamb in a large roasting pan and bake for 30 minutes. Reduce the temperature to 350 degrees and bake for about 2 hours, basting frequently, until the leg moves freely from the body. Keep adding boiling water so that there will be about 2 to 2½ cups drippings.
3. Meanwhile, as the lamb roasts, prepare the artichokes. Trim the artichokes at the base, leaving about 1 inch of stem. Remove all tough outer leaves. Cut off about 1 inch from the top. Cut each artichoke in half lengthwise and scrape away the fuzzy choke. Pare around the stem. Rub the cut portions with juice of 1 lemon. Place each half in a large saucepan of salted cold water to which is added the juice of the remaining 3 lemons and the flour. Bring to the boil and simmer for about 10 minutes until slightly tender.
4. Remove the lamb and set aside in a warm place. Gently place each artichoke half in pan with lamb drippings. Bake the artichokes about ½ hour until tender but not overcooked. Sprinkle with dill and garnish with parsley sprigs.
   Yield: 12 or more servings.

Gigot au Pastis *(Leg of lamb with Pernod or Ricard)*

1. Preheat the oven to 350 degrees.

2. Using a sharp, pointed knife, make slight incisions in the lamb. Press slivers of garlic into the incisions. Rub the lamb all over with oil and sprinkle with salt and pepper to taste, rosemary and thyme.

3. Roast the lamb for 15 minutes a pound if you wish the lamb rare. Roast longer for well-done lamb. Let the lamb rest for 15 minutes after it is removed from the oven. When ready to serve, warm the Pernod or Ricard in a saucepan and pour it over the lamb, igniting it immediately with a match. Slice the lamb and serve with tomato sauce.

Yield: 6 to 8 servings.

1	7-pound leg of lamb, boned and rolled
2	cloves garlic, peeled and cut into slivers
2	tablespoons peanut, vegetable or corn oil
	Salt and freshly ground pepper
½	teaspoon or more dried rosemary
½	teaspoon dried thyme
½	cup Pernod or Ricard
2	cups sauce tomate au pastis (see recipe below)

Heat the oil in a saucepan and add the shallot and onion. Cook, stirring, until the onion is golden brown. Add the remaining ingredients and bring to the boil. Simmer briefly and serve hot in a sauceboat.

Yield: About 2 cups.

Sauce tomate au pastis *(Tomato sauce with Pernod or Ricard)*

1	tablespoon olive or vegetable oil
1	shallot, finely chopped
¾	cup finely chopped onion
2	cups fresh or canned tomato sauce
½	teaspoon dried thyme
½	teaspoon crushed bay leaves
1	teaspoon sugar
	Salt and freshly ground pepper
½	cup Pernod or Ricard

Gigot d'Agneau au Pistou *(Braised lamb with basil and garlic stuffing)*

1. When the lamb is boned, ask the butcher to reserve the bones and crack them.

2. Combine the bacon, garlic, parsley and basil in a food processor or use an electric blender. Blend the ingredients to a fine purée.

3. Sprinkle the lamb inside with salt and pepper. Spread the bacon mixture inside the lamb to fill it. If some of the stuffing oozes out, no matter. Sew up the lamb, tucking in torn pieces of lamb as necessary. Sprinkle the lamb all over with salt and pepper. Rub the lamb with any excess bacon and herb mixture.

4. Place the lamb, fat-side down, in a heavy casserole and

1	5-pound leg of lamb, boned
¼	pound bacon or salt pork
6	cloves garlic, finely minced
3	sprigs fresh parsley
10	fresh basil leaves
	Salt and freshly ground pepper
1	cup coarsely chopped onion
½	cup coarsely chopped carrot
¾	cup dry white wine
2	cups chopped, peeled, fresh or canned tomatoes

arrange the bones around it. The lamb and bones should fit snugly inside the casserole. Brown the lamb on all sides and sprinkle onions and carrots around it. Cover and cook for about 5 minutes.

5. Carefully pour off and discard all fat that has accumulated. Add the wine, tomatoes, salt and pepper to taste. Cover and bring to the boil. Cook over moderate heat for about 2 hours.

6. Remove the lamb and strain the sauce into a saucepan. Bring to the boil and skim the surface as necessary to remove as much fat as possible. Cook the sauce down until it is properly concentrated and saucelike. Slice the meat and spoon a little of the sauce over each serving.

Yield: 8 to 12 servings.

Grilled Boneless Leg of Lamb Indian-style

1   8- to 9-pound leg of lamb, boned
2   medium-size onions
1   piece fresh ginger, about 3 inches long and 1 inch wide
5 to   7 cloves garlic, peeled and coarsely chopped
⅔   cup lemon juice
1   tablespoon ground coriander
1   teaspoon ground cumin
1   teaspoon garam masala (see recipe below)
1   teaspoon ground turmeric
¼   teaspoon ground mace
¼   teaspoon ground nutmeg
¼   teaspoon ground cinnamon
¼   teaspoon ground cloves
1   cup olive oil
2½   teaspoons salt
¼   teaspoon freshly ground pepper
   Cayenne pepper to taste
   Coloring (see note)
12   radishes for garnish

1. Have the butcher "butterfly" the meat, or do it at home. Cut the meat, leaving it in one piece, so that it will lie flat on a grill.

2. Chop 1 onion and put it into the container of a food processor or electric blender. Add the ginger, garlic and ¼ cup lemon juice. Blend to a smooth paste.

3. Pour the mixture into a stainless steel or enamel dish large enough to hold the meat. Add the remaining spices, oil, salt, pepper, cayenne and coloring and blend well.

4. Carefully cut off all fat and tissue from the lamb and use a sharp pointed knife to pierce the flesh at many spots on both sides. Add the meat to the dish and rub in the paste of herbs and spices. Cover and place in the refrigerator. Let stand for 24 hours, turning it occasionally.

5. Grill the meat over charcoal, under the broiler, or on an electric grill. In India the meat is generally cooked until well done. Ideally, it should be quite dark on the outside and slightly pink within, with no juices flowing.

6. As the meat cooks, slice the remaining onion into very thin rounds and drop into ice water. Cover and refrigerate. Clean the radishes and make radish roses if desired. Drop into ice water and refrigerate.

7. When ready to serve, transfer the meat to a warm platter. Garnish with the drained onion slices and radishes.

Yield: 10 to 12 servings.

Note: Ideally, the coloring for this dish is an Indian food coloring in powdered form. A good substitute is about 12 drops of red food coloring, 15 drops of yellow food coloring and 1 tablespoon of mild paprika.

Combine all the ingredients in a small coffee grinder and blend thoroughly. The mixture may be kept for weeks if tightly sealed.
Yield: About 3 tablespoons.

Garam masala

1 tablespoon peeled cardamom seeds
1 2-inch stick cinnamon, crushed
1 teaspoon whole cloves
1 teaspoon whole black peppercorns
1/3 teaspoon grated nutmeg
1 teaspoon cumin seeds, optional

Bhuna Ghost   *(Pan-roasted lamb)*

1. Cut the lamb or have it cut into 1½-inch cubes.
2. Place the lamb in a bowl and add the remaining ingredients. Set aside until ready to cook, for 1 hour or longer.
3. Preheat the oven to 350 degrees.
4. Spoon the lamb into a shallow roasting pan. A recommended size is 16- x 9½- x 2½-inches. Smooth the lamb over and place the pan in the oven, uncovered. Bake for 1 hour and 15 minutes without stirring. The lamb should be quite tender and the pan juices will be quite liquid. Serve with rice.
Yield: 12 servings.

1 4¼-pound lean, skinless, boneless leg of lamb (about 7 pounds before boning)
2 tablespoons finely chopped fresh ginger
3 hot green chilies, chopped, with seeds
1 tablespoon finely chopped garlic
1½ tablespoons chopped fresh coriander leaves
Juice of 1 lemon
Salt to taste
1 teaspoon freshly ground pepper
1 tablespoon peanut, vegetable or corn oil

Leg of Lamb Persian-style

One of the many fine dishes we sampled in the home of Jennifer Manocherian was an excellent roast lamb with yogurt, the meat having been marinated for many hours in yogurt with seasonings. Mrs. Manocherian has rather a solid background in cooking. Her mother was Ann Roe Robbins, who for many years directed one of the best cooking schools in Manhattan, and her husband, Fred, who was born in Teheran, came from a family where fine food was a tradition.

1 6- to 7-pound leg of lamb
1 cup plain yogurt
¼ cup olive oil
½ cup grated onion
Salt and freshly ground pepper

1. Place the lamb in a large plastic bag and add the yogurt, olive oil, onion, salt and pepper to taste. Seal tightly and, using the hands, maneuver the marinade all over the meat. Refrigerate overnight or leave at room temperature for several hours. Leave the lamb in the bag but turn it occasionally to redistribute the marinade.

2. Preheat the oven to 500 degrees.

3. Remove the lamb from the bag and place it in a roasting pan large enough to hold it amply. Pour and squeeze the marinade over the meat and bake, uncovered, until the meat is very brown on top, 30 to 40 minutes. As the meat bakes, add ½ cup or so of water to the roasting pan to prevent sticking. There should be about ¼-inch of liquid on the bottom of the pan at all times. When the meat is brown on top, turn it and bake for about 15 minutes on that side. Cover tightly with the lid and reduce the heat to 375 degrees. Bake from 1 to 1½ hours, or until almost fork tender. Serve with the natural pan juices, skimmed of most of the fat.

Yield: 8 to 12 servings.

How to Prepare a Crown Roast of Lamb for Stuffing

If your butcher will not prepare a crown roast of lamb, here is how to go about it. Buy 2 racks of lamb, 7 ribs each. Have them neatly trimmed. Cut and pull away the skin but leave the light layer of fat beneath the skin. The ribs should measure about 4 inches in length. Using a sharp knife, make a slight slit between each rib at the meaty end.

Place the ribs together, fat side touching. Using a heavy needle and string, tie the ends of the racks neatly together.

Stuffed Crown Roast of Lamb

1 ready-to-cook crown roast of lamb
Salt and freshly ground pepper to taste
1 medium-size eggplant, about 1 pound

1. Preheat the oven to 450 degrees.

2. Place the crown roast, meaty side down, on a round, shallow baking dish. Sprinkle the inside with salt and pepper.

3. Trim off the ends of the eggplant and pare away the skin. Cut the eggplant into ½-inch cubes.

4. Heat the oil in a large skillet and add the onion. Cook

briefly and add the eggplant. Cook, stirring, for about 5 minutes and add the garlic. Add the ground lamb and beef and cook, stirring and chopping down with the side of a heavy metal spoon to break up any lumps. Cook for about 5 minutes, or until the meat loses its raw look. Remove from the heat and spoon into a mixing bowl and let cool. Add ½ cup of the bread crumbs, egg and parsley. Blend well.

5. Stuff the center of the crown roast with the filling and sprinkle with remaining 2 tablespoons bread crumbs. Brush the outside of the roast with oil. Dribble a little oil on top.

6. Bake for 30 minutes, or longer if you wish the lamb to be medium- or well-done. Pour off the fat, taking care the roast does not slide off. Add the butter and return the roast to the oven for 1 minute. Add the chicken broth. Stir to dissolve the brown particles. Serve carved lamb with filling.

Yield: 6 to 8 servings.

2	tablespoons olive oil
1	cup finely chopped onion
1	teaspoon finely chopped garlic
¾	pound ground lamb
¼	pound ground beef
½	cup plus 2 tablespoons fresh bread crumbs
1	egg
¼	cup finely chopped parsley
2	tablespoons peanut, vegetable or corn oil
2	tablespoons butter
¼	cup fresh or canned chicken broth

Roast Stuffed Shoulder of Lamb

1. Preheat the oven to 400 degrees.

2. Spread the boned shoulder of lamb fat side up on a flat surface. Sprinkle with salt and pepper.

3. Chop the mushrooms finely or process them in a food processor. They must be finely chopped but not pasty. There should be about 2 cups.

4. Heat the butter in a skillet and add the onion, shallots and garlic. Cook briefly, stirring, until wilted and add the chopped mushrooms, salt, pepper and lemon juice. Cook for about 5 minutes, stirring, and add the bread crumbs. Stir and remove from the heat. Spoon and scrape into a mixing bowl. Add the parsley and thyme.

5. Spread the filling onto and over the opened-up shoulder of lamb. Carefully roll the meat like a jelly roll to enclose the filling. This will be a bit tricky for the filling will spill out. Push it back in as neatly as possible. Tie the roast in several places with string.

6. Brush the roast with oil and place it fat side up in a small roasting pan. Surround it with the onion and carrot halves. Place in the oven and bake for 1 hour to 1 hour and 15 minutes.

7. Remove the roast and place the pan over moderate heat. Add the chicken broth and bring to the boil. Discard the onion and carrot. Untie the roast and slice it. Serve with the pan gravy.

Yield: 8 or more servings.

1	boned shoulder of lamb, about 3½ pounds
	Salt and freshly ground pepper to taste
½	pound fresh mushrooms
1	tablespoon butter
1	cup finely minced onion
1	tablespoon finely minced shallots
1	clove garlic, finely minced
	Juice of ½ lemon
1	cup fine, fresh bread crumbs
2	tablespoons finely chopped parsley
¼	teaspoon fresh or dried thyme
1	tablespoon peanut, vegetable or corn oil
1	onion, peeled
1	carrot, trimmed, peeled and split in half lengthwise
½	cup fresh or canned chicken broth

Breast of Lamb à la Francaise

2 to 2½ pounds breast of lamb
with bones, or lamb riblets
Salt and freshly ground
pepper to taste
1 cup fresh bread crumbs
1 tablespoon finely chopped
shallots
1 tablespoon finely chopped
parsley
1 clove garlic, minced
½ teaspoon chopped rosemary

1. Preheat the oven to 450 degrees.
2. Have most of the fat trimmed from the top of the lamb breast. The breast should preferably be in one or two pieces and not cut into ribs.
3. Place the pieces of lamb, meaty side down, on a baking dish and sprinkle with salt and pepper. Place the lamb in the oven and bake for 30 minutes. Turn and bake for 15 or 20 minutes. Turn again and pour off the fat that has accumulated.
4. Combine the remaining ingredients and blend well. The lamb should be meaty side up. Sprinkle it with the bread crumb mixture and continue baking for 15 to 20 minutes. The crumbs should be appetizingly brown. Cut into pieces.

Yield: 4 servings.

Côtes d'Agneau à l'Anglaise   *(Breaded lamb chops)*

6 loin lamb chops, each about 2
inches thick
½ cup flour
1 egg
1 tablespoon water
Salt and freshly ground
pepper
5 tablespoons plus 1 teaspoon
peanut, vegetable or corn oil
1 cup fine, fresh bread crumbs
3 tablespoons butter

1. Trim off almost all the fat from each chop. Dredge the chops lightly on both sides in flour.
2. Combine the egg, water, salt, pepper and 1 teaspoon of oil in a flat dish. Dip the lamb chops in the mixture and then in bread crumbs to coat both sides. Pat lightly with the flat side of a knife to help the crumbs adhere.
3. Heat the remaining oil in a skillet large enough to hold the chops and add 1 tablespoon of butter. When very hot, add the chops and cook over moderately low heat for about 8 minutes. Turn and cook for about 15 minutes. Transfer to hot plates. Pour off the fat from the skillet and add the remaining 2 tablespoons of butter. Cook until hazelnut brown and pour equal portions of the butter over each chop.

Yield: 6 servings.

Crepinettes d'Agneau   *(Lamb patties)*

1½ pounds ground lamb
2 cups fine, fresh bread
crumbs
1 cup milk
½ cup finely minced onion
¼ teaspoon finely chopped
juniper berries
Salt and freshly ground
pepper to taste

1. Put the lamb in a mixing bowl. Combine the crumbs and milk and let stand briefly. Add this to the lamb. Add the onion, juniper berries, salt and pepper. Blend well.
2. Divide the mixture into 10 portions and shape each portion into a round patty, each 3 or 4 inches in diameter. It may help if you shape the meat with fingers dampened in cold water. If caul fat is available, wrap each patty in a small rectangle of it.

3. Heat half the butter in one large or two smaller skillets and add the patties. Cook for about 3 minutes on one side and turn. Cook for about 5 minutes on the other side. Pour off the fat from the skillet and add the vinegar. Cook and add the remaining butter. Pour this over the patties and serve.

Yield: 5 servings.

Note: Caul fat is available in many butcher shops as well as in Chinese markets.

Caul fat (see note), optional
6 tablespoons butter
1 tablespoon red wine vinegar

Tori Keema *(Spiced ground lamb Indian-style)*

1. The lamb may be cooked in a skillet or wok, but preferably in a wok over a high flame.

2. Crush the coriander and cumin seeds separately. Crush them until they are coarse-fine but not pulverized.

3. Heat the butter in the wok or skillet and, when it is hot but not brown, add the lamb, stirring to break up any lumps in the meat. Cook over high heat, stirring and turning the meat constantly. It will give up a good deal of liquid and some fat. Cook the meat until it loses its raw red color. Drain quickly and return it to the wok.

4. Add the tomato paste, crushed seeds, ginger and garlic, tossing and stirring to blend well. Add the yogurt, stirring and tossing constantly. Add salt and pepper to taste and pepper flakes. Cook, stirring constantly, for about 5 minutes. If the lamb becomes too dry, add a little more yogurt. When ready, stir in the chopped fresh coriander.

5. Serve spooned over hot, steamed, halved zucchini. Serve one or two pieces of zucchini per person. Serve with yogurt and onion relish and chutney.

Yield: 6 or more servings.

Note: To toast the coriander and cumin seeds, put them in a small skillet and cook over moderate heat, stirring and shaking the skillet. Cook until they give off a slight aroma and are lightly browned but not burnt.

1 teaspoon toasted coriander seeds (see note)
1 teaspoon toasted cumin seeds
3 tablespoons butter
2 pounds ground lean lamb
3 tablespoons tomato paste
2 teaspoons finely chopped fresh ginger, or use half the amount powdered dry ginger
2 teaspoons finely chopped garlic
1 cup plain yogurt
Salt and freshly ground pepper
½ teaspoon hot red pepper flakes, or chopped fresh hot green or red pepper
1 tablespoon chopped fresh coriander
Yogurt and onion relish (see recipe below)

Yogurt and onion relish

1. Spoon the yogurt into a small bowl.

2. Thinly slice the onion. Bring enough water to the boil to cover the onion slices when added. Drop in the onion slices. Stir and remove from the heat.

3. Drain immediately in a small sieve and run under cold running water until chilled. Drain once more.

4. Add the onion, salt to taste and cumin to the yogurt. Chill. Serve with Indian foods as a side dish.

Yield: About 2 cups.

1 cup plain yogurt
1 onion, about ¼ pound, peeled
Salt
½ teaspoon roasted, crushed cumin seeds (see note from tori keema recipe)

Turkish-style Grilled Lamb on Skewers

1 pound ground lamb
  Salt and freshly ground
  pepper
1 small egg, lightly beaten
1 small onion
  Oil
¾ cup yogurt
1 clove garlic, finely minced
4 slices hot buttered toast
3 tablespoons hot melted butter
1 teaspoon paprika

1. Prepare a charcoal grill. The grill should be placed about 4 inches above the hot coals.

2. In a mixing bowl combine the lamb, 2 tablespoons salt, pepper and egg. Grate the onion and squeeze it through cheesecloth to make 1 tablespoon of juice. Add it to the lamb. lamb.

3. Divide the mixture into 4 portions and roll each portion out into a sausage shape. It helps if the hands are dampened lighty with water before shaping. Brush the lamb rolls with oil and run one wooden skewer through the center of each roll, lengthwise.

4. Meanwhile, blend the yogurt, garlic, salt and pepper to taste.

5. Grill, turning often, until the lamb is cooked through. Arrange one roll on a slice of toast.

6. Spoon equal amounts of sauce over the lamb rolls and pour melted butter over this. Sprinkle with paprika and serve.

Yield: 4 servings.

Braised Lamb Shanks, Greek-style

6 meaty lamb shanks, about 6¼
  pounds
  Salt and freshly ground
  pepper
1 large onion, halved and thinly
  sliced, about 2 cups
2 cloves garlic, finely minced
2 teaspoons dried, crushed
  oregano
2 green peppers, cored, seeded
  and cut into 2-inch cubes
½ pound fresh tomatoes, cored
  and cut into large cubes,
  about 3 cups
1 eggplant, about 1 pound,
  trimmed and cut into 1½-inch
  cubes
3 zucchini, about ¾ pound,
  halved and cut into 1-inch
  lengths
3 sprigs fresh mint

1. Preheat the oven to 400 degrees.

2. There will probably be a meaty flap attached to each shank. Attach this neatly onto the shank with string. Sprinkle the shanks with salt and pepper to taste. Arrange close together in one layer in a large baking dish. Place in the oven and bake for 30 minutes. Turn the shanks and bake for 15 minutes longer.

3. Scatter the onion, garlic, oregano, peppers, tomato, eggplant, zucchini and mint sprigs over the top of the shanks. Sprinkle with salt and pepper to taste. Continue baking for 30 minutes.

4. Reduce the heat to 350 degrees. Continue baking for 15 minutes or longer until shanks are fork-tender.

Yield: 6 servings.

Lamb with Scallions

1. Place the lamb on a flat surface and, using a sharp knife, cut it against the grain into ¼-inch thick slices. If desired, the lamb may be partly frozen to facilitate slicing.

2. Place the slices in a mixing bowl and add the salt and egg whites. Stir in a circular motion until the whites become a bit bubbly. Stir in 1½ tablespoons cornstarch and 1½ tablespoons oil. Refrigerate, preferably overnight, or for at least 1 hour.

3. Trim the scallions at the white tips, but otherwise leave them whole. Flatten them by pounding lightly with the flat side of a cleaver or heavy knife. Cut the scallions on the diagonal into 1-inch lengths. There should be about 4 cups. Set aside.

4. Chop the garlic coarsely. Set aside.

5. Combine the wine, remaining 1 tablespoon of cornstarch blended with the water, the soy sauce, monosodium glutamate, sugar, vinegar, sesame oil and chicken broth. Stir to blend and set aside.

6. Heat the 4 cups of oil in a wok or skillet and, when it is almost smoking, add the lamb, stirring to separate the slices. Cook, stirring constantly, for a total of 45 seconds, no longer, and drain the meat. Drain the wok completely.

7. Heat the remaining 2 tablespoons of oil in the wok and, when it is very hot, add the scallions and garlic and cook, stirring and tossing, for about 30 seconds. Add the lamb, stirring, and the vinegar mixture. Cook, tossing and stirring, until piping hot and slightly thickened. Serve hot.

Yield: 4 to 8 servings.

1¼	pounds very lean lamb, cut from the leg in one piece
¼	teaspoon salt
2	small egg whites
2½	tablespoons cornstarch
4	cups plus 3½ tablespoons peanut, vegetable or corn oil
30	scallions
3	large cloves garlic
2	tablespoons shao hsing wine, or dry sherry
2	tablespoons water
3	tablespoons soy sauce
⅛	teaspoon monosodium glutamate, optional
½	teaspoon sugar
1	tablespoon red wine vinegar
½	teaspoon sesame oil
⅓	cup fresh or canned chicken broth

Hunan Lamb

This is perhaps the most delectable dish of many prepared in our kitchen by Chef Tsung Ting Wang, conceivably the most successful Chinese chef in the United States. It is a spicy, long-cooked casserole dish, which makes it ideal in Chinese menu planning. Chef Wang, of the Shun Lee Palace and Shun Lee Dynasty restaurants in New York, planned a twelve-course banquet around it. But with a cold appetizer, a hot soup, and one or two stir-fry dishes, it could be the center of a less ambitious but nonetheless outstanding Chinese meal.

3 pounds lean leg of lamb
½ cup peanut oil
12 cloves garlic, crushed
12 hot dried red chili peppers
1 1-inch cube fresh ginger, thinly sliced
2 scallions, cut into 2-inch lengths
½ pound rock sugar (available in Chinese groceries and at times in supermarkets)
2 tablespoons chili paste with garlic (available in bottles in Chinese groceries)
¼ cup dark soy sauce
2 teaspoons salt
1 tablespoon monosodium glutamate, optional
2¼ cups (1½ bottles) beer

1. Cut the lamb into 2-inch cubes.

2. Bring to the boil enough water to cover the lamb. Add lamb and cook for about 3 minutes, stirring occasionally. Drain quickly and run under cold water until thoroughly chilled throughout. Drain.

3. Heat the oil in a wok or skillet and add the garlic. Cook for about 10 seconds and add the chili peppers and ginger. Cook over high heat until garlic and chili peppers are dark brown. Add the scallions and cook, stirring, for about 20 seconds. Add the lamb and cook, stirring, for about 1 minute. Add the rock sugar, chili paste with garlic, soy sauce, salt, monosodium glutamate, if desired, and stir to blend. Transfer the mixture to a casserole and pour in the beer.

4. Cover the casserole and cook until lamb is tender, 45 minutes to an hour.

Yield: 6 to 12 servings.

Roast Loin of Pork with Mustard

1 4-pound loin of pork with bone
Salt and freshly ground pepper
¼ pound caul fat, available in butcher shops or Chinese markets
½ cup imported mustard, such as Dijon or Düsseldorf
6 sprigs fresh thyme, or 1 teaspoon dried
1 onion, about ½ pound
24 very small white onions, peeled
¼ cup water

1. Preheat the oven to 400 degrees.

2. Using a sharp knife, carefully trim away most but not all of the fat from the loin of pork. Sprinkle the pork with salt and pepper to taste.

3. Open up the sheet of caul fat on a flat surface. Place the pork, bone side down, in the center of the caul fat. Smear the mustard all over the pork. Arrange the thyme sprigs at various points over the pork. Or sprinkle with dried thyme. Bring up the edges of the caul fat to enclose the roast completely.

4. Place the roast, bone side down, in a roasting pan and bake, uncovered, for 30 minutes. Split the onion in half and thinly slice it. Scatter the slices around the pork. Arrange the small white onions around the roast.

5. Reduce the oven heat to 375 degrees and bake for 45 minutes. Cover loosely with foil and cook for 15 minutes longer.

6. Remove the foil and cover the roast with a heavy lid. Reduce the oven heat to 350 degrees and bake for 30 minutes.

7. Remove the roast, leaving the juices in the pan. Remove the caul fat from the pork and transfer the roast to a serving dish. Use a slotted spoon and remove the small white onions. Spoon them around the roast as garnish.

8. Put the pan juices through a food mill or sieve into a

saucepan. Skim off the fat. Bring the juices to the boil and add the water. Bring to the boil again. Slice the roast and spoon a little of the sauce over each slice.

Yield: 6 to 8 servings.

Roast Pork with Garlic

1. Preheat the oven to 400 degrees.

2. Cut each clove of garlic into 8 slivers. Make little holes near the bone end of the meat and in the fat. Insert the garlic slivers in the holes. Sprinkle the roast with salt and pepper to taste and rub all over with oil. Arrange the roast, fat side down, in a roasting pan. Add the onion and sprinkle with thyme. Bake for 30 minutes and turn the roast fat side up. Baste well with the pan drippings. Bake for 45 minutes.

3. Pour off the fat from the roasting pan and add the chicken broth, stirring to dissolve the brown particles that cling to the bottom and sides of the pan. Return the roast to the oven and reduce the oven heat to 375 degrees. Continue roasting for about 45 minutes longer.

4. Serve the pan juices separately with the carved roast.

Yield: 6 to 8 servings.

3 large cloves garlic
1 5- to 6-pound center cut pork roast
Salt and freshly ground pepper to taste
1 tablespoon peanut, vegetable or corn oil
1 small onion, peeled and quartered
1 teaspoon thyme
1 cup fresh or canned chicken broth

Confit de Porc *(Pork loin cooked with spices)*

1. If there is a rind on the fat back, slice it off and discard. Grind the fat back, using the fine blade of a meat grinder. You can also grind the fat back in a food processor. Put the ground fat back in a deep, heavy kettle and cook it, stirring with a wooden spoon as it melts. Continue cooking until it is completely rendered of fat. Strain the fat.

2. Using a long, sharp, thin knife, make an incision dead center inside the pork loin. This is for stuffing the loin with spices. A sharpening steel of the sort used for sharpening knives is excellent for this. Make small incisions on the outside of the loin.

3. Put the rosemary, sage and garlic on a flat surface and chop finely. Add salt and pepper.

4. Rub the outside of the loin with the spice and garlic mixture. Push as much of it as possible inside the center incision, using the sharpening steel or another instrument.

5. Fit the loin of pork into a baking dish in which it fits

5 pounds fat back
1 5-pound center cut of pork, boned (about 3 pounds boned weight)
1/4 cup rosemary
1 tablespoon sage
1 large clove garlic
Salt and freshly ground pepper to taste

snugly without crowding. Pour the melted fat over it. The fat should barely cover the loin. Put the loin on the top of the stove and bring the fat to the boil. Let it simmer, uncovered, for 50 to 60 minutes, taking proper precautions that the fat does not catch fire.

6. Let cool. The pork is now ready to be removed from the liquid fat and served sliced. Or it may be kept in the fat, which will harden as it cools. It will keep for months or even a year if it is properly stored in a very cool spot or refrigerated. Preserved pork is also excellent if stored in olive oil. It improves on aging. Before serving, of course, the fat must be melted and the meat removed.

Yield: 16 to 20 servings.

Pork Braisé à l'Ivrogne *(Pork in red wine)*

1　5-pound loin of pork
1　clove garlic, peeled
½　teaspoon paprika
2　cups coarsely chopped onion
1　cup coarsely chopped leeks, optional
¾　cup carrots, cut into rounds
1　bay leaf, crushed
½　tablespoon rosemary
1　teaspoon coriander
　　Salt and freshly ground pepper to taste
2　sprigs fresh thyme, or 1 teaspoon dried
1　bottle dry red wine, preferably Burgundy
3　sprigs fresh parsley
¼　cup flour
½　cup fresh or canned beef broth
¼　teaspoon nutmeg
2　tablespoons butter

1. Rub the pork all over with the clove of garlic. Rub it with paprika and place it in a deep casserole or Dutch oven. Add the onion, leeks, if desired, carrots, bay leaf, rosemary, coriander, salt, pepper, thyme, wine and parsley. Cover and let stand in the refrigerator for 24 hours, turning the meat occasionally.

2. Preheat the oven to 400 degrees.

3. Remove the meat from the marinade. Strain the liquid and reserve both the liquid and the vegetables.

4. Heat a deep casserole or Dutch oven and place the pork loin, fat side down, in it. Cook for about 5 minutes until it is sizzled well. Place the pork in the oven uncovered and bake for 30 minutes. Remove the pork and pour off the fat.

5. Return the pork, fat side up, and scatter the vegetables around it. Return the pork to the oven and bake for 10 minutes uncovered. Sprinkle the vegetables with flour and bake for 5 minutes longer. Stir in the wine marinade and beef broth and cover. Bake for 1 hour.

6. Remove the meat and keep covered. Strain the sauce, pressing to extract as much liquid from the solids as possible. Skim off the fat. Pour the sauce into a saucepan and reduce it over moderate heat for about 20 minutes. Add the nutmeg and swirl in the butter. Slice the meat and serve it with the sauce.

Yield: 8 or more servings.

Pork Chops with Mustard and Green Peppercorns

1. Sprinkle the chops on both sides with salt and pepper to taste. Blend the flour and paprika and dredge the chops with the mixture. Heat the oil in a heavy skillet and brown the chops for about 5 minutes to a side.

2. Pour off the fat from the skillet and sprinkle the chops with the carrots, onion and garlic. Add the bay leaf and thyme. Add the wine and chicken broth and cover. Cook over low heat for about 1 hour. Remove the chops.

3. Stir the mustard into the pan drippings. Bring to the boil but do not boil. Add the peppercorns, capers and parsley. Serve hot over the chops.

Yield: 8 servings.

8	center-cut pork chops, about ½ pound each
	Salt and freshly ground pepper
½	cup flour
1	teaspoon paprika
1	tablespoon peanut, vegetable or corn oil
⅔	cup finely diced carrots
⅔	cup finely diced onion
1	clove garlic, finely chopped
1	bay leaf
1	sprig fresh thyme, or ½ teaspoon dried
1	cup dry white wine
1	cup fresh or canned chicken broth
1	tablespoon imported mustard, such as Dijon or Düsseldorf
1	tablespoon green peppercorns
2	tablespoons capers
1	tablespoon finely chopped parsley

Herb stuffed Pork Chops

1. Preheat the oven to 350 degrees.

2. Open the chops for stuffing "butterfly" fashion. To do this, use a sharp knife and slice the chops through the center down to the bone, top to bottom. Open them up and, using a flat mallet, pound the opened-up flaps to flatten lightly. Do not break the meat, however, in pounding.

3. Drop the pistachios, if used, into boiling water. Let stand a few seconds and drain. Rub off the skins. Set the pistachio meats aside.

4. Cook the ground pork in a saucepan, stirring, until it loses its red color. Add the onion and mushrooms and cook, stirring. Chop the garlic with the parsley and marjoram and add to the pork mixture. Stir in the bread crumbs. Chop the chicken liver and add it, stirring. Add salt and pepper to taste and the pistachios. Cook briefly and remove from the heat. Let cool. Add the egg and blend well.

5. Sprinkle the opened-up chops with salt and pepper to taste. Add equal amounts of the filling to the chops and bring

4	loin, center-cut pork chops, each about 1 inch thick
¼	cup peeled pistachio nuts, optional
¼	pound ground pork
¼	cup finely chopped onion
1	cup thinly sliced mushrooms
1	small clove garlic, peeled
3	tablespoons parsley
½	teaspoon dried marjoram or sage
¼	cup fine, fresh bread crumbs
1	raw chicken liver
	Salt and freshly ground pepper
1	egg, beaten
	Flour for dredging
1	tablespoon butter
1	cup fresh or canned chicken broth

the flaps together to enclose the stuffing. Skewer the ends of each chop with toothpicks or sew with string.

6. Dredge the chops on all sides in flour seasoned with salt and pepper. Heat the butter in a large heavy skillet and brown the chops well on one side, for 5 minutes or longer. Turn and brown on the other side. Cover loosely with aluminum foil.

7. Place the skillet in the oven and bake for 1 hour. Remove the chops briefly and add half the chicken broth to the skillet, stirring it into the brown particles on the bottom of the skillet. Return the chops to the skillet. Cover with foil and bake for 15 minutes longer. Turn the chops in the pan glaze, then transfer them to a hot serving dish. Add the remaining broth to the skillet and cook, stirring, to dissolve the brown particles remaining. Strain this over the chops.

Yield: 4 servings.

Pork Chops Esterhazy

8 thick loin pork chops, about ½ pound each
Salt and freshly ground pepper
2 tablespoons peanut, vegetable or corn oil
½ cup chopped carrots
½ cup chopped celery
1 cup chopped onion
2 tablespoons finely minced garlic
½ teaspoon dried thyme
1 bay leaf
6 sprigs parsley
½ cup dry white wine
1 cup fresh or canned chicken broth
1 tablespoon tomato paste
1 tablespoon imported mustard, such as Dijon or Düsseldorf
1 cup sour cream
¼ cup drained capers

1. Sprinkle the chops with salt and pepper to taste. Heat the oil in a large skillet and add the chops. Brown on both sides, for about 10 minutes each side. Pour off the fat.

2. Scatter the carrots, celery, onion, garlic, thyme, bay leaf and parsley around the chops. Cover and cook for 10 minutes. Add the wine and the chicken broth blended with tomato paste. Cook for 45 minutes and turn the chops. Continue cooking for about 45 minutes, or until the chops are quite tender.

3. Remove the chops and keep them warm. Add the mustard and sour cream and stir. Bring just to the boil, but do not boil or the sour cream will curdle. Put the sauce through a fine sieve, pressing down with a wooden spoon to extract the liquid flavorings from the vegetables. Add this to a small saucepan and stir in the capers. Add salt to taste and reheat gently without boiling. Spoon this over the chops and serve hot.

Yield: 8 servings.

Pork Chops in Mustard and Cream Sauce

1. Preheat the oven to 300 degrees.

2. Place the chops in a baking dish and pour the wine over them. Let stand for an hour or so. Remove the chops and pat dry. Dredge them lightly in a mixture of flour, salt and pepper. Heat the oil in a large skillet and brown the chops on both sides, for about 4 minutes to a side. Transfer the chops to a heavy casserole or Dutch oven and sprinkle with salt, pepper and thyme or sage.

3. Melt the butter in a saucepan and add the garlic. Stir without browning and pour on top of the chops. Place the chops in the oven and cover. Bake for 1½ hours, basting frequently.

4. Meanwhile, pour the cream into a saucepan and boil, uncovered, until reduced to ⅔ cup. Combine the mustard and tomato purée in a mixing bowl and beat with a whisk. Gradually add the reduced cream, beating well. Spoon the sauce over the chops and reduce the oven heat to 250 degrees. Cover and bake for 30 minutes longer. Garnish with the slivered cornichons and watercress.

Yield: 6 servings.

6 loin pork chops, each about 1 inch thick
½ cup dry white wine
¾ cup flour
Salt and freshly ground pepper
¼ cup peanut, vegetable or corn oil
1 teaspoon finely chopped dried thyme or sage
2 tablespoons butter
4 cloves garlic, peeled and split in half
2 cups heavy cream
1 tablespoon powdered mustard
2 tablespoons tomato purée
½ cup thinly slivered cornichons
Watercress for garnish

Breaded Pork Cutlets

1. Season the pork cutlets with salt and pepper. Beat the eggs with the milk and add salt and pepper to taste. Coat the pork cutlets with egg and dip in bread crumbs. Place the cutlets on a flat surface and tap lightly with the flat side of a heavy knife to help crumbs adhere.

2. Heat about ¼ inch oil in a heavy skillet and cook the pork cutlets until golden brown on all sides and cooked through. Serve with lemon wedges, or use in following recipe for pork cutlets parmigiana.

Yield: 4 servings.

1½ pounds boneless pork cutlets, about 8 slices
Salt and freshly ground pepper
2 eggs
3 tablespoons milk
2 cups fresh bread crumbs
Olive oil
Lemon wedges

Pork Cutlets Parmigiana

1½ pounds cooked, breaded
pork cutlets (see preceding
recipe)
1½ cups tomato sauce
4 thin slices mozzarella cheese
Grated Romano or Parmesan
cheese

1. Preheat the oven to 400 degrees.
2. Prepare the pork cutlets. Spoon a little sauce over the bottom of a flat baking dish. Add the cutlets in one layer. Spoon more tomato sauce on top and cover with mozzarella cheese and the remaining sauce. Sprinkle with Romano or Parmesan cheese and bake until piping hot and the cheese is melted.
   Yield: 4 servings.

Braciole di Maiale Ripiena   *(Stuffed pork cutlets)*

If we were to single out the most agreeable meal we sampled in Rome on a recent trip, it would be a two-hour lunch taken at a relatively small and relatively unknown regional restaurant called the Colline Emiliane, on Via Avignonesi. It is a family-style place totally without pretense, with the owner as principal chef and his wife as pasta maker. The pasta, incidentally, was the best we've sampled anywhere.

The main course was braciole di maiale ripiena, boneless rolled pork cutlets stuffed with cheese and ham, breaded and sautéed. It was a truly admirable dish and we hastened to duplicate it in our own kitchen.

8 lean, boneless pork cutlets
taken from the loin, about 1½
pounds trimmed weight
Salt and freshly ground
pepper to taste
¼ pound thinly sliced prosciutto
¼ pound fontina or Gruyère
cheese
⅓ cup flour
2 eggs
2 tablespoons water
1½ cups bread crumbs
Oil for deep frying
Lemon wedges

1. The pork cutlets should be trimmed of all fat. Place them, one at a time, on a flat surface and pound them with a flat mallet or the back of a heavy skillet. Sprinkle one side with salt and pepper.
2. Finely chop the prosciutto. Cut the cheese into ¼-inch cubes. Blend the prosciutto and cheese. Divide the mixture into 8 equal portions and shape each into a ball.
3. Place 1 ball of prosciutto and cheese in the center of each flattened piece of pork. Fold up the bottom of each pork cutlet to partly enclose the filling. Bring the two outside edges over, envelope-fashion. Finally, fold over the top to totally enclose the filling. Press down the seams to seal.
4. Dredge each package in flour. Beat the eggs with water and drop the packages in this. Finally, dredge all over with bread crumbs.
5. Add oil to a depth of about 1 inch in a large, heavy skillet. When hot, add the packages and cook until brown, turning as necessary until cooked through, about 6 minutes. Drain on paper toweling. Serve with lemon wedges.
   Yield: 4 to 8 servings.

Spinach, Pork and Liver Loaf

1. Preheat the oven to 375 degrees.
2. Place the pork in a mixing bowl and set aside.
3. Drop the spinach into a large quantity of boiling water and let boil for about 1 minute. Drain well and run under cold running water. Squeeze to extract most of the moisture. Chop the spinach and add it to the meat.
4. Heat the butter in a saucepan and cook the onion and garlic until the onion is wilted. Let cool slightly and add this to the meat.
5. Add the remaining ingredients and blend well. Pour the mixture into a standard loaf pan (8½- x 4½- x 2½-inches). Smooth it over. Place the pan in a baking dish and pour boiling water around the pan to a depth of about 1½ inches. Bake from 1 to 1¼ hours. Serve hot or cold.

Yield: 8 or more servings.

1	pound ground pork
¾	pound cleaned spinach, or 1 10-ounce package
2	tablespoons butter
1	cup finely chopped onion
1	clove garlic, finely minced
¾	pound chicken livers, chopped
2	egg yolks
1	whole egg
1	tablespoon imported mustard, such as Dijon or Düsseldorf
1	cup fine, fresh bread crumbs Salt and freshly ground pepper
½	teaspoon ground allspice

Bitokes de Porc au Karvi   *(Pork patties with caraway)*

1. Place the pork in a mixing bowl and add the bread crumbs, salt and pepper to taste and the caraway. Blend well with the fingers.
2. Divide the mixture into 12 portions of approximately the same weight. Using the fingers, shape the portions into neat, round, flat patties. Arrange on a baking dish and refrigerate until ready to cook.
3. Heat 2 tablespoons butter and add the onion and garlic. Cook, stirring, until wilted and add the basil, bay leaf, thyme and tomatoes. Bring to the boil and add salt to taste. Simmer for about 20 minutes and stir in 2 more tablespoons of butter.
4. When ready to cook, heat the oil and remaining tablespoon butter in a skillet. Brown the patties on one side, for about 3 minutes. Turn and brown on the other. Continue cooking until done.
5. Serve hot with the tomato sauce spooned over.

Yield: 6 servings.

2	pounds ground pork
1	cup fine, fresh bread crumbs Salt and freshly ground pepper
1	teaspoon crushed caraway seeds, or ½ teaspoon ground caraway
5	tablespoons butter
2	cups chopped onion
1	clove garlic, finely minced
6	fresh basil leaves, or 1 teaspoon crushed dried leaves
1	bay leaf
1	sprig fresh thyme, or ½ teaspoon dried
2	pounds fresh tomatoes, peeled, cored and cubed, about 4 cups, or use an equal amount of crushed, canned imported tomatoes
3	tablespoons peanut, vegetable or corn oil

Braised Pork with Sauerkraut

The braised pork:

3½ pounds boneless pork, cut
 into 2-inch cubes
 Salt and freshly ground
 pepper to taste
1 cup chopped onion
2 tablespoons paprika
2 cloves garlic, finely minced
1 bay leaf
½ cup fresh or canned chicken
 broth

The sauerkraut:

3 pounds sauerkraut
1 tablespoon lard
1 cup finely chopped onion
1 clove garlic, finely minced
1 pound tomatoes, peeled and
 cut into 1-inch cubes, about
 2 cups
 Salt and freshly ground
 pepper to taste
1 teaspoon crushed caraway
 seeds
¾ cup Alsatian, Rhine or
 Moselle wine
¾ cup fresh or canned chicken
 broth

1. Preheat the oven to 400 degrees.
2. Sprinkle the pork with salt and pepper. Arrange in one layer in a large roasting pan and place in the oven. Bake uncovered for 30 minutes.
3. Add the chopped onion, paprika, garlic and bay leaf to the pork and stir. Bake uncovered for 15 minutes. Add the ½ cup chicken broth and bake for 30 minutes.
4. Reduce the oven heat to 350 degrees and bake the pork until fork-tender, 20 to 30 minutes.
5. As the pork bakes, cook the sauerkraut.
6. Drain the sauerkraut well, pressing with the hands to remove excess liquid. Use as is or, if you prefer a blander dish, rinse under cold water and drain well, pressing to remove more liquid.
7. Heat the lard in a saucepan and add the onion and garlic. Cook, stirring often, until onion is browned lightly. Add the tomatoes, salt and pepper.
8. Add the sauerkraut, caraway seeds, wine and broth. Cover and cook for about 45 minutes.
9. Make a layer of the hot sauerkraut on a serving dish and spoon the sauce from the pork over it. Spoon the cubes of pork on top and serve immediately. Serve with plain boiled potatoes.
 Yield: 6 to 8 servings.

Brochette de Porc au Romarin *(Rosemary pork en brochette)*

1¾ pounds lean shoulder or loin
 of pork
2 tablespoons peanut,
 vegetable or corn oil
1 tablespoon red wine vinegar
1 teaspoon chopped rosemary
 Salt and freshly ground
 pepper
1 clove garlic, finely minced
 Devil sauce (see recipe
 below)

1. Cut the pork into 1-inch cubes and place them in a mixing bowl. Add all the remaining ingredients except the devil sauce. Stir occasionally until well seasoned.
2. Arrange the cubed pork on 4 to 6 skewers. If wooden skewers are used, it is best if they are soaked for an hour or so in cold water. Cover the tips with foil to prevent burning.
3. Prepare a charcoal fire in a grill. When the coals and grill are properly hot, brush the grill lightly with oil. Arrange the skewered pork on the grill and cook, turning as necessary, until done, for 30 minutes or longer. Serve with devil sauce.
 Yield: 4 to 6 servings.

Combine all the ingredients in a saucepan and bring to the boil, stirring. Serve hot.

Yield: About ½ cup.

Devil sauce

⅓ cup commercially prepared Escoffier sauce diable, available in fine food specialty shops
1 teaspoon imported mustard, such as Dijon or Düsseldorf
2 tablespoons heavy cream
1 teaspoon Worcestershire sauce
   Salt and freshly ground pepper

Vietnamese Grilled Pork Patties in Lettuce Leaves

1. Combine all the ingredients for the ground pork in a bowl and blend well with the fingers. Place the bowl briefly in the refrigerator. Do not freeze. The chilling will facilitate shaping the patties.

2. Meanwhile, prepare a charcoal fire.

3. With the fingers and palms, shape the pork into 2-inch balls. Make them all approximately the same size. Maneuver each ball into a miniature football shape, approximately 3 inches long. Chill until ready to use.

4. Run a skewer lengthwise through each patty and grill, turning frequently, until browned and cooked through. Serve immediately. The technique for eating the patties is as follows: Open a lettuce leaf and add a sprig of coriander, 1 or 2 mint leaves, chopped scallion and a small spoonful of rice. Add the hot pork patty and wrap the leaf around. Using the fingers, dip the "package" into the nuoc mam sauce and eat with the fingers.

Yield: 4 to 8 servings.

The pork:

2 pounds ground pork
2 cloves garlic, finely chopped or mashed between wax paper
1 teaspoon grated fresh ginger
1 tablespoon shao hsing wine, or dry sherry
2 tablespoons light soy sauce
2 tablespoons peanut, vegetable or corn oil
1 teaspoon sugar
   Salt to taste

The wrapping and garnishes:

24 large Boston lettuce leaves, well rinsed and patted dry
1 cup loosely packed fresh coriander
1 cup loosely packed fresh mint leaves
1 cup chopped scallions
2 cups raw rice cooked without salt until tender and cooled to room temperature
   Nuoc mam sauce (see recipe page 654)

Albondigas   (Mexican meatballs in tomato and chili sauce)

1 pound twice-ground pork
1 egg
1 teaspoon dried oregano
½ teaspoon ground cumin
  Salt and freshly ground
  pepper
1 small zucchini
3 tablespoons finely chopped
  onion
2 cloves garlic, finely minced
3 cups drained imported
  canned tomatoes
2 or 3 chipotle chilies, available
  in tins in Mexican and
  Spanish stores
2 tablespoons peanut,
  vegetable or corn oil
½ cup fresh or canned chicken
  broth
¼ cup finely chopped fresh
  coriander

1. Place the pork in a mixing bowl. Beat the egg, and add the oregano and cumin. Stir and add this mixture to the pork. Add salt and pepper to taste.

2. Trim off the ends of the zucchini. Cut the zucchini into thin slices. Stack the slices and cut them into strips. Cut the strips into fine cubes. There should be about ¾ cup. Add the zucchini, onion and garlic to the meat. Blend well with the hands. Using lightly oiled fingers and palms, shape the mixture into 18 meatballs.

3. Combine the tomatoes and chilies in the container of an electric blender. Blend thoroughly.

4. Heat the oil in a Dutch oven or casserole. Add the tomato mixture. Add salt and pepper to taste and cook, stirring, for about 5 minutes. Add the chicken broth and bring to the boil. Add the meatballs one at a time and bring to the boil. Cover closely and simmer for about 45 minutes. Serve sprinkled with chopped coriander. Serve with hot rice.

Yield: 4 servings.

Lion's Head

8 dried black mushrooms
1¼ pounds ground pork
20 water chestnuts, finely diced
1 teaspoon finely minced fresh
  ginger
3 scallions, chopped
1 teaspoon finely minced
  garlic
  Grated rind of 1 orange
¼ teaspoon sesame oil
1 tablespoon shao hsing wine,
  or dry sherry
1 tablespoon light soy sauce
1 teaspoon salt
1 tablespoon cornstarch
  Peanut, vegetable or corn oil
  for deep frying
  Steamed spinach or broccoli,
  optional

1. Place the mushrooms in a mixing bowl and add hot water to cover. Let stand for 20 minutes or longer until softened.

2. Place the pork in a mixing bowl. Drain the mushrooms and squeeze dry. Chop them. Add them to the pork. Add the water chestnuts, ginger, scallions, garlic, grated orange rind, sesame oil, the wine, soy sauce, salt and cornstarch. Mix well and shape into 8 to 12 balls.

3. Heat the oil for deep frying and add the meatballs. Deep fry until crisp and golden on the outside. Drain well. Place the meatballs in a steamer and steam for 20 to 25 minutes. Serve on a bed of spinach or broccoli.

Yield: 8 servings.

Pine Nut Meatballs with Dark Sauce

This is a celestial dish that can be part of a banquet with many Chinese dishes, as Virginia Lee served it in our home. But it is sumptuous enough to stand almost on its own with only one or two other dishes. An added bonus is that it can be made hours in advance of serving.

30 to	40 large mushrooms, about 2½ pounds
8	large leeks (or use 1 bunch of scallions)
1¼	cups pine nuts
2	pounds fat and lean pork, preferably uncured, unsalted bacon
3	whole eggs
2	tablespoons cornstarch
3	tablespoons dark soy sauce
2	tablespoons shao hsing wine, or dry sherry
	Salt to taste
2	teaspoons plus 1½ tablespoons sugar
2	tablespoons finely minced ginger
6 to	8 tablespoons cold water
4	cups peanut, vegetable or corn oil
4	scallions
4	¼-inch thick slices peeled, fresh ginger
3½	cups fresh or canned chicken broth

1. Trim off the mushroom stems level with the bottoms of the caps. Drop the caps into a basin of cold water and set aside. Discard the stems.

2. Trim off the ends of the leeks about 1 inch from the bottom. Discard the ends or use for soups. Split the leeks halfway to the middle and rinse well under cold water to remove sand. Drop into cold water and set aside.

3. Chop the pine nuts until fine. Set aside.

4. Place the meat in a bowl and add 2 eggs, the cornstarch, soy sauce, wine, salt, 2 teaspoons sugar, minced ginger, 6 tablespoons of cold water and the nuts. Work briskly with the fingers in a circular motion. The more you work the meat the better. Work the mixture for a minimum of 10 minutes. Shape the meat into 6 large balls of equal size.

5. Beat the remaining egg and dip the fingers into it. The fingers and palms should be coated with the egg. Pick up 1 meatball at a time and toss it back and forth from one hand to another until it is smooth and coated and somewhat flat like a thick hamburger rather than round.

6. Heat the 4 cups of oil in a wok or skillet and add half the meatballs. Ladle the hot oil over the exposed portions of the balls. Cook for 2 to 3 minutes and turn. Cook for about 2 minutes longer and drain. They should be golden brown. Cook the remaining meatballs in the same way. Remove. Leave the oil in the wok. Transfer the meatballs to a casserole so that they fit snugly in one layer. Tie each of the 4 scallions into loops and add them. Add the sliced ginger.

7. Add the chicken broth and remaining sugar and bring to the boil. Cover and simmer for 2 hours.

8. Meanwhile, heat the oil in the wok and add half the mushrooms cap-side down. Cook, stirring, for about 5 minutes, turning once. Drain. Add remaining mushrooms to the wok and cook in the same way. Add the leeks and cook, turning occasionally so that they cook evenly. Cook for about 6 minutes, until wilted but not brown. Drain and add to mushrooms.

9. Carefully garnish the tops of the meatball casserole with

the leeks and mushrooms. Do not add the liquid that drained from them. Cover and continue cooking until the leeks are tender, about ½ hour or longer. Serve half a meatball per guest.

Yield: 12 servings with other Chinese dishes.

Barbecued Ribs with Ginger Sauce

1 cup ketchup
1 teaspoon freshly grated ginger
4 teaspoons butter
2 tablespoons Worcestershire sauce
3 tablespoons lemon juice
½ teaspoon finely minced garlic
2 tablespoons honey
1 teaspoon ground coriander
1 rack of spareribs, the meatier and smaller the ribs the better
Salt and freshly ground pepper to taste
¼ teaspoon monosodium glutamate, optional

1. Preheat the oven to 350 degrees.

2. In a saucepan combine the ketchup, ginger, butter, Worcestershire sauce, lemon juice, garlic, honey and coriander. Bring to the boil and stir to blend.

3. Place the spareribs on a rack meaty side up and sprinkle with salt and pepper and monosodium glutamate, if desired. Place in the oven and bake for 30 minutes or until nicely browned.

4. Brush the spareribs with a layer of sauce and bake for 15 minutes longer.

5. Turn the spareribs and brush with sauce. Bake for 15 minutes longer and turn. Brush with sauce. Continue baking for 15 to 30 minutes longer, basting as necessary. Serve hot or cold.

Yield: 4 servings.

Chinese-style Barbecued Pork

2 pounds boneless pork loin in one piece
1 scallion, green part and all, chopped
3 thin slices ginger, finely chopped
2 tablespoons plus 2 teaspoons soy sauce
2½ tablespoons hoisin sauce
2 tablespoons shao hsing wine, or dry sherry
8 drops red food coloring
1 teaspoon sesame oil
¼ cup hot water
1 tablespoon honey
Hot mustard (see recipe page 647)

1. Cut the pork into thin slices. Cut the slices into thin strips. Place the strips of pork in a bowl and add the chopped scallion, ginger, 2 tablespoons soy sauce, hoisin sauce, wine, food coloring and sesame oil. Blend well and let stand for at least 2 hours, or overnight.

2. Preheat the oven to 375 degrees.

3. Fit a rack in a shallow roasting pan and arrange the strips of meat on it. Place in the oven and bake for 30 minutes. Turn the strips and continue baking for 30 minutes.

4. Blend the hot water, honey and remaining 2 teaspoons of soy sauce. Brush the strips of pork on all sides with this sauce. Return the meat to the oven and bake for 10 minutes longer. Let cool for at least 15 minutes before serving. Serve hot or cold with hot mustard, barbecue sauce (made with 3 tablespoons ketchup and 1 teaspoon Worcestershire sauce) and/or soy sauce.

Yield: 12 servings with other Chinese dishes.

Barbecued Country Spareribs

1. Prepare the barbecue sauce and let it stand overnight, or for several hours.

2. Put the spareribs in a saucepan and add the water, soy sauce, pepper and marjoram. Bring to the boil and let simmer for about ½ hour, turning the ribs in the liquid so that they cook evenly. Drain the spareribs and discard the liquid. Combine the spareribs with the barbecue sauce and bring to the boil. Let stand until ready to cook. The ribs may be prepared to this point several hours in advance.

3. Preheat the oven to 350 degrees.

4. Reheat the spareribs in the sauce.

5. Spoon and scrape the ribs into a roasting pan or baking dish. Pour the sauce over them and cover. Bake for about 1 hour. Uncover and bake for 15 to 30 minutes longer, basting often.

Yield: 4 to 6 servings.

Country barbecue sauce (see recipe page 654)

4 to 5 pounds country spareribs, cut into 1- or 2-inch pieces
2 cups water
½ cup imported soy sauce
1 tablespoon freshly ground pepper
1 teaspoon dried marjoram

Deviled Pigs' Feet

1. Place the pigs' feet in a kettle and add water to cover, salt, bay leaf, onion, parsley, peppercorns, carrots and celery. Bring to the boil and simmer for about 3 hours, or until the pigs' feet are quite tender. Let stand until cool.

2. Preheat the oven to 400 degrees.

3. Remove the pigs' feet. Blend the 3 tablespoons of mustard with wine, salt and pepper to taste. Brush the pigs' feet with this. Roll the pigs' feet in fresh bread crumbs and arrange them on a rack. Dribble 2 tablespoons of oil over each pigs' foot. Bake for 30 minutes, or until crisp and golden brown. Serve with mustard on the side.

Yield: 4 servings.

4 pigs' feet, preferably large ones
Salt to taste
1 bay leaf
1 small onion, peeled and stuck with 2 cloves
2 sprigs parsley
12 crushed peppercorns
2 carrots, trimmed and scraped
3 ribs celery, rinsed and quartered
3 tablespoons imported mustard, such as Dijon or Düsseldorf
2 tablespoons dry white wine
Freshly ground pepper to taste
2 cups fresh bread crumbs
8 tablespoons peanut, vegetable or corn oil

Philadelphia Scrapple

4	pounds pigs' knuckles
½	pound not-too-lean pork chop with bone
12	cups water
½	pound beef or calf's liver
	Salt to taste
½	teaspoon freshly ground black pepper
2	small, dried, hot red peppers
1	tablespoon leaf sage
⅛	teaspoon grated nutmeg or mace
2½	cups yellow cornmeal

1. Combine the pigs' knuckles, pork chop, water, liver, salt, black pepper, dried red peppers, sage and nutmeg in a kettle. Bring to the boil and simmer, partly covered, for about 2 hours, or until the knuckle meat is fork-tender.

2. Remove the pigs' knuckles and pork and liver from the kettle. Set aside.

3. Strain the cooking liquid and discard the spices. There should be about 11 cups.

4. Remove the bones from the pigs' knuckles and pork chop. Keep all the meat, fat, skin and so on. Put the pieces of knuckle, pork chop, liver and so on into the container of a food processor. Take care that no trace of bone is added. Or grind the mixture in a food grinder. As it is processed or ground, scrape it into a large kettle. Add 8 cups of the reserved cooking liquid and stir to blend. Bring to the boil.

5. Spoon the cornmeal into a bowl. Add the remaining 3 cups of cooking liquid. Blend well with a wire whisk. Add this to the boiling ground mixture, stirring to prevent lumping. Add salt to taste.

6. Place the kettle on a metal pad and let it simmer over low heat for about 30 minutes. Stir often from the bottom. Cornmeal has a tendency to lump and/or stick as it cooks if it is not stirred often.

7. Pour the mixture evenly into two loaf pans (measuring 9- x 5 x 2¾-inches). Let stand until cool. Refrigerate until set. To cook, cut the loaves into ½-inch thick slices. Dredge lightly in flour and sauté in bacon fat or butter.

Yield: 2 loaf pans.

How to Cook a Smithfield, Virginia or Country Ham

1	14- to 16-pound cured Smithfield, Virginia or country ham
40 to	60 whole cloves
½	cup brown sugar

1. Place the ham in a large kettle, roasting pan or basin and add cold water to cover. Soak overnight. The water may be changed often to get rid of excess salt.

2. Preheat the oven to 300 degrees.

3. Drain the ham and trim or scrape off all mold on the "face" side (this is the side opposite the skin side).

4. It is not essential, but you will facilitate carving the ham after cooking if you run a boning or other knife around the contours of the hipbone on the underside of the ham. Run the

knife down deep around the bone, but do not remove the bone at this time. It will be removed after cooking.

5. Place the ham in a roaster with 10 cups of water and cover closely with a lid or heavy-duty aluminum foil. Place in the oven and bake for 20 to 25 minutes to the pound. Remove the ham from the oven. Do not turn off the oven.

6. Using the fingers, pull against the hipbone that was carved around earlier. Run the carving knife around the bone and pull with the fingers to remove.

7. Increase the oven heat to 425 degrees.

8. Slice away the skin from the ham, leaving a thick layer of fat. Using a sharp knife, score the ham at 1-inch intervals, making a diamond-shaped pattern. Stud the fat with 40 to 60 cloves. Sprinkle the surface with the brown sugar and bake for 15 minutes.

Yield: 12 to 20 servings.

How to Cook a Fresh Ham

1. It is not essential, but you will facilitate carving the ham after cooking if you run a boning or other knife around the contour of the hipbone on the underside of the ham. Run the knife down deep around the bone, but do not remove the bone at this time. It will be removed after cooking.

2. Place the ham, skin side up, on a flat surface. Using a very sharp knife, make ¼-inch deep gashes from the butt end to the shank end, cutting through the skin at 1-inch intervals.

3. Place the ham, skin side up, in a roasting pan and add the salt, onion, carrots, garlic, celery, shallots, parsley sprigs, thyme, bay leaf and peppercorns. Pour the wine over and around the ham. Baste ham on top with all the ingredients. Cover closely with aluminum foil.

4. Place in the refrigerator or a cold place and let stand for 24 hours.

5. Preheat the oven to 400 degrees.

6. Remove the ham, but reserve the marinating liquid and vegetables. Put the ham in a roasting pan, skin side up, and place it in the oven. Bake for 45 minutes and reduce the oven heat to 375 degrees. Bake for 15 minutes and add 1 cup of the reserved marinade—liquid and vegetables—to the roasting pan. Start basting and baste often as the roast cooks. As the roast bakes the basting liquid will evaporate. Continue adding

1	16-pound fresh ham (unsmoked and uncured)
2	tablespoons salt
1	cup halved, thinly sliced onion
1	cup thinly sliced carrots
2	cloves garlic, thinly sliced
1	cup coarsely chopped celery
½	cup coarsely chopped shallots
6	parsley sprigs
1	teaspoon dried thyme
1	bay leaf
12	peppercorns
2	bottles (6 cups) dry white wine, preferably Burgundy

the marinade as necessary. Bake for 2 hours and reduce the heat to 350 degrees. Pour the remaining marinade around the meat. Cover the meat with foil and continue roasting for 2 hours to 2 hours and 15 minutes. The internal temperature should be about 165 degrees. Two bones protrude from the shank end of the ham, one large and one small. If the small upper bone can be removed with a slight pull, it is an indication that the ham is cooked.

7. Remove the ham. Tilt the pan in which the ham cooked and, using a large spoon, skim off all the surface fat. Pour the sauce into a sieve, preferably a sieve of the sort called a chinois in French kitchens. Press the solids with the back of a heavy spoon to extract as many juices as possible.

8. Using the fingers, pull against the hipbone that was carved around earlier. Run the carving knife around the bone and pull with the fingers to remove.

9. After cooking, it is best to let the ham rest for at least ½ hour before carving. If desired, transfer the ham to a serving dish and garnish with watercress.

10. To carve, run the carving knife under the skin of the ham and carve around under it from one side to the other. Leave a coating of fat on top of the ham. Cut away excess fat. Many people like the crisp skin, so reserve it to serve on demand.

11. Place the ham fat side up. Make a perpendicular cut down to the bone about 3 inches from the meaty shank end. After all the top meat has been carved, turn the ham on its side and carve the meat off the sides neatly.

Yield: 12 to 20 servings.

How to Cook a Smoked Ham

1   **13- to 14-pound smoked ham**
48 **whole cloves**
½   **cup granular brown sugar**
½   **cup Madeira**
    Sauce madère (see recipe page 652), optional

1. It is not essential, but you will facilitate carving the ham later if you run a boning or other knife around the contour of the hipbone on the underside of the ham. Run the knife down deep around the bone, but do not remove the bone at this time. It will be removed after cooking.

2. Put the ham, fat side up, in a deep kettle or roaster, preferably on a rack to prevent sticking. Add enough water to cover about 1 inch above the ham and bring to the boil. Simmer for about 2½ hours. As the ham cooks, the water will

evaporate. You must keep replenishing the water so that the ham is continuously covered as it cooks.

3. Remove the ham from the broth and discard the broth. Let the ham cool until it can be handled.

4. Using a carving knife, carefully and neatly trim off the skin all around, leaving a light layer of fat on top. Using the fingers, pull against the hipbone that was carved around earlier. Run the carving knife around the bone and pull with the fingers to remove it.

5. Preheat the oven to 425 degrees.

6. Score the fat of the ham, cutting into the fat to make diamond patterns all over. Stud the points of each diamond with cloves. Sprinkle the ham with sugar, patting it down all over the top surface of the ham.

7. Place the ham scored side up in a roasting pan and pour the wine into the pan. Place in the oven and bake, basting occasionally, for 25 or 30 minutes. Baste often toward the end of the cooking time. Serve, if desired, with sauce madère.

Yield: 12 to 20 servings.

Ham Loaf with Sour Cream and Paprika Sauce

1. Preheat the oven to 400 degrees.

2. Cut the ham into cubes and grind it, using the medium blade of a food grinder or a food processor. Spoon it into a mixing bowl and set aside.

3. Heat the butter in a skillet and add the garlic, onion, mushrooms and celery. Cook briefly until vegetables are wilted. Sprinkle with pepper to taste and cook for about 15 minutes. Add the chicken broth and cook for about 3 minutes. Spoon the mixture into the bowl with the ham. Add the bread crumbs, the egg beaten with the yolk, cream, nutmeg and parsley. Blend well.

4. Butter a 9 x 5 x 2¾-inch loaf pan and add the ham mixture. Smooth over the top and bake for 45 minutes to 1 hour. Remove from the oven and let stand for at least 30 minutes before serving. This is not a firm loaf, but it can be sliced. Serve sliced with sour cream and paprika sauce.

Yield: 6 to 8 servings.

1½ pounds cooked ham
1 tablespoon butter
1 clove garlic, finely minced
1 cup finely chopped onion
¼ pound mushrooms, cut into very small cubes, about 1¾ cups
½ cup finely chopped celery
Freshly ground pepper
1 cup fresh or canned chicken broth
2 cups fine, fresh bread crumbs
2 whole eggs, lightly beaten
1 egg yolk
¾ cup heavy cream
¼ teaspoon finely ground nutmeg
2 tablespoons chopped parsley
Sour cream and paprika sauce (see recipe below)

Sour cream and paprika sauce

1 tablespoon butter
1 small clove garlic
¼ cup finely chopped onion
¾ cup finely chopped green pepper
2 teaspoons paprika
1 tablespoon flour
¾ cup fresh or canned chicken broth
½ cup fresh or canned cooked tomatoes
1 cup sour cream
 Salt
2 tablespoons finely chopped parsley

Heat the butter in a saucepan and add the garlic, onion and green pepper. Cook until vegetables are wilted and add the paprika and flour, stirring with a wire whisk. Add the broth and tomatoes and stir rapidly until thickened and smooth. Stir in the sour cream and salt to taste and heat thoroughly, stirring. Stir in the parsley and serve hot.

Yield: About 2 cups.

Ham and Sauerkraut Balls

4 teaspoons butter
1½ tablespoons flour
½ cup milk
½ pound cooked ham
½ pound sauerkraut
¼ cup finely chopped onion
½ teaspoon caraway seeds
2 teaspoons dry mustard
 Freshly ground pepper
2 egg yolks
1 egg
¼ cup water
 Salt
 Flour for dredging
1½ cups fresh bread crumbs
 Oil for deep frying
 Lemon wedges
 Hot mustard (see recipe page 647), optional

1. Melt 3 teaspoons butter in a small saucepan and add the flour, stirring with a wire whisk. Add the milk, stirring rapidly with the whisk. When blended and smooth, the sauce should be quite thick. Remove from the heat.

2. Chop the ham finely on a flat surface or grind it, using the medium blade.

3. Press the sauerkraut to extract most of the liquid.

4. Heat the remaining teaspoon of butter and add the onion. Cook, stirring, until wilted. Add the sauerkraut and cook briefly, stirring. Add the ham, caraway, dry mustard and pepper to taste. Add the white sauce. Blend thoroughly. Add the egg yolks, stirring rapidly. Cook for about 1 minute, stirring, and remove from the heat. Spoon into a mixing bowl and smooth over the top. Cover with foil or plastic wrap and chill.

5. Using the fingers, shape the mixture into 28 or 30 balls.

6. Beat together the egg, water, salt and pepper to taste.

7. Dredge the balls lightly all over with flour. Dip the balls into the egg mixture to coat well and finally in bread crumbs. Arrange on a rack.

8. When ready to cook, heat the oil for deep frying and cook the balls, turning as necessary, until golden brown and piping hot to the center. Drain and serve hot with lemon wedges and, if desired, hot mustard.

Yield: 6 servings.

Ham Croquettes

1. Prepare the meat and set it aside. The chopped pieces, incidentally, should be no more than ¼ inch in diameter.

2. Melt the butter in a saucepan and add the onion, stirring with a wire whisk. Add the flour, stirring to blend. When blended, add the milk, stirring rapidly with the whisk. When blended and smooth, add the meat. Bring to the boil and remove from the heat.

3. Add the yolks, stirring rapidly with the whisk. Return to the heat and cook briefly. Add the nutmeg, salt (if the ham is salty, do not add salt) and pepper to taste. Spoon the mixture into a dish and cover closely with buttered wax paper. Refrigerate, preferably overnight.

4. Remove the paper and, using the fingers, divide the mixture into 12 to 14 portions. Shape into balls and roll lightly in flour. The portions may be shaped finally into balls or cylinders. When smooth on the surface and neatly coated with flour, dredge in the whole egg combined with 3 tablespoons water and then in bread crumbs. Arrange on a rack and chill until ready to cook.

5. Heat the oil and, when it is hot, add the balls, a few at a time. Cook for 2 or 3 minutes, or until golden and cooked through. Serve hot with tomato sauce.

Yield: 6 to 8 servings.

4 cups coarsely chopped cooked ham (or leftover beef, lamb or pork)
3 tablespoons butter
3 tablespoons finely chopped onion
¼ cup flour
1½ cups milk
3 egg yolks
¼ teaspoon freshly grated nutmeg
Salt and freshly ground pepper
Flour for dredging
1 egg lightly beaten
3 tablespoons water
1½ cups fine, fresh bread crumbs
Peanut, vegetable or corn oil for deep frying
Tomato sauce (see recipe page 650)

Roast Suckling Pig

Two of the best roast suckling pigs we've ever eaten were in Puerto Rico: once, when the animal was hand-turned out of doors for several hours on a wooden spit over hot coals; the second was a decade later in the home of the Governor of Puerto Rico, Carlos Romero-Barcelo and his American-born wife, Kate. Their chef, Jesùs Villalba, cooked the pig in the oven with a minimum of effort, and the results were admirable—a crisp, crusty skin with tantalizing flavor and moist, tender, well-done meat. This is his version, stuffed with rice and fresh pigeon peas.

1 13- to 15-pound suckling pig
½ cup peanut, vegetable or corn oil
¼ cup salt
2 cloves garlic, peeled and mashed to a fine purée
1 tablespoon crushed dried oregano
Freshly ground pepper to taste
Rice with pigeon peas (see recipe below)

1. Wash the pig well and dry inside and out.

2. Blend the oil, salt, garlic, oregano and pepper. Prick the pig all over and massage the pig inside and out with the garlic mixture. Put in a pan, cover with cheesecloth and let stand for several hours.

3. Preheat the oven to 350 degrees. Place the pig in a roasting pan, feet side down, and bake for about 1 hour and 10 minutes. Baste often. If at any point any part of the pig starts to burn (ears, feet, etc.), cover that part with foil.

4. Reduce the oven heat to 250 degrees and bake for about 1 hour and 10 minutes longer, basting often. Increase the oven heat to 400 degrees and bake for 20 to 30 minutes, basting. Remove the pig from the oven. Remove the cheesecloth.

5. Fill the stomach cavity of the pig with the rice mixture. Keep the stuffing intact with a sheet of aluminum foil. There may be an excess of rice. This may be heated later and served on the side.

6. Before serving, preheat the oven once more to 350 degrees. Place the stuffed pig back in the oven on a roasting pan and bake for 20 minutes longer.

Yield: 12 or more servings.

Rice with pigeon peas

2 cups fresh green pigeon peas, or 1 1-pound can, available in Spanish markets
Salt to taste
3 tablespoons olive oil
1 cup finely chopped onion
1 teaspoon finely minced garlic
1 cup chopped, cored, seeded, sweet green pepper
¼ cup diced raw, not-too-lean, cured ham, preferably unsmoked
1 tablespoon chopped fresh coriander leaves
1 cup cubed tomatoes
2 cups fresh or canned tomato sauce, put through a sieve if fresh
1 cup drained pimiento-stuffed green olives
2 tablespoons drained capers
4 cups rice
⅓ cup canned coconut cream, such as Coco Lopez
4 cups fresh or canned beef broth

1. If the peas are fresh, put them in a kettle with water to cover and salt to taste. Bring to the boil and simmer until tender, 45 minutes to 1 hour. If they are canned, drain them.

2. Heat the oil in a skillet and add the onion, garlic, green pepper, ham and coriander leaves. Cook, stirring, until the onion is wilted. Add the tomatoes, pigeon peas, tomato sauce, olives and capers. Stir and add the rice. Stir to blend well and add the coconut cream and beef broth.

3. Cover closely with aluminum foil and bring to the boil. Simmer for 20 minutes. Discard foil. The rice is now ready to be used as a stuffing for roast suckling pig.

Yield: About 8 cups, or enough to use as a stuffing for a small roast suckling pig.

How to Prepare Sausage Casings

Sausage casings, available in specialty pork stores, are normally preserved in salt. When ready to use, put them in a basin of cold water and let stand. Drain and return to the basin of cold water.

Lift up one end of a casing and blow into it. It will expand, balloonlike. This is how you determine if the casings have holes in them. Discard casings with holes or cut the casing at the hole and use the partial casing.

How to Fill Sausage Casings

1. Outfit an electric grinder or a sausage-making machine—either hand-cranked or electric—with a special sausage stuffing attachment.

2. Slide one prepared sausage casing onto the attachment and tie the end of the casing. Grind the meat, holding the casing to permit free entry of the filling into the casing.

3. Fill the casing, making sausages of any desired length. Some sausages, like chipolatas, are only 1 inch long. Others, like chorizos, may be about 6 inches long. Garlic sausages may be about 16 inches long.

4. When the desired amount of filling has been added, pinch the casing at the point where the meat enters. Turn the meat-filled casing to seal. Grind in meat for the second sausage, turn the casing as before and continue until all the sausages of whatever length are made.

Saucisses de Toulouse   (Mild spiced pork sausages)

Chop the pork and pork fat coarsely in a food processor or use a meat grinder equipped with the coarse blade. Spoon and scrape the mixture into a mixing bowl and add the remaining ingredients. Use as a stuffing for sausages to be dried and/or smoked, or made into patties to be fried.

Yield: About 2½ pounds, or 9 or 10 sausage links of about ¼ pound each.

1¾ pounds lean pork, cubed
1 pound pork fat, cubed
   Salt
½ teaspoon freshly ground pepper
¼ teaspoon marjoram
1 teaspoon saltpeter, available in drugstores

Saucissons à l'Ail *(Garlic sausages)*

3 pounds lean pork, cut into cubes
1½ pounds pork fat, cut into cubes
Salt to taste
1 teaspoon freshly ground pepper
½ teaspoon saltpeter, available in drugstores
¼ teaspoon ground nutmeg
½ cup port wine
1 tablespoon finely chopped garlic

1. Put the pork and pork fat through a meat grinder outfitted with the coarsest blade. Put the meat in a mixing bowl and add all the remaining ingredients. Put it once more through the grinder using the coarsest blade.

2. Use to fill sausage casings.

Yield: 6 to 10 16-inch sausage rings.

How to Cook Cotechine or Garlic Sausages

Cotechine (garlic sausages or saucissons à l'ail)
Salt to taste
1 onion, sliced
3 sprigs fresh thyme, or ½ teaspoon dried
1 bay leaf
12 peppercorns

Prick the cotechine in several places. Place in a kettle and add cold water to cover. Add the remaining ingredients and bring to the boil. Simmer the sausages for 40 or 45 minutes. Let stand in the cooking liquid until ready to serve. Serve sliced, hot or cold. Served hot, these are very good with lentils or with hot potato salad.

Saucisses Chablisienne *(Sausages with white wine stuffing)*

4 pounds lean pork, cut into 2-inch cubes
2 pounds solid pork fat, cut into 2-inch cubes
Salt to taste
1 teaspoon freshly ground black pepper
5 dried hot red pepper pods, or about 1 teaspoon ground
1 clove garlic, finely minced
½ cup dry white wine
½ teaspoon saltpeter, available in drugstores

1. Put the pork and pork fat into a large mixing bowl and add the salt and pepper.

2. Grind the hot red pepper pods (without the stems) in a small clean coffee grinder. Add it to the meat.

3. Add the garlic, wine and saltpeter. Mix well with the hands and cover. Let stand in the refrigerator overnight.

4. Put the mixture through à meat grinder fitted with the largest blade. Use to stuff sausage casings.

Yield: 6 to 10 sausage rings, about 16 inches long.

Chorizos   *(Spicy Spanish sausages)*

1. Put the pork meat and fat in a mixing bowl.

2. Heat the coriander seeds in a small skillet until they are lightly toasted. Put them into a mortar or a spice mill and grind them.

3. Add the coriander, salt to taste, paprika, garlic, black pepper, red pepper flakes, cumin, oregano, cloves and vinegar to the meat. Blend well with the hands.

4. Grind the mixture coarsely. To do this, grind briefly in a food processor or in a food grinder outfitted with the coarse blade. To test for seasonings, take a small portion of the stuffing and flatten it, biscuit shape. Fry until cooked in a small skillet. Add more seasonings to taste to the basic mixture.

5. Use the mixture to stuff sausage casings.

Yield: About 5 pounds, or 24 sausages of 5 or 6 inches in length.

3½ pounds lean pork, cut into cubes
1½ pounds pork fat, cut into cubes
1 tablespoon coriander seeds
Salt
3 tablespoons paprika
2 tablespoons finely chopped garlic
1 teaspoon freshly ground black pepper
½ teaspoon crushed red pepper flakes, or cayenne pepper
½ teaspoon ground cumin
2 teaspoons crushed dried oregano
¼ teaspoon ground cloves
3 tablespoons red wine vinegar

Chipolatas   *(Small French sausages)*

1. Using a food processor or a meat grinder equipped with a medium blade, grind the lean pork and pork fat. Or have this done by the butcher.

2. Put the meat in a bowl and add the remaining ingredients. Blend well. Use to stuff sausage casings, preferably very small sheep's casings.

Yield: 90 to 100 sausages measuring 3 inches long and 1 inch wide.

4 pounds very lean pork
2 pounds fresh, unsalted pork fat
2½ teaspoons freshly ground pepper
5 teaspoons salt
1 hot red pepper pod, crumbled
¼ teaspoon grated nutmeg
1 whole clove, pounded with a mallet

Smoked Southern Sausage

It is a pity most people assume that the smoking of food is a highly elaborate and complex function that requires extensive and expensive equipment. This is wholly untrue. You can smoke in almost any confined area, even in an old oil drum, as long as it's equipped with a base for burning wood and a couple of racks. We ourselves own a standard electric smoker that cost about $30 a couple of years ago.

3½ pounds lean pork, cut into 2-inch cubes
2 pounds solid pork fat, cut into 2-inch cubes
2½ tablespoons rubbed sage or more to taste
4 tablespoons sweet paprika
Salt
2 teaspoons finely ground black pepper
12 dried hot red pepper pods, or about 1 tablespoon ground

1. Put the pork and pork fat into a large mixing bowl and add the sage, paprika, salt and pepper.
2. Grind the hot red peppers in a small, clean coffee grinder. Add it.
3. Mix well with the hands, cover and let stand in the refrigerator overnight.
4. Put the mixture through a meat grinder fitted with the largest blade. Use to stuff sausage casings.
5. Hang the sausages in a smoker and smoke according to the manufacturer's instructions.

Yield: 6 to 8 sausage rings, about 16 inches long.

Liverwurst

5 pounds pork liver
5 pounds fresh lean, unsmoked bacon (boneless)
2 teaspoons white pepper
1 teaspoon cardamom
¾ teaspoon powdered ginger
1¼ teaspoons mace
1 teaspoon crushed marjoram
½ teaspoon crushed thyme leaves
¼ cup salt, or to taste
¼ pound onion, chopped (about 1 cup) and blended to a purée
3 tablespoons white corn syrup
1 tablespoon saltpeter, available in drugstores

1. Cut the pork liver and bacon into 1- or 2-inch cubes and blend to a fine purée. This is best done by using a food processor.
2. Pour the mixture into a large bowl and add the remaining ingredients. Blend well.
3. Use the mixture to stuff liverwurst casings.
4. Bring enough water to the boil in a large kettle to cover the sausages when added. The temperature of the water should be approximately 180 degrees. Add the sausages and then add a lid or other contrivance to keep the sausages submerged as they cook. Cook for about 1 hour. Drain and let cool.

Yield: 6 sausages, about 10 or 12 inches long.

Andouillettes   *(French chitterling sausages)*

10 pounds ready-to-cook chitterlings, available in specialty pork stores
½ cup powdered mustard
1 cup finely chopped shallots
½ teaspoon nutmeg
Salt to taste
1 teaspoon freshly ground pepper

1. The chitterlings should be cleaned and ready to cook. Rinse them in numerous changes of cold water and drain well in a colander. Squeeze to extract much of the moisture. Pour the chitterlings into a large mixing bowl.
2. Add the powdered mustard, shallots, nutmeg, about 3 tablespoons of salt, the pepper and wine. Mix well with the hands.
3. Stuff the sausage casings with the seasoned chitterlings.

4. Put the sausages in a large kettle and prick each in several places with a needle. Add cold water to cover, thyme, bay leaf, onion, garlic, cloves, salt and peppercorns. Cover and bring to the boil. Simmer for 2 hours. Drain.

5. Weight the sausages down with heavy, flat weights for at least 2 hours. Remove the weights and refrigerate. When ready to cook, grill the sausages for about 20 minutes. The sausages may be grilled under the broiler but preferably they should be grilled over a charcoal or gas grill. Remember that before grilling the sausages are already cooked, so it is necessary to grill them just until they are golden brown on the outside and piping hot inside. Serve with mustard.

Yield: 24 or more servings.

½	cup dry white wine
½	teaspoon dried thyme
1	large bay leaf
1	large onion, peeled
2	cloves garlic, peeled
6	whole cloves
12	peppercorns
	Prepared mustard, preferably imported, such as Dijon or Düsseldorf

Civet de Lapin   *(Rabbit in red wine sauce)*

1. Preheat the oven to 350 degrees.
2. Sprinkle the rabbit pieces with salt and pepper. Set aside.
3. Drop the salt pork into cold water to cover. Bring to the boil and simmer for about 1 minute. Drain. Cook the pieces in one or two heavy skillets until the slices are rendered of their fat and crisp. Remove the pieces with a slotted spoon and set aside.
4. Add the rabbit pieces to the fat and brown on all sides. If two skillets are used, combine the pieces in one skillet after browning.
5. Add the garlic, onions, mushrooms and carrot and cook, stirring, for about 5 minutes. Tie the bay leaf, thyme sprigs and parsley in a bundle and add it. If blood is not available for later use, sprinkle the flour over all and stir to coat the pieces of rabbit. Add the wine and water and bring to the boil on top of the stove. Cover and place in the oven. Bake for about 45 minutes if the rabbit is small, about 1 hour and 15 minutes if large.
6. If rabbit blood is to be used, add a small amount of the hot sauce to the blood. Gradually stir this mixture into the sauce and simmer gently, stirring, for about 1 minute. Remove the herb bundle and sprinkle the rabbit with the browned pieces of salt pork.

Yield: 4 to 8 servings.

1	2½- to 4-pound rabbit, cut into serving pieces
	Salt and freshly ground pepper to taste
¼	pound thinly sliced salt pork cut into ¼-inch strips
2	teaspoons finely chopped garlic
16	very small white onions, peeled, or 1 cup finely chopped onion
⅓	pound small button mushrooms, left whole, or larger mushrooms quartered and sliced
1	carrot, trimmed, scraped and cut into rounds
1	bay leaf
2	sprigs fresh thyme, or ½ teaspoon dried
3	sprigs parsley
¼	cup flour (to be used only if rabbit blood, indicated below, is not available)
3	cups dry red Burgundy
1	cup water
¾ to	1 cup blood (blended with the juice of ½ lemon to prevent coagulation)

Lapin à la Moutarde *(Rabbit with mustard sauce)*

1 3- to 3½-pound young rabbit, cleaned
¼ pound butter
   Salt and freshly ground pepper to taste
¾ pound carrots, trimmed, scraped and cut into 2-inch lengths
¾ pound small white onions, peeled, about 10
3 tablespoons imported mustard, such as Dijon or Düsseldorf
1 cup plus 2 tablespoons dry white wine
½ pound mushrooms, left whole if small, otherwise sliced or quartered
1 cup fresh or canned chicken broth·
1 bay leaf
1 clove garlic, peeled and left whole

1. Preheat the oven to 425 degrees.
2. Cut the rabbit into 5 large pieces: the forelegs with thighs attached, the hind legs with thighs attached, and the meaty breast portion. Set the liver aside.
3. Melt the butter in a baking dish large enough to hold the rabbit pieces in one layer. Add the rabbit pieces. Sprinkle with salt and pepper and turn the pieces in the butter. Place the rabbit skinned side down.
4. Meanwhile, put the carrots and onions in a saucepan and add cold water to cover and salt to taste. Bring to the boil and simmer for about 5 minutes. Drain and set aside.
5. Put the rabbit in the oven. Do not cover. Bake for 30 minutes and turn the rabbit pieces, skinned side up.
6. Blend the mustard and 2 tablespoons wine in a small mixing bowl. Brush the rabbit all over with half the mustard mixture. Add the liver. Return to the oven and let bake for about 5 minutes. Turn the rabbit pieces.
7. Scatter the mushrooms, the blanched carrots and onions around the rabbit pieces. Brush the rabbit pieces, including the liver, with the remaining mustard. Pour the remaining 1 cup wine and the broth around the rabbit pieces. Add the bay leaf and garlic.
8. Bake for 30 minutes longer, basting occasionally, and reduce the oven heat to 375 degrees. Continue roasting and basting for about 15 minutes or until tender.
   Yield: 6 servings.

Ragout de Lapin *(Rabbit stew)*

1 tender young rabbit, 1½ to 2 pounds
¾ cup onion, coarsely chopped
1 cup carrots, scraped and cut into ½-inch cubes
½ cup coarsely chopped celery
½ cup coarsely chopped leeks, optional
6 sprigs fresh thyme, or ½ teaspoon dried
4 large sprigs parsley
4 juniper berries, crushed
   Salt and freshly ground pepper to taste
2 cups dry red wine

1. Cut the rabbit into serving pieces as follows: The two back legs, the two back thighs, the "saddle," or back, cut in half crosswise into two meaty parts, the two front legs and thighs left together, the meaty "breast" cut in half crosswise, the neck and the head (the head will not be too appetizing to all guests). Discard the lungs. Put the liver into a bowl.
2. Put the rest of the cut-up carcass into another bowl. Add the onion, carrot, celery, leeks, if used, thyme, parsley, juniper berries, salt, pepper and wine. Cover closely with plastic wrap and let stand in the refrigerator or a very cold place for two to three days (if pressed for time, overnight will do). Cover the liver and refrigerate.
3. Drain the rabbit pieces but reserve separately both the marinating liquid and the solids.

4. Heat 2 tablespoons of the butter in a large, heavy skillet and add the rabbit pieces. Brown on all sides, for 5 to 10 minutes. Scatter the reserved solids over and around the rabbit pieces. Stir. Add the liver.

5. Sprinkle with the flour and stir to coat the rabbit pieces evenly. Add the marinating liquid and water. Stir until boiling and thickened. Add salt and pepper to taste. Cover closely and cook for 30 to 45 minutes. Cooking time will depend on the size and age of the rabbit. A very young rabbit will cook in ½ hour.

6. Transfer the rabbit pieces to a casserole large enough to hold them in one layer. Strain the sauce through a fine sieve, pushing to extract as much liquid as possible from the solids. Discard the solids.

7. Heat the remaining butter in a skillet and add the mushrooms. Cook until they give up their liquid. Continue cooking until the liquid evaporates. Add this to the rabbit.

8. Pour the strained sauce over the pieces of rabbit and mushrooms. Serve very hot.

Yield: 4 servings.

3	tablespoons butter
3	tablespoons flour
1	cup water
¼	pound fresh mushrooms, left whole if small, otherwise sliced or quartered

Fillet of Venison Bourguignonne

1. Cut the fillet crosswise in half and put the pieces in a bowl. Add the salt, pepper, celery, onion, leeks, carrots, rosemary, thyme, parsley, bay leaf, marjoram and the wine. Cover closely and refrigerate or place in a very cold place for two to three days (if pressed for time, overnight will do).

2. Remove the venison pieces. Strain the marinating liquid, reserving separately both the marinating solids and the liquid.

3. Heat 1 tablespoon butter in a saucepan and add the reserved solids (vegetables and herbs). Cook for about 5 minutes, stirring often. Add the reserved liquid and let boil over high heat for about 10 minutes, or until liquid is reduced to about ¾ cup.

4. Blend the arrowroot and 2 teaspoons Cognac and stir this into the sauce. Put the sauce through a fine sieve into a small saucepan, pressing to extract as much liquid as possible from the solids. Discard the solids. Set the sauce aside.

5. Heat the remaining butter in a skillet and add the 2 well-drained pieces of venison fillet. Cook to brown one side over high heat for about 2 minutes. Turn and brown quickly on the other side. Reduce the heat to moderate and continue cooking, turning the pieces as necessary so that they cook evenly, for 8 to 10 minutes. Take care that the pieces do not overcook or

1	fillet or boneless loin of venison
	Salt and freshly ground pepper to taste
¾	cup coarsely chopped celery
⅔	cup coarsely chopped onion
¾	cup coarsely chopped leeks
½	cup cubed carrots
2	sprigs fresh rosemary, or 1 teaspoon dried
3	sprigs fresh thyme, or ½ teaspoon dried
2	sprigs fresh parsley
1	bay leaf
½	teaspoon dried marjoram
2	cups dry red wine, preferably a fine Burgundy
3	tablespoons butter
¾	teaspoon arrowroot or cornstarch
2	teaspoons plus 2 tablespoons Cognac
½	cup heavy cream

they will become dry. The meat should remain slightly rare. Transfer the pieces of meat to a serving dish.

6. Pour all the fat from the skillet and add the 2 tablespoons of Cognac. Add the strained sauce and the cream. Bring to the boil, stirring. If desired, strain the sauce through a fine sieve.

7. The venison fillet may be covered with a thin and somewhat tough or fatty layer. Cut this away and discard it. Carve the flesh on the bias into thin slices and serve with the sauce.

Yield: 6 servings.

Ragout of Venison

2	quarts, approximately, marinade for game (see recipe below)
5	pounds shoulder of venison, cut into 2- or 3-inch cubes
2 to	4 tablespoons peanut, vegetable or corn oil
¼	cup flour Salt and freshly ground pepper
4	tablespoons currant jelly
⅓	pound lean salt pork
10	small white onions
1	teaspoon butter
1	teaspoon sugar
½	pound thinly sliced mushrooms

1. Prepare the marinade and add the venison pieces. Stir and cover with foil. Refrigerate for 4 or 5 days, no longer.

2. Preheat the oven to 400 degrees.

3. Remove the meat from the marinade and set it aside. Drain the vegetables, reserving the solids and the liquid. There should be about 4 cups liquid.

4. Heat 2 tablespoons oil in one or two medium-size skillets. Brown one-third of the meat at a time. As the meat is browned, transfer it to a kettle. Use more oil as necessary to cook the meat. The total time for browning the meat should be about 10 minutes.

5. Add a little more oil to a skillet and cook the reserved solids over high heat for about 5 minutes. Add this to the meat.

6. Sprinkle the flour over all and stir to coat the pieces more or less evenly. Cook for about 3 minutes and add the reserved liquid. Add salt and pepper to taste. Bring to the boil and cover. Place the kettle in the oven and bake for 2 hours.

7. Remove from the oven, tilt the kettle and skim off the excess fat from the surface. Add the jelly and stir until dissolved. Simmer for 5 minutes on top of stove.

8. Meanwhile, cut the salt pork into matchlike "batons." Put them in a saucepan, cover with cold water and bring to the boil. Simmer for 1 minute and drain.

9. Peel the onions and combine them in a saucepan with water to barely cover, salt to taste, the butter and sugar. Cook until liquid evaporates and the onions start to take on a brown glaze.

10. Heat a skillet and add the pieces of salt pork. When crisp, remove the pieces with a slotted spoon and set aside. Add the mushrooms to the rendered salt pork fat. Sprinkle

with salt and pepper to taste and cook, stirring as necessary, for about 10 minutes. Drain well and set aside.

11. Put the onions in a skillet and add the salt pork and mushrooms. Cook for about 5 minutes. Sprinkle this mixture over the venison and cook for 10 minutes.

Yield: 12 or more servings.

---

1. Combine in a saucepan ¼ cup of red wine vinegar, the marjoram, juniper berries, bay leaf, rosemary, cloves, thyme and peppercorns. Bring to the boil and simmer for about 5 minutes.

2. Empty the mixture into a stainless steel or enamel bowl and add the remaining ingredients. Use as a marinade for game.

Yield: 2 quarts, approximately, or enough marinade for 5 pounds of venison.

Marinade for game

4¼	cups red wine vinegar
½	teaspoon dried marjoram
4	juniper berries, crushed
1	bay leaf
1	teaspoon rosemary
2	whole cloves
¼	teaspoon thyme
10	peppercorns
1	cup coarsely chopped celery
1	cup thinly sliced carrots
1	cup quartered small onions
2	sprigs parsley
	Salt to taste

VI. Poultry

Roast Chicken with Watercress

1   3-pound chicken
     Salt and freshly ground pepper
     to taste
1   bunch watercress
4   tablespoons butter

1. Preheat the oven to 450 degrees.
2. Sprinkle the inside of the chicken with salt and pepper.
3. Cut off the bottom stems of the watercress, about halfway up the stalks. Stuff the chicken with the stems and reserve the leaves in a plastic bag to keep them fresh. Truss the chicken. Sprinkle the outside with salt and pepper.
4. Lay the chicken on one side in a small baking dish and dot the top side with half the butter. Place in the oven and bake, basting occasionally, for about 15 minutes. When golden, turn the chicken onto the other side. Bake for 15 minutes, basting often. Turn the chicken onto its back and bake for 15 minutes longer, basting.
5. Tip the chicken so that the inside juices run out into the baking dish. Untruss and carve the chicken and arrange on a warm platter. Pour the pan juices over.
6. Heat the remaining butter in a skillet until it is hazelnut brown. Pour over the chicken. Garnish one end of the platter with the reserved watercress leaves. As the chicken and watercress are served, spoon a little of the natural sauce over both chicken and watercress.
    Yield: 4 servings.

Poulets Rotis à la Piperade et Sauce Moutarde   *(Roast chicken with mustard sauce)*

2   3½-pound chickens
3   tablespoons butter
     Salt and freshly ground
     pepper to taste
1   cup water
½   cup heavy cream
4   tablespoons imported
     mustard, such as Dijon or
     Düsseldorf
     Piperade (see
     recipe below)

1. Preheat the oven to 400 degrees.
2. Rub the chickens all over with butter. Sprinkle them inside and out with salt and pepper. Truss. Arrange the chickens on their sides in a shallow roasting pan.
3. Roast the chickens for about 20 minutes and turn them on the other side. Baste often. Continue roasting for about 20 minutes and turn the chickens on their backs. Roast for 20 minutes, or until cavity juices run clear when chickens are lifted so that the juices flow into the pan. Continue roasting, if necessary, until done.

250

4. Remove the chickens and keep warm. Pour off the fat from the pan and add the water, stirring to dissolve the brown particles that cling to the pan. Pour this liquid into a saucepan and cook to reduce by half.

5. Add the cream and cook briefly. Add the mustard and cook, stirring, for about 30 seconds.

6. Serve the chicken sliced with the mustard sauce and piperade.

Yield: 8 to 12 servings.

1. Core and seed the peppers. Cut them into thin strips. There should be about 5 cups. Set aside.

2. Core and peel the tomatoes. Cut them into eighths. There should be about 5 cups. Set aside.

3. Peel the onions and cut them in half. Then cut the onions into very thin slices. There should be about 3 cups. Set aside.

4. Heat ¼ cup of oil in each of 3 skillets. Add the peppers to one skillet, the tomatoes to another and the onions and garlic to the third. Cook the peppers, onions and garlic until they are browned without burning. Cook the tomatoes until they are somewhat reduced and saucelike. Add the peppers and onions to the tomatoes. Add salt and pepper to taste.

5. Heat the remaining tablespoon of oil in a skillet and add the ham. Cook for about 30 seconds and add to the tomatoes. Add the garlic and the bay leaves. Cook for about 15 minutes.

6. Turn the heat to very low and add the eggs one at a time, stirring constantly. The trick is to incorporate the eggs into the tomato sauce, stirring so as to prevent curdling. The heat must be gentle. After the eggs are added, do not cook further but serve immediately.

Yield: 8 to 12 servings.

Piperade *(A tomato and pepper dish)*

5	green peppers, about 1½ pounds
5	large, red, ripe tomatoes, about 2½ pounds
2 or 3	onions, about ¾ pound
1	clove garlic, finely minced Salt and freshly ground pepper to taste
¾	cup plus 1 tablespoon peanut, vegetable or corn oil
⅛	pound thinly sliced prosciutto or other ham, cut into shreds or cubes
1	tablespoon finely minced garlic
2	bay leaves
3	eggs

Chicken Stuffed with Scrambled Eggs

Several years ago we dined on an uncommonly interesting dish in an Italian restaurant in Boston. It was roast chicken with a custardlike stuffing that proved to be extremely palatable, not only because of its delicate flavor but also because of its tender, gossamerlike texture. We honestly don't recall the name of the restaurant, and would not name it if we did, for it was otherwise undistinguished. After numerous tries in our kitchen, we discovered that the filling was nothing more than well-seasoned scrambled eggs, which, when cooked in the bird, achieved that sought-after and notably compelling stuffing.

5 eggs
¼ cup heavy cream
½ teaspoon chopped tarragon
Salt and freshly ground pepper
3½ tablespoons butter
1 2½-pound chicken
1 small onion, peeled

1. Preheat the oven to 450 degrees.

2. Beat the eggs in a mixing bowl until well blended. Add the cream, tarragon and salt and pepper to taste.

3. Heat 1 tablespoon butter in a skillet and add the egg mixture. Cook over low heat, stirring with a rubber spatula, until the eggs are almost set. Do not overcook. Remove from the heat. Stir in ½ tablespoon butter. Cool.

4. Sprinkle the inside of the chicken with salt and pepper and stuff with the egg mixture. Truss the chicken. Sprinkle the outside with salt and pepper to taste.

5. Melt 2 tablespoons of butter in a shallow roasting pan and turn the chicken around in it until coated. Add the onion to the pan. Rest the chicken on one side and place it in the oven. Bake for 15 minutes, basting occasionally. Turn the chicken to the other side and continue baking for about 15 minutes, basting occasionally. Turn the chicken once again and bake for 15 minutes, basting often.

6. Untruss the chicken and carve it. Serve the stuffing on the side.

Yield: 4 servings.

Chicken Albuféra

Black truffles, which are a staple of the classic French kitchen, have an indescribably delicious and subtle perfume and taste when they are used fresh from the earth. Unfortunately, much of this aroma dissipates once the truffles are processed either in cans or other containers. Thus they become an expensive conceit. But there is no substitute for them, either fresh or canned, in chicken albuféra, in which truffles are inserted between the skin and flesh of the chicken to give it a special aroma, or perfume. The dish is attributed to Antonin

Carême, the supreme chef of the eighteenth century, and came to us via George Perrier, the chef and owner of Le Bec Fin, an elegant and superior restaurant in Philadelphia.

1. Preheat the oven to 500 degrees.

2. Separate the skin from the flesh of the breast and thighs of the chicken. To do this, start at the neck opening and run the fingers gradually between the skin and flesh, working the fingers first over the breast and then about halfway down the thighs. This is not difficult to do.

3. Cut half the truffles into thin slices and insert these at intervals between the skin and the flesh of the breast and thighs. Sprinkle the inside of the chicken with salt, pepper and 1 teaspoon each Madeira and Cognac. Set aside.

4. Slice the chicken livers and cut the slices into thin strips. Cut the strips into cubes. Sprinkle with salt and pepper. Heat 2 teaspoons each butter and oil in a small saucepan and, when quite hot, add the livers. Cook, stirring and tossing, about 3 minutes or until done. Drain. Spoon the rice into a mixing bowl and add the drained livers.

5. Cut the remaining truffles into small cubes and add them to the rice. Sprinkle with 1 tablespoon of Madeira and add salt and pepper to taste. Add the foie gras and toss to blend well.

6. Spoon the rice mixture into the chicken. Truss the chicken. Place on one side in a small baking dish and smear with the remaining 3 tablespoons of butter. Sprinkle with remaining tablespoon of oil and bake for 10 minutes. Do not cover. Reduce the oven heat to 450 degrees. Bake for 10 minutes and turn the chicken onto its other side. Bake for 20 minutes and turn the chicken on its back. Bake for about 5 minutes, or until golden brown. Sprinkle with remaining 2 tablespoons of Madeira and add the chicken base.

7. Remove the chicken and bring the pan sauce to the boil. Tilt the pan and skim off any excess fat from the top. Add the cream and bring to the boil, stirring. Put the sauce through a fine sieve, preferably the French sieve known as a chinois. Press with a wooden spoon to extract any liquid from any solids in the sauce. Bring to the boil and serve hot.

8. Untruss the chicken and serve it carved with the rice stuffing and sauce.

Yield: 4 servings.

Note: Pure foie gras is the ultimate ingredient for this dish, but the tinned, far less expensive pâté de foie is acceptable as a substitute. Both are available in fine food stores and in most well-stocked supermarkets.

1	3-pound chicken
2 to	4 black truffles
	Salt and freshly ground pepper to taste
3	tablespoons plus 1 teaspoon Madeira
1	teaspoon Cognac
4	chicken livers
3	tablespoons plus 2 teaspoons butter
1	tablespoon plus 2 teaspoons peanut, vegetable or corn oil
1½	cups baked rice (see recipe page 454)
1	cup foie gras or pâté de foie cut into ½-inch cubes (see note)
½	cup brown chicken base (see recipe page 658)
⅓	cup heavy cream

Moroccan Chicken with Lemon and Olives

2   2½-pound chickens
2   preserved lemons (see instructions below)
2   teaspoons finely chopped garlic
2   teaspoons ground, dried ginger
¾   teaspoon finely ground pepper
¼   teaspoon powdered saffron
½   cup peanut, vegetable or corn oil
4   cups water
¾   cup grated onion (see note)
8   stalks fresh coriander tied with a string
    Salt to taste
24 imported black olives, about 1 cup

1. Wipe the inner cavity of the chicken carefully.

2. Rinse the lemons with cold water. Drain. Remove the pulp from the skins of the lemons. Reserve the skins. Put the pulp in the container of an electric blender or food processor. Add the garlic, ginger, pepper and saffron and start blending. Gradually add the oil. Spoon the mixture into a large mixing bowl.

3. Add the chickens to the bowl and rub them inside and out with the mixture. Add the livers. Cover and let stand overnight in the refrigerator.

4. Transfer the chickens, breast side down, to a kettle in which they will fit neatly and in one layer. Add the livers and the marinating mixture. To the bowl in which the chickens marinated, add the water, stirring to blend with remaining remnants of marinade in the bowl. Add this to the chickens. Add the onion and the coriander. Add salt to taste. Bring the cooking liquid to a boil. Partly cover and simmer for about 30 minutes. Uncover, turn the chickens breast side up and continue cooking for about 15 minutes.

5. Remove the chickens and livers. Place the chickens breast side up in a baking dish. Set aside.

6. Chop and mash the livers to a paste. Add the liver paste to the cooking liquid. Quarter the reserved lemon peel and add the pieces. Add the olives. Cook down the liquid to 4 cups.

7. Place the baking dish containing the chickens in a 500-degree oven to brown. Serve the chicken carved into pieces with the sauce on the side.

Yield: 12 servings.

Note: To grate onions for Moroccan cooking, peel about 1 pound of onions. Cut them into quarters. Blend thoroughly in a food processor. Place a sieve over a bowl and add the onions. Let drain.

Preserved lemons *(This must be made two weeks in advance)*

6 to   10 lemons
       Salt

1. Set each lemon on the flat stem end. Using a sharp knife, cut straight down through the center of each lemon to about ½ inch of the base. Leave each sliced lemon on its base, but give it a quarter turn. Slice down once more to within ½ inch of the base. Continue until all the lemons are prepared.

2. Make a ¼-inch layer of salt in a sterile quart Mason jar.

3. Pack the inside of each lemon with salt. As each lemon is

prepared, add it to the jar, pushing down. Make a layer of lemons, then a layer of salt, pressing down lightly on the lemons to make sure they are snug. They will, of course, give up much of their juices as they are pressed. Continue until the jar is packed full. Press down until juices rise to cover the lemons. Make certain that a little air space is left when the jar is sealed. Let stand in a not too warm place for at least two weeks, until the lemons are firm but tender.

Note: Always rinse the lemons before using. After the jar is opened, refrigerate. These lemons may also be used with baked fish dishes, in salads and in marinades.

Chicken au Poivre

1. Skin, bone and halve the chicken breasts. Sprinkle the pieces with salt and pepper.

2. Melt the butter in a skillet large enough to hold the pieces in one layer. Add the onion, carrots and garlic and cook, stirring, for about 10 minutes without browning. Sprinkle with flour and stir to blend. Arrange the chicken pieces, boned side down, in the skillet and sprinkle with thyme, bay leaf, parsley, celery and leeks, if used. Cover closely and let cook for 5 minutes. Add the vermouth, cream and broth and cover once more. Simmer for 20 minutes.

3. Remove the chicken pieces to a platter and keep warm. Spoon and scrape the sauce into the container of a food processor or blender and blend to a fine purée. Return this sauce to a saucepan and add salt to taste. Add the mustard, stirring, and remove from the heat. Sprinkle with chives and pour the sauce over the chicken. Serve hot.

Yield: 8 servings.

4 large whole chicken breasts, the larger the better
   Salt
1 tablespoon coarsely ground pepper
6 tablespoons butter
1 cup thinly sliced onion
1 cup thinly sliced carrots
1 clove garlic, crushed
2 tablespoons flour
½ teaspoon dried thyme
1 bay leaf
3 tablespoons finely chopped parsley
½ cup coarsely chopped celery
½ cup finely chopped leeks, optional
1 cup dry vermouth
½ cup heavy cream
1 cup fresh or canned chicken broth
1 tablespoon imported mustard, such as Dijon or Düsseldorf
1 tablespoon chopped chives

Boneless Chicken Breasts with Mushrooms and Cheese

2 boneless chicken breasts, about 1 pound, split
  Salt and freshly ground pepper to taste
2 tablespoons butter
½ cup duxelles (see recipe page 503)
4 thin slices Gruyère or Swiss cheese
1 tablespoon finely chopped shallots
¼ cup dry white wine
¾ cup heavy cream

1. Preheat the oven to 400 degrees.
2. Place the chicken breasts skin side down on a flat surface and pound lightly with a flat mallet. Sprinkle with salt and pepper on both sides. Heat the butter in a skillet and add the chicken breasts, skin side down. Cook until golden on one side, about 3 minutes, and turn. Cook for about 2 minutes on the other side. Remove the breasts.
3. Arrange the breasts on a baking dish, skin side up. Cover each breast with about 2 tablespoons of duxelles. Cover each with a slice of cheese.
4. To the skillet in which the chicken cooked, add the shallots and wine, stirring to dissolve the brown particles that cling to the bottom of the skillet. Add the cream and cook over high heat for about 1 minute. Strain this over the chicken breasts.
5. Place the dish in the oven and bake for 5 minutes.
Yield: 4 servings.

Deviled Chicken Breasts

Although highly spiced foods are characteristic of many regional kitchens throughout the world, they have over the centuries generally been eschewed by the French. Perhaps the most piquant dishes contrived in France are those labeled à la diable, which is to say deviled, and even they are pale to the palate compared with the Szechwan dishes of China and the indigenous dishes of Delhi. Dishes à la diable gain their piquancy through the use of mustard.

3 tablespoons imported mustard, such as Dijon or Düsseldorf
3 tablespoons dry white wine
1 teaspoon Worcestershire sauce
4 whole chicken breasts, split, boned and skinned
2½ cups fine, fresh bread crumbs
  Salt and freshly ground pepper

1. Combine the mustard, wine and Worcestershire sauce. Stir to blend.
2. Place the chicken pieces between layers of wax paper and pound lightly with a flat mallet. Sprinkle the chicken pieces with salt and pepper to taste and brush on all sides with the mustard mixture. Dip the pieces to coat all over in bread crumbs. Pat lightly with the flat side of a heavy knife to help crumbs adhere. Place on a rack.
3. When ready to cook, heat equal portions of butter and oil in two skillets. Add the chicken pieces and brown on both sides, for about 5 minutes to a side.

4. Serve with mustard cream sauce.
Yield: 4 to 8 servings.

4 tablespoon butter
4 tablespoons peanut, vegetable or corn oil
Mustard cream sauce (see recipe page 646)

Suprêmes de Volaille Cordon Bleu *(Deep-fried stuffed chicken breasts)*

1. Have the cheese and ham ready for the filling.
2. Place the chicken breasts between sheets of plastic wrap and pound lightly with a flat mallet to make them larger. Sprinkle with salt and pepper.
3. Spoon 1 tablespoon of shredded cheese in the center of each chicken breast. Cover with 1 rectangle of ham. Spoon another tablespoon of cheese on top of each piece of ham. Fold the edges of the chicken breasts over to enclose the filling. Place the stuffed chicken breasts briefly in the freezer before breading them.
4. Beat the eggs with the water in a flat container. Dip the stuffed chicken breasts first in flour to coat well, then in the egg mixture, coating all over. Finally, roll them in bread crumbs.
5. Cook in deep fat until golden brown and cooked through, 10 minutes, more or less, depending on the size of the stuffed pieces.
Yield: 6 servings.

¼ pound shredded Gruyère or Swiss cheese, 1½ cups
¼ pound boiled ham, about ¼ inch thick, cut into 6 rectangles
3 whole or 6 halved chicken breasts, skinned and boned
Salt and freshly ground pepper to taste
2 large eggs
¼ cup water
½ cup flour
3 cups fresh bread crumbs
Oil for deep frying

Chicken à la Kiev

1. Cream the butter with the chives. If unsalted butter is used, beat in salt to taste. Chill briefly. If the chicken breast pieces are small, use the lesser amounts of butter and chives. If quite large, use the greater amounts.
2. Place the chicken breasts between sheets of plastic wrap and pound lightly with a flat mallet to make them larger. Sprinkle with salt and pepper.
3. Put 1½ to 3 tablespoons of filling in the center of each chicken breast. Fold the edges over to enclose the filling. Place the stuffed chicken breasts briefly in the freezer before breading them.
4. Beat the eggs with the water in a flat container. Dip the stuffed chicken breasts first in flour to coat well, then in the egg mixture, coating all over. Finally, roll them in bread crumbs.

¼ to ½ pound butter
1 to 2 tablespoons chopped chives
Salt
3 whole or 6 halved chicken breasts, skinned and boned
Salt and freshly ground pepper to taste
2 large eggs
¼ cup water
½ cup flour
3 cups fresh bread crumbs
Oil for deep frying

5. Cook in deep fat until golden brown and cooked through, 10 minutes, more or less, depending on the size of the stuffed pieces.

Yield: 6 servings.

Chicken Breasts Lucien *(Chicken with vegetagles and cream sauce)*

3 whole chicken breasts, split in half, skinned and boned
Salt and freshly ground pepper to taste
6 tablespoons butter
2½ tablespoons flour
1½ cups fresh or canned chicken broth
½ cup carrots cut into very fine julienne strips
½ cup celery cut into julienne strips
1 cup finely shredded fresh mushrooms
1 cup heavy cream
Fine buttered noodles

1. Sprinkle the chicken breasts with salt and pepper and set them aside.

2. Heat 3 tablespoons of butter in a saucepan and add the flour, stirring with a wire whisk. When blended, add the chicken broth, stirring rapidly with the whisk. When the sauce is thickened and smooth, reduce the heat and cook, stirring frequently, for 30 minutes.

3. Meanwhile, heat 1 tablespoon of butter in a heavy saucepan and add the carrots, celery and mushrooms. Cover and cook until vegetables are wilted, stirring occasionally, about 6 minutes.

4. While the vegetables cook, heat remaining 2 tablespoons of butter in a skillet and add the chicken pieces. Cook on one side and when they start to become golden brown turn and brown lightly on the other.

5. Scatter the mixture of vegetables over the chicken pieces and cover. Cook over low heat for about 15 minutes. The breasts may be kept warm in a very low oven for a few minutes.

6. Add the cream to the sauce and stir as it comes to a boil.

7. Spoon the noodles onto a hot serving dish and arrange the chicken and vegetables over them. Add the sauce to the liquid remaining in the skillet and bring to a boil, stirring. Pour the sauce over the chicken and serve.

Yield: 6 servings.

Chicken Breasts Portugaise

5 tablespoons butter or chicken fat
2 medium-size onions, thinly sliced
3 cups cored, seeded green peppers, cut into thin strips (or use sweet red peppers, if available, to give color)
Salt and freshly ground pepper to taste

1. Preheat the oven to 400 degrees.

2. Heat 1 tablespoon of butter (or use chicken fat) in a saucepan and add the onion, green or red pepper, salt and pepper. Cook, stirring, for about 3 minutes, until crisp-tender. Add the mushrooms and cook, stirring for about 1 minute. Add the garlic, cook for 1 minute, then add the tomatoes. Add salt and pepper to taste and cover. Bake for 20 minutes. Remove the saucepan to the top of the stove and uncover. Cook, stirring occasionally, for about 10 minutes.

3. Melt 2 tablespoons of butter (or more if you think it necessary) in one large or two small heavy skillets. Add the chicken, skinned side down, and cook over moderate heat until that side is a gentle brown, 3 to 5 minutes. Turn the pieces. Cook for 8 to 10 minutes longer until the other side is lightly browned. Do not overcook. Transfer the chicken to a warm platter and cover to keep warm.

4. Add the shallots to the skillet and stir. Pour in the white wine and stir to dissolve any brown particles that may cling to the bottom of the skillet. Let the wine reduce almost completely and add the chicken broth. Let this cook until it is almost totally reduced. Add the tomato sauce and bring to a boil. Swirl in the remaining 2 tablespoons of butter, shaking the skillet. Return the chicken to the skillet and spoon the sauce over. Serve, if desired, with saffron rice on the side. Sprinkle with parsley.

Yield: 8 servings.

3	cups thinly sliced mushrooms
2	tablespoons finely minced garlic
2	cups whole canned tomatoes, preferably Italian plum tomatoes
4	whole chicken breasts, skinned and boned and split in half
2	shallots, finely chopped
1/3	cup dry white wine
1/3	cup fresh or canned chicken broth
	Saffron rice, optional
	Finely chopped parsley for garnish

Paupiettes de Volaille Florentine *(Chicken breasts stuffed with spinach)*

1. Preheat the oven to 375 degrees.
2. Pick over the spinach. Pull off and discard any tough stems. Rinse the leaves thoroughly to remove any trace of sand. Drop the spinach into boiling salted water and cook for about 1 minute, stirring. Drain immediately in a colander. When the spinach is cool enough to handle, press it between the hands to extract excess liquid. Put the spinach on a board and chop it finely with a knife. Set aside.
3. Slice the mushrooms and chop them. Set aside. There should be about 1¾ cups.
4. Cut 2 of the prosciutto slices into thin strips. Chop finely. Set aside.
5. Heat 1 tablespoon of butter in a skillet and add ½ cup onion, 1 small clove of garlic and ½ cup of diced mushrooms. Cook for about 3 minutes and add the chopped prosciutto. Stir in the spinach and rice. Sprinkle with salt and pepper and stir until blended. Set aside to cool.
6. Split each chicken breast in half. Trim away and discard the cartilage and nerve tissues. Place the chicken breast halves skinned side down on a flat surface and pound lightly with a flat mallet or the bottom of a clean skillet. Center a slice of prosciutto on each chicken breast. Spoon equal amounts of filling down the center of each chicken breast half. Roll the end of

1	pound fresh spinach, or 1 10-ounce package
1/4	pound fresh mushrooms
8	very thin slices prosciutto or boiled ham
3	tablespoons butter
1	cup finely chopped onion
2	small cloves garlic, finely minced
1	cup cold cooked rice
	Salt and freshly ground pepper to taste
3	whole, skinless, boneless chicken breasts
	Flour for dredging
1/2	cup finely diced carrot
1/4	cup finely diced celery
2	tablespoons flour
1/2	cup dry white wine
1	cup fresh or canned chicken broth
1	tablespoon tomato paste
1	sprig fresh thyme, or ½ teaspoon dried
1/2	bay leaf

the chicken over to enclose the filling and tuck in the bottom and top. Tie each bundle in 2 places with string. Dredge each bundle in flour seasoned with salt and pepper.

7. Heat the remaining 2 tablespoons of butter in a skillet large enough to hold the pieces and brown them all over, for about 10 minutes.

8. Remove the chicken pieces and add the remaining onion, mushrooms and garlic. Cook briefly and add the carrots and celery, stirring. Sprinkle with 2 tablespoons flour and add the wine, stirring with a wire whisk. Cook 5 minutes and add the broth and tomato paste. Stir to blend and add the thyme and bay leaf. Return the chicken rolls to the skillet. Cover with a round of wax paper and place in the oven. Bake for 30 to 40 minutes, or until chicken is tender.

9. Remove chicken rolls and discard the strings. Serve hot with the sauce spooned over. Leftover chicken rolls are good cold.

Yield: 6 servings

Chicken Breasts Stuffed with Mushrooms

3 whole, skinless, boneless chicken breasts, halved
¼ pound mushrooms
2 teaspoons lemon juice
6 tablespoons butter
2 teaspoons finely chopped shallots
Salt and freshly ground pepper to taste
2¼ cups fresh bread crumbs
1 tablespoon finely chopped parsley
6 thin slices ham, preferably prosciutto
2 eggs
1 teaspoon peanut oil, plus oil for deep frying
Flour for dredging
¼ cup finely chopped chives, optional

1. Preheat the oven to 400 degrees.

2. Place each of the chicken pieces between pieces of plastic wrap and pound to flatten lightly without breaking the meat.

3. Slice, then chop the mushrooms finely or slice and blend until coarse-fine in an electric blender. Add the lemon juice.

4. Heat 2 tablespoons butter in a skillet and add the shallots. Cook briefly and add the mushrooms. Sprinkle with salt and pepper and cook for about 3 minutes. Add ¼ cup bread crumbs and parsley.

5. Remove plastic and sprinkle the chicken pieces with salt and pepper. Center a piece of ham on each. Spoon equal portions of the mushroom mixture in the center and roll to enclose the filling. Place on a tray and chill.

6. Beat the eggs with the teaspoon of oil and salt and pepper to taste.

7. Dip the chicken rolls first in flour, then in beaten egg, and finally coat them all over with remaining bread crumbs.

8. Heat the oil and cook the chicken rolls until golden brown all over. Drain.

9. Place the chicken rolls on a baking dish and dot with remaining butter. Bake, basting frequently, for about 15 minutes. Serve sprinkled with chopped chives.

Yield: 6 servings.

Stuffed Chicken Breasts with Tomato Sauce

1. Preheat the oven to 375 degrees.

2. Skin and bone or have the chicken breasts skinned, boned and halved.

3. Using the fingers, make a pocket on the under or boned side of the chicken breasts for stuffing. Salt and pepper the breasts.

4. Heat 3 tablespoons of butter in a skillet and add the onion. Cook until wilted.

5. Rinse the spinach well and cook, covered in the water that clings to the leaves, stirring so that it cooks evenly, about 1 minute. Drain the cooked spinach and, when cool enough to handle, squeeze to extract excess moisture. Chop finely.

6. Add the spinach to the onions in the skillet. Add the ham, ricotta, egg yolk, Parmesan, nutmeg, sausage, garlic and basil. Blend thoroughly.

7. Stuff the 8 pieces of chicken breast with 2 or 3 tablespoons of the mixture. Fold the ends of the chicken to enclose the filling. It is not necessary to tie the pieces. Arrange the pieces close together in a baking dish, stuffed side down.

8. Melt the remaining 6 tablespoons of butter and dribble it over the chicken. Sprinkle with wine. Do not cover, but bake for 45 minutes to 1 hour, basting often. Serve hot with hot tomato sauce.

Yield: 8 servings.

4	large whole chicken breasts, the larger the better
	Salt and freshly ground pepper
9	tablespoons butter
1/4	cup finely chopped onion
1	pound spinach, or 1 10-ounce package
1	cup ground cooked ham
1	cup ricotta cheese
1	egg yolk
1/2	cup freshly grated Parmesan cheese
1/4	teaspoon grated nutmeg
1/4	pound ground sausage
1	clove garlic, finely minced
1	teaspoon dried basil
1/4	cup dry sherry
	Tomato sauce (see recipe below)

1. Heat the oil in a large saucepan and add the onion. Cook, stirring, until the onion wilts. Add the garlic and cook briefly. Add the tomatoes, wine, basil, thyme, oregano, orange peel, salt, pepper and sugar. Simmer over low heat for about 40 minutes, stirring occasionally to prevent sticking and burning.

2. Pour the sauce into the container of a food processor or electric blender and blend. Return to a saucepan and bring to the boil. Stir in the sour cream and serve.

Yield: About 4 cups.

Tomato sauce

1/4	cup olive oil
3/4	cup finely chopped onion
1 or	2 cloves garlic, finely minced
6	cups crushed, imported, canned, peeled tomatoes with tomato paste
1/4	cup dry white wine
1/2	teaspoon dried basil
1/4	teaspoon dried thyme
1/2	teaspoon dried oregano
1	piece orange peel, white pulp removed
	Salt and freshly ground pepper
1	teaspoon sugar
2	tablespoons sour cream

Chicken Breasts Mexican-style

6 whole chicken breasts, boned, skinned and cut into 1-inch squares
4 cloves garlic, finely minced
1 onion, finely chopped
2 canned peeled green chilies, chopped
3 tablespoons curry powder
½ cup brown beef gravy
1 teaspoon soy sauce
Salt and freshly ground pepper
2 teaspoons chopped fresh coriander, optional

1. Place the chicken pieces in a bowl. Combine the remaining ingredients and add to the chicken. Cover and refrigerate for at least 1 hour.

2. Preheat the broiler for 20 minutes. Arrange chicken in a metal pan large enough to hold the pieces placed close together in one layer. Broil for 6 minutes, or until top is brown. Do not turn the pieces.

Yield: 6 servings.

How to Cut Up a Chicken

French chefs have a much more "elegant" way of cutting up chickens for sautéed dishes than you're likely to get from any butcher. It produces ten separate pieces, including four that contain breast meat.

1. Place the chicken on its back and cut off the wing tip.

2. Place the fingers where the thigh and leg are joined, either left or right. Pull the thigh and leg away from the body and, using a sharp knife, carefully cut through and sever the thigh, cutting the joint where the thigh is joined to the body. Repeat this to remove the second thigh and leg. Cut through the joint where thigh and leg meet to make two pieces.

3. Hold the main wing bone with one hand and, using a small knife, cut through the joint that joins the wing bone to the body. While pulling the wing bone away from the body with the fingers, slice toward the rear of the chicken, cutting away a small strip of breast meat, three or four inches long. Leave most of the breast intact. If desired, cut off but reserve the "second," or middle wing joint. Repeat this on the other side.

4. Turn the breast section on its side. With a sharp knife, cut through both sides, cutting away the back bones and leaving the almost whole breast intact with bones.

5. Place the breast skin side up. Split it in half crosswise.

6. All the pieces are now ready to be sautéed. There are the two legs, two thighs, two wings with small strips of breast meat, two breast pieces and two second wing joints. The wing tips may be discarded.

Sauté of Chicken Antiboise

1. Sprinkle the chicken pieces all over with salt and pepper.

2. Heat 2 tablespoons of oil in a heavy skillet and add the chicken, skin side down. Cook for about 5 minutes over fairly high heat until nicely browned on the skin side. Turn the pieces and reduce the heat to moderate. Continue cooking to brown evenly all over, about 15 minutes, turning the pieces as necessary.

3. Transfer the pieces to a warm platter and cover with foil. Place in a warm place while finishing the sauce.

4. Add the cherry tomatoes and olives to the skillet and cook, stirring gently, to heat through. Spoon out the tomatoes and olives and add them to the chicken.

5. Pour out most of the fat from the skillet, but leave a shallow coating of fat. Add the onion, shallots, garlic, bay leaf and thyme and cook, stirring, for about 1 minute. Add the wine and cook over high heat until it is reduced by about half, stirring with a wooden spoon to dissolve the brown particles that cling to the bottom and sides of the skillet.

6. Add the chicken broth and sprinkle with parsley. Add the hot pepper flakes, if used. Cook down until the sauce is somewhat thickened, about 10 minutes.

7. Sprinkle the remaining oil over the sauce and stir briefly to blend. Add salt and pepper to taste.

8. Uncover the chicken and add any juices that may have accumulated to the sauce. Add the chicken mixture and reheat briefly. Serve the chicken with the sauce spooned over.

Yield: 4 to 6 servings.

1	3-pound chicken, cut into serving pieces
	Salt and freshly ground pepper
2	tablespoons plus 1 teaspoon olive oil
12 to 18	cherry tomatoes
12	stuffed green olives
12	pitted black olives, preferably imported olives, such as Italian or Greek
2	tablespoons finely chopped onion
1	tablespoon finely chopped shallots
1	teaspoon finely minced garlic
1	bay leaf
2	sprigs fresh thyme, or ½ teaspoon dried
½	cup dry white wine
½	cup fresh or canned chicken broth
2	tablespoons finely chopped parsley
½	teaspoon hot red pepper flakes, optional

Chicken Sauté Bourguignonne

1 3-pound chicken, cut into
  serving pieces
  Salt and freshly ground
  pepper
4 tablespoons butter
½ pound mushrooms left whole
  if small, otherwise quartered
  or sliced
½ cup finely chopped onion
2 tablespoons shallots
1 bay leaf
1 clove garlic, unpeeled but
  lightly crushed
2 sprigs fresh thyme, or ½
  teaspoon dried
1 tablespoon flour
½ cup chicken broth
1 cup dry red Burgundy wine

1. Sprinkle the chicken all over with salt and pepper.

2. Heat 2 tablespoons of the butter in a heavy skillet and add the chicken, skin side down. Cook for about 5 minutes over fairly high heat until nicely browned on the skin side. Turn the pieces and reduce the heat to moderate. Continue cooking to brown evenly all over, about 15 minutes, turning the pieces as necessary.

3. Transfer the chicken to a warm serving platter and cover with foil. Place in a warm place while finishing the sauce.

4. Do not pour off the fat from the skillet. Add the mushrooms, salt and pepper to taste and cook, stirring, over fairly high heat until mushrooms start to take on a little color, about 2 minutes. Add the onion, shallots, bay leaf, garlic and thyme. Cook, stirring, for about 1 minute.

5. Sprinkle evenly with flour and add the chicken broth and wine, stirring rapidly with a wire whisk. When smooth, use a wooden spoon to scrape off and dissolve the brown particles that cling to bottom and sides of the skillet. Cook for about 10 minutes.

6. Uncover the chicken and add any juices that may have accumulated around the chicken to the sauce. Stir. Swirl in the remaining butter. Add the chicken and reheat briefly. Serve the chicken with the sauce spooned over.

Yield: 4 to 6 servings.

Chicken Sauté with Watercress

2 bunches crisp, unblemished
  watercress
  Salt
1 3-pound chicken, cut into
  serving pieces
  Freshly ground pepper
3 tablespoons butter
2 tablespoons finely chopped
  shallots
½ cup dry white wine
1 cup heavy cream

1. Trim off and discard ½ inch or so from the watercress stems.

2. Drop the watercress sprigs into boiling salted water to cover. Use more salt than you normally would; it helps keep the sprigs green. When the water returns to the boil, cook for about 3 minutes, no longer. Drain quickly and run under cold running water to chill. Drain well and pat dry with paper towels. Put the watercress in the container of a food processor or electric blender and blend. Do not overblend and make a purée of the watercress. Tiny pieces should be identifiable. Set aside. There should be about ¾ cup.

3. Sprinkle the chicken pieces all over with salt and pepper to taste.

4. Heat 2 tablespoons of the butter in a heavy skillet and add the chicken, skin side down. Cook for about 5 minutes over fairly high heat until nicely browned on the skin side. Turn the pieces and reduce the heat to moderate. Continue cooking to brown evenly all over, about 15 minutes, turning the pieces as necessary.

5. Transfer the pieces to a warm serving platter and cover with foil. Place in a warm place while finishing the sauce.

6. Pour out most of the fat from the skillet, but leave a shallow coating of fat. Add the shallots to the skillet and cook, stirring, for about 1 minute. Add the wine and cook over high heat until it is reduced by about half, stirring with a wooden spoon to dissolve the brown particles that cling to the bottom and sides of the skillet.

7. Add the heavy cream and cook over high heat, stirring, for about 5 minutes. Add the watercress, salt and pepper to taste, stirring.

8. Uncover the chicken and add any juices that may have accumulated to the sauce. Stir. Swirl in the remaining butter. Add the chicken and heat as briefly as possible. Serve the chicken with the sauce spooned over.

Yield: 4 to 6 servings.

Poulet à la Moutarde *(Chicken sauté with mustard sauce)*

1. Sprinkle the chicken on all sides with salt and pepper. Heat the butter in a heavy skillet and add the chicken, skin side down. Cook until golden brown, about 5 minutes, and turn. Cook for about 5 minutes.

2. Pour off the excess fat from the skillet and scatter the carrots, mushrooms and shallots between the chicken pieces. Continue cooking for about 5 minutes. Sprinkle with flour, stirring the pieces to distribute the flour evenly. Add the wine and stir. Add the broth, bay leaf and thyme. Cover and cook for 20 minutes.

3. Turn off the heat. Add the mustard and stir it into the sauce. Do not boil further. Serve immediately.

Yield: 4 to 6 servings.

1 3-pound chicken, cut into serving pieces
Salt and freshly ground pepper to taste
2 tablespoons butter
12 small carrots, about ½ pound, trimmed and scraped
½ pound fresh mushrooms, the smaller the better
2 tablespoons finely chopped shallots
2 tablespoons flour
½ cup dry white wine
1 cup fresh or canned chicken broth
1 bay leaf
3 sprigs fresh thyme, or ½ teaspoon dried
2 tablespoons imported mustard, such as Dijon or Düsseldorf

Poulet Sauté au Vinaigre *(Sautéed chicken with vinegar and tomato sauce)*

It is a commonplace that there are many dishes, mostly imported, that enjoy a tremendous vogue in America. When we first came onto the food scene, curried dishes were the great fad coast to coast. In the intervening years, Americans have adopted such foods as boeuf bourguignonne, steak tartare, quiche lorraine, beef Wellington (for which we hold no high regard) and salmon with sorrel sauce. One of the most recent of these dining diversions is a chicken sauté served in a sauce lighty laced with vinegar.

One man who played no small part in this current vogue is Paul Bocuse, almost indisputably the most famous chef in the world. He has done more to "propagandize" French cooking than anyone else of his generation. When he spent a day in our kitchen, assisted by Pierre Franey and Jacques Pepin, two of America's best-known chefs, we came into an original source for the chicken sauté, which is served at Bocuse's restaurant in Lyons.

2 chickens, about 2½ pounds each, cut into serving pieces
Salt and freshly ground pepper
4 tablespoons butter
6 whole, peeled cloves garlic
6 whole, unpeeled cloves garlic
½ cup red wine vinegar
¾ cup dry white wine
1 cup fresh or canned chicken broth
3 tablespoons tomato paste
1 pound fresh, red, ripe tomatoes, peeled, seeded, and cut into 1-inch cubes, about 2 cups
2 tablespoons tarragon wine vinegar
3 tablespoons chopped fresh tarragon, or 1 tablespoon dried

1. Preheat the oven to 400 degrees.
2. Sprinkle the chicken pieces with salt and pepper.
3. Heat equal amounts of the butter in two heavy skillets and add the chicken pieces, skin side down. Brown on one side, for 6 to 8 minutes, and turn. Add equal amounts of peeled and unpeeled garlic to both skillets. Cook the chicken, turning the pieces often, for about 10 minutes. Using a slotted spoon, transfer the chicken from one skillet to the other. Pour off and discard the fat from the first skillet. Place the skillet containing all the chicken in the oven, uncovered. Let bake for 10 minutes. Remove from the oven and cover.
4. Meanwhile, add the red wine vinegar to the first skillet, stirring to dissolve the brown particles that cling to the bottom and sides of the pan. Cook over high heat until reduced by half and add the wine and chicken broth. Add the tomato paste and stir to dissolve.
5. Cook for about 15 minutes and add the tomatoes and tarragon wine vinegar. Bring to the boil over high heat and cook for 10 minutes. Add the tarragon and cook for about 3 minutes.
6. Pour off the fat from the skillet containing all the chicken. Pour the tomato and tarragon sauce over the chicken and stir to blend. Bring to the boil stirring, making sure the chicken pieces are well coated.

Yield: 6 servings.

Pollo alla Campagnola *(Chicken sauté with prosciutto and mushrooms)*

1. Sprinkle the chicken pieces with salt and pepper and dredge lightly in flour.

2. Heat the oil to a depth of about ⅓ inch in one or two large, heavy skillets. Cook the chicken pieces, turning often, until golden brown all over. Drain.

3. Place the mushrooms in a saucepan and add water to barely cover. Bring to the boil. Simmer for 1 minute and set aside.

4. Heat 8 tablespoons of butter in a skillet and add the garlic, onion and shallots. Cook, stirring, until wilted and add the prosciutto. Cook briefly and sprinkle with tarragon. Cook for about 3 minutes and add the browned chicken pieces.

5. Drain the mushrooms but reserve the cooking liquid. Add the mushrooms, lemon juice and white wine to the chicken. Add a little of the reserved mushroom cooking liquid and stir. Boil gently for about 5 minutes and add the remaining butter. When it melts, stir to blend and serve.

Yield: 8 servings.

2	3½-pound chickens, cut into serving pieces
	Salt and freshly ground pepper
	Flour for dredging
	Oil for shallow frying
¾	cup dried Italian mushrooms
12	tablespoons butter
2	cloves garlic, finely minced
⅓	cup finely chopped onion
¼	cup chopped shallots
¼	pound prosciutto, cut into fine julienne strips
1	tablespoon chopped fresh tarragon, or 2 teaspoons dried
3	tablespoons lemon juice
¾	cup dry white wine

Sautéed Chicken with Sorrel

1. Sprinkle the chicken pieces with salt and pepper. Heat the butter and oil in a heavy skillet with a lid. Add the chicken pieces skin side down and cook for 5 minutes or longer until golden brown. Turn the pieces and reduce the heat. Cook for about 10 minutes, uncovered.

2. Meanwhile, stack the sorrel leaves and cut them into fine shreds. This is called a chiffonade. Set aside.

3. Scatter the shallots around the chicken pieces and cook briefly. Sprinkle the chicken with the chiffonade and add the wine. Cover and cook for about 5 minutes. Uncover and add ½ cup of cream. Turn the chicken pieces in the sauce, but leave them skin side up. Cover and remove from the heat.

4. When ready to serve, uncover. Cook the chicken in the sauce over high heat for about 5 minutes. Remove the chicken to a warm platter. Blend the remaining ⅓ cup of cream with the egg yolk and stir it into the sauce. Cook just until the sauce bubbles up. Do not cook longer or the sauce may curdle. Serve the chicken with the sauce spooned over.

Yield: 6 servings.

2	2½-pound chickens, cut into serving pieces
	Salt and freshly ground pepper
2	tablespoons butter
1	tablespoon olive oil
4 to	5 cups loosely packed sorrel leaves
3	tablespoons finely chopped shallots
1	cup dry white wine
½	cup plus ⅓ cup heavy cream
1	egg yolk

Chicken in Tarragon Cream Sauce

2   3-pound chickens, cut into serving pieces
2   cups dry white wine
2   cups fresh or canned chicken broth
1   tablespoon finely chopped fresh tarragon, or ½ teaspoon dried
     Salt and freshly ground pepper
1   cup heavy cream
1   tablespoon butter
1   tablespoon flour

1. Arrange the chicken pieces skin side down in one layer in a heavy casserole. Add the wine, broth, tarragon, salt and pepper to taste and cover. Bring to the boil and cook for 15 to 20 minutes. Remove the chicken pieces and cover with foil to keep warm.

2. Cook the sauce over high heat until it is reduced by half. Add the heavy cream and cook for 8 to 10 minutes longer over high heat. Add salt and pepper to taste.

3. Blend the butter and flour and add it to the sauce, stirring. Do not boil. Pour hot sauce over the chicken and serve.

Yield: 8 servings.

Chicken and Sausage with Olive and Anchovy Sauce

1½   pounds sweet or hot Italian sausage links
1   3-pound chicken, cut into serving pieces
     Salt and freshly ground pepper to taste
3   tablespoons olive oil
1   cup chopped celery
1   cup chopped onion
½   pound mushrooms, sliced
8   flat fillets of anchovies
½   cup imported black olives, preferably in brine and from Italy or Greece
1   tablespoon drained capers
¼   cup dry white wine
¼   cup tomato sauce or tomato paste

1. Cut the sausage links into 3-inch pieces. Cook them in a heavy skillet, turning until browned all over. Remove, drain and put them in a casserole with a tight-fitting cover. Discard fat.

2. Sprinkle the chicken pieces with salt and pepper. In another skillet, heat the olive oil and brown the chicken pieces lightly on all sides. Add the chicken to the sausage.

3. Meanwhile, put the celery in a saucepan and add water to cover and salt to taste. Bring to the boil and simmer for about 5 minutes, or until crisp-tender. Drain but reserve both the celery and cooking liquid.

4. To the fat remaining in the skillet after the chicken is cooked, add the onion and mushrooms. Cook, stirring, until wilted. Add the anchovies, olives and capers. Add the drained celery, wine and tomato sauce and simmer for about 10 minutes. Add this to the chicken and sausage. Add salt and pepper to taste and cover closely. Simmer on top of the stove for about 30 minutes, or until chicken is tender. As the dish cooks, if it becomes too dry, add a little of the reserved celery liquid or a bit more tomato sauce.

Yield: 6 to 8 servings.

Poulet à l'Étouffée *(Oven-baked chicken with potatoes and mushrooms)*

1. Preheat the oven to 400 degrees.

2. Sprinkle the chicken pieces with salt and pepper. Heat the oil in a large, heavy skillet and add the chicken pieces skin side down. Cook for 8 to 10 minutes until nicely browned.

3. As the chicken cooks, drop the cubed potatoes into cold water. Bring to the boil and drain. Set aside. Cut the mushrooms into quarters. There should be about 1½ cups.

4. When the chicken pieces are browned, turn the pieces skin-side up and scatter the potatoes and mushrooms around them. Add the garlic and sprinkle with marjoram. Bake for 30 minutes.

5. Add the chicken broth and bring to the boil on top of the stove. Remove the chicken pieces to a hot platter. Add the lemon juice to the sauce. Pour the sauce over the chicken and sprinkle with parsley.

Yield: 4 servings.

1   3½-pound chicken, cut into serving pieces
    Salt and freshly ground pepper to taste
2   tablespoons olive oil
2   cups potatoes, cut into 1-inch cubes
6   mushrooms, about ¼ pound
3   cloves garlic, unpeeled
½   teaspoon marjoram or chopped rosemary
    Juice of half a lemon
2   tablespoons chopped parsley

Chicken Parmesan

1. Combine the chicken, oil, oregano, salt, pepper, garlic and 4 tablespoons of grated cheese in a baking pan. The pan must be large enough to hold the chicken pieces in one layer in a not too crowded fashion. Blend well and let stand, covered, until ready to cook.

2. Preheat the oven to 350 degrees.

3. Separate the pieces of chicken in the pan, arranging them skin side up. Leave the marinade in the pan. Sprinkle the chicken with wine. Sprinkle with remaining cheese and place in the oven.

4. Bake for 1 hour, or until the chicken is tender. If desired, run the chicken under the broiler for a second or so to crisp the skin. Spoon some of the pan drippings over the chicken. Pour the remaining drippings over the drained noodles and toss. Serve the chicken with the noodles.

Yield: 4 to 6 servings.

2   broiling or frying chickens, cut into serving pieces
½   cup olive oil
1   teaspoon dried, crumbled oregano
    Salt and freshly ground pepper to taste
1   teaspoon finely chopped garlic
6   tablespoons grated Parmesan cheese
1   cup dry white wine
1   pound noodles cooked to the desired tenderness and drained

Chicken Sauté with Lemon

2 1¾-pound chickens, cut into
   serving pieces
   Salt and freshly ground
   pepper
3 tablespoons butter
¼ cup finely chopped shallots
10 thin lemon slices
½ cup dry white wine

1. Sprinkle the chicken pieces with salt and pepper.

2. Melt the butter in a skillet and brown the chicken skin-side down. When golden, turn the pieces and brown on the other side.

3. Sprinkle with shallots and arrange the lemon slices over the chicken. Cover and cook for 5 minutes. Pour off the fat and add the wine. Cover and cook for 15 minutes, or until tender. Serve with the pan gravy.

Yield: 4 to 6 servings.

Chicken Haitian-style (*A kind of escabeche*)

3 2½-pound chickens,
   quartered
½ lemon or lime
¾ cup tarragon vinegar
2 cloves garlic, finely chopped
½ teaspoon freshly ground
   pepper
   Salt to taste
½ long fresh, hot red or green
   pepper, chopped or cut into
   rings
2 onions, about ¾ pound total
   weight
½ cup coarsely chopped, loosely
   packed parsley
¼ cup peanut or corn oil
½ cup dry white wine
½ cup fresh or canned chicken
   broth
1 teaspoon tomato paste

1. Rinse and drain the chicken pieces well. Rub the pieces all over with half a cut lemon or lime. Place in a mixing bowl. Add the vinegar, garlic, pepper, salt and hot pepper.

2. Cut the onions into ¼-inch slices and break the slices into rings. Add them. Add the parsley and let stand for an hour or so, turning the chicken in the marinade from time to time.

3. Heat the oil in a large, heavy skillet and cook the chicken, a few pieces at a time, until browned on all sides. As the pieces are cooked, transfer them to a Dutch oven large enough to hold them all. When the pieces are transferred, add the marinade to the skillet and stir to dissolve all brown particles that cling to the bottom and sides of the skillet. Cook for about 5 minutes. Add the wine, chicken broth and tomato paste. Add salt to taste.

4. Pour this over the chicken and partly cover. Cook, moving the pieces of chicken around occasionally, for about 45 minutes, or until very tender. Serve the chicken, hot or cold, with the sauce.

Yield: 8 to 12 servings.

Murghi Massala (*Chicken curry*)

1 3-pound chicken, cut into
   serving pieces
⅔ cup peanut, vegetable or
   corn oil

1. Pull off and discard the skin of the chicken or use the skin for soup. It is easy to skin the chicken, using the fingers and a dry clean towel for tugging.

2. Heat the oil in a large, heavy kettle and add the onion.

Cook, stirring, for about 5 minutes until the onion is dry but not brown. Add the cinnamon and cardamom seeds and continue cooking, stirring, until onion is golden brown. Add the garlic and ¼ cup water.

3. Add the yogurt and cook briskly, stirring, for about 5 minutes. Add the ginger pieces, turmeric, paprika, powdered ginger, cumin, coriander and 1 cup of water.

4. Cook, stirring, for about 5 minutes and add the chicken pieces. Add salt to taste. Cook for 20 minutes, stirring frequently.

5. Add the remaining cup of water and cook for about 10 minutes, stirring often. Add the cream and bring to the boil. Cook for about 2 minutes.

Yield: 4 to 6 servings.

1 large onion, coarsely grated, about 1½ cups
1 4-inch piece cinnamon stick
2 whole, unhusked cardamom seeds, or ½ teaspoon ground
1 tablespoon finely minced garlic
2¼ cups water
1 cup yogurt
⅓ cup fresh ginger, cut into pieces the size of match sticks
1 teaspoon turmeric
2 teaspoons sweet paprika
1 teaspoon powdered ginger
½ teaspoon ground cumin
1 teaspoon ground coriander
Salt to taste
½ cup heavy cream

Poulet à la Diable (Broiled chicken with mustard crumbs)

1. Preheat the broiler to high.
2. Sprinkle the chicken with salt and pepper. Brush on all sides with oil. Arrange the chicken pieces, skin side down, on a baking dish. Place the chicken under the broiler 3 or 4 inches from the source of heat. Broil for about 5 minutes and turn the pieces. Broil for about 5 minutes on the second side and remove.

3. Blend the mustard and wine. Place the chicken pieces skin side down. Brush the pieces on top with half the mustard mixture. Sprinkle the chicken with half the bread crumbs using equal amounts for each piece. Return to the broiler and broil for about 1 minute, or until richly browned. Do not let the crumbs burn.

4. Turn the pieces. Brush with the remaining mustard mixture and sprinkle with the remaining crumbs. Return to the boiler and let broil for about 1 minute, or until richly browned on the second side.

5. Immediately turn the oven heat to 350 degrees. Place the chicken in the oven and bake for 10 minutes, or until done.

Yield: 4 servings.

1 3-pound chicken, cut into quarters
Salt and freshly ground pepper to taste
3 tablespoons peanut, vegetable or corn oil
2 tablespoons imported mustard, such as Dijon or Düsseldorf
2 tablespoons dry white wine
4 to 6 tablespoons fine, fresh bread crumbs

Cuisses de Volaille aux Herbes   (*Baked chicken legs with herbs*)

16	chicken legs with thighs attached, about 1 pound each
	Salt and freshly ground pepper to taste
8	tablespoons butter
1½	cups fresh bread crumbs
2	tablespoons finely chopped shallots
2	teaspoons finely chopped garlic
4	tablespoons chopped parsley
1	teaspoon chopped thyme
2	teaspoons chopped fresh rosemary
½	cup dry white wine

1. Preheat the oven to 425 degrees.

2. Sprinkle chicken pieces with salt and pepper. Melt the butter in a baking dish large enough to hold the legs in one layer. Add the chicken legs and turn them in the butter until well coated. Arrange the pieces skin side down in one layer. Place the chicken legs in the oven and bake for 30 minutes.

3. Meanwhile, combine the bread crumbs, shallots, garlic, parsley, thyme and rosemary.

4. Turn the chicken pieces skin side up and sprinkle with the bread crumb mixture. Bake for 30 minutes longer. Pour the wine around (not over) the chicken pieces. Bake for 5 minutes longer and serve.

Yield: 8 or more servings.

Curried Chicken Wings

We have always treasured the writing of Janet Flanner, who for many years wrote a letter from Paris, signed Genêt, for *The New Yorker*. We were delighted to read in an interview that she shared one of our passions. "My favorite dish is chicken wings," she declared. "It's the most refined part of the creature." We can only add bravo and contribute several refined uses for that part of the creature.

18 to	24 chicken wings
3	tablespoons curry powder
¾	cup finely chopped onion
1	tablespoon finely minced garlic
2	apples, cored, peeled, and cut into small cubes (about 2 cups)
1	banana, peeled and cut into small cubes
1½	cups water
1	cup plain yogurt
1	cup drained tomatoes
1	bay leaf
	Salt and freshly ground pepper

1. Cut off and discard the small wing tips of the chicken wings. Leave the main wing bone and second wing bone attached and intact.

2. Heat a large, heavy skillet and, without adding fat, cook the chicken wings, stirring often, to brown. The chicken will brown in its own natural fat. Sprinkle the pieces with curry powder and stir. Cook, stirring often, for about 10 minutes.

3. Add the onion, garlic, apples and banana. Stir and add the water, yogurt, tomatoes, bay leaf, and salt and pepper to taste. Cover and cook for 45 minutes to 1 hour.

Yield: 6 to 8 servings.

Chicken Wings Chasseur

1. Cut off and discard the small wing tips of the chicken wings. Leave the main wing bone and second wing bone attached and intact.

2. Sprinkle with salt and pepper to taste. Heat a large, heavy skillet and, without adding fat, cook the chicken wings, stirring often, to brown. The chicken will brown in its own natural fat. When lightly browned, add the mushrooms, onion, shallots and garlic. Cook, stirring occasionally, for 5 minutes.

3. Sprinkle with flour and stir to coat the pieces of chicken and mushrooms. Add the wine, tomatoes, chicken broth and tarragon. Add salt and pepper to taste. Cover and cook for 35 to 40 minutes, or until chicken wings are thoroughly tender.

Yield: 6 to 8 servings.

18 to 24 chicken wings
Salt and freshly ground pepper
½ pound thinly sliced mushrooms
4 tablespoons chopped onion
2 tablespoons chopped shallots
1 teaspoon minced garlic
¼ cup flour
1 cup dry white wine
1½ cups tomatoes
1 cup fresh or canned chicken broth
1 tablespoon dried tarragon

Chicken Wings with Oyster Sauce

1. Cut off and discard the small wing tips of the chicken pieces. Cut the main wing bone from the second joint and reserve both. Set aside.

2. Put the pieces in a bowl and add 2 teaspoons of the cornstarch, 1 tablespoon of the oil, the dark soy sauce and sugar. Blend well.

3. Heat the remaining 2 tablespoons of oil in a wok or skillet and add the chicken mixture. Cook, stirring, for about 5 minutes, taking care that the sauce does not burn.

4. Add the chicken broth and cover. Cook for about 10 minutes, or until chicken pieces are cooked. Remove the chicken and set aside.

5. Cook down the liquid in the wok and add the ginger and scallion. Cook, stirring, and add the oyster sauce and 2 tablespoons of water.

6. Blend the remaining cornstarch with 1 tablespoon of water and stir this in. Add the wine. Return the chicken wings to the pan and stir over high heat to coat with the sauce.

Yield: 4 servings.

8 chicken wings
3 teaspoons cornstarch
3 tablespoons peanut, vegetable or corn oil
1 tablespoon dark soy sauce
1 teaspoon sugar
¼ cup fresh or canned chicken broth
1 tablespoon finely chopped fresh ginger
⅓ cup chopped scallion, green part and all
2 tablespoons oyster sauce
3 tablespoons water
1 tablespoon shao hsing wine, or dry sherry

Chicken Wings Risotto

8 chicken wings
2 tablespoons butter
Salt and freshly ground pepper to taste
½ cup finely chopped onion
1 teaspoon finely minced garlic
1 green pepper, cored, seeded and cut into ½-inch cubes
½ teaspoon loosely packed stem saffron
½ cup dry white wine
2 cups cored, unpeeled, red, ripe fresh tomatoes, cut into 1-inch cubes
1 zucchini, about ½ pound, trimmed and cut into 1-inch cubes
½ cup long grain rice
1 cup water
1 bay leaf
2 sprigs fresh thyme, or ½ teaspoon dried

1. Cut off the small wing tips of each chicken piece. Cut the main wing bone from the second joint and reserve both.

2. Heat the butter in a skillet and add the chicken pieces, including the small wing tips. Sprinkle with salt and pepper. Cook over moderately high heat, stirring occasionally, for about 5 minutes until golden brown. Remove the wing tips.

3. Add the onion and garlic and stir. Cook until wilted. Add the green pepper and stir. Sprinkle with saffron and stir. Add the wine and cook briefly. Add the tomatoes and zucchini. Blend well and add the rice, water, bay leaf and thyme. Sprinkle with salt and pepper. Stir gently to blend and cover. Bring to the boil and simmer for 20 minutes.

Yield: 4 servings.

Oven-baked Chicken Wings with Honey

18 chicken wings
Salt and freshly ground pepper
2 tablespoons vegetable oil
½ cup soy sauce
2 tablespoons ketchup
1 cup honey
½ clove garlic, chopped

1. Preheat the oven to 375 degrees.

2. Cut off and discard wing tips of chicken wings. Cut the remaining wings in two parts and sprinkle with salt and pepper.

3. Combine remaining ingredients and pour over chicken wings in a greased baking dish. Bake for 1 hour until well done and sauce is caramelized. If chicken starts to burn, reduce the heat and cover with foil.

Yield: 6 servings.

Southern Barbecued Chicken

1 2½-pound chicken
Salt and freshly ground pepper to taste

1. Prepare a charcoal grill and have it ready. The coals must be white hot but not overly plentiful or the chicken will cook too fast. Arrange the grill 6 to 8 inches above the coals.

2. Split the chicken in half for grilling. Place it skin side up on a flat surface and flatten lightly with a mallet. This will help it lie flat on the grill. Sprinkle the chicken with salt and pepper to taste. Sprinkle with oil or rub with lard.

3. Place the chicken skin side down on the grill and cook until browned, about 10 minutes. Brush the top with barbecue sauce and turn. Brush the skin side with sauce. Continue grilling, brushing often with sauce, until chicken is thoroughly cooked, for 30 minutes or less.

4. Give the chicken a final brushing with the sauce and remove to a serving dish.

Yield: 2 to 4 servings.

1 tablespoon oil or, preferably, softened lard
Southern barbecue sauce (see recipe page 653)

Southern Fried Chicken

There are many ways to prepare Southern fried chicken, but this is my favorite. It is my family's recipe for the dish and has a crisp, crunchy crust because the chicken pieces are soaked in milk before coating with flour.

The Viennese fried chicken that follows is essentially the same, except that the chicken is coated with egg and bread crumbs.

Both are good cold to carry along in a picnic basket.

1. Put the chicken pieces in a bowl and add milk to cover. Add the Tabasco sauce and stir. Refrigerate for 1 hour or longer.

2. Combine the flour, salt and pepper (the flavor of pepper is important) in a flat baking dish. Blend well. Remove the chicken pieces, two or three at a time, and dip them into the flour mixture, turning to coat well.

3. Heat the lard and butter in a skillet, preferably a black iron skillet, large enough to hold the chicken pieces in one layer without touching. Heat the fat over high heat. Add the chicken pieces, skin side down, and cook until golden brown on one side. Turn the pieces and reduce the heat to medium low. Continue cooking until golden brown and cooked through. The total cooking time should be 20 to 30 minutes. As the pieces are cooked, transfer them to absorbent paper toweling to drain.

Yield: 4 servings.

1 chicken, 2½ to 3 pounds, cut into serving pieces
Milk to cover
¼ teaspoon Tabasco sauce
1 cup flour
1½ to 2 teaspoons salt
2 teaspoons freshly ground black pepper
1 pound lard, or corn oil for frying
¼ pound butter

Viennese Fried Chicken

1   2½-pound chicken, cut into
    serving pieces
    Salt and freshly ground
    pepper
½   cup flour
2   eggs
2   tablespoons water
2   cups fine, fresh bread crumbs
¾   cup peanut, vegetable or corn
    oil
12 tablespoons butter
½   cup sizzling melted butter
    Lemon wedges, optional
    Parsley sprigs, optional

1. Sprinkle the chicken pieces all over with salt and pepper. Coat them evenly all over with flour. Beat the eggs with the water, salt and pepper to taste. Dip the floured chicken pieces in the egg mixture to coat well. Coat with bread crumbs and pat lightly to help the crumbs adhere. Continue until all pieces are breaded.

2. Heat the oil and 12 tablespoons of butter in a skillet large enough to hold the chicken in one layer. When the fat is quite hot, add the chicken, skin side down. Cook for 10 minutes and turn. Cook for 10 minutes on the other side. When ready, the chicken should be golden brown on both sides and cooked through.

3. Pour the melted butter over the chicken just before serving. Serve hot, garnished, if desired, with lemon wedges and parsley.

Yield: 4 servings.

Note: After the chicken is fried, it may be kept warm for up to 20 minutes in an oven preheated to 200 degrees.

Chicken Pot Pie

This can be one of the great dishes of the world. We are not speaking of the basic and hearty pie of New England and Pennsylvania Dutch territory made with boiled birds. No offense intended, but that is wine from a lesser bottle. What we do speak of is the elegant, when perfectly made, chicken pot pie of England.

The pastry:

2   cups flour
8   tablespoons butter
4   tablespoons lard
    Salt
2 to 3 tablespoons cold water

1. For the pastry, put the flour in a mixing bowl and add the butter, lard and salt to taste. Using a pastry blender, work the mixture until it looks like coarse cornmeal. Add the water a little at a time, working the dough lightly with the fingers. Add just enough water to have it hold together. Shape into a ball and wrap in wax paper. Refrigerate for at least ½ hour.

2. To make the filling, melt 3 tablespoons butter in a skillet and add the chicken, skin side down. Sprinkle with salt and pepper. Cook over low heat without browning for about 5 minutes, turning once. Scatter the carrots, celery and white onions over.

3. Heat the remaining 2 tablespoons of butter in another skillet and add the mushrooms. Cook, stirring, until they give up their liquid. Continue cooking until most of the liquid evaporates. Add the mushrooms to the chicken.

4. In a cheesecloth square tie together the parsley, cloves and thyme. Add it to the chicken. Cook, stirring frequently, for about 10 minutes. Do not burn.

5. Sprinkle with the flour, stirring to distribute it evenly. Add the wine and broth. Add the Tabasco sauce and cover. Simmer for ½ hour.

6. Preheat the oven to 400 degrees.

7. Meanwhile, cut the bacon into 2-inch lengths. Cook the pieces until crisp and brown. Drain.

8. Strain the chicken and pour the cooking liquid into a saucepan. Discard the cheesecloth bag. Arrange the chicken and vegetables in a baking dish (we used a 16- x 10½- x 2-inch oval dish). Cut the eggs into sixths and arrange them over the chicken and vegetables. Scatter the bacon bits over the chicken and vegetables.

9. Skim off and discard the fat from the cooking liquid. Bring the liquid to the boil and add the heavy cream. Bring the sauce to the boil. Simmer for about 20 minutes. Add the Worcestershire sauce, salt and pepper to taste. Pour the sauce over the chicken mixture.

10. Roll out the pastry. Cut a round or oval just large enough to fit the baking dish. Arrange it over the chicken mixture and cut out a small hole in the center to allow steam to escape. Brush with beaten egg. Bake for 30 minutes.

Yield: 6 to 8 servings.

The filling:

5 tablespoons butter
2 2½-pound chickens, cut into serving pieces
   Salt and freshly ground pepper
½ cup coarsely chopped carrots
½ cup coarsely chopped celery
1 cup small white onions, peeled
½ pound mushrooms, thinly sliced
3 sprigs fresh parsley
2 whole cloves
3 sprigs fresh thyme, or ½ teaspoon dried
4 tablespoons flour
1 cup dry white wine
4 cups fresh or canned chicken broth
   A few drops Tabasco sauce
5 strips bacon
3 hard-cooked eggs, peeled
1 cup heavy cream
1 teaspoon Worcestershire sauce
1 egg, beaten

Deep-dish Curried Chicken Pie

Pie pastry (see recipe
  page 608)
¼ cup butter
1 cup finely diced onion
1 teaspoon finely minced garlic
½ cup finely chopped celery
¾ cup finely diced apple
¼ cup flour
2 teaspoons curry powder
  Salt and freshly ground
  pepper to taste
1 bay leaf
3 cups fresh or canned chicken
  broth
3 cups cooked chicken, cut into
  bite-size morsels
1 cup heavy cream
2 tablespoons diced chutney
1 egg yolk

1. Prepare the pastry and set it aside.

2. In a saucepan melt the butter and add the onion, garlic, celery and apple. Cook, stirring, for about 5 minutes. Sprinkle with flour and curry powder. Add salt, pepper and bay leaf. Add the chicken broth, stirring constantly. Cook, stirring, until sauce thickens. Cook over low heat for 10 minutes. Add the chicken, cream and chutney and cook for about 1 minute.

3. Pour the mixture into a 2-inch deep 2-quart casserole. The curried chicken must fill the casserole to keep the pastry from sagging when it is added. Let cool.

4. Preheat the oven to 375 degrees.

5. Roll out the pastry to fit the top of the baking dish, leaving a 1- or 2-inch margin.

6. Brush around the outer rim and sides of the baking dish with the yolk beaten with a little water.

7. Neatly fit the pastry over the dish, letting the overlapping margin hang down. Press gently around the pastry to seal it against the yolk mixture. Trim off the bottom of the pastry to make it neat.

8. Cut small slits or one round on top of the dough to allow steam to escape. You may gather scraps of dough together and roll it out to make a pattern on top of the pie. Brush spots where cutout will be applied with yolk mixture before adding. Brush the top and sides of the dough with yolk mixture.

9. Place the dish on a baking sheet (this will facilitate turning the dish in the oven for even browning). Place in the oven and bake until piping hot and the pastry is nicely browned, about 45 minutes.

Yield: 6 or more servings.

Bitokes de Volaille au Persil (*Chicken patties with parsley*)

2 pounds skinned, boneless
  chicken breasts
2 tablespoons finely chopped
  shallots
1 cup fine, fresh bread crumbs
  plus bread crumbs for
  dredging

1. Finely grind or have ground the chicken breasts. This is easily done with a food processor.

2. Put the chicken in a mixing bowl and add the shallots, 1 cup bread crumbs, cream, salt and pepper to taste and the parsley. Blend well with the fingers.

3. Divide the mixture into 12 portions of approximately the same weight. Using the fingers, shape the portions into neat,

round, flat patties. Arrange on a baking dish and refrigerate until ready to cook.

4. Dredge the patties evenly on all sides with bread crumbs, patting lightly so that the crumbs adhere.

5. When ready to cook, heat 3 tablespoons of oil and 1 tablespoon butter. Brown the patties on one side, for about 3 minutes. Turn and brown on the other. Continue cooking to the desired degree of doneness (alternatively, after browning, the patties may be partly cooked and transferred to an oven preheated to 250 degrees to finish cooking, for about 10 minutes).

6. Transfer the patties to a platter. Heat the remaining butter in a skillet until it is light brown (noisette) and pour this over the patties.

Yield: 6 servings.

½ cup heavy cream
   Salt and freshly ground pepper
3 tablespoons finely chopped parsley
3 tablespoons peanut, vegetable or corn oil
5 tablespoons butter

Capillotade *(A French chicken hash)*

1. Preheat the oven to 425 degrees.

2. Remove the flesh from the chicken bones. Pull off the skin. Add both skin and bones to the broth in which the chicken cooked and continue cooking for 20 minutes or longer.

3. Cut the chicken into bite-size pieces. There should be about 2 cups.

4. Finely chop the mushrooms. There should be about 2 cups.

5. Heat 1 tablespoon of butter in a skillet and add the onion. Cook until wilted. Add the mushrooms, salt and pepper to taste. Cook for about 2 minutes and add the wine. Cook over high heat until reduced by half. Add the chicken and stir to blend. Cook for about 4 minutes and set aside.

6. Heat remaining 3 tablespoons butter in a 1-quart saucepan. Add the flour and stir to blend with a wire whisk. Add 2 cups of the simmering stock, stirring rapidly with the whisk. Strain and reserve remaining stock for another use. Add the cream, nutmeg and cayenne. Add about ⅔ of this to the chicken mixture. Simmer for about 5 minutes.

7. To the remaining sauce add the egg yolk and stir. Bring just to the boil, stirring rapidly, but do not cook further.

8. Pour the chicken mixture into an oval baking dish and spoon the remaining sauce over all. Sprinkle with cheese and bake until browned in the oven, for about 10 minutes.

Yield: 8 to 10 servings.

1 3-pound chicken, simmered in chicken broth until done
½ pound fresh mushrooms
4 tablespoons butter
¼ cup finely chopped onion
   Salt and freshly ground pepper
½ cup dry white wine
¼ cup flour
1 cup heavy cream
⅛ teaspoon freshly grated nutmeg
   Pinch of cayenne pepper
1 egg yolk
3 tablespoons grated Gruyère or Swiss cheese

Chicken or Turkey Croquettes

It has long been our contention that some of the best dishes in the world are those that bear the unseemly and unpalatable label "leftovers." Two of the merest cases in point are roast turkey and roast beef. We like them piping hot from the oven, but how much more delectable we find them the day after, thinly carved and tucked between slices of a decent loaf of bread, the slices smeared with freshly made mayonnaise. That and a pickle. Omar, the tentmaker, probably never knew his "paradise enow." Our enthusiasm for leftovers is evidenced by this heartily endorsed recipe for chicken or turkey metamorphosed into croquettes to be served with a fresh mushroom sauce.

3½ cups coarsely chopped cooked chicken or turkey meat, including skin
2 tablespoons butter
3 tablespoons finely minced onion
3 tablespoons flour
1½ cups fresh or canned chicken broth
Salt and freshly ground pepper
¼ teaspoon freshly grated nutmeg
3 drops Tabasco sauce
3 egg yolks
Flour for dredging
1 egg, lightly beaten
3 tablespoons water
1½ cups fine, fresh bread crumbs
Peanut, vegetable or corn oil for deep frying
Mushroom sauce (see recipe page 647)

1. Prepare the chicken or turkey and set aside. The chopped pieces should be no more than ¼ inch in diameter.
2. Melt the butter in a saucepan and add the onion, stirring to wilt. Sprinkle with flour and stir with a wire whisk until blended. Add the broth, stirring rapidly with the whisk. Stir in the chicken. Add salt and pepper to taste, nutmeg and Tabasco. Remove the sauce from the heat and add the yolks, stirring vigorously with the whisk. Cook briefly, stirring, and remove from the heat.
3. Spoon the mixture into a dish (one measuring 8- x 8- x 2-inches is convenient) and smooth it over. Cover with a piece of buttered wax paper and refrigerate, preferably overnight.
4. Remove the paper and, using the fingers, divide the mixture into 12 to 14 portions. Shape into balls and roll lightly in flour. The portions may be shaped finally into balls or cylinders. When smooth on the surface and neatly coated with flour, dredge in the whole egg combined with the 3 tablespoons water, and then in bread crumbs. Arrange on a rack and chill until ready to cook.
5. Heat the oil and, when it is hot, add the balls or cylinders, a few at a time. Cook for 2 or 3 minutes or until golden and cooked through. Serve hot with mushroom sauce.

Yield: 6 to 8 servings.

Chicken Loaf with Watercress Sauce

2 pounds skinless, boneless chicken breasts

1. Preheat the oven to 400 degrees.
2. Cut the chicken into cubes; place it in a food processor or electric blender and blend, stirring down as necessary.

3. Scrape the mixture into a mixing bowl and add the remaining ingredients, except for sauce. Blend well. Pour into a 6-cup loaf pan and cover with wax paper. Add a close-fitting lid.

4. Set the mold inside a larger heat-proof utensil and pour boiling water around it. Bake for 1½ hours, or until set and cooked through. Serve sliced and hot with watercress sauce.

Yield: 6 to 8 servings.

1 cup finely chopped onion
2 egg yolks
2 cups fine, fresh bread crumbs
⅔ cup heavy cream
1 cup finely chopped watercress
¼ teaspoon grated nutmeg
Salt and freshly ground pepper to taste
Watercress mayonnaise sauce (see recipe page 648)

Mousseline of Chicken with Mushroom Sauce

1. Carefully trim the chicken breasts of any nerve fibers. Refrigerate the chicken and the liver, if used. They must be cold when preparing this dish.

2. In a skillet, combine the flour and water and cook, stirring briskly and constantly with a wire whisk, mashing down as necessary with a plastic spatula. Cook for about 10 minutes in all. When ready, the mixture must be totally free of lumps. Spoon and scrape it into a small mixing bowl and cover with a light layer of oil to prevent a skin from forming on the surface. Let cool. Cover closely with a layer of plastic wrap and chill thoroughly. This mixture is called a panade.

3. Melt the butter in a small saucepan and remove from the heat. Let cool but do not chill. The butter must remain liquid.

4. Preheat the oven to 375 degrees.

5. Cut the chicken and liver into cubes and put them in the container of a food processor or blender. If a blender is used, this will have to be done in two or three steps. Add the butter and salt and pepper to taste.

6. Add the panade, cream, egg yolks, nutmeg and cayenne. Blend until smooth.

7. Beat the whites until stiff and fold them into the mixture.

8. Butter a 6-cup ring mold. Spoon and scrape the chicken mixture into the mold, smoothing the surface with a spatula. Cover closely with a round of wax paper.

9. Set the mold in a basin of boiling water and bring to the boil on top of the stove. Place the basin with the mold in the oven and bake for about 35 minutes, or until puffed and cooked.

10. Unmold onto a round plate and serve sliced with mushroom sauce.

Yield: 8 or more servings.

1 pound skinless, boneless chicken breasts
1 chicken liver, optional
⅔ cup flour
⅔ cup water
Oil
2 tablespoons butter
Salt and freshly ground pepper to taste
1 cup heavy cream
4 egg yolks
⅛ teaspoon freshly grated nutmeg
⅛ teaspoon cayenne pepper
2 egg whites
Mushroom sauce (see recipe page 647)

Pon Pon Chicken

2 cups shredded cooked
chicken
1 lettuce leaf
1 tablespoon chopped scallion
1 teaspoon or more chopped
garlic
1½ teaspoons finely chopped
fresh ginger
3 tablespoons well-stirred
sesame paste (see note)
1½ tablespoons soy sauce,
preferably dark soy sauce
1 tablespoon white vinegar,
preferably rice vinegar
1 teaspoon sugar
1 teaspoon monosodium
glutamate, optional
Salt
1 tablespoon chili paste with
garlic (see note)
1 tablespoon sesame oil (see
note)

Place the chicken in the lettuce leaf on a serving dish. Blend the remaining ingredients and pour the sauce over the chicken. Serve at room temperature.

Yield: 6 to 12 servings.

Note: These ingredients are widely available in Chinese grocery stores.

Shredded Chicken with Bean Sprouts

2 or 3 large chicken breasts,
about 2 pounds
Salt
3½ tablespoons shao hsing
wine, or dry sherry
2 egg whites
3 tablespoons cornstarch
4 cups plus 1½ tablespoons
peanut, vegetable or corn oil
⅓ pound bean sprouts, about 3
cups
2 tablespoons water
⅛ teaspoon sugar
½ teaspoon sesame oil
⅓ cup fresh or canned chicken
broth

1. Skin and bone the chicken breasts. Place on a flat surface and, using a sharp knife, cut them against the grain into thin slices. Cut the slices into very thin shreds. There should be about 2 cups. If desired, the chicken may be partly frozen to facilitate the slicing and shredding.

2. Place the meat in a mixing bowl and add salt, 1½ tablespoons wine and the egg whites. Stir in a circular motion until the whites become a bit bubbly. Add 2 tablespoons of cornstarch and 1½ tablespoons of oil. Stir to blend well. Refrigerate, preferably overnight, or for at least 1 hour.

3. Ideally, the tips of the bean sprouts should be plucked, leaving only the firm white center portion. This is tedious, however, and is not necessary. Set aside.

4. Combine the remaining 2 tablespoons of wine, remaining 1 tablespoon of cornstarch mixed with the water, salt, sugar, sesame oil and chicken broth. Stir to blend. Set aside.

5. Heat the remaining 4 cups of oil in a wok or skillet and add the chicken mixture. Cook over high heat, stirring constantly and vigorously to separate the shreds, for about 1 minute. Drain almost completely, leaving about 1 tablespoon of oil in the wok.

6. Add the scallions and ginger, stir for a second and add the bean sprouts. Cook, stirring vigorously, for about 15 seconds. Add the chicken, sesame oil mixture and vinegar and cook, stirring, until piping hot and lightly thickened. Serve hot.

Yield: 4 to 8 servings.

2	tablespoons chopped scallions
1	teaspoon chopped fresh ginger
1	teaspoon white vinegar

Chicken Soong *(Cubed chicken in lettuce leaves)*

1. Core the lettuce and separate it into leaves. Pile on a platter and set aside.

2. Place the chicken breast on a flat surface and, holding a sharp kitchen knife almost parallel to the cutting surface, cut the breast into the thinnest possible slices. Stack the slices and cut into shreds. Cut the shreds into tiny cubes. There should be about 2 cups. Place the chicken meat in a mixing bowl and add the egg white, salt and 1 tablespoon cornstarch. Blend well with the fingers. Refrigerate for 30 minutes.

3. Core the chilies. Split them in half and shred them. Cut the shreds into small cubes. There should be about ½ cup.

4. Slice the water chestnuts thinly. Cut the slices into small cubes. There should be about ½ cup. Combine the chopped chilies, water chestnuts, celery, carrots and ginger. Set aside.

5. In another bowl, combine the garlic and scallion and set aside.

6. Combine the wine, soy sauce, chili paste with garlic, sugar, monosodium glutamate, if used, and set aside.

7. Combine the remaining 1 tablespoon of cornstarch and the water and stir to blend. Set aside.

8. Heat the peanut oil in a wok or skillet and, when it is hot, add the chicken, stirring constantly to separate the cubes. Cook for about 1½ minutes and drain. Set aside.

9. Return 2 tablespoons of the oil to the wok and add the celery and water chestnut mixture. Cook, stirring, for about 30 seconds and add the scallion and garlic. Cook, stirring, for about 10 seconds and add the chicken. Cook, stirring, for about 30 seconds, or until the chicken is piping hot. Add the wine and soy sauce mixture and the sesame oil. Stir the corn-

1	head iceberg lettuce
1	large, boned chicken breast, about 1 pound
1	egg white
½	teaspoon salt
2	tablespoons cornstarch
2	long green chilies, hot or mild
10 or	12 water chestnuts
½	cup finely diced celery
3	tablespoons finely diced carrots
1	teaspoon chopped fresh ginger
2	teaspoons or more finely chopped garlic
3	tablespoons finely chopped scallion
2	tablespoons shao hsing wine, or dry sherry
½	tablespoon soy sauce
½	tablespoon chili paste with garlic (see note)
1	teaspoon sugar
1	teaspoon monosodium glutamate, optional
1	tablespoon water
2	cups peanut, vegetable or corn oil
½	teaspoon sesame oil (see note)

starch mixture until smooth and add it quickly. Stir rapidly for about 30 seconds and transfer to a hot platter.

10. Serve the chicken with the lettuce on the side. Let each guest help himself, adding a spoonful or so of the chicken mixture to a lettuce leaf, folding it before eating.

Yield: 6 to 12 servings.

Note: These ingredients are widely available in Chinese grocery stores.

Sesame Chicken with Asparagus Ring

3 to 4 whole chicken breasts
3 tablespoons sesame paste (see note)
2 tablespoons thin (light) soy sauce
¼ teaspoon hot oil (see note)
¼ cup plus ⅓ cup corn oil
¼ cup water
¼ cup Szechwan peppercorns (see note)
Salt to taste
1 pound asparagus
4 thin slices fresh ginger
Freshly ground pepper to taste
½ tablespoon shao hsing wine, or dry sherry
¼ teaspoon sugar
¾ cup loosely packed leaves of coriander

1. Place the chicken breasts in a kettle and add water to cover. Bring to the boil and simmer for 10 to 15 minutes, depending on size. Turn off the heat and let stand until cool.

2. Drain the chicken and pull the skin and meat from the bones. Shred the skin and meat. There should be about 5 cups.

3. Combine the sesame paste, soy sauce, hot oil, ¼ cup corn oil and water.

4. Place the peppercorns in a small skillet and cook briefly, shaking the skillet until the peppercorns give off a pleasant roasted aroma. Pour out onto a flat surface and crush lightly. Hold a sieve over the sauce and add the peppercorns to the sieve. Sift the fine, loose particles into the sauce. Reserve the coarse peppercorns for another use.

5. Scrape the asparagus with a swivel-bladed vegetable knife. Cut the stalks and tips on the bias into 2-inch lengths.

6. Heat the remaining ⅓ cup of corn oil in a wok or skillet and add the ginger. When it is quite hot but not smoking, add the asparagus pieces and immediately add the pepper, wine and sugar. Cook, stirring constantly, for about 30 seconds. Cover with the wok cover for about 15 seconds. Uncover and cook, stirring, for about 15 seconds longer. Take care not to overcook. Scoop out the asparagus.

7. When ready to serve, make a border of asparagus around an oval or round serving dish.

8. Add the coriander leaves to the sesame sauce and stir. Pour this over the chicken and toss to blend. Spoon the

chicken into the center of the asparagus. Garnish with sprigs of fresh coriander. Serve at room temperature.

Yield: 8 to 12 servings.

Note: These ingredients are widely available in Chinese grocery stores.

Spicy Jellied Chicken

1. Place the pork rind in a saucepan or small kettle, add cold water to cover and simmer for 10 minutes. Drain and run under cold running water. Drain and slice away the fat from the rind. Discard the fat and reserve the rind.

2. Drop the chicken into boiling water and turn it occasionally for about 3 minutes. Drain. Rinse well under cold water inside and out. Drain.

3. Place the chicken in a kettle and add the pork rind and all remaining ingredients except coriander sprigs. Cover and cook over low heat for about 1½ hours. Turn the chicken and uncover. Continue cooking, basting often, for about ½ hour longer.

4. Remove the chicken and drain the inside into the kettle. Continue cooking the liquid with the bony parts for about 45 minutes. Strain and skim off all fat. Discard the solids. If more than 2 cups of liquid remain, return it to the kettle and continue cooking until reduced to 2 cups.

5. When the chicken is cool enough to handle, pull away and discard the bones, large and small. Do not skin the chicken, but cut or pull away all excess or peripheral fat and discard it.

6. Arrange the chicken pieces compactly in a bowl such as a soufflé dish measuring about 7½ inches wide and 3 inches deep. Pour the sauce over the chicken and let cool. Chill until firm.

7. Unmold the dish onto a flat surface. Cut the mold into thirds. Cut each portion into slices about ½ inch thick. Arrange neatly on a serving dish and garnish with sprigs of fresh coriander.

Yield: 12 servings with other Chinese dishes.

½ pound pork rind
1 4-pound chicken
1 meaty, bony chicken back
4 chicken necks or wings
3 pieces star anise, available in Chinese grocery stores
1 2-inch piece cinnamon
½ cup dark soy sauce
¼ cup shao hsing wine, or dry sherry
4 cups water
2½ tablespoons sugar
Salt to taste
3 whole scallions
2 ½-inch pieces unpeeled ginger, crushed
Fresh coriander sprigs for garnish

Lemon Chicken

The chicken:

2 skinned, boned chicken breasts
2 tablespoons soy sauce
2 teaspoons shao hsing wine, or dry sherry
½ cup plus 1 tablespoon cornstarch
¼ teaspoon sugar
1 egg yolk
4 cups plus 1 tablespoon peanut, vegetable or corn oil
Salt and freshly ground pepper
¼ cup flour

The lemon sauce:

1½ tablespoons salted black beans
1 tablespoon water
3 tablespoons fresh lemon juice
½ cup fresh or canned chicken broth
3 tablespoons sugar
½ teaspoon sesame oil
2 teaspoons cornstarch
Salt to taste
Drops yellow food coloring
2 tablespoons peanut, vegetable or corn oil
2 cloves garlic, finely minced
¼ teaspoon crushed red pepper flakes

1. Place the chicken breasts on a flat surface and cut into thin (¼-inch thick) slices about 2 inches wide and 1½ inches long. Put them in a mixing bowl. Add the soy sauce, wine, 1 tablespoon of cornstarch, sugar, egg yolk, 1 tablespoon of oil, salt and pepper to taste. Let stand for 10 minutes or longer.

2. Blend remaining ½ cup of cornstarch with the flour. Coat each piece of chicken in this mixture.

3. Heat remaining 4 cups of oil for deep frying (400 degrees). Add the chicken, stirring to separate the pieces. Cook for about 30 seconds, or until chicken is golden brown. Drain well and transfer to a platter. Keep warm until the sauce is made.

4. Crush the black beans and add 1 tablespoon of water. Let stand until ready to use.

5. Blend the lemon juice, chicken broth, sugar, sesame oil, cornstarch, salt and food coloring in a small bowl. Heat 1 tablespoon of oil in a saucepan and add the garlic. Stir in the lemon sauce. Bring to the boil, stirring, and add the black beans and red pepper flakes. When clear and thickened, sprinkle with the remaining 1 tablespoon of oil. Pour this over the chicken and serve hot.

Yield: 6 servings.

Sesame Chicken with Garlic Sauce

The chicken:

6 chicken thighs
1 egg yolk
1 tablespoon soy sauce
1 clove garlic, finely minced

1. Bone the thighs or have them boned. Slice the thighs into 4 or 6 squares of approximately the same size. Place the pieces in a bowl and add the egg yolk, 1 tablespoon soy sauce and minced garlic. Let stand.

2. Sift the flour, cornstarch and baking powder into a bowl. Stir in the water, eggs, 2 teaspoons oil and sesame seeds.

3. To prepare the sauce, heat 1 tablespoon of oil and add the garlic and ginger. Cook briefly and add the chicken broth, sugar, soy sauce, ground pepper and monosodium glutamate, if desired. Simmer for about 5 minutes.

4. Add the chicken to the batter.

5. Heat 4 cups of oil in a wok or skillet and add the batter-coated chicken pieces, one at a time. Do not add all the chicken pieces at once. Cook, stirring to separate the pieces, for about 1 minute, or until golden brown. Drain each batch as they cook. Pour out the oil after cooking the chicken pieces. Return the chicken pieces to the wok.

6. Add the garlic sauce and blend well. Stir in the chopped scallions and sesame seeds and heat through.

Yield: 4 servings.

The batter:

 1 cup plus 2 tablespoons flour
 3 tablespoons cornstarch
 1¼ teaspoons baking powder
 ¾ cup cold water
 2 eggs, lightly beaten
 2 teaspoons peanut, vegetable or corn oil
 1 tablespoon sesame seeds

The garlic sauce:

 1 tablespoon peanut, vegetable or corn oil
 4 cloves garlic, finely minced
 1 teaspoon finely chopped fresh ginger
 ½ cup fresh or canned chicken broth
 1½ teaspoons sugar
 2 tablespoons dark soy sauce
 ¼ teaspoon freshly ground pepper
 ¼ teaspoon monosodium glutamate, optional
 4 cups peanut, vegetable or corn oil
 ¾ cup chopped scallions, green part and all
 1 tablespoon sesame seeds

Brochette de Volaille à l'Origan *(Skewered oregano chicken)*

1. There will, of course, be 6 chicken breast halves. Cut each half crosswise into 4 pieces. This will yield 24 cubes.

2. Place the chicken in a dish and add the remaining ingredients except the Mexican tomato and chili sauce. Turn the cubes occasionally so that they are well seasoned. Let stand until ready to cook.

3. Arrange the pieces on 4 to 6 skewers. If wooden skewers are used, it is best if they are soaked for an hour or so in water. Cover the tips with foil to prevent burning.

4. Prepare a charcoal fire in a grill. When the coals and grill are properly hot, brush the grill lightly with oil. Arrange the skewered chicken on the grill and cook, turning as necessary,

 3 chicken breasts, split in half and boned, but preferably with the skin left on
 1 teaspoon oregano
 Salt and freshly ground pepper
 2 tablespoons lime juice
 2 tablespoons peanut, vegetable or corn oil
 2 tablespoons finely chopped parsley
 Salsa cruda (see recipe page 651), or melted butter

until done, 20 minutes or longer. Serve with Mexican tomato and chili sauce or melted butter poured over. Serve, if desired, with mushroom rice with turmeric (see recipe page 456).

Yield: 4 to 6 servings.

Murghi Tikka *(Skewered chicken Indian-style)*

1	2½- to 3-pound chicken, cut into serving pieces
1	cup plain yogurt
	Salt to taste
¼	teaspoon turmeric
1	clove garlic, finely minced
1	teaspoon freshly grated ginger, or ½ teaspoon powdered
6	drops yellow food color

1. Pull off and discard the skin of the chicken or use the skin for soup. It is easy to skin the chicken, using the fingers and a dry clean towel for tugging when necessary. Using a paring or boning knife, cut the meat of the chicken from the bones in as large portions as possible. Save the bones for soup. Cut the meat into 2-inch cubes and set aside.

2. Combine the remaining ingredients and stir to blend. Add the chicken chunks and stir to coat. Cover and let stand for several hours, or overnight.

3. Skewer the chunks on a spit and grill over hot charcoal (see note) just until cooked through and still moist inside. Do not overcook or the chunks will become dry. Cooking time will vary, but 10 minutes is average.

Yield: 4 to 6 servings.

Note: The skewered chicken is preferably cooked by turning it on the spits over direct charcoal heat without using a grill. If necessary, however, the chicken may be cooked on the grill, turning frequently so that it cooks evenly.

Chicken Indonesian-style

10 to	12 chicken thighs
	Salt and freshly ground pepper
½	teaspoon ground mace
4	tablespoons butter
1	large onion, finely chopped, about 3 cups

1. Preheat the oven to 325 degrees.

2. Skin the chicken thighs and place them in a bowl. Sprinkle with salt, pepper and mace and rub to coat well. Heat the butter in a skillet and brown the chicken pieces lightly. Transfer the chicken pieces to a baking dish.

3. Meanwhile, combine the onion, garlic, lemon juice,

sugar, cumin, coriander, meat seasoning, hot chili paste and ketjap manis.

4. Add the onion and spice mixture to the skillet in which the chicken cooked. Cook, stirring, for 8 to 10 minutes.

5. Combine the grated coconut and water and let stand briefly, kneading with the hands. Squeeze the mixture through cheesecloth or a potato ricer. Add 1 cup of the coconut milk to the onion and spice mixture and stir to blend. Discard the coconut. Bring to the boil. Pour over the chicken and bake, uncovered, until the chicken is tender, 20 to 30 minutes. Turn the chicken pieces once as they cook.

Yield: 5 to 6 servings.

Note: These are Indonesian names of the various spices, which are available at outlets that sell imported spices.

1	clove garlic, crushed
1	tablespoon lemon juice
1	tablespoon dark brown sugar
1½	teaspoons ground cumin (djinten) (see note)
1½	teaspoons ground coriander (ketumbar) (see note)
2	teaspoons bottled imported meat seasoning (bumboe sesate) (see note)
½ to 1	teaspoon imported hot chili paste (sambal oelek) (see note)
½	cup ketjap manis (see recipe page 655)
2	ounces dried grated coconut (klapper) (see note)
1½	cups hot water

Chicken Korma

1. Cut the chicken into 2-inch cubes. There should be about 5 cups.

2. Heat ¼ cup of the oil in a heavy saucepan or small casserole and add the onion, garlic and ginger. Cook, stirring often, until the mixture is dark caramel colored. This may take 45 minutes or even longer and care must be taken that the mixture does not stick or burn.

3. Heat the remaining oil in a Dutch oven or heavy casserole and add 1 cup of the onion mixture. Add the water, paprika, salt, tomato paste and crushed cardamom seeds. Add the chicken and stir to blend. Add the chopped chili peppers and cover. Cook for 12 to 15 minutes, just long enough so that the chicken pieces are cooked through without drying out. Remove from the heat and let stand until ready to serve. When ready to serve, reheat briefly. Sprinkle with fresh coriander.

Yield: 8 to 12 servings.

3½	pounds skinned, boned chicken breasts
⅔	cup oil
8	cups chopped onion
3	cloves garlic, finely minced
1	2-inch piece ginger, finely grated
¾	cup water
2	teaspoons paprika
	Salt to taste
½	cup tomato paste
1	teaspoon crushed green cardamom seeds taken out of the pods
2 to 4	chopped fresh, hot green chili peppers
1	tablespoon chopped fresh coriander leaves

Yakitori (*Japanese skewered chicken*)

Yakitori could be described as the Japanese equivalent of hamburger, but in its variety and nature it is infinitely more sophisticated. There seems to be almost universal sides-taking in Tokyo as to the superiority of one fin bec's choice of yakitori restaurant over that of another. Yaki means grilled; tori means birds. And the bird of choice is usually chicken, cut into boneless cubes and arranged on skewers before grilling.

Bone the light and dark meat of a chicken, setting aside the heart, liver, gizzard and so on. Cut the light and dark meat into bite-size cubes. Arrange the cubes on skewers. If desired, arrange one- or two-inch lengths of scallions alternately on some skewers with the chicken pieces.

Trim and cut away the tough, muscular parts of the gizzards, if used. Arrange the tender gizzard pieces on skewers. Arrange the liver and heart on skewers. Grill the unseasoned chicken pieces, brushing as necessary with yakitori-no-tare (see recipe). Cook, turning often, until the chicken pieces are done. Remove from the heat, sprinkle with lemon and serve hot.

Yield: A varying number of servings, depending on the quantity of chicken used.

Note: Although strictly speaking only chicken or other fowl is used for yakitori, many restaurants also include other skewered foods: mushroom caps, asparagus wrapped in bacon, steak bits and so on.

Yakitori-no-tare (*Sauce for yakitori*)

Chicken bones, optional
½ cup sake
½ cup mirin (sweet sake), available in Japanese markets
⅓ cup or slightly more coarsely cracked rock sugar (see note)
1 cup dark soy sauce (see note)
2 to 3 tablespoons honey

1. If chicken bones are used, cook them over a charcoal fire, turning often and without burning. Crack them and put them in a saucepan. Add the sake, mirin, rock sugar and soy sauce. Bring to the boil and cook for 3 minutes.

2. Stir in the honey and boil 2 minutes longer. Strain before using. Use to brush chicken on skewers as it is grilled.

Yield: About 2½ cups.

Note: Rock sugar and dark soy sauce are available in Oriental food shops.

Brochette de Foies de Volaille *(Chicken livers en brochette)*

1. Pick over the chicken livers and trim them to remove veins and connecting tissues. Cut the livers in half. Place them in a mixing bowl. Add the soy sauce, sherry, sugar, garlic, monosodium glutamate, if used, and pepper flakes. Let stand until ready to cook.

2. Cut the bacon in half crosswise. Wrap 1 chicken liver half in half a bacon strip and arrange on 4 to 6 skewers. If wooden skewers are used, it is best if they are soaked for an hour or so in cold water. Cover the tips with foil to prevent burning.

3. Prepare a charcoal fire in a grill. When the coals and grill are properly hot, brush the grill lightly with oil. Arrange the skewered chicken livers on the grill and cook, turning as necessary, for 10 minutes or longer, according to the desired degree of doneness.

Yield: 4 to 6 servings.

¾ pound chicken livers
¼ cup soy sauce
4 teaspoons sweet sherry wine
1 tablespoon sugar
1 clove garlic, finely minced
⅛ teaspoon monosodium glutamate, optional
⅛ teaspoon crushed red pepper flakes
10 or more bacon strips

Chicken Livers in Madeira Sauce

1. Pick over the livers to remove any tough veins. Cut each liver in half. Set aside.

2. Heat 1 tablespoon butter in a saucepan and add the shallots, Madeira, brown sauce, salt and pepper. Simmer for 15 minutes. Add the remaining 1 tablespoon of butter and swirl it around until blended.

3. Heat the oil in a skillet and, when it is very hot, add the livers. Cook, turning the livers quickly, for about 1 minute. Drain in a sieve and add the livers to the Madeira sauce. Serve piping hot.

Yield: 4 servings.

½ pound chicken livers
2 tablespoons butter
2 tablespoons chopped shallots
2 tablespoons Madeira
½ cup brown sauce, or canned beef gravy
Salt and freshly ground pepper to taste
¼ cup peanut, vegetable or corn oil

Chicken Liver Sauté with Paprika

1. Pick over the chicken livers to remove tough membranes. Cut the livers in half. Sprinkle with paprika, salt and pepper, stirring to coat evenly.

2. Heat 1 tablespoon of butter and the oil in a small skillet. When very hot, add the livers. Cook over high heat, stirring the livers and turning them so that they cook evenly, for about 2 minutes. Drain.

3. Melt the remaining butter in the skillet and return the

½ pound chicken livers
1 teaspoon paprika
Salt and freshly ground pepper to taste
2 tablespoons butter
1 tablespoon peanut, vegetable or corn oil
2 to 4 slices buttered toast

livers to the skillet. Cook, shaking the skillet and stirring, for about 45 seconds. Serve on toast.

Yield: 2 to 4 servings.

Gâteau de Foies Blonds *(A baked mousse of chicken livers)*

The mousse of chicken livers:

¼ pound firm, fresh marrow (see note)
⅔ pound chicken livers, picked over to remove any veins and connecting tissue
1 very small clove garlic
1 cup whole eggs, about 4
⅔ cup egg yolks, about 8
2⅔ cups heavy cream
Salt and freshly ground pepper

The sauce:

1 cooked 2-pound lobster (see recipe below)
¼ cup butter, preferably lobster butter (see recipe below)
Salt and freshly ground pepper to taste
3 tablespoons Cognac or Armagnac
1 cup heavy cream
¼ cup whipped cream
3 egg yolks
2 tablespoons water
½ pound melted butter

1. Preheat the oven to 350 degrees.
2. To make the mousse, blend the marrow with the chicken livers and garlic clove in the container of a food processor. Beat lightly the whole eggs and egg yolks and stir the chicken liver mixture into the egg mixture. Add the cream, salt and pepper to taste and strain the mixture through a very fine sieve.
3. Butter a 6-cup mold and pour in the mixture (two 3-cup molds could be used). Line a deep baking dish large enough to hold the mold or molds with a layer of paper. Pour in boiling water. Place the mold in the dish and place in the oven. Bake for 1 hour or longer until the custard is slightly firm in the center. A straw inserted in the center will come out clean when withdrawn.
4. As the custard cooks, prepare the sauce.
5. Remove the meat from the tail and claws of the lobster and cut the meat into slices.
6. Heat the butter in a saucepan and add the lobster slices, salt and pepper. Add the Cognac and ignite. Add the heavy cream and whipped cream and bring just to the boil.
7. Prepare the egg yolks like a hollandaise. Place them in a saucepan and add the water. Cook, beating vigorously over high heat or hot water until they are thickened and pale yellow. Gradually spoon the clear liquid from the melted butter into the sauce, beating constantly. Pour out the white milky residue. Stir this into the lobster and heat without boiling.
8. Unmold the mold and spoon the lobster sauce over each serving.

Yield: 8 to 10 servings.

Note: If you wish to butcher your own, buy marrow bones and carefully crack them with a cleaver so that they break in half and the marrow can be easily removed. It will take about 1½ pounds of marrow bones to produce ¼ pound of marrow.

1. Combine the water, onions, carrots, garlic, parsley, thyme, salt and peppercorns in a kettle large enough to hold the lobster and bring to the boil. Simmer for 10 minutes.

2. Add the wine and return to the boil. Cook for 5 minutes.

3. Add the lobster and simmer for 20 minutes, covered. Remove from the heat and let stand for 10 minutes longer. Drain.

Boiled lobster

4 quarts water
3 onions, peeled and quartered
3 carrots, scraped and quartered
4 cloves garlic, unpeeled and lightly crushed
6 sprigs fresh parsley
2 sprigs fresh thyme, optional
  Salt to taste
12 peppercorns, crushed
1 bottle (3 cups) dry white wine
1 2-pound live lobster

1. Pound the carcass with a mallet and/or chop it finely with a cleaver. Add it to the container of a food processor and add the butter. Blend well.

2. Scrape the mixture into a saucepan and heat, stirring. Cook, stirring, until a nice "brown" or nutty smell comes from the saucepan. Add water to cover to a depth of about 1 inch over the top of the butter mixture. Bring to the boil and remove from the heat.

3. Strain the mixture through a fine sieve, using a wooden spoon to extract as much liquid from the solids as possible.

4. Let cool, then chill. The butter will harden on top. Remove the butter and discard the water. This butter will keep for more than a week in the refrigerator and can be frozen.

Yield: About ¾ pound.

Lobster butter

1 cooked lobster carcass, plus any excess trimmings, coral and so on
¾ pound butter at room temperature
6 cups water, approximately

Roast Turkey

1. Preheat the oven to 450 degrees.

2. Stuff with any desired stuffing and truss the turkey. Place it in a shallow roasting pan. Brush the turkey with oil and sprinkle with salt.

3. Roast the turkey for about 50 minutes until it is nicely browned. Turn the pan in the oven occasionally to brown evenly. When browned, cover loosely with a sheet of aluminum foil. Continue roasting, basting at intervals. After 2 hours, reduce the oven heat to 375 degrees. Continue roasting for about 1 hour longer, or until the turkey is done (a ther-

1 12- to 16-pound turkey
4 tablespoons peanut, vegetable, or corn oil
  Salt

mometer inserted in the dressing should register about 160 degrees).

4. Remove the turkey and pour off any fat that may have accumulated. Add about ½ cup of water to the roasting pan and stir to dissolve the brown particles clinging to the bottom and sides of the pan. Add this to the giblet gravy, if desired. Let the turkey rest for 20 to 30 minutes. Remove the trussing strings. Carve the turkey and serve with dressing and gravy.

Yield: 12 to 20 servings.

Corn bread stuffing

12	tablespoons butter
2	cups finely chopped onion
1	cup finely chopped green pepper
1½	cups finely chopped heart of celery
4	cups finely crumbled Southern corn bread (see recipe page 554)
3	cups crumbled toast
2	hard-cooked eggs, coarsely chopped
	Freshly ground pepper to taste
½	cup fresh or canned chicken broth
3	raw eggs
	Salt to taste

1. Melt 4 tablespoons butter and add the onion, green pepper and celery. Cook, stirring, until vegetables are crisp-tender. Set aside.

2. Place the corn bread and toast in a mixing bowl and add the hard-cooked eggs and the celery mixture. Add a generous amount of pepper and the remaining ingredients. Stir to blend well.

Sausage stuffing

	Turkey liver, gizzard and heart
½	pound sliced bacon, cut into small squares
½	pound sausage meat
2	cups finely chopped onion
3	cloves garlic, finely minced
1	teaspoon rubbed sage
4	tablespoons butter
4	cups fresh bread crumbs
3	hard-cooked eggs, coarsely chopped
½	cup chopped parsley
	Salt and pepper to taste

1. Place the turkey liver in the container of a food processor or electric blender. Cut away and discard the tough fibrous membrane from the gizzard and add the gizzard to the container. Rinse the heart well to remove blood and add the heart. Blend thoroughly.

2. Cook the bacon in a large skillet and, when it is rendered of fat, add the sausage meat. Cook until both are rendered of fat. Add the chopped onion and garlic and cook until onion is wilted. Add the puréed liver mixture and sage. Cook until liver mixture loses its red color. Add the butter, bread crumbs, eggs, parsley, salt and pepper. Cool.

1. Put the meat in a deep saucepan or small casserole. Cook, stirring with the side of a heavy metal spoon to break up lumps. Cook until meat loses its red color.

2. Add salt, pepper, bay leaf and thyme. Cook for about 5 minutes, stirring. Add the onion and garlic and stir to blend. Cover and cook for about 15 minutes. Add the wine. Stir. Cover and cook for 15 minutes longer.

3. Meanwhile, twist each link sausage at mid-point to make twenty-four miniature sausages. Add these to a skillet and fry them as usual, turning and shaking the skillet so that they brown evenly. Cook until done. Drain on absorbent toweling.

4. Spoon and scrape the ground pork mixture into a mixing bowl. Drain the sausages and add them.

5. Put the turkey liver on a flat surface. Chop it and add it to the stuffing. Add the chestnuts, parsley, salt and pepper and blend well.

1. Pour the rice into a saucepan and add water and salt to taste. Bring to the boil and simmer for 6 minutes, no longer. Drain.

2. Melt the butter in a large skillet and add the onion. Cook, stirring, until wilted. Add the rice, raisins, nuts and ground meat. Stir frequently, using the side of a heavy metal kitchen spoon to break up lumps in the meat. Add the cloves, cinnamon, salt and pepper and remove from the heat. Let cool.

3. Use the stuffing to fill the cavity of a 12- to 16-pound turkey. If there is leftover stuffing, set it aside.

4. Roast the bird in the usual fashion. Skim off most of the fat from the roasting pan. Spoon and scrape the stuffing from inside the turkey into the pan drippings. Add any reserved stuffing. Mix well and bake for 30 minutes longer at the same temperature used for the roasting.

1. Cut the neck into 1-inch lengths and set aside.

2. Cut away and discard the tough casing from the tender part of the gizzard. Place the gizzard pieces in a saucepan. Cut the heart in half and add it. Add the liver and cold water to cover. Add salt to taste and bring to the boil. Simmer for 30 minutes. Remove from the heat and drain. Set aside.

3. Meanwhile, heat the 1 tablespoon oil in a saucepan and

Ground pork and chestnut stuffing

2 pounds ground boneless shoulder of pork
Salt and freshly ground pepper to taste
1 large bay leaf
¼ teaspoon dried thyme
2 cups finely chopped onion
1 teaspoon finely chopped garlic
1 cup dry white wine
12 breakfast sausages in links, about ¾ pound
1 turkey liver
3 cups peeled, cooked whole chestnuts (canned may be used)
½ cup finely chopped parsley

Hamburger and nut stuffing à la Grecque

½ cup uncooked rice
1½ cups water
Salt
¼ pound butter
2 cups finely chopped onion
1 cup seedless raisins
¾ pound peeled, cooked chestnuts
½ cup pine nuts
1½ pounds ground top-quality beef
1 teaspoon ground cloves
2 teaspoons ground cinnamon
Salt and freshly ground pepper to taste

Giblet gravy

1 turkey neck
1 turkey gizzard
1 turkey heart
1 turkey liver
Salt to taste

1 tablespoon peanut, vegetable or corn oil
Freshly ground pepper to taste
1¼ cups finely chopped onion
½ cup finely chopped carrots
¾ cup finely chopped celery
1 clove garlic, coarsely chopped
3 tablespoons flour
1 bay leaf
2 sprigs fresh thyme, or 1 teaspoon dried
3 cups chicken broth
2 sprigs parsley
1 tablespoon tomato paste
1 tablespoon butter

add the neck, salt and pepper to taste. Cook, stirring frequently, over medium heat until the neck is golden brown, about 20 minutes. Add ¾ cup onion, the carrots, celery and garlic and stir. Sprinkle with flour and stir until neck pieces are evenly coated. Add the bay leaf, thyme, broth, parsley and tomato paste. Stir until the sauce reaches the boil. Continue cooking for about 1½ hours. Strain the sauce. Discard all solids.

4. Slice the giblets and cut them into slivers. Cut the slivers into fine dice.

5. In a saucepan, heat the 1 tablespoon of butter and add the remaining ½ cup of chopped onion. Add the chopped giblet mixture and cook, stirring occasionally, for about 5 minutes. Add the strained sauce and bring to the boil. Simmer for about 5 minutes and add salt and pepper to taste.

Yield: About 3 cups.

Canard Roti à Plat (*A basic recipe for roasting a duck*)

1 4- to 5-pound duckling
Salt and freshly ground pepper to taste
1 large clove garlic
¼ cup dry white wine
½ cup fresh or canned chicken broth
2 tablespoons butter, optional

1. Preheat the oven to 375 degrees.

2. Truss the duck with string and sprinkle it inside and out with salt and pepper. Chop the neck into 1- or 2-inch lengths. Cut away the tough outer membrane of the gizzard. Sprinkle the pieces of neck and gizzard with salt and pepper.

3. Place the duck on its back in a roasting pan. Surround it with the neck and gizzard. Place in the oven and bake for 30 minutes.

4. Remove the pan and pour or spoon off the accumulated fat. Turn the duck on its side and return to the oven. Roast for 30 minutes.

5. Remove the pan and spoon or pour off the fat. Take care not to pour off the nonfat liquid in the pan.

6. Increase oven heat to 400 degrees. Turn the duck breast side down and return to the oven. Bake for 30 minutes.

7. Turn the duck on its other side and bake for 30 minutes.

8. Remove the pan. Remove and discard the trussing string from the duck. Transfer the duck, back side down, to another roasting pan. If desired, rub the skin all over with the garlic. Return to the oven for 10 minutes. As it roasts, rub it once more all over with garlic.

9. Meanwhile, place the original roasting pan on top of the stove and add the wine, stirring with a wooden spoon to dis-

solve the brown particles that cling to the bottom and sides. Cook until reduced by half and add the chicken broth. Bring to the boil and strain the sauce. Reheat.

10. Traditionally, this sauce is enriched before serving by adding browned butter to it. This is optional, however. To make the butter, place it in a skillet and swirl it around and around over high heat until it foams up and then becomes hazelnut brown. Do not burn. Quickly add this to the sauce.

11. Cut the duck into quarters or carve it as desired. Serve with the hot sauce.

Yield: 4 servings.

Canard à l'Orange *(Roast duck with oranges)*

1. Preheat the oven to 375 degrees.

2. Using a swivel-bladed vegetable peeler, peel off and reserve the extreme outer yellow surface of 1 orange. Discard any of the white pulp that may cling to this "zest." Cut the zest, or yellow strips, into very fine shreds (julienne). Drop the shreds into boiling water and let simmer for about 30 seconds. Drain and set aside.

3. Completely peel all the oranges and carefully section them, cutting between the membranous intersections around each section. There should be about 1½ cups of sections. Set these aside.

4. Truss the duck with string and sprinkle it inside and out with salt and pepper. Chop the neck into 1- or 2-inch lengths. Cut away the tough outer membrane of the gizzard. Sprinkle the pieces of neck and gizzard with salt and pepper.

5. Place the duck on its back in a roasting pan. Surround it with the neck and gizzard. Place in the oven and bake for 30 minutes.

6. Remove the pan and pour or spoon off the accumulated fat. Turn the duck on its side and return to the oven. Bake for 30 minutes.

7. Remove the pan and spoon or pour off the fat. Take care not to pour off the nonfat liquid in the pan.

8. Increase oven heat to 400 degrees. Turn the duck breast side down and return to the oven. Bake for 30 minutes.

9. Turn the duck on its other side and bake for 30 minutes.

10. Remove the pan. Remove and discard the trussing string

4	whole seedless oranges
1	4- to 5-pound duckling
	Salt and freshly ground pepper to taste
¾	cup fresh or canned chicken broth
¼	cup sugar
¼	cup red wine vinegar
1	teaspoon cornstarch
1	tablespoon water
2	tablespoons Grand Marnier

from the duck. Transfer the duck, back side down, to another roasting pan. Return to the oven for 10 minutes longer.

11. Meanwhile, place the original roasting pan on top of the stove and add the chicken broth, stirring and scraping with a wooden spoon to dissolve the brown particles that cling to the bottom and sides of the pan. Bring to the boil. Strain into a pan.

12. Blend the sugar and vinegar in a very small saucepan and cook, watching carefully, until large bubbles form on the surface. Continue cooking until the syrup is thickened and slightly caramelized. This is called a gastrique. Add the sauce from the roasting pan. Bring to the boil.

13. Blend the cornstarch and water and stir it into the sauce.

14. Just before serving, add the zest and Grand Marnier to the sauce. Drain the orange sections and add them. Cook, stirring gently, just until sections are thoroughly hot. Do not break them in stirring and do not overcook or they will become mushy.

15. Serve the duck cut into quarters or carved. Pour a little of the sauce over the duck and serve the remainder separately.

Yield: 4 servings.

Canard Vasco da Gama *(Roast duck with green peppercorns)*

1	4- to 5-pound duckling
	Salt and freshly ground
	pepper to taste
¼	cup Calvados, applejack or
	Cognac
½	cup water
1	cup fresh or canned chicken
	broth
1	tablespoon green peppercorns
	(or more if you like it hot)
2	tablespoons butter

1. Preheat the oven to 375 degrees.

2. Sprinkle the duck inside and out with salt and pepper and truss with string. Chop the neck into 1- or 2-inch lengths. Cut away the tough outer membrane of the gizzard. Sprinkle the pieces of neck and gizzard with salt and pepper.

3. Place the duck on its back in a roasting pan. Surround it with the neck and gizzard. Place in the oven and bake for 30 minutes.

4. Remove the pan from the oven and pour or spoon off the accumulated fat. Turn the duck on its side and return to the oven. Bake for 30 minutes.

5. Again, remove the pan from the oven and spoon or pour off the accumulated fat, being careful to guard the nonfat liquid in the pan.

6. Increase oven heat to 400 degrees. Turn the duck breast side down and return to the oven. Bake for 30 minutes.

7. Turn the duck on its other side and bake for 30 minutes more.

8. Remove the pan from the oven. Remove and discard the

trussing string from the duck. Transfer the duck, back side down, to another roasting pan. Return to the oven for 10 minutes more.

9. Pour or spoon off all the fat from the roasting pan. Add the Calvados and flame it. Add the water and broth and stir with a wooden spoon, scraping to dissolve the brown particles that cling to the bottom and sides of the pan. Strain the sauce into a saucepan and add salt and pepper to taste and the green peppercorns. Bring to the boil. Skim off any fat. There will be very little.

10. Carve the duck into serving pieces.

11. Swirl the butter into the sauce and serve it with the carved duck.

Yield: 4 servings.

Canard au Citron *(Roast duck with lemon)*

---

1. Preheat the oven to 375 degrees.

2. Sprinkle the duck inside and out with salt and pepper. Truss the duck with string and arrange breast side up in a roasting pan. Place in the oven and bake for 30 minutes.

3. Remove the pan from the oven and pour or spoon off the accumulated fat. Turn the duck on its side and return to the oven. Bake for 30 minutes.

4. Again, remove the pan from the oven and spoon or pour off the accumulated fat, being careful to guard the nonfat liquid in the pan.

5. Increase oven heat to 400 degrees. Turn the duck breast side down and return to the oven for another 30 minutes. Turn the duck on its other side and bake for 30 minutes more.

6. Meanwhile, cut or chop the duck neck and wing tips into 1-inch lengths. Cut the gizzard into quarters. Place these in a heavy saucepan without additional fat and cook, stirring frequently, until nicely browned, about 10 minutes. Sprinkle with salt and pepper. Add the carrots, celery and onion to the saucepan and continue cooking, stirring frequently, for about 10 minutes.

7. Add the chicken broth, parsley, thyme, bay leaf, peppercorns, salt and pepper. Cook, skimming the surface as necessary to remove foam and scum, for about 45 minutes. Strain and reserve. There should be a bit less than 2 cups.

8. Carefully peel 1 lemon, removing only the yellow outer

1	4- to 5-pound duckling
	Salt and freshly ground pepper to taste
½	cup coarsely chopped carrots
⅔	cup coarsely chopped celery
¾	cup coarsely chopped onion
3	cups fresh or canned chicken broth
3	sprigs fresh parsley
3	sprigs fresh thyme, or ½ teaspoon dried
1	bay leaf
4	peppercorns
1	lemon
¼	cup sugar
¼	cup wine vinegar
½	cup sweet sherry or Madeira
1	tablespoon cornstarch
1	tablespoon water
¼	cup Grand Marnier

skin. Cut the skin into very thin strips (julienne). Use the peeled lemon for juice to be added later.

9. Drop this skin into a small saucepan of boiling water. Boil about 1 minute and drain. Set aside.

10. Blend the sugar and vinegar in a wide-mouth saucepan and cook over high heat, watching carefully, until the mixture is dark amber and large bubbles form on the surface. Take care that it does not burn or it will be bitter. This is called a gastrique.

11. Remove the duck from the oven. Remove and discard the trussing string from the duck. Transfer the duck, back side down, to another roasting pan. Return to the oven for 10 minutes more.

12. Pour off the fat from the original roasting pan. Place the pan on the stove and add the sherry, stirring with a wooden spoon to dissolve the brown particles that cling to the bottom and sides of the pan. Strain into the gastrique.

13. Blend the cornstarch and water and stir this into the sauce. Cook for 5 minutes and add the juice of 1 lemon. Cook 1 minute and add salt and pepper to taste.

14. Add the julienne strips of lemon and bring to the boil. Add the Grand Marnier.

15. Serve the duck cut into quarters or carved. Pour the sauce over the duck.

Yield: 4 servings.

Duck in Red Wine Sauce

2 oven-ready ducks, 5 to 6 pounds each
Salt and freshly ground pepper
1 tablespoon butter
⅓ cup coarsely chopped shallots
¾ cup coarsely chopped onion
½ bay leaf
½ clove garlic
2 sprigs parsley
¼ cup flour
1 bottle (3 cups) dry red wine, preferably Burgundy
1 cup fresh or canned chicken broth

1. Preheat the oven to 450 degrees.

2. Remove and discard the inner fat from the ducks. Sprinkle the ducks inside and out with salt and pepper.

3. Arrange the ducks back side down in a roasting pan (a rack is not necessary) and bake for 30 minutes. Remove the ducks and pour off the fat from the pan. Return the ducks to the oven and bake for 30 minutes longer. The ducks should now be fairly crisp and free of skin fat. If they are not, return to the oven for 10 minutes or so.

4. Remove the ducks from the oven and, when they are cool enough to handle, carve them as follows: Carve away and separate the legs and thighs. Carve on either side of the breast bone, carving the breast halves in whole pieces and leaving the main wing bone attached. Cut off and reserve the second

joint and wing tip from the wing bone. Trim off and discard any excess fat but leave the skin intact.

5. As the ducks are carved, arrange the pieces, skin side up, in one layer in a heavy casserole. Cover with a round of wax paper, then with the casserole lid, and set aside.

6. Chop the neck and carcass and other reserved bones of the ducks. Set aside. Discard any excess fat.

7. Heat the butter in a deep, heavy saucepan and add the shallots, onion, bay leaf, garlic and parsley. Cook, stirring frequently, until the vegetables start to take on color. Add the chopped duck bones and cook, stirring often, for about 10 minutes. Sprinkle the vegetables and bones with flour and stir until the bones are well coated. Add the wine and broth and stir well. Bring to the boil and add salt and pepper to taste. Cook, uncovered, for about 1 hour. Strain the sauce over the duck pieces. Press to extract juices from the solids. Discard the solids.

8. Cover the casserole and simmer gently for about 30 minutes. Serve if desired, with buttered wild rice (see recipe page 456).

Yield: About 8 servings.

Duck with Green Peppercorn Sauce

1. Prepare the duck stock and the crème fraîche at least one day in advance.

2. Bone the duck carefully, working the knife around the breast bones and thigh bones to keep the meat as nearly intact and in one piece as possible. Save the duck carcass to make soup or another batch of duck stock. Do not cut the fat covering the breast meat and thighs, but discard all remaining excess duck fat.

3. Cut the boned duck into 4 pieces as follows: 2 breast halves and 2 completely boned thighs. Carefully and neatly trim around the breast pieces and the thighs to remove all peripheral fat. Sprinkle the pieces on all sides with salt and pepper.

4. Use a heavy skillet and, when it is hot, add the duck pieces fat side down. Cook until the skin starts to become crisp and the meat immediately adjacent to the fat starts to lose its reddish color, about 3 minutes.

5. Turn the duck pieces and cook for about 2 minutes on the other side. The outside should be nicely browned but the in-

½ cup condensed duck stock (see recipe below)

6 tablespoons crème fraîche (see recipe page 653)

1 4- to 5-pound fresh duck
Salt and white pepper

2 teaspoons water-packed green peppercorns

side of the flesh should remain rare. Tastes vary, however, so cook it like steak to any desired degree of doneness.

6. Transfer the duck pieces to a warm platter and let rest briefly while preparing the sauce. Add the duck stock to a small, heavy saucepan and bring to the boil. Add the crème fraîche and stir until thoroughly blended and smooth. Bring to the boil. Crush the peppercorns and stir them in. Strain through a sieve, if desired.

7. Using a sharp knife, cut the duck pieces on the diagonal into ¼-inch-thick slices. Arrange them overlapping on 4 or 6 warm plates. Spoon the hot sauce over each serving.

Yield: 4 to 6 servings.

Condensed duck stock

1	duck carcass, including the heart and gizzard (the liver may be used for another purpose)
4 to	6 carrots, about 1 pound
2	leeks, well trimmed and washed
4 to	6 onions, about 1 pound
2	ribs celery
6	parsley sprigs
1	bay leaf
¼	teaspoon dried thyme
1	clove garlic, unpeeled and left whole
1	tablespoon duck fat, chopped
5	quarts water

1. Chop the duck carcass into 2-inch pieces. Set aside.

2. Coarsely chop the carrots, leeks, onions and celery. Set aside.

3. Tie the parsley, bay leaf, thyme and garlic in a cheese-cloth bag.

4. Brown the pieces of duck carcass and the chopped vegetables with the duck fat in a heavy skillet or kettle. It is not necessary to add additional fat. When well browned, add the water and cheesecloth bag. Do not add salt and pepper. Bring to the boil and simmer, skimming the surface as necessary, for about 4 hours. Strain. Discard the solids.

5. Put the stock in a saucepan and cook it down to 1½ cups.

Yield: 1½ cups.

Note: Leftover duck stock can be frozen.

Charcoal-grilled Duck, French-style

1	whole, cleaned, 4½- to 5-pound duck with giblets
½	bay leaf
	Salt and freshly ground pepper to taste
¼	teaspoon dried thyme
1	tablespoon peanut, vegetable or corn oil
3	tablespoons butter
1	clove garlic, peeled and crushed
2	tablespoons chopped parsley

1. In this method of grilling duck, the breast is cut away in two neat, flat pieces without skin or bone. The legs and thighs are left more or less intact with skin on and bones in. The legs and thighs are cooked first because they require the longest cooking, about 30 minutes. The breast meat is grilled just before serving because it cooks quickly like a small, thin steak or scaloppine.

2. Place the duck back side down on a flat surface. Rub a sharp knife such as boning knife along the breast bone, cutting through the skin and down to the bone. Carefully run the knife between the skin and the meat, pulling the skin with the

fingers to expose the smooth breast meat. Cut off and discard the skin. Now, carefully run the knife between the breast meat and the carcass, using the fingers as necessary. Remove the 2 pieces of breast meat.

3. Cut or carve off the 2 thighs, leaving the legs attached. Use the carcass for another purpose such as soup. Place the legs and thighs on a flat surface, skin side down, and carefully cut away the excessive peripheral skin fat that borders the thighs.

4. Sever the bone joint between the legs and thighs. This will facilitate cooking, but do not cut the legs and thighs in two.

5. Chop together the bay leaf, salt, pepper and thyme, chopping until the bay leaf is quite fine. Rub this mixture on the legs and thighs and over the breast and giblets. Brush all with oil.

6. Arrange the breast pieces, ends touching, in a flat dish. Cover with giblets and neatly arrange the legs and thighs, skin side up, over all. Let stand until ready to cook.

7. Prepare a charcoal grill and have it ready. The coals must be white hot but not too plentiful or the meat will cook too fast. Arrange the bed of coals about 6 inches from the grill that will hold the duck for broiling. Arrange the giblets on a skewer and add them to the grill.

8. Place the legs and thighs, skin side down, on the grill. Grill the legs and thighs, turning as often as necessary, until skin is crisp and flesh is cooked. If necessary, brush the food with a little more oil as it cooks. Grill the giblets until done, turning as often as necessary. About 5 minutes before these foods are done, add the breast meat and cook, for 1 or 2 minutes to a side, until done. Ideally, the breast meat should be served a bit rare.

9. Transfer the pieces to a serving platter. Slice the breast meat on the bias and cut legs and thighs in half where they join.

10. Heat the butter and garlic and pour over the grilled pieces. Sprinkle with chopped parsley and serve immediately.

Yield: 2 to 4 servings.

Vietnamese Grilled Lemon Duck

1   4½- to 5½-pound duck, cut into quarters
4   scallions, trimmed and finely chopped
1   teaspoon grated fresh ginger
2   teaspoons powdered turmeric
2   tablespoons dark soy sauce
1   teaspoon sugar
    Salt and freshly ground pepper to taste
½   teaspoon grated lemon rind
    Lemon wedges
    Nuoc mam sauce (see recipe page 654)

1. Quarter the duck or have it quartered. If the backbone is removed it will lie flatter on the grill. It will also cook more evenly if the wing tip and second wing bone are removed. Use a sharp knife and trim away all peripheral and excess fat.

2. Combine the scallions, ginger, turmeric, soy sauce, sugar, salt, pepper and lemon rind. Rub the mixture into the duck. Let stand for 4 hours or so, turning the duck in the marinade.

3. Meanwhile, prepare a charcoal fire. When the fire is ready, place the duck fat side down. Cook about 1 hour, turning the duck frequently and as necessary until it is evenly cooked and the skin crisp. Serve with lemon wedges. Serve individual small bowls of nuoc mam sauce on the side as a dip for the duck.

Yield: 4 servings.

Fosenjohn   *(Duck and meatballs in walnut sauce)*

The food of Persia has many combinations of meat with fruit, and often combined meat flavors within one dish. So it is with this quite outrageously good duck and meatball combination cooked in a sauce made with pomegranate syrup, raisins and walnuts.

The duck and sauce:

½   pound walnut meats
1   15-ounce box dark raisins
    Salt and freshly ground pepper to taste
6   cups fresh or canned beef broth
1   cup pomegranate molasses (see note)
⅓   cup water
1   4- to 5-pound duck

The meatballs:

2   pounds ground round steak
2½ cups coarsely chopped onion
6   tablespoons roasted chick-pea powder (see note), or fine dry bread crumbs

1. Using the fine blade of a meat grinder, grind the walnuts and raisins. Put them into a casserole large enough to hold the duck and sprinkle with salt and pepper. Add the beef broth and cook, stirring occasionally, for about 10 minutes. Add a small clean piece of iron such as the grinder blade. This will give a dark color to the sauce.

2. Add the pomegranate molasses and water. Cook, stirring frequently, for about 30 minutes.

3. Meanwhile, heat a heavy skillet and add the duck, breast side down. The duck will brown in its own fat. When the duck is brown on one side, turn it. Continue turning the duck and cooking until it is well seared and brown on all sides. This should take about 20 minutes.

4. Remove the duck. Reserve the rendered duck fat, if desired, for another use. Add the duck, back side down, to the walnut and raisin sauce. Ladle the sauce over the duck and into the cavity. Add as much sauce as the cavity will hold. Continue cooking.

5. Put the ground meat into a mixing bowl.

6. Put the onions into the container of a food processor or electric blender and blend to a thin purée. Add them to the meat. Add the chick-pea powder or bread crumbs. Add salt and pepper to taste. Blend well and add the milk. Work the mixture with the fingers until it is smooth and thoroughly blended. If you like spicy dishes, knead in more black pepper. Shape the mixture into meatballs about the size of golf balls. There should be 24 to 30 of them. Drop them around the duck into the walnut and raisin sauce. Cover and cook for about 30 minutes.

7. Skim off most of the fat from the sauce and turn the meatballs in the sauce. Cover and cook for 1 hour longer.

8. Remove the duck to a serving platter and surround it with the meatballs and sauce. Remove the piece of iron.

Yield: 8 to 12 servings.

Note: Available in shops that specialize in Middle Eastern foods.

Salt and freshly ground pepper
½ cup milk

Yuan Pao (Braised duck with leeks)

1. Remove and discard any cavity fat from the duck. Cut off the wing tips but leave the main wing bone and second joint intact.

2. Slice the skin of the duck from head to tail. Using a sharp cleaver, hack the duck's backbone from head to tail to open up the inside of the duck.

3. Open up the duck's inside, placing it skin-side down on a flat surface. Trim and pull away dark pulpy matter, veins and so on. Rinse the duck and drain. Pat dry.

4. Place the duck skin side up and, using a small trussing needle, skewer the skin of the tail section together neatly and firmly. Brush the duck skin all over with 3 tablespoons dark soy sauce. If the head is still on, loop a long, heavy string around the neck to facilitate turning it in hot oil.

5. Heat the oil in a wok or other utensil large enough to hold the duck with the body flattened. Add the duck, skin side down, and cook over high heat for about 3 minutes. Turn, spooning oil over the head so that it cooks, too. Cook for 3 minutes longer and remove. Pour out the oil and wipe out the wok. Reserve the oil. Return the duck to the wok, skin side up. Add the wine. Turn the duck skin side down and add 2 tablespoons of dark soy sauce and 6 cups of water. Add 1 ta-

1 5-pound duck, preferably with head left on, available in Chinese poultry markets
6 tablespoons dark soy sauce
6 cups oil
6 tablespoons shao hsing wine, or dry sherry
6 cups water
1 tablespoon plus 1 teaspoon salt
2 tablespoons plus 1 teaspoon sugar
6 leeks

blespoon of salt and 2 tablespoons of sugar. Cover and cook over low heat for about 45 minutes. Turn duck and cook 1 hour. (The duck may be cooked to this point and left to stand.)

6. Meanwhile, trim off the end of the leeks. Cut off the tops of the leeks but leave leeks 7 or 8 inches long. Split leeks in half and rinse well under cold water. A spoonful of salt added to the water helps in cleaning. Drain the leeks.

7. Heat reserved oil for deep fat frying in a wok or kettle and add the leeks. Cook for about 4 minutes. Remove and drain.

8. About ½ hour before serving, reheat the duck and add the leeks. Cover and cook for 15 minutes.

9. Remove the duck to a platter skin side up and remove the string from the neck. Cover the duck with the leeks. Add remaining tablespoon of dark soy sauce, remaining 1 teaspoon salt and remaining teaspoon sugar to the sauce and boil down until syrupy. Pour it over the duck and serve hot.

Yield: 8 servings with other Chinese dishes.

Sliced Duck with Young Ginger Root

1 4- to 5-pound duck, the smaller the better

1 teaspoon salt

1 tablespoon plus 4 teaspoons cornstarch

6 water chestnuts, sliced, about 1½ cups

1 sweet red pepper, cored, seeded and cut into ½-inch cubes, about ½ cup

2 scallions, trimmed and cut into ½-inch lengths, about ½ cup

5 pieces bottled young ginger root in syrup, available in 1-pound jars in Chinese markets

15 whole fresh asparagus spears for garnish, optional

4 cups peanut, vegetable or corn oil

¾ cup fresh or canned chicken broth

¼ teaspoon monosodium glutamate, optional

1. Using a sharp knife, carefully remove and discard the skin from the duck. Bone the duck, reserving the bones, if desired, for soup. To facilitate slicing, the duck meat may be partly frozen. In any event, cut the duck meat into very thin slices, about 3 cups. To this, add ½ teaspoon salt and 4 teaspoons of cornstarch and blend well.

2. Prepare the water chestnuts, sweet peppers and scallions and set aside.

3. Rinse off the ginger and slice thinly. There should be about ⅔ cup. Set aside.

4. Scrape the asparagus spears, if used, leaving the tips intact. Drop the spears into boiling water for about 50 seconds. Drain and immediately run under cold water to crisp. Drain thoroughly.

5. Heat 2 cups of oil in a wok or skillet and add the asparagus. Cook for about 45 seconds and drain completely. Reserve the oil. Add ½ cup chicken broth to the wok and the asparagus. Cook for about 10 seconds and sprinkle with remaining salt and monosodium glutamate, if used. Drain and transfer to a platter.

6. Combine the wine, remaining cornstarch blended with the water, soy sauce, vinegar, sesame oil and remaining ¼ cup chicken broth. Set aside.

7. Heat the remaining oil, including reserved oil, in a wok or skillet and add the water chestnuts. Cook for about 10 seconds and add the duck, stirring and tossing constantly. Cook for about 30 seconds. Add the sweet red peppers and ginger pieces and cook, stirring, for about 10 seconds. Drain completely.

8. To the wok add 2 teaspoons of hot pepper oil and add the scallions and fresh ginger. Add the duck mixture and the vinegar mixture, stirring rapidly. Cook until piping hot and until the duck pieces are thoroughly coated. Serve on the platter with the asparagus spears as a garnish.

Yield: 4 to 8 servings.

2 tablespoons shao hsing wine, or dry sherry
2 tablespoons water
2 tablespoons soy sauce
½ teaspoon white vinegar
½ teaspoon sesame oil
1 tablespoon finely chopped fresh ginger
2 teaspoons hot pepper or chili oil, available in bottles in Chinese markets

Confit d'Oie (*Preserved goose*)

One of the glories of the French table is a dish that has received little notice in America. Except for some rare and special occasions, it is almost nonexistent in the nation's French restaurants. Confit d'oie, or preserved goose, is a delicacy of consummate goodness that is easily, if a trifle expensively, made. The goose is cut into large pieces, seasoned and marinated overnight. The following morning it is cooked in a boiling bath of goose fat and lard. The goose is then cooled and stored for up to a year.

Those Americans who may be conversant with the dish know it best as the classic ingredient for some of the traditional cassoulets of France. It is an essential taste that is often missing in cassoulets in this country, but one that is well worth the effort.

But preserved goose, sliced and cooked until it is crisp and golden brown and served with thin sliced potatoes cooked in hot goose fat is paradise enough.

1. Cut off and discard the wing tips of the goose. Cut off and reserve the second wing joints. Cut or pull away any solid goose fat and reserve it.

2. Carefully cut off the thighs and legs of the goose, leaving each leg and thigh attached.

3. Carefully bone away the breast of the goose in two sections, left and right, but leaving the main wing bone attached and unboned. Reserve the gizzard.

1 12- to 14-pound oven-ready goose
Salt and freshly ground pepper
1 bay leaf
½ teaspoon dried thyme
½ teaspoon saltpeter, available in drugstores
3 pounds lard (see note)

4. Use the bony carcass of the goose for making soup. Cut off and reserve any additional pieces or scraps of goose skin.

5. Sprinkle the goose pieces—the leg and thigh pieces, the breast halves and the second wing joints—with salt and pepper, using a fairly generous amount of salt. Rub it in on all sides.

6. Place the bay leaf on a flat surface. Using a sharp heavy knife, chop it finely. Add the thyme and chop it. Add the saltpeter. Rub the mixture into the goose pieces on all sides. Pack the pieces into a mixing bowl or other utensil. Cover closely and refrigerate for 24 hours.

7. Heat one or two large, heavy, deep skillets, flameproof casseroles or Dutch ovens and add the breast and thigh pieces, skin side down, in one layer. Add the second wing joints, gizzard and the reserved goose fat and skin. Add the lard and bring to a boil. The goose will be cooked in fat without any additional liquid. The goose pieces must be totally immersed in fat when the fat melts. Cover and cook for 2 hours.

8. Using a two-pronged fork, carefully remove the goose pieces (thighs with legs, breast halves, and second wing joints). Reserve the cooking fat.

9. Arrange equal portions of the goose pieces in two earthenware terrines or casseroles. The pieces should be arranged as compactly as possible.

10. Strain enough of the cooking fat over both terrines so that the goose parts are completely submerged in fat. If the goose pieces are not completely covered, it will be necessary to add more lard and pour it over. Let stand until thoroughly cool. Refrigerate. Cover closely. Properly refrigerated or stored in a cold, dry place, preserved goose should keep for weeks and even months.

Yield: 1 preserved goose.

Note: It is a minor point, but it would be preferable if all goose fat rather than lard were used for cooking the goose. For example, if you were cooking 3 geese (roasting or whatever) during the winter season, the extra fat in each goose could be reserved and frozen until ready to make the confit d'oie.

Roast Goose with Fruit Stuffing

1. Preheat the oven to 400 degrees.

2. Fill the cavity of the goose with the stuffing. Truss the goose and sprinkle it all over with salt and pepper.

3. Place the goose breast side up in a shallow roasting pan. Place it in the oven and bake for 1 hour, basting occasionally.

4. Pour off the fat from the roasting pan and scatter the onion, celery, carrots, garlic and bay leaf around the goose. Add the neck and cook for 1 hour. Baste often. At the end of 2 hours of cooking time, or before if the goose becomes too brown, cover with foil.

5. Continue roasting for 1 hour, a total of 3 hours. Remove the goose to a warm platter. Pour off the fat from the roasting pan and add the cup of water, stirring to dissolve the brown particles on the bottom and around the sides of the pan. Strain the pan liquid and serve as sauce.

6. Remove and discard the trussing string from the goose. Carve the goose and serve.

Yield: 10 or more servings.

1	19-pound goose
	Fruit stuffing (see recipe below)
	Salt and freshly ground pepper to taste
1	cup coarsely chopped onion
1	cup coarsely chopped celery
¾	cup coarsely chopped carrots
1	whole clove garlic, unpeeled
1	bay leaf
1	cup water

1. Trim off and discard the tough outer coating of the gizzard. Pick over the liver and remove the veins. Put the gizzard, liver and heart pieces into the container of a food processor or electric blender and blend thoroughly.

2. Heat the butter in a large, heavy skillet and add the celery and onion. Cook until wilted and add the puréed liver mixture. Stir and add the garlic, wine, sage, thyme, bay leaf and parsley. Cook, stirring, for about 5 minutes. Add the remaining ingredients and blend well with the hands.

Fruit stuffing for goose

	Goose gizzard, liver and heart
3	tablespoons butter
2	cups finely chopped celery
2½	cups finely chopped onion
1	clove garlic, finely chopped
1	cup dry white wine
1	tablespoon chopped sage
¼	teaspoon chopped thyme
1	bay leaf
1	cup finely chopped parsley
1	12-ounce package pitted prunes, chopped
6	cups peeled, seeded apples, cut into thin wedges
2	cups coarse fresh bread crumbs
	Salt and freshly ground pepper to taste
2	egg yolks, lightly beaten

Roast Capon with Nut Stuffing

1 8- to 10-pound capon, cleaned weight
1 cup pecans or walnuts
½ pound fresh mushrooms
½ pound chicken livers
2 tablespoons butter
1 cup finely chopped onion
2 cloves garlic, finely minced
2 teaspoons chopped fresh thyme, or 1 teaspoon dried
½ cup coarsely chopped parsley
  Salt and freshly ground pepper
1 pound sausage meat
2 eggs
2 cups bread crumbs
¾ cup coarsely chopped onion
¾ cup coarsely chopped celery
½ cup coarsely chopped carrots
1 whole garlic clove
½ bay leaf
2 sprigs fresh thyme, or ½ teaspoon dried
1 cup fresh or canned chicken broth

1. Preheat the oven to 425 degrees.

2. Remove the inner fat from the cavity of the capon. Set aside with the liver, neck, gizzard and heart.

3. Place the pecans or walnuts on a baking dish and bake until crisp. Take care not to burn them. Remove and let cool.

4. Cut or chop the mushrooms into very small dice.

5. Cut both the capon liver and chicken livers into small pieces.

6. Heat the butter and add the finely chopped onion. Cook until wilted and add the minced garlic and mushrooms. Cook briefly, stirring, until mushrooms give up their liquid. Continue cooking until liquid evaporates. Add the chopped livers, chopped thyme, parsley, salt and pepper to taste.

7. Cook until the liver changes color. Add the sausage meat, stirring to break up the sausage with the side of a spoon. Add the eggs and bread crumbs and blend well. Crumble the nuts and add them. Cool.

8. Stuff the capon both in the cavity and in the neck and truss.

9. Rub the roasting pan with reserved capon fat and add the capon, breast side up. Scatter the coarsely chopped onion, celery, carrots, garlic clove, bay leaf and thyme sprigs around it. Add the capon neck, gizzard and heart. Do not add liquid. Sprinkle the capon with salt and pepper to taste.

10. Place the pan, uncovered, in the oven and bake for 45 minutes, basting often. Cover loosely with a large sheet of aluminum foil. Reduce the oven heat to 400 degrees and continue cooking for 45 minutes, basting often.

11. Reduce the oven heat to 375 degrees. Remove the foil or let it remain, depending on the brownness of the bird. Continue roasting and basting for about 1 hour longer. The total cooking time is approximately 20 minutes per pound. When the capon has cooked for about 2 hours, carefully pour off all the fat from the roasting pan. Add the chicken broth. Continue cooking until done.

12. Remove the capon and strain the liquid from the pan into a saucepan. Reduce slightly and serve hot with the carved capon.

Yield: 8 to 12 servings.

Cailles aux Raisins *(Quail with grapes)*

1. Sprinkle the quail with salt and pepper. It is not necessary to truss them.

2. Heat the butter in a large, heavy skillet and, when it is hot and almost browning, add the quail. Brown the birds on all sides, turning occasionally to brown evenly, for about 5 minutes.

3. Add the grapes. Have a cover ready that will fit the skillet snugly. Add the Cognac. Cover quickly so that the Cognac does not flame. Cook for 4 to 5 minutes. Uncover and serve immediately.

Yield: 3 to 6 servings.

6 ready-to-cook quail, about 1¼ pounds total weight
Salt and freshly ground pepper to taste
3 tablespoons butter
2 cups fresh seedless grapes
2 tablespoons Cognac

Faisan Smitane *(Roast pheasant with sour cream sauce)*

1. Preheat the oven to 425 degrees.

2. Truss the pheasant and sprinkle it with salt and pepper. Arrange it on one side in a roasting pan. Split the gizzard in half. Put the gizzard and heart around the bird. Place in the oven and bake for 15 minutes, basting occasionally. Turn the bird to the other side and continue baking and basting for about 15 minutes.

3. Turn the pheasant on its back and reduce the oven heat to 400 degrees. Continue roasting and basting for about 10 minutes. Add the liver and continue roasting and basting for about 10 minutes longer.

4. Transfer the pheasant to a serving dish. Pour the fat from the pan. Add the onion and stir until wilted. Add the wine and stir to dissolve the brown particles that cling to the bottom and sides of the pan. Let most of the wine evaporate and add the heavy cream. Cook, stirring, until cream is reduced by half. Turn off the heat and stir in the sour cream. Bring to the boil, stirring until smooth. Pour any liquid that has accumulated in the cavity of the bird into the sauce. Add salt and pepper to taste. Strain the sauce, using a fine sieve.

5. Untruss and carve the pheasant and serve with the sauce.

Yield: 4 servings.

1 plucked, cleaned, ready-to-cook pheasant, about 2½ pounds.
Salt and freshly ground pepper to taste
2 tablespoons butter
⅓ cup finely chopped onion
½ cup dry white wine
½ cup heavy cream
½ cup sour cream

Pheasant au Chambertin

4 pheasant, 1¾ to 2 pounds each
2 tablespoons peanut, vegetable or corn oil
½ cup chopped carrot
¾ cup chopped onion
½ cup chopped celery
1 cup chopped mushrooms
12 juniper berries, crushed
2 bay leaves
4 shallots, thinly sliced
3 cups Charmes-Chambertin or other Burgundy wine
2 cups fresh or canned chicken broth
4 cups water
Salt and freshly ground pepper
10 tablespoons butter
½ cup Cognac
2 tablespoons flour

1. Cut the pheasant as follows: Separate the legs from the thighs; split the breasts in half; bone the breast halves, but leave the main wing bone attached. Reserve all the bones.

2. Heat the oil in a heavy skillet and add the reserved bones. Cook, stirring frequently, until golden brown on all sides, about 30 minutes. Pour off the fat.

3. Add the chopped carrot, onion, celery, mushrooms, juniper berries, bay leaves and shallots. Cook, stirring often, for about 15 minutes. Add half the wine, the chicken broth, water and salt and pepper to taste. Cover and cook for 1 hour.

4. In another heavy skillet, heat 8 tablespoons butter and add the meaty pheasant pieces, skin side down. Cook, turning as necessary, until golden brown all over. Pour the Cognac over the pheasant pieces and ignite it.

5. Strain the bone and wine sauce, pushing the solids with the back of a wooden spoon to extract as much liquid as possible. Discard the solids. Add the sauce to the pheasant pieces. Add the remaining wine and partly cover. Simmer for about 45 minutes if the pheasant are young and tender. Cook longer if necessary.

6. If desired, remove the pheasant and strain the sauce again. Bring the sauce to the boil. Blend the remaining 2 tablespoons butter with the flour and add it gradually to the sauce, stirring constantly. Return the pheasant to the sauce and serve hot.

Yield: 8 to 12 servings.

Stuffed Squab Derby

What would you command if you were allowed one last great meal on this earth? We have our answer. The menu would move blissfully from caviar with vodka to, in due course, a fine fat squab stuffed with truffles and foie gras. It would end with an elegant grapefruit ice. Now, preferences in food are highly subjective and there may be those who would question our choice of squab. But to our mind, squab is one of the most sumptuous of birds and for the last go-round at table we would not willingly accept a substitute.

8 squab, each about ¾ pound cleaned weight
5 tablespoons butter

1. The squab should be cleaned and ready for roasting, but reserve the necks, feet and gizzards for the brown sauce. Reserve the livers for the stuffing.

2. Preheat the oven to 425 degrees.

3. Heat 1 tablespoon butter in a small skillet and add the livers. Cook over high heat, shaking the skillet and stirring, about 1 minute. The livers must cook quickly or they will be tough. Add the livers to the rice.

4. Cube the foie gras. Add the foie gras and chopped truffles to the rice and stir to blend well.

5. Sprinkle the inside of the squab with salt and pepper to taste and stuff them with the rice mixture. Truss the squab. Sprinkle with salt and pepper.

6. Melt 3 tablespoons of butter in a heavy roasting pan large enough to hold the squab. Turn the squab in the butter until coated on all sides. Place squab on their sides and bake for 15 minutes. Baste often. Turn onto other side and bake for 15 minutes, basting frequently. Place squab on their backs and continue roasting and basting for another 10 to 15 minutes. Remove to a warm platter and cover with foil.

7. Skim off all fat from the roasting pan, leaving the squab drippings. Add 2 tablespoons Cognac and ignite it. Pour in the brown sauce and stir to blend. Put the sauce through a fine sieve and bring it to the boil. Swirl in the remaining tablespoon of butter. Add the remaining Cognac and serve piping hot with the squab. Garnish each squab with a truffle slice before serving.

Yield: 8 servings.

8	squab livers, each cut in half
2	cups cooked rice
1¼	ounces pure foie gras, available in tins in fine specialty food markets
1	tablespoon chopped truffles
	Salt and freshly ground pepper
3	tablespoons Cognac
1½	cups brown sauce for squab (see recipe below)
8	truffle slices

1. Heat the oil in a small, heavy saucepan and add the necks, feet and gizzards. Sprinkle with salt and pepper. Cook, stirring frequently, until parts are nicely browned all over. Drain.

2. Return the squab pieces to the saucepan and add the celery, onion, carrots, thyme, parsley and bay leaf. Continue cooking, stirring occasionally, for about 5 minutes.

3. Sprinkle with flour and stir until all pieces are well coated. Cook, stirring occasionally, for about 5 minutes. Add the remaining ingredients and stir rapidly until blended. Bring to the boil and simmer, uncovered, for 1½ hours. Put the sauce through a fine sieve, pressing the solids with the back of a wooden spoon to extract as much of the liquid as possible. Discard the solids. Put the sauce in a small saucepan and simmer, uncovered, for about 30 minutes longer.

Yield: 1½ cups.

Note: If the squab have been trimmed, bony chicken pieces such as necks may be substituted.

Brown sauce for squab

1	tablespoon oil
	Necks, feet and gizzards from 8 squab (see note)
	Salt and freshly ground pepper to taste
¼	cup chopped celery
½	cup chopped onion
½	cup chopped carrots
3	sprigs fresh thyme, or ½ teaspoon dried
3	sprigs parsley
½	bay leaf
2	tablespoons flour
½	cup dry white wine
1	cup fresh or canned chicken broth
1	cup water
1	tablespoon tomato paste

Piccioni alla Contadina *(Squab peasant-style)*

8 or 10 pieces dried black mushrooms, preferably imported Italian mushrooms
4 fresh, cleaned squab, split in half
Salt and freshly ground pepper
½ cup olive oil
1 clove garlic, thinly sliced
1 cup finely chopped onion
1 teaspoon dried rosemary
½ cup dry red wine
2 cups crushed fresh or canned tomatoes
1 cup thinly sliced mushrooms
¼ cup tomato paste
⅓ cup water

1. Soak the mushrooms in cold water to cover for 1 hour or longer.

2. Sprinkle the squab halves with salt and pepper to taste. Set aside and reserve the squab livers.

3. Heat all but 2 tablespoons of oil in a large heavy skillet and add the squab, split-side down. Brown over high heat, turning, and add the garlic, onion and rosemary. Add the wine, tomatoes, salt and pepper to taste. Squeeze the black mushrooms to extract most of the moisture and add them.

4. In another skillet, heat the remaining 2 tablespoons of oil and cook the fresh mushrooms until wilted. Add them to the squab and cook for 5 minutes.

5. Blend the tomato paste with water and add it. Cover closely and cook for 30 minutes. Add the squab livers and continue cooking for about ½ hour. Serve with hot polenta.

Yield: 8 servings.

B'steeya or Pastilla *(Moroccan squab or poultry pie)*

One of the great main courses of the world is this buttery, fragile-crusted pigeon pie that comes out of Morocco. It is a curious dish but infinitely gratifying. Curious, because it contains, in addition to shredded cooked flesh of squab (Cornish game hens make an admirable substitute), ground almonds, confectioners' sugar and cinnamon.

I first tasted the dish in 1942 when I was stationed as a third-class petty officer aboard the U.S.S. *Augusta* in the harbor of Casablanca. I timidly requested to stay with the admiral in charge of the amphibious forces and, a day or so after the cease-fire, I found myself in a place of pure enchantment. I fell in love with Morocco and, naturally, Moroccan cooking.

Years later, we recreated the dish in our kitchen. Although the recipe may seem long, it isn't complicated. And it is well worth the effort.

1. Rub the squab or game hens inside and out with salt and pepper to taste. Heat the butter in a large casserole or Dutch oven and brown the squab lightly on all sides, turning as necessary. Do not burn the butter. Scatter the onion around the birds and cook until wilted. Add the garlic, turmeric, saffron,

ginger, coriander, hot red pepper, parsley, peppercorns, cinnamon sticks and water. Bring to the boil. Simmer, covered, for 45 minutes to 1 hour. When ready, the birds should be quite tender.

2. Remove the birds to a platter and let cool. Let the cooking liquid reduce over high heat to about half the volume. Let this cool.

3. As the birds cook, brown the almonds in a skillet containing the oil. Cook, shaking the skillet and stirring, until the nuts are evenly browned. Drain on absorbent toweling and let cool. Chop or blend them coarsely with a rolling pin. Blend them with the sugar and cinnamon and set aside.

4. Remove the flesh from the birds. Discard the skin and bones. Shred the flesh and set aside.

5. Put the eggs in a mixing bowl and add the lemon juice and about ¾ cup of the reduced liquid. Discard the remaining liquid. Beat the eggs with a whisk until thoroughly blended.

6. Heat about 2 tablespoons butter in a large skillet and add the egg mixture. Stir with a rubber spatula, scraping the bottom and sides as for making scrambled eggs. Continue cooking until eggs are fairly firm but not dry. Some of the liquid may separate. Ignore it. Remove from the heat and let cool.

7. Preheat oven to 475 degrees. Generously butter a 10- x 10-inch or slightly larger cake pan.

8. Lay out the 18 squares of phyllo pastry on a flat surface. At this point it is best to work as a team of two with one person brushing clarified butter on the pastry, the other transferring the leaves as they are prepared. Work quickly.

9. Brush the top pastry copiously with melted butter. Transfer it quickly to the buttered pan. It should be situated symmetrically. Press the center down gently inside the pan. Butter another sheet and repeat. Continue until a total of 10 generously buttered pastry layers are piled on top of each other.

10. Add a light layer of the shredded squab or game hens to the pastry-lined pan. Add the scrambled egg mixture, leaving the liquid, if any, in the skillet. Add the remaining squab, smoothing it over to the edges of the pastry. Sprinkle all but ¼ cup of the almond mixture over the squab. Dribble a little butter on top.

11. Butter 4 more sheets of pastry and cover the top of the "pie" as before. Bring up the edges and corners of the pastry, folding them inward to enclose the filling. Butter 4 more sheets of pastry and arrange these buttered side up. Quickly and with great care, tuck and fold these under the entire pie, lift-

The squab or game hens:

5 squab or, more economically, 4 Cornish game hens
Salt and freshly ground pepper
2 tablespoons butter
2 cups chopped onion
1 large clove garlic, unpeeled but crushed
1½ teaspoons ground turmeric
½ teaspoon stem saffron
5 small slices fresh ginger, or ½ teaspoon ground ginger
1 teaspoon crushed coriander seeds
1 small hot dried red pepper
6 sprigs fresh parsley
12 peppercorns, crushed
2 cinnamon sticks, each about 2 inches long
4 cups water

The almond, cinnamon and sugar filling:

1 cup blanched almonds
2 tablespoons peanut, vegetable or corn oil
1½ tablespoons confectioners' sugar
½ teaspoon ground cinnamon

The egg mixture:

8 large eggs
¼ cup lemon juice
2 tablespoons butter

The final assembly:

18 to 24 squares (see note) phyllo pastry
1 cup clarified butter (see instructions below)

The garnish:

3 tablespoons confectioners' sugar

ing the pie up with the fingers so that, when ready, it nestles neatly inside the cake pan.

12. Place the pie in the oven and bake for 20 minutes, brushing the top occasionally with more butter. When nicely browned on top, cover loosely with foil and continue baking for about 20 minutes longer.

13. Or, preferably, when the pie has baked the first 20 minutes and is nicely browned, place a rimmed but otherwise flat pan, like a pizza pan, over the pie. Hold it over a basin to catch any drippings. Invert quickly, turning the pie out. Now, invert a similar rimmed but otherwise flat pan over the pie and turn it over once more. This way the pie has its original crust side up. Return it to the oven. Cover loosely with a sheet of aluminum foil and continue baking until the sides are nicely browned, about 20 minutes.

14. Immediately sprinkle the top of the pie with confectioners' sugar and the remaining ¼ cup of the almond mixture.

15. Serve the pie hot. Traditionally, this pie is eaten with the fingers in Morocco. It is admirably complemented by two Moroccan salads—spicy orange salad and spicy tomato salad—recipes for which appear elsewhere in the book.

Yield: 6 servings.

Note: To make this pie, use a minimum of 18 pastry sheets. A few additional sheets of pastry will not matter. Note, too, that there will probably be leftover butter, which can be reserved for another use.

A note about working with phyllo pastry. Reasonable caution must be taken to prevent its drying out. This is easily done by keeping the sheets covered with a damp cloth as you work. Do not be afraid of tearing the pastry. It can be repaired with another sheet.

Clarified butter

Place ¾ pound of butter (the quantity is arbitrary) in a 1-quart measuring cup and let it stand on an asbestos pad over very low heat, or place it in a 200-degree oven until melted. Do not disturb the liquid. Let cool, then refrigerate. The clarified butter will harden between two soft, somewhat liquid or foamy layers. Scrape off the top layer. Invert the cup so the clarified butter comes out in one solid piece (you may have to encourge this with a fork or knife). Wipe off the clarified butter with paper toweling. This butter will keep for weeks in the refrigerator. Melt the butter before each use.

VII. Fish and Shellfish

Poached Striped Bass

1. Wrap the fish in a cheesecloth or a clean dish towel. Tie it with string in three or four places.

2. Set the rack of the fish poacher in place. Add the water, wine, onion, celery, carrot, parsley, bay leaves, garlic, salt, peppercorns and red pepper to the fish poacher. Cover and bring to the boil. Let simmer for 20 minutes. Remove from the heat and let the liquid cool.

3. Put the fish in the poacher and cover. Bring gently to the boil. At the boil, cook for 8 minutes. Remove from the heat. Uncover and let stand (see note) until the fish and cooking liquid become lukewarm.

4. Lift up the rack and let the fish drain. Cut off and discard the string. Unwrap the cheesecloth or towel enclosing the fish. Using a paring knife, neatly and carefully pull and scrape away the line of bones along the back side of the fish. Use the knife and fingers to pull and scrape away the skin from the topside of the fish. Scrape and pull away the small bones at the belly (underside) of the fish. The fatty, brownish-gray flesh on top of the fish should be scraped away also. It has an oily taste.

5. Lift up the cheesecloth or towel on which the fish rests. Transfer the fish, skinned side down, onto a serving platter. Remove and discard the cheesecloth. Repeat the skin removal from the other side of the fish. Scrape away the brownish-gray flesh and so on. Remove the skin from the cheek of the fish. Clean the rim of the platter.

6. Decorate the fish with one or more garnishes such as lemon wedges, tomato wedges and so on. Serve with a sauce based on mayonnaise, such as anchovy mayonnaise, cucumber mayonnaise, sauce rémoulade.

Yield: 6 or more servings.

Note: The fish could be served hot after standing in the cooking liquid for about 10 minutes after the heat is turned off. Serve with hollandaise sauce or simply melted butter, lemon and herbs.

1	3-pound (cleaned weight) striped bass, with head and tail left on but with gills removed.
14	cups water
1	cup dry white wine
2	cups coarsely chopped onion
1½	cups coarsely chopped celery
1	cup coarsely chopped carrots
4	sprigs fresh parsley
2	bay leaves
3	small cloves garlic, left whole
	Salt to taste
8	peppercorns
1	small dried, hot, red pepper Tomato wedges, hard-cooked egg wedges, parsley, lemon wedges, dill sprigs and so on for garnish

317

Baked Whole Fish Stuffed with Clams

The fish:

1 large 6-pound fish, such as
   striped bass, weakfish (sea
   trout) and so on, gills
   removed but head and tail left
   intact
   Salt and freshly ground
   pepper

The stuffing:

½ pound fresh mushrooms
8 tablespoons butter
1 cup finely chopped onion
3 tablespoons finely chopped
   shallots
½ feaspoon finely minced garlic
½ bay leaf
1 sprig fresh thyme, or ½
   teaspoon dried
2 hard-cooked eggs, peeled and
   chopped
3 cups fine, fresh bread crumbs
12 cherrystone clams, or 1 can
   minced clams
½ cup finely chopped parsley
1 egg, lightly beaten
   Salt and freshly ground
   pepper

The roasting:

8 tablespoons butter
   Salt and freshly ground
   pepper
½ cup finely chopped onion
¼ cup finely chopped shallots
1 clove garlic, finely minced
2 sprigs fresh thyme, or ½
   teaspoon dried
1 bay leaf
4 sprigs parsley

The sauce:

4 tablespoons butter

1. Preheat the oven to 350 degrees.

2. Rinse the fish and pat it dry inside and out. Sprinkle the cavity with salt and pepper to taste.

3. Chop the mushrooms finely. There should be about 2 cups.

4. Heat the 8 tablespoons of butter in a large skillet and add the onion, shallots and ½ teaspoon minced garlic. Cook until wilted. Add the mushrooms. Chop the bay leaf and thyme. Add this to the mushrooms. Cook until the mushrooms give up their liquid and then cook until most of the liquid evaporates. Add the hard-cooked eggs and bread crumbs.

5. Shuck the clams. Save both the clams and their liquid. Set the liquid aside. Chop the clams. There should be about ⅔ cup. Add the clams and parsley to the mushroom mixture. Add the lightly beaten egg, salt and pepper to taste. Blend well.

6. Stuff the cavity of the fish with the mushroom mixture. Using lengths of string, tie the flaps of the fish together to enclose the stuffing.

7. Select a roasting pan (not too deep) large enough to hold the fish. Rub the bottom of the pan with 1 tablespoon butter. Sprinkle the pan with salt and pepper. Add the fish. Scatter the ½ cup chopped onion, shallots, garlic, thyme, bay leaf cut in half and parsley around the fish. Cut 7 tablespoons butter into thin slices and arrange them on top of the fish. Sprinkle with salt and pepper to taste. Add the reserved clam juice. Cover the fish closely with heavy-duty aluminum foil.

8. Place in the oven and bake for 1 hour. Uncover. Remove the foil and cut away strings.

9. Pour the pan liquid from around the fish into a saucepan. Cook the liquid down until reduced by half. Strain it through a fine sieve into another saucepan, pushing with a rubber spatula to extract liquid from the solids. Swirl in the 4 tablespoons butter and heat, stirring, but do not boil. Serve the sauce with the fish. Garnish the fish platter with lemon halves and parsley sprigs.

Yield: 10 servings.

Baked Whole Fish à la Grecque

1. Preheat the oven to 400 degrees.
2. Sprinkle the fish inside and out with salt and pepper to taste. Place in a roasting pan and pour the olive oil over it. Arrange the lemon slices on top and cover with the sprig of thyme.
3. Scatter the onion rings around the fish and add the garlic and oregano.
4. Place the roasting pan on top of the stove to heat the bottom briefly without cooking the fish. Place the fish in the oven and bake for 10 minutes.
5. Pour the wine around the fish. Continue baking, basting often, for about 10 minutes. Add the clams and bake for 20 minutes longer, basting.

Yield: 6 servings.

1   4- to 5-pound whole fish, such as striped bass, sea bass or weakfish (sea trout)
    Salt and freshly ground pepper
¼   cup olive oil
4   lemon slices
1   sprig fresh thyme, or ½ teaspoon dried
1   medium-size onion, peeled and thinly sliced, about 2 cups
1   clove garlic, finely minced
1   teaspoon dried oregano
⅔   cup dry white wine
12   littleneck clams, the smaller the better, optional

Striped Bass with Sorrel

1. Preheat the oven to 425 degrees.
2. Butter a baking sheet with 2 tablespoons butter.
3. Sprinkle the fish inside and out with salt and pepper to taste. Place the fish on the baking sheet and dot it with 3 tablespoons butter. Scatter the mushrooms, shallots and onion around the fish. Place the bay leaf, thyme and parsley in the cavity of the fish.
4. Pour the wine over and around the fish and cover closely with heavy-duty aluminum foil. Place in the oven and bake for 20 to 30 minutes. Remove the foil and continue baking for 20 to 30 minutes longer.
5. Pour the cooking liquid and the vegetables with herbs into a saucepan. Cover the fish and keep it warm while preparing the sauce.
6. Reduce the cooking liquid to ½ cup. Strain it into a skillet. Add 1½ cups heavy cream and cook, stirring, for about 15 minutes. The sauce should be reduced to about 1 cup.
7. Meanwhile, heat the remaining tablespoon of butter and add the sorrel. Cook until the sorrel is wilted. Add this to the suace.
8. Blend the remaining ½ cup cream with the egg yolk. Add it to the sauce and cook briefly without boiling.
9. To serve the fish, it is preferable to remove the small bone

6   tablespoons butter
1   4- to 6-pound striped bass, scaled, cleaned and gills removed
    Salt and freshly ground pepper
3   mushrooms, sliced
½   cup thinly sliced or chopped shallots
½   cup chopped onion
1   bay leaf
3   sprigs fresh thyme, or 1 teaspoon dried
6   sprigs parsley
2   cups dry white wine
2   cups heavy cream
2   cups shredded sorrel
1   egg yolk

line down the back of the fish plus the skin of the fish. Both are easily removed simply by pulling and scraping neatly with the fingers. Serve the fish in individual portions with a little of the hot sauce spooned over.

Yield: 6 to 10 servings.

Grilled Fish in Foil

1 5½-pound fish, such as striped bass or bluefish, cleaned and gills removed but with head and tail left intact
Oil or melted butter for brushing the fish
Salt and freshly ground pepper
1 teaspoon grated fresh ginger
Wild bayberry (laurel) leaves for stuffing
1 small lemon, thinly sliced

1. Prepare a charcoal fire for grilling.
2. Place the fish on a flat surface and score the skin in a diamond pattern. Brush with oil, salt and pepper inside and out. Rub the scored portion with fresh ginger.
3. Stuff the mouth and stomach cavity of the fish with leafy sprigs of wild bayberry. Garnish one side of the fish with overlapping slices of lemon. Wrap the fish securely in heavy-duty aluminum foil, taking care to seal the edges of the foil tightly.
4. Place the fish on the grill and grill for about 20 minutes on one side. Turn and grill for about 20 minutes on the other. Serve hot or lukewarm with watercress mayonnaise, if desired.

Yield: 10 or more servings.

Scandinavian Fish Stuffed with Sauerkraut

1 4- to 5-pound white fish, such as striped bass or baquata, a West Coast fish
10 tablespoons butter
Salt and freshly ground pepper
2 tablespoons chopped shallots
3 or 4 cups cooked sauerkraut
2 cups dry white wine
Juice of 1 lemon
2 bay leaves
10 peppercorns
20 sprigs fresh dill, rinsed and patted dry
¼ cup white vinegar

1. Preheat the oven to 375 degrees.
2. To prepare this dish properly, the fish must be boned, opening up the body from the stomach and working to the backbone. This can be done by any professional fish man. The head can be removed.
3. Butter a metal baking dish large enough to hold the fish with 2 tablespoons of butter. Sprinkle with salt, pepper and shallots. Place the fish in the dish and open up the center. Sprinkle with salt and pepper and brush with 2 tablespoons of melted butter. Scatter the sauerkraut inside the fish, making about a 1-inch layer. Fold the fish over to enclose the stuffing and skewer the opening.
4. Dot the top of the fish with 4 tablespoons of butter. Sprinkle with salt and pepper. Pour over it 1½ cups of white wine and the lemon juice. Surround the fish with bay leaves, pep-

percorns and dill. Cover closely with foil. Bring the cooking liquid to a boil on top of the stove. Place the fish in the oven and bake for 45 minutes to 1 hour, or until the fish flakes easily and is not dry.

5. Pour off the cooking liquid into a saucepan. Bring to the boil and cook rapidly to reduce slightly, about 5 minutes.

6. Meanwhile, combine the remaining ½ cup of wine, vinegar and sugar. Cook, stirring, until slightly syrupy and reduced by half.

7. Blend 2 tablespoons of butter with the flour and add this gradually to the sauce, stirring rapidly with a whisk. Stir in the syrup. Blend the cream and egg yolk and add it, off heat, to the sauce, stirring rapidly.

8. Serve the fish sliced with the sauce spooned over it.

Yield: 4 to 6 servings.

4	tablespoons sugar
2	tablespoons flour
½	cup heavy cream
1	egg yolk

Pescado Veracruzano *(Striped bass with onions, tomatoes and peppers)*

1. Place the fish on a dish and prick the skin all over with a fork. Sprinkle all over with the juice of the limes. Stuff the cavity of the fish with the lime shells. Let stand for 3 hours. Remove the lime shells.

2. Preheat the oven to 375 degrees.

3. Sprinkle the fish all over with salt and pepper and place it on a large baking dish. It may be necessary to cut off the head to make the fish fit the pan.

4. Heat the oil in a saucepan and add the onion and garlic. Cook until wilted. Add the tomatoes, capers, olives, jalapeno peppers, oregano, bay leaf, salt and pepper to taste. Simmer for about 10 minutes.

5. Pour the sauce over the fish and place in the oven. Bake, uncovered, for about 30 minutes. Turn the fish carefully and continue baking for 30 to 40 minutes longer, or until the flesh flakes easily when tested with a fork. Serve garnished with lime wedges and coriander sprigs, if desired.

Yield: 8 or more servings.

1	4-pound fish, such as striped bass, red snapper or weakfish (sea trout) with head left on but gills removed
2	limes Salt and freshly ground pepper to taste
3	tablespoons olive oil
2	cups thinly sliced onion
3	tablespoons finely chopped garlic
4	cups diced, peeled tomatoes
3	tablespoons drained capers
20 to	24 stuffed green olives
2 or	more jalapeno peppers, drained, seeded and coarsely chopped
1	teaspoon chopped fresh oregano, or half the amount dried
1	bay leaf Lime wedges for garnish Fresh coriander sprigs for garnish, optional

Striped Bass in Phyllo Pastry

5 cups loosely packed spinach leaves
2 tablespoons finely chopped chervil, parsley or fresh sage leaves
1 tablespoon olive oil
¼ cup finely chopped shallots
¾ cup shucked, drained oysters, about 12
   Salt and freshly ground pepper
¾ cup clarified butter (see note)
12 leaves phyllo pastry
6 teaspoons fine, fresh bread crumbs, approximately
6 center-cut fillets of striped bass with skin on, about ½ pound each

1. Preheat the oven to 450 degrees.

2. Pick over the spinach leaves to remove any tough stems. Rinse and drain well. Combine with the chervil.

3. Heat the oil in a large heavy skillet and add the shallots. Cook briefly, stirring. Add the spinach and cook, stirring, until spinach is wilted. Spoon out onto a chopping block.

4. Add the oysters, salt and pepper to taste. Chop finely using a heavy knife.

5. Brush a baking dish with butter.

6. Arrange the phyllo pastry in one stack on a clean cloth. Brush with butter. Sprinkle with crumbs. Turn pastry sheet over and bruh with butter. Sprinkle with crumbs. As you work, keep pastry sheets covered with a lightly dampened cloth to prevent them from drying out.

7. Arrange the fish fillets one at a time on a flat surface, skin side down. Slice them crosswise and slightly on the bias. Make four parallel gashes almost but not to the skin.

8. Arrange one fish fillet, skin side down, on the center of 2 sheets of the pastry. Spoon 1 tablespoon or so of the oyster and spinach mixture inside each gash. Sprinkle with salt and pepper. Lift up the pastry and fold it over and over to enclose the fillet. Cut off excess pastry, leaving about 2 inches of phyllo to fold under. Fold the edges under, envelope fashion. Repeat with the other fillets. Brush the top of the "packages" with butter and arrange them on the buttered baking dish.

9. Place in the oven and bake for 20 minutes, or until "packages" are well puffed and browned.

Yield: 6 servings.

Note: To clarify butter, place the butter in a heatproof glass measuring cup and let it melt slowly in a 200-degree oven. Do not stir the butter. Pour off the clear, golden liquid on top, leaving the white milky substance at the bottom. The clear liquid is clarified butter.

Striped Bass Fermière

2 skinless and boneless striped bass fillets, about 5½ pounds
2 or 3 small carrots

1. Cut the fish fillets slightly on the bias into 8 "steaks." Refrigerate.

2. Trim and scrape the carrots and cut them into very thin rounds.

3. Heat 8 tablespoons of butter in a heavy casserole large enough to hold all the pieces of fish in one layer. Add the carrots, shallots, celery and mushrooms. Add ⅓ cup of dry white wine. Cook until all the wine has been reduced, about 10 minutes. Add another ⅓ cup of wine and cook until it is reduced, about 10 minutes. Add another ⅓ cup of wine and cook until it is reduced, about 10 minutes.

4. Sprinkle the fish pieces with salt and pepper and arrange them in one layer over the vegetables. Pour the remaining ½ cup of wine over the fish and bring to the boil. Simmer for about 6 minutes. Sprinkle with lemon juice.

5. Melt 2 tablespoons of butter in an oval serving dish large enough to hold the fish in one layer. Transfer the fish and cover to keep warm.

6. To the casserole add the cream and bring it to a boil over high heat, shaking the skillet so that it blends with the vegetable flavors, about 3 minutes. Add remaining 7 tablespoons of butter, bit by bit, while shaking the casserole. Pour this over the fish and serve immediately.

Yield: 8 servings.

17	tablespoons butter
1	cup thinly sliced shallots
1½	cups thinly sliced celery
4	mushrooms, thinly sliced
1½	cups dry white wine
	Salt and freshly ground pepper to taste
	Juice of ½ lemon
1	cup heavy cream

Striped Bass Marechiare

1. Cut each fillet crosswise into 8 pieces of approximately equal size. Coat the pieces with flour.

2. Heat the oil and, when it is hot but not smoking, add the fish pieces. This may have to be done in two steps. Deep fry for 6 or 7 minutes. The pieces should be half cooked. Drain on towels.

3. Arrange the pieces of fish in one layer in a baking dish. Arrange the clams and mussels around the fish. Spoon the crushed tomatoes over the fish and sprinkle with garlic and parsley, salt, pepper and basil. Sprinkle with oil. Cover and simmer on top of the stove for about 5 minutes. Sprinkle with clam juice. Continue simmering for about 20 minutes or longer, until fish flakes easily when tested with a fork.

Yield: 8 servings.

2	fillets of striped bass with skin left on, about 4 pounds
	Flour for dredging
	Oil for deep frying
12	cherrystone clams
12	well-cleaned large mussels
2	cups crushed imported tomatoes
4	cloves garlic, finely slivered
1	tablespoon finely chopped parsley
	Salt and freshly ground pepper to taste
2	tablespoons snipped fresh basil leaves, or 1 teaspoon dried
½	cup salad oil
¾	cup fresh or bottled clam juice

Escalopes de Bar Rayé aux Huitres *(Striped bass fillet with oysters)*

It is obvious that in our profession we are occupied with the sheer pleasure of dining well. Once in a while, one is faced with a moment of daring, a new experience, a quickened emotion not unlike diving into a cold swimming pool before the sun has prepared you for it.

When we dined at the Restaurant Girardet in the small town of Crissier in Switzerland, we had such an experience. Freddy Girardet has become one of the great creative forces in the world of chefs today, and our meal was unforgettable, not a dish to be faulted. We dined on an elaborate succession of his creations, one of which was loup de mer aux huitres, or loup de mer with oysters. When Pierre Franey recreated the Girardet dishes in our kitchen, he substituted striped bass for the loup de mer, which is not available in American waters. It remains just as glorious.

1 1½-pound skinless, boneless fillet of striped bass
1 tablespoon butter
  Salt and freshly ground pepper to taste
½ cup carrot cut into very fine julienne strips (approximately the size of toothpicks)
¼ cup leeks cut into very fine julienne strips
½ cup celery root (or use stalk celery) cut into very fine julienne strips
1 cup dry white wine
1 cup fish stock (see recipe page 659)
24 shucked oysters with their liquid
1 cup heavy cream
1 tablespoon finely chopped chives

1. Cut the fillet into 6 portions of approximately equal weight, slicing slightly on a diagonal. Place the pieces on a flat surface and pound lightly with a flat mallet.

2. Butter a baking dish with 1 tablespoon of butter and sprinkle with salt and pepper. Arrange the fish pieces over the bottom. Sprinkle with salt and pepper. Refrigerate until ready to cook.

3. Prepare the vegetables and drop them into boiling salted water. Simmer for about 5 minutes and drain.

4. Preheat the oven to 450 degrees.

5. In a heated saucepan heat the wine and fish stock and liquid from the oysters if there is any. Bring to the boil.

6. Pour 1½ cups of the wine mixture over the fish and place in the oven. Bake for 3 to 5 minutes. Do not overcook. Pour off and add the cooking liquid to the original wine mixture. Keep the fish covered with foil.

7. Add the oysters to the liquid and cook briefly, about 1 minute. Scoop out the oysters and arrange equal amounts of them over the portions of fish.

8. Meanwhile, reduce the cooking liquid to about 1 cup. Add the cream and boil over high heat for about 5 minutes. Add the drained vegetables and chopped chives. Spoon the sauce over the oysters and fish and serve piping hot.

Yield: 6 servings.

Bar Rayé à la Nage *(Striped bass in court bouillon with cream)*

1. In a kettle, combine the onions, carrots, leek, garlic, wine, broth, bay leaf, thyme, salt and peppercorns. Add the fish bones and trimmings, if available. Bring to the boil and simmer 30 minutes. Carefully remove all bones and trimmings, but leave the vegetables in the broth.

2. Preheat the oven to 400 degrees.

3. Butter an oval or rectangular metal baking dish.

4. Cut each fillet into 3 pieces and arrange them on the baking dish. Spoon the court bouillon over the fish and bring it to the boil on top of the stove. Cover with foil and bake for 20 minutes.

5. Carefully remove the fish to a hot serving dish or onto individual warm plates and keep warm. Bring the liquid in the baking dish to the boil and reduce it over moderately high heat, about 5 minutes. Add the cream and continue cooking for about 5 minutes. Swirl in the butter and serve the court bouillon with the vegetables spooned over the fish. Sprinkle with chopped parsley.

Yield: 6 servings.

3 small white onions, cut into slices about ⅛ inch thick (about 1 cup loosely packed)
2 carrots, scraped and cut into ⅛-inch slices
1 leek, rinsed well and chopped (about 1 cup)
1 clove garlic, sliced
2 cups dry white wine
2 cups fish broth, or use half water, half bottled clam juice
1 bay leaf
3 sprigs fresh thyme, or ½ teaspoon dried
  Salt to taste
16 peppercorns
  Bones and trimmings from a striped bass, if available
2 striped bass fillets, about 3 pounds
½ cup heavy cream
2 tablespoons butter
  Chopped parsley for garnish

Sea Bass with Fresh Fennel

1. Heat the butter in a baking dish large enough to hold the fish. Stir in the olive oil and garlic. Let cool briefly and add the fish, turning it in the mixture. Sprinkle with salt and pepper.

2. Cut off enough of the fennel leaves to stuff the fish lightly. Add this to the cavities.

3. Cut off the tops of the fennel bulb and trim the base. Pull off and discard the tough outer leaves. Cut the bulb into quarters and arrange these around the fish.

4. When ready to cook, preheat the oven to 375 degrees. Place the fish in the oven and bake for 30 minutes, basting both the fish and fennel frequently. Cook until the fish flakes easily when tested with a fork.

Yield: 6 to 8 servings.

12 tablespoons butter
3 tablespoons olive oil
6 cloves garlic, finely minced
2 1½- to 2-pound sea bass or other small whole fish, cleaned and with head intact but with gills removed
1 fennel bulb with leaves
  Salt and freshly ground pepper

Sea Bass with Tomato Sauce

1 2-pound, cleaned but
   unscaled sea bass, preferably
   with head left on and gills
   removed
   Salt and freshly ground
   pepper
2 pounds fresh seaweed, or 1
   package dried laver (seaweed),
   available in Chinese and
   other Oriental markets
⅓ cup water
   Sauce vierge (see recipe
   below)

1. Sprinkle the fish with salt and pepper. If fresh seaweed is available, place a bed of seaweed in a heavy casserole large enough to hold the fish. If dried laver is used, soak it briefly in hot water and arrange half the laver over the casserole. Place the fish on top and add the remaining seaweed or laver. Add the water and cover closely. Steam for 10 minutes.

2. Remove the fish. Remove the fish bones and skin. Place the fish on a serving dish and spoon lukewarm sauce vierge over. Serve lukewarm.

Yield: 2 servings.

Sauce vierge

1 cup crushed, peeled, seeded,
   red ripe tomatoes
3 tablespoons olive oil
1 crushed, unpeeled garlic clove
1 tablespoon chopped fresh
   chervil, or 1 teaspoon dried
1 teaspoon each chopped fresh
   parsley and tarragon
½ teaspoon ground coriander
   Salt and freshly ground
   pepper

1. Mash the tomatoes to a pulp or blend in a food processor or electric blender. Pour and scrape the mixture into a mixing bowl.

2. Beat in the oil and add the remaining ingredients. Let sit in a warm but not hot place until lukewarm. Serve with the fish.

Yield: About 1¼ cups.

Poached Whole Cod

1 8- to 10-pound codfish,
   cleaned and with head on but
   gills removed
2 cups dry white wine
12 cups water
1 teaspoon dried rosemary
1 bay leaf
½ cup coarsely chopped onion
1 hot red pepper
4 sprigs fresh parsley
10 sprigs fresh dill
   Salt to taste
12 peppercorns

1. Prepare the cod and set it aside.

2. Combine the remaining ingredients in a fish cooker and bring to the boil. Simmer for 15 minutes and let cool.

3. Add the codfish and bring to the boil. Simmer for 15 to 20 minutes. Let stand until ready to serve. Serve, if desired, with orange and dill mayonnaise.

Yield: 10 to 12 servings.

Poached Cod with Mustard and Parsley Sauce

1. Arrange the fish steaks in one layer in a casserole in which they fit comfortably. Add the milk and water. The liquid should cover the steaks, but barely. Add the salt, pepper, parsley, bay leaf and peppercorns. Bring to the boil. Let simmer for 5 minutes and turn off the heat. Let stand for 3 minutes or longer until ready to serve.

2. Combine the shallots and vinegar in a very heavy, small saucepan and cook until most of the vinegar evaporates. Let cool briefly and add the water. Start adding the butter gradually, beating vigorously and rapidly with a wire whisk. Take care that the sauce does not boil at any point because it will curdle, but it must be very hot, just below the boiling point. If it starts to get too hot, remove the saucepan from the heat. When it is creamy and smooth and lightly thickened, add the mustard and parsley.

4. Carefully drain the steaks and serve with the sauce spooned over.

Yield: 4 servings.

4	cod steaks, about ¾ pound each and about 1 inch thick
½	cup milk
3	cups water
	Salt and freshly ground pepper to taste
8	parsley sprigs tied with string
1	bay leaf
8	peppercorns, crushed
2	tablespoons finely chopped shallots
2	tablespoons red wine vinegar
1	tablespoon cold water
8	tablespoons butter
1	tablespoon imported mustard, such as Dijon or Düsseldorf
4	tablespoons finely chopped parsley

Cod Florentine

1. Preheat the oven to 375 degrees.

2. Prepare the mornay sauce and set aside.

3. If bulk spinach is used, pick it over well. Discard any tough stems. Wash the leaves thoroughly to rid them of all sand. Drop the spinach into boiling water to cover. Return to the boil and simmer for about 2 minutes. Drain and run the spinach under cold running water. Squeeze the spinach between the hands to extract excess moisture. Chop the spinach coarsely. Set aside.

4. Butter a baking dish with 2 tablespoons of butter. Sprinkle with shallots, salt and pepper.

5. Cut the cod into 6 pieces of appoximately the same weight. Arrange the pieces neatly over the baking dish. Sprinkle with salt and pepper and the wine. Cover with foil. Bring the wine to the boil on top of the stove, then put the dish in the oven. Bake for 12 to 15 minutes, or just until the fish flakes easily when tested with a fork.

6. Meanwhile, heat the remaining 1½ tablespoons of butter in a skillet and add the onion. When it wilts, add the chopped

2½	cups mornay sauce (see recipe page 645)
2	pounds or 2 10-ounce packages fresh spinach
3½	tablespoons butter
1	tablespoon finely chopped shallots
	Salt and freshly ground pepper
1¾ to	2 pounds skinless, boneless cod or striped bass fillets
½	cup dry white wine
3	tablespoons chopped onion
3	tablespoons freshly grated Parmesan cheese

spinach, salt and pepper. Cook for about 1 minute, no longer.

7. Spoon the spinach into an oval baking dish and smooth it over the bottom. Carefully transfer the baked cod pieces to the spinach, arranging them neatly over it. Cover and keep warm.

8. Pour the wine liquid from the baked fish into a saucepan and reduce it quickly over high heat to about ¼ cup. Add this to the mornay sauce and stir. Bring to the boil.

9. Spoon the hot sauce over the fish, smoothing it to coat the fish evenly. Sprinkle with Parmesan cheese and bake, uncovered, until bubbling throughout and the fish is nicely browned on top.

Yield: 6 servings.

Broiled Cod Fillets

2 cod fillets or codfish steaks
4 tablespoons butter
  Salt and freshly ground pepper
½ cup fresh bread crumbs
½ teaspoon paprika

1. Preheat the oven to 450 degrees.

2. Grease the bottom of a baking dish with 1 tablespoon of butter.

3. Arrange the fillets, skin side down, on the dish and sprinkle with salt and pepper.

4. Scatter the bread crumbs on a piece of wax paper. Hold a small sieve over the crumbs. Put the paprika through the sieve and blend paprika and crumbs. Sprinkle the fish fillets with the crumbs and melt and dribble the remaining 3 tablespoons butter over all. Broil about 6 inches from the heat until golden brown. Then bake for 5 to 10 minutes.

Yield: 2 servings.

Morue Boulangère *(Baked cod with potatoes)*

10 to 14 tablespoons butter
  Salt and freshly ground pepper to taste
4 cod steaks with skin on, each about 2 inches thick
1½ pounds baking potatoes
1 small onion, thinly sliced, about ½ cup

1. Preheat the oven to 400 degrees.

2. Butter a large metal baking dish with 2 or 3 tablespoons butter. The dish should be large enough to hold the fish and potatoes in one layer (we used an oval dish that measured 10- x 16-inches). Sprinkle with salt and pepper. Arrange the cod steaks in one layer on the bottom.

3. Peel and thinly slice the potatoes, plunging the slices im-

mediately into cold water to prevent them from discoloring. Drain the potatoes in a colander. Neatly scatter the potato slices around and between the pieces of fish, not on top. Scatter the onion slices over the potatoes. Salt and pepper the fish and vegetables. Generously dot everything with the remaining butter. Do not add liquid; the fish provides its own.

4. Place the baking dish on top of the stove and bring to the boil. When it starts to boil, put the dish in the oven and bake uncovered for 15 minutes. Baste the fish and potatoes and continue baking for 20 minutes longer, basting occasionally.

5. Meanwhile, blend the garlic, parsley and fresh bread crumbs in the container of an electric blender and sprinkle the mixture over the fish and vegetables. Bake for 10 minutes longer, or until crumbs are brown.

Yield: 4 to 6 servings.

1 small clove garlic, finely chopped
3 tablespoons chopped parsley
3 tablespoons fresh bread crumbs

Cod Dugléré au Pernod

1. Cut the cod into 6 or 8 serving pieces. Set aside.

2. Melt 2 tablespoons of butter in a skillet large enough to hold the cod in one layer. Add the shallots, onion and garlic. Cook until wilted. Add the wine and cook until most of it evaporates. Add lemon juice, parsley and the tomatoes. Add salt and pepper to taste. Cook for 10 minutes.

3. Add the cod in one layer. Sprinkle with salt and pepper and cover. Bring to the boil and simmer for about 5 minutes. Add the cream and shake the skillet gently to blend. Handle the cod with care as it tends to flake and break. Cook for about 3 minutes.

4. Carefully pour the sauce from the skillet into a saucepan. Boil it down for about 5 minutes and add the Pernod. Swirl in the remaining butter and pour this over the fish. Serve in hot soup plates. Serve sprinkled with chopped parsley.

Yield: 6 servings.

2¾ pounds cod steaks, each about 1 inch thick, skinned and boned
4 tablespoons butter
2 tablespoons finely diced shallots
2 tablespoons finely chopped onion
1 clove garlic, finely minced
½ cup dry white wine
Juice of ½ lemon
1 tablespoon finely chopped parsley
1 cup peeled fresh or canned tomatoes
Salt and freshly ground pepper to taste
½ cup heavy cream
1 tablespoon Pernod, Ricard or other anise-flavored liqueur
Freshly chopped parsley for garnish

Frituras de Bacalao *(Codfish fritters)*

¼ pound dried salt cod
2 cups flour
½ teaspoon black pepper
   Salt to taste
1 teaspoon crushed, dried oregano
1½ cups cold water, approximately
1 tablespoon chopped hot, or mildly hot, green or red fresh chilies
1 tablespoon chopped coriander leaves (see note)
   Peanut, vegetable or corn oil for shallow frying

1. Put the cod in a bowl and add cold water to cover. Let stand for several hours or overnight, changing the water if the cod is very salty. Drain well. Flake the cod with the fingers, discarding any bones. Chop the flesh finely. There should be about ½ cup.

2. Put the flour in a bowl and add the black pepper (the taste of pepper should be bit pronounced). Add salt and oregano. Gradually add the cold water, stirring with a whisk to prevent lumping. This batter should not be runny, nor too thick. Add the chopped cod, chilies and coriander leaves. Stir and refrigerate for several hours.

3. Heat about ⅛ inch of oil in a skillet. Add the batter, about 1 tablespoon to a fritter. Cook until golden brown on one side. Turn and cook until golden brown on the other side. Drain on absorbent toweling.

Yield: About 24 fritters.

Note: In Puerto Rico, cooks use equal amounts of culantro and fresh coriander leaves. The flavors are similar but culantro, a dark green serrated leaf, is more pungent. Culantro leaves are available in Puerto Rican vegetable and produce markets. If you can't find them, use all fresh coriander leaves.

Fried Eel

1 or 2 skinned and cleaned eel, about 1¼ pounds total weight
   Milk to cover
   Salt and freshly ground pepper to taste
¼ teaspoon Tabasco sauce
½ cup flour
   Oil for deep frying
1 large bunch parsley
   Lemon wedges
   Tartar sauce (see recipe page 643)

1. Cut the eel into 3-inch lengths. Place in a mixing bowl and add milk to cover, salt, pepper and Tabasco sauce.

2. Drain well. Dredge the eel pieces in flour seasoned with salt and pepper.

3. Heat the oil in a deep fryer or a skillet and, when it is hot and almost smoking, add the eel pieces. Cook, stirring occasionally and turning the pieces, until golden brown and cooked through. Drain on paper toweling.

4. Trim off and discard the parsley stems. If the parsley is totally clean, do not wash it. If it is rinsed, it must be patted thoroughly dry. Add the parsley and deep fry until crisp. It will darken as it cooks. Drain well and serve with the eel pieces. Serve with lemon wedges and tartar sauce.

Yield: 6 or more servings.

Matelote of Eel

1. Cut each of the eel into 3-inch lengths. Dredge the pieces in ¼ cup flour seasoned with salt and pepper.

2. Heat the oil in a heavy skillet and brown the eel pieces on all sides, turning often, about 5 minutes. Pour off fat.

3. Scatter the onion, garlic and carrots between the eel pieces and cook for about 3 minutes.

4. Add the wine, thyme, bay leaf and simmer for about 10 minutes.

5. Meanwhile, combine the mushrooms in a saucepan with 1 tablespoon of the butter, water, anchovy paste, lemon juice, salt and pepper to taste. Bring to the boil and simmer, stirring, for about 5 minutes. Add the mushroom liquid to the eel. Set the mushrooms aside. Simmer the eel in the sauce for 5 minutes longer.

6. Remove the eel pieces and keep warm.

7. Blend the remaining butter with the remaining flour. Add it bit by bit to the sauce, stirring. Strain the sauce through a sieve into another skillet and bring to the boil. Simmer for about 5 minutes. Add the eel pieces and mushrooms.

8. Toast the French bread slices and rub on all sides with garlic. Serve the eel and mushrooms hot with the sauce poured over on the toast. Serve with boiled potatoes.

Yield: 6 to 8 servings.

2	cleaned, skinned eel, about 2½ pounds total weight
¼	cup plus 1½ tablespoons flour
	Salt and freshly ground pepper to taste
3	tablespoons peanut, vegetable or corn oil
1	cup finely chopped onion
2	cloves garlic, chopped
¾	cup finely diced carrots
2½	cups dry red wine
½	teaspoon dried thyme, or 2 sprigs fresh thyme
1	bay leaf
½	pound mushrooms, preferably button mushrooms (if the mushrooms are large, slice them)
3½	tablespoons butter
¼	cup water
1	tablespoon anchovy paste
	Juice of ½ lemon
6 to	8 slices French bread
1	clove garlic, peeled and cut in half

Anguilla Scarpione *(Fried eel with oil and vinegar)*

1. Cut off and discard the heads and small tail ends of the eel. Cut the eel into 2-inch pieces. Sprinkle the pieces with salt and pepper to taste and dredge lightly in flour. Shake off excess.

2. Heat the oil in a skillet and brown the eel on all sides, a few pieces at a time. Drain the pieces as they cook. Transfer them to a platter.

3. Pour off the oil but do not wipe out the skillet. Add the onion and cook, stirring, until wilted. Add the bay leaves, salt and pepper to taste, vinegar and wine. Cook for 5 minutes and pour this over the eel.

Yield: 12 servings.

12	fresh, skinned eel, each weighing about ¾ pound
	Salt and freshly ground pepper
	Flour for dredging
1	cup olive oil
4	cups thinly sliced onion
6	bay leaves
⅓	cup white vinegar
⅔	cup dry white wine

Broiled Eel with Mustard Butter

The eel:

1   1¼- to 1½-pound skinned eel
    (cleaned weight)
3   tablespoons butter
    Salt and freshly ground
    pepper to taste

The mustard butter:

4   tablespoons butter at room
    temperature
    Juice of ½ lemon
2   teaspoons imported mustard,
    such as Dijon or Düsseldorf
3   tablespoons finely chopped
    parsley
¼   teaspoon Worcestershire sauce
    Tabasco sauce to taste
    Salt and freshly ground
    pepper to taste

1. Preheat the broiler to its highest heat.
2. Using a sharp knife, score the eel flesh top and bottom. To do this, make shallow ⅛-inch parallel incisions at ½-inch intervals. Cut the eel into 6-inch lengths.
3. In a baking dish, gently melt the 3 tablespoons butter and add the eel pieces. Sprinkle with salt and pepper and turn the eel pieces in the butter until coated all over.
4. Place the dish of eel 4 to 6 inches from the source of heat and broil for 1½ to 2 minutes. Turn the pieces and cook for 2 to 3 minutes longer. Pour off all the fat that has accumulated in the pan. Serve immediately with the mustard butter.
5. To make the mustard butter, combine all the ingredients for the butter and beat rapidly with a whisk or wooden spoon until well blended. Spoon equal amounts over the fish sections and serve immediately.

Yield: 6 servings.

Finnan Haddie

Since we first encountered finnan haddie on a breakfast menu at the Connaught Hotel in London more than twenty-five years ago, it has been our long-held notion that this smoked-fish delicacy is one of the consummate breakfast foods. Give us a platter of choice finnan haddie, freshly cooked in its bath of water and milk, add melted butter, a slice or two of hot toast, a pot of steaming Darjeeling tea and you may tell the butler to dispense with the caviar, truffles and nightingales' tongues.

The proper way to poach finnan haddie is to place it (defrosted if frozen) in a skillet with water to barely cover. Add about ½ cup milk and, if desired, 1 bay leaf, 2 cloves and 2 slices of onion. Bring to the boil but do not boil. Let the haddock simmer gently for about 2 minutes, or until the fish is piping hot. Do not cook long or it will toughen and become fibrous. Drain the fish, spoon it onto hot plates and pour hot melted butter over it. Serve immediately with lemon halves on the side and a pepper mill for those who wish it. After a first course of freshly squeezed orange juice, serve the fish with buttered, boiled potatoes, buttered toast, marmalade and tea or champagne. Breakfast coffee is not a suitable drink with smoked fish.

Finnan Haddie à la Crème

1. Cut the finnan haddie into 6 pieces more or less the same size.

2. Prepare the sauce before cooking the haddie. Melt 3 tablespoons of the butter in a saucepan and stir in the flour, using a wire whisk. When blended, add 2½ cups of milk, stirring constantly with the whisk. When the sauce is blended and smooth, add salt and pepper to taste. Cook, stirring frequently, for 20 to 30 minutes.

3. When the sauce is almost done, place the fish pieces in a large dish for poaching and add water to cover (the fish will swell slightly as it cooks). Do not add salt. Add the remaining milk, onion slice and bay leaf. Bring to a boil and cook briefly, just until the fish is piping hot throughout. Do not cook for an extended period, because the fish will toughen.

4. Just before serving, finish the sauce. Add to the sauce 1 cup of liquid in which the fish cooked and the ½ cup of cream. Add nutmeg and cayenne and stir to blend. When the sauce returns to the boil, remove from the heat and swirl in the remaining 2 tablespoons of butter.

5. Drain the fish, one piece at a time, using a slotted spoon. Transfer one piece at a time to a hot dinner plate and spoon the sauce over. Serve with grilled tomatoes and buttered "new" potatoes, if desired.

Yield: 6 servings.

2½ to 3 pounds finnan haddie
5 tablespoons butter
4 tablespoons flour
3½ cups milk
  Salt and freshly ground pepper
1 onion slice, about ½ inch thick
1 bay leaf
½ cup cream
¼ teaspoon freshly grated nutmeg, or more to taste
⅛ teaspoon cayenne pepper, or Tabasco sauce to taste

Fish and Chips

4 large Idaho potatoes, about 2
pounds
6 cups peanut, vegetable or
corn oil
½ cup flour
Salt and freshly ground
pepper to taste
8 small, skinless, boneless
flounder or other fish fillets,
about 2 pounds
Batter for fish (see recipe
below)
Oil for deep frying
Malt vinegar

1. Trim the potatoes with a swivel-bladed vegetable scraper. Drop them into cold water to prevent discoloration. Cut the potatoes into ½-inch-thick slices. Cut the slices into ½-inch strips. Drop into cold water and drain.

2. Heat about 6 cups of oil in a deep fryer. A Chinese wok is also good for this. Drop a few strips of potato into the hot oil and cook for 1½ to 2 minutes. Drain on absorbent toweling. Continue until all the strips have been precooked and drained.

3. Blend the flour, salt and pepper. Dredge the fillets in flour. Dip the fish fillets, one at a time, in the batter and drop them into the oil (preheated to 350 degrees). You may cook three or four fillets at one time. Cook until puffed and browned. Turn the pieces as they cook. Total cooking time for each fillet is 1½ to 2 minutes. Please note that after a few pieces of fish are cooked, you should let the oil come back to its original heat. As the fish pieces are added, the oil heat is diminished. Continue until all the fish is cooked and drained.

4. Before cooking the potatoes a second time, bring the oil temperature to about 400 degrees (slightly higher than for the fish). Add the potatoes, one batch at a time. Cook for 1½ to 2 minutes, or until crisp. Drain. Continue cooking and draining until all the potatoes are used. Serve the batter-fried fish with the potatoes.

5. Serve with malt vinegar and salt on the side so that guests may flavor the fish according to their own tastes.

Yield: 4 servings.

Batter for fish

1 cup cold water
½ teaspoon pure yellow food
coloring
2 tablespoons corn oil
1 teaspoon salt
1 cup flour
1 teaspoon baking powder

1. Combine the cold water, food coloring, oil and salt in a mixing bowl. Gradually add the flour, stirring rapidly with a wire whisk.

2. Just before using, stir in the baking powder, making certain it is evenly blended in the batter.

Yield: Enough batter for 8 fish fillets.

Flounder Fillets à la Moutarde

1. Preheat the broiler to high.
2. Place the fillet halves on a flat surface. Sprinkle with salt and pepper and brush with oil. Arrange the fillets on a baking sheet. Blend the mayonnaise, mustard and parsley. Brush it evenly over the fillets.
3. Place the fillets under the broiler, 3 or 4 inches from the source of heat. Broil for about 1 minute, or until golden brown on top and the fish is just cooked through. Serve with lemon wedges.

Yield: 4 servings.

8 small, skinless, boneless flounder fillets, about 1 pound
Salt and freshly ground pepper to taste
1 tablespoon peanut, vegetable or corn oil
2 tablespoons mayonnaise, preferably homemade
1 tablespoon imported mustard, such as Dijon or Düsseldorf
2 teaspoons finely chopped parsley
4 lemon or lime wedges

Frogs' Legs Provençale

1. To keep the frogs' legs flat as they cook, insert one leg in between the two muscles of the lower part of the other leg.
2. Put the legs in a dish and add cold milk to cover.
3. Put the tomatoes in a small saucepan with salt and pepper to taste. Bring to the boil and simmer for 20 minutes. Remove from the heat.
4. Meanwhile, blend the flour with salt and pepper. Remove one pair of legs at a time from the milk and add them to the flour, turning to coat well.
5. Heat the oil in a large skillet and add 4 tablespoons of butter. When it is quite hot, add the legs, cooking until golden on one side. Turn and cook until golden on the other side. Transfer the legs to a warm serving dish, arranging them neatly in one layer. Heat the tomato sauce and spoon it over the legs.
6. Pour off the fat and wipe out the skillet. Add the remaining butter and the garlic. When the butter is hot and foaming, pour it over the tomato sauce and frogs' legs. Serve sprinkled with chopped parsley.

Yield: 4 servings.

12 large pairs or 24 small pairs frogs' legs
Cold milk to cover
2 cups crushed tomatoes
Salt and freshly ground pepper
Flour for dredging
½ cup peanut, vegetable or corn oil
12 tablespoons butter
1 tablespoon finely chopped garlic
¼ cup finely chopped parsley

Gefilte Fish

2 pounds each (approximately)
of carp, pike and white fish,
filleted to give about 3½
pounds skinned fish; reserve
heads, bones and skins
3 onions
3 carrots
Sprig of parsley
Salt and freshly ground
pepper
2 cloves garlic, optional
4 eggs, lightly beaten
½ cup water

1. Rinse the fish heads, bones and skins and place in a saucepan with 1 onion, 2 carrots cut in quarters, parsley, salt and pepper to taste and 1 clove garlic, if used. Cover with about 2 quarts water.

2. Bring to a boil, cover and simmer for 1 hour or longer. Strain broth and reserve. Discard bones.

3. Grind the fish fillets and remaining onions and remaining garlic clove, if used, through the finest blade of a meat chopper. Grind a second time and then chop in a bowl or on a board until the mixture is very fine. Transfer to a bowl if on a board.

4. Beat in the eggs, water, salt and pepper to taste to give a fine, smooth mixture.

5. Shape the fish mixture into about 20 medium-size balls. Heat the reserved, strained broth in a large skillet or sauté pan. Gently drop the balls of fish into the simmering, but not boiling, liquid. Partly cover and simmer very gently for 1½ to 2 hours. Slice the remaining carrot thickly and add during the last 30 minutes of cooking time.

6. Drain and place the fish balls on a platter, cool slightly, cover and refrigerate. Remove carrot pieces and reserve for a garnish. Strain the broth into a bowl, cool, and chill overnight.

7. Serve the gefilte fish garnished with carrot pieces and with jellied broth or aspic.

Yield: 20 medium-size gefilte fish.

Maquereaux au Vin Blanc Provençale *(Mackerel with white wine and tomatoes)*

2 tablespoons olive oil
1 cup thinly sliced onion
¼ cup thin carrot rounds
2 cloves garlic, finely minced
Salt and freshly ground
pepper
2 tablespoons white vinegar
2 cups dry white wine
3 whole cloves
1 bay leaf
1 cup fresh or canned peeled
tomatoes

1. Preheat the oven to 400 degrees.

2. In a saucepan, heat 1 tablespoon oil and add the onion. Cook, stirring, until wilted. Add the carrot rounds, garlic, salt and pepper to taste, vinegar, white wine, cloves, bay leaf and tomatoes. Cook for 20 minutes and let cool.

3. Select a baking dish large enough to hold the mackerel in one layer. Rub the bottom of the dish with the remaining 1 tablespoon oil and sprinkle with salt and pepper. Arrange the mackerel in the dish. Arrange the lemon slices over the fish and sprinkle with lemon juice. Sprinkle with salt and pepper to taste.

4. Spoon the tomato and wine sauce over the fish and cover with a piece of buttered wax paper cut to fit the baking dish. Bake for 15 to 20 minutes, just until the fish flakes easily when tested with a fork. Baking time will depend on the size of the fish.

Yield: 10 or more servings.

Note: Mackerel fillets may be used in this recipe, but time will have to be adjusted accordingly.

5 pounds cleaned whole mackerel (see note)
10 thin lemon slices
3 tablespoons lemon juice

Poached Salmon

1. Combine all the ingredients for the court bouillon in a fish cooker or a kettle large enough to hold the fish. Bring to the boil and simmer, covered, for about 20 minutes. Let cool.

2. Wrap the whole salmon or salmon piece in cheesecloth or a clean towel and tie neatly with string. Lower it into the fish cooker and cover. Bring to the boil and simmer gently for exactly 20 minutes. The cooking time will be the same for a whole salmon or a large center section. Let stand briefly and serve hot, or let cool completely until ready to use if it is to be served at room temperature.

3. Remove the salmon and untie it. Remove the cheesecloth or towel. Place the salmon carefully on a flat surface and pull and scrape away the skin. Scrape away the thin dark brown flesh that coats the main pink flesh.

4. Decorate and garnish the salmon as desired. As a suggestion, drop large tarragon sprigs in boiling water and drain immediately. Chill instantly in ice water. Pat dry. Garnish surface of salmon with halved cherry tomatoes and tarragon leaves. Arrange around the salmon small Boston lettuce cups filled with quartered hard-cooked eggs wedged neatly between quartered small tomatoes. Serve with lemon wedges and mayonaise sauces such as cucumber mayonnaise, mustard mayonnaise, anchovy mayonnaise or sauce verte and cucumber salad with dill.

Yield: 12 to 24 servings, depending on size of salmon and whether served as an appetizer, buffet dish or main course.

The court bouillon:

24 cups water
1 bottle dry white wine
1½ cups coarsely chopped carrots
1½ cups coarsely chopped celery
3 cups chopped onion
4 cloves garlic, unpeeled but cut in half
1 hot red pepper
10 dill sprigs
6 sprigs fresh parsley
Salt to taste
1 bay leaf
1½ cups coarsely chopped leeks

The salmon:

1 whole, cleaned salmon, up to 7½ pounds, or use 1 large section of salmon such as the tail section or center cut, about 3½ pounds

The garnishes:

Tarragon sprigs
Cherry tomatoes, halved
Boston lettuce
Hard-cooked eggs, quartered
Small tomatoes, quartered
Lemon wedges

Saumon Grillé Mirabeau (Grilled salmon steaks with anchovy butter and olives)

The salmon:

6   1-inch-thick slices fresh
     salmon, with bone in
     Oil
     Salt and freshly ground pepper
     to taste

The anchovy butter:

8   flat fillets of anchovy, chopped
     (about 1½ tablespoons)
8   tablespoons butter at room
     temperature

The garnish:

6   lemon slices, seeds removed
6   flat fillets of anchovy
6   jumbo pitted green olives
6   tiny sprigs fresh parsley

1. Prepare a fire of charcoal or wood for grilling the fish. Or preheat the broiler to high.

2. Place the steaks in a flat dish such as a jelly roll pan and brush lightly with oil on all sides. Sprinkle with salt and pepper. Set aside.

3. Put the chopped anchovies in a small mixing bowl and add the butter. Blend well. Put the mixture through a fine sieve. Spoon it into a small serving bowl. Let stand at room temperature unless it is exceedingly hot, in which case keep it in a cool spot.

4. Prepare the lemon slices and set them aside.

5. Wrap 1 fillet of anchovy around the middle of each olive like a belt. The olives should be bottom up. Make a small hole in the bottom of each olive and stick the stem of 1 small sprig of parsley in each olive.

6. Grill the salmon for 4 or 5 minutes to a side until cooked but not dry. To test for doneness, insert the point of a knife somewhat firmly into the center of each small salmon bone. If the knife can be withdrawn removing the center bone, the fish is done.

7. To serve, place the fish steaks on a hot platter. Place 1 anchovy-wrapped olive in each piece where the bone was removed. Garnish with 1 lemon slice. Serve hot with anchovy butter on the side for guests to help themselves.

Yield: 6 servings

Cotelettes de Saumon Pojarski (Salmon cutlets with brown butter sauce)

1½   pounds skinless, boneless
      fillets of fresh salmon
1½   cups (approximately) fine,
      fresh bread crumbs
 1   cup heavy cream
      Salt and freshly ground
      pepper to taste
¼   teaspoon nutmeg, more or
      less to taste
      Pinch of cayenne pepper
 4   tablespoons peanut,
      vegetable or corn oil
 8   tablespoons butter

1. Use the fine blade of a meat grinder and grind the salmon, putting it through once. The salmon should not be put in a blender or food processor because it will be too fine. It could be chopped very fine, using a sharp knife.

2. Put the salmon in a mixing bowl and add ½ cup bread crumbs and ⅓ cup heavy cream, stirring briskly with a wooden spoon. Add salt, pepper and nutmeg. Add cayenne and continue beating rapidly with the spoon. Beat in the remaining ⅔ cup of heavy cream.

3. Lay out a length of wax paper. Divide the mixture into 6 equal portions. Shape each portion first into an oval like a small football, then place each portion on the wax paper and shape each piece to look like a pork chop with bone. The "chop" should be about ¾ inch thick. Arrange the "chops" on

a jelly roll pan or other utensil and refrigerate until ready to cook.

4. Coat cutlets on all sides with the remaining bread crumbs. Heat 2 tablespoons of oil and 2 tablespoons of butter in each of two skillets and, when it is hot, add the salmon. Cook on one side for about 4 minutes, until golden brown, and turn. Cook for 3 to 4 minutes longer until golden brown on the second side. Transfer salmon to a warm platter.

5. Add the remaining 4 tablespoons of butter to one of the skillets and cook, shaking the skillet, until the butter starts to brown, no longer. Do not let the butter burn. Pour the hot butter over the salmon.

Yield: 6 servings.

Saumon à l'Oseille *(Salmon with sorrel sauce)*

Le Francais, the enormously popular restaurant outside Chicago, ranks on any count with the finest French restaurants in America. It is the culinary offspring of Jean Banchet, a highly skilled and innovative chef who was born in Roanne, best celebrated as the home of the Troisgros restaurant. One of the most popular dishes he serves is a Troisgros creation, now celebrated wherever serious eaters gather, the salmon with sorrel sauce.

1. Cut the fish on the bias like smoked salmon into ¼-inch-thick slices. Flatten gently with a flat mallet. Refrigerate.

2. In a deep skillet, combine the shallots, fish stock, vermouth and white wine. Cook over high heat for about 45 minutes until the liquid is reduced to about ½ cup.

3. Add 2 cups cream, salt and pepper to taste. Bring to the boil and stir in the fish glaze, if used. Cook over high heat for about 2 minutes.

4. Cut the sorrel into very fine shreds (chiffonade). Add to the cream mixture and bring to the boil. Beat the yolks with the remaining cream. Remove the sauce from the heat and stir in the yolk and cream mixture. Swirl in the 2 tablespoons butter. Season with lemon juice. Keep the sauce hot but do not boil or it will curdle.

5. Dredge the fish slices lightly in flour seasoned with salt and pepper.

6. Heat the clarified butter in one or two large skillets. When it is very hot but not smoking, add the fish slices. Cook for about 1 minute on one side until golden brown. Turn and

1	3- to 3½-pound boned, skinned salmon
¼	cup chopped shallots
4	cups fish stock (see recipe page 659)
1½	cups dry vermouth
1	cup dry white wine
2¼	cups heavy cream
	Salt and freshly ground pepper
3	tablespoons fish glaze (see note), optional
¼	pound fresh sorrel
4	egg yolks
2	tablespoons butter
	Juice of ½ lemon
	Flour for dredging
½	cup clarified butter (see note page 322)

cook for about 1 minute on the other. Serve the fish with the sauce spooned over.

Yield: 4 to 6 servings.

Note: Fish glaze is a long-simmered reduction of fish stock. The stock is cooked many hours until it becomes a thick gelatinous, lightly browned mass, like thick, smooth caramel. It is a classic foundation glaze in French kitchens.

Shioyaki *(Salt grilled salmon)*

1½ pounds salmon
1 tablespoon salt
¼ cup sake
6 lemon wedges

1. Place the salmon on a board, preferably wooden, and sprinkle it with salt on all sides. Tilt the board at a small angle so that any liquid given by the fish because of the salt will drain. Let the fish stand in a very cool place for 3 or 4 hours.

2. Cut the salmon into individual serving pieces of about ¼ pound each. Rinse each individual piece quickly in cold water and pat dry.

3. Skewer the fish, preferably using 2 skewers for each serving so that they do not break while cooking. Grill it over hot coals skin side down, for about 2 minutes. Continue grilling, turning the pieces as necessary so that they cook evenly throughout.

4. When cooked, douse the fish with sake and flame it. Serve with lemon wedges.

Yield: 6 servings

Coulibiac of Salmon

It is not easy to explain precisely what a coulibiac of salmon is. The easiest way out would be to define it as a pâté of salmon. Such a definition is woefully inapt. It is no mere trifle, no ordinary pâté, something to be dabbled with while awaiting a second course or third or fourth. A coulibiac is a celestial creation, manna for the culinary gods and a main course unto itself.

A coulibiac admittedly demands patience, time, talent and

enthusiasm, and if you are possessed of these, what a magnificent offering to those invited to your table. Actually, any cook who is skilled enough to prepare a brioche dough, a standard French crêpe and a cream sauce is equal to the task.

1. Have all the ingredients for the coulibiac ready.

2. Remove the salmon and mushroom mixture from the refrigerator. Using a knife, cut it in half lengthwise down the center.

3. Remove the brioche dough from the bowl and with floured fingers shape it into a thick, flat pillow shape. Place the brioche dough on a lightly floured board and roll it into a rectangle measuring about 21 by 18 inches. The rectangle, of course, will have slightly rounded corners. Arrange 8 crêpes, edges overlapping in a neat pattern, over the center of the rectangle, leaving a border of brioche dough.

4. Sprinkle the crêpes down the center with a rectangle of about one-third of the rice mixture. Pick up half the chilled salmon and carefully arrange it, mushroom side down, over the rice mixture. Sprinkle with another third of the rice mixture. Top this, sandwich fashion, with another layer of the chilled salmon filling, mushroom side up. Sprinkle with remaining rice. Cover with 6 overlapping crêpes.

5. Bring up one side of the brioche. Brush it liberally with a mixture of 2 beaten yolks and 2 tablespoons cold water. Bring up the opposite side of the brioche dough to enclose the filling, overlapping the two sides of dough. Brush all over with egg yolk. Trim off the ends of the dough to make them neat. Brush with yolk and bring up the ends, pinching as necessary to enclose the filling.

6. Butter a baking dish with 2 tablespoons of butter. Carefully turn the coulibiac upside down onto the baking dish. This will keep the seams intact. Brush the coulibiac all over with yolk. Using a small, round, decorative cooky cutter, cut a hole in the center of the coulibiac. This will allow steam to escape. Brush around the hole with yolk. Cut out another slightly larger ring of dough to surround and outline the hole neatly. Roll out a scrap of dough and cut off strips of dough to decorate the coulibiac. Always brush with beaten yolk before and after applying pastry cutouts.

7. Roll out a 6-foot length of aluminum foil. Fold it over into thirds to make one long band about 4½ inches in height. Brush the band with 4 tablespoons of melted butter. Arrange the band neatly and snugly around the loaf, buttered side against the brioche. The purpose of the band is to prevent the

Brioche dough (see recipe page 342)
Salmon and mushrooms with velouté (see recipe page 343)
14 7-inch crêpes (see recipe page 344)
Rice and egg filling (see recipe page 344)

Ingredients used in assembly:

2 egg yolks
2 tablespoons cold water
2 tablespoons butter at room temperature
¾ pound plus 4 tablespoons hot melted butter

sides of the loaf from collapsing before the dough has a chance to firm up while baking. Fasten the top of the band with a jumbo paper clip. Run a cord around the center of the foil band to secure it in place. Run the cord around three times and tie the ends. Make certain the bottom of the loaf is securely enclosed with foil. Set the pan in a warm, draft-free place for about 30 minutes.

8. Meanwhile, preheat the oven to 400 degrees.

9. Place the loaf in the oven and bake for 15 minutes. Reduce the oven heat to 375 degrees and bake for 10 minutes longer. Cover with a sheet of aluminum foil to prevent excess browning. Continue baking for 20 minutes (a total baking time at this point of 45 minutes). Remove foil and continue baking for 15 minutes more.

10. Remove the coulibiac from the oven. Pour ½ cup of the melted butter through the steam hole into the filling. Serve cut into 1-inch slices with remaining hot melted butter on the side.

Yield: 16 or more servings.

Brioche dough

¾ cup milk
¼ teaspoon sugar
3 packages granular yeast
4 to 4½ cups flour
Salt to taste
1 cup egg yolks (about 12)
8 tablespoons butter at room temperature

1. Pour the milk into a saucepan and heat it gradually to lukewarm. Remove from the heat. If the milk has become too hot, let it cool to lukewarm.

2. Sprinkle the milk with sugar and yeast and stir to dissolve. Cover with a towel. Let stand about 5 minutes and place the mixture in a warm place (the natural warmth of a turned-off oven is good for this) for about 5 minutes. It should ferment during the period and increase in volume.

3. Place 4 cups of flour with salt to taste in the bowl of an electric mixer fitted with a dough hook, or use a mixing bowl and wooden spoon. Make a well in the center and pour in the yeast mixture, the cup of yolks and butter. With the dough hook or wooden spoon, gradually work in flour until well blended. Then beat vigorously until dough is quite smooth and can be shaped into a ball.

4. Turn the dough out onto a lightly floured board and knead until it is smooth and satiny, about 10 to 15 minutes. As you work the dough, continue to add flour to the kneading surface as necessary to prevent sticking, but take care not to add an excess or the finished product will be tough.

5. Lightly butter a clean mixing bowl and add the ball of dough. Cover with a clean towel and let stand in a warm place for about 1 hour or until double in bulk. Punch the dough down. Turn it out once more onto a lightly floured board.

Knead it for about 1 minute and return it to the clean bowl. Cover closely with plastic wrap and refrigerate overnight.

6. The next morning, punch the dough down again and continue to refrigerate, covered, until ready to use.

1. Preheat the oven to 400 degrees.

2. Using a sharp carving knife, cut each fillet on the bias into slices about ⅓ inch thick. Each fillet should produce about 12 slices.

3. Select a heatproof rectangular baking dish. It should be just large enough to hold two rows of slightly overlapping slices (a dish measuring 13½- x 8½- x 2-inches is suitable). Rub the bottom of the dish with the 2 tablespoons butter and sprinkle with onion, shallots, salt and pepper. Arrange two parallel rows of salmon slices, the slices slightly overlapping, over the onion and shallots. Sprinkle with salt to taste. Sprinkle somewhat liberally with black pepper. Scatter the mushrooms over the salmon. Sprinkle the mushrooms with fresh dill and pour the wine over all. Cover with aluminum foil and bring to the boil on top of the stove. Place the dish in the oven and bake for 15 minutes.

4. Remove the dish, uncover and pour the accumulated liquid into a saucepan. Carefully spoon off most of the mushrooms and transfer them to another dish. Bring the cooking liquid to the boil over high heat. Tilt the dish containing the salmon. More liquid will accumulate as it stands. Spoon or pour this liquid into the saucepan containing the cooking liquid.

5. For the velouté, melt the 2 tablespoons butter in a saucepan and stir in the flour, using a wire whisk. When blended, add the cooking liquid, stirring rapidly with the whisk. Cook for about 5 minutes, stirring often. Add the mushrooms and continue cooking for about 20 minutes, adding any liquid that accumulates around the salmon. Add the cayenne pepper and lemon juice. Beat the yolks with a whisk and scrape them into the mushrooms, stirring vigorously. Cook for about 30 seconds, stirring, and remove from the heat. Add salt and a generous amount of pepper to taste.

6. Spoon and scrape this sauce—it should be quite thick—over the salmon. Blanket the salmon all over with an even layer of the sauce but try to avoid having it spill over the sides of the salmon. Smooth the sauce over. Let cool. Grease a neat rectangle of wax paper with butter. Arrange this, buttered side down, on the sauce-covered salmon and refrigerate until thoroughly cold.

Salmon and mushrooms with velouté

The salmon and mushrooms:

2 skinless, boneless salmon fillets, preferably center-cut, each weighing about 1½ pounds
2 tablespoons butter
2 tablespoons finely chopped onion
2 tablespoons finely chopped shallots
 Salt and freshly ground pepper to taste
¾ pound fresh mushrooms, thinly sliced
¼ cup finely chopped fresh dill
2 cups dry white wine

The velouté:

2 tablespoons butter
3 tablespoons flour
⅛ teaspoon cayenne pepper
3 tablespoons lemon juice
5 egg yolks

Crêpes

1½ cups flour
3 large eggs
Salt and freshly ground
pepper to taste
1¾ cups milk
2 tablespoons melted butter
1 tablespoon finely chopped
parsley
1 tablespoon finely chopped
dill

1. Place the flour in a mixing bowl and make a well in the center. Add the eggs, salt and pepper and, stirring, gradually add the milk.

2. Put the mixture through a sieve, running the whisk around inside the sieve to remove lumps. Add the melted butter, the parsley and dill. Use to make crêpes.

Yield: About 14 7-inch crêpes.

Note: Leftover crêpes may be frozen. Interlayer them with rounds of wax paper, wrap in foil and freeze.

Rice and egg filling

3 hard-cooked eggs
1¾ cups firmly cooked rice
¼ cup finely chopped parsley
1 tablespoon finely chopped
dill
Salt and freshly ground
pepper to taste
1½ cups chopped, cooked vesiga
(see recipe below), optional

Chop the eggs and put them in a mixing bowl. Add the remaining ingredients and blend well.

Vesiga for coulibiac

½ pound vesiga
Salt to taste

One of the classic—but optional—ingredients for a coulibiac of salmon is called vesiga. It is a ropelike, gelatinous substance, actually the spinal marrow of sturgeon. The vesiga, after cleaning, must be simmered for several hours until tender. It is then chopped and looks like chopped aspic. It has a very bland flavor and its principal contribution to the dish is its slightly tender but chewy texture.

Vesiga is by no means a staple item, but it is often available from certain fish stores in metropolitan areas.

1. Wash the vesiga in cold water. Split it as necessary for thorough cleaning. Drain the vesiga and place it in a saucepan. Add water to cover and salt to taste. Bring to the boil.

2. Simmer for 4 hours, replacing the liquid as it evaporates. Drain the vesiga and chop it. It will be translucent and look like chopped aspic.

Sea Trout Grenobloise

1. Cut the fish fillet into 4 serving pieces of equal size.
2. Put the milk in a flat dish and add the fish. Sprinkle with salt and pepper to taste. Turn the fish pieces on all sides in the milk.
3. Lift the pieces from the milk and dip into the flour seasoned with salt and pepper.
4. Heat the oil in a skillet large enough to hold the fish in one layer without crowding. Cook for 3 to 6 minutes, or until golden brown on one side. Cooking time will depend on the thickness of the fish. Turn the pieces and cook for 2 to 3 minutes. Baste occasionally as the pieces cook.
5. Remove the fish to a warm serving platter. Wipe out the skillet.
6. Add the butter to the skillet and heat, swirling the butter around. When it starts to brown, add the capers and cook for about 2 minutes, shaking the skillet occasionally.
7. Add the vinegar and cook for about 10 seconds. Spoon the mixture over the fish. Sprinkle with parsley and serve.

Yield: 4 servings.

1½ pounds sea trout (weakfish) or other fish, filleted but with skin left on
2 tablespoons milk
Salt and freshly ground pepper
¼ cup flour
¼ cup peanut, vegetable or corn oil
4 tablespoons butter
¼ cup drained capers
1 teaspoon red wine vinegar
1 tablespoon finely chopped parsley

Shad Stuffed with Shad Roe Nantaise

1. Preheat the oven to 400 degrees.
2. Cut the shad roe in half, slicing through the membrane. Remove and discard the membrane. Put the roe on a flat surface and add the shallots, coarsely chopped hard-cooked egg and ¼ cup chopped parsley. Chop together to blend well.
3. Put the crumbs in a mixing bowl and add the milk. Stir to blend. Add the roe mixture and salt and pepper to taste.
4. Open up the fillets, skin side down. Sprinkle with salt and pepper. You will note that there are two flaps to each fillet. Open these up and spread one fillet with the roe filling, smoothing it over. Bring up the sides of the fillet. Cover with the other fillet, letting the flaps of the fillet fall down and overlap the stuffed fillet.
5. Tie the "package" neatly with string in four or five places to keep the fillets and filling intact.
6. Butter a baking dish large enough to hold the stuffed fish. Use about 2 tablespoons of the butter. Sprinkle with salt and pepper.
7. Arrange the fish fillets in the dish. Dot with 2 tablespoons

1 pair shad roe
1½ tablespoons finely chopped shallots
1 hard-cooked egg, coarsely chopped
¼ cup finely chopped parsley
1 cup fresh bread crumbs
½ cup milk
Salt and freshly ground pepper
2 shad fillets, about 1½ pounds
5 tablespoons butter
½ cup dry white wine
8 thin slices lemon for garnish
Chopped parsley for garnish

butter. Place in the oven and bake for 15 minutes. Spoon 1 tablespoon of dry white wine over the fish and continue baking, basting often with the pan juices, for about 15 minutes.

8. Pour the remaining wine over all and continue baking and basting for 15 minutes longer. It is imperative that you baste often as the fish cooks.

9. Remove the fish and add the remaining 1 tablespoon of butter to the pan liquid. Remove the strings from the fish. Using the fingers, pull off and discard the skin of the fish from the top. The skin comes off easily. Baste the fish. Garnish with lemon slices and sprinkle with chopped parsley. It is now ready to be carved crosswise and served.

Yield: 6 to 8 servings.

Herbed Maryland Shad *(Oven steamed so you can even eat the bones)*

Shad is, of course, one of the boniest fish to be found in river or ocean. For years, we have been asked about a technique for cooking shad in which the whole fish is baked until the bones are "dissolved" as a result of the prolonged cooking. Only recently did we come across such a recipe in a throwaway brochure from the Seafood Marketing Authority in Annapolis, Maryland.

We tested the recipe in our own kitchen and, much to our surprise, it works admirably. In fact, it drew raves—"melted" bones and all. We added a delicious herb butter sauce.

1	4-pound shad, dressed
	Salt and freshly ground pepper to taste
4 to	5 cups water
1	cup white wine
2	ribs celery, coarsely chopped
1	small onion, chopped
2	bay leaves
	Beurre nantais sauce (see recipe page 648), optional

1. Preheat the oven to 300 degrees.

2. Wash the shad and dry with paper towels. Sprinkle the fish inside and out with salt and pepper.

3. Put the fish on the rack of a baking pan. Add the water and wine to a level just under the fish. Add 4 cups of water and remaining ingredients, except the sauce. If necessary, add the fifth cup of water to prevent burning.

4. Cover tightly and steam for 5 hours. Baste often. Serve sliced crosswise through the bones. Serve, if desired, with herb butter sauce.

Yield: 6 servings.

Note: The secret of softening the bones is to make sure the pan cover fits tightly and to cook the fish for the full amount of time. If these directions are followed exactly, even the large backbone will be soft enough to be eaten, and most of the small splinter bones will disappear.

Broiled Shad Fillet with Roe

1. Preheat the broiler.

2. Lightly oil a baking sheet with 1 teaspoon of oil. Arrange the shad fillet on the baking sheet with the roe next to it. Sprinkle the fish and roe with salt and pepper. Brush with the remaining 2 tablespoons of oil. Sprinkle the fish and roe with paprika, dusting it through a small sieve.

3. Place the fish under the broiler about 4 inches from the source of heat and broil for 6 to 8 minutes.

4. Transfer the fish and roe to a serving dish. Pour the melted butter over all. Garnish with lemon wedges and parsley clusters.

Yield: 2 to 4 servings.

2 tablespoons plus 1 teaspoon peanut, vegetable or corn oil
1 shad fillet, about 1 pound
½ pair shad roe
Salt and freshly ground pepper to taste
½ teaspoon paprika
2 tablespoons hot melted butter
Lemon wedges for garnish
Parsley clusters for garnish

Shad and Roe Véronique

1. Preheat the oven to 400 degrees.

2. Sprinkle the shad fillet and the roe with salt and pepper to taste.

3. Rub the bottom of a baking dish with the 2 tablespoons of butter. Sprinkle with shallots. Arrange the shad fillet, skin side down, on the baking dish. Do not open up the flaps of the fillet where the bones were removed.

4. Arrange the roe half next to the fillet. If fresh seedless grapes are available, remove them from the stems and rinse and drain well. Scatter them around the fish and roe. Cover with buttered wax paper and cook on top of the stove until it sizzles. Place the dish in the oven and bake for 15 minutes.

5. Pour the liquid from the fish into a small skillet. Do not add the grapes. Cook the liquid down until almost evaporated. Add the cream and cook down over high heat. Pour any additional liquid that accumulates around the fish and roe into the cream sauce. Cook down over high heat until it is syrupy and saucelike, about 5 minutes.

6. Put the sauce through a sieve, preferably a seive of the sort known in French kitchens as a chinois. Press the sauce through with the back of a spoon.

7. Reheat the sauce and add the juice of half a lemon. If canned grapes are used, drain them and add to the sauce just to heat through.

Yield: 2 to 4 servings.

1 shad fillet
½ pair shad roe (use the larger portion)
Salt and freshly ground pepper
2 tablespoons butter
1 tablespoon finely chopped shallots
½ cup white seedless grapes, preferably fresh
1 cup heavy cream
Juice of ½ lemon

Shad and Roe Provençale

1 shad fillet, about 1 pound
½ pair shad roe
 Salt and freshly ground
 pepper to taste
¼ cup milk
 Flour for dredging
½ cup peanut, vegetable or corn
 oil
3 tablespoons butter
10 firm but ripe cherry tomatoes
1 clove garlic, finely minced
2 tablespoons chopped parsley

1. The fillet may be cut in half crosswise or left whole. It will be easier to handle if it is cut in half. Place the fillet and roe on a flat dish and sprinkle with salt and pepper. Add the milk and coat the fish and roe with it. Dredge the fish and roe with flour.

2. Heat the oil in a heavy skillet large enough to hold the fillet and roe in one layer. Cook the fillet and roe for about 6 minutes, until crisp and golden brown on one side. The fish and roe should be cooked over relatively high heat. Turn and cook, basting occasionally, until crisp and brown on the other side, about 6 minutes. Transfer to a warm platter.

3. Heat the butter in a skillet and add the cherry tomatoes. Cook for about 3 minutes, shaking the skillet so that the tomatoes heat evenly. Add the garlic and cook briefly. Pour this over the fish and sprinkle with parsley.

Yield: 2 to 4 servings.

Shad and Roe Grenobloise

1 shad fillet, about 1 pound
½ pair shad roe
 Salt and freshly ground
 pepper to taste
¼ cup milk
 Flour for dredging
½ cup peanut, vegetable or corn
 oil
1 lemon
3 tablespoons butter
3 tablespoons drained capers
 Chopped parsley for garnish

1. The fillet may be cut in half crosswise or left whole. It would be easier to handle if it is cut in half. Place the fillet and roe in a flat dish and sprinkle with salt and pepper. Add the milk and coat the fish and roe with it. Dredge the fish and roe with flour.

2. Heat the oil in a heavy skillet large enough to hold the fillet and roe in one layer. Cook the fillet and roe for about 6 minutes, until crisp and golden brown on one side. The fish and roe should be cooked over relatively high heat. Turn and cook the fish and roe, basting occasionally, until crisp and brown on the other side, about 6 minutes. Transfer to a warm platter.

3. As the fish cooks, prepare a lemon. Slice around to remove the rind (including the white pulp). Discard the rind. Cut between the membraneous sections to remove the lemon sections. Set aside.

4. Heat the butter in a skillet and, when it is starting to brown, add the capers. Sprinkle the juice that has accumulated around the lemon sections over the fish. Add the lemon sec-

tions to the capers and butter. Cook until piping hot and bubbling and starting to brown. Pour this over the fish. Sprinkle with chopped parsley and serve.

Yield: 2 to 4 servings.

Shad Roe à la Crème

1. Arrange the shad roe in a saucepan large enough to hold it comfortably. Add water, milk, salt, bay leaf and parsley. Bring to the boil. Simmer for 10 minutes and remove from the heat. Remove the roe and set aside.

2. Strain the liquid. Set aside 1½ cups and discard the rest.

3. Melt the butter in a saucepan and add the flour, stirring with a wire whisk. When blended, add the strained cooking liquid, stirring rapidly with the whisk. When thickened and smooth, add the cream, Tabasco and nutmeg. Add salt and pepper to taste and the wine.

4. Cut the roe into bite-size pieces and add to the sauce. Or spoon the sauce over the pieces of roe. Serve on toast or with rice or boiled potatoes.

Yield: 2 to 4 servings.

1	pair shad roe
2	cups water
½	cup milk
	Salt to taste
1	bay leaf
2	sprigs fresh parsley
2	tablespoons butter
2	tablespoons flour
½	cup heavy cream
	Tabasco sauce to taste
⅛	teaspoon freshly grated nutmeg
	Freshly ground pepper to taste
1	tablespoon dry sherry, optional

Shad Fillets Doria

1. If the fillets are small, cut each one in half. If there is one large fillet, cut into 4 equal-size pieces. Place the pieces in a flat dish. Blend the oil, lemon juice, parsley, bay leaf and thyme. Add salt and pepper to taste. Spoon this evenly over the shad pieces and turn them in it. Let stand for an hour or so.

2. Meanwhile, heat 3 tablespoons of butter in a skillet and add the bread cubes. Cook, stirring and tossing so that the cubes are evenly coated with butter, until golden brown on all sides. Drain well and reserve the butter.

3. Preheat the oven to 400 degrees.

4. Season the flour with salt and pepper. Remove the shad pieces one at a time and dredge on all sides with flour. Dip in egg to coat on all sides.

5. Meanwhile, heat the butter reserved from browning the bread cubes and the remaining 2 tablespoons of butter in a skillet large enough to hold the fish in one layer. As each piece is dipped in egg, add it to the skillet. Cook for about 5 minutes,

2	small shad fillets or 1 large fillet, about 1 pound
¼	cup peanut, vegetable or corn oil
1½	tablespoons lemon juice
2	tablespoons finely chopped parsley
½	bay leaf, finely minced
½	teaspoon chopped fresh thyme, or ¼ teaspoon dried
	Salt and freshly ground pepper
5	tablespoons butter
1	cup small, fresh bread cubes
½	cup flour
1	egg, well beaten
1	cup heavy cream
	Parsleyed cucumber ovals (see recipe page 495)

until golden on one side. Carefully turn the pieces and cook on the other side for about 7 minutes.

6. Arrange the fish on a heat-proof dish and place in the oven.

7. Meanwhile, add the cream to a saucepan or small skillet and cook over high heat until it is reduced to ½ cup. Spoon this evenly over the fillets, sprinkle with the croutons and serve hot. Accompany the fish with the cucumbers.

Yield: 4 servings.

Baked Red Snapper

The fish:

1 4- to 5-pound whole red snapper with head and tail left on
 Salt and freshly ground pepper
 Lime or lemon juice
 Unsalted butter, softened

The stuffing:

2 tablespoons butter
2 tablespoons finely chopped or grated onion
1 tablespoon finely chopped green pepper
1 tablespoon finely chopped celery
½ cup fresh bread crumbs
 Salt and freshly ground pepper
½ teaspoon dried tarragon
1 teaspoon dried basil
1 tablespoon chopped parsley

1. Scale and clean the fish thoroughly. If possible, debone it without disturbing the shape. Place the fish in a shallow oblong baking dish. Sprinkle inside cavity with salt, pepper and a little lime or lemon juice. Spread with unsalted butter.

2. Preheat the oven to 400 degrees.

3. For the stuffing, heat the butter in a skillet and sauté the onion until just transparent. Add the green pepper and celery. Then add bread crumbs, salt, pepper, tarragon and basil. Add parsley and uncooked shrimp. Continue cooking and, when shrimp barely start to turn pink, add bay shrimp and almonds. Add the fish stock. Stuffing is done when the medium-size shrimp are all pink.

4. Place stuffing in fish. Secure cavity with toothpicks or skewers. Sprinkle outside of fish with salt, pepper and a little lime or lemon juice. Dot generously with unsalted butter. Cover with foil pressed around the edges.

5. Place fish in oven and bake for 20 minutes. Uncover and bake for 15 minutes longer, or until fish flakes easily. Remove fish to hot platter.

6. For the sauce, add cornstarch to drippings in pan, stirring. Stir in the ½ cup fish stock. Add salt, pepper, basil and dill. Add the dry white wine or vermouth.

7. Add the 2 raw shrimp and 1 tablespoon tiny bay shrimp

and then the cream. Check for seasoning. Cook until shrimp turn pink. Pour a little sauce over fish, reserving the remainder to be served separately.

Yield: 8 servings.

Note: Large shrimp, cut into small pieces, may be substituted for bay shrimp. Tiny shrimp are available in jars in specialty food shops.

6 medium-size raw shrimp, shelled and deveined, cut into small chunks

7 tablespoons tiny bay shrimp, cooked (see note)

¼ cup chopped or slivered toasted almonds

2 tablespoons fish stock, or bottled clam juice

The sauce:

1 tablespoon cornstarch

½ cup fish stock, or bottled clam juice
Salt and freshly ground black pepper to taste

½ teaspoon dried basil

½ teaspoon chopped fresh dill, optional

½ cup dry white wine or vermouth

2 medium-size raw shrimp, shelled and deveined, cut into small chunks

1 tablespoon tiny bay shrimp, cooked (see note)

¼ cup heavy cream

Sole in White Wine Sauce with Shrimp

There is no fish whose name has a vaguer meaning than sole. The finest and true sole is that whose natural habitat is the English Channel. Legend has it that officials once planted a few of these fish, properly tagged, in American waters. Within a matter of days the fish swam directly back where they came from. On the East Coast of America, various fish from Atlantic waters, such as yellow-tail flounder, gray sole, lemon sole, plus winter and summer flounder (fluke) are legally sold as fillet of sole. On the West Coast, the Pacific yields lemon sole, rex sole and rock sole. Sole in American recipes usually means any flatfish from either coast.

5 tablespoons butter
2 tablespoons finely chopped
  shallots
8 fillets of sole, striped bass or
  other white-fleshed fish,
  about 2 pounds
  Salt and freshly ground
  pepper
2 tablespoons finely chopped
  dill or parsley
½ cup dry white wine
½ pound raw shrimp, shelled
  and deveined
  A few drops Tabasco sauce
1½ cups heavy cream
1 teaspoon lemon juice

1. Preheat the oven to 400 degrees.

2. Select a baking dish large enough to accommodate the fish in one layer. We used an oval baking dish that measured 16- x 10-inches.

3. Grease the dish with 1 tablespoon of butter and sprinkle with the shallots. Place the fish, skinned side down, in one layer. Dot with the remaining 4 tablespoons butter and add salt and pepper to taste. Sprinkle with 1 tablespoon of dill and pour the wine over all. Cover closely with a piece of waxed paper. Place the baking dish on top of the stove and bring to the boil. Place the dish immediately in the oven and bake for 5 minutes. Do not bake much longer, or the fish will become dry.

4. Meanwhile, place the shrimp on a flat surface and cut them into ½-inch pieces.

5. Carefully drain the liquid that has accumulated in the baking dish into a medium-size skillet. Add the shrimp, salt and pepper and a dash of Tabasco. Simmer for about 30 seconds. Using a slotted spoon, remove the shrimp and scatter them over the fish.

6. Reduce the cooking liquid over high heat for about 2 minutes. Add the heavy cream and reduce it over high heat for about 10 minutes, or until the sauce is thickened. Add the lemon juice and a bit more Tabasco, if desired. Add a little more salt and pepper. Spoon the sauce over the fish and shrimp and sprinkle with the remaining tablespoon of chopped dill.

Yield: 8 servings.

Paupiettes de Sole au Porto *(Sole with port wine sauce)*

12 small skinless, boneless
   fillets of sole or flounder,
   about 1½ pounds
2 tablespoons plus 2 teaspoons
  butter
  Salt and freshly ground
  pepper to taste
2 tablespoons finely chopped
  shallots
1 cup port wine, preferably
  white port
2 cups thinly sliced mushrooms
¾ cup heavy cream
2 teaspoons flour

1. Roll the fish fillets like small jelly rolls.

2. Butter the bottom of a baking dish large enough to hold the rolls in one layer with 2 tablespoons butter. Sprinkle with salt, pepper and shallots.

3. Arrange the rolls, seam side down, in the dish and sprinkle with salt and pepper.

4. Pour the wine over the fish and scatter the mushrooms over all. Cover closely and bring to the boil. Simmer for about 5 minutes.

5. Transfer the pieces of fish to a serving dish and cover with wax paper.

6. Return the dish with the cooking liquid to the stove and cook over high heat. Add the cream and continue cooking

down until reduced by half. As it cooks, add any liquid that may accumulate around the fish rolls.

7. Blend the flour and remaining butter and stir this gradually into the sauce. Pour the sauce over the fish and serve.

Yield: 6 servings.

Fillets de Sole Thérèse *(Stuffed fillets of sole)*

1. Place the fillets on a flat surface. There is a thin bone line running lengthwise down the center of each fillet. Run a sharp knife lengthwise on either side of the bone line. Remove it. This will produce 24 fillet halves.

2. Heat 3 tablespoons butter in a small skillet and add the shallots. Cook for about 2 minutes and add the mushrooms. Add the truffles, if used. Cook until mushrooms give up their liquid. Stir occasionally.

3. Add the chopped shrimp and lobster. Cook for about 1 minute and add the cream, salt and pepper to taste. Cook for about 5 minutes.

4. Blend 4 tablespoons butter and 6 tablespoons flour until smooth. Add it, spoonfuls at a time, to the lobster and mushroom mixture, stirring. When thickened and smooth, add the yolk, stirring. Remove from the heat. Let cool.

5. Arrange the fillet halves on a flat surface and pound lightly with a flat mallet. Do not break the flesh. Spoon equal portions of the filling — 3 or 4 tablespoons — on the center of 12 pieces of fillet. Smooth the filling up and down the fish almost but not quite to the ends of each fillet half. Cover each fillet half with another.

6. Arrange the stuffed fillets on a shallow pan and refrigerate.

7. Combine the eggs, 2 tablespoons oil and water in a large baking dish. Add salt and pepper to taste. Beat well to blend.

8. Pour the remaining 1 cup of flour into a large, flat baking dish.

9. Spoon the bread crumbs into another large, flat baking dish.

10. Dip the stuffed sole "packages," one at a time, in flour, then in the egg mixture. Add to the bread crumbs, coating well and pressing down to help crumbs adhere. Set aside.

11. When ready to cook, heat about 2 tablespoons oil and 2 tablespoons butter in each of two skillets. Add as many fish fillets as the skillets will hold. Cook for about 5 minutes on one

12	large, skinless fillets of sole, preferably lemon sole, about 4¼ pounds
¾	cup plus 7 tablespoons butter, approximately
2	tablespoons finely chopped shallots
⅓	pound fresh mushrooms, finely chopped, about 2 cups
3	tablespoons finely chopped truffles, optional
3	large cooked shrimp, finely chopped, about ½ cup
⅓	pound cooked lobster meat, finely chopped, about 1¼ cups
1	cup heavy cream Salt and freshly ground pepper
1	cup plus 6 tablespoons flour
1	egg yolk
2	eggs
½	cup plus 2 tablespoons peanut, vegetable or corn oil
½	cup water
6	cups fine, fresh bread crumbs Juice of 1 lemon Lemon slices for garnish

side; turn and cook for 5 minutes on the other side. Remove to a warm platter. Wipe out the skillet and add more oil and butter as necessary, about 2 tablespoons each oil and butter. To keep the fish warm, place the platter in an oven preheated to about 300 degrees.

12. Heat the remaining 4 tablespoons of butter and add the lemon juice. Pour this over the fish. Serve garnished with lemon slices.

Yield: 12 servings.

Calamari alla Nanni *(Squid in wine sauce)*

⅔ cup olive oil
6 cloves garlic, finely chopped
⅓ cup finely chopped scallions
4 bay leaves
1 2-ounce can flat anchovies
6½ pounds fresh squid, thoroughly cleaned and cut into 1-inch rounds
½ cup chopped fresh parsley
½ cup chopped fresh basil
¾ cup dry white wine
½ teaspoon oregano
1 pound peeled, cored, crushed fresh tomatoes, about 1½ cups, or use canned imported tomatoes
Salt and freshly ground pepper
1 tablespoon Pernod or other anise-flavored liqueur, optional

1. Heat the oil in a large kettle and add the garlic, scallions and bay leaves. Add the anchovies along with the oil in which they are packed. Simmer for about 5 minutes and add the remaining ingredients except the liqueur. Cover and let simmer for 1 hour.

2. Stir in the Pernod, if used, and serve hot with rice.

Yield: 12 or more servings.

Stuffed Squid

2 pounds medium to large squid, cleaned
5 anchovy fillets
3 cloves garlic, crushed
2 tablespoons drained capers

1. Mince together the tentacles, anchovies, 1 clove garlic, capers and Italian parsley. Place mixture in a bowl. Add bread crumbs and 1 tablespoon olive oil and mix well to form a pastelike mixture.

2. Stuff the bodies of the squid about one-third full with the

mixture and skewer with a toothpick. (In cooking, the bodies shrink to about one-third of their original size and the filling expands slightly. If overstuffed, the bodies rupture). Save any remaining filling.

3. Heat the remaining oil in a 10- to 12-inch skillet, one large enough to hold the squid in a single layer. Sauté the remaining garlic cloves in the oil until golden, then discard the cloves.

4. Let the oil cool slightly and add the stuffed squid along with any remaining filling. Sprinkle squid with pepper. Cook gently over moderately low heat for 8 to 10 minutes. Add the wine, bring to a boil and simmer until the wine has reduced to half.

5. If the squid have shrunk a lot, transfer the squid and pan juices to a smaller pan just large enough to hold them. Add about ½ cup water or just enough to barely cover the squid. Cover the skillet and simmer over low heat for 10 minutes. Uncover, taste for seasoning and adjust if necessary. Cook over moderately high heat until the sauce has reduced to about half and has thickened slightly. Serve the squid warm with the sauce and Italian bread. Stuffed squid is also good cold as an appetizer.

Yield: 4 to 6 servings.

1 cup loosely packed Italian flat parsley leaves
4 tablespoons unseasoned dry bread crumbs
5 tablespoons olive oil
⅛ to ¼ teaspoon freshly ground black pepper
1 cup dry white wine

Pesce al Salmoriglio *(Fish steaks with oil and lemon sauce)*

1. Preheat the broiler or prepare charcoal for grilling.
2. Have the fish ready and set it aside.
3. Blend the lemon juice, salt and crushed dried oregano. Gradually add the oil while stirring with a fork. Add a generous amount of black pepper. This sauce is known as a salmoriglio sauce.
4. When the broiler or charcoal grill is quite hot, place the fish under the broiler or on the grill. The fish should be quite close to the source of heat. It must cook quickly. Cook for about 1 minute on one side. Turn carefully but quickly and cook for 1 minute or slightly longer on the other side. Do not overcook or the fish steaks will become dry.
5. Transfer the fish to a warm platter and ladle the salmoriglio sauce over it.

Yield: 4 servings.

2 pounds swordfish, salmon or tile fish, cut crosswise into ½-inch-thick steaks
Juice of half a lemon (at least 2 tablespoons)
Salt to taste
1 teaspoon dried oregano
¼ cup olive oil
Freshly ground pepper to taste

Sautéed Swordfish in Cream Sauce

2 pounds swordfish, about 1
   inch thick
   Salt and freshly ground pepper
   to taste
   Flour for dredging
6 tablespoons butter
2 tablespoons finely chopped
   shallots
3 tablespoons Cognac
1 cup heavy cream

1. Cut the swordfish into 4 or 6 individual servings. Sprinkle the pieces with salt and pepper and dredge on all sides in flour.

2. Heat 4 tablespoons of the butter in a heavy skillet large enough to hold the fish in one layer. Brown on one side for 3 to 5 minutes and turn with a spatula. Cook on the second side for about 7 minutes, or until cooked through.

3. Push the fish pieces to one side of the skillet and add the shallots. Cover and cook for about 3 minutes. Do not overcook or the fish will become dry.

4. Transfer the fish to a warm serving platter and add the Cognac to the skillet. Ignite it and add the cream. Cook over high heat for about 2 minutes. Add the remaining butter to the skillet and swirl it in. Return the fish to the skillet. Spoon the sauce over and serve hot.

Yield: 4 to 6 servings.

Paupiettes of Trout Mousse with Leeks

6 skinless, boneless fillets of
   rainbow trout, about 1½
   pounds
3 or 4 very large leeks
   Salt
2 egg whites
1 cup heavy cream
   Butter for greasing a pan
   and foil
5 tablespoons fish broth, or
   use canned clam juice
1 cup shallot butter (see recipe
   below)
   Freshly ground pepper to
   taste
2 tablespoons olive oil

1. Preheat the oven to 400 degrees.

2. Cut the trout into 1-inch cubes and chill. The fish must be very cold.

3. You will need 12 large outer leaves of leeks. Remove the leaves from the leeks and rinse well. Bring enough water to the boil in a large kettle to cover the leek leaves when they are added. Add salt to taste and the leaves. Let simmer for about 2 minutes and drain. Run cold water over the leaves until well chilled. Drain, then pat dry on clean toweling.

4. Sprinkle the trout with salt. Put the trout in the container of a food processor. Add the egg whites while blending. With the motor still running, gradually add the cream.

5. Open up the leek leaves and arrange them on a flat surface. Neatly trim off the top and bottom of each leek to make them about 9 inches long.

6. Add a mound of trout mousse (about 3 tablespoons) near the base of each leek. Roll up each leaf to enclose the mousse.

7. Butter a metal baking dish (a dish that measures about 14- x 8-inches) and arrange the rolls, seam side down, on the dish. Pour the fish broth around the rolls.

8. Butter a sheet of aluminum foil and arrange it, buttered side down, over the rolls. Place on top of the stove and, when pan liquid comes to the boil, place the dish in the oven. Bake for 15 minutes or less, until the mousse is cooked through. Spoon the shallot butter over the center of the rolls. Sprinkle each paupiette with a generous grinding of black pepper and 2 tablespoons of olive oil.

Yield: 6 servings.

Shallot butter

1. Combine the vinegar and water in a saucepan and bring to the boil. Add the shallots and cook until most of the liquid evaporates.

2. Add the butter bit by bit to the saucepan, beating rapidly with a wire whisk over moderate heat. The sauce must be thoroughly hot but it must not boil. When ready, the sauce should be thickened and creamy.

Yield: About 1 cup.

- 2 tablespoons vinegar
- 2 tablespoons water
- 2 tablespoons finely chopped shallots
- ½ pound butter at or near room temperature

Pan-fried Trout

1. Sprinkle the trout on all sides with salt and pepper. Dredge lightly in flour.

2. Meanwhile, heat the oil in a large iron skillet over a hot charcoal fire. Or heat it on the stove.

3. When the oil is hot and almost smoking, add the fish and cook until crisp and golden brown on one side. Turn and cook until crisp and golden on the other side. Continue cooking until the fish is cooked through. Cooking time will depend on the size of the fish.

4. As the fish cook, push them to one side and add the potatoes and onions. Cook, turning the potatoes and onion slices until browned and golden on both sides. Remove the fish and serve with lemon wedges. Serve with the potatoes and onions.

Yield: 4 servings.

- 4 trout, 8 to 10 ounces each, cleaned but with head and tail on
  Salt and freshly ground pepper to taste
  Flour for dredging
- ⅓ cup peanut, vegetable or corn oil
- 3 partly cooked, peeled potatoes, cut into ¼-inch slices, about 3 cups
- 1 small onion, peeled and sliced
  Lemon wedges

Trout Meunière with Pecans

4 10-ounce trout (see note)
¼ cup milk
  Salt and freshly ground
    pepper to taste
½ cup flour
¼ cup peanut, vegetable or corn
    oil
5 tablespoons butter
½ cup pecan halves
  Juice of 1 lemon
2 tablespoons finely chopped
    parsley

1. Using a pair of kitchen shears, cut off the fins from the back and sides of the trout. Leave the head and tail intact.

2. Place the trout in a large pan and add milk, salt and pepper. Turn the trout in the mixture.

3. Remove the trout without patting dry and dredge on all sides in flour seasoned with salt and pepper.

4. Heat the oil and 1 tablespoon of the butter in a large, heavy skillet and add the trout, lining them up neatly in the pan. Cook for about 8 minutes, or until golden and cooked on one side. Turn and cook for 8 minutes longer. Baste often. The basting is important to keep the trout juicy.

5. Remove the trout to a warm platter. Sprinkle with salt and pepper.

6. Pour off the fat from the pan and wipe out the skillet. Add the remaining 4 tablespoons of butter and, when melted, add the pecans. Cook, shaking the pan and stirring, until the butter becomes the color of hazelnuts. Do not burn. Add the lemon juice and pour the sauce over the fish. Serve sprinkled with chopped parsley.

Yield: 4 servings.

Note: The 10-ounce weight specified here is arbitrary. Larger or smaller trout may be cooked in the same manner, but adjust the cooking time accordingly.

Deep-fried Trout

4 10-ounce trout
¼ cup milk
  Salt and freshly ground
    pepper to taste
½ cup flour
  Oil for deep frying
  Tartar sauce (see recipe page
643)
  Lemon wedges for garnish

1. Using a pair of kitchen shears, cut off the fins from the back and sides of the trout. Leave the head and tail intact.

2. Place the trout in a large pan and add milk, salt and pepper. Turn the trout in the mixture.

3. Remove the trout without patting dry and dredge on all sides in flour seasoned with salt and pepper.

4. Heat the oil for deep frying, about 325 degrees. Add the trout and fry until golden brown and cooked through, about 8 minutes.

5. Remove the trout. Drain on absorbent toweling. Sprinkle with salt and serve with tartar sauce on the side and lemon wedges as a garnish.

Yield: 4 servings.

Truites au Bleu *(Trout cooked in court bouillon)*

1. Using a pair of kitchen shears, cut off the fins from the back and sides of the trout. Leave the head and tail intact.

2. Using a long needle such as a trussing needle, run a string through the eyes of the trout, then through the tail. Tie the head and tail together. The reason for this is simply appearance. When trout are freshly caught, they are killed and dressed and dropped into boiling water immediately. These trout will curve naturally through muscle and nerve reaction.

3. Combine the water and vinegar in a fairly wide casserole. There should be enough liquid to cover the trout when they are added. Add the bay leaf, salt and peppercorns. Bring to the boil and simmer for 10 minutes.

4. Drop the trout into the simmering water. Simmer for 5 minutes. Drain the trout and serve with lemon wedges and hot melted butter or hollandaise sauce.

Yield: 4 servings.

4	10-ounce trout
4	quarts water
1	cup white vinegar
1	bay leaf
	Salt to taste
10	peppercorns
	Lemon wedges
	Melted butter or hollandaise sauce (see recipe page 644)

Panché de Poisson *(Mixed steamed fish fillets with vegetables)*

The word panaché means mixed or assorted. When this dish is prepared at the Troisgros restaurant in Roanne, an assortment of fish is used and three or more kinds of fish are served with each portion. If you can find a mixture of fish for the recipe, well and good; otherwise, simply use one or two kinds of fish.

1. Cut the fish into 8 or more individual portions, enough to serve 2 or more portions per person. The pieces should be of more or less equal size. Arrange the pieces, skin side down, in a steamer (steamers such as used in Chinese or other Oriental cookery are good for this). Arrange the fish pieces in one layer. You will probably need two tiers to hold the fish.

2. Sprinkle the fish with salt and pepper. Put water into the bottom of the steamer and set the tier or tiers in place. Set aside until ready to cook.

3. Drop the peas into boiling salted water and cook for about 30 seconds, no longer. Drain and put immediately into cold water to chill quickly. Drain. Set aside.

4. Pick over the snow peas, if used, and pull off any "strings" from top and bottom of each pea. If green beans are to be used, trim off the ends. Cut the beans into 1½-inch

2½	pounds nonoily, white-fleshed fish fillets, boneless but with skin left on
	Salt and freshly ground pepper to taste
1	cup shelled fresh new peas, or 1 package frozen green peas
⅓	pound fresh snow peas, if available, or use an equal weight of fresh green beans
2	large carrots, about ½ pound
2	large red, ripe, unblemished tomatoes, about 1 pound
	Beurre nantais (see recipe page 648)

lengths. Drop the snow peas or green beans into boiling salted water. Cook the snow peas for about 30 seconds; cook the green beans slightly longer. Drain and put immediately into cold water to chill quickly. Drain. Set aside.

5. Cut the carrots into 1½-inch lengths. Cut the pieces into ¼-inch slices. Stack the slices and cut each slice into ¼-inch strips (julienne). Discard the center strips or core of each carrot. There should be about 1 cup when ready. Drop the strips into boiling salted water and cook for 30 seconds, no longer. Drain and put them immediately into cold water to chill quickly. Drain.

6. Core and peel the tomatoes. Cut them into slices and then into ½-inch cubes. There should be about 1½ cups.

7. When ready to serve, bring enough water to cover the vegetables to the boil. Add salt to taste.

8. Set the steamer over moderate heat and bring water in the bottom of the steamer to the boil. Remember that the fish when steamed cooks very quickly, 30 seconds to 1 minute. If the fish steams longer, it will be dry.

9. Prepare the butter sauce and set aside.

10. When the fish is properly cooked, drop all the vegetables, including the tomatoes, into the boiling water. This is just to heat them through. Do not cook or the tomatoes will disintegrate. Drain quickly and well.

11. Arrange the fish on individual serving dishes and spoon equal amounts of vegetables over the pieces. Spoon hot butter sauce over each serving.

Yield: 4 to 6 servings.

Fish Mousse

1¼ pounds skinless, boneless, white-fleshed, nonoily fish such as striped bass, flounder, fluke, sole or blackfish
2 large eggs
Salt and freshly ground pepper to taste
⅛ teaspoon grated nutmeg
Pinch of cayenne pepper
1½ cups heavy cream
Sauce Dugléré (see recipe page 651)
Chopped parsley

1. Preheat the oven to 375 degrees. Generously butter a 4½- to 5-cup ring mold.

2. Cut the fish into 1- or 2-inch cubes and put in the container of a food processor. Add the eggs, salt, pepper, nutmeg and cayenne. Blend until coarse.

3. Gradually add the cream, pouring it through the funnel, while blending. Spoon the mousse into the ring mold. Smooth it over and cover with a ring of buttered wax paper cut to fit.

4. Place the mold in a basin of water and bring the water to the boil on top of the stove. Place in the oven and bake for 35 to 45 minutes, or until set. Let stand for 5 to 10 minutes. Unmold onto a round platter and serve with sauce Dugléré. Serve sprinkled with chopped parsley.

Yield: 6 to 8 servings.

Pain de Poisson *(A French fish loaf to be served hot or cold)*

1. Preheat the oven to 400 degrees.

2. It is best to prepare this dish in two batches, using a food processor if available. If an electric blender is used, it will have to be done in several batches.

3. Cut the fish into cubes and add half of it to the container of a food processor. Add 1 yolk, salt and pepper to taste, nutmeg and Tabasco to taste and blend. Continue blending while gradually adding half the cream. Repeat this step. As the fish mixture is prepared, transfer it to a mixing bowl.

4. Blend the green peppers coarse-fine. Blend the carrots similarly. Squeeze out and discard excess liquid from the vegetables. Add the pulp to the fish mixture.

5. Spoon the mixture into a 7- or 8-cup ring mold. Smooth over the surface and cover with a round of wax paper cut to fit directly over the fish. Place the mold in a baking dish and pour boiling water around it.

6. Bake for about 35 minutes, or until set. The inner temperature should register between 150 and 160 degrees. Serve hot with the tomato sauce. Or chill and serve cold with a flavored mayonnaise.

Yield: 8 to 12 servings.

1¾ pounds white-fleshed, nonoily fish fillets such as fluke, flounder or blackfish

2 egg yolks
Salt and freshly ground pepper

¼ teaspoon freshly grated nutmeg
Tabasco sauce

1½ cups heavy cream

3 small green peppers, cored and seeded and cut into 1-inch cubes

¼ pound carrots, trimmed and scraped and cut into 1-inch lengths
Sauce Dugléré
(see recipe page 651)

Fish Creole

1. Preheat the oven to 450 degrees.

2. Cut the fish into 6 individual serving pieces and set aside.

3. Melt half the butter in a saucepan and add the onion. Cook, stirring, until wilted and add the garlic and sweet peppers. Sprinkle with salt and pepper to taste. Toss well and add the tomatoes, capers, Tabasco to taste and parsley. Cover and cook for 15 minutes. Uncover and cook for 5 minutes longer.

4. Rub a baking dish with half the remaining butter and sprinkle with salt and pepper. Add the fish pieces and dot with the remaining butter. Spoon the sauce over and bake for 15 minutes.

Yield: 6 servings.

1¾ pounds skinless, boneless fish fillets such as sea trout, sea bass, cod, red snapper or hake

6 tablespoons butter

1 cup thinly sliced onion

1 teaspoon chopped garlic

3 cups chopped green and red sweet peppers
Salt and freshly ground pepper

2 cups chopped fresh tomatoes, or one 17-ounce can imported peeled tomatoes, preferably with tomato paste and basil

2 tablespoons capers
Tabasco sauce

¼ cup finely chopped parsley

Fish and Seafood Andalouse

4   pounds red and/or green
      sweet peppers
5   tablespoons butter
      Salt and freshly ground
      pepper
1   tablespoon flour
1   cup fish stock, or bottled clam
      juice
1   pound shrimp
1   pound fresh skinless and
      boneless sea trout or sea bass
      fillets or other white-fleshed,
      nonoily fish fillets
½   pound scallops
1   tablespoon chopped shallots
1   teaspoon loosely packed stem
      saffron, or ½ teaspoon
      powdered saffron, optional
½   cup chopped, drained, canned
      tomatoes, preferably imported
      plum tomatoes

1. Core and seed the peppers. Cut the peppers into ½-inch strips. There should be about 4 cups loosely packed.

2. Heat 2 tablespoons butter in a large skillet and add the peppers and salt and pepper to taste. Cook quickly, tossing and stirring, for about 8 minutes. When ready, the peppers should be crisp but tender. Set aside.

3. Heat 1 tablespoon of butter and add the flour. Stir with a whisk until blended. Add the fish stock, stirring rapidly with the whisk. When the sauce is thickened and smooth, season to taste with salt and pepper. Set aside.

4. Peel and devein the shrimp. If they are large, cut them in half lengthwise. Set aside.

5. Cut the fish fillets into 1½-inch cubes. Set aside.

6. If bay scallops are used, leave them whole. If ocean scallops are used, cut them in half or quarter them. Set aside.

7. Heat remaining 2 tablespoons butter in a large skillet and add the shallots. Cook, stirring, and add the shrimp, fish, scallops and peppers. Sprinkle with salt and pepper and cook, stirring as necessary, for about 2 minutes. Add the saffron, if used, and tomatoes. Stir in the fish sauce.

8. Add salt and pepper to taste. Cover and cook for about 3 minutes, no longer. Serve immediately with rice.

Yield: 8 to 10 servings.

Sesame Seed Fish

¾   pound fish fillets, preferably
      flounder or fluke
1½   tablespoons shao hsing
      wine, or dry sherry
      Salt to taste
1¾   teaspoons sugar
¾   teaspoon ground white
      pepper
2   egg whites
4   tablespoons cornstarch
½   cup sesame seeds
½   cup fine, fresh bread crumbs
6 or   more sprigs fresh coriander
      for garnish
½   cup finely shredded ginger

1. Place the fish on a flat surface and cut it into 2-inch pieces. Place fish in a bowl and add the wine, salt, ¾ teaspoon sugar and pepper. Stir to coat the fish well and set aside.

2. Blend the egg whites with the cornstarch and salt to taste.

3. Blend the sesame seeds and bread crumbs.

4. Dip one piece of fish at a time in the egg white mixture to coat all over. Dip into the sesame seed mixture to coat and arrange on a plate. Continue this until all the pieces are coated. If necessary, use more sesame seeds and crumbs.

5. Drop the coriander leaves, if used, into cold water and let stand. Drain and pat dry.

6. Combine the ginger, vinegar, remaining 1 teaspoon sugar and salt and stir to blend. Let stand until ready to use and then drain the ginger. Discard the marinade.

7. When ready to cook, heat the oil in a wok or skillet and add the fish pieces. Turn off the heat. This will prevent the sesame seeds from exploding. Turn on the heat and continue cooking the fish until nicely browned and crisp, turning as necessary in the oil. Drain.

8. Arrange the fish on a platter. Garnish one end of the platter with coriander leaves and the other with the drained ginger.

Yield: 12 servings with other Chinese dishes.

1	tablespoon red wine vinegar
6	cups peanut, vegetable or corn oil

Bean Sauce Hot Fish

1. Prepare the rice two days before as indicated in the recipe.

2. Rinse the fish and pat dry.

3. Heat the oil in a wok or casserole large enough to hold the fish. When it is almost smoking, add the fish and cook for about 1 minute. Drain and set aside. Pour off and reserve the oil.

4. Heat ½ cup of reserved oil in a wok or skillet and add the pork, stirring to break up lumps. When the meat changes color, add the ginger, garlic and red pepper, stirring. Add the chili paste and bean paste. Cook for about 1 minute and add the cup of fermented rice and salt. Cook, stirring, over high heat and add ½ cup of water. Cook over high heat, stirring, for about 10 minutes.

5. Meanwhile, heat 2 tablespoons of oil in a pan large enough to hold the fish and add the fish. Add remaining 1 cup of water and cover. Steam for 8 to 10 minutes. Drain. Transfer the fish to a serving dish.

6. Add the scallions to the pork sauce and pour the sizzling hot sauce over the fish. Serve.

Yield: 8 servings with other Chinese dishes.

1	cup fermented rice (see recipe below)
1	1¾- to 2-pound red snapper Peanut, vegetable or corn oil for deep frying
½	pound ground pork
½	cup finely chopped ginger
2½	tablespoons finely chopped garlic
¼	pound hot, fresh, red peppers, seeded and chopped, about ¾ cup
1½	tablespoons chili paste with garlic, available in Oriental markets
½	cup bean paste, available in Oriental markets
	Salt to taste
1½	cups water
1	cup chopped scallions

1. Soak the rice overnight in cold water to cover, then drain.

2. Line a steamer top or a colander with cheesecloth and add the drained rice. Cover and steam for 1 hour.

3. Crush the wine ball or cube on a flat surface, using a mallet or rolling pin. When it is crushed fine like a powder, blend well with the flour. Set aside.

4. Rinse the rice delicately in lukewarm water, working gently with the hands to separate the grains. The rice should be at about body temperature when it is ready. If it is too

Fermented rice

¾	pound glutinous rice
½	wine ball, or wine cube (available in Oriental markets)
1½	teaspoons all-purpose flour

warm at this time, it will ferment too quickly. If it is cold, it will not ferment.

5. When the rice is right, drain it well. Sprinkle with the wine ball and flour mixture and work gently to mix thoroughly. Spoon the rice into a thin bowl and smooth the top with the fingers.

6. Using the fingers, make a hole or well in the center, about 1 inch in diameter. Pat the top of the rice with wet fingers to smooth it, but do not disturb the hole. You will see later when you uncover the rice that the hole accumulates liquid as the rice stands.

7. Cover the bowl well and then carefully wrap it in blankets. Set the blanket-covered bowl in a warm (but not too warm) place and let it stand for 24 hours. If properly made and all the elements are right, liquid will have accumulated in the hole.

8. Spoon the rice and liquid into mason jars and seal loosely. Let stand until room temperature, then refrigerate. The fermented rice keeps for weeks in the refrigerator, but you should loosen the tops occasionally to make sure too much gas is not accumulating inside the jars.

Yield: 1½ pints.

Crystal Fish

½ pound shrimp
2 tablespoons cornstarch, plus cornstarch for dredging
½ egg white (beat the egg white lightly and measure it)
2½ teaspoons salt
½ teaspoon sugar
¼ teaspoon monosodium glutamate, optional
1 tablespoon shao hsing wine, or dry sherry
1½ tablespoons finely chopped scallions
1½ tablespoons finely diced, soaked, black mushrooms
2 flounder fillets, about ¾ pound total weight
2 tablespoons crab roe, optional

1. Shell and devein the shrimp. Chop to a pulp on a flat surface or blend in a food processor or electric blender. Spoon into a bowl and add 1 tablespoon cornstarch, ½ egg white, 1 teaspoon salt, sugar, monosodium glutamate, if used, and wine. Blend well. Add scallions and mushrooms and blend again. Set aside.

2. Place the flounder fillets, skinned side down, on a flat surface. Brush the top side liberally with cornstarch. With dampened fingers, smear each fillet with equal amounts of the shrimp mixture. Smooth over with a rubber spatula. Dot the top of both with bits of crab roe, if used.

3. Lay out 2 rectangles of caul fat and place one fillet, shrimp side up, in the center of each. Carefully and neatly fold the edges of caul fat over the fillet to enclose it completely.

4. Combine the flour, remaining 1 tablespoon cornstarch, remaining 1½ teaspoons salt, 4 teaspoons oil and baking powder in a mixing bowl. Add enough water to make a

smooth but not too thin paste, about 9 tablespoons. Dip the coated fish in the batter, using the fingers to coat top and bottom liberally.

5. Heat enough oil to barely cover the fish. Add one fillet and ladle the oil over, turning the fish as necessary so that it cooks evenly. Cook for about 5 minutes. Remove and drain. Add other fish and cook. Drain.

6. Cut the fillets widthwise into 1½-inch rectangles. Serve hot, garnished with sprigs of Chinese parsley. Serve the Szechwan peppercorn mixture on the side as a dip.

Yield: 8 servings with other Chinese dishes.

2	large rectangles (about 14- x 11-inches) caul fat, available in pork stores and Chinese markets
11	tablespoons flour
4	teaspoons peanut, vegetable or corn oil, plus oil to cover fish
1	tablespoon baking powder
9	tablespoons water, approximately
	Chinese parsley sprigs for garnish
	Szechwan peppercorn dip (see recipe below)

Combine all the ingredients and use as a dip for crystal fish.

Szechwan peppercorn dip

1	tablespoon finely ground Szechwan peppercorns
1	tablespoon salt
1	tablespoon sugar
¼	teaspoon monosodium glutamate, optional

Clam Fritters

1. To prepare the clams, chop them on a flat surface or put them through a food grinder, using the medium blade. Put the clams in a mixing bowl.

2. Add the egg, lemon juice, parsley, baking soda and flour and stir.

3. Blend the clam juice and milk and add this gradually to the clam mixture, sitrring constantly. Add only enough of the clam juice and milk to make a batter that is not too runny. Add the butter, cayenne and pepper.

4. Heat an eighth of an inch of oil in a skillet and drop the batter, about 2 tablespoons, into the oil. Continue adding batches of batter without letting the sides touch. Turn the fritters as they brown and continue cooking until cooked through. Continue cooking until all the batter is used. Serve hot with shrimp sauce.

Yield: 4 servings.

1	cup chopped clams
1	egg, lightly beaten
1	teaspoon lemon juice
1	tablespoon finely chopped parsley
1	teaspoon baking soda
1	cup flour
¼	cup clam juice
¼	cup milk
4	teaspoons melted butter
	Pinch of cayenne pepper
	Freshly ground pepper to taste
	Oil for shallow frying
	Shrimp sauce (see recipe page 649)

Wash-boiler Clambake

Blessed are those who live by the sea, for theirs is the kingdom of shellfish and seaweed, the two principal ingredients of an old-fashioned clambake. Clambakes where we live in East Hampton come in two sizes: the large, traditional, back-breaking affair with pits to dig and rocks to fire and sand to sweep; and the more recently evolved wash-boiler clambake for smaller gatherings. The latter, of course, may lack the color of the original, but we can state emphatically that the results are more or less equal. And there is one vast and important difference. The marvelous old-fashioned clambake demands 600 pounds of seaweed. With the wash-boiler type, you can settle for a child's portion—twenty-four pounds.

24	pounds wet seaweed, or enough to fill an 18-gallon wash boiler
2	3½- to 4-pound chickens, quartered
	Peanut, vegetable or corn oil
2	teaspoons paprika
	Salt and freshly ground pepper to taste
24 or	more cherrystone or littleneck clams
17	red-skinned, "new" potatoes, about 2½ pounds
3 or	4 quahog or chowder clams (for flavor only)
8	1¼-pound lobsters
16	ears fresh corn, unshucked
½	pound butter, melted
4	lemons, cut into wedges
	Tabasco sauce
	Worcestershire sauce

1. Gather the seaweed and have it ready.

2. Make a large wood fire in a grill, improvised if need be, on which the wash boiler will sit.

3. Make a charcoal fire for grilling the chicken pieces.

4. Place the chicken in a large dish and add enough oil to coat the pieces. Sprinkle with paprika, salt and pepper and rub well. Grill the chicken pieces quickly first on one side, then the other until they are golden brown but not cooked. Tie 2 pieces of chicken in each of 4 cheesecloth bags.

5. Make individul cheesecloth packages of clams, 3 or more per serving.

6. Put about a sixth of the seaweed in the bottom of the wash boiler. Add the chicken in cheesecloth. Cover with the same amount of seaweed and add all but one of the potatoes. Add more seaweed and the packaged clams. Add the quahogs. Add more seaweed and the lobsters. Add more seaweed and the corn. Add a final layer of seaweed and place the reserved potato directly in the center. Cover closely with a lid. Weight the lid down with heavy stones. Cook over a good fire for 1¼ to 1½ hours, or until the potato on top is tender without being mushy.

7. Serve all the foods simultaneously with melted butter, lemon wedges and the sauces. Cold beer, but of course. Plus ice cream or watermelon.

Yield: 8 servings.

Broiled Maryland Crab Cakes

1. Preheat the broiler to moderate.

2. Handle the crabmeat as little as possible to avoid breaking up the large, firm lumps. Remove any pieces of shell or cartilage, however.

3. Blend the mayonnaise, egg white and cracker crumbs in a mixing bowl. Add the crab and fold gently to blend without breaking up the lumps of meat. Using slightly moistened fingers, divide the mixture into 8 equal portions. Shape each portion into a patty. Coat the patties all over with bread crumbs, pressing to make the crumbs adhere. Refrigerate until ready to use.

4. Heat 1 tablespoon butter in a skillet large enough to hold the crab cakes. Turn them in the butter to coat top and bottom. Place under the broiler and broil about 4 inches from the flame, turning once, until nicely browned and cooked through, about 5 minutes. Serve 2 crab cakes with equal portions of melted butter.

Yield: 4 servings.

1 pound crabmeat, preferably lump or backfin
1 cup freshly made mayonnaise
1 egg white
3 to 4 tablespoons very fine cracker crumbs
½ cup fine, fresh bread crumbs, or cracker crumbs
1 tablespoon butter
1 cup hot melted butter

Deep-fried Crab Cakes

Follow the instructions for broiled Maryland crab cakes. Instead of broiling them, drop them into hot fat to cover and cook until golden brown. Drain on absorbent paper towels.

Deep-fried Soft-shell Crabs

1. Sprinkle the crabs on all sides with salt and pepper.

2. Break the egg into a flat dish and add the water, salt and pepper to taste. Beat to blend well.

3. In a separate flat dish place the flour, salt and pepper to taste. Blend.

4. Place the bread crumbs in a third flat dish.

5. Dip the crabs first in egg, then in flour and finally in crumbs, turning and patting so that the crumbs adhere.

6. Heat the fat for deep frying and add the crabs. Cook, turning as necessary, until crisp and golden brown. Drain on absorbent toweling. Serve hot with lemon wedges and tartar sauce.

Yield: 4 servings.

4 soft-shell crabs
Salt and freshly ground pepper
1 egg
3 tablespoons water
½ cup flour
1½ cups fresh bread crumbs
Fat for deep frying
Lemon wedges
Tartar sauce (see recipe page 643)

Soft-shell Crabs Meunière

4   soft-shell crabs
¼   cup milk
    Salt and freshly ground
    pepper
½   cup flour
½   cup peanut, vegetable or corn
    oil
    Juice of ½ lemon
4   thin slices from a peeled
    lemon, seeds removed
2   tablespoons chopped parsley
3   tablespoons butter

1. Put the crabs in a shallow dish in one layer and add the milk, salt and pepper. Turn the crabs in the milk.

2. Season the flour with salt and pepper.

3. Heat the oil in a heavy skillet large enough to hold the crabs in one layer.

4. Dip the crabs immediately from the milk into the flour, turning to coat well.

5. Heat the oil until quite hot and add the crabs, belly side up. Cook for 4 to 5 minutes (more or less depending on the size of the crabs) and turn. Cook until golden on both sides and cooked through. Transfer the crabs to a warm serving platter and sprinkle with lemon juice. Garnish neatly with lemon slices and sprinkle with parsley.

6. Wipe out the skillet with a clean cloth and add the butter. When melted and bubbling, pour the butter over the crabs.

Yield: 4 servings.

How to Steam Hard-shell Crabs

Place any suitable number of hard-shell blue crabs in a basin or sink and run cold water over them to cover. Add ¼ cup salt (or more, depending on the number of crabs) and let stand for at least 1 hour. This will rid the crabs of their sediment. Drain the crabs and rinse under more cold water.

Transfer the crabs to the top of a bamboo, stainless steel or other steamer and steam, closely covered, for 20 minutes. Serve hot or cold.

Crab Imperial

1½   cups crabmeat, preferably
    lump or backfin
1   teaspoon butter
1   cup chopped green pepper

1. Preheat the oven to 425 degrees.

2. Handle the crabmeat as little as possible to avoid breaking up the large, firm lumps. Remove any pieces of shell or cartilage, however.

3. Heat the butter in a small skillet and add the green pepper. Cook, stirring and shaking the skillet, until pepper is crisp but slightly wilted. Set aside.

4. Put the mayonnaise in a mixing bowl. Beat the cream until almost stiff. Fold this into the mayonnaise. Add crabmeat and green pepper and gently fold and stir until well blended.

5. Arrange the crab mixture in 8 individual ramekins or, preferably, crab shells.

6. Place in the oven and bake for 15 minutes, or until bubbling hot throughout and nicely browned.

Yield: 4 to 8 servings.

1 cup freshly made mayonnaise
¼ cup heavy cream

Stuffed Crabs Caribbean-style

1. Preheat the oven to 400 degrees.

2. Melt 8 tablespoons butter in a wide, shallow saucepan or skillet. When melted, add the scallions, garlic and chili. Add the curry powder and blend. Add the crabmeat. Add the coriander leaves, if desired, and parsley. Add salt and pepper to taste. Add enough crab liquid to moisten properly. If you want a richer—and better—dish, add 2 to 4 more tablespoons butter. Add bread crumbs and blend well.

3. Remove from the heat and use the mixture to fill 4 to 8 clam shells.

4. Bake for 10 to 15 minutes, until piping hot and nicely brown. Serve with lime wedges, sliced or halves.

Yield: 4 to 8 servings.

8 tablespoons butter, approximately
4 scallions, chopped
1 teaspoon chopped garlic
1 hot green chili, finely chopped, seeds optional, or use dried red pepper flakes to taste
1 tablespoon curry powder
¾ to 1 pound crabmeat, finely shredded (This does not have to be lump or fancy crab. Snow crab, flaked crabmeat or even canned crab may be used.)
2 tablespoons finely chopped fresh coriander leaves, optional
2 tablespoons finely chopped parsley
Salt and freshly ground pepper
6 to 8 tablespoons crab liquid, or bottled clam juice
2 cups fresh bread crumbs
Lime wedges for garnish

Crab Fritters

1½ cups flour
　　Salt and freshly ground
　　pepper
　2 tablespoons olive oil
¼ teaspoon grated nutmeg
　　Tabasco sauce
　2 eggs, separated
　1 cup milk
　1 cup finely chopped scallions
　1 pound crabmeat, lump or
　　backfin, picked over well
½ cup peanut, vegetable or
　　corn oil
　　Tomato sauce (see recipe
　　page 650)

1. Put the flour in a mixing bowl and add salt and pepper to taste, olive oil, nutmeg and Tabasco to taste. Add the yolks of the eggs and gradually add the milk, stirring constantly with a whisk. Add the scallions and fold in the crabmeat. Beat the egg whites until stiff and fold them in.

2. Heat the ½ cup of oil in a heavy skillet and add spoonfuls of the crab mixture. The quantity of each spoonful is optional. The fritters may be very small, only a tablespoon or so, or rather large, 4 tablespoons. Cook until brown on one side, turn and cook until brown on the other. Drain on paper towels. Serve with tomato sauce.

Yield: 20 to 40 fritters.

Flowers Around the Snow *(Stir-fried crab)*

　8 large egg whites, about 1¼
　　cups
1½ tablespoons cornstarch
1¼ cups milk
　2 teaspoons salt
　2 teaspoons sugar
¾ pound fresh, picked-over
　　crabmeat (see note)
½ cup chives cut into ½-inch
　　lengths, preferably Chinese
　　chives (available in Chinese
　　markets), which are flatter
　　and more flavorful than
　　Western chives
½ cup peanut, vegetable or
　　corn oil, plus oil for deep
　　frying
　1 2-ounce package bean
　　threads (cellophane noodles)
　1 tablespoon dried rose petals,
　　optional

1. Put the whites in a mixing bowl. Beat lightly with a fork or chopsticks.

2. Separately blend the cornstarch with ½ cup of milk, a little at a time. When blended, add this to the eggs. Add the remaining milk. Add the salt and sugar and beat well. Add the crab and half of the chives and blend well. Set aside.

3. When ready to serve, heat the fat for deep frying. Break the bean threads into three portions. Set one portion aside for another use. Add the other portions, one at a time, to the hot fat. Cook for about 2 seconds on one side and turn. Cook for about 2 seconds and turn. Quickly lift from the fat and place on a round serving platter. Repeat with the second portion.

4. Heat ½ cup of oil in a wok and, when hot, add the egg white mixture. Cook, using a flat stirring spoon and stir gently and slowly, pushing the mixture from the outside toward the center. Use a lifting and folding motion. Cook, stirring and lifting gently from the bottom, for 3 or 4 minutes.

5. Transfer to the center of the fried bean threads. Garnish with the rose petals, if desired, and the remaining chives.

Yield: 8 servings with other Chinese dishes.

Note: It is preferable to use part crab roe from female crabs, but this is generally found only in crabs that you steam and pick out yourself.

Lobster Cooked on Seaweed

1. Preheat the oven to 500 degrees.
2. Select a tray large enough to hold the lobsters in one layer.
3. Place half the seaweed on the tray and place the lobsters shell side up. Cover with the remaining seaweed and place the tray in the oven. Bake for 15 minutes.
4. Remove the tray and quickly split in half the tail of each lobster. Do not split the carcass or main body portion at this time. Return the lobsters to the tray, shell side up, and bake for 30 minutes longer.
5. Meanwhile, put the butter in a saucepan and let it melt. Add the salt and garlic and heat until piping hot.
6. Remove the lobsters from the oven and use a sharp, heavy knife to split the main body portions in two. Serve half a lobster to each guest along with the hot sauce (and nutcrackers for the claws).

Yield: 6 to 12 servings.

6	1¼- to 1½-pound lobsters
6 to	8 quarts freshly harvested, wet seaweed
½	pound sweet butter
	Salt to taste
2	cloves garlic, smashed

Baked Lobster with Herb Butter

1. Preheat the oven to 450 degrees.
2. Turn the lobster on its back and split it lengthwise. Remove and discard the small sac inside the lobster near the eyes.
3. Arrange the lobster halves, split side up, in a baking dish and brush with oil. Sprinkle with salt and pepper.
4. Bake for 15 minutes and remove.
5. Combine the butter with the remaining ingredients. Using a fork, lift up the tail sections from the shell. Spoon the butter into the shell and replace the tails in the shells. Serve immediately.

Yield: 1 to 2 servings.

1	1- to 1½-pound lobster
1	teaspoon olive oil
	Salt and white pepper
½	cup butter
1	tablespoon finely chopped shallots
1	tablespoon finely chopped parsley
1	teaspoon finely chopped fresh tarragon

Navarin de Homards *(Baked lobsters with vegetables)*

1½	cups small potatoes, peeled and quartered or cut into chunks
	Salt
¾	pound green beans, trimmed at the ends and cut into 1-inch lengths
1	cup shelled peas, the fresher the better
1½	cups carrots cut into bâtonnets (see note)
1	cup fresh turnips cut into bâtonnets (see note)
3 or	4 live lobsters, about 1½ pounds each
6	tablespoons butter
¼	cup olive oil
⅓	cup finely chopped shallots
8 to	10 very small white onions, peeled and cut into quarters or eighths
	Freshly ground pepper
¾	cup dry white wine
1¼	cups chicken broth, preferably freshly made
3	tablespoons flour

1. In a saucepan, bring to the boil enough water to amply cover the potatoes. Add salt to taste and a bit more than seems logical. Add the potatoes and simmer until cooked but still a bit firm to the bite, 10 to 15 minutes. Drain well.

2. In a saucepan, bring to the boil enough water to cover the green beans amply. Add salt as indicated above. Add the beans and cook until tender but still a bit firm to the bite, about 10 minutes. Drain and rinse under cold water until well chilled. Drain well.

3. Bring enough water to the boil to cover the peas thoroughly. Add salt as indicated above. Add the peas and simmer for 4 minutes or longer, until tender but still firm. Drain and rinse under cold running water. Drain well.

4. Combine the carrots and turnips and add cold water to cover. Add salt to taste and bring to the boil. Cook as above, about 10 minutes. Drain and rinse until cold. Drain well.

5. Plunge a knife into the center of each lobster where the tail and body meet. This will kill the lobster instantly. Cut the lobsters in half at midsection between the carcass and tail. Cut the tail section into 3 pieces. Cut the carcasses in half lengthwise. Remove and reserve the soft coral and liver portion of the lobster. Discard the sac. Crack the claws.

6. Heat 4 tablespoons of butter and the oil in a large, heavy casserole or Dutch oven and add all the lobster pieces. Cook for 3 to 4 minutes. Add the shallots and onions and stir. Add the blanched vegetables—potatoes, green beans, peas, carrots and turnips. Add salt and pepper to taste. Cook for about 5 minutes, stirring to blend the flavors.

7. Add the wine and broth and cover. Cook for about 10 minutes. Remove from the heat. Using a lid to hold the solids in place, drain off the liquid into a large, heavy saucepan. Bring liquid to the boil and let simmer for about 15 minutes.

8. Meanwhile, add remaining 2 tablespoons butter to the coral and liver and blend well with the fingers. Add the flour and blend well. Add to the sauce, stirring vigorously. Bring to the boil and cook, stirring constantly, for about 5 minutes.

9. Pour this mixture over the lobster mixture and bring to the boil. Cook, stirring, for about 5 minutes. Serve.

Yield: 10 servings.

Note: In French cooking, bâtonnets are vegetables that are cut into the size of tiny *bâtons*. Vegetables cut bâtonnet-style include carrots, turnips, celery and others that are first cut into any given small length, such as an inch or two, and then cut into small rectangles about ¼ to ½ inch on all sides.

Ragout de Homard aux Primeurs *(Lobster in cream sauce with vegetables)*

1. Plunge the lobsters head first into a large quantity of boiling salted water. Cook for 5 minutes and drain. Pierce the lobsters between the eyes and suspend the lobsters head down so that they drain further. Let cool.

2. Quarter the carrot lengthwise. Cut the quarters into 1½-inch lengths. There should be about ½ cup. Set aside.

3. Cut the turnip into ½-inch slices. Stack the slices. Cut the slices into ½-inch strips. Cut the strips into ½-inch lengths. There should be about 18 bâttonets thus prepared, about ⅔ cup.

4. Slice the green beans in half lengthwise. Cut the strips into ½-inch lengths. There should be about ½ cup.

5. Drop the carrot and turnip pieces into boiling salted water and cook until crisp-tender, about 5 minutes. Drain and set aside.

6. Separately, drop the beans into boiling salted water and cook until crisp-tender, 2 to 3 minutes. Drain and combine with the carrots and turnips.

7. Meanwhile, cut or tear off the claws and tail sections of the lobster. Crack them and pull out the meat. Set the meat aside in a bowl. Reserve the shell.

8. Split the body section in half and remove the coral and liver of the lobster. Set aside.

9. Coarsely chop and set aside all the pieces of lobster shell. In our own case, we prefer to do this using a food processor. We find it in no way damages the blades or motor.

10. Heat the butter in a kettle and add the shallots and chopped carcass. Cook, stirring, and add the wine and half the basil. Add salt and pepper to taste and cook for about 15 minutes. Add the reserved coral and liver and cook 1 minute, no longer.

11. As the carcass cooks, slice the lobster meat into large bite-size morsels. Place in a saucepan and add the vegetable mixture. Do not cook.

12. When ready, add the cream to the simmering carcass. Let boil for about 5 minutes. Put the mixture, carcass and all, through a food mill and into a saucepan, extracting as much liquid as possible. Discard the solids. Cook the sauce, un-

2 1½-pound lobsters, preferably female
Salt to taste
1 carrot, trimmed and scraped
1 small turnip, peeled
6 to 8 small green beans, the smaller the better, ends trimmed
2 tablespoons butter
1 tablespoon finely chopped shallots
1 cup dry white wine
½ cup finely shredded fresh basil, loosely packed
2 cups heavy cream

covered, over high heat for about 12 minutes. Strain it through a sieve with the finest mesh possible, preferably the kind known in French as a chinois. Add salt and pepper to taste.

13. Pour the sauce over the lobster and vegetables and add the remaining shredded basil. Bring just to the boil until bubbling and hot. Do not cook but a moment or two or the lobster will toughen. Serve immediately.

Yield: 4 servings.

Homard à la Nage *(Boiled lobster on a bed of vegetables)*

The court bouillon and lobsters:

16 cups water
2 cups dry white wine
1 cup chopped carrots
1 cup sliced celery
1 cup green part of leeks
3 cloves garlic, lightly pounded
1 hot red pepper
½ cup loosely packed parsley sprigs
1 bay leaf
½ teaspoon dried thyme
12 peppercorns
  Salt
6 live lobsters, about 1½ pounds each

The garnish:

5 tablespoons butter
½ cup thinly sliced small white onions
½ cup thinly sliced shallots
1 cup carrots, cut into very thin rounds
1 cup thinly sliced heart of celery
1 cup thinly sliced leeks
½ cup dry white wine
2 tablespoons finely chopped parsley

1. In a kettle large enough to hold 6 lobsters, combine the ingredients for the court bouillon. Cover and let simmer for about 20 minutes. Add the lobsters and cover. Let cook for about 15 minutes.

2. Drain the lobsters, but save about ½ cup of the cooking liquid. Hang the lobsters by the tail upside down to drain.

3. When cool enough to handle, proceed as follows: Break off the large claws and tear off the small pincer of each claw. Crack the large claws widthwise in the center, hacking the claw shell neatly top and bottom. This will permit removing the top half and leave the claw meat intact in the bottom half. Set aside and continue. Take care to save all the liquid that emanates from the lobsters as they are cracked.

4. Tear off the tail section of each lobster. Crack the shell by gripping it in the palm of the hand and using a slight force. Remove the meat. Discard the tail shell but shove the tail section back in place inside the body section. This permits serving the lobsters without the shell but resembling the lobster in its original state. As the lobsters and claws are prepared, put them on a warm platter and add about ½ cup of reserved cooking liquid to keep them moist. Cover with foil while the garnish is finished. Strain the liquid that has accumulated from the cracked lobsters.

5. Heat 1 tablespoon of butter in a saucepan and add the onions and shallots as indicated in the garnish. Cook briefly and add the carrots, celery and leeks. Cover and cook for about 5 minutes. Add the liquid that has accumulated as the lobsters were cracked and the wine. Cook down slightly, about 5 minutes. Swirl in the remaining 4 tablespoons of butter and add the parsley.

6. Arrange the hot vegetable garnish on 6 hot plates. Add 1

lobster and 2 claws to each serving and serve with hot melted butter flavored with lemon juice.

Yield: 6 servings.

The butter:

¾ cup melted butter
Juice or ½ lemon

Homard au Whiskey

1. Plunge a knife into each lobster where the body and tail section meet to sever the spinal chord. This will kill the lobster instantly. Break off the tail and set aside in a large bowl. Break off the large claws and add to the bowl. Cut off the small feeler claws and add to the bowl. Pull out and discard the interior of the chest portion of the lobster. But by all means reserve the coral and liver (the soft portions that are gray, black and sometimes red). Put this into a bowl by itself and set aside.

2. In a large deep kettle heat the oil and 2 tablespoons of butter. When the oil and butter are quite hot but not brown, add the lobster tails, claws and so on. Do not add the coral and liver. Stir the lobster pieces around briefly and add salt and pepper, the celery, carrot, onion, shallots, bay leaf, thyme and garlic. Cook for about 5 minutes, stirring occasionally. Carefully pour off and discard any liquid that may have accumulated from the cooking (use the kettle lid to keep the lobster and other ingredients from falling out of the kettle as the liquid is poured off).

3. Return the kettle to the stove and add ½ cup of whiskey. Do not cover. Stir briefly and add the tomato paste. Cook, stirring, for about 5 minutes and add the fish stock. Cover and simmer for 20 minutes.

4. Uncover and transfer the claws and tails of the lobster to a platter to cool. Continue to cook the remaining pieces of lobster over moderate heat for about 5 minutes.

5. Add the heavy cream and turn the heat to high. Stir briefly and cook, uncovered, for about 10 minutes to reduce the cream.

6. Add the flour and 4 tablespoons of butter to the coral and liver and stir to blend well with a whisk. Add this to the kettle and simmer for about 3 minutes, stirring. Pour the contents of the kettle into a food mill (this may have to be repeated several times if the food mill is small). Press to extract as much liquid

4 to 6 lobsters, about 7 pounds
¼ cup peanut, vegetable or corn oil
8 tablespoons butter
Salt and freshly ground pepper to taste
¼ cup finely chopped celery
½ cup finely chopped carrot
⅓ cup finely chopped onion
⅓ cup finely chopped shallots
1 bay leaf
2 sprigs fresh thyme, or ½ teaspoon dried
1 teaspoon finely minced garlic
¾ cup bourbon whiskey
4 tablespoons tomato paste
1 cup fish stock, or fresh or bottled clam juice
2 cups heavy cream
2 tablespoons flour
2 tablespoons chopped parsley

as possible from the solid pieces of lobster shell. Discard lobster shells. Pour the sauce into a saucepan and let simmer.

7. Remove the meat from the tail and claws. Cut each tail portion into 3 pieces. Discard the shell.

8. Heat 1 tablespoon of butter in a large skillet and, when hot, add the lobster meat. Add the remaining ¼ cup of whiskey and cook briefly, shaking the skillet. Add half the sauce. Let the remaining sauce continue to simmer. Add remaining 1 tablespoon of butter to the lobster and sauce mixture and swirl it in. Sprinkle with parsley. Serve in a rice ring or with rice on the side. Serve the remaining sauce on the side.

Yield: 6 servings.

Moules Marinière   *(Mussels in white wine)*

One of the most fascinating discussions we ever engaged in took place while mussel gathering one gray day on Duxbury Bay in Massachusetts with C. Graham Hurlburt. Mr. Hurlburt, in addition to being director of administrative services at Harvard, is an expert on the edible blue mussel and experiments in cultivation. The thing that really intrigued us was the gentleman's comparison of mussels and T-bone steaks. The protein content of both is virtually the same, he informed us. Steak, however, has four times more calories than mussels and eighteen times more fat. How, we've been pondering ever since, can anything so positively nutritious be so positively delectable.

2½ pounds (about 2 quarts) cleaned mussels
2 tablespoons butter
2 tablespoons finely chopped onion
1 tablespoon finely chopped shallots
1 small clove garlic, finely minced
2 tablespoons finely chopped parsley
   Freshly ground pepper
¾ cup dry white wine

1. Run the mussels under cold running water, rubbing the shells together to remove any foreign matter that may still cling to them. Drain well.

2. Heat the butter in a kettle and add the onion, shallots and garlic. Cook until wilted and add the mussels. Add half the parsley, pepper to taste and wine. Cover closely and cook for about 5 minutes, or until the mussels are opened. Serve in soup bowls sprinkled with remaining parsley.

Yield: 2 to 4 servings.

Moules Provençale *(Steamed mussels with tomatoes)*

1. Scrub the mussels thoroughly under cold running water. Drain.

2. Heat the oil in a small kettle and add the onion and garlic. Cook until the onion is wilted and add the tomatoes and wine. Cook over high heat to reduce slightly and add the mussels. Cover closely and steam until mussels are opened, about 5 minutes. Sprinkle with parsley and basil.

3. Arrange one or two crusts in the bottom of each of 4 soup bowls. Spoon the mussels into the bowls and serve piping hot.

Yield: 4 servings.

3	quarts (3½ pounds) fresh mussels
5	tablespoons olive oil
¼	cup finely chopped onion
2	cloves garlic, finely minced
1	cup fresh, peeled, chopped tomatoes
1	cup dry white wine
2	tablespoons finely chopped parsley
1	tablespoon finely chopped fresh basil, or 1 teaspoon dried
4 to	8 provençale crusts (see instructions below)

Preheat the oven to 400 degrees. Brush 4 to 8 thin rounds of French bread with olive oil on both sides. Place on a baking sheet and bake until crisp, turning once.

Provençale crusts

Moules au Safron *(Mussels with saffron cream)*

1. Scrub the mussels thoroughly. Drain and set aside.

2. Melt the butter in a kettle and add the leeks, onion, garlic and shallots. Cook for about 1 minute and add the saffron. Cook about 2 minutes, stirring, and add the vinegar and mussels. Add salt and pepper to taste and cover closely. Cook for about 1 minute.

3. Add the parsley and cream and cover. Cook for about 5 minutes, or until the mussels open. Serve in hot soup bowls.

Yield: 4 servings.

3	pounds (about 2½ quarts) cleaned mussels
2	tablespoons butter
3	tablespoons finely chopped leeks
2	tablespoons finely chopped onion
1	clove garlic, finely minced
1	tablespoon finely chopped shallots
1	teaspoon loose stem saffron
2	tablespoons wine vinegar
	Salt and freshly ground pepper
¼	cup finely chopped parsley
½	cup heavy cream

Moules à la Moutarde *(Mussels in mustard cream sauce)*

4 tablespoons butter
4 tablespoons finely chopped
   shallots
1 teaspoon finely minced garlic
2 quarts (about 2½ pounds)
   well-scrubbed mussels
   Freshly ground pepper
1 cup heavy cream
2 tablespoons imported mustard,
   such as Dijon or Düsseldorf

1. Heat the butter in a kettle and add the shallots and garlic. Add the mussels and pepper to taste. Cover and cook until the moisture in the kettle starts to steam.

2. Add the cream and cover and cook, stirring often, for about 3 minutes. Uncover and continue to cook, stirring often, until the mussels open.

3. Using a slotted spoon, transfer the mussels to 4 to 6 soup bowls. Stir the mustard into the sauce while heating without boiling. Spoon equal portions of sauce over the mussels and serve immediately.

Yield: 4 to 6 servings.

Mussels Vinaigrette

5 pounds clean, well-scrubbed
   mussels, the smaller the
   better
½ cup wine vinegar
2 sprigs thyme, or ½ teaspoon
   dried
1 bay leaf
   Freshly ground pepper
1½ cups chopped red onion
⅓ cup chopped parsley
¾ cup peanut, vegetable or
   corn oil

1. Place the mussels in a kettle and add ¼ cup vinegar, thyme and bay leaf. Cover and steam until the mussels open, 5 to 10 minutes. Drain.

2. Empty the warm mussels into a large serving dish or mixing bowl. Toss with the remaining ingredients, including the remaining ¼ cup of vinegar and pepper to taste.

Yield: 12 or more servings.

Deep-fried Oysters, Southern-style

For each 18 oysters, season 1 cup of yellow cornmeal with salt and pepper to taste. Drain the oysters and dredge them, one at a time, in the cornmeal. Heat 4 cups of peanut, vegetable or corn oil in a skillet or deep fat fryer. Add the oysters and cook until nicely browned, about 1 minute. Serve, if desired, with tartar sauce.

Stir-fry Oysters and Shrimp

For years we had heard of Danny Kaye's prowess as a chef, particularly in the province of Chinese cooking, but tended to regard it with some skepticism. One more touch of Hollywood, we mused. His talents, however, wildly exceed his billing. With only one helper in what is undoubtedly the finest Chinese kitchen of any private home anywhere, he regaled us with a banquet of surpassing excellence. This stir-fry oyster and shrimp dish and the batter-fried scallops are just two of our favorites from Danny's repertory.

1. Place the oysters in a bowl and add the flour and water to cover. Stir the oysters in the liquid. Drain well and run under several changes of cold water. Drain well. The flour will both cleanse and plump the oysters. They must be rinsed well before draining.
2. Drop the oysters into barely simmering water. Turn off the heat. Let stand for 1 minute and drain. Set aside. Repeat with the shrimp.
3. Heat the oil in a wok or skillet over high heat. Add the ginger and scallions and cook, stirring, for about 5 seconds. Add the oysters and shrimp and stir rapidly. Cook for about 15 seconds. Add the soy sauce, sesame oil, salt and pepper to taste, stirring constantly.
4. Blend the cornstarch with water and stir it into the dish. Cook for 15 seconds, stirring quickly, and serve.

Yield: 8 servings with other Chinese dishes.

1 cup raw oysters
¼ cup flour
½ pound shrimp, shelled and deveined
2 tablespoons peanut, vegetable or corn oil
1 2-inch piece fresh ginger, peeled and cut into fine shreds
5 scallions, trimmed and cut into 2-inch lengths
1 teaspoon light soy sauce
¼ teaspoon sesame oil
Salt and freshly ground pepper
1½ tablespoons cornstarch
1½ tablespoons water

Broiled Scallops

1. Preheat the broiler to high.
2. Select a large, flat baking dish with a low rim. Put the butter in it and place under the broiler until butter melts and is bubbling hot without browning.
3. Add the scallops and stir to coat with butter. Add the crumbs, salt and pepper and stir until scallops are coated with crumbs.
4. Place the scallops about 3 inches from the source of heat and broil. Do not close the broiler door as the scallops cook. Broil for 5 minutes without stirring or turning. Serve hot with lemon wedges.

Yield: 4 servings.

3 tablespoons butter
1 pound scallops
2 tablespoons fine, fresh bread crumbs
Salt and freshly ground pepper to taste
Lemon wedges

Batter-fried Scallops

2 cups whole bay scallops, or quartered ocean scallops
½ cup flour
½ cup cornstarch
1 egg white
1 tablespoon peanut, vegetable or corn oil
1 tablespoon white vinegar
1 teaspoon baking soda
½ cup or more water
Flour for dredging
Peanut, vegetable or corn oil for deep frying
2½ cups sweet and sour sauce (see recipe below)

1. Rinse and drain the scallops well.
2. In a mixing bowl, combine the flour, cornstarch, egg white, 1 tablespoon oil, vinegar and baking soda. Mix well.
3. Gradually add the water, stirring constantly with a wire whisk. Add enough water to make a thick, pancakelike batter.
4. Dredge the scallops in flour.
5. Heat the oil almost to smoking and, if desired, test one scallop by dipping it in the batter and frying to determine if the batter is too thick. If so, stir in a little more water.
6. Add the scallops to the batter and quickly drop them one at a time into the hot oil. Deep fry, stirring and turning with a strainer, making sure that the scallops do not stick together. Remove and drain well. Pour onto a serving dish. Pour the heated sweet and sour sauce over and serve.

Yield: 8 servings.

Sweet and sour sauce

1 cup sugar
¾ cup white vinegar
½ cup plus 3 tablespoons water
¾ cup pineapple juice
1½ tablespoons cornstarch
½ teaspoon red food coloring

1. Combine the sugar, vinegar, ½ cup water and pineapple juice in a saucepan. Bring to the boil and simmer, stirring, until sugar dissolves.
2. Blend the cornstarch with the remaining water and stir into the sauce. Stir in food coloring.

Yield: About 2½ cups.

Breaded Scallops

1 pound scallops
1 egg
1 teaspoon peanut, vegetable or corn oil
Salt to taste
1 tablespoon water
Flour for dredging
1 cup fine, fresh bread crumbs
Oil for deep frying
Lemon wedges

1. If the scallops are freshly opened, rinse and drain them.
2. Combine the egg, 1 teaspoon oil, salt and water in a dish, such as a pie plate.
3. Dredge the scallops lightly on all sides in flour. Turn them in the egg mixture until coated. Dredge them on all sides in the bread crumbs. Arrange them on a rack so that they do not touch. The scallops may be prepared to this point about an hour in advance or they may be cooked immediately.
4. Heat the oil for deep frying and add the scallops. Cook them quickly, stirring with a slotted spoon, until golden brown. Drain on absorbent toweling. Serve with cucumber mayonnaise, tartar sauce or a cocktail sauce. Serve garnished with lemon wedges.

Yield: 4 to 6 servings.

Scallops with Shallot Butter and Pine Nuts

1. Preheat the oven to 450 degrees.
2. Rinse the scallops and pat them dry.
3. Work the butter with the fingers until it is soft. Add the shallots, salt to taste, pine nuts, parsley, bread crumbs and lemon juice.
4. Add equal amounts of scallops to each of 8 scallop shells or ramekins. Top the scallops with equal portions of the butter. Place on a baking dish and bake for 10 minutes, or until piping hot and bubbling.

Yield: 8 servings.

1	pound fresh bay scallops
12	tablespoons butter
3	tablespoons finely chopped shallots
	Salt
2	tablespoons pine nuts
1	tablespoon chopped parsley
⅓	cup fine, fresh bread crumbs
1	tablespoon lemon juice

Coquilles St. Jacques *(Scallops with mushrooms in cream sauce)*

1. Melt 1 tablespoon of the butter in a saucepan and add the shallots. Cook briefly, stirring, and add the mushrooms. Cook until wilted and add salt, pepper and wine.
2. Add the scallops and bring to the boil. Cook until all the scallops are heated through, stirring gently as necessary. Take care not to let the scallops overcook or they will toughen.
3. Using a slotted spoon, remove and set aside the scallops and mushrooms. Reserve the liquid. There should be about ¾ cup of liquid.
4. Melt 2 tablespoons of butter in a saucepan and add the flour, stirring rapidly with a wire whisk. When blended add the reserved liquid, stirring until thickened and smooth. Add the milk and 1 cup of cream. Cook for about 5 minutes. Add salt and pepper to taste and a pinch of cayenne pepper.
5. Whip the 2 tablespoons of heavy cream. Fold it into the sauce.
6. Use 6 individual scallop shells or ramekins. Spoon equal portions of the scallops and mushrooms into each shell. Spoon the sauce over the scallop mixture.
7. Preheat the broiler to high. Place the filled shells under the broiler about 6 inches from the source of heat and bake until a nice brown glaze forms on top. As the scallops broil, turn occasionally for even browning, about 5 minutes. Serve immediately.

Yield: 6 servings.

4	tablespoons butter
1	tablespoon finely chopped shallots
2	cups thinly sliced mushrooms
	Salt and freshly ground pepper to taste
½	cup dry white wine
1	pound scallops
2	tablespoons flour
½	cup milk
1	cup plus 2 tablespoons heavy cream
	Pinch of cayenne pepper

Sauté of Scallops Doria

1 cucumber, about ½ pound
2 tablespoons butter
1 tablespoon finely chopped
   shallots
1 pound fresh scallops
   Salt and freshly ground
   pepper
2 tablespoons tomato purée
¾ cup heavy cream
2 teaspoons lemon juice
1 tablespoon finely chopped
   dill

1. Trim off the ends of the cucumber. Cut the cucumber into 1½-inch lengths. Trim the pieces, discarding the skin and soft center section with the seeds. There should be about 1 cup.

2. Heat the butter in a large heavy skillet and cook the shallots, stirring, for about 1 minute. Add the scallops, salt and pepper to taste. Cook over high heat for about 30 seconds, shaking the skillet. Add the cucumber pieces. Cook for about 1 minute and add the tomato purée and cream, salt and pepper to taste. Bring to the boil and simmer for about 2 minutes.

3. Using a slotted spoon, transfer the scallops to a warm bowl and set aside. Cook down the liquid with the cucumbers over high heat for about 2 minutes, or until thickened and sauce-like. Add the lemon juice. Return the scallops to the sauce and sprinkle with dill.

Yield: 4 servings.

Scallops Florentine

1 pound spinach in bulk, or 1
   10-ounce package
1 pound scallops
1 tablespoon finely chopped
   shallots
4 tablespoons butter
   Salt and freshly ground
   pepper to taste
¼ cup wine
2 tablespoons flour
1 cup milk
½ cup heavy cream
⅛ teaspoon freshly grated
   nutmeg
2 tablespoons freshly grated
   Parmesan cheese

1. If the spinach is in bulk, pick it over to remove and discard any tough stems or blemished leaves. Rinse the spinach and drain well. Cook the spinach briefly until the leaves wilt. Drain well and chop. Set aside.

2. Combine the scallops, shallots, 1 tablespoon of butter, salt, pepper and wine. Bring just to the boil. Do not cook further. Using a slotted spoon, remove the scallops and set aside. Reserve the cooking liquid.

3. Melt 2 tablespoons of butter in a saucepan and add the flour, stirring with a wire whisk. When blended, add the milk and stir rapidly until thickened and smooth. Add the scallop liquid, stirring. Add the cream and simmer for about 5 minutes.

4. Meanwhile, heat the remaining butter in a skillet and add the spinach. Toss briefly just to heat through. Add salt, pepper and nutmeg. Toss.

5. Spoon the mixture into an oval gratin dish and spread it out evenly. Cover with an even layer of scallops. Spoon the sauce over and sprinkle with the grated cheese. Run the dish under a preheated broiler and cook just to glaze the top. Or bake at 450 degrees for about 5 minutes.

Yield: 4 to 6 servings.

Scallop Mousse

1. Preheat the oven to 375 degrees.

2. Heat 1 tablespoon butter in a skillet. Add the chopped shallots and cook briefly. Add 1 cup of scallops, salt and pepper to taste. Cook briefly, about 40 seconds, over high heat. Add the wine and cook for about 1 minute.

3. Remove the scallops with a slotted spoon. Reserve the liquid in the skillet. As the cooked scallops stand, liquid will accumulate around them. Always add this to the skillet liquid. This liquid will be used in the sauce to be served with the mousse.

4. Put half the remaining scallops in the container of a food processor. Add salt, pepper and a touch of nutmeg. Add 1 egg yolk. Stir it around with a spatula to keep it from spattering when the processor is turned on. Blend the ingredients, stopping the motor once in a while and stirring down and scraping the side of the processor. When the scallops are well blended and with the cover still on, gradually add 1 cup of cream. Process to a creamy purée, about 1 minute in all. Scrape the mixture into a mixing bowl and set aside.

5. Add the second batch of scallops and repeat the above blending process with the addition of salt, pepper, nutmeg, 1 egg yolk and another cup of cream.

6. Combine the two batches of mousse mixture and add the drained cup of cooked scallops. Fold them in with a rubber spatula.

7. Brush the inside of a 7- or 8-cup mold with 1 tablespoon of butter. Spoon and scrape the mousse mixture into the mold. Smooth the surface. Butter a ring of wax paper and place it buttered side down over the mousse.

8. Set the mold in a basin of hot water and bring to the boil on top of the stove. Place in the oven and bake for 45 minutes. Remove the mousse. It will have puffed and browned on top. Remove the wax paper and pull off the brown "skin" from the surface. It pulls off evenly.

9. Unmold the mousse. Liquid will quickly accumulate around the base of the mousse. Add this liquid to the sauce Duglére. Spoon the sauce over the mousse and down the center. Sprinkle with chopped parsley. Serve the mousse sliced with the sauce.

Yield: 8 or more servings.

4 cups scallops, preferably bay scallops, about 2 pounds. If sea scallops are used, cut them into quarters.
2 tablespoons butter
1 tablespoon finely chopped shallots
Salt and freshly ground pepper
½ cup dry white wine
Freshly grated nutmeg
2 egg yolks
2 cups heavy cream
2 tablespoons chopped parsley
Sauce Duglére (see recipe page 651)

Scallops and Shrimp on Skewers

20 scallops, about ¾ pound
20 shrimp, about ¾ pound
    Salt and freshly ground
    pepper
 2 tablespoons peanut, vegetable
    or corn oil
    Tabasco sauce to taste
 1 teaspoon dried rosemary
 2 tablespoons lemon juice
 1 clove garlic, finely minced
 1 slice lemon
½ cup fine, fresh bread crumbs
    Melted butter for basting
    Lemon wedges

1. Place the scallops and shrimp in a mixing bowl and add salt and pepper to taste, oil and Tabasco sauce. Chop the rosemary and add it. Add the lemon juice, garlic and lemon slice. Blend well and refrigerate for at least ½ hour.

2. Arrange the scallops and shrimp alternately on 4 skewers. Dredge in bread crumbs.

3. To grill, brush a hot, fired grill with oil and add the skewers. Brush occasionally with melted butter. Turn after 2 minutes and continue to turn frequently while grilling, a total of about 12 minutes.

4. To broil, place the skewers on a baking dish and broil 6 inches more or less from the source of heat. Broil for about 5 minutes and turn. Brush frequently with melted butter. Broil for 10 to 12 minutes. Serve with lemon wedges.

Yield: 4 servings.

Batter-fried Shrimp

Many years ago, when we attended a hotel school in Switzerland, we first discovered the miracle known as a beer batter. Although a can of flat beer may be the bane of those who dote on a frosty and lively brew, it is a liquid of considerable merit to a knowledgeable cook. It yields a crisp, puffy, gossamer coating to such good things as shrimp, brains and assorted vegetables.

1½ pounds shrimp
    Beer batter (see recipe page
    207)
1½ tablespoons cornstarch
 1 tablespoon dry sherry
 2 tablespoons finely chopped
    parsley
    Salt
    Peanut, vegetable or corn oil
    for deep frying
    Lemon wedges

1. Peel and devein the shrimp but leave the last tail segment intact. Refrigerate until ready to use.

2. Prepare the beer batter well in advance.

3. Combine the shrimp with the cornstarch, sherry, parsley and salt to taste.

4. When ready to cook, heat the oil. Add a few shrimp at a time to the batter and, using a 2-pronged fork, drop them, one at a time, into the hot oil. Cook, turning as necessary, to brown evenly. Drain on paper towels. Sprinkle with salt.

5. Serve immediately with lemon wedges and any desired sauce such as hot mustard, marmalade and mustard sauce, soy and ginger dip.

Yield: 4 to 6 servings.

Shrimp Steamed in Beer with Dill

Do not peel the shrimp. Put them in a saucepan or deep small skillet and add the remaining ingredients. Cover and bring to the boil. Bring to a rolling boil and remove from the heat. Serve the shrimp with melted butter.

Yield: 2 to 4 servings.

1 pound shrimp, about 30
1 bay leaf
6 sprigs fresh dill
1 clove garlic
8 whole peppercorns, crushed
1 teaspoon allspice
1 dried hot red pepper pod
½ to 1 cup beer
Salt to taste
2 small ribs celery with leaves

Shrimp with Sorrel

1. Peel and devein the shrimp. Rinse well and pat dry. Reserve the shrimp shells.

2. Pick over the sorrel; remove and discard any tough stems. Rinse well and pat dry. On a flat surface, cut the sorrel into fine shreds (chiffonade). Set aside.

3. Heat 2 tablespoons butter in a small, deep skillet and add the shrimp shells, stirring. Cook briefly and add the onion and shallots. Cook for about 2 minutes, stirring frequently, and sprinkle with flour, stirring. Add the wine and tomato paste, stirring until well blended. Cook for about 5 minutes.

4. Add the cream and cook for about 5 minutes over high heat. Strain through a sieve, pushing down to extract as much liquid as possible from the solids.

5. Heat 1 tablespoon of butter in a small saucepan and add the sorrel. Cook, stirring, just until wilted.

6. Heat the remaining butter in a saucepan and add the shrimp. Sprinkle with salt and pepper and cook briefly, stirring, just until the shrimp change color. Add the Cognac and ignite it. When the flame dies down, stir in the cream sauce and sorrel. Bring to the boil and simmer about 1 minute.

7. Beat the yolks and add a little of the hot sauce, stirring constantly. Return the mixture to the sauce and stir without

1¾ pounds shrimp
1 pound fresh sorrel (see note)
5 tablespoons butter
⅓ cup finely chopped onion
3 tablespoons finely chopped shallots
1 tablespoon flour
1 cup dry white wine
3 tablespoons tomato paste
2 cups heavy cream
Salt and freshly ground pepper
¼ cup Cognac or bourbon
2 egg yolks
Toast rounds (see note)

boiling. Remove from the heat immediately. Serve on toast rounds.

Yield: 6 to 8 servings.

Note: If sorrel is not available, substitute 1 tablespoon chopped fresh tarragon or dill, but do not cook the herb before adding. Or sprinkle with chopped chives before serving.

The best way to make toast rounds is to cut fresh white bread slices with a bread cutter. Brush with butter and bake in a 400-degree oven until toasted.

Shrimp Creole au Pernod

1½ pounds shrimp
4 tablespoons plus 1 teaspoon butter
1½ cups coarsely chopped onion
1 cup coarsely chopped celery
1 green pepper, cored, seeded and cut into 1-inch cubes
3 cloves garlic, finely minced
3 cups peeled, red, ripe tomatoes, preferably the Italian plum tomatoes if canned ones are used
2 tablespoons chopped fresh basil, or 1 teaspoon dried
2 teaspoons thyme
1 bay leaf
   Tabasco sauce to taste
1 teaspoon grated lemon rind
   Salt and freshly ground pepper to taste
1 teaspoon flour
3 tablespoons finely chopped parsley
   Juice of ½ lemon
1½ tablespoons Pernod or Ricard

1. Peel the shrimp and split them down the back. Rinse away the black vein. Set aside.

2. Melt 4 tablespoons of butter in a saucepan and add the onion. Cook, stirring, until they are wilted and add the celery, green pepper and garlic. Cook, stirring briefly, for about 3 minutes. Do not overcook, for the vegetables should remain crisp.

3. Add the tomatoes, basil, thyme, bay leaf, Tabasco, lemon rind, salt and pepper. Cook uncovered for about 15 minutes.

4. Add the shrimp and cover. Cook for about 3 minutes, no longer.

5. Blend the remaining teaspoon of butter and the flour and add it bit by bit to the simmering sauce, stirring constantly. Cook for about 1 minute and add the parsley and lemon juice. Add the Pernod, heat and serve.

Yield: 4 servings.

Shrimp à la Moutarde de Meaux

2 pounds shrimp
5 tablespoons butter
4 tablespoons flour
2 cups milk

1. Preheat the oven to 450 degrees.

2. Shell the shrimp and split them down the back. Rinse away the black vein. Drain and cut each shrimp in half crosswise. Set aside.

3. In a saucepan, melt 3 tablespoons butter and stir in the flour, using a wire whisk. Add the milk, stirring rapidly with the whisk. Season with salt, pepper and cayenne. Simmer, stirring occasionally, for 15 minutes.

4. In another saucepan, combine the shallots, wine and chopped parsley. Cook over high heat until the wine is almost totally reduced. Add the white sauce and cook, stirring occasionally, for about 10 minutes.

5. Beat the egg yolk lightly and add it to the sauce, stirring rapidly. Remove the sauce from the heat and add 3 tablespoons mustard.

6. Melt remaining 2 tablespoons butter in a skillet and add the shrimp. Cook just until the shrimp turn red. Add remaining tablespoon mustard and stir to coat well. Add a third of the sauce to the shrimp and stir to coat.

7. Spoon the shrimp into 8 individual ramekins or large scallop shells. Spoon an equal amount of the sauce over each serving. Sprinkle with an equal amount of Parmesan cheese and bake for 10 to 15 minutes, until piping hot.

Yield: 8 servings.

Salt and freshly ground pepper to taste
⅛ teaspoon cayenne pepper
3 tablespoons finely chopped shallots
½ cup dry white wine
¼ cup finely chopped parsley
1 egg yolk
4 tablespoons moutarde de Meaux, or use another imported mustard, such as Dijon or Düsseldorf
¼ cup freshly grated Parmesan cheese

Curried Shrimp with Noodles

1. Peel the shrimp and remove the dark vein down the back. Rinse. Drain the shrimp and set aside.

2. Heat 2 tablespoons of butter in a saucepan and add the onion and garlic. Cook until the onion is wilted and add the celery and apple. Sprinkle with curry powder and stir to blend thoroughly. Add the tomatoes, fish broth, bay leaves, salt and pepper. Bring to the boil and add the banana. Cook for about 20 minutes.

3. Heat the remaining butter in a small skillet and add the shrimp. Sprinkle with salt and pepper. Cook, stirring and shaking the skillet, for about 1 minute. Add the sauce and bring to the boil. Simmer for 5 minutes.

4. Serve on a bed of noodles.

Yield: 4 servings.

1½ pounds shrimp
4 tablespoons butter
1 cup finely chopped onion
1 teaspoon finely minced garlic
¾ cup finely chopped celery
1 cup peeled, cored, finely cubed apple
4 tablespoons curry powder
1 cup crushed tomatoes
2 cups fish broth, or use 1 cup bottled clam juice diluted with 1 cup of water
2 bay leaves
Salt and freshly ground pepper to taste
¾ cup peeled, finely cubed, ripe but firm banana
½ pound hot, buttered, freshly cooked noodles

Garides mi Feta *(Shrimp baked with feta cheese)*

3 cups imported canned Italian plum tomatoes
1 pound shrimp, about 24
¼ cup olive oil
1 teaspoon finely chopped garlic
¼ cup fresh fish broth, or bottled clam juice
1 teaspoon crushed dried oregano
1 teaspoon dried red pepper flakes
2 tablespoons drained capers
Salt and freshly ground pepper
3 tablespoons butter
¼ pound feta cheese
¼ cup ouzo, a Greek anise-flavored liqueur widely available in wine and spirits shops, optional

1. Preheat the oven to 350 degrees.
2. Put the tomatoes in a saucepan and cook until reduced to about 2 cups. Stir often to prevent burning and sticking.
3. Shell and devein the shrimp and set aside.
4. Heat the olive oil in another saucepan or deep skillet and add the garlic, stirring. Add the tomatoes, using a rubber spatula to scrape them out.
5. Add the fish broth, oregano, pepper flakes, capers and salt and pepper to taste.
6. Heat the butter in a heavy saucepan or skillet and add the shrimp. Cook briefly, less than 1 minute, stirring and turning the shrimp until they turn pink.
7. Spoon equal portions of half the sauce in 4 individual baking dishes and arrange 6 shrimp plus equal amounts of the butter in which they cooked in each dish. Spoon remaining sauce over the shrimp.
8. Crumble the cheese and scatter it over all. Place the dishes in the oven and bake for 10 to 15 minutes, or until bubbling hot.
9. Remove the dishes from the oven and sprinkle each dish with 1 tablespoon ouzo, if desired, and ignite it. Serve immediately.
Yield: 4 servings

Mousse of Shrimp

1½ pounds shrimp, shelled and deveined
Salt and freshly ground pepper
¼ teaspoon cayenne pepper
¼ teaspoon grated nutmeg
2 eggs
2½ cups heavy cream
3 cups sauce Joinville (see recipe page 649)

1. Preheat the oven to 375 degrees.
2. In the container of a food processor, combine the shrimp, salt, pepper, cayenne and nutmeg. Blend for about 30 seconds, stopping the motor and stirring down with a rubber spatula if necessary.
3. Add the eggs and blend, stopping the motor and stirring down as necessary, for about 20 seconds or until the mousse mixture is smooth. Add the cream slowly while blending. Blend for about 30 seconds. To taste for seasoning, drop a small spoonful of the mixture into a small saucepan with boiling water. Cook briefly and taste. Add more salt, pepper, nutmeg or cayenne if desired.

4. Generously butter a round, 6-cup ring mold and spoon the mixture into it. Cover with a buttered round of wax paper cut to fit over the top of the mousse. Place the mold in a basin of water and bring to a boil on top of the stove.

5. Bake for 30 to 40 minutes. To test for doneness, insert a long needle into the center of the mousse. If it comes out clean, the mousse is done. Do not overbake.

6. Unmold the mousse onto a round serving platter. If any liquid seeps from the mousse, drain it off. Dribble some of the sauce Joinville over and around the mousse and serve the remainder on the side.

Yield: 8 to 12 servings.

Quenelles de Crevettes *(Shrimp quenelles)*

Quenelles are one of the greatest inventions of French chefdom—gossamer, lighter-than-air ovals of fish, seafood, meat or poultry, delicately seasoned, poached briefly and served with any of a number of sauces. Quenelles of any sort were always enormously tedious to prepare, but with a food processor they are quite simple. An electric blender may be used, but the process will require much more time and patience.

1. Shell and devein the shrimp. Reserve the shells to be used in making the sauce. Cut the flounder or fluke into cubes. Add the shrimp and fish to the container of a food processor or electric blender. If a blender is used, this will have to be done in at least two steps.

2. Blend the mixture briefly and add salt and pepper to taste, a pinch each of cayenne pepper and ground nutmeg. Add the egg yolk and blend.

3. While blending, add the cream gradually.

4. Butter a heatproof dish, one that is large enough to hold the quenelles when they are shaped. There will be 18 or 20 oval-shaped quenelles of equal size. To shape the quenelles, use 2 large soup spoons. Have ready a bowl filled with hot water. Pick up a heaping spoonful of the shrimp mixture with one spoon.

5. Dip the second spoon into the hot water and run it around under the shrimp mixture, starting on top of the mix-

¾   pound shrimp
½   pound fillet of flounder or
      fluke
      Salt and freshly ground
      pepper
      Pinch of cayenne pepper
      Pinch of nutmeg
1   egg yolk
1½ cups heavy cream
      Sauce aux crevettes (see recipe
      below)

ture and turning the second spoon inside the first spoon. This should produce a smooth, neat, oval quenelle.

6. As the quenelles are shaped, transfer them to the buttered dish. Arrange them close together and in a neat pattern.

7. Cut a sheet of wax paper into a pattern that will fit neatly over the quenelles. Butter it and place it buttered side down over the quenelles.

8. Meanwhile, bring a large quantity of water to the boil and add salt to taste. Gently ladle water over the wax paper so that it will flow gradually into the dish. Continue adding water until the quenelles are barely covered.

9. Bring to the boil on top of the stove and simmer as gently as possible for from 5 to 10 minutes, or until the quenelles are piping hot. Do not overcook.

10. Remove the quenelles carefully and quickly, using a slotted spoon, and drain them briefly on absorbent toweling. Serve immediately with piping hot shrimp sauce spooned over.

Yield: 6 servings.

Sauce aux crevettes

¼ pound shrimp, plus shells from the shrimp used in making quenelles
2½ tablespoons butter
1 tablespoon finely chopped shallots
1 tablespoon finely minced onion
2½ tablespoons flour
1 cup dry white wine
1 cup fish broth, or bottled clam juice
1½ tablespoons tomato paste
½ cup crushed, skinned, fresh or canned ripe tomatoes
½ tablespoon finely chopped fresh tarragon, or ½ teaspoon dried
Pinch of cayenne pepper
Salt and freshly ground pepper to taste
1 cup heavy cream
1 tablespoon Cognac

1. Shell and devein the shrimp. Cut them into small pieces and set aside. Combine the shells with the shells reserved from making the quenelles.

2. Heat 1 tablespoon of butter in a saucepan and add the shallots and onion. Add the reserved shrimp shells. Sprinkle with flour and stir to blend. Add the wine and broth, stirring rapidly with a whisk. Continue stirring until blended. Bring to the boil and add the tomato paste, tomatoes, tarragon, cayenne, salt and pepper. Simmer for 30 minutes.

3. Pour and spoon the mixture, including the shells, into the container of a food processor (see note). This will probably have to be done in two steps. Blend until the shrimp shells are coarsely blended. Strain the sauce, pressing with the back of a wooden spoon to extract as much juice as possible from the solids.

4. Return the mixture to a saucepan and add the cream. Cook, stirring, for 10 to 15 minutes.

5. Heat ½ tablespoon of butter in a skillet and add the shrimp pieces. Cook just until the shrimp change color, about 1 minute. Add the Cognac and ignite it. Add the shrimp to the sauce. Add the remaining tablespoon of butter and swirl it in. Serve hot.

Yield: About 2 cups of sauce.

Note: Take care not to overwork the motor of the food processor. The shells should not be finely pulverized.

Hunan Shrimp

1. Peel the shrimp and split them in half. Rinse well to remove the dark vein. Pat dry.

2. Place the shrimp in a mixing bowl and add 1½ tablespoons wine, the egg whites and 1½ tablespoons oil. Stir in a circular motion until whites become bubbly and add half the salt and 1½ tablespoons cornstarch. Stir to blend.

3. Prepare the scallions and ginger and set aside.

4. Combine the remaining 3 tablespoons wine, remaining 1 tablespoon cornstarch blended with the water, soy sauce, vinegar, sugar, remaining salt, sesame oil and chicken broth.

5. Heat remaining 4 cups of oil in a wok or skillet and add the shrimp, one at a time. Cook about 1 minute and scoop out, leaving the oil in the wok continuously heating. Return the shrimp to the oil and cook for about 30 seconds. Drain wok completely.

6. Return about 1 tablespoon of oil to the wok and add the scallions and ginger, stirring constantly. Cook for about 5 seconds and add the shrimp and the vinegar mixture. Toss and stir until piping hot and the shrimp are coated evenly. Serve garnished with coriander leaves if desired.

Yield: 4 to 8 servings.

10	giant shrimp, about 1¼ pounds, available in Chinese fish markets
4½	tablespoons shao hsing wine, or dry sherry
2	egg whites
4	cups plus 1½ tablespoons peanut, vegetable or corn oil
½	teaspoon salt
2½	tablespoons cornstarch
2	scallions, white part only, trimmed and shredded
5	very thin slices fresh ginger, shredded
2	tablespoons water
2	tablespoons soy sauce
2½	tablespoons white vinegar
2	tablespoons sugar
½	teaspoon sesame oil
⅓	cup chicken broth
½	cup loosely packed fresh coriander, optional

Cold Shrimp, Cucumber and Tree Ears with Sweet and Sour Sauce

1. Place the shrimp in a bowl and add water to cover and salt to taste. Let stand about ½ hour. Drain. Drop the shrimp into boiling water to cover. When the water returns to the boil, drain and run under cold water to chill. Peel the shrimp and slice in half. Rinse once more to remove the intestinal vein. Pat dry and refrigerate.

2. Pour boiling water over the tree ears and let stand about ½ hour. Drain. Drop the tree ears into boiling water to cover. When the water returns to the boil, drain and chill under cold running water. Drain and pat dry.

3. Trim off and discard the ends of the cucumbers. Do not peel the cucumbers. Split them in half lengthwise and scoop out the seeds with a melon ball cutter or spoon. Split each half in two widthwise. Slice the cucumbers quite thinly and set aside. There should be about 3 cups.

4. In a wok, combine the dried peppers, peppercorns, ses-

¾	pound unpeeled shrimp, about 20
	Salt
⅓	cup tree ears, available in Chinese grocery stores
2	firm, unblemished cucumbers, about ½ pound each
12	small or 3 large hot, dried, red peppers
2	tablespoons Szechwan peppercorns, available in Chinese grocery stores
¼	cup sesame oil
1	tablespoon corn oil
½	cup red wine vinegar
¾	cup sugar

ame oil and corn oil. Heat thoroughly and cook, stirring, for about 4 minutes. Cook until the red peppers start to turn black-red. The mixture may smoke slightly. Remove from the heat and drain off the hot seasoned oil. Discard the spices.

5. Wipe out the wok and add the seasoned oil. Blend the vinegar and sugar and add it. Add salt to taste. Bring to the boil and let bubble up, stirring, for about 3 minutes. Pour the mixture into a cup or saucepan and let cool.

6. Arrange the cucumbers on the bottom of a round serving dish. Add a layer of tree ears, then the shrimp. Cover with plastic wrap and chill until ready to serve.

7. Uncover the salad and pour the sauce over. Serve cold.

Yield: 12 servings with other Chinese dishes.

Shrimp and Crabmeat Szechwan-style

½ pound small shrimp, the smaller the better
1 egg white
2 tablespoons cornstarch
½ pound fresh crabmeat, picked over to remove all trace of shell and cartilage
½ cup chopped scallion
2 teaspoons chopped garlic
¼ cup chopped fresh ginger
3 tablespoons chopped coriander, optional
4 hot dried red chili peppers, chopped
2 tablespoons shao hsing wine, or dry sherry
4 teaspoons dark soy sauce
1 teaspoon sugar
¾ teaspoon ground white pepper
1 teaspoon monosodium glutamate, optional
1 tablespoon chili paste with garlic, available in Chinese grocery stores
1 tablespoon water
2 cups or more peanut, vegetable or corn oil

1. Shell and devein the shrimp. Put the shrimp in a mixing bowl and add the egg white and 1 tablespoon cornstarch. Blend well with the fingers. Refrigerate for 30 minutes or longer.

2. Have the crabmeat ready.

3. Combine the scallion, garlic, ginger, coriander and dried red peppers. Set aside.

4. Combine the wine, dark soy sauce, sugar, white pepper, monosodium glutamate, if used, and chili paste with garlic. Set aside.

5. Blend the remaining tablespoon of cornstarch and the water. Set aside.

6. Heat the oil in a wok or skillet. There must be enough oil to completely cover the shrimp when they are added. When the oil is hot but not smoking, add the shrimp and stir rapidly to separate them. Cook for only 30 seconds, or just until the shrimp are separated. Drain quickly.

7. Return about 2 tablespoons of oil to the wok and add the scallion and garlic mixture. Cook, stirring, for about 5 seconds and add the crab mixture. Cook, stirring, just until heated through, for about 20 seconds, and add the shrimp. Add the wine and soy sauce mixture. Stir the cornstarch mixture until smooth and add it quickly. Stir rapidly for about 30 seconds and spoon the mixture onto a hot serving platter.

Yield: 6 to 12 servings.

Sambal Goreng Udang *(Shrimp in coconut milk)*

1. Prepare the shrimp and set aside.

2. Heat the oil and add the garlic, onion and chili. Cook, stirring, for about 30 seconds. Add the shrimp and stir until they redden.

3. Add the salam leaves and laos root and stir. Add the salt, sugar and tamarind liquid. Cook, stirring, for about 1 minute.

4. Add the coconut cream and bring to the boil. Add the tomato wedges and simmer for about 5 minutes. Do not overcook.

Yield: 6 or more servings with other Indonesian dishes.

Note: To make tamarind liquid, blend 2 tablespoons tamarind seeds (available in Oriental food shops) with ¼ cup water. Let stand for 30 minutes. Using the fingers, work the mixture until the soft solids loosen from the seeds. Put through a strainer, pushing as much of the soft solids through as possible.

1 pound small shrimp, peeled and deveined
1 tablespoon peanut, vegetable or corn oil
1 clove garlic, very thinly sliced
1 small onion, halved and thinly sliced, about ½ cup
1 mild or hot fresh green chili, cut on the diagonal into thin slices, about ⅓ cup
2 salam leaves, available in Oriental food shops
1 thin slice laos root, available in Oriental food shops
  Salt to taste
1 teaspoon sugar
1 tablespoon tamarind liquid (see note)
½ cup coconut cream (see recipe below)
1 tomato, cut into wedges, about ¾ cup

Coconut cream

Using a hammer, crack one small coconut at four or five points. This should produce four or five large pieces. Discard inner coconut liquid. Rest one piece at a time, shell side down, over a gas or electric burner. Let stand over moderately low heat for about 1 minute. Using a towel to protect the fingers, lift the coconut and lift the fleshy part from the shell. It should come off easily. Using a swivel-bladed vegetable scraper, scrape away the dark exterior, leaving only the white meat. Cut the meat into small cubes. There should be about 3 cups.

Put these cubes into the container of a food processor or electric blender. Add 2 cups of hot tap water. Blend until coconut meat is finely pulverized. Pour the liquid through a sieve into a bowl. Press and squeeze to extract excess liquid. Reserve both the grated coconut and the liquid. There should be about 2 cups of squeezed-out pulp and 2 cups of liquid. The liquid is coconut cream. If you add more water to the pulp and squeeze a second time, you will have a thinner liquid, which is coconut milk.

Jingha Tarhi *(Prawn curry)*

2¼ pounds large shrimp
½ cup peanut, vegetable or corn oil
1 large onion, coarsely chopped, about 1½ cups
½ teaspoon celery seed
1 tablespoon finely minced garlic
½ cup water
Salt to taste
1 teaspoon turmeric
2 teaspoons ground coriander
1 teaspoon ground cumin
2 teaspoons paprika
½ cup yogurt
2 tablespoons chopped fresh coriander leaves, optional
Juice of ½ lemon

1. Shell and devein the shrimp. Rinse and drain well and set aside.

2. Heat the oil in a deep saucepan and add the onion. Cook for about 10 minutes, stirring often. When the onion starts to turn a golden brown, add the celery seed, garlic and half the water. Cook for about 3 minutes and add the salt, turmeric, ground coriander, cumin and paprika. Cook, stirring, for about 3 minutes, and add the yogurt and remaining water.

3. Cook for about 4 minutes and add the shrimp. Cook for 8 to 10 minutes, stirring frequently. Cover and cook for about 10 minutes. Sprinkle with fresh coriander, if desired, and lemon juice. Serve hot.

Yield: 6 or more servings.

Tempura

2 egg yolks
2 cups ice water
2 cups plus about 3 tablespoons flour, sifted
Oil for deep frying
Foods to be deep fried (see below)
Salt to taste
Lemon wedges for garnish
Tempura dip (see recipe below)

It has been observed that all the world's cuisines can be categorized according to their most characteristic cooking medium: Chinese cooking is based on oil, French on butter and Japanese on water. It has long been a source of puzzlement that, where the Japanese kitchen is concerned, there is one outstanding exception, and that is tempura. On a trip to Osaka, we found out why. Shizuo Tsuji, the distinguished head of the largest hotel school in Japan, told us that tempura was brought into Japan by Portuguese priests who came to Japan in the sixteenth century. Tempura's original form was probably what the French call beignets and the English call fritters.

1. Place yolks in a mixing bowl and beat well, preferably with chopsticks.

2. Add the ice water, stirring constantly. When well blended, add 2 cups of flour all at once, stirring. Do not overblend. The batter, when ready, should be fairly lumpy.

3. Heat oil to the depth of about 2 inches in a utensil suitable for deep frying. When it is very hot but not smoking, add any combination of the ingredients listed below and prepared

as indicated. Cook batter-coated foods until golden but not browned.

4. Lift from the fat and drain on absorbent paper towels. As the foods are added and cooked, it is important to skim the surface of the fat to remove any loose bits of batter and particles of food that rise to the top. If the batter seems too thin at any point, sprinkle the surface with a tablespoon of flour and stir briefly, leaving it lumpy.

5. Continue cooking until all the foods are deep fried. Sprinkle the tempura lightly with salt and garnish with lemon wedges. Serve with the tempura dip.

Yield: Any number of servings, depending on quantity of foods cooked.

The single essential ingredient of any tempura is shrimp. All the other batter-fried foods are side dishes. Here are some of the ingredients that may be dipped in batter and deep fried for the tempura in the recipe above:

Shrimp: Peel the shrimp but leave the last tail segment intact. Make slight gashes in the shrimp at ½-inch intervals on the underside. When ready to cook, dip lightly in flour, then in batter and deep fry. Drain and serve hot.

Squid: Clean the squid thoroughly or buy them cleaned. All the inner digestive tract should be eliminated as well as all bone or cartilage. The outer mottled skin, as well as the very fine, transparent under skin, should be pulled away and discarded. Rinse the flesh and pat it dry. Cut the squid into strips measuring about 4 inches by 1 inch. Score on the underside. When ready to cook, coat lightly in flour and dip in batter. Deep fry, drain and serve hot.

Fresh mushrooms: In Japan there are numerous varieties of wild mushrooms included in an elaborate tempura. They include matsutake or pine tree mushrooms; enikodake, delicate, long-stemmed, white-fleshed mushrooms with a tiny cap, generally fried in bundles, and shiitake, the large black mushroom caps common in Japanese and Chinese cookery, which, if not available fresh, may be soaked from the dried state, squeezed and patted dry. They may then be floured, dipped in batter and deep fried. Drain and serve hot.

Fish: Almost any white-fleshed, nonoily fish may be cut into bite-size pieces and used. Conger eel, which is quite fatty, is, on the other hand, a frequent addition to a tempura. Sometimes the skinless, boneless eel is used, sometimes whole small fillets. Very small fish are frequently used whole, while some small fish are sometimes butterflied, boned and used.

Foods to be deep fried

All these are dipped in flour, then in batter and deep fried, drained and served hot.

Onions: Cut onions into ½-inch-thick slices, skewer with toothpicks to keep the rings intact, dip in flour, then batter and fry. Drain and serve hot.

There are also special and banquet type foods—deep fried without batter—that may be added to an elaborate tempura:

Shrimp: Peel the shrimp, leaving the last tail segment intact. Dip peeled portion in flour, then in egg white, then liberally in a choice of crushed almonds, fine cracker crumbs, white sesame seeds or finely chopped bean thread (cellophane noodles). Deep fry, drain and serve hot.

Small fish fillets with green noodles: Break enough Japanese green noodles (green soba) into fine pieces to make ½ cup. Dip fillets in flour, then egg white, then coat with noodles. Deep fry. This gives a porcupine effect. Serve hot.

Small fish fillets with egg noodles: Break enough Japanese egg noodles (udon) into fine pieces to make ½ cup. Dip fillets in flour, then in egg white, then coat with noodles. Deep fry. This gives a porcupine effect. Serve hot.

Miniature eggplant: The eggplant must be very small (no more than 3 inches in length). Leave the eggplant whole and with stems on. Slice them from bottom to center, about half way up, at ¼-inch intervals. Deep fry until cooked through.

Miniature hard-shell crab (very small soft-shell crabs could be substituted): If the miniature crabs are available, break off and discard the tiny "apron" on the front of each. Drop the crab into very hot fat. Cook about 30 seconds or less and drain. Serve as is.

Scallops: Use bay scallops or cut ocean scallops into bite-size pieces. Skewer or not, as desired. Dip in flour, then in egg white, then liberally in a choice of crushed almonds, fine cracker crumbs, white sesame seeds or finely chopped bean thread (cellophane noodles). Deep fry, drain and serve hot.

Shrimp "toast" sandwiches: Blend enough raw shrimp to make ½ cup of purée. Stir in half an egg yolk, salt to taste and dash of monosodium glutamate (optional). Cut trimmed white bread slices in half or into quarters. Spread one piece with the shrimp mixture, cover with another slice, sandwich fashion, and cook in very hot oil until brown on one side. Turn and brown on the other. Drain, cut into small squares and serve hot.

Japanese cooks also prepare deep fried gingko nut meats stuffed with the same shrimp mixture as for toast. The gingko nuts are sliced down the center without cutting through. The opening is sprinkled lightly with flour and filled with a small portion of the shrimp mixture. The gingko nut meats are skewered and deep fried.

Combine the dashi, dark soy sauce and mirin and bring to the boil. Add the katsuobushi and stir. Remove from the heat immediately. Let stand for about 30 seconds, skimming the surface as necessary. Add a dash of monosodium glutamate, if desired, and strain. Serve with grated radish on the side so that guests may add their own.

Yield: About 3½ cups.

Tempura dip

2½ cups dashi (see recipe page 659)

½ cup dark soy sauce

½ cup mirin (sweet sake), available in wine and spirit shops near Oriental communities

1 cup well-packed katsuobushi, shaved bonito flakes, available in most Japanese grocery stores
Monosodium glutamate, optional
Grated Japanese white radish, available in Oriental markets

VIII. Stews and Casseroles

A couple of decades of observing the cooking and dining patterns of Americans has led me to the conclusion that cooks have one need that, if met, would put them in a state of absolute nirvana in the kitchen. Particularly those cooks with a desire to entertain guests and relax over cocktails with them. The need is for a dish, subtly seasoned and tempting, that can be made hours or even days in advance, or, for that matter, frozen and defrosted on schedule. The answer, of course, is stews, braised dishes and casseroles. Many in this chapter will also feed a crowd, a boon during holiday seasons.

Boeuf Braisé au Vin Rouge *(Beef braised with red wine)*

The braised beef:

- 1 3½- to 4-pound boneless chuck roast, tied with string
  Salt and freshly ground pepper
- 1 tablespoon peanut, vegetable or corn oil
- 1 large onion, cut into ½-inch cubes, about 1 cup
- 1 carrot, trimmed, scraped and cut into ½-inch cubes, about 1 cup
- 2 ribs celery, trimmed, cut in half and cut into ½-inch cubes, about 1 cup
- 1 clove garlic, finely minced
- 2 cups dry red wine

1. Preheat the oven to 400 degrees.

2. Sprinkle the beef on all sides with salt and pepper to taste. Heat 1 tablespoon oil in a deep, heavy casserole or Dutch oven. Brown the meat on all sides for about 15 or 20 minutes, turning often. When ready, the beef should have a nice mahogany color without being burned.

3. Scatter the cubed onion, carrot, celery and garlic around the meat. Stir and add the wine, beef broth, bay leaf, thyme, parsley and cloves. Cover closely and place in the oven. Bake for 1½ hours.

4. Reduce the oven heat to 350 degrees. Continue baking for ½ hour.

5. Meanwhile, combine the onions, turnips, carrots and celery to be used for the garnish in a kettle of cold water to cover and salt to taste. Bring to the boil. Simmer for about 2 minutes and drain.

6. Heat the butter in a large kettle and cook the sautéed veg-

398

etables and mushrooms, swirling the skillet and stirring the vegetables, for about 5 minutes, or until they start to take on a golden color.

7. Remove the meat from the oven and cool the meat briefly. Pour off the cooking liquid and strain through a sieve, pressing the vegetables with the back of a wooden spoon to extract as much of the juices as possible.

8. Remove the string from the meat and return the meat to the casserole. Add the vegetables and the strained sauce. Cover and return to the oven. Bake for 30 minutes longer.

Yield: 6 servings.

1 cup fresh or canned beef broth
1 bay leaf
3 sprigs fresh thyme, or ½ teaspoon dried
4 sprigs fresh parsley
2 whole cloves

The vegetable garnish:

10 or 12 small white onions, about ½ pound, peeled
2 or 3 white turnips, about ½ pound, peeled and quartered
3 carrots, about ½ pound, trimmed, scraped, halved and cut into 2-inch lengths
2 ribs celery, trimmed, quartered lengthwise and cut into 2-inch lengths
1 tablespoon butter
¼ pound fresh mushrooms, halved, quartered or left whole, depending on size

Beef Stew

1. Cut the meat into 2-inch cubes.

2. Using a large skillet, heat the oil and add the beef cubes. Add salt and pepper and cook, stirring and turning the pieces often, for about 10 minutes.

3. Add the garlic and onion and cook, stirring occasionally, for about 10 minutes. Sprinkle with flour and stir to coat meat evenly.

4. Add the wine and stir until mixture boils and thickens. Stir in the water. Add the cloves, bay leaf, thyme and parsley. Cover closely and simmer for 1 hour.

5. Meanwhile, cut the carrots into 1-inch lengths. If the pieces are very large, cut them in half lengthwise. Add them to the beef. Cover and continue cooking for 30 minutes, or until the carrots are tender. Serve sprinkled with chopped parsley.

Yield: 8 or more servings.

4 pounds lean, boneless chuck steak
¼ cup olive oil
Salt and freshly ground pepper to taste
1 tablespoon finely chopped garlic
2 cups coarsely chopped onion
6 tablespoons flour
4 cups dry red wine
2 cups water
4 whole cloves
1 bay leaf
½ teaspoon thyme
6 sprigs parsley, tied in a bundle
6 large carrots, about 1½ pounds, trimmed and scraped

Carbonnade Flamande *(Beef cooked in beer)*

3 pounds boneless chuck in one piece
¼ pound lean bacon
3 large onions, about 1½ pounds
3 tablespoons butter
3 cloves garlic, finely chopped
  Salt and freshly ground pepper to taste
2 sprigs fresh thyme, or ½ teaspoon dried
2 bay leaves
1 tablespoon brown sugar
2 cups light beer
1 cup fresh or canned beef broth
3 slices French bread, crusts removed
3 tablespoons imported mustard, such as Dijon or Düsseldorf
2 tablespoons red wine vinegar

1. Preheat the oven to 325 degrees.

2. Place the meat on a flat surface. Cut it into slices about ¾ inch thick. Cut the slices into strips about 2 inches wide. Cut the strips into 2-inch lengths. Set aside.

3. Cut the bacon into small pieces. Cook the pieces in a large skillet until lightly browned and crisp. Using a perforated spoon, transfer the pieces to a large, heavy casserole, leaving the fat in the skillet.

4. Peel and quarter the onions. Cut each quarter into thin slices. There should be about 7 cups. Set aside.

5. Add the butter to the fat in the skillet. Add one-quarter of the cubed meat and cook over high heat, turning the pieces so that they cook evenly. As the meat browns, transfer the pieces to the casserole. Add more meat and continue cooking until all the meat is browned and added to the casserole.

6. Add the onions to the skillet and cook, stirring occasionally, until lightly browned. Add the onions to the meat.

7. Add the garlic, salt, pepper, thyme, bay leaves, sugar, beer and broth.

8. Spread the bread on both sides with the mustard. Place the slices on top of the stew. Cover closely. Bring to the boil. Place in the oven and bake for 1½ to 2 hours. Cooking time will depend on the tenderness of the meat.

9. Stir the vinegar into the sauce and place on top of the stove. Simmer for about 2 minutes. Pour the stew into a sieve and strain the sauce into a saucepan. Skim off the fat and bring back to the boil. Arrange the meat on a warm serving platter and spoon the sauce over the meat.

Yield: 6 servings.

California Casserole

1 pound ground round steak
1 tablespoon peanut oil
1 clove garlic, finely minced
  Salt and freshly ground pepper
1 large onion, finely chopped
1 green pepper, cored, seeded and chopped

1. Preheat the oven to 350 degrees.

2. Cook the meat in oil until it loses its red color. Add the garlic, salt, pepper, onion, green pepper and chili powder. Cook for 5 minutes, or until onion is wilted.

3. Add Worcestershire, Tabasco, tomatoes, kidney beans and rice and turn into a buttered 2-quart casserole. Bake, uncovered, for 45 minutes.

4. Sprinkle with olives and cheese and bake for 15 minutes longer, or until cheese is melted.
Yield: 8 servings.

1 tablespoon chili powder
1 tablespoon Worcestershire sauce
  Tabasco sauce to taste
1 1-pound can Italian plum tomatoes
1 1-pound can kidney beans
¾ cup rice
¼ cup chopped stuffed green olives
¾ cup shredded Cheddar cheese

Beef, Eggplant and Noodle Casserole

1. Trim off and discard the ends of the eggplant. Peel the eggplant and cut it into ¾-inch cubes. There should be about 6 cups. Toss with a teaspoon of salt and set aside.

2. Heat a skillet. Do not add oil. Add the meat and stir, chopping down with the side of a heavy kitchen spoon to break up lumps. Add the onion, garlic, cinnamon and bay leaf and continue cooking, breaking up any lumps. The meat will give up a good deal of liquid. Continue cooking until most of this liquid evaporates. Add the eggplant and stir to blend. Cook for about 5 minutes and add the tomatoes and hot pepper, salt and pepper to taste.

3. Cook for about 30 minutes, stirring often.

4. As the meat cooks, heat the butter in a saucepan and add the flour, stirring with a wire whisk. When blended, add the milk, stirring rapidly with the whisk. When thickened and smooth, add salt and pepper to taste.

5. Blend the cornstarch and water and stir it into the simmering sauce. Cook for about 1 minute. Remove the sauce from the heat and add the yolks, stirring rapidly with the whisk. Cook, stirring briskly, for about 1 minute. Remove from the heat.

6. Cook the noodles in boiling salted water until tender. Drain and add them to the meat sauce.

7. Meanwhile, preheat the oven to 400 degrees.

8. Spoon and scrape the meat mixture into a baking dish (a dish measuring about 10- x 16- x 2-inches is good for this). Smooth over the top. Spoon the sauce over all and smooth this over. Sprinkle with cheese and place in the oven. Bake for about 20 minutes, or until piping hot and browned on top.
Yield: 6 to 8 servings.

1 eggplant, about 1¼ pounds
  Salt
2 pounds ground beef, preferably chuck
2 cups finely chopped onion
2 cloves garlic, finely minced
½ teaspoon ground cinnamon
1 bay leaf
2 pounds tomatoes, cored, peeled and chopped, about 4 cups, or use canned Italian plum tomatoes
1 hot dried red pepper, optional
  Freshly ground pepper
3 tablespoons butter
3½ tablespoons flour
2 cups milk
2 teaspoons cornstarch
2 tablespoons water
2 egg yolks
½ pound noodles, fine or medium
¼ cup freshly grated Parmesan cheese

Picadillo *(A meat stew with olives and capers)*

1 cup dried currants
4 tablespoons peanut, vegetable or corn oil
3 cups finely chopped onion
2 to 4 tablespoons finely chopped garlic
3 cups chopped green peppers
1 10-ounce jar stuffed green olives
3 3½-ounce jars capers, drained
½ cup white vinegar
  Salt
1 tablespoon freshly ground pepper
¾ teaspoon cinnamon
1 teaspoon ground cloves
2 bay leaves
  Tabasco sauce
6 pounds ground round or chuck
12 cups peeled, chopped tomatoes
  Freshly cooked rice

1. Place the currants in a bowl and add warm water to cover. Let stand until they "plump," about ½ hour.

2. Meanwhile, heat half the oil in a very large kettle and add the onion, garlic and green peppers. Cook, stirring, until wilted. Add the green olives, capers, vinegar, salt to taste, pepper, cinnamon, cloves, bay leaves and Tabasco sauce to taste. Cook, stirring, for about 10 minutes.

3. In a large casserole or Dutch oven heat the remaining oil and add the meat. Cook, stirring with the side of a metal kitchen spoon to break up all lumps. Cook only until the meat loses its red color.

4. Add the green olive mixture and stir to blend.

5. Drain the currants and add them.

6. Add the tomatoes and cook, stirring often, for about 1 hour. Skim off the fat as it rises to the surface. Serve hot with rice.

Yield: 18 or more servings.

Macaroni and Beef Casserole

1½ cups elbow macaroni
3½ tablespoons butter
¾ cup chopped onion
¼ cup finely chopped green pepper
1 pound chopped ground chuck or round
1 teaspoon basil
1 teaspoon oregano
½ cup drained tomatoes
3 tablespoons flour
2 cups milk
2 cups (about 10 ounces) cubed Cheddar cheese
  Salt and freshly ground pepper

1. Preheat the oven to 450 degrees.

2. Drop the macaroni into boiling salted water and simmer until macaroni is barely tender. Do not overcook because the dish will bake later in the oven. Drain in a colander and place under cold running water.

3. In a skillet, heat 1½ tablespoons butter and add the onion and green pepper. Cook, stirring, until onion is wilted. Add meat. Cook, stirring, until meat loses its red color. If there is an accumulation of liquid fat in the skillet, drain well in a large sieve. Return the meat mixture to the skillet. Add the basil, oregano and tomatoes. Cook for 3 minutes.

4. In a saucepan, heat the remaining 2 tablespoons of butter and stir in the flour, using a wire whisk. Add the milk, stirring rapidly with the whisk. Cook, stirring, for about 5 minutes. Remove the sauce from the heat and stir in the Cheddar

cheese. Stir until it melts. Add salt and pepper to taste, nutmeg and cayenne.

5. Spoon the macaroni into a baking dish. Ours measured 7- x 10- x 2½-inches. Spoon the meat mixture over the macaroni and pour the cheese sauce over all. Sprinkle with Parmesan cheese and bake for 30 minutes, or until hot and bubbling throughout. Run under the broiler briefly to glaze.

Yield: 4 to 6 servings.

¼	teaspoon grated nutmeg
	Cayenne pepper to taste
	Grated Parmesan cheese

Queue de Boeuf Forestière *(Oxtail ragout with mushrooms)*

1. Preheat the oven to 375 degrees.

2. The oxtail pieces should be well trimmed, leaving only a light layer of fat all around each piece. Sprinkle with salt and pepper. Use one or two large, heavy skillets and add the oxtail pieces, fat side down. It is not necessary to add additional fat. Brown the pieces well on all sides, turning the pieces often, for 40 to 45 minutes.

3. Transfer the pieces to a large, deep casserole or Dutch oven and continue cooking, without adding liquid or fat, for about 10 minutes longer, stirring and turning the pieces in the casserole. Pour off any fat that accumulates.

4. Add the onion, celery, garlic, thyme and bay leaf and stir to distribute the ingredients. Sprinkle the flour evenly over the surface and stir to coat the ingredients. Add the wine, water, beef broth, tomatoes, salt, pepper, cloves and parsley.

5. Cover and bring to the boil on top of the stove. Place the casserole in the oven and bake for 2 hours.

6. Meanwhile, trim and scrape the carrots. Quarter the carrots lengthwise and cut the pieces into 1½-inch lengths. There should be about 4 cups. Drop the carrots into boiling salted water to cover and cook for about 5 minutes. Drain and set aside.

7. If the mushrooms are large, quarter or slice them. Heat the butter in a skillet and add the mushrooms with salt and pepper to taste. Cook, stirring, for about 5 minutes. Set aside.

8. When the oxtail is tender, remove the pieces to a large bowl. Add the carrots and mushrooms. Put the sauce in which the oxtails cooked through a fine sieve, pushing the solids through as much as possible. Return the sauce to the casserole, add the oxtails and vegetables and cook briefly until piping hot.

Yield: 8 to 12 servings.

6	pounds oxtail, cut into pieces
	Salt and freshly ground pepper to taste
2	cups coarsely chopped onion
2	cups coarsely chopped celery with leaves
2	cloves garlic, finely minced
1	teaspoon dried thyme
1	bay leaf
6	tablespoons flour
1	bottle (3 cups) dry red burgundy
2	cups water
3	cups fresh or canned beef broth
1	cup whole tomatoes, peeled and crushed
4	whole cloves
6	sprigs fresh parsley
10 or	12 whole carrots, about 1¼ pounds
1	pound mushrooms, preferably button mushrooms
2	tablespoons butter

India House Lamb Curry

6 pounds lean, boneless shoulder of lamb, cut into 1½-inch cubes
½ cup peanut, vegetable or corn oil, approximately
¾ pound carrots, scraped, quartered and thinly sliced, about 2 cups
5 celery ribs without leaves, coarsely chopped, about 2 cups
½ pound onions, coarsely chopped, about 2 cups
2 large, tart apples, about ½ pound, peeled, cored and cut into ½-inch cubes, about 4 cups
½ cup canned sweetened, shredded, dried coconut
1 tablespoon finely chopped garlic
4 bay leaves
1 teaspoon dried thyme
8 tablespoons curry powder, more or less to taste
½ cup flour
7 tablespoons tomato paste
8 cups fresh or canned chicken broth
1 cup chutney
1 cup heavy cream

1. Preheat the oven to 400 degrees.

2. Use two skillets for this, one to brown the meat in batches, the other to receive the meat after the cubes are browned.

3. Pour about ¼ cup of oil into the first skillet to brown the meat. Add about one-quarter of the cubed meat and cook to brown on all sides. When browned, transfer the pieces to the second skillet. Continue cooking in the second skillet. Add a second batch of meat, cook to brown and so on until all the pieces are browned. Add more oil as necessary to the first skillet.

4. When all the pieces are browned, add any remaining oil, or 2 tablespoons, to the first skillet. Add the carrots, celery and onions and cook, stirring occasionally.

5. As the vegetables cook in the first skillet, add the cubed apples and coconut to the meat. Add the cooked vegetables, garlic, bay leaves, thyme, curry powder, flour and tomato paste to the meat. Stir to blend well. Add the chicken broth and stir to blend. Add the chutney. Bring to the boil. Cover and place in the oven.

6. Bake for 1 hour. Transfer the pieces of lamb to a casserole.

7. Put the sauce, a little at a time, into the container of a food processor or blender and blend to a fine purée. As the sauce is processed and smooth, add it to the lamb pieces. Bring to the boil and add the cream. Bring to the boil again and serve hot.

Yield: 12 to 16 servings.

Lamb with Sour Cream and Dill

3½ pounds lamb, cut into 1½-inch cubes
Salt and freshly ground pepper to taste
1 tablespoon butter
1 cup finely chopped onion
1 clove garlic, finely minced
1 cup dry white wine

1. Sprinkle the lamb with salt and pepper. Heat the butter in a large kettle and cook the lamb, stirring, until it loses its red color. It will give up considerable liquid.

2. Add the onion and garlic and cook briefly. Add the wine and broth. Cut off the tops of the dill but reserve both the leaves and stems. Tie the stems in a small bundle and add to the lamb. Set the leaves aside.

3. Cover and cook for about 1¼ hours, or until the lamb is tender. Add the heavy cream. Stir in the sour cream and dill leaves. Remove the lamb with a slotted spoon. Cook down the sauce for about 10 minutes. Strain the sauce through a fine sieve.

4. Meanwhile, put the mushrooms in a saucepan and add the lemon juice. Add salt and pepper to taste. Cover and cook for about 5 minutes.

5. Cook the peas in boiling salted water until tender.

6. Return the lamb to the sauce. Add the mushrooms and peas. Reheat and serve with rice.

Yield: 6 to 8 servings.

2	cups fresh or canned chicken broth
1	bunch fresh dill, or 1 tablespoon dill weed
1	cup heavy cream
¼	cup sour cream
½	pound mushrooms, left whole if small, otherwise quartered or sliced
	Juice of ½ lemon
1½	cups freshly shelled peas, or 1 10-ounce package frozen

Navarin d'Agneau   *(A ragout of lamb)*

1. Sprinkle the meat with salt and pepper and set aside.

2. Trim the carrots, celery, turnips and potatoes, peeling as necessary. Quarter the carrots and cut them into 1½-inch lengths. Cut the celery into pieces of the same size. Cut the turnips into ½-inch slices. Cut the slices into pieces the same size as the carrots.

3. Cut the potatoes into ½-inch slices. Cut the slices into "sticks" the size of french fried potatoes. Drop into cold water.

4. Heat a skillet large enough to hold the meat in one layer. Do not add fat. The meat has enough fat. Add the cubes of meat and cook to brown well on all sides, turning as necessary as the pieces give up fat. The browning will take from 10 to 15 minutes.

5. Transfer the pieces of meat to a heavy casserole and heat briefly, stirring.

6. Pour off the fat from the kettle in which the meat was browned. Add 1 cup of water and stir to dissolve the brown particles that may cling to the bottom and sides of the kettle. Set aside.

7. Add the onion and garlic to the meat and stir. Add the wine and cook briefly. Add the skillet liquid. Add the remaining cup of water, tomato paste, bay leaf and thyme. Bring to the boil and cook for 1 hour.

8. Meanwhile, cover the carrots, celery and turnips with cold water and bring to the boil. Drain and set aside.

9. Drain the potatoes. Put them in a saucepan, cover with cold water and bring to the boil. Drain.

2¼	pounds lean shoulder of lamb, cut into 2-inch cubes and including a few rib bones
	Salt and freshly ground pepper to taste
2	carrots
2	ribs celery
1 or 2	white turnips
2	potatoes
2	cups water
½	cup chopped onion
1	clove garlic, finely minced
½	cup dry white wine
2	tablespoons tomato paste
1	bay leaf
2	sprigs fresh thyme, or ½ teaspoon dried
½	cup frozen peas (reserve the remaining peas for another use)

10. When the stew has cooked for 1 hour add the carrots, celery and turnips. Cook for 20 minutes. Add the potatoes and cook for 5 minutes longer. Add the peas and continue to cook for 5 minutes, or until the potatoes are tender.

Yield: 6 to 8 servings.

Lamb Stew Marocaine

4 pounds lamb, cut into 2-inch cubes
  Salt and freshly ground pepper to taste
1 large onion, peeled and cut into 1-inch cubes, about 2 cups
2 zucchini, trimmed and cut into 1-inch cubes, about 3 cups
1 eggplant, trimmed, peeled and cut into 1½-inch cubes, about 4 cups
1 small hot dried red pepper
1 teaspoon ground cumin
1 teaspoon crushed coriander seeds
2 cups canned tomatoes with tomato paste
3 cups water

1. Heat a large heavy skillet or wide casserole until very hot. Do not add fat. Add the lamb and cook over high heat, stirring the pieces to prevent sticking. Cook for about 10 minutes, stirring often, until meat is nicely browned.

2. Transfer the meat to another dish. Add the onion to the skillet. Cook for about 5 minutes, stirring. Add the zucchini, eggplant, hot pepper, salt and pepper. Cook, stirring, for about 2 minutes.

3. Return the meat to the skillet and stir. Add the cumin, coriander, tomatoes, water, salt and pepper to taste. Cover closely and cook over low heat for about 1 hour.

4. Uncover and cook for about 5 minutes longer to reduce the sauce a bit.

Yield: 6 or more servings.

Haricot d'Agneau   *(Lamb stew with beans)*

1 pound small white dried beans, preferably California small white beans or Minnesota pea beans
2¼ pounds lean shoulder of lamb, cut into 2-inch cubes and including a few rib bones
  Salt and freshly ground pepper to taste
¾ cup chopped onion
2 cloves garlic, finely minced
1 14-ounce can tomatoes with tomato paste

1. Soak the beans overnight in cold water to cover to a depth of 2 inches.

2. Sprinkle the lamb with salt and pepper. Heat a skillet large enough to hold the meat in one layer. Do not add fat. The meat has enough fat. Add the cubes of meat and cook to brown well on all sides, turning as necessary as the pieces give up fat. The browning will take from 10 to 15 minutes.

3. Transfer the pieces of meat to a heavy casserole and sprinkle with onion and garlic. Cook briefly. Add the tomatoes, 2 cups water, thyme, 1 bay leaf, salt and pepper. Cover and cook for about 1½ hours.

4. Pick over the beans to remove any foreign material. Put the beans in a saucepan and add 8 cups water, half a bay leaf,

onion stuck with cloves and whole carrot. Bring to the boil and simmer 1 to 1½ hours, skimming the surface as necessary. Test for doneness.

5. When the lamb is tender and cooked, drain the beans and remove the bay leaf and thyme sprigs. Remove carrot and cut it into ½-inch dice. Add the beans and carrot to the lamb stew. Cover and cook for 10 minutes.

Yield: 8 servings.

2   sprigs fresh thyme, or ½ teaspoon dried thyme
1½ bay leaves
1   small onion stuck with 2 cloves
1   large carrot, trimmed and scraped

Shepherd's Pie

1. Prepare the lamb and set it aside.
2. Heat 1 tablespoon butter in a casserole and add the onion, garlic and thyme. Cook briefly until onion wilts. Add the meat and bay leaf. Cook, stirring to break up lumps in the meat. Add salt and pepper to taste and sprinkle with flour. Add the tomatoes and water, stirring. Cover and cook for 30 minutes. Add the parsley.
3. Meanwhile, peel the potatoes. Cut them into quarters and put them in a saucepan. Cover with cold water and salt to taste. Bring to the boil and simmer until tender, for about 20 minutes.
4. Drain the potatoes and put them through a food mill. Bring the milk to the boil. Add the milk to the potatoes and beat in the remaining butter.
5. Spoon the lamb stew into a baking dish (a dish measuring about 8½- × 13½- × 2-inches is a suitable size). Top with the mashed potatoes and smooth them over. Sprinkle with cheese.
6. When ready to cook, preheat the oven to 400 degrees.
7. Bake for 20 minutes. Run under the broiler to glaze. Serve hot.

Yield: 6 to 8 servings.

2½ pounds raw or cooked ground lamb
3   tablespoons butter
2   cups chopped onion
2   teaspoons finely chopped garlic
½   teaspoon thyme
1   bay leaf
    Salt and freshly ground pepper
2   tablespoons flour
1   cup crushed tomatoes
½   cup water
¼   cup finely chopped parsley
2   pounds potatoes
2   cups milk
½   cup grated Gruyère or Swiss cheese

Couscous

People of taste who dote on Moroccan cooking tend to find it among the most sensual foods on earth. It is without question one of the world's great cuisines. A steaming platter of perfectly prepared couscous, to our palate, is about as close as one need come to feasting on heavenly manna.

The name involves two things. Couscous is a fine, blond-colored cereal that resembles grain. It is also the finished dish in which these grains are cooked and served with a sweet and savory meat sauce. This version, with lamb and pumpkin, is from Paula Wolfert, who lived for ten years in North Africa and has written extensively on Moroccan cuisine.

2¾ pounds meaty but bony parts of lamb, such as neck or shoulder, but preferably the shank, cut into 2-inch pieces with bone

10 medium-size onions, about 2½ pounds

1½ tablespoons salt

4 quarts cold water

4 teaspoons finely ground black pepper

2 teaspoons ground dried ginger

¼ teaspoon ground saffron

½ pound butter

3 pounds medium-grain couscous

3 teaspoons olive oil, approximately

1 3-pound whole, fresh pumpkin, or use acorn squash

2 pounds carrots

1 pound seedless raisins

1 can (2 cups) chick-peas

½ cup sugar

¼ pound butter at room temperature

1. Put the lamb in a kettle, preferably into the bottom of a couscousière (couscous cooker).

2. Peel the onions and cut them in half lengthwise. Place each half cut side down and cut them into slices about ½ inch thick. There should be 7 or 8 cups. Add the onions to the kettle. Add the salt, water, black pepper, ginger and saffron. Cook and bring to the boil. Cook for 45 minutes.

3. Meanwhile, put the couscous in a large bowl and add cold water to cover, stirring constantly with the hands to prevent the grains from sticking and to thoroughly moisten all the grains. Immediately pour the couscous into the top steamer of the couscousière, or into a colander that will fit closely inside a kettle, and let drain. Some of the grains may fall through. Empty the grains into a very large, open bowl. Let dry for about 10 minutes.

4. The grains will cake together. Using the fingers, break up the grains, working well to break up all lumps so that all the grains are totally separate.

5. Remove the cover from the stew. Add the steamer to the top of the couscousière. When the steam starts to rise in the holes of the steamer, add about one-fourth of the couscous grains. When the steam is again apparent, add the remaining couscous. Cook for 15 minutes.

6. Remove the steamer from the stew and transfer the couscous once more to the large bowl.

7. Blend 1 cup of cold water and salt to taste. Spoon this over the couscous and, using a large metal spoon, toss the grains and spread them out so that the grains will cool quickly. Let stand for ½ hour.

8. Grease the hands with oil and toss the grains, breaking up any lumps. Do this three times, oiling the hands each time before working the grains.

9. Return the couscous to the steamer and replace it over the stew. Let steam for 30 minutes. Remove the couscous again, and, using the back of the spoon, spread out once more in the large bowl. Let dry once more.

10. Cut the pumpkin into eighths. Peel it. Scrape away and discard the seeds. Cut the pumpkin flesh into 3-inch pieces. There should be about 8 cups.

11. Trim and scrape the carrots. Depending on size, cut the carrots into 2-inch lengths, or split in half and cut into

pieces about 2 inches long. There should be about 6 cups.

12. At this point the stew may be taken off the stove and set aside for several hours until ready for a final cooking. Cover the couscous with damp paper towels.

13. When ready for the final cooking, add the pumpkin, carrots, raisins, chick-peas and sugar to the stew. Add more salt and pepper to taste. Bring to the boil and cook for 10 minutes. Put the steamer on the kettle. Add the couscous. Steam for 20 minutes.

14. Distribute the butter over the top of the couscous and let it melt down.

15. Pour and spoon the couscous out into a large (very large) round or oval platter. Make a well in the center and spoon about one-third of the stew in the center. Spoon some of the outside couscous onto the stew. Add more couscous. More stew. Spoon up more couscous. More stew and so on.

16. Serve with any leftover stew on the side (there will be quite a bit).

Yield: 12 or more servings.

Pork and Green Chili Stew

1. Sprinkle the pork with salt and pepper.

2. Heat the lard in a large, heavy skillet in which the cubed pork will fit in one layer. When the fat is very hot, add the pork and cook, stirring the pieces often, over very high heat. Cook until browned on all sides.

3. Add the onion and garlic and cook, stirring, until the onion is wilted. Sprinkle with oregano and stir.

4. Drain the tomatoes. Blend with the chilies in a food processor or electric blender. Add this to the stew. Add the chopped coriander leaves.

5. Add salt and pepper to taste. Add the broth and bring to the boil. Cover and cook for 1¼ hours, or until the pork is fork-tender.

6. Garnish with sprigs of fresh coriander. Serve with sour cream on the side.

Yield: 8 or more servings.

3 pounds lean pork, cut into 2-inch cubes
Salt and freshly ground pepper to taste

2 tablespoons lard or vegetable oil

2 cups finely chopped onion

1 tablespoon finely chopped garlic

1 tablespoon crumbled dried oregano

2 15¼-ounce cans tomatoes verdes (green tomatoes), available in Spanish markets

1 4-ounce can chopped green chilies, available in Spanish markets

2 tablespoons finely chopped fresh coriander leaves plus whole coriander leaves for garnish

2 cups fresh or canned chicken broth
Sour cream

Pork and Potato Stew

4 links sweet or hot Italian
    sausage
2 pounds pork neck bones (see
    note), cut into 3- or 4-inch
    pieces
2 shoulder pork chops, each cut
    into thirds
1 1-pound 1-ounce can whole
    tomatoes, preferably Italian
    peeled tomatoes
1 cup water
4 carrots, thinly sliced
    Salt and freshly ground
    pepper
5 potatoes, about 1½ pounds,
    peeled and cut into 1½-inch
    cubes
2 onions, about ½ pound,
    thinly sliced
½ teaspoon dried basil
½ teaspoon dried oregano

1. Cook the sausages in a heavy casserole or Dutch oven. When they start to give up their fat, add the neck bones and pork chops. Cook, stirring and turning, to brown well.

2. Add the tomatoes, water, carrots, salt and pepper to taste and cook for 45 minutes. Add the remaining ingredients and cook for another 45 minutes, or until all the meats are tender.

Yield: 4 to 6 servings.

Note: Pork chops, boneless pork, or spareribs, all cut into 2- or 3-inch cubes, may be substituted for the neck bones.

Jambalaya

¼ pound salt pork, cut into
    small cubes
¾ pound chorizos or hot Italian
    sausages
4 cups finely chopped onion
3 cups finely chopped celery
3 tablespoons finely minced
    garlic
4 cups chopped sweet green
    peppers
1 cup chopped sweet red
    peppers, or use an additional
    cup of chopped green
    peppers
3 pounds porkette, available
    in supermarkets, or a cooked
    ham in one thick slice
3 bay leaves

1. Using a large kettle or Dutch oven, cook the salt pork cubes, stirring often, until rendered of fat.

2. Cut the sausages into ½-inch-thick slices and add them. Cook for about 8 minutes, stirring occasionally, and add the onion. Cook, stirring often, until wilted and add the celery, garlic, green pepper and red pepper.

3. Cut the porkette or ham into 1-inch cubes and add it. Add the bay leaves, thyme, tomatoes, parsley, salt, pepper and Tabasco sauce to taste. Continue cooking. Drain the oysters and add their liquor. Set the oysters aside.

4. Add half the fish broth and half the water. Cook, stirring once or twice from the bottom, for about 10 minutes.

5. Add the rice and stir gently. Cover and cook for about 15 minutes. If necessary, add a little more broth and water to prevent sticking.

6. Add the remaining broth and water, the shrimp, scallops

and oysters. Cook, stirring often from the bottom, for 15 to 20 minutes. If necessary, add more liquid to prevent scorching and drying out.

7. Serve with a bottle of Tabasco sauce on the side.

Yield: 24 or more servings.

3 sprigs fresh thyme, or 1 teaspoon dried

1 35-ounce can tomatoes, preferably Italian plum tomatoes

1 cup finely chopped parsley
Salt and freshly ground pepper
Tabasco sauce

1 quart oysters with their liquor

4 cups, approximately, fish broth, or use fresh or canned clam juice

4 cups water

3 cups raw rice

5 pounds fresh shrimp, shelled and deveined

1½ pounds fresh bay scallops

Choucroute Garnie

1. Drain the sauerkraut and press to extract most of the liquid. If you wish a milder dish, run cold water over it and drain again, pressing. Set aside.

2. Heat the lard in a large, heavy skillet.

3. Sprinkle the spareribs with salt and pepper. Add them to the lard and brown on all sides. Scatter the onion and garlic between the ribs and cook briefly, stirring.

4. Put the sauerkraut over and around the ribs. Pour the broth and wine over all. Place the pork butt in the center of the sauerkraut.

5. Add the cloves, juniper berries or gin, caraway seeds, bay leaf, salt and pepper. Bring to the boil and cover. Cook for about 30 minutes and add the potatoes. Cover again and cook for 15 minutes longer.

6. Add the kielbasa and cover again. Cook for 15 minutes longer, or until sausage is piping hot throughout.

Yield: 6 to 8 servings.

4 pounds sauerkraut

2 tablespoons lard, bacon fat or vegetable oil

2 pounds country-style spareribs
Salt and freshly ground pepper to taste

1 cup finely chopped onion

1 clove garlic, finely minced

2 cups fresh or canned chicken broth

1 cup dry white wine

2 whole cloves

2 pounds smoked pork butt

8 juniper berries, or ½ cup dry gin

½ teaspoon caraway seeds

1 bay leaf

12 small white potatoes, scrubbed and peeled

1¼ pounds kielbasa (Polish sausage)

Cassoulet

2 pounds dried pea beans marked "no soaking necessary"
3 quarts water
1 onion stuck with 4 cloves
1 bay leaf
1 carrot, trimmed and scraped
  Salt and freshly ground pepper
¾ pound slab of lean salt pork with rind
1 garlic sausage (cotechine)
3 tablespoons goose fat or peanut oil
1 tablespoon finely chopped garlic
2 cups chopped onion
1 2-pound 3-ounce can tomatoes
  Lamb stew (see recipe below)
½ preserved goose in its fat (see recipe page 307)
  Roast pork (see recipe below)
3 tablespoons bread crumbs made from toasted bread
4 tablespoons melted butter

1. Pick over the beans and wash them well. Place the beans in a kettle with the water, onion, bay leaf, carrot, salt, pepper and salt pork. Prick the garlic sausage in several places with a 2-pronged fork and add it. Bring to the boil and simmer for 30 minutes.

2. Remove the garlic sausage and set aside. Continue cooking the beans for 30 minutes and remove the salt pork.

3. Slice off and reserve the salt pork rind. Cut the rind into ¼-inch dice and set aside. Return the salt pork meat to the kettle.

4. Heat the goose fat in a saucepan and add the diced pork rind. Add the garlic and chopped onion. Cook for about 10 minutes without browning. Add the tomatoes and let simmer, stirring often, for about ½ hour.

5. When the beans are tender, drain them but reserve the beans, salt pork and cooking liquid. Discard the whole onion and bay leaf. Put the beans in a kettle and add the tomato sauce and the lamb stew, including both meat and sauce. Stir to blend and add salt and pepper to taste. Cover and simmer for about 10 minutes.

6. Cut the salt pork into neat, ¼-inch-thick slices and set aside.

7. Skin the garlic sausage and cut into neat, ¼-inch-thick slices and set aside.

8. Heat the goose, including the gizzard and wing if they are present. Remove the pieces and cut or pull the meat from the bones. Slice the meat as neatly as possible.

9. Cut the pork from the bones and slice it neatly. Save the pan juices from the roasting pan. Pour off the fat.

10. Spoon about a third of the beans into a large casserole and arrange the pork slices over all. Add the pan juices.

11. Add a cup of the bean liquid to the remaining beans. Spoon half the remaining beans over the pork. Arrange the sliced preserved goose over all. Add all the remaining beans. Arrange the sliced salt pork and garlic sausage over the top. Scatter the bread crumbs over the top and dribble the butter over.

12. When ready to cook, preheat the oven to 400 degrees and bake for 30 minutes. If the casserole seems too dry, add a little more bean liquid as the cassoulet cooks. When ready to serve, the cassoulet should be piping hot and bubbling throughout.

Yield: 12 or more servings.

1. Use a heavy skillet and brown the lamb on all sides in the oil. Sprinkle with salt and pepper to taste and add the onion and garlic. Stir to blend. Carefully pour off all fat.

2. Return the skillet to the heat and add the remaining ingredients.

3. Cover closely and cook for 1 hour and 15 minutes, or until the lamb is fork-tender.

Yield: 6 to 8 servings, or enough for one large cassoulet.

Lamb stew

3 pounds shoulder of lamb with bone, cut into 2-inch cubes
2 tablespoons oil or goose fat
   Salt and freshly ground pepper
1 cup finely chopped onion
2 cloves garlic, finely minced
1 cup dry white wine
2 cups water
3 tablespoons tomato paste
1 sprig fresh thyme, or 1 teaspoon dried
4 sprigs parsley
½ bay leaf

1. Preheat the oven to 425 degrees.

2. Sprinkle the pork all over with salt and pepper. Place the pork, fat side down, in a baking dish and bake for about 20 minutes. Turn the pork and continue cooking for about 20 minutes. If it starts to brown too quickly, cover loosely with a sheet of aluminum foil. Continue baking for about 20 minutes, or until thoroughly cooked and tender.

Yield: 4 servings, or enough for one large cassoulet.

Roast pork

1 3-pound center-cut pork loin
   Salt and freshly ground pepper

Baked Mushrooms, Noodles and Ham Mornay

1. Preheat the oven to 450 degrees.

2. Heat 2 tablespoons of butter in a saucepan and add the flour, stirring with a wire whisk. When blended, add the milk, stirring rapidly with the whisk.

3. Add salt and pepper to taste, nutmeg, cayenne and the Cheddar, stirring until the cheese melts. Add the cream and bring to the boil. Remove from the heat.

4. Melt the remaining 1 tablespoon of butter in a skillet and add the onion, stirring. When wilted, add the mushrooms and cook until wilted. Add the ham and heat through.

5. Meanwhile, cook the noodles according to package directions until tender. Take care not to overcook, for they will cook briefly later.

6. Add the cheese sauce to the ham mixture and add the wine. Bring to the boil. Drain the noodles well and add them to the mixture. Stir gently to blend.

3 tablespoons butter
3 tablespoons flour
3 cups milk
   Salt and freshly ground pepper
⅛ teaspoon ground nutmeg
⅛ teaspoon cayenne pepper
½ pound grated Cheddar cheese
1 cup heavy cream
¼ cup finely chopped onion
¼ pound mushrooms, cut into small cubes, about 2 cups
½ pound cooked ham, cut into ½-inch cubes, about 1¾ cups
¾ pound broad noodles
2 tablespoons port wine
¼ cup grated Parmesan cheese

7. Put the mixture into a baking dish (an oval dish measuring about 8- x 14-inches is appropriate). Sprinkle with the grated Parmesan. Bake for 5 to 10 minutes. Run briefly under the broiler until nicely glazed.
Yield: 6 to 8 servings.

Blanquette de Veau

Blanquettes and fricassees are stews that are enriched with cream and egg yolks. The word blanquette derives from blanchir, which in French means to cook without browning. With a fricassee, from fricasser, which means to cut up and fry, on the other hand, the meat is cooked until it starts to brown.

One of the most unusual blanquettes we've ever sampled came to us from Aline Landais, a young Frenchwoman living in America. It is made with veal and cauliflower, a distinctive combination that we have tried on several occasions and each time the result has been uncommonly appealing.

5	pounds boneless shoulder of veal, cut into 1½- or 2-inch cubes
7	cups fresh or canned chicken broth, approximately
1	medium onion stuck with 4 cloves
2	whole cloves garlic, unpeeled
1	bay leaf
	Salt
½	teaspoon freshly grated nutmeg
1	teaspoon peppercorns
½	teaspoon dried thyme
1	medium-size head of cauliflower
16 to	24 small white onions, the smaller the better, peeled
1	cup celery, cut into small sticks measuring about ½ inch thick and 1½ inches long
½	pound fresh mushrooms, left whole if small, or cut into halves or quarters if large

1. Preheat the oven to 350 degrees.

2. Place the meat in a kettle and add cold water to cover. Bring to the boil. When the water boils vigorously, drain the meat and run under cold running water until thoroughly chilled.

3. Return the meat to the kettle and add 5 cups of chicken broth. Add the onion stuck with cloves, whole garlic cloves, bay leaf, salt to taste and half the nutmeg. Tie the peppercorns and thyme in a cheesecloth bag and add it. Bring to the boil on top of the stove.

4. Cover and place in the oven. Bake for 1 hour.

5. Meanwhile, cut away and discard the core from the cauliflower. Break the cauliflower into flowerets, each piece about 1¼ inches in diameter. Set aside.

6. Prepare the small onions and celery in separate batches. Prepare the mushrooms and sprinkle with lemon juice to prevent discoloration.

7. Put the cauliflower in a saucepan and add enough of the chicken broth to barely cover. Simmer briefly until tender but still firm to the bite. Drain but reserve the liquid. Similarly, cook the onions and celery in separate batches but always saving and using the same liquid.

8. Put the mushrooms in a saucepan and cover with the same liquid. Bring just to the boil and drain.

9. After the veal has cooked for 1 hour, add the carrot

rounds and celery. Bake for 30 minutes longer, or until meat is tender.

10. Pour the cooking liquid from the kettle into a saucepan. There should be 4 cups. Cook over high heat and reduce the liquid to 3 cups. Add 1 cup of heavy cream. Combine this with the meat, cauliflower, onions, celery and mushrooms. Bring to the boil.

11. Blend the sour cream with the beaten egg yolks. Add the remaining nutmeg, lemon and lime juices and cayenne pepper. Stir this into the liquid around the meat, stirring over gentle heat just until the sauce comes to the boil. Do not boil for more than a few seconds or the sauce will curdle. Remove the cheesecloth bag.

Yield: 8 to 12 servings.

Juice of ½ lemon
1 cup thin carrot rounds
1 cup heavy cream
½ cup sour cream
4 egg yolks, lightly beaten
1 tablespoon lemon juice
1 tablespoon lime juice
⅛ teaspoon cayenne pepper

Fricassee of Veal

1. Cut the breast of veal into 2-inch cubes, chopping through the bone. Or have this done by the butcher. The bone is important.

2. Place the cubed breast of veal and the stewing veal in a large mixing bowl and place under the cold water tap. Let the water run in a trickle for 1 hour. This will whiten the meat. Drain.

3. Heat the butter in a heavy casserole and add the meat. Cook for 5 minutes and sprinkle with salt and pepper to taste. Add the chopped onion, half the nutmeg and the garlic. Tie the thyme, bay leaf, parsley and cloves in a cheesecloth bag and add it. Add the chicken broth, wine and cayenne and cover closely. Bring to the boil and cook 45 minutes.

4. Add the carrots, whole onions and mushrooms and cook for 45 minutes longer.

5. Drain off about 4 cups of the cooking liquid and bring it to the boil. Cook over high heat until reduced almost by half.

6. Blend the cream with the egg yolks, salt and pepper to taste and the remaining nutmeg.

7. Add the reduced hot mixture to the egg and cream mixture, stirring rapidly. Return this to the veal, stirring, but do not boil or it will curdle. Bring just to the boil, however. Remove the cheesecloth bag.

Yield: 10 to 12 servings.

1 4-pound breast of veal
4 pounds stewing veal, cut into 2-inch cubes
4 tablespoons butter
Salt and freshly ground pepper
1 onion, finely chopped
¼ teaspoon nutmeg, or more to taste
1 clove garlic, finely minced
6 sprigs fresh thyme, or 1 teaspoon dried
1 bay leaf
6 sprigs parsley
2 cloves
2 cups fresh or canned chicken broth
1 cup dry white wine
⅛ teaspoon cayenne pepper
3 carrots, scraped, quartered and cut into 2-inch lengths
36 small white onions, the smaller the better, peeled and left whole
¾ pound fresh mushrooms, quartered if large or left whole if small
1 cup heavy cream
6 egg yolks

Veal Stew with Eggplant

3 pounds lean veal, cut into 2-inch cubes
Salt and freshly ground pepper to taste
½ cup peanut, vegetable or corn oil
2 cups onion cut into 1-inch cubes
1 tablespoon finely chopped garlic
¼ cup flour
4 cups eggplant cut into 2-inch cubes
2 cups zucchini cut into 1-inch rounds
3 cups green peppers cut into 1½-inch cubes
3 cups tomatoes cut into 1-inch cubes
1 cup dry white wine
2 cups fresh or canned chicken broth
3 tablespoons tomato paste
1 sprig fresh thyme, or 1 teaspoon dried
1 cup water

1. Sprinkle the veal with salt and pepper.

2. Heat the oil in a large, heavy skillet. It should be large enough to hold the meat in one layer. Brown the meat on all sides, turning the pieces as necessary. This will take 15 or 20 minutes.

3. Add the onion and garlic. Cook briefly, stirring, and sprinkle with flour. Stir so that meat is coated evenly.

4. Add the eggplant, zucchini and green peppers. Stir and add the tomatoes, wine and chicken broth. Add salt and pepper to taste. Stir in the tomato paste, thyme and water. Bring to the boil. Cover and cook for 1 hour and 15 minutes.

Yield: 8 or more servings.

Hungarian Veal Goulash

2 tablespoons lard, corn oil or butter
4 cups halved and sliced onion, about 1 pound
4 pounds boneless veal or pork, cut into 2-inch cubes
1 to 3 tablespoons paprika (see note)
2 tablespoons finely chopped garlic
Salt and freshly ground pepper
2 tablespoons flour
2½ cups fresh or canned chicken broth
1½ cups cored, seeded green

1. Preheat the oven to 350 degrees.

2. Heat the lard in a Dutch oven or deep, heavy saucepan and add the onion. Cook, stirring, until wilted. Add the veal and stir. Cook, stirring often, until the veal loses its red color.

3. Sprinkle with the paprika and stir. Cook for 5 minutes and sprinkle with garlic and salt and pepper to taste. Stir briefly and sprinkle with flour. Stir to coat the pieces of meat and add the chicken broth. Bring to the boil. Cover with a round of wax paper and put the lid on. Place in the oven and bake from 1½ to 2 hours. Cooking time will depend on the quality of the veal. Best-quality veal cooks more rapidly than that of a lesser quality. Pork cooks quickly.

4. Meanwhile, drop the green pepper strips into boiling water and blanch for about 15 seconds. Drain immediately and set aside.

5. Thirty minutes before the stew is fully cooked, sprinkle with the pepper strips. Continue cooking until veal is tender.

6. If desired, add the sour cream. Preferably, it should be beaten with a whisk before adding and stirred in gradually. Serve the stew, if desired, with spaetzli (see recipe below).

Yield: 8 or more servings.

Note: The best Hungarian paprika is available in bulk. It comes in three strengths: sweet, medium and hot. It should be added to taste.

peppers cut into 1-inch strips
1 cup sour cream at room temperature, optional

1. Place the flour in a mixing bowl. Beat the eggs and add them to the flour, stirring with a wire whisk or an electric beater. Gradually add the milk, beating or stirring constantly. Add salt and nutmeg.

2. Bring a large quantity of water to a boil in a kettle and add salt. Pour the spaetzli mixture into a colander and hold the colander over the boiling water. Press the mixture through the holes of the colander with a rubber spatula or large spoon. The spaetzli are done when they float on the top. Drain the noodles and spoon them onto a clean towel or paper towels to dry briefly.

3. Heat the butter in a skillet and, when it is hot, add the spaetzli, tossing and stirring 3 to 5 minutes. Serve hot.

Yield: 4 to 6 servings.

Spaetzli

2 cups sifted flour
3 eggs
⅔ cup milk
Salt
⅛ teaspoon grated nutmeg
2 tablespoons butter

Chicken and Sausage Casserole

1. Place the tomatoes in a saucepan and cook them down until reduced to 2 cups. Taste and, if they seem acid, stir in the sugar.

2. Sprinkle the chicken with salt and pepper. Heat the oil in a skillet and add the chicken pieces skin side down. Prick the sausages with a fork and add them. Cook, turning the ingredients, until browned on all sides, about 15 minutes. Carefully pour off all fat.

3. Scatter the onion, mushrooms, green pepper and garlic between the pieces of chicken and sausages. Sprinkle with oregano.

4. Add the tomatoes, chicken broth and wine and stir to dissolve any brown particles on the bottom of the skillet. Cover closely and cook for 20 minutes.

Yield: 4 to 6 servings.

4 cups peeled Italian plum tomatoes
1 teaspoon sugar, optional
1 2½-pound chicken, cut into serving pieces
Salt and freshly ground pepper to taste
1 tablespoon olive oil
6 sweet or hot Italian sausages, about 1 pound
1 cup coarsely chopped onion
1 cup sliced mushrooms
1 large green pepper, cored, seeded and cut into 1-inch cubes
1 clove garlic, finely minced
1 teaspoon oregano
½ cup chicken broth
½ cup dry white wine

Chicken Lokri *(Chicken and rice Caribbean-style)*

1 3-pound chicken, cut into
   serving pieces
   Salt and freshly ground
   pepper to taste
3 tablespoons lime juice
4 tablespoons butter
1 tablespoon tomato paste
1 teaspoon sugar
¾ cup finely chopped onion
½ cup finely chopped celery
1 teaspoon finely minced garlic
2 teaspoons Worcestershire
   sauce
1 cup chopped fresh or canned
   tomatoes
3 cups fresh or canned chicken
   broth
1 cup rice
1 pound cabbage, cored and
   chopped or finely shredded,
   about 4 cups

1. Put the chicken in a dish and massage with salt, pepper and lime juice.

2. Heat 2 tablespoons butter in a large, heavy skillet and add the chicken, skin side down. As it starts to brown, add the tomato paste and sugar and continue cooking over high heat until lightly browned, about 10 minutes. Turn the pieces as they cook.

3. Add the onion, celery and garlic and cook for about 1 minute. Add the Worcestershire sauce. Stir and cook for about 5 minutes. Add the tomatoes. Cook for about 15 minutes. Add half the broth and stir. At boil, set aside.

4. Meanwhile, combine the rice and remaining chicken broth in a separate saucepan and bring to the boil. Cover and cook for about 15 minutes, or until liquid is absorbed.

5. As the chicken and rice cook, heat the remaining 2 tablespoons butter in a small skillet and add the chopped cabbage. Cook and stir over low heat for about 10 minutes, until cabbage is tender. Take care that it does not burn.

6. Before serving, add the rice and cabbage to the chicken. Stir to blend. Bring to the boil and serve.

Yield: 4 to 6 servings.

Chicken, Broccoli and Noodle Casserole

1 3-pound chicken
   Salt to taste
12 crushed peppercorns
2 ribs celery, quartered
1 small onion, peeled and
   stuck with 2 cloves
3 sprigs fresh parsley
1 carrot, trimmed and
   quartered
8 tablespoons butter
6½ tablespoons flour
2½ cups chicken broth from the
   cooked chicken
1½ cups heavy cream
1 bunch broccoli, about 2¼
   pounds

1. Place the chicken in a kettle and add water to cover, salt, peppercorns, celery, onion, parsley and carrot. Bring to the boil and simmer for 30 minutes, or until chicken is tender but not dry. Set aside. Remove the chicken and cook down the broth to about 3 cups. Strain it.

2. Preheat the oven to 400 degrees.

3. Melt 5 tablespoons of butter in a saucepan and add the flour, stirring with a wire whisk. Add the 2½ cups of broth, stirring rapidly with the whisk. When thickened and smooth, stir in the cream. Cook, stirring often, for about 10 minutes longer.

4. Meanwhile, break the broccoli into flowerets. Drop them into boiling salted water and simmer for about 2 minutes. Drain. Run under cold running water to chill. Drain well.

5. Pull the chicken meat from the bones. Remove and dis-

card the skin. Cut the chicken into bite-size pieces. There should be about 4 cups.

6. Melt 2 tablespoons of butter in a heavy skillet and add the broccoli. Sprinkle with salt, pepper and nutmeg. Cook, tossing and stirring the broccoli, for about 1 minute. Add the chicken. Add 2 cups of the sauce and stir gently to blend.

7. Add the egg yolk to the remaining sauce. Reheat, stirring rapidly and constantly. Cook for about 30 seconds and remove from the heat.

8. Cook the noodles in boiling water with salt to taste. Drain well. Toss with remaining butter, salt and pepper.

9. Arrange the noodles over the bottom of a baking dish (an oval dish measuring about 14- x 8- x 2-inches is good for this). Spoon the chicken and broccoli mixture neatly over the noodles.

10. Spoon the sauce over all and smooth it over. Sprinkle the cheese on top and place in the oven. Bake for 15 minutes until piping hot throughout. If desired, run the dish under the broiler to obtain a richer glaze on top.

Yield: 6 servings.

Freshly ground pepper to taste
⅛ teaspoon nutmeg
1 large or two small egg yolks
¼ pound fine or medium noodles
¼ cup grated Gruyère or Parmesan cheese

Ragout of Chicken Giblets

1. Pick over the giblets. Rinse and drain well.
2. Heat the butter and add the giblets, salt and pepper. Cook for about 10 minutes, stirring occasionally. Add the onion and garlic and cook briefly. Sprinkle with flour and stir in the wine, water, tomato paste, thyme and bay leaf.
3. Cover and cook for about 5 minutes. Add the remaining ingredients, cover again and let simmer for about 1 hour, or until tender.

Yield: 8 servings.

1¾ pounds combined chicken giblets and hearts
2 tablespoons butter
Salt and freshly ground pepper to taste
1 cup finely chopped onion
1 clove garlic, finely minced
2 tablespoons flour
½ cup dry white wine
3 cups water
2 tablespoons tomato paste
2 sprigs fresh thyme, or 1 teaspoon dried
1 bay leaf
2 turnips, about ½ pound, cut into eighths
2 ribs celery, trimmed, halved and cut into 1½-inch lengths
3 carrots, trimmed, quartered and cut into 1½-inch lengths
2 potatoes, about 1 pound, cut into 1½-inch pieces to resemble french fries

Xin Xin *(Brazilian chicken stew)*

2 cups dried peeled shrimp (see note)

2 2½- to 3-pound chickens, cut into serving pieces
Salt and freshly ground pepper to taste

2 cloves garlic, finely chopped or mashed to a pulp with mortar and pestle

2 teaspoons ground coriander seeds

1 cup dende oil (see note)

2 cups thinly sliced, loosely packed onion

2 Tabasco peppers, fresh or bottled, chopped

½ cup finely chopped, tightly packed parsley

3 cups water

1. Place the shrimp in a mixing bowl and add cold water to cover. Let stand overnight until softened.

2. Sprinkle the chickens with salt and pepper and rub the pieces with garlic. Put the seasoned chicken pieces in a heavy kettle or Dutch oven.

3. Drain the shrimp well and put them into the container of a food processor or electric blender. Blend well, stirring down with a plastic spatula as necessary.

4. Add the shrimp to the chicken. Add the coriander seeds, dende oil (shake the bottle well before adding), onion, chopped Tabasco peppers and parsley.

5. Add the water and cover. Bring to the boil and cook, stirring gently once in a while, for about 1 hour, or until chicken is thoroughly tender.

Yield: 8 or more servings.

Note: Dried peeled shrimp are available in plastic bags in Chinese groceries and supermarkets.

Olive oil plus about 1 tablespoon of paprika would be a vague but acceptable substitute for the dende oil.

Brunswick Stew

1 9- to 10-pound capon, or use 2 or 3 chickens with 10 pounds total weight, cut into serving pieces
Salt and freshly ground pepper

¼ cup butter

3 cups thinly sliced onion

2 cups diced sweet green peppers, seeded

2 cups diced celery

1 tablespoon finely minced garlic

2 dried, hot, red pepper pods

3 bay leaves

1 cup coarsely chopped parsley

8 cups water

1. Sprinkle the chicken pieces with salt and pepper. Heat the butter in two large skillets and brown the chicken pieces on all sides. Or use one skillet and do this in several steps.

2. Remove the chicken and add the onion, peppers, celery and garlic. Cook until the vegetables give up their liquid. Cook until liquid evaporates and the vegetables start to brown.

3. Return the chicken to the skillet or skillets and add the hot pepper pods, bay leaves, parsley, water, tomatoes and okra. Cover and cook for 15 minutes.

4. Meanwhile, drop the corn into boiling water and cover. When the water returns to the boil, remove it from the heat. Let stand, covered, for 5 minutes. Drain and let cool.

5. Add the lima beans to the stew and continue cooking for 15 minutes. Uncover and continue cooking for 10 minutes, or until beans are tender.

6. Cut and scrape the kernels off the cob. There should be about 6 cups. Add this to the stew. Add salt and pepper to taste. Stir in the Worcestershire sauce and serve piping hot.

Yield: 18 or more servings.

4 cups peeled, chopped tomatoes

2 10-ounce packages frozen cut okra

10 or more ears fresh corn on the cob, or use 3 10-ounce packages frozen whole kernel corn

4 cups shelled baby lima beans, or use 3 10-ounce packages frozen baby lima beans

¼ cup Worcestershire sauce

My Mother's Chicken Spaghetti

Curiously, the first Thanksgiving dinner I recall in sum was a non-turkey dinner when I was a child in Mississippi and my mother had a boardinghouse.

At the time of my birth, my father had been a fairly prosperous plantation owner. Shortly before I reached my teens, he lost everything, as the family saying went. Although my mother fancied herself every bit the Southern belle, which she was, in those days Southern belles could open boardinghouses and still maintain status and face. Hers was probably the most elegant table in the entire Mississippi Delta. It was set with her family silver (it had been buried under the smokehouse the day the Yankees came). Each place at the large oval table, which could accommodate twelve to fourteen, was set with a silver goblet in which ice water and sometimes iced tea were served. My father, meanwhile, resorted to raising animals for milk and food.

There were two holidays each year when my mother stipulated that meals would not be served to boarders, all of whom went to visit relatives or friends anyway. Christmas and Thanksgiving.

The non-turkey Thanksgiving came about because the three children in the family announced that they were bored with the daily diet of poultry. Chicken was the least expensive food item in the South and it was served at my mother's table almost invariably once and sometimes twice a day. A vote was taken. Almost in unison we asked for mother's baked spaghetti, a dish made with chicken, ground beef, mushrooms, cheese, tomatoes and a cream sauce. Thus we had spaghetti fresh from the oven for Thanksgiving dinner, reheated for supper.

1 3½-pound chicken with
   giblets
   Fresh or canned chicken
   broth to cover
   Salt
3 cups imported Italian peeled
   tomatoes
7 tablespoons butter
3 tablespoons flour
½ cup heavy cream
⅛ teaspoon grated nutmeg
   Freshly ground pepper
½ pound fresh mushrooms
2 cups finely chopped onion
1½ cups finely chopped celery
1½ cups chopped green pepper
1 tablespoon or more finely
   minced garlic
¼ pound ground beef
¼ pound ground pork
1 bay leaf
½ teaspoon hot red pepper
   flakes, optional
1 pound spaghetti or
   spaghettini
½ pound Cheddar cheese,
   grated, 2 to 2½ cups
   Freshly grated Parmesan
   cheese

1. One of the stipulations in the original recipe for this dish is that the spaghetti and all the ingredients be combined at least 4 hours before baking.

2. Place the chicken with neck, gizzard, heart and liver in a kettle and add chicken broth to cover and salt to taste. Bring to the boil and simmer until the chicken is tender without being dry, 35 to 45 minutes. Let cool.

3. Remove the chicken and take the meat from the bones. Shred the meat, cover and set aside. Return the skin and bones to the kettle and cook the stock down for 30 minutes or longer. There should be 4 to 6 cups of broth. Strain and reserve the broth. Discard the skin and bones.

4. Meanwhile, put the tomatoes in a saucepan and cook down to half the original volume, stirring.

5. Melt 3 tablespoons of butter in a saucepan and add the flour, stirring to blend with a wire whisk. When blended and smooth, add 1 cup of the reserved hot broth and the cream, stirring rapidly with the whisk. When thickened and smooth add the nutmeg, salt and pepper to taste. Continue cooking, stirring occasionally, for about 10 minutes. Set aside.

6. If the mushrooms are very small, leave them whole. Otherwise, cut them in half or quarter them. Heat 1 tablespoon of butter in a small skillet and add the mushrooms. Cook, shaking the skillet occasionally and stirring the mushrooms, until they are golden brown. Set aside.

7. Heat 3 tablespoons of butter in a deep skillet and add the onion. Cook, stirring, until wilted. Add the celery and green pepper and cook, stirring, for about 5 minutes. Do not overcook. The vegetables should remain crisp-tender.

8. Add the garlic, beef and pork and cook, stirring and chopping down with the edge of a large metal spoon to break up the meat. Cook just until the meat loses its red color. Add the bay leaf and red pepper flakes, if desired. Add the tomatoes and the white sauce made with the chicken broth. Add the mushrooms.

9. Cook the spaghetti or spaghettini in boiling salted water until it is just tender. Do not overcook. Remember that it will cook again when blended with the chicken and meat sauce. Drain the spaghetti and run under cold running water.

10. Spoon enough of the meat sauce over the bottom of a 5- or 6-quart casserole to cover it lightly. Add about one-third of the spaghetti. Add about one-third of the shredded chicken, a layer of meat sauce, a layer of grated Cheddar cheese and another layer of spaghetti. Continue making layers, ending with a layer of spaghetti topped with a thin layer of meat sauce and grated Cheddar cheese.

11. Pour in up to 2 cups of the reserved chicken broth or enough to almost but not quite cover the top layer of spaghetti. Cover and let the spaghetti stand for 4 hours or longer. If the liquid is absorbed as the dish stands, add a little more chicken broth. Remember that when this dish is baked and served, the sauce will be just a bit soupy rather than thick and clinging.

12. When ready to bake, preheat the oven to 350 degrees.

13. Place the spaghetti casserole on top of the stove and bring it just to the boil. Cover and place it in the oven. Bake for 15 minutes and uncover. Bake for 15 minutes longer, or until the casserole is hot and bubbling throughout and starting to brown on top. Serve immediately with grated Parmesan cheese on the side.

Yield: 12 or more servings.

Shahi Biryani   (A chicken and rice casserole)

1. The chicken should be cut into flat pieces, each about a 3-inch square.	2 pounds skinned, boneless chicken breasts
2. Heat ½ cup of oil in a casserole and cook the chicken pieces sprinkled with salt and paprika until they lose their raw look. Set aside.	1½ cups peanut, vegetable or corn oil Salt to taste
	¼ teaspoon paprika
3. Heat the remaining cup of oil in a heavy casserole and cook the onion, stirring, until golden brown, about 20 minutes.	4 cups thinly sliced onion
4. Wash the rice well and cover with cold water. Let stand for ½ hour.	3 cups short-grain rice, preferably purchased in Indian markets
5. Cover the raisins with cold water and let stand.	¾ cup raisins
6. Place the casserole with onions on low heat. Add cumin seeds, bay leaves, whole cloves, garlic slivers and drained raisins. Cook, stirring, for 3 minutes. Add the yogurt and salt to taste.	1 tablespoon crushed cumin seeds
	6 bay leaves
	6 whole cloves
	½ teaspoon slivered garlic
7. Drain the rice and add it to the casserole along with the chicken pieces and any liquid that may have accumulated. Add the crushed cardamom seeds and chicken broth. Sprinkle with kewra, if desired. Cover and cook for 15 minutes.	¼ cup thick yogurt (see instructions below)
	1 teaspoon crushed cardamom seeds
8. Meanwhile, preheat the oven to 250 degrees.	4¼ cups chicken stock (see recipe below)
9. Do not uncover and do not stir, but pick up the casserole firmly with both hands and toss to redistribute the chicken and the rice. Or, if the casserole is too heavy and seems unwieldy, uncover it and gently stir the rice with a rubber spatula to redistribute it.	½ teaspoon kewra (see note), optional

10. Place the casserole in the oven and bake for 30 minutes.

11. It is preferable to scoop the rice mixture from the casse-

role to a rice dish with a saucer so that the rice grains do not become sticky.

Yield: 8 to 12 servings.

Note: Kewra is a white spirit that smells vaguely and pleasantly like nasturtiums. It is available in bottles in Indian stores.

Thick yogurt

Line a bowl with cheesecloth. Empty the contents of 1 pint of plain commercial yogurt into the cheesecloth. Bring up the edges of the cheesecloth and tie with a long string. Suspend the cheesecloth bag with the string over the bowl. Let stand for about 2 hours.

Chicken stock Indian-style

The bones of a 3-pound chicken
Water to cover
Salt to taste
2 cinnamon sticks, each about 1½ inches
4 crushed brown cardamom pods

Combine all the ingredients in a saucepan. Bring to the boil and cook, uncovered, for about 45 minutes. Strain.

Yield: About 5 cups.

Red Beans and Rice

2 cups dried red or kidney beans
1½ cups thinly sliced Polish (garlic) sausage
1½ cups thinly sliced leeks
1½ cups chopped fennel bulb, optional
½ teaspoon dried thyme
Salt to taste
1 small dried hot red pepper, crushed
1 tablespoon vinegar
1 cup rice
2¼ cups fresh or canned chicken broth
½ cup finely chopped parsley
½ teaspoon lemon juice
½ teaspoon salt
1 cup diced, cooked chicken
Chopped green pepper for garnish

1. Soak the beans overnight in cold water to cover.

2. Drain the beans and add enough cold water to cover to a depth of 1 inch above the top of the beans. Add the sausage, leeks, fennel, if desired, thyme, salt, pepper and vinegar. Cover and cook for 30 to 45 minutes, or until beans are done and most of the liquid has been absorbed. Add more liquid as necessary or uncover to reduce the amount of liquid.

3. Meanwhile, combine the rice with the broth, parsley, lemon juice, salt and chicken. Cover and bring to the boil. Cook until all the liquid is absorbed, 12 to 14 minutes.

4. Combine the rice and beans and serve hot garnished with chopped green peppers.

Yield: 6 to 8 servings.

Fish, Spinach and Noodle Casserole

1. Preheat the oven to 400 degrees.

2. Split each fillet lengthwise down the main centerline. Fold each fillet in half.

3. If fresh bulk spinach is used, trim off and discard any tough stems and blemished leaves. Rinse and drain the spinach well. Drop the spinach into boiling water and cook for 2 minutes. Drain well. When cool enough to handle, squeeze the spinach between the hands to remove excess moisture. Chop the spinach coarsely. There should be about 1½ cups.

4. Butter with 1 tablespoon butter a baking dish large enough to hold the folded fish fillets in one layer. Sprinkle with shallots, salt and pepper. Arrange the fillets over this and sprinkle with the wine.

5. Cover the fish and bring to the simmer on top of the stove. Place in the oven and bake for 5 minutes, no longer. Transfer the fish fillets to a platter and cover. Keep warm. Cook the pan liquid down by about half.

6. Melt 3 tablespoons of butter in a saucepan and add the flour, stirring with a wire whisk. When blended, add the milk, stirring rapidly with the whisk. When the mixture is thickened and smooth, season with salt, pepper, Tabasco sauce and nutmeg. Add the liquid in which the fish cooked. Continue cooking the sauce for about 5 minutes. Remove it from the heat and stir in 2 egg yolks. Cook briefly, stirring rapidly, and remove from the heat.

7. Cook the noodles until tender and drain. Toss with 1 tablespoon of butter, salt and pepper to taste.

8. Heat remaining 1 tablespoon of butter in a skillet and add the chopped spinach, salt and pepper to taste. Cook for about 3 minutes, stirring often.

9. Spoon the noodles over the bottom of a baking dish (an oval dish measuring about 14- x 8- x 2-inches is good for this). Add the spinach, distributing it evenly.

10. Arrange the fish fillets over the spinach in a neat layer, the pieces close together. Spoon the sauce over the fish. Sprinkle with cheese and place in the oven. Bake for 15 minutes.

Yield: 6 servings.

6 fish fillets, such as sole or flounder, about 1½ pounds
1 pound fresh spinach, or 1 10-ounce package
6 tablespoons butter
2 tablespoons finely chopped shallots
Salt and freshly ground pepper to taste
½ cup dry white wine
4 tablespoons flour
2 cups milk
A few drops Tabasco sauce
⅛ teaspoon nutmeg
2 egg yolks
¼ pound fine or medium noodles
2 tablespoons freshly grated Parmesan cheese

Seafood, Mushroom and Noodle Casserole

½ pound cooked seafood, such as crabmeat, shrimp or lobster, cut into small bite-size pieces (if small shrimp are used, leave them whole)
¼ pound mushrooms, preferably button mushrooms
2 hard-cooked eggs
3 tablespoons butter
1½ tablespoons finely chopped shallots
Salt and freshly ground pepper to taste
1 tablespoon flour
1½ cups milk
1 egg yolk
Tabasco sauce
2 teaspoons dry sherry
½ pound fine, buttered, freshly cooked noodles
⅓ cup grated Gruyère, Swiss or Parmesan cheese

1. Preheat the oven to 450 degrees.
2. Prepare the seafood and set aside.
3. If the mushrooms are very small, leave them whole. Otherwise, slice or quarter them. Set aside.
4. Peel and slice the hard-cooked eggs. Set aside.
5. Melt 2 tablespoons butter in a saucepan and add the shallots. Cook briefly and add the mushrooms. Sprinkle with salt and pepper. Cook for about 5 minutes, stirring occasionally.
6. Sprinkle with flour and stir with a wire whisk until mushroom pieces are coated. Add the milk and cook, stirring constantly, until sauce thickens. Cook for about 5 minutes, stirring occasionally.
7. Remove the sauce from the heat and add the egg yolk, stirring rapidly. Add a dash of Tabasco and the sherry.
8. Meanwhile, cook the noodles until tender in boiling salted water. Drain and add the remaining tablespoon of butter, salt and pepper to taste.
9. Spoon the noodles into a baking dish (one that measures 14- x 8- x 2-inches is suitable). Scatter the pieces of seafood over and arrange the egg slices over all. Spoon and scrape the sauce over this, distributing it evenly and smoothing it over. Sprinkle with cheese and place in the oven. Bake for 15 to 20 minutes.

Yield: 4 to 6 servings.

Paella

¼ cup olive oil
4 cloves garlic, thinly sliced
¾ cup coarsely chopped onion
1½ cups unpeeled tomatoes, cored and cut into cubes
3 chorizos or Spanish sausages, cut into ¼-inch slices
2 cups raw, shelled and deveined shrimp

1. Heat the oil in a paella pan or a wide, shallow, heatproof casserole. When it is very hot, add the garlic and cook, stirring, until it is golden brown. Remove the garlic with a slotted spoon and discard it.
2. Add the onion and cook, stirring, for about 3 minutes. Depending on the source of heat, it will be necessary to shift the pan around so that the foods cook evenly.
3. Add the tomatoes and cook, stirring, for about 5 minutes. Add the sausages and cook for about 1 minute, stirring. Add

the shrimp and cook until they turn bright red. Add the capers and tomato paste. Stir briefly and add the clams and scallops. Add the oysters and cook, stirring, for about 2 minutes. Add 5 cups of the chicken broth, bay leaves and oregano.

4. Gradually sprinkle the rice into the pan so that it is evenly distributed. After the rice is added, the paella must be stirred constantly until the dish is finished. But do not stir the rice in a circular fashion. Instead, using a wooden spoon, dip it into the paella and stir gently back and forth in a small area. Move the spoon to another part of the pan and stir gently back and forth. Continue, taking care that all areas of the paella are stirred. Add the Tabasco.

5. After the rice has been cooking for 8 or 10 minutes, add 2 more cups of hot chicken broth and continue stirring in the above-mentioned fashion. Cook for about 5 minutes and distribute the chicken over the rice, pushing it into the stew.

6. Continue cooking and stirring and, if the dish seems to become dry, add more hot broth gradually. The dish should not be soupy. The paella is ready when the rice is tender. Remove the bay leaves. Garnish the paella and serve.

Yield: 12 to 18 servings.

¼	cup capers
⅓	cup tomato paste
12	cherrystone clams
1½	cups bay scallops
1	cup drained oysters
7 to	8 cups fresh hot chicken broth (see recipe below)
2	bay leaves
1	teaspoon oregano
2½	cups long-grain rice
	Tabasco to taste
6	cups cubed, shredded chicken (see recipe below)
	Garnish (see directions below)

1. Place the chicken in a kettle and add the remaining ingredients. Bring to the boil and simmer until the chicken is tender.

2. Strain and reserve the broth and the chicken.

3. Remove the meat from the chicken and discard the bones. Cut the meat into bite-size pieces and set aside.

Yield: About 8 cups of broth and 1 chicken.

Chicken and broth for paella

1	3-pound chicken
9	cups unsalted chicken broth made from the bony parts of chicken, or use water
½	teaspoon freshly ground pepper
	Salt to taste
½	teaspoon chopped Spanish saffron
2	large onions, cut into quarters
2	ribs celery with leaves

How to garnish paella

The traditional garnishes for a paella include pimientos, generally cut into lozenges or strips; cooked green peas; Spanish olives stuffed with pimientos, and hard-cooked eggs, cut into wedges. The egg yolks may be put through a sieve and sprinkled over all. A piece of seafood such as a clam in the shell is centered in the pan. It is surrounded with wedges of egg white like the spokes of a wheel, with lozenges of pimiento in between. A cup of cooked peas generally serves as a border around the paella. The olives, approximately a cup, are scattered at random.

Vatapá Jodo *(Brazilian shrimp with coconut)*

1 pound dried peeled shrimp (see note page 420)
1½ loaves French bread, approximately
1½ cups milk
⅓ cup olive oil
1 cup chopped onion
1 clove garlic, finely minced
  Salt to taste
1 cup chopped green pepper
2¾ cups tomatoes
2 cups fresh or canned, unsweetened coconut cream or milk (see recipe page 393)
1 cup water
1½ pounds fresh shrimp, peeled and deveined
1 cup dende oil (see note page 420)
6 ounces unsalted cashew nuts
1 teaspoon ground coriander, or 1 tablespoon finely chopped fresh coriander leaves
  Freshly ground pepper to taste
¾ cup finely chopped loosely packed parsley
¾ cup chopped scallions
1 or more very hot small peppers (see note), or according to taste

1. Place the dried shrimp in a mixing bowl and add water to cover. Let stand several hours or overnight. Drain but reserve the soaking liquid. There should be about 6 cups drained shrimp.

2. Remove the crusts from the bread and slice the bread. Put it in a mixing bowl and add the milk. Let stand for an hour or so.

3. In a large casserole, heat the oil and add the onion. Crush the garlic with 1 teaspoon salt with mortar and pestle. Add it. Cook, stirring, until onion starts to brown.

4. Add the soaked dried shrimp and green pepper and cook, stirring, for about 4 minutes. Add the tomatoes and cook over high heat for about 5 minutes.

5. Add about 2½ cups of the reserved liquid in which shrimp soaked. Cook for about 10 minutes, stirring occasionally. Cover and cook for about 30 minutes longer.

6. Put the ingredients in the container of a food processor and blend briefly.

7. Mash the soaked bread (about 5 cups in all) with a spoon to make a mush. Add it to the shrimp mixture and blend until the mixture is pastelike. Scrape out into a mixing bowl.

8. Add the coconut milk, water and fresh shrimp and stir to blend the shrimp without crushing into the pastelike mixture.

9. Gradually stir in the dende oil, stirring constantly.

10. If the cashew nuts are salted, rinse them off and pat dry. In any event, put them into the container of the food processor or electric blender and blend. Add them to the casserole. Add the coriander, salt, pepper, parsley, scallions and peppers. Bring to the boil and turn off the heat. Do not boil. If the casserole must be reheated, stir constantly.

Yield: 8 to 12 servings.

Note: The traditional peppers used in this recipe are malagueta peppers, which are very small, fiery hot chilies from Brazil. Substitute fresh hot green or red peppers or canned Mexican chilies, such as pickled serrano peppers. Use them according to taste.

Crab Gumbo

1. Drop the corn into boiling water to cover and return the water to the boil. Remove from the heat and let stand for 5 minutes. Drain. Cut the kernels from the cob and set aside.

2. Heat the bacon fat in a skillet. Cut the okra, fresh or frozen, into ½-inch lengths. Add to the skillet and cook, stirring often, for 10 to 15 minutes, or until it is quite dry.

3. Meanwhile, heat the butter and add the onion, garlic, celery and green pepper. Cook, stirring, until the onion is wilted.

4. Add the tomatoes, salt and pepper to taste, Worcestershire sauce, broth and water. Add Tabasco to taste and bring to the boil. Simmer for 40 minutes.

5. Stir in the crab and corn and heat thoroughly.

6. When ready to serve, add the wine and parsley. Heat thoroughly and serve with hot cooked rice.

Yield: 6 or more servings.

4 to 6 ears corn
2 tablespoons bacon fat
¾ pound fresh young okra, or use 1 10-ounce package frozen
2 tablespoons butter
¾ cup finely chopped onion
1 teaspoon finely chopped garlic
¾ cup finely chopped celery
½ cup finely chopped green pepper
4 tomatoes, cored and chopped, about 4 cups
Salt and freshly ground pepper
1 teaspoon or more Worcestershire sauce
2 cups fish broth, or use 2 cups bottled clam juice
1 cup water
Tabasco sauce
½ pound or more crabmeat, preferably lump or backfin
5 tablespoons dry sherry
¼ cup finely chopped parsley

Crab and Noodles au Gratin

1. Preheat the oven to 450 degrees.

2. Pick over the crab, if necessary, to remove all traces of shell and cartilage. Set aside.

3. Melt 4 tablespoons butter in a saucepan and add the flour, stirring with a wire whisk. When blended, add the milk, stirring rapidly with the whisk. Add salt and pepper to taste, the cayenne, nutmeg and cream. Bring to the boil and simmer, stirring occasionally, for about 5 minutes.

4. Remove the sauce from the heat and add the yolk, stirring rapidly with the whisk. Add the wine.

5. Meanwhile, cook the noodles in boiling salted water until just tender. Do not overcook, for they will be baked later.

6. Drain the noodles and return them to the kettle. Stir in the remaining 2 tablespoons of butter and about ½ cup of

1 pound lump or backfin crabmeat
6 tablespoons butter
3 tablespoons flour
3 cups milk
Salt and freshly ground pepper
⅛ teaspoon cayenne pepper
¼ teaspoon nutmeg
½ cup heavy cream
1 egg yolk
⅓ cup sherry, preferably medium sweet
¾ pound fine noodles
¼ cup grated Parmesan cheese

sauce. Spoon the noodles into a baking dish and smooth them over. Scatter the crabmeat over the noodles. Spoon the remaining sauce over all. Sprinkle with cheese and bake for 25 minutes, or until piping hot. Run the dish under the broiler to get a brown glaze.

Yield: 4 to 6 servings.

IX. Pasta

There is probably not one person in a thousand in this country who knows that the countless sauces destined for pasta cannot, in the classic sense, be used arbitrarily with all pasta regardless of shape, size, color and texture. Put otherwise, you cannot serve, indiscriminately, all sauces with any kind of pasta.

The rules for which sauce goes with which shape pasta cannot be reduced to a simple, absolute formula. But generalizations are very much in order, particularly when they come from Marcella Hazan, an expert on Italian cuisine who has frequently visited our kitchen and shared her knowledge and enthusiasm.

Generally speaking, she says, sauces that contain pieces of things—things like chopped meat, peas, ham and so on—go well with a pasta that has a hole (like macaroni), or a shape that catches pieces, spiral shapes for example, and shells.

Very thin sauces are destined for pasta like spaghetti or vermicelli. But there is one exception. If the sauce has a base of olive oil and contains clams, scallops, chopped fish or seafood, pasta strands such as spaghetti would be quite suitable. Think of linguine with clam sauce.

Homemade pastas go best with sauces that must be absorbed, which is to say sauces that cling. Like the cream and cheese sauce tossed with fettucine and known as Alfredo. You would never—or shouldn't—serve packaged spaghetti with that sauce.

Like most Italian cooks, Mrs. Hazan is firm in her belief that homemade pasta rolled by hand is superior to that prepared by machine. As a concession, she agreed to prepare pasta in my kitchen using a machine.

Homemade Pasta

1. Empty the flour onto a wooden or Formica surface. Make a well in the center and neatly build up a "wall" to surround the eggs. Start beating the eggs with a fork, gradually incorporating the flour.

1¾ cups semolina (durum wheat flour)
3 large eggs (¾ cup)

2. Do not let the eggs overflow; keep the wall built around by pushing with the fingers toward the center. Continue stirring and incorporating flour until all flour is added.

3. When the eggs have lost their fluidity (will not overflow the walls), start pushing the flour into the egg mixture, kneading gently, and continue working the flour all over the surface to incorporate all the flour.

4. Remove the pasta. Wash and dry the board and start kneading again by hand. It will get more elastic. Turn the ball of dough as it is kneaded until it has the texture of satiny, nonsticky modeling clay. Wrap in plastic. Let it rest 8 minutes. When you open it, the pasta will seem sticky again. Do not add more flour.

5. Remove the pasta from the plastic wrapping and shape it into a ball. Cut it into 5 pieces of more or less equal size. Set the pasta machine opening to wide (No. 6). Flatten each of the 5 pieces of pasta dough. Run the pieces through the machine, one at a time, without changing the setting. Arrange them on a clean cloth as they are put through. Reduce the setting to the next smaller opening and put the pieces through. When the pasta has gone through the No. 4 opening, stop rolling.

6. Cut each strip of pasta crosswise at the center point. This will make 10 pieces. Reduce the opening by half and put the 10 strips of pasta through the opening. Let them dry on the cloth, turning from time to time. Let dry for 30 minutes, more or less (see note). Put the sheets of pasta through any desired cutter to produce the shape and/or width you desire. The sheets of pasta when rolled out fine may also be cut by hand for widths the cutters cannot accommodate.

Yield: 1 pound of pasta, or 4 to 6 servings.

Note: One way to test whether the pasta is dry enough is to put one small sheet of pasta through the fine cutter of the machine. If the strands stick together and have to be pulled apart with the fingers, the pasta should be allowed to dry longer.

Sugo di Canestrelli *(Pasta with scallops)*

1½	pints scallops
⅓	cup plus 4 tablespoons olive oil
2	teaspoons finely chopped garlic

1. Cut each scallop into quarters. Set aside.

2. Heat the ⅓ cup of oil in a wide saucepan and add the garlic. Cook briefly, stirring, without browning. Add the scallop pieces and parsley and 3 tablespoons of oil, stirring. Add

the salt and hot red pepper flakes. Cook for about 1 minute and set aside.

3. Toss the pasta with the scallops and add the remaining tablespoon of oil. Serve sprinkled with toasted bread crumbs.

Yield: 8 servings.

2½ tablespoons finely chopped flat leaf parsley
Salt to taste
¼ teaspoon finely chopped hot red pepper flakes
2 pounds homemade tonnarelli (see recipe below and double it), or use spaghetti or vermicelli, cooked to the desired degree of doneness and drained
¼ cup toasted bread crumbs

Homemade tonnarelli (*A fine cut pasta*)

Prepare the recipe for homemade pasta. When the sheets of pasta have been dried briefly as indicated, put them through the fine cutter of the machine. If the pasta is not to be used immediately, take a few strands of pasta and wrap them around the fingers, bird's nest fashion. Let stand until thoroughly dry like store-bought pasta. They will later be easier to handle.

To cook, drop the pasta into boiling salted water. Cook until just tender, less than a minute after the water returns to the boil. Drain.

Yield: 1 pound of tonnarelli.

Sugo alla Saffi (*Penne with ham and asparagus*)

1. Using a swivel-bladed vegetable scraper, scrape the sides of the asparagus, starting about 2 inches from the top. Cut off the ends of the spears about 1 inch from the bottom.

2. Split the ham slice in half. Cut the halves into ½-inch-thick strips.

3. Bring enough water to the boil to cover the asparagus spears when they are added. Add the asparagus and cook for about 2 minutes and drain. When cool enough to handle, cut the asparagus into 1-inch lengths.

4. Heat half the butter in a small skillet and add the ham. Cook, stirring and shaking the skillet, until ham is piping hot.

5. Heat the remaining butter in a skillet and add the asparagus. Cook briefly, stirring, until all liquid evaporates, no longer. Add the cream and bring to the boil. Cook for about 5 minutes until sauce is thickened. Add the ham.

6. Cook the pasta to the desired degree of doneness. Serve tossed with the pasta sauce and grated Parmesan cheese.

Yield: 8 servings.

1½ pounds fresh asparagus
1 6-ounce boiled ham slice, about ¼ inch thick
2 tablespoons butter
1 cup heavy cream
1½ pounds penne (a tubular pasta with ends cut on the diagonal), available where fine Italian imported foods are sold
Grated Parmesan cheese

Spaghetti Primavera

This inspired blend of pasta and crisp-tender vegetables, such as zucchini, mushrooms, broccoli and green beans, is a creation of Italian origin that flourishes in one of New York's most popular luxury French restaurants, Le Cirque. Although the dish is called spaghetti primavera—spaghetti with a springtime air—it is served all year long at Le Cirque and can be reproduced easily in the home.

1 bunch broccoli
2 small zucchini
4 asparagus spears, each about 5 inches long
1½ cups green beans, trimmed and cut into 1-inch lengths
Salt
½ cup fresh or frozen green peas
¾ cup fresh or frozen pea pods, optional
1 tablespoon peanut, vegetable or corn oil
2 cups thinly sliced mushrooms
Freshly ground pepper
1 teaspoon chopped hot, fresh, red or green chilies, or about ½ teaspoon dried red pepper flakes
¼ cup finely chopped parsley
6 tablespoons olive oil
1 teaspoon finely chopped garlic
3 cups red, ripe tomatoes cut into 1-inch cubes
6 fresh basil leaves, chopped, about ¼ cup, or about 1 teaspoon dried basil
1 pound spaghetti or spaghettini
4 tablespoons butter
2 tablespoons fresh or canned chicken broth
½ cup heavy cream, approximately
⅔ cup grated Parmesan cheese
⅓ cup pine nuts

1. Trim the broccoli and break it into bite-size flowerets. Set aside.

2. Trim off and discard the ends of the zucchini. Do not peel the zucchini. Cut the zucchini into quarters. Cut each quarter into 1-inch or slightly longer lengths. There should be about 1½ cups, no more. Set aside.

3. Cut each asparagus spear into thirds. Set aside.

4. Cook each of the green vegetables separately in boiling salted water to cover. The essential thing is to cook each vegetable so that it remains crisp-tender. Cook the broccoli, zucchini, green beans and asparagus for about 5 minutes. Drain well, run under cold water to chill and drain thoroughly. Combine them in a mixing bowl.

5. Cook the peas and pea pods for about 1 minute if fresh, or 30 seconds if frozen. Drain, chill and drain again. Combine all the vegetables in the mixing bowl.

6. Heat the peanut oil in a skillet and add the mushrooms. Add salt and pepper to taste, shaking the skillet and stirring. Cook for about 2 minutes. Add the mushrooms to the vegetables. Add the chopped chilies and parsley.

7. Heat 3 tablespoons olive oil in a saucepan and add half the garlic, the tomatoes, salt and pepper to taste. Cook for about 4 minutes, stirring gently so as not to break up the tomatoes more than is essential. Add the basil, stir and set aside.

8. Heat the remaining 3 tablespoons olive oil in a large skillet and add the remaining garlic and the vegetable mixture. Cook, stirring gently, just to heat through.

9. Drop the spaghetti into boiling salted water. Cook until almost but not quite tender. That is to say, al dente. The spaghetti when ready must retain just a slight resilience in the center. Drain well.

10. Melt the butter in a utensil large enough to hold the drained spaghetti and vegetables. Add the chicken broth, ½

cup cream and cheese, stirring constantly. Cook gently on and off the heat until smooth. Add the spaghetti and toss quickly to blend. Add half the vegetables and pour in the liquid from the tomatoes, tossing and stirring over very low heat.

11. Add the remaining vegetables and, if the sauce seems to dry, add about ¼ cup more cream. The sauce should not be soupy. Add the pine nuts and give the mixture one final tossing.

12. Serve equal portions of the spaghetti mixture in 4 to 8 hot soup or spaghetti bowls. Spoon equal amounts of the tomatoes over each serving. Serve immediately. Four portions will serve as a main course; 6 to 8 as an appetizer.

Yield: 4 to 8 servings.

Fettucelle Alfredo

Alfredo Viazzi came to professional cooking relatively late in life, but is now one of the most successful chefs and restaurant owners in New York. He has demonstrated his Merlin-like ways with pasta many times in our kitchen, and we include here three of his specialties.

1. Heat the oil and 2 tablespoons of butter in a casserole. Add the garlic and cook briefly without browning. Add the anchovies and stir. Add the tomatoes and pepper to taste and cook for about 10 minutes.

2. Add the capers, olives and tuna. Stir to blend. Add the remaining butter and cook for about 10 minutes. Add parsley and, if desired, add salt to taste.

3. Cook the fettucelle and drain. Serve with the sauce.

Yield: 4 servings.

3 tablespoons olive oil
8 tablespoons butter
1 tablespoon chopped garlic
8 fillets of anchovy, minced
1 cup drained, crushed, peeled imported Italian plum tomatoes
Freshly ground pepper
⅓ cup drained capers
¾ cup pitted, imported red olives, such as Greek calamati, Spanish Alfonso or Italian gaeta
1½ cups canned, undrained tuna
1 tablespoon finely chopped parsley
Salt, optional
1 pound fettucelle or cavatelli

Tagliarini Verdi Ghiottona *(Green noodles with chicken livers and prosciutto)*

½ pound butter
½ cup finely chopped onion
¼ cup finely diced carrots
Salt and freshly ground
  pepper
2 tablespoons chopped parsley
⅛ teaspoon grated nutmeg
½ pound ground meat,
  preferably veal, although
  pork or beef might be used
¼ pound chicken livers, cut into
  ½-inch cubes
1 tablespoon dry sherry
⅓ cup fresh or canned chicken
  broth
1 cup drained, crushed, peeled,
  imported Italian plum
  tomatoes
1 tablespoon olive oil
¼ pound prosciutto or other
  ham, shredded, about 1 cup
  loosely packed
1 pound pasta, preferably green
  tagliarini, although
  spaghettini or spaghetti could
  be used, cooked according to
  taste

1. Heat the butter in a skillet or casserole and add the onion and carrots. When bubbling, sprinkle with salt and pepper to taste. Cook gently and without browning for about 8 minutes.

2. Add the parsley and nutmeg. Add the veal and cook, stirring to break up any lumps. When the meat loses its red color, add the chicken livers and cook, stirring, for about 1 minute. Add salt to taste and the sherry. Cook for about 1 minute, stirring, and add the chicken broth. Simmer for about 3 minutes. Add the tomatoes and cook for about 5 minutes.

3. Heat the oil in another skillet and cook the prosciutto for about 3 minutes, stirring. Add to the sauce and continue to cook for about 20 minutes. Serve hot with the cooked pasta.

Yield: 4 to 6 servings.

Tagliarini Verdi ai Quattro Formaggi *(Green tagliarini with four cheeses)*

½ pound butter
¼ teaspoon freshly ground
  white pepper
¼ pound fontina cheese, cubed,
  available in Italian markets
¼ pound gorgonzola cheese,
  cubed, available in Italian
  markets
¼ pound bel paese cheese,
  cubed

1. Melt the butter in a deep saucepan and add the pepper. Add the fontina, gorgonzola and bel paese cheeses. Stir until the cheeses melt. Stir in the Parmesan cheese and heavy cream.

2. Drop the tagliarini into salted boiling water and cook, stirring frequently, until tender, 7 to 12 minutes. Drain the tagliarini and toss in the cheese mixture.

Yield: 4 to 6 servings.

¾ cup grated Parmesan
cheese
1 cup heavy cream
1 pound green tagliarini, or
spaghetti
Salt

Penne or Rigatoni Modo Mio *(Pasta with cauliflower and ham)*

The "mio" in this recipe title is one of our most prized acquaintances, Ed Giobbi. Ed's kitchen is one of those places we always visit with bounding enthusiasm and keen appetite because, although he is a painter and sculptor by profession, he is a splended and inventive cook who goes about his hobby with the cool dexterity of a croupier shuffling cards. He also believes that pasta can be one of the most gratifying and healthy ways to eat economically. This and the following four recipes are ample and delicious proof of his thesis.

1. Have all the ingredients cut, chopped, measured and ready to cook before starting this dish. Have a kettle of water at the boil for the pasta.

2. Heat the butter and oil in a skillet and add the onions. Cook, stirring, until golden. Add the garlic, ham, basil, parsley, wine, salt and pepper to taste and continue cooking.

3. Simultaneously, as soon as the onions start to cook, add the penne or rigatoni and potatoes to the boiling water. Add salt and pepper to taste. Let return to the boil, stirring often so that the pasta does not stick. Let cook for about 4 minutes.

4. Add the cauliflower and continue cooking for 4 to 5 minutes, or until the pasta is just cooked. Do not overcook. When done, drain immediately and add the pasta mixture to the ham mixture. Toss with half the grated Parmesan cheese. Serve with the remaining cheese on the side.

Yield: 8 servings.

2 tablespoons butter
2 tablespoons olive oil
2 cups thinly sliced onions
1 teaspoon finely chopped garlic
1½ cups boiled ham, cut into ½-inch cubes
2 tablespoons chopped fresh basil, or half the amount dried
2 tablespoons chopped fresh parsley
1 cup dry white wine
Salt and freshly ground pepper
½ pound penne or rigatoni
2 cups peeled, raw potatoes cut into ½-inch cubes
4 cups cauliflower (1 small), broken or cut into flowerets
½ cup grated Parmesan cheese

Pasta con Asparagi *(Pasta with asparagus)*

1½ pounds fresh asparagus
3 tablespoons butter
Salt and freshly ground pepper
2½ tablespoons olive oil
2 whole cloves garlic
2 cups canned Italian plum tomatoes put through a sieve
1 tablespoon finely chopped fresh parsley
1 teaspoon dried basil, or 1 tablespoon finely chopped fresh basil
¾ pound penne, rigatoni or other tubular pasta
2 eggs plus 1 egg yolk, beaten well with a fork
½ cup grated Parmesan cheese

1. Have all the ingredients for this recipe prepared and ready to cook before starting to cook. Bring about 3 quarts of water to the boil and have it ready for the pasta.

2. Cut the asparagus into lengths about 2 inches long. If the stalks are thick, cut them in half or quarter them. Leave the tips intact. Heat the butter in a skillet and add the asparagus pieces, salt and pepper to taste. Cook for 4 to 5 minutes, or until crisp-tender and lightly browned. Remove from the heat.

3. Heat the oil in a deep skillet and add the garlic. Cook until lightly browned and remove and discard the garlic. Add the tomatoes, parsley, basil, salt and pepper to taste. Cook, stirring, for about 10 minutes.

4. Meanwhile, add the pasta and salt to the water and, when it returns to the boil, cook for about 7 minutes or until tender. Do not overcook.

5. Just before the pasta is done, turn off the heat under the tomatoes and add the beaten eggs, stirring vigorously so that they blend in the sauce without curdling. Do not boil the sauce after the eggs are added.

6. Add the asparagus to the tomato sauce and stir to blend.

7. Drain the pasta immediately. Add the tomato sauce and asparagus, toss with half the cheese. Serve piping hot with the remaining cheese on the side.

Yield: 8 or more servings.

Pasta with Broccoli

½ pound fresh broccoli (see note)
½ pound spaghettini or linguine
5 tablespoons olive oil
2 to 3 cloves garlic, finely chopped
½ teaspoon hot red pepper flakes, approximately
2 cups water, approximately
Salt to taste
Grated Parmesan cheese

1. This recipe is incredibly easy to make, but there are a couple of pitfalls that must be guarded against. When the pasta and vegetables are cooked, the pasta must be stirred often to keep the strands from sticking to themselves and to the bottom of the pan. It is best to stir gently but often with a plastic spatula to prevent this.

2. Trim off and reserve the bud clusters at the top of the broccoli stems. Leave part of the stem attached to the base of each cluster. If the clusters are very large, cut them in half. Reserve the stems as well.

3. Unless the broccoli is very young and tender, pare or peel off the outer skin of the stems. If the stems are large, slice

them in half lengthwise. In any event, cut the stem sections into 2-inch lengths. Combine and set aside the prepared broccoli pieces.

4. Break the pasta into 2- or 3-inch lengths. Set aside.

5. Heat the oil in a heavy, not too large skillet or casserole, about 9 or 10 inches in diameter. Add the garlic and cook briefly. Add the hot pepper flakes, pasta and broccoli. Add 1 cup of water and, when it boils, stir the ingredients to make certain the pasta does not stick to itself or the bottom of the pan.

6. Cover the pan and continue cooking but stirring often and adding water as it is absorbed, about ¼ cup at a time. Add salt to taste. When this dish is ready, the pasta will be cooked, the broccoli crisp-tender and most of the liquid will be absorbed. The "sauce" that clings to the pasta will be minimal. The total cooking time is 10 to 12 minutes. Do not overcook or the pasta will become mushy.

7. Serve immediately in hot soup plates with Parmesan cheese on the side.

Yield: 4 appetizer servings or 2 main dishes.

Note: Broccoli di rape, a tender, delicious and somewhat bitter Italian green, which is becoming more available in America, may be substituted for the broccoli.

Cold Pasta and Broccoli with Pesto

1. Prepare the pesto and have it ready.

2. Cut the broccoli into small flowerets. Trim the stalks and stems of the broccoli and cut the stems and stalks into bite-size lengths. Steam the broccoli pieces over boiling water or cook in boiling salted water until crisp-tender. Do not overcook. Set aside.

3. Cook the rigatoni in boiling salted water more or less according to package directions, but take care not to overcook. The pasta must be tender and in no sense mushy. Drain but reserve a little of the boiling pasta water to dilute the pesto.

4. Heat the oil in a saucepan and add the garlic and blanched broccoli. Sprinkle with pepper flakes. Cook, stirring gently, just to heat through. Remove from the heat.

5. Meanwhile, core the tomato and cut the tomato into bite-size wedges.

6. Put the rigatoni in a bowl. Add 1 or 2 tablespoons of the hot pasta water to the pesto and stir until slightly thinned. Do

4 to 6 tablespoons pesto genovese (see below)
1 bunch of broccoli
Salt
1 pound rigatoni or any tubular pasta, preferably imported
3 tablespoons olive oil
1 clove garlic, finely chopped
½ teaspoon or more hot red pepper flakes, optional
1 firm red, ripe tomato

not make it soupy. Pour this over the rigatoni. Add salt to taste. Add the broccoli and tomato and toss to blend. Serve at room temperature.

Yield: 8 to 10 servings.

Pesto Genovese *(Basil and nut sauce for pasta)*

2 cups fresh basil
½ cup olive oil
2 tablespoons pine nuts (pignoli)
2 cloves garlic, peeled
Salt to taste
½ cup grated Parmesan cheese
2 tablespoons grated Romano pecorino cheese (or increase the quantity of Parmesan by this amount)
3 tablespoons butter at room temperature

1. Remove all tough stems from the basil. To measure, pack the leaves gently but somewhat firmly in a measuring cup without crushing the leaves.

2. Empty the basil into the container of a food processor or electric blender. Add the olive oil, pine nuts, garlic and salt and blend on high speed. Using a rubber spatula, scrape the sides down occasionally so that it blends evenly. Pour the mixture into a bowl and beat in the grated cheeses by hand. Beat in the softened butter.

3. Let stand until the pesto is at room temperature. When the pasta is cooked, and before draining, quickly add and stir 1 or 2 tablespoons of the hot pasta water into the pesto. Toss with the hot drained pasta and serve.

Yield: Enough sauce for 1 pound pasta.

How to freeze pesto

Prepare the above recipe for pesto. Spoon it into a plastic container or freezer jar, filling the container almost to the brim. Seal and freeze. When ready to serve, defrost overnight in the refrigerator.

Spaghetti Carbonara

¼ pound pancetta or lean bacon (see note)
2 medium-size onions, finely chopped
3 tablespoons olive oil
Salt and freshly ground pepper to taste
5 tablespoons chopped parsley, Italian if available
½ cup chopped prosciutto
½ pound diced fontina or fontinella cheese
1 pound spaghetti
4 eggs, beaten
Grated Parmesan cheese

1. Cut the pancetta or bacon into 1-inch pieces. Cook in a small skillet until crisp. Drain on paper towels and set aside.

2. Sauté onions in the olive oil. When wilted, add salt, pepper, parsley, prosciutto, pancetta and fontina. (If fontinella is used, add to sauce the last few minutes). Cover and simmer over low heat, stirring often, for 5 to 10 minutes.

3. Cook the spaghetti in boiling salted water until tender but firm to the bite, al dente. Drain, place in a serving bowl, add eggs and toss well. Add sauce and toss again. Serve immediately with grated Parmesan cheese.

Yield: 6 servings.

Note: Pancetta is available in Italian pork stores.

Paglia e Fieno alla Romano *(Straw and hay noodles)*

1. Grill, broil or cook the sausages in a skillet until done. Peel off and discard the sausage skin. Cut the meat into 1-inch cubes.

2. Warm the cream and have it ready.

3. Cook the pasta in boiling salted water for 3 to 5 minutes. Drain and empty it into a warm deep dish. Add the butter, 1 tablespoon at a time, tossing. Add the sausage and cream, tossing. Add salt and pepper to taste. Spoon the cheese in, tossing, and serve immediately.

Yield: 4 servings.

1 pound sweet or hot Italian sausages
½ cup heavy cream
½ pound green noodles
½ pound white noodles
8 tablespoons butter, at room temperature
Salt and freshly ground pepper
1 cup grated Parmesan cheese

Pasta with Ginger and Garlic

One of the oddest, tastiest and most intriguing recipes for pasta we've found in a long time was sent to us by Joe Famularo, an executive with McGraw-Hill publishers and a cook book author. Joe, a fine cook, dispatched the recipe to us pursuant to one more suggestion that noodles may have first been created in China. "I don't know the origin of this dish," he wrote, "but my father cooked it religiously and swore it was an old ancestral recipe from Potenza in Italy. I often accused him of inventing it, however, for he was born on Mott Street—a street that quietly divided Little Italy from Chinatown."

1. Heat the water in a kettle in which the pasta will boil.

2. Meanwhile, heat the oil in a saucepan and add the carrot. Cook for about 3 minutes, stirring occasionally. Add the garlic, ginger, scallion, oregano, salt, pepper flakes and vermouth. Cook for about 5 minutes. Add the 1 cup of water. Bring to the boil and simmer until the pasta is cooked (do not cook the sauce more than 15 minutes total cooking time).

3. Cook and drain the pasta and return it to the kettle. Add the butter. Add three-quarters of the ginger sauce. Toss.

4. Serve the pasta in hot bowls, with about 1 tablespoon of remaining sauce spooned on top. Serve Parmesan cheese separately.

Yield: 4 to 6 servings.

1 pound vermicelli, spaghettini or spaghetti
½ cup olive oil
½ cup finely diced carrot
1 tablespoon finely chopped garlic
2 tablespoons finely chopped fresh ginger
2 tablespoons chopped scallion
1 teaspoon dried oregano
Salt to taste
¼ to ½ teaspoon hot red pepper flakes
½ cup dry vermouth
1 cup water
4 tablespoons butter
Grated Parmesan cheese

Spaghetti with Eggplant

5	tablespoons olive oil
2	cloves garlic, finely minced
4	cups peeled tomatoes, preferably imported if canned
4	tablespoons tomato paste
¾	cup water
1	teaspoon sugar
	Salt and freshly ground pepper
½	cup chopped parsley
1	tablespoon finely chopped fresh basil, or ½ teaspoon dried
1½	pounds eggplant
½	pound or more spaghetti
¾	cup grated Parmesan cheese

1. Heat 1 tablespoon of oil in a saucepan and add the garlic. Cook, stirring, without browning and add the tomatoes, tomato paste, water, sugar, salt and pepper to taste, parsley and basil. Stir to blend. Partly cover and cook, stirring frequently, for about 45 minutes.

2. Meanwhile, cut off the ends of the eggplant. Peel the eggplant and cut it into ½-inch cubes.

3. Heat the remaining oil in a large skillet and, when it is very hot, add the eggplant and salt to taste. Cook the eggplant, tossing, until it is nicely browned and tender. Add the eggplant to the tomato sauce and cover. Cook for 30 to 40 minutes, or until the eggplant blends with the sauce.

4. Cook the spaghetti to the desired degree of doneness and drain. Serve hot with the sauce. Serve grated Parmesan cheese on the side. This sauce is excellent when reheated.

Yield: 6 to 8 servings.

Palle di Pasta *(Deep-fried fettucine balls)*

3	tablespoons butter
3	tablespoons flour
1	cup milk
½	cup heavy cream
	Salt and freshly ground pepper
¼	teaspoon grated nutmeg
¼	cup grated Parmesan cheese
6	ounces (½ package) fettucine, preferably imported (see note)
2	eggs, lightly beaten
2	tablespoons water
1½	cups fresh bread crumbs
	Oil for deep frying
	Ragu bolognese (see recipe below)

1. Melt the butter in a saucepan and add the flour, stirring with a wire whisk. When blended, add the milk, stirring rapidly with the whisk. Add the cream and continue stirring until blended and smooth and simmering. Add salt and pepper to taste and the nutmeg. Stir in the cheese. Let cool for about ½ hour.

2. Drop the fettucine into boiling salted water and cook until tender. Take care not to overcook, however, or the pasta will become mushy. Drain the pasta well.

3. Fold the pasta into the cream sauce. Let cool. Chill overnight.

4. With the hands, scoop up equal amounts of the pasta mixture. Shape into balls, rolling between the palms. There should be about 10 balls.

5. Beat the eggs with salt, pepper and water. Dredge the balls all over with the egg mixture, then in bread crumbs.

6. Heat the oil and, when quite hot, add the balls. Cook, turning often and controlling the heat as necessary so that the balls cook properly and are crisp and golden all over without becoming too dark. Total cooking time should be about 8 min-

utes. Serve with ragu bolognese and, if desired, additional Parmesan cheese.

Yield: 5 to 10 servings.

Note: Fresh noodles made with about 1 cup of flour may be used for this dish. If used, cook briefly, less than a minute, or until tender.

1. Blend the beef and pork. Chop the pancetta until fine and add it.

2. Heat the butter in a large heavy skillet and add the meat mixture, stirring to break up any lumps. Cook briefly and add the onion, celery and carrot. Continue cooking, stirring often, until the meat is nicely browned. Add salt and pepper to taste. Add the wine and cook, stirring occasionally, until wine is reduced.

3. Add 1 cup of broth and cook until most of the liquid disappears. Add the remaining broth and cook until that has cooked down and little liquid remains. Add the tomato paste and cook briefly.

4. Meanwhile, heat the milk almost but not quite to boiling. Add it to the meat and simmer until most of the milk is absorbed.

Yield: 4 to 6 servings.

Ragu bolognese

½ **pound ground beef**
½ **pound ground pork**
¼ **pound rolled, salt pancetta (see note on page 440), or use lean salt pork**
4 **tablespoons butter**
1 **cup finely chopped onion**
⅓ **cup finely chopped celery**
½ **cup finely chopped carrot**
 Salt and freshly ground pepper
½ **cup dry red wine, preferably Italian**
2 **cups fresh or canned beef broth**
2 **tablespoons tomato paste**
½ **cup milk**

Linguine and Clam Sauce

1. Open and drain the clams and reserve both clams and juice. Chop the clams. There should be about 1 cup of clams and 1½ cups of juice.

2. Pour the juice into a kettle and add the water and salt. This is for cooking the linguine or spaghetti. When ready to cook, bring the liquid to the boil and add the linquine. The clam sauce requires less time than the linguine.

3. As the linguine cooks, heat the cream in a saucepan just to the boil.

4. Meanwhile, heat half the butter in another saucepan and add the clams, garlic, parsley, basil, thyme and pepper. Do not add salt at this time. Add the cream.

5. When the linguine is done, drain it in a colander. Pour it onto a large hot platter and add the sauce immediately, tossing. Add the remaining butter, cheese and salt to taste, tossing with a fork and spoon. Serve very, very hot with a pepper mill on the side.

Yield: 4 to 6 servings.

18 **cherrystone clams**
4 **cups water**
 Salt to taste
1 **pound linguine**
1 **cup heavy cream**
8 **tablespoons butter**
1 **tablespoon finely chopped garlic**
4 **tablespoons finely chopped parsley**
3 **tablespoons finely chopped basil**
1 **teaspoon chopped fresh thyme leaves, or ½ teaspoon dried**
 Freshly ground pepper to taste
½ **cup grated Parmesan cheese**

Pasta with Sausages and Pork

2 links hot Italian sausage
4 links sweet Italian sausage
1 ready-to-cook braciole, about ¾ pound
1 pound spareribs, cut into 3- or 4-inch squares, or 1 pound boneless pork, left whole
1 2-pound 3-ounce can tomatoes, preferably Italian peeled tomatoes
1 6-ounce can tomato paste
¾ cup water
½ cup finely chopped onion
2 cloves garlic, finely minced
Salt and freshly ground pepper
½ teaspoon hot red pepper flakes, more or less to taste
2 teaspoons dried oregano
1 pound pasta such as ziti, fusilli, shells or rigatoni
½ cup grated cheese, preferably Romano

1. In a large, heavy skillet, brown the sausages. When they start to give up their fat, add the braciole and spareribs. Cook until all the meats are well browned on all sides.

2. Meanwhile, strain the tomatoes and add them to a kettle large enough to hold the meats. Add the tomato paste. Rinse the can out with the water and add the water.

3. Transfer the meats to the kettle and pour off all but 2 tablespoons of fat from the skillet. Add the onion and cook until transparent. Add the garlic and brown lightly. Add this to the kettle. Add the salt, pepper, pepper flakes and oregano. Partly cover. Cook, stirring often from the bottom to prevent sticking and burning, for a total of 2½ hours, skimming the surface as necessary to remove fat and scum.

4. Cook the pasta to the desired degree of doneness. Drain the pasta and return it to the pot. Add a little sauce and ½ cup cheese. Toss lightly to coat.

5. Place the meat on a platter. Spoon a cup or so of sauce on the bottom of a hot, deep serving dish. Add the pasta and spoon a little more sauce on top. Serve the remaining sauce on the side. Serve, if desired, with additional grated cheese.

Yield: 6 to 10 servings.

Spaghetti alla Puttanesca con Vongole *(Spaghetti whore's-style with clams)*

¼ cup olive oil
1 tablespoon finely minced garlic
4 cups peeled, chopped tomatoes, preferably fresh, or imported Italian plum tomatoes
⅓ cup finely chopped parsley
2 tablespoons finely chopped fresh basil, or 1 tablespoon dried
1 teaspoon dried oregano
½ teaspoon red pepper flakes, or more to taste
2 tablespoons drained capers
18 pitted black olives (see note)
2 2-ounce cans flat anchovies

1. Heat the oil in a deep heavy skillet and add the garlic. Cook without browning, for about 30 seconds. Add the tomatoes, half the parsley, basil, oregano, red pepper flakes, capers and olives. Cook over moderately high heat for about 25 minutes. Stir frequently.

2. Meanwhile, drain the anchovies and chop them coarsely. Wash the clams under cold running water until clean.

3. When the sauce is ready, add the anchovies and remaining parsley. Cook, stirring, for about 1 minute.

4. Add the clams and cover the skillet closely. Cook for about 5 minutes, or until all the clams are opened.

5. Serve piping hot with freshly cooked spaghetti.

Yield: 6 servings.

Note: By all means use imported black olives for this dish, not the insipid California verison. Imported black olives are available in most specialty food shops as well as in Italian,

Greek and Spanish markets. We use a cherry pitter to remove the pits, but a paring knife will do.

The clams may be omitted from this dish and it will still be excellent.

24 littleneck clams, the smaller the better

1 pound spaghetti, cooked to the desired degree of doneness

Ragu Abruzzese (A meat and tomato sauce for pasta)

The chefs of Italy are equally as chauvinistic about distinguishing the places of their birth as gastronomic spawning places as are the French. Just as French chefs claim that the gastronomic center of France (if not the universe) is Lyons, so do many Italian chefs claim that the mountainous Abruzzi region of Italy has produced the preponderance of great Italian chefs.

Luigi Nanni, whom we consider to be one of the best Italian chefs in Manhattan, is from Abruzzi and maintains that poor regions tend to produce fine cooks who must exercise the greatest skill with such bounty as they have. Signor Nanni, chef-padrone of Nanni's and Il Valetto in Manhattan, led us though a blissful meal in our home that proved his great skill. One of the dishes was an exceptional pasta bathed in his Abruzzese tomato sauce.

1. Heat the oil in a heavy kettle and add the bones. Sprinkle with salt and pepper and cook, stirring occasionally, until nicely browned, about 10 or 15 minutes.

2. Add the meat and cook, stirring occasionally, for about 30 minutes, or until browned. Pour off fat from kettle.

3. Add the butter, celery, onion, shallots, garlic and bay leaves. Cook for about 20 minutes, stirring occasionally. Add the wine and simmer for 10 minutes. Add the tomatoes, tomato paste and water. Cook for about 30 minutes and add the rosemary. Cook for about 1 hour longer.

4. Remove the bones. The meat clinging to the bones is excellent for nibbling on.

5. Remove and discard the bay leaves and cheesecloth bag.

6. Cover the mushrooms with water and bring to the boil. Simmer about 1 minute. Drain and add to the tomato sauce. Cook briefly. This sauce is now ready to be served with almost any form of pasta. The meat may be served with the sauce or separately after the pasta course. This sauce will keep for several days in the refrigerator and much longer if reheated occasionally. It freezes well.

Yield: About 4 quarts of sauce.

1 cup vegetable oil

2½ pounds veal and beef bones, preferably a few marrow bones included
Salt and freshly ground pepper

2¼ pounds flank steak, cut into ½-inch-thick rectangles, measuring about 2 by 4 inches

½ pound butter

¾ cup finely chopped heart of celery

1½ cups chopped onion

½ cup chopped shallots

3 cloves garlic, chopped

3 bay leaves

2 cups dry red wine

4 quarts tomatoes, put through a sieve or food mill to eliminate seeds

1 cup tomato paste

1½ cups water

1 sprig fresh rosemary, or 1 tablespoon dried, tied in a cheesecloth bag

¾ cup dried Italian mushrooms

Marinara Sauce

6 cups canned Italian plum
   tomatoes
2 tablespoons olive oil
1 tablespoon finely chopped
   garlic
2 teaspoons dried oregano
3 tablespoons chopped parsley
   Salt and freshly ground pepper

1. Place the tomatoes in a saucepan and cook until reduced by half. Stir often to prevent sticking.

2. Heat the oil in another saucepan and add the garlic. Cook briefly and add the tomatoes, oregano, parsley, salt and pepper to taste.

Yield: About 3 cups.

Penne Arrabbiata *(Tomato and hot chili sauce with pasta)*

1 pound, about 1½ cups,
   dried Italian mushrooms
4½ cups fresh or canned
   tomatoes
6 to 8 fresh basil leaves, optional
1 hot, dried red pepper (see
   note)
   Salt and freshly ground
   pepper to taste
4 to 6 strips bacon (see note)
¼ cup olive oil
1 or 2 teaspoons finely minced
   garlic
1 pound penne or other
   tubular pasta
   Grated Parmesan cheese

1. Place the mushrooms in a mixing bowl and add warm water to cover. Let stand, stirring occasionally, until softened.

2. Meanwhile, put the tomatoes and basil in a saucepan and bring to the boil. Add the hot, dried red pepper, salt and pepper. Some cooks recommend puréeing the tomatoes in a food mill or food processor before or after cooking down. Others prefer mashing them down with a spoon as they cook for a bulkier texture.

3. Cook, stirring occasionally from the bottom to prevent sticking, for about 45 minutes, or until reduced to about 3½ cups. If the sauce becomes too thick as it cooks down, add some of the mushroom liquid or water.

4. Double the bacon strips over themselves and cut the strips crosswise into ⅛-inch strips.

5. Heat the oil in a small, deep skillet and add the bacon pieces. Cook, stirring, until rendered of fat but not crisp.

6. Add the garlic and stir. Cook briefly. Meanwhile, squeeze the soaked mushrooms to extract most of the liquid and add them, stirring. Cook, stirring, for about 3 minutes. Add the cooked-down tomatoes, salt and pepper to taste. If desired, add hot crushed red pepper flakes. For a richer sauce stir in 1 or 2 more tablespoons of olive oil.

7. Cook and drain the penne. Serve with the sauce and grated Parmesan cheese.

Yield: Four to six servings.

Note: The whole pepper may be eliminated, in which case add hot red pepper flakes to the sauce when it is almost ready.

Generally, in Italy, guanciale (salted or otherwise cured pork cheeks) or pancetta (salted or otherwise cured pork belly) is used in preference to bacon. These products are available in Italian pork stores.

Rigatoni al Forno

1. Heat 3 tablespoons of butter in a heavy skillet and add the onion. Cook, stirring, until wilted. If the mushrooms are tiny, leave them whole. Otherwise, quarter them or slice them, depending on size. Add the mushrooms to the onion and cook, stirring frequently, until the mushrooms give up their liquid. Cook further until the liquid evaporates.

2. In a separate skillet, cook the pork or sausage meat (take the skins off) until rendered of its fat. Use a wooden spoon to break up any lumps. Add the meat to the mushroom mixture and stir it in. Sprinkle with garlic, fennel (omit the fennel if sausages are used), basil, sage, oregano and red pepper. Cook for about 3 minutes, stirring. Add the tomatoes, salt, pepper, water and chicken broth. Simmer for 1 hour, stirring frequently.

3. Add the chopped parsley and simmer for 15 minutes longer. Stir in the olive oil and set aside to cool.

4. Drop the rigatoni or ziti into a large quantity of boiling salted water and cook, stirring rapidly to make certain that the pieces of pasta float free and do not stick to the bottom. Cook for about 8 minutes. Do not cook longer because the pasta will be baked later. Immediately drain the pasta in a colander and run cold water over it. Drain well.

5. Preheat the oven to 400 degrees.

6. Spoon a thin layer of sauce into a 13½- x 8¾- x 1¾-inch baking dish. Add a single layer of rigatoni. Scatter half the mozzarella over it and sprinkle with 1 tablespoon Parmesan. Continue making layers of sauce, pasta, mozzarella and Parmesan, ending with a layer of sauce and Parmesan. Use only about ½ cup of Parmesan for the dish. The remainder will be served with the finished dish.

7. Dot the casserole with the remaining butter and bake, uncovered, for 30 minutes, or until bubbling hot throughout. Run the dish briefly under the broiler to give it a nice brown glaze. Serve the dish cut into squares with Parmesan cheese on the side.

Yield: 8 to 12 servings.

7 tablespoons butter
2 cups chopped onion
1 pound mushrooms
1 pound ground pork or Italian sausages
1 teaspoon finely minced garlic
¾ teaspoon fennel seeds
1 tablespoon finely chopped fresh basil, or 1 teaspoon crushed dried basil
¾ teaspoon crushed sage
¾ teaspoon crushed oregano
1 dried red pepper, chopped, optional
6 cups peeled Italian plum tomatoes
Salt and freshly ground pepper to taste
1 cup water
1 cup fresh or canned chicken broth
¼ cup finely chopped parsley
2 tablespoons olive oil
1 pound rigatoni or ziti
½ pound mozzarella cheese, cut into ½-inch cubes
2 cups grated Parmesan cheese

Lobster with Tomatoes and Tarragon *(For spaghetti)*

3 live lobsters, about 1¼ pounds each
4 tablespoons butter
Salt and freshly ground pepper
¼ cup olive oil
⅓ cup finely diced onion
3 tablespoons finely minced shallots
½ teaspoon chopped garlic
⅓ cup finely diced celery
¼ cup finely diced carrots
1 tablespoon finely chopped fresh tarragon, or 2 teaspoons dried
2 tablespoons tomato paste
¼ cup Cognac
1⅓ cups finely diced or chopped fresh or canned tomatoes
1 cup dry white wine

1 Plunge a knife into each lobster where the body and tail section meet, to sever the spinal cord. This will kill the lobster instantly. Save all juices that flow from the bodies. Break off the tails and cut each tail crosswise into 3 pieces. Crack the claws. Discard the tough sac near the eyes. Split the carcass in half widthwise. Remove the lobster liver and coral and place in a bowl. Add 2 tablespoons butter and set aside.

2. Sprinkle the lobster with salt and pepper to taste.

3. Heat the oil in a large, heavy skillet or casserole and add the lobster. Cook, stirring, for about 2 minutes or until shell starts to turn red. Add the onion, shallots, garlic, celery, carrots, half the tarragon and tomato paste. Stir to blend and cover. Cook for about 3 minutes. Flame with the Cognac.

4. Add the tomatoes, any liquid from the lobster and wine. Add salt and pepper to taste. Cover and cook for about 5 minutes. Total cooking time should be about 10 minutes.

5. Remove the lobster pieces from the skillet. When cool enough to handle, remove the lobster meat from the tail and claws and set aside.

6. Blend the coral and liver with the butter and stir it into the sauce. Bring to the boil over high heat. Put the sauce through a food mill, pressing to extract as much liquid as possible from the solids. Discard the solids. Return the sauce to the skillet and add the lobster pieces. Sprinkle with the remaining tarragon and swirl in the remaining butter. Serve with hot spaghetti.

Yield: 4 to 6 servings.

Chicken Lasagne with Meatballs

1 2½-pound chicken, boiled, with reserved broth
28 to 32 meatballs (see recipe below)
3 cups tomato sauce (see recipe page 450)
6 tablespoons butter
2 tablespoons flour

1. Preheat the oven to 400 degrees.

2. Cook the chicken and, when it is cool enough to handle, remove the skin and bones. Add the skin and bones to the broth and continue cooking. Shred the meat. There should be about 2 cups. Set aside.

3. Prepare the meatballs and simmer them in the tomato sauce for about 20 minutes, or until sauce is thickened.

4. Melt 2 tablespoons of butter in a saucepan and add the flour, stirring with a wire whisk. When blended and smooth, add 1 cup of strained, reserved chicken broth, stirring rapidly with the whisk. (Reserve the remaining strained broth for another purpose.) Stir this sauce into the tomato and meatball mixture. Set aside.

5. Cook or parboil the lasagne according to the package directions and have it ready. Do not cook it far in advance of using.

6. Spoon a little of the tomato sauce (do not add meatballs at this time) over the bottom of a lasagne pan measuring approximately 13- x 8- x 2-inches. Add a layer of lasagne with edges slightly overlapping. Spoon in half the tomato and meatball mixture and smooth it over. Add a layer of chicken, half the ricotta, smoothing it over, half the mozzarella slices and a generous sprinkling of Parmesan.

7. Add another layer of lasagne, meatballs in sauce (reserving ½ cup of sauce without meatballs for topping), ricotta, mozzarella, another sprinkling of Parmesan and ricotta. Spoon over the reserved ½ cup of sauce and 3 tablespoons of Parmesan. Melt the remaining 4 tablespoons of butter and pour it over. Bake for 15 to 20 minutes, or until the lasagne is bubbling throughout and golden brown. Serve cut into squares with additional Parmesan cheese.

Yield: 8 to 12 servings.

Note: Generally speaking, half of a 1-pound package of lasagne is sufficient for a platter of lasagne. This recipe used 10 or 12 "ribbons" of lasagne.

1 package lasagne (see note)
1 pint ricotta cheese
1 12-ounce package mozzarella cheese, thinly sliced
1 cup grated Parmesan cheese

Combine all the ingredients except the oil in a mixing bowl. Shape the mixture into 28 to 32 small meatballs. Heat the oil in a skillet and brown the meatballs on all sides. The meatballs are now ready to be added to a sauce for further cooking.

Yield: 28 to 32 meatballs.

Meatballs for lasagne

½ pound ground pork, beef or veal, or any combination of the three
¼ cup fine, fresh bread crumbs
¼ cup grated Parmesan cheese
1 egg yolk
2 tablespoons heavy cream
⅛ teaspoon grated nutmeg
½ teaspoon chopped garlic
2 tablespoons chopped parsley
Salt and freshly ground pepper
3 tablespoons corn, peanut or olive oil, approximately

Tomato sauce

2 tablespoons olive oil
6 tablespoons butter
1½ cups chopped onion
1 tablespoon chopped garlic
¼ pound fresh mushrooms, finely chopped
¾ cup finely chopped carrots
2 tablespoons finely chopped fresh parsley
1 tablespoon finely chopped fresh basil, or 1 teaspoon dried
6 sprigs fresh thyme, or 1 teaspoon dried
1 teaspoon sugar
1 whole clove
½ cup dry white wine
4 cups chopped fresh or canned tomatoes
Salt and freshly ground pepper to taste

1. Heat the oil and 2 tablespoons of butter in a heavy casserole and add the onion, garlic, mushrooms, carrot, parsley, basil, thyme, sugar and clove. Cook, stirring, until the mixture is almost dry but still moist, about 10 minutes.

2. Add the wine and cook, stirring, over high heat until wine evaporates. Add the tomatoes, salt and pepper and bring to the boil. Partly cover and simmer for 1 hour.

3. Put the mixture through a food mill, pushing through as much of the vegetable solids as possible. Stir in the remaining butter and bring to the boil.

Yield: About 3 cups.

Lasagne with Ricotta and Sausages

1 pound sweet or hot Italian sausages
1 tablespoon olive oil
1 clove garlic, finely minced
½ pound ground lean pork
½ cup dry white wine
3 cups tomato sauce (see recipe above)
Salt and freshly ground pepper
12 lasagne strips
2 cups ricotta cheese
¼ cup hot water
1 cup grated Parmesan cheese
¼ cup melted butter

1. Preheat the oven to 375 degrees.

2. Remove and discard the skins from the sausages. Heat the oil in a skillet and add the sausage meat. Cook, stirring to break up the meat. When the sausage has given up its fat, drain off all but about 1 tablespoon of oil from the skillet. Add the garlic and pork to the sausage, stirring to break up the pork. Cook, stirring, until pork turns white. Add the wine and bring to the boil over high heat. Cook, stirring, until wine evaporates. Add the tomato sauce, salt and pepper to taste.

3. Bring a large quantity of salted water to the boil and add the lasagne strips, one at a time. Cook until almost tender. Add a quart of cold water to the pot. Drain and spread the strips on a damp cloth.

4. Lightly grease a lasagne pan measuring approximately 13- x 8- x 2-inches. Add a layer of lasagne.

5. Beat the ricotta with the hot water to make it spreadable. Spread about ⅓ of the ricotta over the lasagne. Spread a layer of the meat sauce over this and sprinkle with about ¼ of the cheese. Continue making layers, ending with a layer of lasagne sprinkled with a final quarter of the cheese. Pour the

melted butter over all and bake for 15 to 20 minutes, or until the lasagne is piping hot and bubbling throughout.

Yield: 4 to 6 servings.

Spinach Ravioli

1. Place the flour in a mixing bowl and make a well in the center. Beat the eggs lightly and add them to the well. Sprinkle with salt to taste. Add the water. Work well with the fingers until the dough can be handled easily. Wrap in wax paper and refrigerate.

2. Drop the spinach into boiling water to cover and cook for about 1 minute. Drain immediately. When cool enough to handle, squeeze the spinach until most of the moisture is pressed out. There should be about ¾ cup of spinach. Put in a mixing bowl.

3. Add the egg, parsley, ricotta, nutmeg and the ¾ cup Parmesan cheese. Add the garlic, salt and pepper to taste and blend well with the fingers.

4. Divide dough into 4 pieces. Roll out the dough by hand, if you are expert in pasta-making, or use a pasta machine and roll out the dough according to the manufacturer's instructions.

5. There are numerous techniques for filling pasta for ravioli. The simplest is to use a ravioli-maker that can be purchased in stores where first-class cooking equipment is sold. The commonest has 12 metal indentations. The surface should be lightly floured. As the dough is rolled out, a rectangle of dough is laid over the surface and a small amount of filling, about 1½ teaspoons, is spooned into the dough-covered indentations. Another rectangle of dough is laid over, stretching the dough gently, if necessary, to cover the entire pan, and a small rolling pin is run over this to seal the filling while simultaneously cutting out patterns of ravioli, which may be separated. Or, the dough can be rolled out, small mounds of filling added at intervals. This can be covered with another sheet of dough and a ravioli cutter used to outline the dumplings.

6. As the ravioli are made, arrange them in one layer on a dry floured kitchen towel.

7. When ready to serve, drop the ravioli into rapidly boiling salted water. Cook until ravioli rise to the top, stirring gently on occasion. Partly cover and continue to cook for 10 to 15 minutes. Cooking time will depend on thickness of dough. Drain well.

The dough:

4 cups flour
5 large eggs, or 1¼ cups, plus 2 egg yolks
Salt
½ to 2 tablespoons cold water

The filling:

¾ pound bulk spinach, or 1 10-ounce package fresh spinach
1 large egg, beaten
2 tablespoons finely chopped parsley
1 cup ricotta cheese
¼ teaspoon grated nutmeg
¾ cup grated Parmesan cheese
¼ teaspoon finely minced garlic
Salt and freshly ground pepper

The service:

¼ pound butter
5 leaves fresh or dried sage, snipped in half
Grated Parmesan cheese

8. As the ravioli cook, heat the butter in a saucepan. Pour off about 3 tablespoons into another saucepan and add the sage. Cook for about 30 seconds. Add the remaining butter and pour hot over the ravioli. Serve Parmesan cheese on the side.

Yield: 8 dozen ravioli, or 6 to 8 servings.

Gnocchi Parisienne   *(Italian dumplings with mornay sauce)*

1 cup water
8 tablespoons butter
  Salt
⅛ teaspoon grated nutmeg
1 cup flour
4 eggs
6 tablespoons grated Parmesan cheese
  Mornay sauce (see recipe page 645)

1. Put the cup of water in a saucepan and add the butter, salt to taste and nutmeg. Bring to the boil.

2. Add the flour all at once, stirring vigorously and thoroughly in a circular fashion. Stir until a ball is formed and the mixture cleans the sides of the saucepan.

3. Add the eggs, one at a time, beating vigorously until they are well blended with the mixture. This mixture is known as a pâte à choux.

4. When all the eggs are added, add the cheese, beating vigorously until it is well blended.

5. Bring 2 quarts of water to the boil. Spoon the pâte à choux into a pastry bag fitted with a round tip (Number 6). Hold the tip over the boiling water. Squeeze the pâte à choux out of the bag and, using a small knife, cut it off into 1½-inch lengths or cylinders. Let the cylinders fall directly into the water, which should be barely simmering. Let cook for 3 or 4 minutes.

6. Drain. If the pieces are not to be used immediately, drop them into a basin of ice water. When ready to use, drain again on absorbent paper toweling. These cylinders are known as gnocchi.

7. Pour the gnocchi into a baking dish (an oval dish measuring about 8- x 14- x 2-inches is suitable) and spoon mornay sauce over all. Bake in an oven preheated to 400 degrees for about 15 minutes.

Yield: 6 to 8 servings.

Gnocchi with Tomato Sauce

  Gnocchi (see recipe for gnocchi parisienne above)
2½ cups fresh or canned tomatoes
  Salt and freshly ground pepper

1. Prepare the gnocchi and set aside.

2. Put the tomatoes in the container of a food processor or blender. Process until liquid. Pour this into a kettle and add salt and pepper to taste. Bring to the boil and simmer for about 5 minutes.

3. Add the cream and cook for about 5 minutes. Remove from the heat and add the egg yolk, stirring rapidly.

4. Spoon the gnocchi into a baking dish (an oval dish measuring about 8- x 14- x 2-inches is suitable) and spoon the sauce over. Sprinkle with cheese and melted butter.

5. When ready to bake, preheat the oven to 400 degrees. Place the dish in the oven and bake for 15 minutes.

Yield: 6 to 8 servings.

1	cup heavy cream
1	egg yolk
2	tablespoons grated Gruyère or Parmesan cheese
2	tablespoons melted butter

Gnocchi di Patate

1. Place the potatoes in a kettle and add cold water to cover. Add salt to taste and bring to the boil. Simmer until the potatoes are tender but not mushy. Drain and let cool.

2. Peel the potatoes. Put them through a ricer, or food mill. Or put them through a meat grinder using the medium blade. Add egg yolks and blend well.

3. Scoop the flour onto a flat surface. Start kneading the potatoes, adding the flour gradually. Add only enough flour to make a firm, soft and delicate dough. If too much flour is added they become tough when cooked. Knead thoroughly, then shape the dough, rolling with the palms to make a thick sausage shape about 12 inches long. Using a knife or pastry scraper cut the roll into 11 equal slices. Roll each slice into a long cigar shape. Cut each cigar into 18 or 19 pieces. These pieces will resemble miniature pillows. Flour the pieces and set aside until ready to cook.

4. Drop the pieces of dough, half of them at a time, into a large quantity of boiling salted water and let cook until they rise to the surface. Drain quickly and chill under cold running water. Drain well.

5. When ready to serve, drop the pieces once more into a large quantity of boiling salted water. When they float the second time, drain them and return them to the pot. Add the melted butter and cheese. Add the sauce and sprinkle with pepper. Serve with additional sauce on the side.

Yield: 6 or more servings.

3	large potatoes, preferably Idaho potatoes, about 1¾ pounds
	Salt to taste
2	egg yolks
1¾ to 2	cups flour
6	tablespoons melted butter Grated Parmesan cheese
2	cups tomato and onion sauce (see recipe below) Freshly ground pepper

1. Using the hands, crush the tomatoes.

2. Heat the lard and add the onions. Cook, stirring often, until the onions are golden brown, about 20 minutes.

3. Add the ham and cook for 5 minutes. Add the tomatoes and cook for about 2 hours, stirring often to prevent sticking. Add salt, pepper and basil.

Yield: About 6 cups of sauce.

Tomato and onion sauce

8	cups canned tomatoes, preferably imported from Italy
¼	pound lard
3	cups thinly sliced onions
⅓	pound ham, preferably prosciutto, cut into very thin strips, about 1½ cups Salt and freshly ground pepper to taste
¼	cup freshly snipped basil leaves, or 1 tablespoon dried

X. Rice, Potatoes and Beans

A Perfect Batch of Rice

Producing a perfect dish of rice Western-style requires a certain attention to detail—the proportion of rice to liquid and the cooking time should be exact. But these two requirements are easy to learn because they are constant, no matter what the other ingredients. The liquid should measure one and one-half times the quantity of rice, and it should be cooked on top of the stove or baked in the oven for exactly seventeen minutes. Ignore those package directions that sometimes call for twice as much liquid as rice. It defeats the purpose of properly cooked rice.

3 tablespoons butter
½ cup finely chopped onion
2 cups rice
   Salt
   Cayenne pepper or Tabasco sauce
3 cups fresh or canned chicken broth
   Parsley
1 bay leaf
1 sprig fresh thyme, or ½ teaspoon dried

1. Preheat the oven to 400 degrees.
2. Heat 2 tablespoons butter in a saucepan and add the onion. Stir and cook until onion wilts.
3. Add the rice and stir until grains are coated.
4. Add salt to taste. Add a pinch of cayenne pepper or Tabasco sauce.
5. Add a bouquet garni consisting of a small bundle of parsley sprigs, bay leaf and thyme.
6. Let the broth come to the boil. At the boil, cover closely and place in the oven. Set a kitchen timer for exactly 17 minutes and bake the rice for precisely that long.
7. Remove and discard the bouquet garni. Add 1 tablespoon of butter and toss to blend.

Yield: 8 servings.

Note: The rice can also be cooked for the same amount of time on top of the stove, provided the saucepan has a tight cover.

This recipe is easily divided simply by reducing all ingredients by half. The basic formula is 1 cup of rice for each 1½ cups liquid.

Rice variations

Saffron rice: Crumble 1 teaspoon of loosely packed stem saffron. Add it to the saucepan and stir just before adding the raw rice.

454

Cumin rice: Use 1 clove finely minced garlic and 1 teaspoon of ground cumin. Add it to the saucepan and stir just before adding the raw rice.

Rice Valenciana

1. Heat the butter in a saucepan and add the sweet pepper. Cook, stirring, for about 5 minutes. The cubes must remain crisp-tender. Add the diced ham and cook to heat through, for about 1 minute. Add the peas and remove from the heat.

2. Pour and scrape the rice into a hot bowl. Add the ham mixture and toss to blend evenly.

3. If desired, spoon and scrape the mixture into a 5-cup mold, packing it down firmly with the back of a wooden spoon. When filled, pack down one final time with a spoon or spatula.

4. Invert a round plate over the mold. Turn the mold and plate over. Tap the mold with a piece of metal or wood. Do not unmold until ready to serve. Lift up the mold and serve immediately or the rice will fall apart as it stands.

Yield: 8 servings.

1 tablespoon butter
1⅓ cups sweet red or green pepper, cut into small cubes
⅔ cup diced ham
1 cup cooked fresh or frozen peas
2 cups cooked rice

Risotto

1. Heat 2 tablespoons of butter in a fairly large casserole. Add the onion and garlic and cook until onion is wilted. Add the rice, saffron, salt and pepper and stir to coat the grains.

2. Meanwhile, heat the broth and keep it at the simmer.

3. Add the wine to the rice and cook, stirring occasionally, until all the wine has evaporated.

4. Add 1 cup of the hot broth to the rice mixture and cook, stirring occasionally and gently, until all that liquid has been absorbed. Add ½ cup more of the broth and cook, stirring occasionally, until it is absorbed.

5. Continue cooking the rice in this fashion, adding ½ cup of broth each 3½ to 4 minutes, just until each ladle is absorbed. Remember that the rice must cook gently.

6. When all the broth has been added and absorbed, fold in the remaining butter and the cheese. When the rice is done, it should be tender but retain a small bite. The total cooking time should be from 25 to 28 minutes.

Yield: 8 servings.

6 tablespoons butter
3 tablespoons finely chopped onion
1 clove garlic, finely minced
2 cups rice
1 teaspoon chopped stem saffron
Salt and freshly ground pepper
5 cups fresh or canned chicken broth
½ cup dry white wine
¾ cup grated Parmesan cheese

Mushroom Rice with Turmeric

¾ pound mushrooms
4 tablespoons butter
½ cup finely chopped onion
1 clove garlic, finely minced
½ teaspoon ground turmeric
1 cup rice
1 bay leaf
1¼ cups fresh or canned chicken broth
    Salt and freshly ground pepper

1. Preheat the oven to 400 degrees.
2. Remove the stems from the mushrooms. Cut the mushroom caps into ½-inch cubes. There should be about 2 cups.
3. Heat 2 tablespoons of butter in a saucepan with a tight-fitting lid and add the onion and garlic. Cook for about 2 minutes and add the mushrooms. Cook for about 5 minutes, stirring. Sprinkle with turmeric and add the rice and bay leaf. Stir until the rice is coated and add the chicken broth, salt and pepper to taste. Cover closely and bring to the boil on top of the stove.
4. Bake for exactly 17 minutes. Remove the cover and discard the bay leaf. Using a 2-pronged fork, stir in the remaining butter while fluffing the rice.
Yield: 4 to 6 servings.

Buttered Wild Rice

1 cup wild rice
2 cups boiling water
   Salt and freshly ground pepper
3 tablespoons butter

1. Place the rice, water, salt and pepper to taste and 1 tablespoon of butter in the top of a double boiler.
2. Cover and steam the rice for 1 hour. Fluff the rice with a fork, stirring in the remaining butter.
Yield: 6 to 8 servings.

Rice with Dill Persian-style

2 cups long-grain rice
¼ cup salt
1 10-ounce package frozen baby lima beans
12 tablespoons butter
2 tablespoons water
1 or 2 Idaho potatoes
1¾ cups chopped fresh dill leaves (1 large bunch, tough stalks discarded)

1. Several hours before cooking the rice, wash it and rinse several times. Place it in a mixing bowl and add cold water to a depth of about 1 inch above the top of the rice. Add the salt and let stand about 1½ hours before cooking.
2. Drain the water into a large, heavy kettle. Add about 3 more quarts of water and bring to a vigorous boil. Add the drained rice and lima beans. Bring back to a boil and cook for 5 to 7 minutes, testing the grains frequently for state of doneness. The grains are ready when they are tender on the outside but have a tiny hard core in the center. Drain immediately or the rice will overcook.

3. Meanwhile, melt the butter with the 2 tablespoons water in a saucepan. Set aside.

4. Similarly, as the rice cooks, peel the potato or potatoes and cut into ¼-inch slices. There should be enough slices to cover the bottom of the same heavy kettle when the slices are placed snugly together without overlapping and in one layer.

5. Pour enough melted butter into the kettle to barely cover the bottom and arrange the potatoes over it. Spoon about one-fourth of the rice over the potatoes and add about one-fourth of the dill. Carefully stir the rice with a spoon to blend in the dill.

6. Do not disturb the potatoes at any point until the dish is fully cooked. Continue adding rice and dill layers, stirring to blend after each addition. Shape the rice-dill mixture into a cone-shaped mound. Pour the remaining butter evenly over the rice. Place the kettle on the heat and cook over medium heat for 5 minutes, or until steam comes through the center. Cover with a heavy bath towel folded so that it fits the top of the pot. Cover this with the lid and place a weight over the lid so that no steam can escape as the rice cooks. Reduce the heat and cook for 45 minutes to 1 hour.

7. When ready to serve, spoon the rice onto a large platter and garnish with the potato slices, bottom side up. The bottoms should be golden brown and crisp. Test the potatoes before removing. If the potatoes haven't browned, uncover and cook over medium heat for a few minutes until browned.

Yield: 8 servings.

Note: This rice can be cooked ahead of time and reheated by pouring a little boiling water over the rice and steaming for 15 minutes longer.

Lontong *(Indonesian rice rolls)*

1. Combine the rice and water in a saucepan. Do not add salt. Bring to the boil and let simmer for about 15 minutes. Remove the saucepan from the heat and let stand for 10 minutes. Let cool.

1 cup rice
3 cups water

2. Cut out 6 squares of aluminum foil, each measuring about 12 inches to a side. Place the squares on a flat surface. Scoop equal amounts of the rice onto each square, patting each into a thick sausage shape measuring about 6 inches long and 1½ inches in diameter. Roll up the rice tightly inside the foil, always keeping the fat sausage shape. Twist the ends firmly to seal.

3. Place the rolls in a kettle containing boiling water to cover

and cook for 45 minutes. Take care that the water covers the rolls at all times.

4. Drain and let the rolls stand for ½ hour. Open and cut into ½-inch-thick slices. Serve with Indonesian dishes. These rolls refrigerate well and may be reheated in boiling water for 10 minutes.

Yield: 6 rice rolls.

Puréed Potatoes

2 pounds potatoes
  Salt to taste
1 cup milk
4 tablespoons butter at room temperature
¼ teaspoon grated nutmeg

1. Peel the potatoes and quarter them or cut them into 2-inch cubes. Place the potatoes in a saucepan and add cold water to cover and simmer for 20 minutes, or until tender.

2. Drain the potatoes and put them through a food mill or ricer. Return them to the saucepan.

3. Meanwhile, bring the milk to the boil.

4. While the milk is being heated, use a wooden spoon and add the butter to the potatoes while beating. Add salt and nutmeg and beat in the hot milk.

Yield: About 6 servings.

Potatoes Mont d'Or

6 potatoes, about 2 pounds
  Salt to taste
1 cup milk
6 tablespoons butter
  Freshly ground pepper to taste
⅛ teaspoon nutmeg
2 eggs, separated
3 tablespoons grated Parmesan cheese

1. Preheat the oven to 350 degrees.

2. Peel the potatoes and cut them into thirds. Drop them into a saucepan with cold water to cover and salt to taste. Bring to the boil and simmer for about 20 minutes until tender.

3. Drain the potatoes well, leaving them in the saucepan. Place the potatoes in the oven to dry for about 5 minutes.

4. Meanwhile, bring the milk just to the boil.

5. Press the potatoes through a food mill into a saucepan and beat in the butter, salt, pepper and nutmeg.

6. Add the egg yolks and beat them in. Beat in the hot milk.

7. Beat the whites until stiff and fold them into the potatoes. Spoon the mixture into a baking dish (we used an oval dish that measured 8- x 14- x 2-inches) and smooth the top. Or, if you want to be fancy, spoon half the mixture into a baking dish and pipe the remainder through a pastry tube. Sprinkle with cheese and bake for 20 minutes. Brown under the broiler until glazed. Serve piping hot.

Yield: 8 or more servings.

Straw Potatoes

1. Peel the potatoes and drop them into cold water to cover.

2. Cut the potatoes into about ⅛-inch-thick slices with a knife or potato slicer. Stack the slices, a few at a time, and cut the potatoes into shreds about ⅛ inch thick. Drop the shreds into cold water as they are prepared.

3. Drain the potatoes well into a colander.

4. Heat the oil to about 360 degrees in a cooker for deep frying. Add the potatoes, a few handfuls at a time, and cook them, stirring frequently, until they are crisp and golden brown. Drain on absorbent toweling and sprinkle with salt.

Yield: 8 servings.

4 large potatoes (about 1½ pounds)
Oil for deep frying
Salt

Sautéed Potatoes

1. Rinse the potatoes and put them in a kettle. Add cold water to cover and salt. Simmer for 30 to 45 minutes, or until tender. Drain immediately.

2. Peel the potatoes. Cut each in half and cut each half into slices about ⅓ inch thick.

3. In a large, heavy skillet, heat the oil and butter. Add the potatoes, salt and pepper. Cook, tossing and stirring with care, until the potatoes are golden brown, 15 to 20 minutes. Sprinkle with garlic, toss and spoon onto a hot dish. Serve sprinkled with chopped parsley.

Yield: 8 or more servings.

3 pounds fairly large potatoes
Salt
¼ cup peanut, vegetable or corn oil
3 tablespoons butter
Freshly ground pepper
1 teaspoon finely minced garlic
1 tablespoon chopped parsley

Crumb Potatoes

1. Peel the potatoes and drop them into cold water. Remove them one at a time and cut a slice off all four sides plus a slice off each end. This will yield a potato with a boxlike shape. Reserve the outside slices for another purpose or discard them.

2. Cut the "boxes" into neat ¼-inch-lengthwise slices. Stack the slices, a few at a time, and cut the slices, lengthwise into ¼-inch-thick sticks.

3. Stack the sticks and cut them into ¼-inch cubes. Drop the cubes into cold water to prevent discoloration.

4. When ready to cook, drain the cubes into a colander. Run

2½ pounds potatoes
⅓ cup peanut, vegetable or corn oil
5 tablespoons butter
Salt

very hot, almost boiling water over them for about 10 seconds. Drain well.

5. Heat the oil and 1 tablespoon butter in a large, shallow skillet. Add the potatoes and salt to taste. Cook, shaking the skillet and stirring the potatoes, for about 8 minutes. Drain well. Wipe out the skillet.

6. Heat the remaining butter in the skillet and add the potatoes. Cook, shaking the skillet and stirring, for 6 to 8 minutes longer, or until the cubes are nicely browned and crisp. Drain and serve hot with salt.

Yield: 6 to 8 servings.

Potatoes Château Chinon

5 potatoes, about 1¾ pounds
Salt
2 eggs, lightly beaten
2 tablespoons flour
⅛ teaspoon grated nutmeg
½ cup Gruyère or Swiss cheese, cut into the finest possible dice
4 tablespoons oil

1. Peel the potatoes and grate them, using the fine blade of the grater. Spoon the potatoes into cheesecloth and squeeze to extract most of the moisture. There should be about 1¾ cups of pulp remaining.

2. Empty the potato pulp into a bowl and add salt to taste, the eggs, flour, nutmeg and cheese and blend well.

3. Heat the oil in a skillet and drop the potato mixture into the skillet, using about 3 tablespoons at a time. Cook until golden on one side; turn and cook on the other side.

Yield: 6 to 8 servings.

Gratin Dauphinoise   *(Baked sliced potatoes with Gruyère cheese)*

2½ pounds potatoes
Butter
2 cloves garlic, peeled
2 cups milk
1 cup heavy cream
Salt and freshly ground pepper to taste
Grated nutmeg to taste
1 cup grated Gruyère or Swiss cheese

1. Preheat the oven to 375 degrees.

2. Peel the potatoes and cut them into very thin slices. As they are sliced, drop them into cold water. Drain. There should be 6 or 7 cups.

3. Rub a baking dish (an oval one measuring about 14- x 8- x 2-inches is convenient) with a peeled clove of garlic. Crush both cloves of garlic lightly and put them in a saucepan.

4. Add the milk, cream, salt, pepper and nutmeg to the garlic cloves and bring to the boil. Strain this mixture over the potatoes. Discard the garlic. Sprinkle the top with the grated cheese. Place in the oven over a baking sheet to catch any drippings. Bake for about 1 hour, or until potatoes are tender and the cheese is golden.

Yield: 8 or more servings.

Pommes Soufflées I *(The traditional method)*

It is said that pommes soufflées came about quite by accident in the kitchen of the Pavillon Henri IV in Saint Germain-en-Laye, that splendid suburb of Paris. The story goes that when the chef got word that a trainload of dignitaries was en route from Paris, he tossed some potatoes into a kettle of hot fat. Moments later, word came that the train was delayed. The chef quickly removed the partly cooked potatoes and drained them. When the guests finally were assembled, he gave the potatoes a second frying—voila!—perfectly puffed potatoes.

1. Use two kettles, each containing peanut, vegetable or corn oil for deep frying.

2. Heat one kettle of fat to 275 degrees, the other to 375 degrees.

3. Peel 6 potatoes, about 2½ pounds. Rinse in cold water and pat as dry as possible. Using a slicing machine or a mandoline (a French slicing device), cut the potatoes into thin uniform slices measuring about ⅛ inch thick. It is important that the slices be as uniform as possible.

4. Pat the slices dry with a kitchen towel. Drop the potatoes all at once into the kettle with the lowest heat, but take care that they do not stick together. Cook, stirring constantly with a mesh or perforated strainer with a handle. Do not allow the potatoes to brown. Let them cook for 8 to 10 minutes, keeping the temperature below 300 degrees. The slices will rise to the surface bubbling. When that bubbling ceases, remove them from the fat.

5. Immediately transfer them to the kettle with the higher temperature and they should puff immediately (some of them may not). Do not let them brown, but remove them with the strainer onto a sheet lined with cloth or paper toweling. At this point they may be left to stand for hours before the final cooking.

6. When ready for the final cooking—and remember that the potatoes must be cooked and served immediately—reheat a kettle of fat to 375 degrees. Add the potatoes all at once and cook until they are well-puffed, brown and crisp. Remove, drain and serve immediately, sprinkled with salt, on a clean, starched linen napkin. If left to stand, the potatoes will become cool and limp.

Yield: 6 servings.

Pommes Soufflées II (*A quick method*)

1. Use only one kettle containing peanut, vegetable or corn oil for deep frying. Heat the oil to 275 degrees.

2. Peel 6 potatoes, about 2½ pounds. Rinse in cold water and pat as dry as possible. Using a slicing machine or a mandoline (a French slicing device), cut the potatoes into thin uniform slices measuring about ⅛ inch thick. It is important that the slices be as uniform as possible.

3. Pat the slices dry with a kitchen towel. Drop the potatoes all at once into the kettle, but take care that they do not stick together. Cook, stirring constantly with a mesh or perforated strainer with a handle. Do not allow the potatoes to brown. Let them cook for 8 to 10 minutes, keeping the temperature below 300 degrees. The slices will rise to the surface bubbling.

4. When the bubbling ceases, remove the potatoes from the fat, using a mesh or perforated strainer, onto a sheet lined with cloth or paper toweling. At this point they may be left to stand for hours before cooking.

5. When ready for the final cooking—and remember that the potatoes must be cooked and served immediately—reheat the kettle of fat to 375 degrees. Add the potatoes all at once and cook until they are well-puffed, brown and crisp. Remove, drain and serve immediately, sprinkled with salt, on a clean, starched linen napkin. If left to stand, the potatoes will become cool and limp.

Yield: 6 servings.

Janssons Frestelse (*Potatoes with anchovy sprats and cream*)

2 pounds potatoes
3 medium-size onions, about ½ pound, peeled
8 to 10 anchovy sprats, available in cans in specialty food stores, or use canned flat anchovy fillets or matjes herring fillets cut into small pieces
2 tablespoons butter
Freshly ground pepper
1 tablespoon liquid from anchovy sprats can

1. Preheat the oven to 375 degrees.

2. Peel the potatoes. As they are peeled, drop them into cold water to prevent discoloration. Cut the potatoes into slices about ½ inch thick or less. Stack the slices and cut them into ½-inch strips like french fries. Let stand in cold water until ready to cook.

3. Cut the onions in half crosswise. Thinly slice each half. There should be about 2 cups.

4. If anchovy sprats are available, remove them from the can. Skin and bone the sprats to produce 16 to 20 fillets. Cut each fillet in half.

5. Butter a baking dish (a rectangular dish measuring about

8½- x 12½- x 1½-inches is suitable). Make a layer, using one-third of the potatoes. Dot this with half the anchovy pieces and sprinkle with half the onions. Sprinkle with pepper to taste. Make another layer of potatoes, anchovies and onions. Make a final layer of potatoes and sprinkle with pepper and anchovy liquid.

6. Pour the cream over all. Sprinkle with bread crumbs and place in the oven. Bake for 45 minutes.

Yield: 6 to 8 servings.

1½ cups heavy cream
3 tablespoons fresh bread crumbs

Roast Potatoes with Fresh Mint

1. Preheat the oven to 400 degrees.
2. Peel the potatoes, leave whole and rinse. Place in a baking pan and add salt and pepper to taste and lemon juice. Add hot gravy and butter and bake until tender. Garnish with mint leaves and serve.

Yield: 12 or more servings.

24 small potatoes
  Salt and freshly ground pepper to taste
  Juice of 1 lemon
1 cup natural gravy from roast lamb
¼ pound butter
  Sprigs of fresh mint

Suki Bhaji *(Spiced potatoes)*

1. Prepare the potatoes and set them aside.
2. Heat the oil in a kettle and add the mustard seeds. When they crackle, add the lentils and cook for about 30 seconds.
3. Add the hing, ginger, chilies, curry leaves, turmeric and salt. Cook, stirring, for about 30 seconds. Add the potatoes and stir gently until they are coated. Turn carefully so as not to break up the potato pieces.
4. Sprinkle with lemon juice and half the coriander. Toss gently to blend. Serve sprinkled with more fresh coriander.

Yield: 8 servings.

7 cups peeled, cooked potatoes cut into 1-inch cubes
¼ cup sesame oil purchased from a health food store
2 teaspoons black mustard seeds
2 teaspoons urad dal (small white lentils)
⅛ teaspoon hing, available where imported spices are sold
1 teaspoon chopped fresh ginger
¼ cup coarsely chopped, mildly hot, fresh chilies
5 to 6 curry leaves, available in Indian food shops
¼ teaspoon turmeric
2 teaspoons salt
2 teaspoons lemon juice
2 tablespoons chopped fresh coriander leaves

Falafel

½ pound dried chick-peas
1 large clove garlic
1 large onion, about ⅓ pound, peeled and thinly sliced
½ teaspoon ground cumin
½ teaspoon ground coriander
1 tablespoon chopped fresh coriander leaves, optional
6 sprigs fresh parsley
Salt and freshly ground pepper
⅛ teaspoon cayenne pepper
¼ teaspoon baking powder
Oil for deep frying

1. Put the peas in a bowl and add water to cover to a depth of about 2 inches above the peas. Soak overnight.

2. Put half the peas in the container of a food processor and add portions of garlic, onion, cumin, ground coriander, fresh chopped coriander, if used, and parsley. Add salt and pepper to taste, cayenne pepper and baking powder.

3. Blend one portion at a time to a fine purée. Empty the mixture into a mixing bowl and proceed with another batch. Continue until all the ingredients are used. The mixture will be manageable but moist.

4. Shape the mixture into balls about the size of a walnut. Flatten the pieces to make biscuit shapes.

5. Heat the oil for deep frying. Add the falafel and cook, turning once, until nicely browned and cooked throughout.

Yield: About 36 pieces.

Fau   *(A Russian purée of beans)*

2 20-ounce cans cannelini beans, undrained
4 yellow onions, about 1 pound, peeled
⅓ cup peanut, vegetable or corn oil
Cayenne pepper according to taste

1. Put the beans through a food mill or use a food processor to blend.

2. Pour the purée into a bowl.

3. Cut the onions in half and slice each half as thinly as possible. There should be about 4 cups loosely packed.

4. Heat the oil in a skillet and add the onions. Cook, stirring, until the onions are nicely browned. Spread the onions evenly over the puréed beans. Sprinkle lightly or heavily with cayenne and serve at room temperature.

Yield: 4 to 6 servings.

Flageolets

1 pound dried flageolets
7 cups water
Salt
1 bay leaf

1. Put the flageolets in a mixing bowl and add cold water to cover to a depth of about 1 inch above the top of the beans. Let soak for several hours or overnight.

2. Drain the beans and put them in a saucepan. Add the

7 cups of water. Add salt to taste, bay leaf, carrot, whole clove of garlic and onion. Bring to the boil and cook until tender. This may take from 1 to 1½ hours, depending on the age of the beans and soaking time.

3. Remove and discard the bay leaf, carrot, whole clove of garlic and onion. Add the minced garlic, parsley and butter. Bring to the boil, uncovered, and cook for 5 minutes.

Yield: 8 or more servings.

1	carrot, scraped
1	clove garlic, peeled but left whole
1	onion, peeled and stuck with 2 cloves
1	clove garlic, finely minced
2	tablespoons finely chopped parsley
3	tablespoons butter

Lentil Purée

1. Combine the lentils, potatoes, onion, garlic, bay leaf, water, salt and pepper to taste in a saucepan. Bring to the boil and simmer for 30 minutes or until the lentils are tender. Drain.

2. Pour the lentil mixture into a food mill and pass it through into a saucepan. Discard any solids left in the food mill.

3. Add ¾ cup heavy cream, butter and salt to taste. Beat well to blend. Smooth the surface and pour the remaining ¼ cup of cream on top to prevent a skin from forming. When ready to serve, heat thoroughly and stir to blend.

Yield: 8 to 10 servings.

1	pound lentils
¾	pound potatoes, peeled and cut into eighths
1	small onion, stuck with 2 cloves
1	clove garlic, peeled
1	bay leaf
6	cups water
	Salt and freshly ground pepper
1	cup heavy cream
4	tablespoons butter

Lentils Côte d'Azur

1. Heat 1 tablespoon butter in a small kettle or deep saucepan and add the ham and coarsely chopped onion. Cook briefly until the onion wilts.

2. Add the lentils, water, broth, bay leaf, thyme, salt and pepper and simmer for 30 to 40 minutes. Discard the bay leaf and ham.

3. Meanwhile, heat the remaining butter in a saucepan and add the leek and finely chopped onion. Add the garlic and cook, stirring, for about 5 minutes. Add the tomatoes and cover. Simmer for about 15 minutes.

4. Combine the lentils with the tomato sauce. Cover and cook for about 15 minutes. Serve sprinkled with chopped parsley and sliced cotechini, or garlic sausage, if desired.

Yield: 6 to 8 servings.

3	tablespoons butter
¼	pound smoked ham slice, fat left on, cut into quarters
¼	cup coarsely chopped onion
½	pound dried lentils
2	cups water
4	cups fresh or canned chicken broth
½	bay leaf
1	sprig fresh thyme, or ¼ teaspoon dried
	Salt and freshly ground pepper to taste
1	finely diced leek
½	cup finely chopped onion
1	clove garlic, finely minced
1	cup tomatoes, fresh or canned
	Chopped parsley for garnish

Limbo Dal *(Lemon lentils)*

Dal, the traditional lentil dish of India, is described by Ismail Merchant as a "rich man's, poor man's dish and every household has its own version. It is a must with any meal, and if you don't offer it, something is wrong." Mr. Merchant, a Bombay-born movie producer and one of the best Indian cooks in Manhattan, offered us his version of dal, made special with lemon.

1¼ cups peanut, vegetable or corn oil
2 onions, halved and thinly sliced, about 1½ cups
4 2-inch pieces of cinnamon stick
2 pounds red lentils, available in specialty food stores
1 tablespoon chopped fresh ginger root
5 cups fresh or canned chicken broth
5 cups water
  Salt
1 teaspoon cayenne pepper
  Juice of 1 lemon
  The squeezed, seeded shell of 1 lemon including skin and pulp
½ cup chopped onion
1 clove garlic, finely minced
1 hot green chili, chopped, with seeds
4 bay leaves
½ cup chopped fresh coriander leaves

1. Heat ¾ cup of the oil in a large saucepan and add the sliced onions. Cook to wilt and add the cinnamon pieces and lentils. Add the ginger and cook, stirring often, for about 10 minutes. Add the broth and water, salt to taste and cayenne pepper. Bring to the boil and simmer for about 10 minutes.
2. Add the lemon juice and lemon shell and cook for about 50 minutes longer, stirring often.
3. Heat the remaining ½ cup of oil and add the onion, garlic, chili and bay leaves. Cook, stirring, until onion is browned. Add this mixture including the oil to the lentils. Sprinkle with chopped coriander leaves and serve hot.

Yield: 12 or more servings.

Pinto Beans

1 pound dried pinto beans
1 large onion, chopped
½ pound chunk salt pork
  Salt

Soak the beans in water to cover for about 1 hour, then drain them. Cover again with water about 2 inches above the beans, add the onion and salt pork and simmer until the beans are tender, about 2 hours. Add salt to taste.

Yield: 8 servings.

Frijoles Rancheros

1. Set the beans and bean liquid aside.
2. Heat the oil in a saucepan and add the onion and garlic. Cook until the onion wilts. Add the green pepper and chopped chilies and cook, stirring, for about 1 minute. Add the beans and bean liquid. Add the tomatoes, cinnamon, clove, salt and pepper to taste. Cover and simmer for 20 minutes.

Yield: 4 to 6 servings.

1	cup drained, cooked pinto beans (see preceding recipe)
¼	cup liquid in which beans cooked
¼	cup olive oil
1	cup finely chopped onion
2	teaspoons finely minced garlic
¾	cup cored, seeded, diced, sweet green pepper
2	tablespoons chopped hot, fresh chilies, preferably jalapenos
2	cups cored, unpeeled, diced tomatoes
1	1-inch piece stick cinnamon, or ½ teaspoon powdered
1	whole clove
	Salt and freshly ground pepper

Roman Beans with Oil

1. Put the beans in a bowl and add water to cover to a depth of about 2 inches above the top layer of beans. Soak overnight.
2. Heat the oil and add the garlic. Cook briefly. Drain the beans and add them. Add the water, sage, salt and pepper to taste. Cook, uncovered, for about 1 hour. Serve as a vegetable with a generous amount of olive oil sprinkled over each serving. Serve the beans with their pot juice spooned over.

Yield: 6 to 8 servings.

1	pound dried Roman, or cranberry, beans
¼	cup olive oil plus more olive oil for garnish
1	tablespoon finely minced garlic
6	cups cold water
2 to	4 sage leaves, the number will depend on size and potency of leaves
	Salt and freshly ground pepper

Frijoles de Olla *(Black beans in a pot)*

1 pound black turtle beans,
  available in stores that
  specialize in Spanish foods
⅛ pound lean salt pork, cut into
  1-inch cubes
½ onion, coarsely chopped
10 cups water
  Salt

1. Wash the beans and drain them. Put them in a kettle with the pork, onion and water. Do not add salt. Bring to the boil and simmer for 1 hour.

2. Add salt to taste and continue cooking for about 2 hours longer.

Yield: About 8 servings.

Note: These beans are best if they are allowed to simmer a while the second day.

XI. Vegetables

How to Cook Whole Artichokes for Vinaigrette

Cut off the stems of the artichokes, using a sharp knife, to produce a neat, flat base. As the artichokes are cut, rub any cut surfaces with lemon to prevent discoloration. Slice off the top "cone" of the artichoke, about 1 inch from the tip.

Using a pair of kitchen scissors, cut off the sharp tips of the leaves, about ½ inch down.

Place in a kettle and add cold water to cover and salt to taste. For each 2 quarts of water, add the juice of 1 lemon. Cover and bring to the boil. Cook for 45 minutes.

Drain the artichokes. Using a melon ball scoop, hollow out the fuzzy choke in the center. Arrange them bottom side up on a rack to drain. Let cool. Chill. They are now ready to be served with cold sauces such as vinaigrette or mayonnaise.

How to Prepare Whole Artichokes for Stuffing

Cut off the stems of the artichokes, using a sharp knife, to produce a neat, flat base. As the artichokes are cut, rub any cut surface with lemon to prevent discoloration. Slice off the top "cone" of the artichoke about 1 inch from the tip.

Using a pair of kitchen scissors, cut off the sharp tips of the leaves, about ½ inch down.

Use a melon ball scoop and hollow out the fuzzy choke in the center, taking care to remove all of it. Turn the artichokes upside down and press down to open up the center and facilitate stuffing. Turn right side up and stuff as desired.

Artichauts Farcis *(Stuffed artichokes)*

4	large artichokes prepared for stuffing (see instructions)
3	tablespoons olive oil
1½	cups finely chopped onion
½	pound ground pork
2	cloves garlic, finely minced
3	tablespoons finely chopped parsley
1	small bay leaf
	Salt and freshly ground pepper to taste
½	teaspoon dried thyme
1½	cups fresh bread crumbs
	Hot red pepper flakes to taste
2	slices bacon, cut into small pieces
1½	cups fresh or canned chicken broth

1. Prepare the artichokes for stuffing and preheat the oven to 350 degrees.

2. Heat 1 tablespoon oil in a skillet and add 1 cup of onion. Cook, stirring, until wilted. Add the pork and 1 clove of minced garlic. Cook, stirring, until meat changes color. Add the parsley, bay leaf, salt, pepper, thyme, bread crumbs and red pepper flakes. Blend well. Stuff the artichokes throughout, that is to say, in the hollowed-out cavity and between the leaves, pushing the stuffing down toward the bottom.

3. Cook the bacon in a casserole large enough to hold the artichokes in one layer. When rendered of fat, add the remaining ½ cup onion and remaining 1 clove minced garlic. Add the artichokes, bottom side down. Dribble the remaining oil over the artichokes and pour the chicken broth around them. Sprinkle with salt and pepper. Bring to the boil and cover closely. Place in the oven and bake for 1 hour.

Yield: 4 servings.

Artichokes Stuffed with Sausage

⅓	pound sausage links, pepperoni, ham or prosciutto
1	teaspoon olive oil
1½	cups fresh bread crumbs
2	tablespoons chopped fresh parsley
2	cloves garlic, finely minced
3	eggs
¼	cup milk
6	tablespoons olive oil
	Salt and freshly ground pepper
6	large artichokes prepared for stuffing (see instructions)
½	cup peeled, drained tomatoes, crushed
4	cups water
2	whole garlic cloves, peeled

1. Cut the meat into small pieces or slices. Heat the oil in a small skillet and cook the meat briefly, shaking the skillet and stirring. Drain and put in a mixing bowl. Add the bread crumbs, parsley and minced garlic. Toss well. Beat the eggs with the milk and 2 tablespoons of olive oil. Add the mixture to the bread crumb mixture. Add salt and pepper to taste. Stir to blend.

2. Stuff the artichokes with the mixture, starting with the center of each artichoke, then stuffing between the leaves more or less at random. Push the stuffing down, as it is added, toward the bottom.

3. Select a casserole large enough to hold the artichokes snugly in one layer. Arrange them in the casserole and spoon equal amounts of tomatoes on the top of each. Pour the water around the artichokes and add the whole garlic cloves to the water. Sprinkle the artichokes with the remaining quarter cup of olive oil. Cover closely and bring to the boil. Reduce the heat and simmer until the artichoke bottoms are tender, 45

minutes to 1 hour. To test for doneness, pull off an outside leaf; if it comes off easily, the artichokes are done.

Yield: 6 servings.

Note: If the artichokes do not fit closely together, it is advisable to tie them around the center with string to help retain their shapes.

How to Prepare Artichoke Bottoms

Cut off the stems of the artichokes, using a sharp knife to produce a neat, flat base. As the artichokes are cut, rub any cut surface with lemon to prevent discoloration.

Using a sharp knife, trim all around the sides and base of the artichoke until the base is smooth and white with the green exterior pared away.

Place 1 artichoke at a time on its side on a flat surface. Using the knife, slice off the top of the artichoke, leaving a base about 1½ inches deep. Using a paring knife, trim all around the sides and bottom to remove the green exterior that remains. Do not remove the fuzzy choke at this time. This comes out easily when the artichokes are cooked.

The artichokes are now ready to be cooked in what is called a blanc légume, or vegetable whitener, a blend of water and flour. Enough blanc légume is used to barely cover the artichoke bottoms as they cook.

For each 6 cups of water to be used, use ¼ cup flour.

Place an ordinary kitchen sieve over the kettle in which the artichokes will be cooked. Add the flour. Pour cold water over the flour, rubbing to dissolve the flour in the water. Add salt to taste. Add the artichoke bottoms and bring to the boil. Cover the kettle closely and cook for about 25 minutes, or until bottoms are tender. Remove the kettle from the heat. If the artichokes are not to be used immediately, let them rest in the cooking liquid until ready to use. Before using, drain the bottoms and pull or scrape out the fuzzy chokes.

Fonds d'Artichauts Provençale *(Artichoke bottoms stuffed with tomatoes)*

6 to 8 cooked artichoke bottoms
(see instructions)
4 tablespoons butter
1 pound red, ripe tomatoes,
peeled and chopped, or use
an equal amount of
imported canned tomatoes
Salt and freshly ground
pepper to taste
1 clove garlic, finely minced
2 tablespoons finely chopped
parsley

1. Prepare the artichoke bottoms. Heat 1 tablespoon butter in a saucepan and add the tomatoes, salt and pepper. Bring to the boil and simmer for about 10 minutes, stirring often from the bottom to prevent sticking.

2. Preheat the oven to 350 degrees. Arrange the hollowed-out artichoke bottoms on a baking dish and brush with butter. Bake until piping hot, about 10 minutes. Fill the hot artichoke bottoms with equal portions of boiling tomato mixture.

3. Heat the remaining butter in a small skillet and add the garlic. When foamy but not browned, add the parsley. Pour this mixture over the tomatoes and serve immediately.

Yield: 6 to 8 servings.

Fonds d'Artichauts Clamart *(Artichoke bottoms stuffed with fresh green peas)*

6 to 8 cooked artichoke bottoms
(see instructions)
1 cup shelled fresh peas,
about 1½ pounds unshelled
⅓ cup shredded Boston lettuce
1 small white onion, chopped,
about 3 tablespoons
1 tablespoon butter
Salt and freshly ground
pepper to taste
¼ teaspoon sugar
1 tablespoon water

1. Prepare the artichoke bottoms.

2. Combine the remaining ingredients in a heavy saucepan and cover closely. Bring to the boil and cook over low heat for 5 to 10 minutes, or until the peas are tender.

3. Preheat the oven to 350 degrees. Arrange the hollowed-out artichoke bottoms on a baking dish and brush with butter. Bake until piping hot, about 10 minutes. Fill the hot artichoke bottoms with hot peas and serve.

Yield: 6 to 8 servings.

Artichoke Bottoms and Mushrooms Bordelaise

4 cooked artichoke bottoms (see
instructions)
4 large mushrooms, about ¼
pound
2 tablespoons butter
Salt and freshly ground pepper
to taste
2 tablespoons chopped shallots
2 tablespoons finely chopped
parsley

1. Drain and hollow out the cooked artichoke bottoms. Place the bottoms, hollowed-out side down, on a flat surface. Cut in half, holding the knife at a slight diagonal. Cut each half into thirds, once more holding the knife at a slight diagonal. Set aside. Slice the mushrooms similarly and set aside.

2. Heat 1 tablespoon of butter in a skillet and add the mushrooms, salt and pepper. Toss and stir until browned. Add the artichokes, the remaining 1 tablespoon butter, shallots and parsley. Cook, stirring and tossing the ingredients, until piping hot.

Yield: 4 to 6 servings.

Asparagus Milanese

1. Preheat the broiler. Using a swivel-bladed vegetable peeler, scrape the asparagus, starting about 2 inches from top of tips. Line up the tips of the asparagus spears uniformly on a flat surface. Cut off the ends 3 or 4 inches from the bottom. Discard the ends.

2. Place the asparagus in a skillet large enough to hold them and add cold water to cover. Add salt to taste. Bring to the boil and simmer from 1 to 5 minutes. Cooking time will depend on the size of the asparagus and how crisp you wish them to remain. Preferably they should be crisp-tender, not limp. Drain immediately.

3. Arrange the asparagus uniformly in a heatproof dish. Sprinkle with butter and cheese. Sprinkle with pepper to taste and glaze them until golden brown under the broiler.

Yield: 6 to 8 servings.

24 to 32 asparagus spears
Salt
4 to 6 tablespoons melted butter
½ to ¾ cup grated Parmesan cheese
Freshly ground pepper to taste

Asparagus with Horseradish Sauce

Combine the horseradish and water in a saucepan and stir. Do not boil but heat almost to the boiling point. Add the butter, piece by piece, and swirl it around until the sauce is well blended and smooth. Serve the hot sauce over the asparagus.

Yield: 4 to 6 servings.

1 tablespoon fresh horseradish
2 tablespoons water
8 tablespoons butter, cut into 8 pieces
16 to 18 hot, freshly cooked asparagus spears

Asperges Polonaise   *(Asparagus with chopped eggs and buttered crumbs)*

1. Using a swivel-bladed vegetable peeler, scrape the asparagus spears starting about 2 inches from the top. Line up the asparagus spears and cut off about 1 inch of the tough bottom portions. Discard the ends. In a skillet bring enough water to the boil to cover the asparagus when added. Add the asparagus and salt to taste and bring to the boil. Simmer until crisp-tender, 3 to 6 minutes, depending on the size of the asparagus. Drain.

2. While hot, arrange the asparagus on a serving dish. Sprinkle neatly with the chopped or sieved egg and salt and pepper. Heat the butter in a heavy skillet and add the bread crumbs. Cook over high heat, swirling the crumbs in the but-

3 pounds asparagus spears, about 30
Salt to taste
1 hard-cooked egg, sieved or finely chopped
Freshly ground pepper to taste
8 tablespoons butter
½ cup fine, fresh bread crumbs
Finely chopped parsley for garnish

ter until the crumbs and butter are hazelnut brown. Pour the mixture over the asparagus and serve sprinkled with chopped parsley.

Yield: 6 servings.

Chinese New Year Bean Sprouts

If you eat large bean sprouts at the beginning of the Chinese New Year, "no matter how rough the road, your path will be smoothed." That's what Virginia Lee says, and we wouldn't question her.

3	cups large bean sprouts
10	dried black mushrooms
1 or	2 pieces bamboo shoot
3	tablespoons plus 1 teaspoon peanut, vegetable or corn oil
½	cup chicken broth
¼	teaspoon monosodium glutamate, optional
1½	teaspoons salt
1	tablespoon shao hsing wine, or dry sherry
1	teaspoon sugar
½	teaspoon dark soy sauce

1. Rinse the bean sprouts and drain well.

2. Pour boiling water over the mushrooms and let stand for about 20 minutes. Drain and squeeze dry. Trim off stems.

3. Cut the bamboo shoots into 12 pyramid shapes, each about 1½ inches tall. Rinse and drain.

4. Heat 3 tablespoons oil in a wok or skillet and add the bean sprouts. Cook for about 30 seconds and add the mushrooms. Cook for 20 seconds and add the bamboo shoots. Add the chicken broth, monosodium glutamate, if used, salt, wine, sugar and dark soy sauce. Cook over high heat, stirring, for about 6 minutes. Turn off heat.

5. Arrange the pieces of bamboo shoot in an oval on a small oval serving dish. Arrange the bean sprouts in the center. Leave the mushrooms in the wok.

6. Add remaining 1 teaspoon of oil to the wok and cook the mushrooms for about 45 seconds. Arrange the mushrooms over the bean sprouts and serve.

Yield: 8 servings with other Chinese dishes.

Purée of Green Beans

1¼	pounds green beans
	Salt
1	pound potatoes
4	tablespoons butter
2	tablespoons heavy cream
¼	teaspoon grated nutmeg

Trim off the ends of the beans. Drop them into boiling salted water to cover. Cook for 5 to 10 minutes, depending on tenderness of beans. Do not overcook. Peel the potatoes and halve, quarter or cut them into eighths, depending on size. Place them in a saucepan and add cold water to cover and salt to taste. Bring to the boil and simmer for 15 to 20 minutes, or until tender. Drain the beans and potatoes and blend them in a food processor. Add the butter, cream, nutmeg and salt to taste. Serve piping hot.

Yield: 6 to 10 servings.

Green Beans with Mustard Sauce

1. Cut or snap off the ends of the beans, but leave the beans whole. Let stand in cold water until ready to use. Drain the beans and, preferably, steam them in a vegetable steamer for about 5 minutes. Or cook them briefly in a large quantity of boiling water about the same length of time. The important thing is not to overcook them. They must remain crisp-tender.

2. As the beans cook, spoon the mustard into a small bowl and add the salt, pepper and lemon juice. Stir to blend and whisk in the oil. Drain the beans. Add the mustard sauce to the beans and toss to coat well. Serve piping hot in a hot serving dish.

Yield: 12 servings.

2	pounds green beans
1	tablespoon imported mustard, such as Dijon or Düsseldorf
	Salt and freshly ground pepper
	Juice of one lemon
1/3	cup olive oil

Haricots Verts à la Paysanne Landaise *(Green beans peasant-style)*

1. Cut or snap off the ends of the beans. Cut or snap the beans into 2-inch lengths. There should be about 5 cups. Add the beans to a basin of cold water and let stand until ready to use. Thinly slice the salt pork and cut the slices into small strips about the size of paper matches. Set aside.

2. Bring the water to the boil and add the salt. That volume of salt will help keep the beans green. Drain the beans and add them. When the water returns to the boil, cook the beans over high heat for about 5 minutes. Take care not to overcook. The beans must remain crisp. Drain them and put them into a basin of cold running water. Let chill in the water. Drain well.

3. Heat the butter in a large saucepan and add the salt pork. Cook until quite crisp. Add the shallots and beans and stir. Cook for about 2 minutes to heat the beans thoroughly. Add the garlic and parsley, toss and serve.

Yield: 8 to 12 servings.

1½	pounds green beans
1/8	pound salt pork
1	gallon water
½	cup salt
3	tablespoons butter
2	tablespoons finely chopped shallots
1	teaspoon finely chopped garlic
¼	cup chopped parsley

Beets in Sour Cream and Mustard Sauce

1¼ to 1½ pounds fresh beets
Salt to taste
2 small red onions
1 tablespoon imported mustard, such as Dijon or Düsseldorf
2 teaspoons white vinegar
½ cup sour cream
Freshly ground pepper to taste

1. Cut off the leaves of the beets, but leave an inch or so of the beet top intact. Do not cut off the root ends. Wash the beets well and place in a kettle. Add cold water to cover and salt to taste. Bring to the boil and simmer until beets are tender. This may take anywhere from 20 minutes to 1 hour depending on the size and age of the beets.

2. Drain the beets and let cool. When cool, trim off and discard the ends of the beets. Peel the beets and cut them into ¼-inch-thick or slightly smaller slices. Place the slices in a mixing bowl. Peel and slice the onions and add them to the bowl. Combine the remaining ingredients and blend well. Pour this mixture over the beets and toss well.

Yield: 6 to 10 servings.

Buraki   (Beets Polish-style)

7 or 8 fresh beets, about 2 pounds
3 tablespoons butter
2 teaspoons lemon juice
Salt to taste
¼ cup sour cream
Freshly ground pepper to taste
¼ teaspoon sugar, optional

1. Trim off the ends of the beets. Peel the beets with a knife or swivel-bladed vegetable peeler. If the beets are very large, cut them into quarters. Cut small beets in half. If they are very small, leave them whole. Put the beets in a large saucepan and add water to cover. Bring to the boil and simmer for 30 to 45 minutes, or until tender. Drain.

2. Mash or blend the beets. Do not make them into a fine purée. The texture should be a little coarse. Add the butter, lemon juice and salt to taste. Stir in the sour cream and pepper. If the beets are not sweet enough, add the sugar. Serve warm.

Yield: 6 to 10 servings.

Broccoli Timbales

One of the characteristics of la nouvelle cuisine, the cooking as practiced by the younger generation of chefs who now rule the great kitchens of France, is an absence of the superfluous garnishes that an older generation felt essential to their art. Gone are the excesses of Duchesse potatoes used to border the silver serving platters, the dazzling floral displays in wax and the puff-pastry crescents.

But the presentation of food remains an important element

in good gastronomy. Molded vegetables are an example of garnishes in good taste that please the eye as well as the palate.

1. Preheat the oven to 375 degrees. Bring enough water to the boil to cover the broccoli when added. Add salt to taste. Add the broccoli and simmer for about 5 minutes. Drain and chop coarsely. The broccoli should not be too fine.

2. Put the eggs and yolks in a mixing bowl. Beat with a whisk and add the cream, salt and pepper to taste and nutmeg. Add the broccoli and blend well.

3. Generously butter 8 timbales or other individual molds and ladle or spoon the custard mixture into the molds. Place the molds in a baking dish and pour boiling water around them. Bring the water to the boil on top of the stove and place in the oven. Bake for about 20 minutes, or until set. Remove. Run a knife between the custard and mold. Unmold and serve hot.

Yield: 8 servings.

3	pounds broccoli, broken into flowerets, about 8 cups
	Salt
3	egg yolks
3	whole eggs
1	cup heavy cream
	Freshly ground pepper
⅛	teaspoon grated nutmeg

Broccoli di Rape

1. If the broccoli di rape is bright green, young and tender, it may be simply trimmed at the base and cooked. If it is a bit large and starting to lose its bright green color, it will be necessary to scrape the outside of the stems. The stems, if small, may be left whole. Or they may be cut in smaller pieces.

2. Rinse the broccoli di rape and drain without patting dry. It will steam in the water that clings to the leaves without adding more liquid. Put the broccoli di rape in a heavy kettle with a tight-fitting lid and add the remaining ingredients. Cover closely and simmer over low heat for about 5 minutes. Serve immediately and, if desired, with lemon wedges.

Yield: 4 servings.

1¼	pounds broccoli di rape (also sold as plain rabe or rapi)
	Salt and freshly ground pepper to taste
½	teaspoon hot red pepper flakes
¼	cup olive oil
1	clove garlic, finely chopped

Brussels Sprouts in Cream

1. Preheat the oven to 375 degrees. Pull off and discard any tough outer leaves from the sprouts. Trim the bottom of the sprouts and make a shallow incision in the form of a cross on the stem end. Place the sprouts in a skillet and add cold water to cover and salt to taste. Bring to the boil and simmer for 10 to 15 minutes, or until the sprouts are crisp-tender. Drain.

2. Melt 2 tablespoons of butter in a saucepan and add the flour, stirring with a whisk. When blended and smooth, add

2	10-ounce packages fresh brussels sprouts
	Salt
3	tablespoons butter
3	tablespoons flour
1	cup cream or milk
1	egg yolk
¼	cup grated Parmesan cheese

the cream, stirring vigorously with the whisk. When thickened and smooth, remove from the heat and add the egg yolk, stirring. Add salt to taste.

3. Select a casserole large enough to hold the sprouts in one layer. Melt the remaining tablespoon of butter in the casserole and add the sprouts. Carefully spoon the sauce over each sprout until they are all coated. Sprinkle with cheese and bake for 10 to 12 minutes. Run the dish under the broiler briefly until nicely glazed.

Yield: 6 to 8 servings.

Cabbage au Gratin

1   **3-pound cabbage**
6   **tablespoons butter**
3   **tablespoons flour**
2   **cups milk**
1½   **cups grated sharp Cheddar cheese**
     Salt and freshly ground pepper to taste
½   **cup finely chopped onion**
1   **clove garlic, finely minced**
½   **cup dry white wine**
½   **teaspoon ground cloves**
½   **teaspoon ground allspice**
3   **tablespoons grated Parmesan cheese**

1. Pull off and discard the tough outer leaves of the cabbage. Discard any outside blemished leaves. Cut away and discard the core of the cabbage. Cut the cabbage into quarters. Cut each quarter into 1-inch-thick slices. Cut each slice into slices 3 inches wide. Separate the cabbage pieces. Bring a large quantity of water to the boil and add the cabbage. Cook for about 2 minutes. Drain.

2. Melt 2 tablespoons butter in a saucepan and add the flour, stirring with a wire whisk. When blended, add the milk, stirring rapidly with the whisk. Remove from the heat and add the cheese and stir until melted and smooth. If necessary, reheat. Add salt and pepper to taste. Set aside.

3. Heat the remaining butter in a large heavy skillet and add the onion and garlic. When wilted, add the drained cabbage, wine, cloves and allspice. Sprinkle with salt and pepper. Partly cover and cook, stirring occasionally, until the liquid evaporates. Add half the cheese sauce and blend. Spoon the mixture into an oval baking dish and smooth it over. Add the remaining cheese sauce and smooth over. Sprinkle with Parmesan cheese.

4. When ready to serve, preheat the oven to 400 degrees. Add the cabbage and bake for 15 to 20 minutes, or until bubbling throughout and nicely browned on top.

Yield: 6 to 8 servings.

Stuffed Cabbage Creole

1. Melt the butter for the filling in a saucepan and add the onion and garlic. Cook until wilted and add the tomatoes, salt and pepper. Cook, stirring occasionally, for about 10 minutes. Let cool. Put the meat in a mixing bowl and add the tomato mixture and the remaining filling ingredients. Blend well with the hands.

2. Cut away and discard the core from the cabbage. Drop the cabbage into boiling water to cover and let simmer for about 15 minutes, turning the cabbage in the water occasionally. Remove the cabbage but let the water continue to simmer in case the cabbage leaves do not come off easily and the cabbage has to be cooked again briefly. Drain the cabbage well, letting it stand core side down. When the cabbage is cool enough to handle, pull off the large leaves down to the white heart. Use the heart for salad or soup.

3. Place a large square of cheesecloth opened up on a flat surface. Place a large cabbage leaf, cupped side up, in the center of the cheesecloth. Add a smaller cabbage leaf to reinforce it. Sprinkle with salt and pepper. Add about 3 tablespoons of filling to the center and bring up the corners of the cheesecloth. Twist the corners, carefully cupping the cabbage leaves to seal in the filling. Squeeze the filled cabbage bundle gently. Untwist the cheesecloth and remove the filled bundle. Continue until all the filling is used. Preheat the oven to 375 degrees.

4. Heat the butter in a skillet. Add the onion, celery, garlic, green pepper, bay leaf, thyme, salt and pepper. Cook for about 5 minutes. Scatter this mixture over the bottom of a baking dish large enough to hold the cabbage bundles in one layer. Add the tomatoes. Arrange the stuffed cabbage bundles seam side down over all. Sprinkle with salt and pepper and add the chicken broth. Bring to the boil and cover closely with foil.

5. Place the dish into the oven and bake for 1¼ hours. If necessary, reduce oven heat to 350 degrees as cabbage bakes. Remove the foil and continue cooking, basting often, for about 15 minutes. Remove from the oven. Transfer the stuffed cabbage to a hot platter. Pour the sauce into a saucepan and skim the surface to remove the fat. Cook down briefly. Blend the cornstarch and water and stir it into the simmering sauce. Spoon the sauce over the cabbage and serve sprinkled with parsley.

Yield: 18 to 24 pieces.

The filling:

- 1 tablespoon butter
- 1 cup finely chopped onion
- 1 clove garlic, finely minced
- 1¾ cups cubed, peeled tomatoes, preferably fresh Salt and freshly ground pepper to taste
- 1 pound ground chuck
- 1 cup bread crumbs
- ¼ cup finely chopped parsley
- 1 egg, lightly beaten

The cabbage:

- 1 4-pound green cabbage

The braising:

- 2 tablespoons butter
- 1 cup thinly sliced onion
- 1 cup finely chopped celery
- 1½ teaspoons finely minced garlic
- 1 cup chopped green pepper
- 1 bay leaf
- ¼ teaspoon dried thyme Salt and freshly ground pepper to taste
- 2 cups peeled, cubed fresh or canned tomatoes
- 1 cup fresh or canned chicken broth
- 2 tablespoons cornstarch
- 3 tablespoons water Chopped parsley for garnish

Veal and Dill-stuffed Cabbage Rolls

The filling:

2 tablespoons butter
1 cup finely chopped onion
1 clove garlic, finely minced
1 pound ground veal
1 cup bread crumbs
½ cup heavy cream
2 tablespoons finely chopped dill
¼ teaspoon grated nutmeg
Salt and freshly ground pepper to taste
1 egg, lightly beaten

The cabbage:

1 4-pound head green cabbage

The braising:

8 tablespoons butter
2 tablespoons chopped dill
1 cup finely chopped onion
Salt and freshly ground pepper to taste
4 crushed allspice
¾ cup dry white wine
½ cup fresh or canned chicken broth
1 unpeeled clove garlic, crushed
Sour cream for garnish
Chopped dill for garnish

1. Heat the butter for the filling in a skillet and add the onion and garlic. When wilted, remove from the heat. Let cool briefly. Put the veal in a mixing bowl and add the onion mixture and remaining filling ingredients. Blend well with the hands.

2. Cut away and discard the core from the cabbage. Drop the cabbage into boiling water to cover and let simmer for about 15 minutes, turning the cabbage in the water occasionally. Remove the cabbage but let the water continue to simmer in case the cabbage leaves do not come off easily and the cabbage has to be cooked again briefly. Drain the cabbage well, letting it stand core side down. When the cabbage is cool enough to handle, pull off the large leaves down to the white heart. Use the heart for salad or soup.

3. Place one cabbage leaf at a time, cupped side up, on a flat surface. Sprinkle with salt and pepper. If the stem end seems tough, slice off part of it at the base. Add about 2 tablespoons of filling to the center of the cabbage leaf. Roll up from the bottom. Fold over the left and right sides of the leaf, then roll upward to enclose the filling compactly. Continue until all filling is used. Preheat the oven to 400 degrees.

4. Grease a baking dish large enough to hold the cabbage rolls in one layer with half the butter. A rectangular dish measuring about 15½- x 9- x 2½-inches is suitable. Sprinkle with chopped dill, onion, salt, pepper and allspice. Arrange the cabbage rolls symmetrically in the dish, seam side down. Dot the cabbage rolls with the remaining butter. Sprinkle with wine and broth. Add the crushed garlic. Cover closely with foil and bring to the boil on top of the stove. Bake for 45 minutes and transfer the rolls to a hot serving platter. Pour off the sauce into a saucepan and reduce by half. Pour the sauce over the rolls and serve with sour cream blended with chopped dill.

Yield: 18 to 24 cabbage rolls.

Pork-stuffed Cabbage Caprice

1. Cook the salt pork in a saucepan or skillet and, when it is rendered of fat and starting to brown, add the onion and garlic. Cook until wilted. Let cool slightly. Put the pork in a mix-

ing bowl and add the onion. Put the livers in the container of a food processor or blender. Blend to a purée. Add this to the pork. Add the remaining filling ingredients and blend well with the hands.

2. Cut away and discard the core from the cabbage. Drop the cabbage into boiling water to cover and let simmer for about 15 minutes, turning the cabbage in the water occasionally. Remove the cabbage, but let the water continue to simmer in case the cabbage leaves do not come off easily and the cabbage has to be cooked again briefly. Drain the cabbage well, letting it stand core side down. When the cabbage is cool enough to handle, pull off the large leaves down to the white heart. Chop the heart coarsely.

3. Lay out a large square of cheesecloth and arrange 7 of the largest cabbage leaves in the center. Arrange them in a circle with the edges overlapping. Arrange them with the core ends extending outward. Sprinkle with salt and pepper. Arrange 1 cup of filling in the center of the leaves and spread it out. Sprinkle with some of the chopped heart. Arrange another layer, using 5 cabbage leaves, over this in a smaller circle and with core ends outward. Sprinkle with salt and pepper. Add more filling and spread it out. Sprinkle with some of the chopped heart. Continue making layers until all of the filling is used. Bring up the edges of the cheesecloth neatly to enclose the stuffed leaves. The object is to reshape the leaves with the filling enclosed so that the bundle will resemble a whole cabbage. Twist the top and press around the bundle to make it compact. Tie the twisted cheesecloth with string. Cut off just above the string to make a topknot. Preheat the oven to 375 degrees.

4. Heat the butter in a kettle large enough to hold the cabbage bundle and add the salt pork slices in one layer. Cook briefly and add the sliced carrot, garlic, onion slices, bay leaf, thyme, cloves and parsley. Add the cabbage, topknot side down.

5. Pour the wine, beef broth, tomato paste and brown sauce around the cabbage. Cover closely and bring to the boil. Place in the oven and bake for 1½ hours. Watch carefully and, if necessary, reduce the oven heat to 350 degrees.

6. Remove the cabbage. Put the sauce through a fine sieve, pressing to extract as much liquid from the solids as possible. Reheat the sauce. Skim the surface to remove the fat. Remove the cabbage from the cheesecloth. Cut into wedges and serve with the hot sauce and sour cream.

Yield: 8 or more servings.

The filling:

¼	pound lean salt pork, ground, about ⅓ cup
1	cup finely chopped onion
1	clove garlic, finely minced
½	pound ground pork
½	pound chicken livers
1	cup bread crumbs
⅓	cup finely chopped parsley Salt and freshly ground pepper to taste
2	eggs
2	sprigs thyme, finely chopped, or ½ teaspoon dried

The cabbage:

1	3½-pound head green cabbage

The braising:

2	tablespoons butter
3	slices lean salt pork, each about ¼ inch thick
1	small carrot, scraped and thinly sliced on the bias, about ½ cup
1	clove garlic, finely minced
1	onion, peeled and cut into 6 ¼-inch slices
1	bay leaf
¼	teaspoon dried thyme
2	whole cloves
3	sprigs parsley
½	cup dry white wine
1	cup fresh or canned beef broth
2	tablespoons tomato paste
1½	cups brown sauce (see recipe page 658), or canned brown beef gravy Sour cream for garnish, optional

Scandinavian Stuffed Cabbage

½ cup raw rice
1½ cups milk
1 3-pound head of cabbage
½ pound ground lean veal or beef
½ pound ground lean pork (or substitute an equal amount of veal or beef)
2 tablespoons grated onion
1 egg, lightly beaten
2 tablespoons flour
Salt and freshly ground pepper
⅛ teaspoon grated nutmeg
¼ teaspoon ground allspice
7 tablespoons melted butter
½ teaspoon paprika
2 tablespoons dark molasses
1 cup fresh or canned beef broth

1. Preheat the oven to 400 degrees.

2. Combine the rice with 1 cup of milk in a saucepan. Cover and bring to the boil over low heat, preferably on an asbestos mat or Flame-Tamer. The heat must be low as the rice cooks or it will tend to overflow. Cook the rice for 15 to 20 minutes, or until tender and the milk absorbed. Remove from the heat, uncover and let cool, fluffing the rice with a fork.

3. Using a sharp paring or boning knife, cut away the center core of the cabbage. A melon ball cutter can also facilitate this. Drop the cabbage into boiling water and cook, turning occasionally in the water, until the center is tender, about 10 minutes. The leaves must be able to be easily separated and removed whole without tearing them. Remove the cabbage and drain it.

4. Place the meats in a mixing bowl and add the rice (add only half the rice for a less starchy dish), grated onion, egg, 1 tablespoon flour, salt, pepper, nutmeg, allspice and the remaining ½ cup of milk. Blend thoroughly. When cool enough to handle, separate the cabbage leaves, using 10 to 12 of the large outer leaves as a base for the stuffing. Arrange these leaves on a flat surface, curve side up. Use a sharp knife and cut away the tough center vein of each leaf. Overlap the cut portion and add equal portions of the filling to each leaf. Cover the filling with smaller center leaves, center vein removed. Roll the leaves to enclose the filling, tucking in the edges neatly.

5. Pour about 2 tablespoons of melted butter over the bottom of a baking dish measuring about 8- x 14- x 2-inches. As the cabbage rolls are prepared, arrange them in the dish close together. Sprinkle with salt, pepper and paprika. Pour all but 1 tablespoon of butter over the cabbage rolls. Pour the molasses in a thin, even stream over the cabbage rolls and add the cup of beef broth. Cover with foil and place in the oven. Let bake until the liquid around the cabbage rolls is boiling rapidly. Reduce the oven heat to 350 degrees. Bake for 30 minutes. Remove the foil and turn the cabbage rolls in the cooking liquid. Cover with foil and bake for about 15 minutes longer. Remove the foil and bake for 15 minutes longer.

6. Pour the pan liquid into a saucepan and bring to the boil. Cover the cabbage rolls and keep warm. Reduce the liquid to about 1 cup. Combine remaining 1 tablespoon of butter with the remaining 1 tablespoon of flour and blend well. Add this,

stirring constantly, to the sauce. Cook, stirring, until the sauce is thickened and smooth. Spoon the sauce over the cabbage rolls. Serve with puréed potatoes and lingonberries or cranberries, if desired.

Yield: 5 to 6 servings.

Lahanodolmathes Avgolemono *(Stuffed cabbage with egg and lemon sauce)*

Lemon is the vanilla of Greek cooking. We have certain Greek friends who would sooner do without salt than the juice of a freshly squeezed lemon. This fondness is nowhere more apparent in the Greek kitchen than in those celebrated dishes that bear the name avgolemono (avgo, meaning egg, plus lemon). One of the best uses to which it can be put is as a sauce for a delectable stuffed cabbage.

1. Pull off the tough outer leaves from the head of cabbage. Use a knife to cut away the tough white center core. Drop the cabbage into boiling salted water to cover and let cook for about 5 minutes, or until the leaves separate easily. Invert the cabbage in a colander and let stand until cool and thoroughly drained.

2. Combine 1 cup of the milk and the rice in a small saucepan and bring to the boil. Stir and cover. Cook over low heat until all the liquid is absorbed and the rice very soft. Stir as necessary. Uncover and let cool. Combine the lamb with the rice, finely chopped onion, dill, cinnamon, salt and pepper to taste, 2 tablespoons olive oil, remaining ½ cup of milk and oregano.

3. Separate the leaves of cabbage and pat dry. Use a sharp knife to make a V cut at the tough center end of each large leaf. Leave the tender smaller leaves intact. Rinse out a large square of cheesecloth in cold water, then squeeze dry and place on a flat surface. In the center place a large cabbage leaf, curly edge up. Arrange a smaller cabbage leaf in the center of the large leaf. Spoon 1 or 2 tablespoons of the filling into the center of the small leaf.

4. Bring the 4 corners of cheesecloth together and twist the ends together over a bowl. This will shape the leaves into a compact round. Remove the cabbage ball from the cheesecloth. It will not be necessary to use any string. Continue making the balls until all the cabbage leaves and filling are used. Shred any remaining cabbage leaves.

2 heads cabbage, about 2 pounds each
  Salt
1½ cups milk
¼ cup raw rice
1 pound ground lamb
⅓ cup finely chopped onion
3 tablespoons chopped fresh dill, or 1 teaspoon dried
½ teaspoon ground cinnamon
  Freshly ground pepper
6 tablespoons olive oil
1 teaspoon dried oregano
2 cloves garlic, chopped
½ cup coarsely chopped onion
2½ cups fresh or canned chicken broth
3 egg yolks
⅓ cup lemon juice

5. Heat the remaining 4 tablespoons of oil in a heavy casserole or Dutch oven large enough to hold the stuffed cabbage rolls in one layer. Add the garlic, coarsely chopped onion, salt to taste and shredded cabbage. Arrange the stuffed cabbage seam side down and sprinkle with salt and pepper to taste. Add the chicken broth and bring to the boil. Cover and cook until the cabbage is tender, 1 to 1½ hours.

6. Pour off and save the cooking liquid. Keep the cabbage warm. Skim fat from cooking liquid. Pour reserved cooking liquid into a saucepan and reduce it to about 1½ cups. Beat the yolks and lemon juice together. Add them, off heat, to the sauce, stirring rapidly. Return sauce to the burner and bring it just to the boil, stirring, but do not boil or it will curdle. Serve the sauce over the cabbage.

Yield: 16 to 18 cabbage rolls.

Chinese Vegetable Casserole

It is as basic as chopsticks to say that the greatest obstacle in the preparation of a Chinese dinner is the ability to organize dishes in a manner that permits the home cook to join guests at table while maintaining a cool presence. Our friend and colleague, Virginia Lee, suggests this vegetable casserole as one of the dishes for such a dinner because it simmers for almost an hour, leaving the cook free to attend the wok for other dishes to be stir fried just before serving.

14 dried mushrooms (see note)
1 2½- to 3-pound Chinese cabbage
1 cup peanut, vegetable or corn oil
Salt to taste
1 teaspoon sugar
3 fat pads fresh bean curd
1 large piece chicken fat, or melted chicken fat or corn oil

1. Place the mushrooms in a bowl and add boiling water to cover. Let stand ½ hour or longer. Drain and cut off and discard the tough stems. Set the whole mushrooms aside.

2. Pull off and discard a few of the large outer leaves of the cabbage. Pull off the remaining leaves and stack them 2 at a time on a flat surface. Neatly trim the leaves into rectangles, trimming away the tops, bottoms and sides of the leaves. Cut the leaves into long strips about 1 inch wide.

3. Heat half the oil in a large wok or skillet and add the cabbage strips. Cook over high heat, stirring and turning the cabbage, for about 5 minutes. Add the salt and sugar and cook briefly, stirring, for about 1 minute longer. The cabbage should remain crisp-tender. Transfer the pieces of cabbage to a casserole, arranging them neatly. Add the cabbage juices.

4. Cut each bean curd pad into 4 slices.

5. Wipe out the wok and add the remaining oil. Heat the oil until quite hot and add the bean curd slices. Cook for about 5 minutes over high heat until golden brown on one side (it will look like pale French toast or a slightly overcooked omelet). Turn the slices and drain.

6. Arrange the bean curd slices, edges slightly overlapping, around the rim of the cabbage. Arrange the mushrooms in a layer and piled in the center of the bean curd. If a piece of chicken fat is available, place it over the mushrooms to prevent them from drying out. Or brush with melted chicken fat or oil. Cover closely and let simmer for about 50 minutes.

Yield: 12 servings with other Chinese dishes.

Note: Dried mushrooms are available in Chinese markets and many supermarkets.

Red Cabbage Alsatian-style

Pull off and discard any tough or wilted outer leaves from the cabbage. Trim away and discard the core from the cabbage. Shred the cabbage finely. There should be about 10 cups. Heat the oil in a heavy skillet and add the cabbage. Cook, stirring, to wilt. Add the cloves, vinegar, sugar, salt and pepper. Cook for 10 to 15 minutes, stirring often. Stir in the butter and serve.

Yield: 10 or more servings.

2 pounds red cabbage
3 tablespoons peanut, vegetable or corn oil
2 whole cloves, crushed
1 tablespoon red wine vinegar
2 tablespoons brown sugar
Salt and freshly ground pepper to taste
3 tablespoons butter

Braised Red Cabbage with Chestnuts

1. Preheat the oven to 450 degrees.

2. Pull off and discard any blemished outer leaves from the cabbage. Quarter the cabbage and shred it finely.

3. Using a sharp paring knife, make an incision around the perimeter of each chestnut, starting and ending on either side of the "topknot" or stem end. Place the chestnuts in one layer in a baking dish just large enough to hold them. Place them in the oven and bake for about 10 minutes, or until they open. Let the chestnuts cool just until they can be handled. Peel them while they are hot.

4. Heat the salt pork in a heavy saucepan large enough to hold the cabbage. When the salt pork is rendered of its fat, add the onion and cook briefly.

1 3-pound red cabbage
12 chestnuts
¼ pound salt pork, cut into small cubes
¼ cup finely chopped onion
3 cooking apples, about 1 pound
1 cup dry white wine
Salt and freshly ground pepper
2 tablespoons dark brown sugar
2 tablespoons butter
1 tablespoon red wine vinegar

5. Meanwhile, peel and core the apples and cut them into quarters. Thinly slice the apple quarters. There should be about 4 cups. Add the apples to the saucepan. Add the wine and bring it to the boil. Add the cabbage, salt and pepper to taste. Add the brown sugar and chestnuts and cover. Simmer for 10 minutes, stirring occasionally. Make sure that the mixture does not stick and burn.

6. Place the saucepan in the oven and bake for 30 minutes. Reduce the oven heat to 375 degrees and bake for 1 to 1¼ hours, or until cabbage is thoroughly tender. Stir occasionally as it cooks. Stir in the butter and vinegar and blend well. Serve piping hot.

Yield: 8 to 12 servings.

Bengalese Cabbage with Mustard Seeds and Coconut

⅓ cup (loosely packed) freshly grated coconut
6 tablespoons mustard oil (see note)
1 teaspoon whole black mustard seeds (see note)
2 bay leaves
1 medium-size cabbage (3 to 3½ pounds), cored and finely shredded
¾ teaspoon salt
1 hot green pepper, cut into fine, long strips resembling cabbage strips

1. When buying a coconut, shake it and make sure it has liquid inside. This liquid is not needed in the recipe, but it insures a moist interior. Crack the coconut open with a hammer and pry away the meat by sliding a pointed knife between it and the hard shell. Cut off the brown skin of the meat and discard it. Wash the white meat and grate it finely.

2. Heat the oil in a wide, casserole-type pot over a medium-high flame. When the oil is hot, add the mustard seeds and bay leaves. As soon as the bay leaves darken and the mustard seeds begin to pop (this takes just a few seconds), add the shredded cabbage. Turn the heat to medium. Stir and cook for about 5 minutes, or until the cabbage wilts. Add the salt and hot pepper strips. Stir and cook for 3 to 5 minutes more. Turn off the heat. Sprinkle with grated coconut, mix well and serve.

Yield: 4 to 6 servings.

Note: Mustard oil and black mustard seeds are available at Indian food shops.

How to Make Sauerkraut

50 pounds white cabbage
1 pound pure granulated salt (noniodized)

1. Remove and discard the outer leaves and any other bruised or otherwise blemished leaves of the cabbage. Cut the cabbage into halves, then into quarters. Cut away the white tough center cores. Using a shredder or sharp slicer, cut the cabbage into fine shreds about the thickness of a penny.

2. In a kettle combine 5 pounds of the shreds with 3 tablespoons of salt. Blend well and let stand for 15 minutes or so,

until the cabbage wilts and gives up part of its liquid. Transfer this to a large sterilized crock. Add alternate layers of cabbage and salt, pressing down gently but firmly after each layer is added until the juice comes to the surface. Continue until the crock is filled to within 3 or 4 inches of the top.

3. Cover the cabbage with a clean white cloth such as a double layer of cheesecloth, tucking in the sides against the inside of the container. Add a free-floating lid that will fit inside the crock and rest on the cabbage. Failing this (perhaps even preferably), add a clean, heavy plastic bag containing water to rest on top of the cabbage. Whatever method is used, the lid or covering should extend over the cabbage to prevent exposure to the air. Air will cause the growth of film yeast or molds. The lid will also act as a weight and should offer enough weight to keep the fermenting cabbage covered with brine. Store the crock at room temperature. The ideal temperature is from 68 to 72 degrees.

4. When fermentation occurs, gas bubbles will be visible in the crock. Total time of fermentation is 5 to 6 weeks.

Yield: Enough for about 18 quarts.

When the sauerkraut has fermented sufficiently, empty it into a large kettle and bring it just to the simmer. Do not boil. The correct simmering temperature is from 185 to 210 degrees. Remove the sauerkraut from the heat and pack it into hot sterilized jars. Cover with hot juice to about ½ inch from the top of the rim. Close and seal the jars with a lid and screw top. Put in a water bath and boil pint jars for 15 minutes, quart jars for 20 minutes. The sauerkraut is now ready to be stored. It will keep on the shelf for months.

How to preserve fresh sauerkraut

Sauerkraut with Caraway

1. Put the sauerkraut in a colander and squeeze or press to remove most of the liquid.

2. Melt the lard in a heavy casserole and add the onion and garlic. Cook, stirring, until the onion is translucent. Add the sauerkraut, sugar, caraway seeds, chicken broth, salt and pepper. Cover and cook for 45 minutes.

3. Peel and grate the potato. There should be about ⅓ cup. Stir this into the sauerkraut. Cover and cook for 15 minutes longer.

Yield: 6 servings.

2 pounds sauerkraut
2 tablespoons lard or other fat
1 cup finely chopped onion
1 clove garlic, finely minced
1 tablespoon sugar
2 teaspoons crushed caraway seeds
2 cups fresh or canned chicken broth
Salt and freshly ground pepper to taste
1 small raw potato

Carrot Purée

2 pounds carrots, trimmed and
scraped
Salt to taste
2 tablespoons butter
½ cup heavy cream
Freshly ground pepper to
taste
⅛ teaspoon grated nutmeg

1. Cut the carrots into ¾-inch lengths. There should be about 6 cups. Place the carrots in a saucepan and add cold water to cover and salt to taste. Bring to the boil and simmer for 20 to 25 minutes, or until the pieces are tender without being mushy.

2. Put the carrots through a food mill, food ricer or food processor to make a fine, smooth purée. Return them to a saucepan. Place over very low heat while beating in butter, cream, salt, pepper and nutmeg.

Yield: 8 or more servings.

Molded Carrots à la Crème

1½ pounds carrots
Salt
⅛ teaspoon nutmeg
½ cup heavy cream
3 eggs
Freshly ground pepper

1. Preheat the oven to 375 degrees.

2. Trim the carrots and scrape them with a swivel-bladed vegetable scraper. Cut them into 2-inch lengths and put them in a saucepan. Add water to cover and salt to taste. Bring to the boil and simmer for about 15 minutes, or until tender without being mushy.

3. Drain and blend the carrots in a food processor or electric blender. Do not blend to a purée. They should be thoroughly blended but still retain some crunchy texture. Empty them into a mixing bowl. There should be about 3 cups. Add the nutmeg. Blend the cream and eggs and add them. Add salt and pepper to taste and blend well.

4. Butter a 4-cup charlotte mold and line the bottom of the mold with a round of wax paper. Butter the paper on top. Pour in the carrots. Set the mold in a baking dish containing hot water. Bring the water to the boil on top of the stove. Place in the oven and bake until set, for about 45 minutes. Unmold the carrots and serve hot.

Yield: 8 or more servings.

Creamed Carrots and Celery

4 large carrots, about 1 pound
5 or 6 ribs celery, about ¾
pound
Salt

1. Trim and scrape the carrots and celery. Cut the carrots into ¼-inch slices lengthwise. Cut each slice into 1½-inch lengths. There should be about 2½ cups. Cut the celery ribs into ¼-inch strips lengthwise and cut the strips into 1½-inch

lengths. There should be about 3½ cups. Place the carrot and celery pieces in a saucepan and add water to cover and salt to taste. Bring to the boil and simmer for about 10 minutes. Do not overcook. The pieces must remain crisp-tender. Drain well.

2. Heat the butter in a heavy saucepan and add the vegetables. Add salt and pepper to taste and nutmeg. Add the heavy cream and cover. Cook, tossing and stirring the vegetables so they cook evenly, for about 5 minutes. Serve piping hot.

Yield: 8 to 10 servings.

6 tablespoons butter
Freshly ground pepper
¼ teaspoon grated nutmeg
½ cup heavy cream

Vichy Carrots

Equip a food processor with the slicing blade. Slice the carrots. There should be about 4 cups. You may, of course, slice them very thin by hand. Put them in a skillet and add salt and pepper to taste, sugar, water (Vichy water if you want to be authentic) and butter. Cover with a round of buttered wax paper and cook over moderately high heat, shaking the skillet occasionally. Cook for about 10 minutes, or until carrots are tender, the liquid has disappeared and they are lightly glazed. Take care they do not burn. Serve sprinkled with chopped parsley.

Yield: 6 servings.

1½ pounds carrots, trimmed and scraped
Salt and freshly ground pepper
1 teaspoon sugar
¼ cup water
4 tablespoons butter
Chopped parsley

Cauliflower Polonaise

1. Trim the cauliflower and put it in a kettle with cold water to cover about 1 inch above the top of the cauliflower. Add the milk and salt and bring to the boil. Simmer, uncovered, for 15 minutes, or to the desired degree of doneness. By all means do not overcook the cauliflower. It must be tender and not mushy. Drain the cauliflower and put it on a hot serving dish.

2. Melt the butter in a small skillet and, when it is quite hot, add the bread crumbs. Cook, shaking the skillet, until they start to brown. Add the egg. Cook, tossing everything, for about 10 seconds and add the parsley. Cook, tossing and stirring, for about 1 minute. When ready, the mixture should be thick and foamy. Do not let it burn. Pour the sauce over the cauliflower and serve.

Yield: 6 to 8 servings.

1 medium-size head of cauliflower
Water to cover
½ cup milk
Salt to taste
4 tablespoons butter
½ cup fine, fresh bread crumbs
1 hard-cooked egg, finely chopped
1 tablespoon chopped parsley

Cauliflower with Mornay Sauce

1   2-pound head cauliflower
½   cup milk
1   tablespoon butter
    Salt and freshly ground
    pepper to taste
3   cups mornay sauce (see recipe
    page 645)
2   tablespoons grated
    Parmesan cheese

1. Break the cauliflower into large flowerets. Put them into a kettle and add cold water to cover and the milk. Add salt to taste. Bring to the boil and simmer for 15 minutes or until tender without being mushy. Drain well.

2. Meanwhile, preheat the oven to 375 degrees. Grease the bottom of a baking dish with butter and sprinkle with a little salt and pepper. Arrange the cauliflower over the bottom, stem side down. Sprinkle with a little more salt and pepper. Spoon the sauce over all. Sprinkle with grated Parmesan cheese. Bake for about 15 minutes, or until browned on top.

Yield: 6 to 8 servings.

Puréed Cauliflower

1   2-pound head cauliflower
½   cup milk
    Salt and freshly ground
    pepper to taste
2   tablespoons butter
⅛   teaspoon ground nutmeg
¾   cup heavy cream

Break the cauliflower into large flowerets. Put them into a kettle and add cold water to cover and the milk. Add salt to taste. Bring to the boil and simmer for 15 minutes, or until tender without being mushy. Drain well. Put the pieces, a few at a time, into the container of a food processor and blend well. Or put the cauliflower through a food mill. Spoon the purée into a saucepan. Heat gently and add the remaining ingredients. Stir until well blended.

Yield: 6 to 8 servings.

Vegetable Koorma

1   cup cauliflower cut into
    small flowerets
1   cup fresh or frozen green
    peas
1   cup string beans cut into ½-
    inch lengths
1   cup carrots cut into ½-inch
    dice

1. Cook each batch of vegetables in boiling salted water until just tender. Drain each batch as it is cooked and combine in a mixing bowl. Set aside.

2. Put the cashews into the container of a food processor or blender and blend to a purée. Add the yogurt, coconut and water and blend to a paste.

3. Heat the oil in a large saucepan and, when it is quite hot

but not smoking, add the cloves, small pieces of cinnamon and cardamom seeds. Add the onion and cook until wilted. Add the tomatoes and stir. Cook for about 5 minutes. Add the turmeric, ground coriander, cumin and salt.

4. Add the cooked vegetables and the yogurt and cashew mixture. Stir in half the fresh coriander. Cover and heat gently until piping hot throughout, about 5 minutes. Serve sprinkled with more fresh coriander.

Yield: 8 servings.

Note: Available in Indian shops.

1	cup potatoes, peeled and cut into ½-inch dice
¾	cup unroasted peeled cashew nuts (see note)
¾	cup yogurt
1	cup unsweetened finely shredded coconut (see note)
¼	cup water
6	tablespoons sesame oil, available in health food stores
6	whole cloves
5	small broken pieces cinnamon stick
3	small cardamom seeds
1½	cups coarsely chopped onion
2	cups unpeeled tomatoes cut into ½-inch cubes
¼	teaspoon turmeric
½	teaspoon ground coriander
½	teaspoon ground cumin
2	teaspoons salt
4	tablespoons chopped fresh coriander leaves

Céleri à la Crème

1. Trim the ribs of celery top and bottom. Cut the ribs into 1-inch lengths (if the pieces are very wide, cut them in half). There should be about 6 cups of cut celery.

2. Place the pieces in a saucepan and add cold water to cover. Bring to the boil, add salt to taste and simmer for about 10 minutes. Do not overcook. The pieces must remain crisp-tender. Drain, but save 2½ cups of the cooking liquid.

3. Heat 4 tablespoons of butter and add the flour, stirring with a wire whisk. Stir in the reserved celery liquid. Cook, stirring, for about 5 minutes. Add the nutmeg, Tabasco and cream and bring to the boil. Add salt and pepper to taste.

4. Heat the remaining 2 tablespoons of butter in a skillet and add the celery. Cook quickly, 1 minute or less, tossing the pieces in the skillet. Add this to the sauce and stir to blend.

Yield: 8 to 10 servings.

2	pounds celery ribs
	Salt
6	tablespoons butter
5	tablespoons flour
⅛	teaspoon nutmeg
⅛	teaspoon Tabasco sauce
1	cup heavy cream
	Freshly ground pepper

Buttered Whole Chestnuts

2 pounds chestnuts
3 tablespoons butter
  Salt
¾ cup fresh or canned chicken
  broth
1 tablespoon sugar

1. Preheat the oven to 400 degrees.

2. Using a sharp paring knife, make an incision around the perimeter of each chestnut, starting and ending on either side of the "topknot" or stem end. Place the chestnuts in one layer in a baking dish just large enough to hold them. Place them in the oven and bake for about 10 minutes. Let the chestnuts cool just until they can be handled. Peel them while they are hot.

3. Place the chestnuts in a saucepan and add the butter, salt to taste, broth and sugar. Cover and cook over low heat, stirring frequently, for 10 to 15 minutes. Place them in the oven and bake, stirring occasionally, for 25 to 30 minutes, or until thoroughly tender.

Yield: 6 to 8 servings.

Purée of Chestnuts

2 pounds chestnuts
  Salt
2 cups fresh or canned chicken
  broth
1 rib celery, quartered
1 small fennel bulb, halved
  (optional)
2 tablespoons butter
1 cup hot milk
½ cup hot heavy cream

1. Using a sharp paring knife, make an incision around the perimeter of each chestnut, starting and ending on either side of the "topknot" or stem end. Put the chestnuts in a skillet with water to cover and salt to taste. Bring to the boil and simmer for 15 to 20 minutes, or until the shells can be easily removed with the fingers. Drain. When cool enough to handle, peel the chestnuts. Remove both the outer shell and the inner peel.

2. Return the chestnuts to the saucepan and add the chicken broth, celery and fennel, if desired. Simmer, covered, for 20 to 30 minutes, or until chestnuts are done. Drain.

3. Put the chestnuts through a food mill or ricer and, while they are still hot, beat in the butter and hot milk and cream. Serve hot.

Yield: 8 to 12 servings.

How to Cook Corn on the Cob

Put enough water in a kettle to cover the shucked corn. Do not add salt. Bring the water to the boil and add the corn and cover. When the water returns to the boil, remove the kettle from the heat. Let the corn stand in the water for at least 5 minutes and serve immediately.

The corn may stand in the water for as long as 20 minutes without damage to its flavor and quality.

Corn and Pimientos Vinaigrette

Cut and scrape the kernels of corn from the cob. There should be about 2 cups. Put in a mixing bowl. Add the pimientos, onion, garlic and parsley. Blend the remaining ingredients with a wire whisk. Pour over the corn mixture and toss to blend.

Yield: 4 to 6 servings.

4 ears cooked corn (see recipe)
½ cup pimientos cut into ¼-inch cubes
½ cup finely chopped onion
½ teaspoon minced garlic
¼ cup finely chopped parsley
1 teaspoon imported mustard, such as Dijon or Düsseldorf
1 tablespoon red wine vinegar
  Juice of ½ lemon
5 tablespoons olive oil
  Salt and freshly ground pepper

Corn Pudding

Although there is nothing more delectable than fresh corn on the cob slathered with sweet butter, we have, since childhood, had a special fondness for grated corn dishes and corn pudding.

1. Preheat the oven to 375 degrees.
2. Grate and scrape the corn off the cob. There should be about 2½ cups. Put the corn pulp in a mixing bowl and add the cream, yolks, whole eggs, cheese, nutmeg, salt, pepper and green chilies. Beat well.
3. Butter a baking dish with the butter (we used a 9-inch ceramic pie plate) and pour in the corn batter. Bake for 25 minutes. Serve hot.

Yield: 6 servings.

8 to 10 ears uncooked corn
½ cup heavy cream
2 egg yolks
2 whole eggs
½ cup grated Cheddar cheese
⅛ teaspoon grated nutmeg
  Salt and freshly ground pepper
1 to 2 tablespoons diced green chilies (available in 4-ounce cans in many groceries and supermarkets), optional
1 tablespoon butter

Corn, Zucchini and Cheese Pudding

4 ears uncooked corn
1 tablespoon butter
½ cup finely chopped onion
1 teaspoon garlic
3 zucchini, about 1 pound, trimmed and cut into ¼-inch-thick rounds
2 egg yolks
1 large egg
½ cup milk
½ cup heavy cream
Salt and freshly ground pepper to taste
⅛ teaspoon nutmeg
¼ pound grated Muenster or Cheddar cheese, about 1 cup

1. Preheat the oven to 375 degrees.
2. Using a knife or another tool (special gadgets for scraping corn off the cob are sold in certain housewares outlets), scrape the corn off the cob. There should be about 2 cups. Set aside.
3. Melt the butter in a skillet and add the onion and garlic. Cook until wilted and add the zucchini. Cook, shaking the skillet, until zucchini is slightly wilted. Remove from the heat.
4. Blend the yolks, whole egg, milk, cream, salt, pepper and nutmeg. Add the corn and cheese and stir. Pour this over the zucchini and stir to blend.
5. Pour the mixture into a 4½- to 5-cup baking dish (an oval baking dish measuring 1½- x 7- x 11½-inches is suitable). Set the dish in a shallow pan and pour about ½ inch of boiling water around it. Place in the oven and bake for 25 minutes, or until custard is set in the center.
Yield: 4 to 6 servings.

Curried Corn with Green Peppers

6 ears cooked corn (see recipe)
3 tablespoons butter
¼ cup finely chopped green pepper
1 teaspoon curry powder
Salt and freshly ground pepper
¼ cup heavy cream

Cut and scrape the corn off the cob. There should be about 1½ cups. Heat 2 tablespoons of butter in a skillet and add the green pepper. Cook, stirring, for about 1 minute. Sprinkle with the curry powder and cook, stirring, for about 30 seconds. Add the corn and salt and pepper to taste. Add the remaining 1 tablespoon of butter and the heavy cream. Serve hot.
Yield: 2 to 4 servings.

Corn and Zucchini au Gratin

1½ pounds zucchini
7 or 8 ears cooked corn (see recipe)
3 tablespoons butter
3 tablespoons flour
1¾ cups milk
⅓ cup heavy cream
⅛ teaspoon grated nutmeg
Cayenne pepper

1. Preheat the oven to 350 degrees.
2. Trim off the ends of the zucchini. Split them lengthwise into halves, then into quarters. Cut each quarter into ½-inch or bite-size pieces. Place the zucchini in the top of a steamer over boiling water. Cover closely and steam for 5 minutes. Do not overcook. The pieces must remain firm and not mushy.
3. Using a sharp knife, cut the corn kernels from the cob. There should be about 2¼ cups.

4. Melt 2 tablespoons butter in a saucepan and add the flour, stirring with a wire whisk. When blended, add the milk all at once, stirring rapidly with the whisk. When thickened and smooth, add the cream, nutmeg and cayenne. Cook for about 5 minutes, stirring occasionaly. Add the Cheddar cheese, stirring, and turn off the heat. Add salt and pepper to taste.

5. Fold the zucchini and corn into the cream sauce. Pour the mixture into a baking dish and sprinkle with Parmesan. Dot with the remaining 1 tablespoon butter and bake for 25 to 30 minutes, or until golden brown and bubbling throughout. If desired, run the casserole under the broiler to get a better glaze on top.

Yield: 6 servings.

3   tablespoons grated Cheddar or Gruyère cheese
Salt and freshly ground pepper
¼   cup grated Parmesan cheese

Parsleyed Cucumber Ovals

Trim off the ends of the cucumbers. Cut the cucumbers into 2-inch lengths. Quarter each section lengthwise. Using a paring knife, carefully trim the pieces, cutting away the green skin and the seeds and leaving only the firm flesh. The pieces are now ready to cook, although if you want to "turn" them, as French chefs do, neatly round the ends of each piece with a knife. Place the pieces in a saucepan and add boiling water to cover and salt. Cook for 1 minute and drain. Return the cucumbers to the saucepan and add butter, salt and pepper to taste. Toss until butter melts. Sprinkle with parsley. Serve hot.

Yield: 4 servings.

2   large, firm, fresh cucumbers
Salt to taste
1   tablespoon butter
Freshly ground pepper
2   tablespoons finely chopped parsley

Kani Kiyuri Ikomi   *(Cucumber stuffed with crab in vinegar sauce)*

1. Peel the cucumbers. Sprinkle a flat surface with salt. Place the cucumbers on the salt bed and, using the palms of the hand, roll the cucumbers in salt. This will soften the cucumbers. Trim off about ½ inch from each end of the cucumbers. Using the small end of a melon ball cutter, scoop out the seeds. Or push out the seedy portions with chopsticks.

2. Shred the crabmeat, discarding cartilage portions. Blend the crab with the sanbaizu. Drain and push the crab mixture into the cucumbers to fill compactly. Cut the cucumbers into ½-inch rounds and arrange on a serving dish. Garnish with shreds of ginger and serve.

Yield: 6 or more servings.

2   small cucumbers
Salt
1   can (about 5½ ounces) imported crabmeat
9   tablespoons sanbaizu sauce (see recipe page 654)
1   teaspoon shredded ginger in salt (beni-shoga)

Eggplant au Gratin

1	eggplant, about 1 pound
	Salt
½	pound fresh mushrooms
3½	tablespoons butter
	Juice of ½ lemon
1½	tablespoons flour
½	cup milk
¼	cup heavy cream
	Freshly ground pepper
¼	teaspoon nutmeg
	Tabasco sauce
1	egg, lightly beaten
2	tablespoons bread crumbs
2	tablespoons grated Parmesan cheese

1. Preheat the oven to 425 degrees.

2. Peel the eggplant and cut the flesh into 1-inch cubes, more or less. Drop the cubes into boiling salted water and cook about 5 minutes. Drain well.

3. Meanwhile, slice the mushrooms. There should be about 3 cups. Heat 1 tablespoon of butter in a skillet and add the mushroom slices. Sprinkle with salt and about 1 teaspoon lemon juice. Cook, stirring and tossing, until wilted and the juices come out. Continue cooking until the liquid evaporates. Set aside.

4. Melt 1½ tablespoons of butter in a saucepan and add the flour, stirring with a wire whisk. Add the milk and cream, stirring rapidly with the whisk. When blended and smooth, add salt and pepper to taste, the remaining lemon juice, nutmeg and Tabasco to taste. Stir in the mushrooms and eggplant. Stir in the egg. Spoon the mixture into a baking dish (we used an 8- x 1-inch pie plate). Sprinkle with a mixture of crumbs and cheese and dot with the remaining tablespoon of butter. Bake for 30 to 40 minutes and then brown under the broiler.

Yield: 4 to 6 servings.

Melanzane Ripieni   *(Stuffed eggplant)*

The eggplant:

1½	pounds eggplant
	Flour for dredging
3	large eggs
2	tablespoons finely chopped parsley
	Oil for deep frying

The filling:

½	pound mozzarella cheese
½	cup finely shredded ham, preferably prosciutto
1	egg
2	cups ricotta cheese

1. Preheat the oven to 500 degrees.

2. Trim off the ends of the eggplant and cut the eggplant lengthwise into 12 center-cut slices. Discard the trimmings. Dredge the slices in flour to coat on all sides. Shake off excess. Beat the eggs with parsley and dip the slices in egg to coat well. Fry the slices, a few at a time, in hot oil, for about 3 minutes for each batch. Drain well.

3. Cut the mozzarella into ¼-inch slices. Cut the slices into ¼-inch strips. Cut the strips into ¼-inch cubes. Combine the mozzarella with the remaining ingredients for the filling except the marinara sauce.

4. Place the fried eggplant slices on a flat surface. Add equal amounts of filling toward the base of each slice. Roll to enclose the filling. Spoon about ½ inch of marinara sauce over a baking dish large enough to hold the stuffed slices. Arrange them

over the sauce. Cover with more sauce and place in the oven.
Bake for about 10 minutes.
Yield: 8 to 12 servings.

¼	cup grated Parmesan cheese
1	tablespoon finely chopped parsley
	Salt and freshly ground pepper to taste
2 to	3 cups marinara sauce (see recipe page 446)

Bangan Bartha *(Spiced eggplant)*

1. Place the eggplant on a hot charcoal grill or wrap them in heavy-duty aluminum foil and bake in a very hot (500-degree) oven for about 20 minutes. If the eggplant are grilled, turn them often over the hot coals. Cook until the eggplant are cap-sized and thoroughly tender throughout. Remove and let stand until cool enough to handle.

2. Melt the butter in a saucepan. When the eggplant are cool, pull away the skin, scraping off and saving the tender inside pulp. Scoop the tender pulp into the saucepan with the butter. Discard the skins. Add the onion to the eggplant and cook for 10 minutes, stirring often and taking care that the mixture does not stick to the bottom and burn.

3. Add salt and the tomatoes. Add the ginger, peppers and paprika and cook, stirring often while scraping the bottom to prevent scorching. Cook for about 15 minutes and remove from the heat. Add the chopped coriander. Serve hot, luke-warm or at room temperature.
Yield: 4 to 8 servings.

2	eggplant, about 1 pound each
8	tablespoons butter
2	cups finely chopped onion
	Salt to taste
1	cup red, ripe tomatoes, cored and cut into thin wedges
½	cup fresh ginger, cut into small cubes or thin sticks the size of match sticks
¾	cup sliced hot green peppers, or use hot red pepper flakes to taste
1	teaspoon sweet paprika
3	tablespoons chopped fresh coriander leaves, optional

Deep-fried Eggplant with Almonds

1. Cut off the ends of the eggplant. Peel the eggplant and cut into slices about ⅛ inch thick. Cut the eggplant slices into small rectangles, measuring about 1 by 1½ inches. Put the pieces into a mixing bowl and sprinkle with salt. Toss lightly. Let stand for about 30 minutes. Add the milk to the eggplant and let stand for about ½ hour. Drain well and discard milk.

2. Dredge the eggplant pieces in flour. Heat the oil for deep

1¼	pounds eggplant
	Salt
1	cup milk
1	cup flour
	Oil for deep frying
4	tablespoons butter
½	cup slivered, blanched almonds

frying to 375 degrees and add the eggplant pieces. Cook, stirring constantly, until very crisp, for 3 to 5 minutes. Remove the pieces with a slotted spoon and let drain on absorbent paper toweling. Sprinkle lightly with salt and transfer to a hot serving dish.

3. Heat the butter in a skillet and, when it is hot and starting to brown, add the almonds, stirring constantly. When the butter is hazelnut colored, pour the almonds and butter over the eggplant. Serve piping hot.

Yield: 4 to 6 servings.

Braised Endive

16 heads Belgian endive
Juice of 1 lemon
4 tablespoons butter
Salt to taste
½ cup water
1 tablespoon sugar

1. Preheat the oven to 450 degrees.

2. Trim off and discard any discolored leaves from the endive. Place the endive in a kettle and add the lemon juice, 2 tablespoons butter, salt, water and sugar. Cover and bring to the boil on top of the stove. Place the kettle in the oven and bake for 30 to 40 minutes. Drain well.

3. Melt the remaining 2 tablespoons of butter in a skillet large enough to hold the drained endive in one layer. Add endive and brown on one side. Turn and brown on the other side. Serve hot.

Yield: 8 servings.

Fennel au Gratin

Fennel is a crisp, aromatic vegetable that is more closely identified with the Italian table than any other. It is established that it was known in England, however, long before the Norman Conquest and that for centuries it has been traditional throughout Europe for use with both fresh and salted fish. Although it is delicious eaten out of hand as a cold appetizer, it is an enormously versatile vegetable when cooked.

3 to 6 fennel bulbs
4 tablespoons butter
Salt and freshly ground pepper

1. Preheat the oven to 400 degrees.

2. Cut off the tops of the fennel bulbs and trim the base. Pull off and discard any tough outer leaves. Cut the remaining fennel into quarters if they are large, or in half if they are small.

Drop the fennel into enough boiling water to cover and, when the water returns to the boil, simmer for 15 to 20 minutes, or until almost tender.

3. Drain the fennel and arrange the pieces symmetrically, cut side down, on a baking dish. Dot with butter. Add salt, pepper and chicken broth. Sprinkle with cheese and bake for 30 minutes.

Yield: 6 to 8 servings.

1 cup fresh or canned chicken broth
½ cup grated Parmesan cheese

Fried Fennel

1. Cut off the tops of the fennel bulbs and trim the base. Pull off and discard any tough outer leaves. Cut remaining fennel into slices slightly less than ½ inch thick. Rinse well and drain.

2. Bring 3 quarts of water to the boil and add salt to taste. Add the fennel slices. Cook until tender yet firm, 6 to 10 minutes. Drain and cool.

3. Dip the slices first in egg, then in bread crumbs. Heat about ½ inch of oil in a heavy skillet and, when the oil is quite hot, add the slices. Do not crowd them but cook as many as possible at one time. Cook until golden brown on one side, turn and cook until golden on the other. Drain on paper toweling. Sprinkle with salt and serve hot.

Yield: 4 servings.

3 fennel bulbs
Salt
2 eggs, beaten
1½ cups fine, dry, unflavored bread crumbs
Oil for frying

How to Prepare Leeks for Cooking Whole

Trim off the root ends of the leeks at the very base. Cut off the tops of the leeks crosswise at the center. Remove any bruised outside leaves. Split lengthwise, inserting a knife about 1 inch from the base. Give it a ¼-inch turn and make another lengthwise cut. This allows the leaves to be opened up. Drop the leeks into a basin of cold water and let stand until ready to use.

Shake the leeks to make certain they are cleared of inner dirt or sand. Tie with string into bunches. Bring enough salted water to the boil to cover the leeks. Add the leeks and cook for 10 minutes. Drain in a colander and let cool. Do not refrigerate.

Leeks au Gratin

6 cooked leeks
3 tablespoons butter
1 tablespoon plus 2 teaspoons flour
1½ cups milk
 Salt and freshly ground pepper to taste
⅛ teaspoon grated nutmeg
 A pinch of cayenne pepper
2 egg yolks
¼ cup grated Gruyère, Swiss or Parmesan cheese

1. Preheat the oven to 450 degrees.
2. Drain the leeks well and let them cool.
3. Melt 2 tablespoons of butter and add the flour, stirring with a wire whisk. When blended, add the milk, stirring rapidly with the whisk. Add salt, pepper, nutmeg and cayenne and blend. Remove from the heat and add the yolks, stirring briskly.
4. Arrange the leeks close together in a row and cut them crosswise into 4 pieces of equal length. Heat the remaining 1 tablespoon butter in a skillet and add the pieces of leeks. Sprinkle with salt and pepper. Cook briefly, tossing to heat evenly. Arrange the leeks in a baking dish (a dish that measures 6½- x 10- x 1½-inches is suitable). Spoon the sauce over and sprinkle with cheese. Bake for 10 minutes, or until piping hot and bubbling throughout. They should be nicely glazed on top.
   Yield: 4 to 6 servings.

Leeks with Cotechine

1 cooked cotechine (see recipe page 242)
2 tablespoons butter
10 cups trimmed, cleaned leeks chopped into 1-inch cubes
1 cup heavy cream
 Salt and freshly ground pepper to taste
⅛ teaspoon nutmeg, or to taste
3 tablespoons fresh bread crumbs
2 tablespoons melted butter

1. Preheat the oven to 425 degrees.
2. Heat the butter in a large saucepan and add the leeks. Cook, stirring occasionally, until wilted. Add the cream, salt, pepper and nutmeg. Cook over high heat for 5 to 10 minutes, or until leeks are tender but not mushy.
3. Carefully slit the skin of the cotechine and pull it away, leaving the cotechine whole. Cut it on the bias into about 24 slices.
4. Pour the creamed leeks into a baking dish (an oval dish that measures 14- x 8- x 2-inches is suitable). Smooth them over and arrange the cotechine slices over all. Sprinkle the top evenly with bread crumbs and pour the melted butter over all. Place the dish in the oven and bake for 15 to 20 minutes, or until piping hot and bubbling throughout. The crumbs should be golden brown. If not, run the dish briefly under the broiler.
   Yield: 4 to 6 servings.

Mushrooms with Herbs

If there is any doubt that American cookery took a lightning-bolt leap forward in sophistication these past few years, one has only to consider the past and current status of fresh mushrooms. Twenty years ago, the total annual production of mushrooms in the United States was a mere 75 million pounds. Today, that figure is well over 310 million pounds. The term lightning bolt is not used loosely here. Legend has it that the ancients believed mushrooms were created by lightning bolts.

1. Slice the mushroom caps thinly. There should be about 8 cups. Set aside.

2. Heat 4 tablespoons of butter in a skillet and add the shallots and garlic. Cook until shallots are wilted and start to brown. Add the parsley, chives, coriander, dill and chervil. Cook for about 1 minute, stirring often. Do not brown and do not let the green color darken. Remove from the heat and keep warm.

3. Heat 6 tablespoons of butter in a skillet. Add the mushrooms and cook, shaking the skillet and stirring so that the mushrooms cook evenly. Add salt and pepper to taste. Remove and discard the garlic from the herb mixture. Combine the mushrooms and herb mixture. Blend well and serve.

Yield: 6 servings.

1	pound mushrooms
10	tablespoons butter
½	cup shallots cut into wafer-thin slices
3	large cloves garlic, peeled and left whole
½	cup finely chopped parsley
½	cup finely chopped chives
½	cup finely chopped fresh coriander leaves
3	tablespoons chopped fresh dill
¼	cup finely chopped chervil, optional
	Salt and freshly ground pepper to taste

Champignons à la Crème *(Creamed mushrooms)*

Melt the butter in a saucepan and add the shallots. Cook, stirring, for about 3 minutes and add the mushrooms and lemon juice. Sprinkle with salt, pepper and nutmeg and cook, stirring often, until mushrooms give up their liquid. Cook until the liquid evaporates. Add the port wine, stirring briefly. Add the cream, stir and bring to the boil. Serve hot.

Yield: 6 to 8 servings.

2	tablespoons butter
1	tablespoon finely chopped shallots
1¼	pound mushrooms, thinly sliced
	Juice of ½ lemon
	Salt and freshly ground pepper to taste
¼	teaspoon grated nutmeg
2	tablespoons port wine
¾	cup heavy cream

Champignons Provençale *(Mushrooms with shallots and parsley)*

1	pound fresh mushrooms
¼	cup peanut, vegetable or corn oil
	Salt and freshly ground pepper to taste
2	tablespoons butter
1½	tablespoons finely chopped shallots
1	tablespoon chopped parsley
¼	cup fine, fresh bread crumbs

1. Wash and drain the mushrooms. Cut them into quarters. Heat the oil in a heavy skillet and, when it is hot and almost smoking, add the mushrooms. Add salt and pepper. Cook over high heat, shaking the skillet and stirring, until the mushrooms are nicely browned all over. Drain in a sieve.

2. Heat the butter in a clean, heavy skillet and add the mushrooms, shallots, parsley and bread crumbs. Cook, tossing and stirring, for about 1 minute. When ready, the crumbs should be dry and crisp. This is an excellent accompaniment for grilled lamb, poultry or steak and also goes well with grilled tomatoes.

Yield: 4 servings.

Sautéed Mushrooms

12 or	more mushrooms, about ½ pound
3	tablespoons butter
	Salt and freshly ground pepper to taste
2	teaspoons Worcestershire sauce
	Juice of ½ lemon

1. Trim off the stems from the mushroom caps. Reserve both stems and caps. Rinse the caps and stems in cold water and drain immediately. Pat dry.

2. Heat the butter in a skillet large enough to hold the mushroom pieces in one layer. Add the mushroom pieces and cook, stirring and shaking the skillet, turning the pieces so that they cook evenly. Sprinkle with salt and pepper. Cook until nicely browned all over. They will give up liquid. Cook until this liquid evaporates. Sprinkle with Worcestershire sauce, stirring and shaking the skillet. Sprinkle with lemon juice. Toss quickly and serve hot.

Yield: 2 to 4 servings.

Creamed Mushrooms with Dried Beef

½	pound mushrooms
4	tablespoons butter
3	tablespoons flour
2	cups milk
2	2½-ounce jars thinly sliced dried beef (chipped beef)
1	2-ounce jar pimientos, drained and cut into strips
2	cups grated Cheddar cheese
⅛	teaspoon grated nutmeg

1. Wash and dry the mushrooms. Cut them into slices, then into fine strips (julienne).

2. Melt 2 tablespoons of butter and add the flour, stirring with a whisk. When blended, add the milk, stirring rapidly with the whisk. Do not add salt.

3. Melt the remaining butter and add the mushrooms. Cook until they are wilted and give up their liquid. Add the sauce, dried beef and pimientos.

4. Remove from the heat and immediately add the cheese, nutmeg and cayenne. Taste the dish and add salt if desired.

Sprinkle with pepper and stir. Serve on toast or toasted English muffin halves.

Yield: 4 to 6 servings.

Pinch of cayenne pepper
Salt, if desired, and freshly ground pepper

Champignons Farcis Bonne Femme *(Mushrooms stuffed with duxelles and sausage)*

1. Preheat the oven to 400 degrees.
2. Cut off the mushroom stems and prepare the duxelles. Let cool briefly and add the sausage and parsley. Blend well. Stuff the mushroom caps with the sausage mixture. Sprinkle with a blend of crumbs and cheese. Dot with butter.
3. Grease a baking dish and arrange the caps stuffed side up. Bake for about 20 minutes, basting occasionally, or until piping hot and browned. Serve hot or cold.

Yield: 4 servings.

12 large mushrooms, about ¾ pound
½ cup duxelles (see recipe below), made with the stems of the mushrooms
¼ pound sausage meat
1 tablespoon finely chopped parsley
2 tablespoons fresh bread crumbs
2 tablespoons grated Parmesan cheese
1 tablespoon butter

Duxelles

1. Remove the stems from the mushrooms and chop the stems finely. There should be about 1 cup. Use the mushroom caps for stuffing. Place the stems in a clean cloth and squeeze like a tourniquet to extract most of the liquid.
2. Heat the butter and oil in a skillet. Add the onion and shallots and cook to wilt. Add the squeezed mushroom stems and stir. Sprinkle with lemon juice, salt and pepper to taste. Cook, stirring, until all of the moisture has evaporated.

Yield: About ½ cup.

12 large mushrooms, about ¾ pound
1½ teaspoons butter
1 teaspoon oil
1 tablespoon finely chopped onion
1 tablespoon finely chopped shallots
Juice of ½ lemon
Salt and freshly ground pepper

Mushrooms Stuffed with Spinach and Anchovies

1. Preheat the oven to 400 degrees.
2. Remove stems and reserve the caps from the mushrooms. Chop the stems. There should be about 1 cup.
3. Pick over the spinach to remove any tough stems. Rinse the leaves well and drop them into boiling water to cover. Simmer for about 1 minute and drain in a colander. Chill under cold running water and drain. Press the spinach between the hands to remove most of the moisture. Chop spinach. There should be about 1 cup.
4. Empty the oil from the anchovy can into a saucepan and

12 large mushrooms
1 pound fresh spinach
1 2-ounce can anchovies
½ teaspoon chopped garlic
½ cup heavy cream
3 tablespoons melted butter
¼ cup grated Parmesan cheese

add the chopped mushroom stems. Cook, stirring, for about 5 minutes and add the spinach and garlic. Chop the anchovies and add them. Stir to blend thoroughly. Stir in the cream and bring just to the boil. Remove from the heat and let cool.

5. Meanwhile, place the mushrooms, hollow side down, in a buttered baking dish. Brush with half the melted butter and place in the oven for 10 minutes. Remove and let cool.

6. Stuff the cavity of each mushroom with the mixture, heaping it up and smoothing it over. Arrange the mushrooms in the baking dish and sprinkle with Parmesan cheese and the remaining melted butter. Place in the oven and bake for 20 minutes.

Yield: 6 servings.

Funghi Trifolati   *(Mushrooms with garlic, oil and parsley)*

½   **ounce dried Italian mushrooms**
½   **cup olive oil**
2   **teaspoons finely chopped garlic**
3   **tablespoons finely chopped parsley**
1   **pound fresh mushrooms, sliced, about 6 cups**
    Salt and freshly ground pepper

1. Put the dried mushrooms in a mixing bowl and add warm water to cover. Let stand for ½ hour or longer until mushrooms are soft. Remove the soaked mushrooms but save all their liquid. Squeeze to extract as much liquid as possible but save this liquid, too. Line a sieve with one layer of a kitchen towel. Strain the liquid. Chop the soaked mushrooms on a flat surface. They should be chopped fairly fine. Combine the strained mushroom liquid and the chopped mushrooms in a skillet. Bring to the boil and cook until all the liquid has evaporated.

2. Heat the olive oil in a deep skillet or casserole and add the garlic. Cook, stirring, without browning. Add the parsley. Add the fresh mushrooms and cook for about 1 minute, stirring. Add the dried mushrooms. Add salt and pepper to taste. Cook until the mushrooms give up their liquid. Continue cooking until the liquid (not the oil) evaporates. Serve as a vegetable or with pasta (see recipe below).

Yield: 4 to 6 servings.

Funghi trifolati with pasta

Prepare the funghi trifolati, but chop the fresh mushrooms finely. Increase the oil from ½ cup to ⅔ cup. Serve tossed with fettucini, spaghetti or vermicelli.

Oignons Farcies *(Stuffed onions)*

1. Preheat the oven to 400 degrees.
2. Peel the onions. Cut off a thin slice from the bottom and top of each onion. Using a melon ball cutter, hollow out the center of each onion, leaving a shell about ½ inch thick all around and on the bottom. Drop the onions into boiling water and simmer for about 10 minutes. Drain. Sprinkle the inside of each onion with salt and pepper to taste.
3. Meanwhile, cook the bacon in a skillet until rendered of fat. Add the chopped onion and garlic and cook until wilted. Remove from the heat and add the ham, 4 tablespoons crumbs, cream, egg, nutmeg, parsley, salt and pepper to taste. Return to the heat, stirring, for about 1 minute, or until heated through. Do not cook. Let the filling cool slightly.
4. Stuff the cavities of the onions with the filling, piling it up over the top. Sprinkle with a blend of remaining bread crumbs and cheese and sprinkle with oil. Arrange the onions on a buttered baking dish and pour the broth around them. Place in the oven and bake for 45 minutes, basting occasionally. If necessary, cover loosely with foil to prevent over-browning.

Yield: 4 servings.

8 onions, about ½ pound each
Salt and freshly ground pepper
8 slices bacon, cut into ½-inch cubes
¼ cup finely chopped onion
2 teaspoons finely chopped garlic
¼ pound finely chopped ham
6 tablespoons fine, fresh bread crumbs
1 tablespoon heavy cream
1 egg, lightly beaten
¼ teaspoon grated nutmeg
¼ cup finely chopped parsley
2 tablespoons grated Parmesan cheese
2 tablespoons peanut, vegetable or corn oil
¼ cup chicken broth

Onions à la Grecque

1. Tie the coriander, marjoram, oregano, thyme, bay leaf and garlic in a cheesecloth bag. Put the bag in a saucepan and add the water, lemon juice, olive oil, salt and pepper to taste.
2. Peel the onions and add them to the saucepan. Bring to the boil. Cover and cook over high heat for about 10 minutes. Uncover and cook over high heat for 5 minutes longer.
3. Spoon the onions, cooking liquid and cheesecloth bag into a mixing bowl and cover. Let cool. Chill overnight. Discard the cheesecloth bag and serve the onions cold or at room temperature. Garnish with lemon or parsley.

Yield: 6 servings.

1 teaspoon coriander seeds
½ teaspoon marjoram
½ teaspoon dried oregano
½ teaspoon dried thyme
1 bay leaf, broken
1 large clove garlic, crushed but unpeeled
1½ cups water
¼ cup lemon juice
2 tablespoons olive oil
Salt and freshly ground pepper
28 to 30 small white onions, about ¾ pound
Lemon wedges or parsley for garnish

Okra Guadeloupe-style

2 10-ounce packages frozen
okra, defrosted
1 small onion, about ¼ pound
Salt to taste
½ cup tarragon wine vinegar
½ cup water
½ teaspoon red pepper flakes,
more or less to taste

Place the okra in a skillet. Peel and cut the onion into thin strips. Add it. Add the remaining ingredients and let stand, stirring occasionally, about 1 hour. Cover and bring to the boil. Cook 7 minutes. No longer. Serve at room temperature or chilled.

Yield: 4 to 6 servings.

Garden Peas à la Menthe

2½ to 3 cups freshly shelled
peas
6 tablespoons butter
Salt and freshly ground
pepper to taste
2 tablespoons water
2 teaspoons chopped fresh
mint

Put the peas in a heavy saucepan and add 4 tablespoons of butter, salt, pepper and water. Cover closely and cook for about 5 minutes, or until peas are just tender. Sprinkle with the mint and swirl in the remaining butter.

Yield: 6 servings.

Snow Peas and Abalone Mushrooms

½ pound snow peas
¼ cup thinly sliced bamboo
shoots
1 10-ounce can abalone
mushrooms (see note)
1 10-ounce can golden
mushrooms (see note)
¾ cup fresh or canned chicken
broth
1 tablespoon cornstarch
¼ cup oyster sauce
1 teaspoon sugar
½ teaspoon monosodium
glutamate, optional
1 tablespoon dark soy sauce
7 tablespoons peanut, vegetable
or corn oil

1. Trim the snow peas and rinse well. Drain. Combine with the bamboo shoots. Set aside.

2. Rinse and drain the two kinds of mushrooms. Set aside.

3. Blend the chicken broth with the cornstarch. Set aside.

4. Blend the oyster sauce, sugar, monosodium glutamate, if used, and soy sauce. Set aside.

5. Heat 6 tablespoons of oil in a wok or skillet and, when very hot, add the bamboo shoots and snow peas. Cook over very high heat for about 30 seconds. Using a slotted spoon, scoop out the vegetables. Add the mushrooms to the wok and cook, stirring, over very high heat for about 45 seconds. Scoop the mushrooms out with the spoon. Add the remaining table-spoon of oil to the wok and add the oyster sauce mixture. Add the chicken broth and cornstarch mixture. When it boils up, add the snow pea and mushroom mixtures. Stir to blend and serve.

Yield: 4 to 6 servings.

Note: Both the mushrooms are available in cans in Chinese markets.

Sautéed Sweet Peppers

Using a sharp knife, cut the peppers down the sides to produce large slices. Discard the core and seeds and inner veins. Stack a few slices at a time and cut them into very fine, julienne strips. There should be about 4 cups. Heat the oil in a very heavy skillet and add the peppers. Do not add salt or other seasonings. Cook over very high heat, tossing and stirring until peppers are crisp and piping hot, a minute or longer.

Yield: 6 servings.

3	sweet red peppers
3	sweet green peppers
2	tablespoons peanut, vegetable or corn oil

Tarragon and Pork-stuffed Peppers

1. Split the peppers in half lengthwise. Sprinkle the insides with salt and pepper.

2. Put the pork through a meat grinder fitted with a coarse blade, or chop it finely. There should be about 4 cups. Put the meat in a mixing bowl.

3. Put the mushrooms through the grinder. Melt 1 tablespoon of butter in a skillet or saucepan and add the mushrooms, 1 cup of onion and half the garlic. Cook, stirring, until the mushrooms give up their liquid. Cook until most of the liquid evaporates. Add the thyme, bay leaf, parsley and tarragon.

4. Add the mushroom mixture to the pork. Add the rice, eggs, salt and pepper to taste, and the pine nuts. Blend well. Stuff the pepper halves with the mixture and sprinkle with bread crumbs and cheese.

5. With 3 tablespoons of butter, grease a flameproof baking dish large enough to hold the peppers. Add the remaining ½ cup of onion and garlic and sprinkle with salt and pepper. Arrange the peppers in the dish. Blend the tomatoes in an electric blender and pour them around the peppers. Add the chicken broth. Sprinkle salt and pepper over all. Melt the remaining 2 tablespoons of butter and dribble it over the peppers.

6. Preheat oven to 350 degrees. Bring the dish to the boil on top of the stove, then place it in the oven. Bake for 45 minutes. Serve the peppers with the natural tomato sauce in the pan.

Yield: 8 servings.

4	large green peppers
	Salt and freshly ground pepper
1	pound leftover roast pork
¼	pound fresh mushrooms, rinsed and drained
6	tablespoons butter
1½	cups finely chopped onion
2	cloves garlic, finely minced
2	sprigs fresh thyme, finely chopped, or ½ teaspoon dried
½	bay leaf, finely chopped
2	tablespoons finely chopped parsley
1	tablespoon finely chopped fresh tarragon, or 1 teaspoon dried, crushed
1	cup cooked rice
2	eggs
½	cup pine nuts, optional
¼	cup fresh bread crumbs
¼	cup grated Parmesan cheese
2	cups peeled tomatoes, preferably Italian plum tomatoes if canned ones are used
½	cup chicken broth

Ratatouille

5 tablespoons olive oil
1 eggplant, about ¾ pound, cut into 1-inch cubes
1 or 2 zucchini, about ¾ pound, cut into 1-inch cubes
2 or 3 onions, about ¾ pound, coarsely chopped
2 or 3 green peppers, about ½ pound, cut into 1-inch cubes
1 tablespoon chopped garlic
2 sprigs fresh thyme, or ½ teaspoon dried
1 bay leaf
Salt and freshly ground pepper
3 or 4 tomatoes, about 1½ pounds, cut into cubes

1. Heat 4 tablespoons of oil in a large, heavy skillet or casserole and, when it is quite hot, add the eggplant. Cook, stirring, for about 3 minutes. Remove with a wooden spoon and put it in a colander. Add the zucchini to the skillet and cook, stirring, for about 3 minutes. Add it to the eggplant.

2. Add the remaining oil to the skillet and add the onion. Cook, stirring, until wilted and add the green peppers. Cook, stirring, for about 3 minutes. Add the garlic, thyme and bay leaf. Add the eggplant and zucchini, salt and pepper to taste. Cook, stirring, for about 5 minutes. Add the tomatoes and stir. Cover closely and cook for 20 minutes.

3. Uncover and cook for about 10 minutes to reduce the liquid that will have accumulated. Serve hot or cold.

Yield: 6 to 8 servings.

Steamed Rutabaga

1½ pounds rutabaga
4 tablespoons butter
3 cups water
3 tablespoons lemon juice
Chopped parsley for garnish

Pare the rutabaga and cut into 1-inch cubes. There should be about 5 cups. Place the rutabaga in a saucepan and add the butter and water. Cover as tightly as possible. Bring the liquid to the boil and cook over low heat until all the liquid has evaporated and the rutabaga is tender. Check occasionally to make certain the rutabaga does not burn toward the end. Pour the lemon juice over the rutabaga. Turn the rutabaga out into a serving dish and sprinkle with parsley.

Yield: 6 to 8 servings.

Baked Rutabagas à la Crème

7 pounds rutabaga
2 pounds potatoes
Salt to taste
4 tablespoons butter
1 cup heavy cream

1. Preheat the oven to 400 degrees.

2. Peel the rutabagas and potatoes. Cut the rutabagas into 2½-inch cubes. Slice the potatoes into approximately the same size. Place the vegetables in a kettle and add cold water to cover and salt to taste. Bring to the boil and cook fo 25 to 30 minutes, or until tender. Drain and put through a food mill.

3. Return the vegetables to the kettle and add the butter. Beat it in over low heat. Bring the cream to the boil and beat it in with a whisk. Spoon the mixture into a baking dish. Bake for about 20 minutes, or until bubbling hot throughout. Brown briefly under the broiler.

Yield: 12 or more servings.

Pain d'Épinards (*A spinach loaf*)

1. Preheat the oven to 350 degrees.

2. Pick over the spinach. Remove and discard any tough stems or blemished leaves. Wash the spinach thoroughly in cold water and drain. Drop the spinach into a kettle of boiling water and add salt to taste. Simmer for about 5 minutes. Drain well. Let cool. Press the spinach between the hands to extract most of the excess moisture. There should be about 2 cups. Place the spinach on a flat surface and chop finely with a heavy knife.

3. Heat 1 tablespoon of butter in a skillet and add the spinach. Cook, stirring briefly, and add salt, pepper and nutmeg. Add 1 cup cream. Stir and bring to the boil. Remove from the heat.

4. Melt the remaining 2 tablespoons of butter in a saucepan and add the flour, stirring with a wire whisk. Add the milk, stirring with the whisk and, when thickened and smooth, add the spinach mixture, salt and pepper to taste. Beat the eggs and add them. Cook briefly, for about 30 seconds. Remove from the heat.

5. Butter the inside of a 5- to 6-cup charlotte mold and line the bottom with a round of wax paper. Butter the paper. Pour in the mixture and place the mold in a baking dish. Pour boiling water around the mold and bring this to the boil on top of the stove. Place the baking dish with the mold in the oven and bake for about 45 minutes, or until set.

6. Pour the remaining 1 cup cream into a saucepan and add salt, pepper and ⅛ teaspoon nutmeg. Bring to the boil and simmer, stirring occasionally, for about 5 minutes.

7. Unmold the spinach loaf onto a round dish. Serve with the cream sauce.

Yield: 8 or more servings.

2½ pounds fresh spinach, or 2 10-ounce packages
Salt to taste
3 tablespoons butter
Grated nutmeg to taste
2 cups heavy cream
2 tablespoons flour
1 cup milk
3 large eggs

Spinach Purée

3 pounds fresh spinach, or 3 10-ounce packages
4 cups water
Salt to taste
2 tablespoons butter
Freshly ground pepper to taste
½ cup heavy cream
⅛ teaspoon grated nutmeg

1. Pick over the spinach. Tear off and discard any tough stems. Discard any blemished leaves. Rinse the spinach well and drain.

2. Bring the 4 cups of water to the boil and add salt to taste. Add the spinach and cook, stirring often, for about 5 minutes. Drain well and let cool. Squeeze the spinach between the hands to remove the excess moisture. Divide it into 4 balls. Blend in a food processor or electric blender. There should be about 3 cups.

3. Heat 2 tablespoons butter and add the spinach, salt, pepper and cream. Add the nutmeg and serve piping hot.

Yield: 8 or more servings.

Acorn Squash with Green Peas

6 unblemished acorn squash
4 tablespoons butter at room temperature
Salt and freshly ground pepper to taste
4 tablespoons light brown sugar
3 cups buttered, cooked fresh peas, or use 2 packages frozen peas, cooked

1. Preheat the oven to 450 degrees.

2. Split the squash in half lengthwise. Scoop out and discard the seeds. Cut off and discard a small slice from the bottom of each squash half so they will sit flat. Arrange the squash halves in a large dish. Brush the cavities and tops with butter. Sprinkle with salt and pepper. Sprinkle 2 teaspoons of brown sugar around the inside of each squash. Bake for 45 minutes to 1 hour. Spoon equal amounts of peas into each cavity and serve hot.

Yield: 12 servings.

Grilled Tomatoes with Oregano

4 large or 8 small tomatoes
3 or more cloves garlic
4 teaspoons fresh or dried oregano
Salt and freshly ground pepper
Olive oil

1. Preheat the broiler to high.

2. Rinse and dry the tomatoes. Do not core or peel them. Split the tomatoes in half and arrange the halves on a baking dish. Cut the garlic into thin slivers. Insert the slivers at various points over the cut surface of the tomato halves.

3. Chop the oregano coarsely and sprinkle the cut surface of the tomatoes with it. Sprinkle with salt and pepper to taste. Dribble the olive oil over all.

4. Place the tomatoes under the broiler, 4 or 5 inches from the flame, and broil for 3 minutes or longer, until the garlic is

browned and the tomatoes are soft but firm. Remove the pieces of garlic and serve the tomatoes hot.

Yield: 8 servings.

Stuffed Tomatoes

1. Preheat the oven to 375 degrees.

2. Remove the stems from the tomatoes. Split the tomatoes in half for stuffing. Gently squeeze each tomato half, letting the seeds, juice and pulp fall into a small bowl. Reserve. Sprinkle each tomato half with salt and pepper to taste and set aside.

3. Remove the sausage meat from the casings. Heat the oil in a skillet and add the onion and garlic. Cook briefly and add the sausage meat, breaking up any lumps with the side of a heavy kitchen spoon. Cook until the meat changes color. Add the reserved tomato seeds, juice and pulp. Cook until liquid evaporates. Let cool briefly. Add the rice, parsley, basil, pine nuts and half the cheese. Add the egg, salt and pepper to taste and blend well. Let cool.

4. Lightly oil a baking dish. Arrange the tomato halves cut side up. Spoon the filling into and over the tops of the tomato halves, piling it up and rounding it with the fingers. Sprinkle with the remaining cheese. Bake for 30 minutes. Serve hot or cold.

Yield: 6 to 12 servings.

6	small, red, ripe, firm tomatoes, about 1½ pounds
	Salt and freshly ground pepper
½	pound sweet or hot Italian sausages, about 4
1	tablespoon olive oil
½	cup finely chopped onion
1	clove garlic, finely minced
1½	cups cooked rice
2	tablespoons finely chopped parsley
1	tablespoon finely chopped basil
3	tablespoons pine nuts
¼	cup grated Parmesan cheese
1	egg, lightly beaten

Fried Tomatoes and Zucchini

1. Core the tomatoes and cut them into ½-inch-thick slices. Trim off the ends of the zucchini and cut the vegetable on the bias into ½-inch-thick slices. In separate batches, sprinkle the tomatoes and zucchini with salt and pepper then coat on all sides with flour, shaking to remove excess.

2. Heat ½ cup of oil in a large heavy skillet and fry the tomatoes on one side and then the other until golden brown. Drain on absorbent toweling. Add the remaining oil to the skillet and fry the zucchini until nicely browned on both sides, draining the slices as they are cooked. Arrange the slices of tomato and zucchini slightly overlapping on a serving dish.

3. Heat the butter in a skillet until it is hazelnut brown. Add

4	red, ripe but firm tomatoes, about 1¼ pounds
3	zucchini, about 1 pound
	Salt and freshly ground pepper to taste
	Flour for dredging
¾	cup peanut oil
3	tablespoons butter
1	clove garlic, finely minced
¼	cup finely chopped parsley

the garlic, stir and remove from the heat. Pour this over the vegetables. Sprinkle with parsley and serve.

Yield: 8 servings.

Stuffed Tomatoes and Zucchini Moroccan-style

12	medium-size red, ripe tomatoes
3	zucchini, about 2 pounds
1½	pounds lean ground lamb
1½	teaspoons freshly ground pepper
1½	teaspoons ground ginger
⅛	teaspoon ground cinnamon
2	teaspoons finely chopped garlic
½	cup rice
¼	teaspoon dried crushed mint
1½	cups grated onion (see method below)
8	tablespoons butter
3	tablespoons finely chopped parsley
3	tablespoons chopped fresh coriander
3	cups water
	Salt
¼	cup lemon juice
	Butter
10	eggs
2	tablespoons chopped coriander
2	tablespoons chopped parsley

1. Cut away the core and enough of the inside of each tomato to leave an almost hollow shell. Sprinkle with salt and invert the tomatoes on a rack to drain. Let stand for 1 hour or longer.

2. Cut the zucchini into 2-inch lengths. Using an apple corer or a vegetable peeler, hollow out each length of zucchini, leaving a shell about ¼ inch thick. Set aside.

3. In a saucepan combine the lamb, 1 teaspoon of pepper, ginger, cinnamon, garlic, rice, mint, onion, butter, parsley, coriander, water and salt to taste. Bring to the boil and cook for about 30 minutes, or until almost all the liquid has evaporated. Add the lemon juice. Remove from heat and let cool.

4. Stuff the tomatoes and the zucchini pieces with the lamb mixture, leveling off the ends or tops. Butter a baking dish and arrange the stuffed tomatoes, bottom side down, on it. Stand the zucchini pieces on end around the tomatoes. Spoon any leftover filling between the stuffed vegetables.

5. When ready to cook, preheat the oven to 350 degrees. Sprinkle the stuffed vegetables with salt and ½ teaspoon pepper. Cover closely with heavy-duty aluminum foil. Prick the foil in several places with a fork to allow steam to escape. Place the dish in the oven and bake for 30 minutes. Remove.

6. Beat the eggs with the coriander and parsley. Add salt and pepper to taste. Increase oven heat to the highest temperature. Pour the beaten egg evenly over the vegetables. Bake for 10 minutes, or until eggs set.

Yield: 12 servings.

Grated onions for Moroccan cooking

Peel about 1 pound of onions. Cut the onions into quarters. Blend thoroughly in a food processor. Place a sieve over a bowl and add the onions. Let drain.

Yield: About 1½ cups.

Zucchini with Summer Herbs

1. Rinse the zucchini and pat dry. Trim off the ends, but do not peel. Cut the zucchini into thin slices about ⅛ inch thick. There should be about 6 cups.
2. Heat the oil in a skillet and, when it is quite hot, add the zucchini. Cook over relatively high heat, shaking the skillet, tossing and stirring gently with a spatula to turn the slices. Add salt and pepper to taste. Cook for about 5 minutes. Drain in a sieve. Do not wipe out the skillet.
3. Add the butter to the skillet. When melted and hot, return the zucchini to the skillet. Add the garlic and herbs. Add salt and pepper to taste. Toss and serve hot.

Yield: 6 servings.

- 1½ pounds zucchini
- 4 tablespoons olive oil
- Salt and freshly ground pepper
- 2 tablespoons butter
- 2 teaspoons chopped garlic
- 1 tablespoon chopped parsley
- 1 tablespoon chopped chives
- 1 tablespoon chopped dill
- 1 teaspoon chopped tarragon
- 1 tablespoon finely chopped fresh basil

Zucchini à l'Italienne *(Baked zucchini with herbs and cheese)*

1. Preheat the oven to 400 degrees.
2. Trim off the ends of the zucchini and cut the zucchini on the bias into ½-inch slices. Sprinkle the slices with salt and pepper. Heat ⅓ cup of oil in a skillet and cook the slices until golden brown on one side. Turn and brown on the other. This may take several steps. Arrange the slices slightly overlapping on a baking dish in which they will fit neatly.
3. Blend the garlic, bread, parsley and rosemary in a food processor or blender. Sprinkle this over the zucchini and sprinkle with the cheese. Dribble the remaining oil over all and bake for 20 minutes, or until bubbling. If desired, run under the broiler to brown further.

Yield: 6 to 8 servings.

- 3 or 4 medium-size zucchini, about 1¾ pounds
- Salt and freshly ground pepper
- ⅓ cup plus 2 tablespoons olive oil
- 1 clove garlic
- 1 cup white bread trimmed of crust and cut into 1-inch cubes
- 6 sprigs fresh parsley
- ½ teaspoon rosemary leaves
- ⅓ cup grated Parmesan cheese

Zucchini Fritti

1. Trim off the ends of the zucchini. Cut the zucchini into 3-inch lengths. Cut each length into ¼-inch slices. Cut the slices into ¼-inch strips. Drop the strips into cold water and let stand briefly.
2. Drain the zucchini well. Place in a bowl, sprinkle with enough flour to coat the pieces and toss well with the hands. Put the eggs in a large bowl. Add the floured zucchini and mix well with the hands until the pieces are coated.

- 3 zucchini, about ½ pound each
- Flour for dredging
- 3 eggs, beaten
- Oil for deep frying

3. Heat the oil until it is hot and almost smoking. Add a portion of the zucchini, half of it or less at a time, and cook, stirring to separate the pieces, for about 6 or 7 minutes, or until crisp. Drain on a clean towel. Serve hot sprinkled with salt.

Yield: 6 or more servings.

Zucchini in the Style of Provence

½ pound onions
2 pounds zucchini
1 teaspoon loosely packed oregano
2 tablespoons olive oil
½ teaspoon finely minced garlic
3 eggs
Salt and freshly ground pepper to taste
Nutmeg

1. Peel the onions and cut them in half. Slice each half thinly. There should be about 2½ cups.

2. Trim off the ends and peel the zucchini. If they are small, cut them in half lengthwise. Cut each quarter or half into 1-inch pieces. There should be about 6 cups.

3. Place the oregano in a small skillet and toast over moderate heat, shaking the skillet and stirring to prevent burning. Cook just until lightly toasted. Do not burn or the oregano will be bitter. Crush or grind the oregano and set it aside.

4. Heat the oil in a heavy saucepan and add the onions. Cover closely and cook without browning, stirring occasionally, for about 20 minutes. Add the zucchini and the garlic. Cover and cook very gently, stirring often to prevent scorching, for about 45 minutes. By that time the vegetables will be very tender. Stir vigorously with a spoon to make a purée.

5. Beat the eggs and add them. Cook for about 2 minutes over moderate heat, stirring, and turn off the heat. Add salt, pepper and nutmeg to taste. Stir in the toasted oregano and serve piping hot.

Yield: 6 to 8 servings.

Mushroom and Cheese-stuffed Zucchini

14 small zucchini, each about 6 inches in length
¾ cup olive oil
1½ cups chopped onion
1½ cups finely diced fresh mushrooms

1. Preheat the oven to 350 degrees.

2. Cut the zucchini in half lengthwise. Using a melon ball scoop or a spoon, scoop out the flesh of each zucchini half, leaving a shell about ¼ inch thick. Set the zucchini halves aside. Chop the pulp and set aside.

3. Heat the oil and add the onion. Cook, stirring often, until onion is wilted. Add the mushrooms and garlic. Cover and cook until mushrooms give up their juices. Add chopped zucchini pulp. Cook over high heat, uncovered, stirring until the liquid evaporates. Add the cream cheese, eggs, 1½ cups of Parmesan cheese, parsley, salt, pepper and hot chilies. Cook, stirring often, for about 10 minutes. Let cool.

4. Stuff the zucchini shells with equal parts of the mixture. Sprinkle with the remaining ½ cup Parmesan. Arrange in a baking dish and bake for 10 minutes, or until piping hot. Run under the broiler to brown briefly.

Yield: 14 to 28 servings.

3 cloves garlic, finely minced
1 cup cream cheese
3 eggs
2 cups grated Parmesan cheese
2 cups finely chopped parsley
Salt and freshly ground pepper
4 hot chilies, chopped, optional

Stuffed Zucchini Boats

1. Preheat the oven to 425 degrees.

2. Trim off a small portion of stem from each zucchini. Split the zucchini in half lengthwise. Using a melon ball scoop, scoop out the center seed portion of each zucchini, leaving a casing to be stuffed. Chop the scooped-out flesh. There should be about 1 cup.

3. Heat 2 tablespoons of oil in a large saucepan and add the onion and garlic. Cook until the onion is wilted. Add the meat and cook, stirring down with a heavy wooden spoon to break up lumps. Cook until the meat loses its red color. Add the reserved chopped zucchini pulp and cook for about 3 minutes, stirring often.

4. Add ½ cup bread crumbs and stir to blend. Add salt and pepper to taste. Add the yolk, parsley and dill. Heat briefly, stirring, until the mixture is slightly thickened. Do not overcook or the egg yolk will curdle.

5. Sprinkle the insides of the zucchini with salt and pepper. Stuff the zucchini halves with equal portions of meat filling, smoothing over the tops. Blend the cheese and remaining bread crumbs. Sprinkle this over the top. Dribble the remaining oil over all and bake for 30 minutes. Serve with fresh tomato sauce.

Yield: 4 servings.

2 zucchini, about 1¼ pounds
4 tablespoons olive oil
½ cup chopped onion
1 clove garlic, finely minced
¼ pound ground veal
¼ pound ground pork
½ cup plus 1 to 2 tablespoons fresh bread crumbs
Salt and freshly ground pepper
1 egg yolk
2 tablespoons finely chopped parsley
3 tablespoons finely chopped dill
1 to 2 tablespoons freshly grated Parmesan cheese
Fresh tomato sauce (see recipe page 650)

Zucchini and Tomatoes Gujarati-style

8 cups thinly sliced zucchini, about 1¼ pounds

1 cup cored tomatoes cut into ½-inch cubes

3 tablespoons sesame oil, purchased in health food stores

2 teaspoons whole cumin seeds

¼ teaspoon hing, available in Indian food shops

1½ teaspoons ground coriander

1½ teaspoons ground cumin

¼ teaspoon turmeric

1 tablespoon paprika

1 teaspoon garam masala (see recipe page 213)

1 teaspoon salt

2 tablespoons water

4 teaspoons chopped fresh coriander leaves

1. Prepare the zucchini and tomatoes and set aside.

2. Heat the oil in a kettle and, when it starts to smoke, add the cumin seeds. Stir briefly and add the hing, coriander, cumin, turmeric, paprika, garam masala and salt. Add the zucchini and tomatoes and stir gently to blend without breaking the slices. Add the water and cover. Cook over gentle heat for 10 minutes. Serve sprinkled with chopped fresh coriander.

Yield: 8 servings.

XII. Salads

We don't often write about nutrition because we believe that any well-planned meal, by definition, will be well balanced in the nutritional sense. Salads are part and parcel of good nutrition and, with rare exceptions, should have a place in almost every major meal year in and year out. Someone is bound to ask what the exceptions are and one answer is: following a platter of sauerkraut.

Basic Salad Sauce

Combine all the ingredients in a small jar. Close and shake until thoroughly blended. Serve over salad greens.

Yield: About ⅓ cup.

2 tablespoons red wine vinegar or lemon juice
6 to 8 tablespoons peanut, vegetable or olive oil
Salt and freshly ground pepper

Piquant salad sauce

Add 1 teaspoon of prepared imported mustard to the basic sauce, plus 1 clove garlic, finely chopped, and a few drops of Tabasco sauce.

Vinaigrette sauce

To the basic sauce add 1 teaspoon capers, 1 teaspoon chopped sour pickles (preferably the imported French pickles known as cornichons), 1 teaspoon of finely chopped onion, 1 tablespoon of finely chopped parsley. Other flavors might include a teaspoon of chopped chives and a teaspoon of chopped chervil.

Ravigote sauce

To the vinaigrette sauce add half a hard-cooked egg, coarsely chopped, and, if desired, 1 tablespoon of red, ripe tomato cut into small cubes.

517

Creamy Salad Dressing

1 egg yolk
2 or 3 teaspoons imported
mustard, such as Dijon or
Düsseldorf
Dash of Tabasco sauce
½ teaspoon finely chopped
garlic
Salt and freshly ground
pepper
1 teaspoon vinegar
½ cup olive oil
1 or 2 teaspoons fresh lemon
juice
1 teaspoon heavy cream

1. Beat the egg yolk and put 1 teaspoon of it in a mixing bowl. Add the mustard, Tabasco, garlic, salt, pepper and vinegar.

2. Using a wire whisk, beat vigorously to blend the ingredients. Still beating, gradually add the oil. Continue beating until thickened and well blended.

3. Add the lemon juice and beat in the heavy cream. Taste the dressing and add more salt, pepper, mustard or lemon juice to taste.

Yield: ¾ cup.

Russian Dressing

½ cup mayonnaise
1 tablespoon chili sauce or
tomato ketchup
1 teaspoon finely grated or
chopped onion
½ teaspoon horseradish
¼ teaspoon Worcestershire sauce
1 tablespoon finely chopped
parsley
1 tablespoon black or red
caviar, optional

Combine all the ingredients in a mixing bowl. Blend well.
Yield: About ½ cup.

Green Beans Vinaigrette

1 pound fresh green beans
Salt
1 tablespoon finely chopped
shallots
1 tablespoon imported mustard,
such as Dijon or Düsseldorf
Freshly ground pepper
1 tablespoon red wine vinegar

1. Trim off the ends of the green beans. Cut the beans into 2-inch lengths. Drop them into boiling salted water and simmer for 2 to 5 minutes. The important thing is not to overcook them. They must remain crisp-tender. Drain well.

2. Meanwhile, combine all the remaining ingredients except the dill in a small saucepan and heat over very low heat, stirring with a whisk, until sauce is lukewarm. Do not cook and do not heat too far in advance.

3. Arrange the warm beans on 4 salad plates and spoon equal amounts of sauce over. Sprinkle with dill, if desired. Serve warm.

Yield: 4 servings.

6 tablespoons peanut, vegetable or corn oil
¼ cup finely chopped fresh dill, optional

Black Bean Salad

1. Bring 3 quarts of water to the boil. Add the beans and return to the boil. Remove from the heat and let stand for 1 hour.

2. Return the beans to the boil and simmer for 1½ to 2 hours, until beans are soft but not mushy.

3. Meanwhile, cook the salt pork in a heavy skillet until the fat is rendered and the pork is crisp. Remove the pork with a slotted spoon and set aside. To the fat in the skillet add the onion and cook for 5 minutes, stirring. Add the green pepper, garlic and oregano and continue cooking, stirring, until onion is golden. Add this to the beans. Add the red wine and bring to the boil. Simmer for ½ hour. Let cool.

4. Combine the ingredients for the vinaigrette sauce and stir it into the beans. Add more salt and pepper to taste, if desired, and chill.

Yield: 8 to 12 servings.

The beans:

2 pounds dried black beans, preferably turtle beans
½ pound salt pork, cut into small cubes
2 cups finely chopped onion
1 cup chopped green pepper
1 tablespoon finely chopped garlic
½ teaspoon dried oregano
1 cup dry red wine

The vinaigrette sauce:

2 tablespoons red wine vinegar
6 tablespoons olive oil
1 clove garlic, finely minced
1 teaspoon Dijon mustard
Salt and freshly ground pepper

Three-Bean Salad

Empty the beans and drain well. Place the beans in a mixing bowl. Add the sugar and vinegar and toss until sugar is dissolved. Add all the remaining ingredients. Toss well and chill until ready to serve.

Yield: About 6 cups.

1 16-ounce can cut wax beans
1 16-ounce can cut green beans
1 16-ounce can kidney beans
¼ cup sugar
½ cup cider vinegar
Salt and freshly ground pepper to taste
¼ cup peanut, vegetable or corn oil
¼ cup finely chopped onion
2 tablespoons finely chopped parsley

Pickled Beets and Onions

1 pound raw beets, trimmed
  Salt and freshly ground
  pepper to taste
2 teaspoons sugar
2½ tablespoons wine vinegar
1 red onion, about ½ pound

1. Place the beets in a saucepan and add cold water to cover. Add salt to taste and bring to the boil. Partly cover and simmer until beets are tender throughout. The cooking time will vary from 15 to 45 minutes or longer, depending on size and age of beets. Let cool in the cooking liquid.

2. Remove the beets and slip off the skins under cold running water. Slice the beets. There should be about 2 cups. Place them in a mixing bowl.

3. Add about 1 teaspoon of salt, pepper to taste, sugar and vinegar and stir until sugar is dissolved. Taste the marinade and add more salt, sugar or vinegar to taste.

4. Peel and slice the red onion. Add it to the mixing bowl and stir until beets and onions are well intermingled.

Yield: 3 to 4 cups.

Moroccan Carrot Salad

1 pound carrots, trimmed and
  scraped
¼ cup olive oil
3 tablespoons lemon juice
1 clove garlic, finely minced
½ teaspoon cumin
¼ teaspoon dried mint leaves
  Salt and freshly ground
  pepper to taste
½ teaspoon confectioners' sugar,
  or more to taste
¼ teaspoon cayenne pepper

1. Use the julienne cutter of a food processor to cut the carrots into fine shreds. Or cut the carrots on a flat surface into ⅛-inch-thick slices. Stack the slices and cut them into very fine strips. There should be about 6 cups.

2. Blend the remaining ingredients and pour the sauce over the carrots. Toss to blend.

Yield: 10 or more servings.

Cucumber à la Russe

1 large cucumber
  Salt
2 tablespoons rice vinegar
2 tablespoons olive oil
1½ teaspoons sugar
½ cup thinly sliced scallions
2 tablespoons chopped fresh
  dill

1. Peel the cucumber and slice it thinly. Put in a mixing bowl and add salt to taste. Let stand for ½ hour.

2. Drain the cucumber and add the remaining ingredients. Add more vinegar, oil or sugar according to taste.

Yield: 4 servings.

Cucumber Salad with Dill

1. If the cucumbers are new and unwaxed, there is no need to peel them. Otherwise, peel them. Cut into thin slices and put in a mixing bowl. There should be 6 cups. Add 6 tablespoons vinegar, ½ cup sugar, 3 teaspoons salt and the dill. Cover and refrigerate for 1 hour or longer.

2. Drain. Add the remaining 1 tablespoon vinegar, 1 teaspoon salt and 1 teaspoon sugar. Blend well.

Yield: 12 or more servings.

2 to 4 large cucumbers
7 tablespoons white wine vinegar
½ cup plus 1 teaspoon sugar
4 teaspoons salt
2 tablespoons chopped fresh dill

Herbed Cottage Cheese Salad

Place the cottage cheese in a mixing bowl. Add the mayonnaise and blend. Add the remaining ingredients and blend well.

Yield: About 4 cups.

3 cups curd-style cottage cheese
½ cup mayonnaise
¾ cup finely chopped scallions
2 tablespoons finely chopped onion
¼ cup chopped chives
¼ cup finely chopped parsley
1 cup finely diced cucumber
1 tablespoon chopped fresh basil, optional
½ cup coarsely chopped radish
Lemon juice to taste
Salt and freshly ground pepper to taste

Angourosalata me Yiaourti (*Cucumber and yogurt salad*)

1. Line a bowl with cheesecloth and empty the yogurt into it. Bring the edges of the cheesecloth together and tie to make a bag. Suspend the bag over the bowl and let drain for 1 hour or longer. The yogurt will become thick like sour cream.

2. Empty the yogurt into a clean bowl and add the remaining ingredients. Blend thoroughly. Chill well.

Yield: 4 to 6 servings.

3 cups plain yogurt
1 cup peeled, seeded, diced cucumber
Salt
2 cloves garlic, finely minced
1 tablespoon chopped fresh dill
¼ cup olive oil
2 teaspoons wine vinegar

Hot Spicy Cucumber Salad

2 large cucumbers
1½ teaspoons salt
3 tablespoons soy sauce
½ teaspoon monosodium glutamate
½ teaspoon crushed red pepper, or ¼ teaspoon cayenne pepper
1 teaspoon sesame oil
1 tablespoon vinegar

1. Wash the cucumbers and pat dry. Pound the cucumbers lightly all over with a cleaver.
2. Trim off the ends. Peel the cucumbers and cut them lengthwise into quarters. Cut or scrape away and discard the seeds.
3. Cut each cucumber strip into 1½-inch lengths. Trim the corners of each piece to make them neater. Put the pieces in a bowl and add 1 teaspoon of salt. Let stand for 10 minutes.
4. Drain the cucumbers well and add the remaining ingredients. Chill and serve.
Yield: 4 servings.

Belgian Endive and Fennel Vinaigrette

6 heads Belgian endive
1 fennel bulb
2 tablespoons fresh lemon juice
1 tablespoon imported mustard, such as Dijon or Düsseldorf
6 tablespoons olive oil
Salt and freshly ground pepper

1. Trim off the bottoms of the endive. Cut the endive into 1-inch lengths or cut it lengthwise into thin shreds. Drop the pieces into cold water. This will keep them from turning dark. Drain and spin dry or pat dry. Put in a plastic bag and chill.
2. Trim the fennel and slice it thinly. Cut the slices into fine pieces. Rinse, drain and spin or pat dry. Chill.
3. Combine the fennel and endive in a chilled mixing bowl. Blend the remaining ingredients and pour it over all. Add more lemon juice or oil to taste. Toss and serve on chilled salad plates.
Yield: 4 to 6 servings.

Fennel and Avocado Vinaigrette

2 fennel bulbs
1 tablespoon finely chopped garlic
1 teaspoon crushed dried oregano
7 teaspoons red wine vinegar
6 tablespoons olive oil
Salt and freshly ground pepper

1. Cut off the tops of the fennel bulbs and trim the base. Pull off and discard any very large, tough outer leaves. Cut the remaining fennel lengthwise into about 12 ½-inch slices. Arrange the slices in one layer in a serving dish.
2. Blend the garlic, oregano, vinegar, oil, salt and pepper to taste. Beat rapidly with a whisk or fork. Add the tomato cubes. Set aside.
3. Arrange 1 anchovy fillet on each of the fennel slices.

When ready to serve, peel the avocado and slice in half. Discard the pit. Cut the avocado lengthwise into ½-inch-thick slices and arrange these around the fennel. Add the olives. Beat the sauce lightly and pour it over all.

Yield: 4 to 6 servings.

1 cup cubed, peeled, seeded fresh tomatoes, optional
12 flat fillets of anchovies
1 ripe, unblemished avocado
24 black olives

Leeks Vinaigrette with Anchovy and Pimiento

Arrange the leeks on a serving dish. Pour the vinegar and oil in a small mixing bowl and beat briskly with a wire whisk. Add the anchovies, garlic, salt and pepper and beat well to blend. Fold in the pimiento and parsley and spoon the sauce over the leeks.

Yield: 4 servings.

8 cooked leeks
2 teaspoons red wine vinegar
4 tablespoons olive oil
3 anchovies, chopped
1 clove garlic, finely minced
Salt and freshly ground pepper to taste
2 tablespoons diced pimiento
2 tablespoons finely chopped parsley

Lentil Salad

1. Combine the lentils, onion, carrot, whole garlic clove, thyme, bay leaf, parsley sprigs, water, salt and pepper to taste. Bring to the boil and simmer for 30 minutes, or until tender. Drain.

2. Remove the carrot and cut it into cubes. Set aside.

3. Remove and discard the bay leaf, parsley, thyme sprigs, if used, the onion stuck with clove and the whole garlic clove.

4. Spoon the lentils into a mixing bowl and add the cubed carrot, the chopped onion, chopped parsley, chopped garlic, wine vinegar and oil. Add salt and pepper to taste. Toss to blend well. Serve garnished with tomato wedges.

Yield: 8 or more servings.

½ pound dried lentils labeled "no soaking necessary"
1 small onion stuck with 1 clove
1 carrot, trimmed and scraped
1 clove garlic, peeled and left whole
2 sprigs fresh thyme, or ½ teaspoon dried
1 bay leaf
3 sprigs fresh parsley
3 cups water
Salt and freshly ground pepper
½ cup finely chopped onion
4 tablespoons finely chopped parsley
1 clove garlic, finely minced
1 tablespoon wine vinegar
4 tablespoons olive oil
Tomato wedges for garnish

Mushrooms à la Grecque

1 teaspoon coriander seeds
½ teaspoon oregano
½ teaspoon dried marjoram
½ teaspoon dried fennel seeds
1 teaspoon dried sage leaves, crushed
½ teaspoon dried thyme
1 bay leaf, broken
1 large garlic clove, crushed but unpeeled
¼ cup water
2 tablespoons lemon juice
3 tablespoons olive oil
1 tablespoon distilled white vinegar
Salt and freshly ground pepper
1 pound mushrooms, the smaller the better
Lemon wedges or parsley for garnish

1. Crush the coriander seeds and put them in a saucepan large enough to hold the mushrooms. Add the oregano. Tie the marjoram, fennel, sage, thyme, bay leaf and garlic in a small square of cheesecloth. Add the cheesecloth bag to the saucepan and add the water, lemon juice, olive oil, vinegar, salt and pepper to taste. Bring to the boil and cook over high heat for 5 minutes.

2. Meanwhile, rinse the mushrooms in cold water and drain them well. If the mushrooms are very small, leave them whole. Otherwise, cut them in half or quarter them, depending on size.

3. Add the mushrooms to the saucepan and return to the boil. Cover and cook over high heat for 7 to 8 minutes, shaking the saucepan to redistribute the mushrooms so that they cook evenly. Uncover and cook for about 5 minutes longer over high heat.

4. Spoon the mushrooms, cooking liquid and cheesecloth bag into a mixing bowl and cover. Let cool. Chill overnight. Remove and discard the cheesecloth bag. Serve cold or at room temperature. Garnish, if desired, with lemon wedges or parsley.

Yield: 6 to 8 servings.

Mushrooms à la Russe

1 pound fresh mushrooms, the smaller the better
1 cup water
½ cup white vinegar
⅓ cup olive oil
Salt to taste
1 teaspoon dried tarragon
2 sprigs fresh thyme, or 1 teaspoon dried
1 bay leaf
3 shallots, thinly sliced

1. This dish is best made at least one day ahead and refrigerated until ready to serve.

2. Rinse the mushrooms and drain them well.

3. Combine the remaining ingredients in a saucepan and bring to the boil. Add the mushrooms and simmer for 30 minutes. Let cool in the liquid and refrigerate. When ready to serve, drain.

Yield: 4 to 8 servings.

Hearts of Palm Salad

1. Drain the hearts of palm. Cut the pieces into ¾-inch rounds and put them in a salad bowl.

2. Slice the mushrooms thinly and add them. Add the tomatoes, onion rings, garlic, lime juice, olive oil, parsley, salt and pepper to taste. Toss and, if desired, add more oil.

Yield: 6 to 8 servings.

2 14-ounce cans hearts of palm
½ pound fresh mushrooms
20 cherry tomatoes, cut in half
1 small red onion, peeled and cut into thin slices
1 small clove garlic, finely minced
¼ cup lime juice
½ cup olive oil or more to taste
¼ cup finely chopped parsley
Salt and freshly ground pepper

Potato Salad with Fines Herbes

There is nothing in the world wrong with the traditional potato salad that grandma used to make. Tossed with some homemade mayonnaise, a bit of celery and onion, it makes a grand addition, as it has for many generations, to picnics and church socials, to backyard barbecues and covered-dish suppers. But there are potato salads and potato salads. Infinitely more sophisticated than grandma's version are the "warm" potato salads, made sometimes with a splash of dry white wine, sometimes with oil and vinegar, sometimes with bacon, and often with an unexpected piquant herb such as tarragon. They add a bit of class to an informal meal, indoors or out.

1. Put the potatoes in a kettle and add cold water to cover and salt to taste. Bring to the boil and cook until tender, 15 to 20 minutes. Remove from the heat and drain.

2. As soon as the potatoes are cool enough to handle, peel them. Cut them into ¼-inch-thick slices and put them in a mixing bowl.

3. Add the shallots, garlic, chives, parsley, tarragon, wine, vinegar, oil, salt and pepper to taste. Toss well. Garnish with heart of romaine lettuce leaves or other greens.

Yield: 6 to 8 servings.

Note: Walnut oil is available in specialty shops that deal in fine imported foods.

2 pounds "new" red-skinned potatoes
Salt
¼ cup finely chopped shallots
1 clove garlic, finely minced
2 tablespoons chopped fresh chives
3 tablespoons finely chopped parsley
1 tablespoon chopped fresh tarragon, or 1 teaspoon dried
¼ cup dry white wine
1 teaspoon red wine or herb vinegar
3 tablespoons walnut oil (see note), or use peanut, vegetable or corn oil
Freshly ground pepper
Lettuce leaves for garnish

Potato Salad with Bacon and Onion

2 pounds "new" red-skinned
   potatoes
   Salt
6 slices lean bacon
4 tablespoons finely chopped
   onion
3 tablespoons finely chopped
   parsley
   Freshly ground pepper
1 tablespoon wine or herb
   vinegar
5 tablespoons peanut, vegetable
   or corn oil
   Lettuce leaves for garnish

1. Put the potatoes in a kettle and add cold water to cover and salt to taste. Bring to the boil and cook until tender, 15 to 20 minutes. Remove from the heat and drain.

2. As soon as the potatoes are cool enough to handle, peel them. Cut them into ¼-inch-thick slices and put them in a mixing bowl.

3. Meanwhile, cook the bacon until crisp. Drain on absorbent paper towels. Chop coarsely. Set aside.

4. Add the onion, parsley, salt and pepper to taste to the potatoes. Add the vinegar and oil and half the bacon and toss.

5. Spoon into a salad bowl and garnish with the remaining bacon bits and small heart of romaine lettuce leaves or other greens

Yield: 6 to 8 servings.

Sweet Potato Salad

1½ pounds sweet potatoes
   (about 3 large)
   Juice of 4 limes
2 large apples
1 cup thinly sliced and then
   chopped celery
6 ounces coarsely chopped
   cashews or pecans
1 cup freshly made
   mayonnaise, approximately

1. Cook the sweet potatoes until soft; drain and cool enough to peel. Quarter lengthwise, then cut into cubes. Place in a mixing bowl and sprinkle with lime juice. Chill.

2. Peel, core and dice the apples. Add to potatoes together with the celery and nuts. Add enough mayonnaise to coat well. Chill before serving.

Yield: 4 to 6 servings.

Sliced Tomatoes with Herbed Vinaigrette Sauce

2 red, ripe, unblemished
   tomatoes
   Salt and freshly ground pepper
1 tablespoon red wine vinegar
3 tablespoons olive oil
1 tablespoon finely chopped
   chives
1 tablespoon finely chopped
   parsley

1. Cut away and discard the core from the tomatoes. Slice the tomatoes and arrange them in a serving dish. Sprinkle with salt and pepper to taste.

2. Blend the remaining ingredients, adding salt and pepper to taste. Pour over the tomatoes and serve.

Yield: 4 servings.

Tomatoes and Onions with Gorgonzola Salad Dressing

1. Core the tomatoes and slice them thickly. Peel the onion and cut it into thick slices. Arrange alternate and slightly overlapping slices of tomatoes and onion on a serving dish.

2. Combine the vinegar, oil, salt and pepper in a bowl and blend well. Add the cheese and cut it into the dressing, which should be slightly lumpy. Pour the salad dressing over all and serve.

Yield: 4 servings.

2 or 3 large, red, ripe tomatoes, about 1½ pounds
1 large Bermuda onion, about 1 pound
1 tablespoon vinegar
3 tablespoons olive oil
Salt and freshly ground pepper
¼ pound Gorgonzola cheese at room temperature

Spicy Tomato Salad Moroccan-style

1. Core the tomatoes and cut them into 1½-inch cubes. Put them in a salad bowl.

2. Trim the celery and chop it coarsely. Add to the tomatoes. Add the parsley and capers.

3. Trim the green peppers and chop them. Chop the cherry peppers and cut the lemon, if used, into ½-inch pieces. Add this to the salad bowl.

4. Blend the salt to taste, cayenne, paprika and olive oil and pour over the salad. Toss to blend well.

Yield: 4 to 8 servings.

3 or 4 large red, ripe tomatoes
3 or 4 tender ribs of celery with a few leaves
½ cup chopped parsley
⅓ cup drained capers
1 to 3 long, hot green peppers
3 to 5 bottled hot cherry peppers, or pickled jalapenos
½ preserved lemon (see recipe page 254), optional
Salt
¼ teaspoon cayenne pepper
1 teaspoon paprika
¼ cup olive oil

Spicy Orange Salad Moroccan-style

1. Peel the oranges, paring away all the exterior white pulp. Cut the oranges into eighths. Cut each segment into 1-inch pieces. Set aside.

2. Place the cayenne, paprika, garlic, olive oil, vinegar, salt and pepper to taste in a salad bowl and blend well with a wire whisk. Add the oranges, parsley and olives. Toss gently to blend and serve cold or at room temperature.

Yield: 4 servings.

3 large, seedless oranges
⅛ teaspoon cayenne pepper
1 teaspoon paprika
½ teaspoon garlic
3 tablespoons olive oil
1 tablespoon vinegar
Salt and freshly ground pepper
⅓ cup freshly chopped parsley
12 pitted black olives, preferably imported Greek or Italian olives

Cooked Tomato and Green Pepper Salad, Moroccan-style

20 red, ripe tomatoes, about 10
   pounds
10 large sweet green peppers,
   about 3½ pounds
¼ cup olive oil
2 teaspoons finely chopped
   garlic
2 teaspoons paprika
⅛ teaspoon or more cayenne
   pepper
   Salt to taste

1. Cut away the core from each tomato and drop all the tomatoes into a basin of boiling water. Let stand for about 12 seconds and drain well. Split the tomatoes in half and squeeze to remove most of the seeds. There will be about 12 cups. If not, add enough canned tomatoes to make 12 cups.

2. Place a sheet of aluminum foil in a broiler pan. Put the peppers on the foil and broil, turning often. When the skins are slightly charred, transfer them to a brown paper bag and close tightly. This will create steam and facilitate peeling.

3. Peel the peppers and cut away and discard the cores. Split the peppers in half and chop them. There should be 4 to 5 cups.

4. In a large, heavy skillet heat the oil and add the tomatoes, stirring. Cook, stirring occasionally, until thickened, about 45 minutes. When ready, the tomatoes will start to bubble as if they are frying. Add the peppers, garlic, paprika, cayenne and salt.

5. Continue cooking, stirring often and taking care that the mixture does not stick or burn. Cook for about 15 minutes. When ready, the olive oil will start to surface and the mixture will be like a thick jam. Serve cool.
   Yield: 12 servings.

Vegetables à la Russe

1 potato, about ⅓ pound
   Salt
1 small cauliflower
1 small bunch broccoli
¼ pound green beans,
   approximately
¼ pound carrots, approximately
¼ pound zucchini,
   approximately
1 cup green peas
¾ cup chopped celery
1 cup chopped scallions, green
   part and all
2 tablespoons chopped parsley
1 tablespoon chopped chives
1 cup mustard mayonnaise (see
   recipe below)

1. Place the potato in a saucepan and add cold water to cover and salt to taste. Bring to the boil and simmer 25 minutes, or until tender. Drain and let cool. Peel the potato and cut it into neat, uniform cubes, each about an inch or slightly less in diameter. Set aside.

2. Break off enough flowerets from the cauliflower to make 1 cup. The pieces should be bite-size morsels.

3. Break off enough flowerets from the broccoli to make 1 cup. Use the remaining cauliflower and broccoli for another meal.

4. Cut the green beans, carrots and zucchini into small cubes, about ½ inch thick. Keep each set of vegetables in separate batches.

5. Cook the cauliflower and broccoli pieces, the cubed green beans, carrots and zucchini in separate batches of boiling salted water until crisp-tender. Cook the peas until barely ten-

der. Take care not to overcook any of the vegetables. As each batch is cooked, drain immediately in a sieve or colander and chill under cold running water. Drain well.

6. Combine the cubed potato, cauliflower, broccoli, green beans, carrots, zucchini and green peas in a mixing bowl. Add the chopped celery, scallions, parsley and chives. Add the mayonnaise and toss gently but well.

Yield: 8 or more servings.

Put the mustard, egg yolk, Worcestershire sauce, vinegar, salt and pepper to taste and Tabasco in a mixing bowl. Beat with a wire whisk. When blended, gradually beat in the oil. Add the lemon juice and blend well. Add more mustard, if desired, to make the mayonnaise more piquant.

Yield: About 1¼ cups.

Mustard mayonnaise

1 tablespoon prepared mustard, such as Dijon or Düsseldorf
1 egg yolk
½ teaspoon Worcestershire sauce
1 teaspoon white vinegar
Salt and freshly ground pepper
Several drops Tabasco sauce
1 cup peanut, vegetable or corn oil
Juice of ½ lemon

Greek Salad

1. Rub a large salad bowl with salt and garlic. Discard the garlic.

2. In the salad bowl, combine the lettuce, celery, radishes, scallions, cucumber, green pepper, olives and cheese.

3. Beat the olive oil with the lemon juice and pour over the salad. Toss and season with salt and pepper. Sprinkle the salad with the oregano and parsley.

4. Arrange the anchovy fillets radiating from the center with the tomato wedges. Garnish with parsley sprigs.

Yield: 12 or more servings.

Salt
1 clove garlic
2 heads Boston lettuce, shredded
1 romaine lettuce, shredded
3 celery hearts, diced
6 radishes, sliced
1 bunch scallions, sliced
1 cucumber, thinly sliced
1 green pepper, cut into thin rings
12 oil-cured black olives
½ pound feta cheese, diced
½ cup olive oil
Juice of 2 lemons
Salt and freshly ground pepper to taste
½ teaspoon oregano
1 tablespoon minced parsley
8 anchovy fillets
3 tomatoes, cut into wedges
Parsley sprigs for garnish

Acar *(Indonesian garden salad)*

1 large onion, peeled and cut into thin slices, about 2 cups loosely packed
5 cups cabbage sliced as thinly as possible and loosely packed
1¼ cups carrot shredded as finely as possible
2 cups thinly sliced, unpeeled cucumber
½ cup cold water
½ cup white vinegar
1 slice fresh ginger, crushed
3½ tablespoons sugar
1 tablespoon salt

1. Prepare the onion, cabbage, carrot and cucumber.
2. In a large salad bowl, combine the water, vinegar, crushed ginger, sugar and salt. Add the cabbage, carrot, onion and cucumber and stir to blend thoroughly. Refrigerate for at least 1 hour before serving.
Yield: 8 or more servings.

Rice Salad with Chicken

1 cup blanched almonds
1 whole chicken breast
Chicken broth to cover
2 cups cooked rice
1 tablespoon grated onion
Salt and freshly ground pepper
4 tablespoons chopped chives and/or parsley
A few drops Tabasco sauce
2 tablespoons red wine vinegar
6 tablespoons peanut, vegetable or corn oil
2 tablespoons lemon juice
1 teaspoon sesame oil, optional

1. Preheat the oven to 425 degrees.
2. Toast the almonds by placing them on a baking sheet and baking for 5 to 10 minutes, watching carefully so that they do not overcook. When done, they should be golden brown. Remove from the oven and let cool.
3. Place the chicken breast in a saucepan and add the broth to cover. Bring to the boil and simmer for 20 minutes. Let stand in the cooking liquid until cool. Remove the chicken and skin and bone it. Cut into small, bite-size cubes. There should be about 2 cups.
4. Spoon the rice into a mixing bowl and add the toasted almonds, cubed chicken and the remaining ingredients. Toss well and serve at room temperature.
Yield: 8 to 12 servings.

Fish Salad in Mayonnaise

3½ cups poached fish, skinned, boned and broken into bite-size morsels
¾ cup carrots cut into small cubes

1. Prepare the fish and set it aside.
2. Cook the carrots, turnips, celery and peas in separate saucepans in boiling salted water to cover until crisp-tender, 5 minutes or less. Frozen peas will cook in less than 1 minute. Drain. Chill under cold running water and drain again.

3. Blend the fish and vegetables. Add the mayonnaise, shallots and chives and blend. Spoon onto a serving dish and garnish with tomato and egg wedges.

Yield: 6 or more servings.

¾ cup turnips cut into small cubes
¾ cup celery cut into small cubes
1 cup fresh or frozen peas
Salt to taste
1 cup freshly made mayonnaise
¼ cup finely chopped shallots
2 tablespoons chopped chives
Tomato wedges and hard-cooked egg wedges for garnish

Chiffonade of Lobster Chez Denis

1. If live lobsters are used, drop them into vigorously boiling salted water and cover. Cook for 10 minutes and remove from the heat. Let stand for about 15 minutes. Drain and let cool.

2. When the lobsters are cool enough to handle, crack them and remove the meat from the claws and tail. Reserve and set aside any red coral. There should be about 2 cups of meat and coral. Refrigerate until ready to use.

3. Place the yolk in a mixing bowl and add the vinegar, mustard, tomato paste, salt and pepper to taste, and cayenne. Gradually add the oil, beating vigorously with a wire whisk. Beat in the lemon juice, tarragon and Cognac.

4. Add the lobster, foie gras, if desired, and tomatoes to the mayonnaise and fold them in with a rubber spatula. This may be done in advance and refrigerated for an hour or so.

5. When ready to serve, stack the romaine lettuce leaves and cut them into the finest possible shreds, using a heavy sharp knife. There should be about 2 cups loosely packed shreds. Add this to the salad and fold it in. Serve immediately before the shreds wilt.

Yield: 6 to 8 servings.

2 1½-pound live lobsters, or 2 cups cubed cooked lobster meat
1 egg yolk
1 tablespoon white wine vinegar
1 tablespoon prepared imported mustard, such as Dijon or Düsseldorf
1 tablespoon tomato paste
Salt and freshly ground pepper
⅛ teaspoon cayenne pepper or Tabasco sauce to taste
1 cup olive oil
Juice of ½ lemon
1 teaspoon chopped fresh tarragon, or ½ teaspoon dried, chopped
2 teaspoons Cognac
½ cup cubed foie gras, optional
¾ cup cubed, seeded tomatoes
6 to 12 leaves fresh, crisp unblemished romaine lettuce leaves, rinsed and patted dry

Lobster Salad à l'Aja

3 cups cubed lobster meat
2 cups cored, peeled, seeded tomatoes cut into ½-inch cubes
2 cups cubed firm but ripe avocado
Juice of 1 lime
2 cups freshly made mayonnaise
Salt and freshly ground pepper
1 hard-cooked egg, finely chopped
Finely chopped red coral from the lobsters, if available
Dill or parsley sprigs for garnish

1. Combine the lobster meat, tomatoes, avocado, lime juice, mayonnaise, salt and pepper to taste. Toss well.

2. Arrange the salad on a platter and sprinkle with the chopped egg and chopped coral. Garnish with dill or parsley sprigs.

Yield: 8 to 12 servings.

Cold Shrimp Salad à la Grecque

12 thin slices red onion
24 cooked shrimp, shelled and deveined
½ cup crumbled feta cheese
1 bunch watercress, trimmed, rinsed and shaken dry
24 cherry tomatoes, or 16 wedges of standard-size, red, ripe tomatoes
3 tablespoons finely chopped fresh dill, optional
3 tablespoons fresh lemon juice
3 tablespoons olive oil
Salt and freshly ground pepper to taste
1 clove garlic, finely minced
Tabasco to taste

1. Arrange the onion rings in the bottom of a salad bowl. Arrange the shrimp over the onions. Sprinkle with feta cheese and cover with watercress.

2. Drop the cherry tomatoes into boiling water to cover and let stand for exactly 12 seconds. Drain quickly and run under cold water. Drain well. Use a small paring knife and pull away the skin of each tomato. Garnish the salad bowl with the tomatoes.

3. Combine the remaining ingredients in a bottle and shake well. Pour the dressing over the salad and toss well.

Yield: 4 servings.

Shrimp, Oranges and Anchovies

1. Put the shrimp in a saucepan and add the allspice and salt to taste. Add cold water to barely cover and bring to the boil. Turn off the heat and let the shrimp stand until they are room temperature. Drain, shell and devein. Set aside.

2. Peel and cut the onions into ¼-inch-thick slices. Place them in a small bowl and pour boiling water over them. Stir for about 15 seconds and drain immediately. Drop them into a small bowl containing cold water and a few ice cubes. When thoroughly chilled, drain and set aside.

3. Peel the oranges and slice them. Arrange an equal number of slices on 4 salad plates. Arrange the shrimp on the oranges and scatter onion rings over each serving. Garnish each with 2 anchovy fillets. Spoon the sauce vinaigrette with rosemary over each serving and add the black olives. Serve immediately.

Yield: 4 servings.

24	fresh shrimp in the shell
6	whole allspice
	Salt
2	small onions, preferably the red-skin variety
3 or 4	seedless navel oranges
8	flat anchovy fillets
½	cup sauce vinaigrette with rosemary (see recipe below) Black olives, preferably imported Greek olives

Place the mustard in a small mixing bowl and add salt and pepper to taste, garlic and vinegar. Use a wire whisk and gradually add the oil, stirring vigorously with the whisk. Stir in the rosemary and serve.

Sauce vinaigrette with rosemary

2	teaspoons imported mustard, such as Dijon or Düsseldorf Salt and freshly ground pepper
½	teaspoon chopped garlic
4	teaspoons red wine vinegar
½	cup peanut, vegetable or corn oil
1	teaspoon chopped fresh rosemary, or ½ teaspoon dried

Salade de Boeuf Gribiche *(Beef salad with herb mayonnaise)*

The meat:

24 to 36 thin slices freshly cooked boiled beef (see recipe below)

The sauce:

1 hard-cooked egg, put through a sieve
1 egg yolk
1 tablespoon imported mustard, such as Dijon or Düsseldorf
1 tablespoon white vinegar
3 tablespoons finely chopped onion
2 tablespoons finely chopped shallots
1 tablespoon finely chopped parsley
1 teaspoon chopped fresh tarragon, or ½ teaspoon dried
1 cup peanut, vegetable or corn oil
3 drops Tabasco sauce
½ teaspoon Worcestershire sauce
  Salt and freshly ground pepper
1 tablespoon cold water

The garnish:

1 hard-cooked egg, chopped
  Finely chopped parsley

1. Arrange the meat with overlapping slices in a symmetrical pattern.
2. To prepare the sauce, put the sieved egg, egg yolk, mustard, vinegar, onion, shallots, parsley and tarragon in a mixing bowl.
3. Using a wire whisk, stir to blend, then gradually add the oil, stirring vigorously and continuously. It should thicken like a mayonnaise.
4. Season the sauce with the Tabasco, Worcestershire, salt and pepper to taste and thin it by beating in the water.
5. Spoon all or part of the sauce over the meat. Garnish with chopped egg and parsley and serve cold.

Yield: 4 to 6 servings.

Boeuf bouilli   (Boiled beef for summer salads)

5 pounds lean brisket of beef, or boneless shin of beef
5 pounds beef bones, such as shin bones, cracked

1. Combine all the ingredients in a large kettle and add water to cover, about 1 gallon. Cook, carefully skimming the surface as necessary to remove foam and scum. After about 1

hour, cover closely and continue cooking for 1½ hours longer, or until the meat is tender.

2. Prepare the beef for salad while still lukewarm. Use the broth for soups.

Yield: About 6 servings.

1	large onion (about ½ pound), stuck with 4 cloves
3 to	6 carrots (about 1 pound), trimmed and scraped, but left whole
3	large ribs celery, trimmed and broken in half
2 or	3 leeks, trimmed and tied together, optional
6	sprigs parsley
4	whole cloves garlic, peeled
2	bay leaves
	Salt and freshly ground pepper
½	teaspoon thyme
2	small turnips, peeled, optional

Salade de Boeuf Vinaigrette

1. This dish can be made well in advance, inasmuch as it is served at room temperature.

2. Place the meat in a mixing bowl.

3. Trim the celery and cut it into 1-inch lengths. Cut each length into very fine matchlike strips (julienne). There should be 1 cup or slightly less.

4. Peel the onion, cut in half and slice each half as thinly as possible. There should be slightly less than 1 cup.

5. Peel and core the tomatoes. Cut them in half and squeeze each half gently to extract the seeds. Cut each half into small cubes. There should be about 1 cup.

6. Trim off the ends of the cornichons. Cut the cornichons into fine matchlike strips (julienne). There should be about ⅓ cup.

7. Add the celery, onion, tomatoes, cornichons, garlic and parsley to the meat.

8. To make the sauce, place the mustard, vinegar, salt and pepper into a cold mixing bowl. Gradually add the oil, stirring rapidly with a whisk. The mixture should mound like a thin mayonnaise, but if it doesn't, no matter. Whisk it and pour it over the beef. Toss to blend. Serve at room temperature.

Yield: About 6 servings.

The salad:

4	cups freshly cooked boiled beef cut into neat, bite-size cubes (see preceding recipe)
2	ribs celery
1	onion, preferably red
2	medium-size tomatoes (about ½ pound)
4 to	6 cornichons
1	clove garlic, finely minced
2	tablespoons finely chopped parsley

The sauce:

1	tablespoon imported mustard, such as Dijon or Düsseldorf
2	tablespoons red wine vinegar
	Salt and freshly ground pepper
⅔	cup peanut, vegetable or corn oil, chilled

Grilled Beef and Romaine Salad Thai-style

The salad:

- 1 large head romaine lettuce, about 1½ pounds
- 1 large or 2 medium-size cucumbers, peeled and thinly sliced, about 1 cup
- 1 red onion, peeled and sliced
- 10 to 12 firm radishes, trimmed and thinly sliced, about 1 cup
- 2 red ripe tomatoes, cored and cut into eighths, or sliced
- 1 bunch scallions, trimmed and cut into 1-inch lengths, about ¾ cup
- 16 mint leaves
- 16 basil leaves
- ½ cup loosely packed fresh coriander leaves

The sauce:

- ½ cup fish sauce, available in Chinese markets
- ⅓ cup freshly squeezed lime juice
- 1 tablespoon finely chopped garlic
- 2 teaspoons grated fresh ginger
- ½ to 1 teaspoon hot red powdered chilies, available in Chinese markets, or cayenne pepper

The meat:

- 8 thin slices top round, sirloin or club steak, about 1½ pounds
  Salt and freshly ground pepper to taste
- ¼ cup peanut, vegetable or corn oil

1. Prepare a charcoal or other grill for cooking the meat. This should be done before starting to prepare the ingredients.

2. Combine all the ingredients for the salad.

3. Combine all the ingredients for the sauce and blend well. Set aside.

4. Sprinkle the meat with salt and pepper. Grill the meat on both sides, for about 2 minutes to a side or longer, depending on the desired degree of doneness.

5. Quickly, while the meat is still hot, cut the slices into ½-inch strips and add them to the greens. If there are any accumulated meat juices, add them to the sauce. Pour the sauce over all and toss. Serve immediately with hot rice or long loaves of bread.

Yield: 8 servings.

Salade de Poulet Troisgros *(Green salad with sautéed sliced chicken)*

When Jean Troisgros comes to your home and prepares a salad as the first course, it belies the notion that salad served before the main course is an enormously unsophisticated and childish concept, as we once wrote. Here was this titan of the kitchen, one of the most celebrated chefs of Europe, giving the gastronomic lie to such a thought. But this was no mundane tossing together of a few lettuce leaves. It was an inspired orchestration of greens and herbs and quickly sautéed thin medallions of chicken.

1. Cut the whole chicken into serving pieces, separating the legs and thighs. Remove the skin and bone from the breast meat. Remove the skin and bone from the thigh meat. Cut the liver, if used, into ½-inch cubes. Use the wings, carcass and legs for another purpose, such as soup.

2. Set the pieces of chicken (or the skinless, boneless chicken breasts) on a flat surface and pound lightly. Cut the pieces on the bias into very thin slices. As the slices are cut, arrange them in one layer on a sheet of wax paper. Cover with another sheet of wax paper and pound lightly with a flat mallet. Do not break the meat. Set aside.

3. Prepare the salad sauce in a salad bowl.

4. Add the salad greens to the salad bowl and sprinkle with tarragon, basil and chervil.

5. When ready to serve, sprinkle the cubed liver and the chicken slices with salt and pepper.

6. Heat 2 teaspoons of oil in a small skillet and, when it is very hot and almost smoking, add the liver pieces. Cook quickly, tossing and stirring until lightly browned all over, for about 30 seconds. Add the scallions and 2 teaspoons vinegar. Stir quickly over high heat and pour this over the salad greens. Add the truffles and truffle juice, if desired. Toss well. Spoon the greens onto 4 or 6 salad plates. Set aside.

7. Heat the remaining oil in a large skillet and add the chicken slices. Cook for about 30 seconds on one side and turn the pieces. Cook for about 30 seconds on the other side. Arrange equal amounts of chicken neatly over each serving of salad.

8. Add the remaining vinegar to the skillet. Stir. At the boil, pour this over the salad and serve.

Yield: 4 to 6 servings.

1   4-pound chicken, or 2 pounds skinless, boneless chicken breasts

⅓   cup salad sauce, approximately (see recipe below)

16 cups mixed, loosely packed salad greens (use any tender greens in season such as oak leaf lettuce, red leaf lettuce, romaine, watercress and so on)

2   teaspoons coarsely chopped fresh tarragon leaves

2   teaspoons coarsely chopped fresh basil leaves

1   teaspoon finely chopped fresh chervil or parsley
Salt and freshly ground pepper to taste

5   teaspoons peanut, vegetable or corn oil

¼   cup chopped scallions

4   teaspoons red wine vinegar

1   small black truffle, cut into fine strips, optional

2   teaspoons truffle liquid, optional

Salad sauce

½ teaspoon finely minced garlic
Salt and freshly ground
pepper to taste
1 tablespoon imported mustard,
such as Dijon or Düsseldorf
5 teaspoons red wine vinegar
5 tablespoons oil, preferably
walnut oil

Combine the garlic, salt, pepper, mustard and vinegar in a salad bowl large enough to contain 16 cups of salad greens when tossed. Using a wire whisk, gradually add the oil, stirring.

Yield: ⅓ cup, approximately

Chicken and Mushroom Mayonnaise

1 7-pound chicken, simmered
in broth until tender
½ pound fresh mushrooms,
preferably button mushrooms
Chicken broth to cover
1 tablespoon drained green
peppercorns out of a bottle or
can
4 tablespoons drained capers
1 cup freshly made mayonnaise
Juice of 1 lemon
Finely chopped parsley for
garnish

1. When the chicken is cool, remove it from the kettle. Take the meat from the bones. Remove the skin from the meat. Return the bones and skin to the kettle and continue cooking to reduce the broth to any desired strength. Use a little broth to cook the mushrooms. Reserve the rest for another use.

2. Cut the chicken into bite-size pieces and put in a bowl.

3. If the mushrooms are small, leave them whole; otherwise quarter them or cut them into eighths. Drop them into a saucepan with chicken broth to cover. Simmer for 5 minutes and drain well. Cool and add them to the chicken.

4. Add the peppercorns, capers, mayonnaise and lemon juice. Toss well to blend. Before serving, sprinkle with chopped parsley.

Yield: 8 or more servings.

Calf's Brains and Winter Greens

If you have to sit out a blizzard, do it with Joseph Renggli, chef of the Four Seasons restaurant. Seppi, as he prefers to be called, drove for five hours to get to our house in the Great Blizzard of '78, and in the course of eight hours produced one of the most dazzling array of dishes we've ever seen. All, by the way, with only candlelight.

One dish of his own invention was an incredibly tasty and inspired salad with deep-fried calf's brains and no fewer than ten greens. It's a pity no guests could get to the house to share it.

1½ pairs calf's brains (about
1¼ pounds)

1. The calf's brain consists of a pair of lobes. Place them in a mixing bowl and add cold water to cover. Let them stand for several hours, changing the cold water frequently.

2. Drain and pick over the brains to remove the outer membranes, the blood and other extraneous matter.

3. All the greens should be rinsed well in cold water and well drained to extract excess water.

4. Combine the egg yolks and 3 tablespoons mustard in a mixing bowl and beat with a whisk to blend.

5. Cut the brains into 1½-inch cubes and add to the mustard mixture. Stir to coat.

6. Spread 1 cup bread crumbs over the bottom of a pan and put the pieces of brain over the crumbs. Sprinkle with remaining crumbs. Gently roll brain pieces in crumbs to coat thoroughly. Remove the breaded pieces to a platter and set aside.

7. To prepare the salad dressing, put the remaining 1 tablespoon of mustard in a mixing bowl and add salt and pepper to taste. Add the walnut oil gradually, beating rapidly with a whisk. Beat in the wine vinegar, olive oil and herb vinegar. Add salt and pepper to taste.

8. Heat the peanut oil in a skillet and add the capers. Cook, stirring, for about 2 minutes and drain well.

9. Heat the butter in a skillet and add the breaded pieces of brain. Cook for 1 to 2 minutes to a side, turning once. The brains should be nicely browned.

10. Put the salad greens in a large bowl and add the dressing. Toss the greens. Arrange the brains over the greens. Sprinkle with the capers. Scatter the shredded carrots and leek over all and garnish with truffle slices, if desired.

Yield: 6 to 8 servings.

Note: These ingredients are available where fine specialty foods are sold.

1 head Belgian endive, trimmed and cut into bite-size pieces
2 cups loosely packed spinach cut into bite-size pieces
1 cup loosely packed watercress sprigs, large bottom stems removed
1 cup limestone lettuce cut into bite-size pieces
1 cup chicory (curly endive) cut into bite-size pieces
1 cup escarole cut into bite-size pieces
1 cup heart of romaine cut into bite-size pieces
1 cup "red" or "leaf" lettuce cut into bite-size pieces
¼ cup loosely packed fresh coriander leaves
¼ cup loosely packed fresh chervil leaves, optional
2 egg yolks
4 tablespoons imported mustard, preferably Maille brand mustard with three herbs (see note)
2 cups fine, fresh bread crumbs
  Salt and freshly ground pepper
3 tablespoons walnut oil (see note)
2 tablespoons wine vinegar, preferably sherry wine vinegar
3 tablespoons olive oil
1 teaspoon herb vinegar such as tarragon
½ cup peanut, vegetable or corn oil
½ cup well-drained capers
4 tablespoons butter
½ cup carrots cut into the finest possible shreds, optional
½ cup white part of leek cut into the finest possible shreds, optional
1 truffle, thinly sliced, optional

Moroccan Brains Salad

2 pairs calf's brains, about 1½ pounds
1 teaspoon cumin, preferably freshly ground
½ cup finely chopped parsley
½ cup finely chopped fresh coriander
2 teaspoons finely chopped fresh garlic
2 teaspoons paprika
¼ teaspoon cayenne pepper
½ cup olive oil
3 cups water
1 teaspoon salt
⅔ cup fresh lemon juice
2 preserved lemons (see recipe page 254)

1. Place the brains in a mixing bowl and add cold water to cover. Let stand for several hours. Drain well.

2. Pick over the brains to remove the fine transparent membrane surrounding them. Put in a saucepan and add the cumin, parsley, coriander, garlic, paprika, cayenne, olive oil, water and salt. Bring to the boil and simmer for 30 minutes, or until half the cooking liquid evaporates. Add the fresh lemon juice and stir to break up the brains. (Ideally, the brains should be mashed at intervals while they are cooking.) Cook until most of the liquid evaporates.

3. Rinse the preserved lemons and drain. Cut into small cubes and add them. Cook over gentle heat for about 5 minutes. Remove from the heat and let cool. Refrigerate. Serve very cold.

Yield: 12 servings.

XIII. Breads

French Bread Dough

This French bread dough is easily made and produces some of the best bread we've encountered from home ovens. The recipe was evolved from one given to us by Jane Phalen, a friend and neighbor. She, in turn, got the recipe from the chef-owner of a one-star restaurant, the Chateau Philip in St. Nicolas de la Balerme. We used it for long loaves and also for pain de mie, the French sandwich bread that is made in black tin pans with sliding lids.

7	cups flour, approximately
½	cup milk
2	cups water
1½	tablespoons salt
4	tablespoons butter
2	envelopes granular yeast

1. Place 7 cups of flour in a mixing bowl or, preferably, in the bowl of an electric mixer outfitted with a dough hook.

2. Combine the milk and 1¾ cups of water in a saucepan. Add the salt and butter and heat, stirring, just until the butter melts. Do not boil. Let cool.

3. Combine the yeast with the remaining ¼ cup of lukewarm water and stir to dissolve. Add the yeast to the flour, stirring constantly with the dough hook or with a wooden spoon.

4. Add the liquid, stirring constantly with the dough hook or beating vigorously with the spoon. Knead with the dough hook for about 5 minutes. Or turn the dough out onto a lightly floured board and knead for about 10 minutes, adding flour as necessary, but always using as little flour as possible.

5. Shape the dough into a ball and put it in a large, clean mixing bowl. Stretch plastic wrap over the bowl and place in a warm place until double in bulk, 2 to 3 hours.

6. Shape and bake the dough according to any method outlined below.

French bread baked in oval molds

Prepare the dough as outlined. When double in bulk, turn it out onto a lightly floured board and knead briefly. Divide in half or in thirds and shape it into 2 or 3 long ropes, approximately the same length as the bread molds.

Grease the molds lightly and arrange one length of bread in each. Cover loosely with a clean dry kitchen towel and let rise in a warm place until double in bulk, about 1 hour. Remove the towel and give the dough 3 parallel and diagonal slashes across the top with a razor or very sharp knife.

Preheat the oven to 450 degrees. Bake for 45 minutes for the double-loaf mold or for 40 minutes for the triple-loaf mold, turning the molds as necessary so that the loaves brown evenly. Remove from the oven and place the loaves on a rack to cool.

Yield: 2 or 3 loaves.

Note: This bread is improved by introducing steam into the oven. You may use a pan on the bottom of the oven and pour boiling water into it the moment the mold is placed in the oven.

French sandwich loaves

Prepare the dough as outlined. When double in bulk, turn it out onto a lightly floured board and knead briefly. Divide it in half and shape into 2 oval loaves. Place each of these into buttered sandwich bread pans (see note), measuring about 10½- x 3¾- x 3½-inches, and seal with the lids. Let rise until the pan is filled with dough, about 1 hour. Do not open the pans, but slide the lid gently just a fraction of an inch and you can tell if dough is sticking to the top. Preheat the oven to 450 degrees. Bake for 45 minutes. Remove cover, unmold onto a rack and let cool.

Yield: 2 loaves.

Note: French sandwich bread pans are available in good kitchen supply stores.

French bread rolls

Prepare the dough as outlined. When double in bulk, turn it out onto a lightly floured board and knead briefly. Sprinkle two baking sheets liberally with cornmeal. Cut or pull off pieces of dough, about ½ cup or slightly more in volume. Shape these into smooth rounds and arrange them on the baking sheets. Cover loosely with a clean, dry towel. Let rise until double in bulk.

Preheat the oven to 450 degrees. Remove the towel. Using a razor or very sharp knife, cut a cross in the top of each bread roll. Place in the oven and bake until browned and cooked through, 35 to 40 minutes. Remove from the oven and remove the rolls. Place on a rack to cool.

Yield: 16 to 20 bread rolls.

Note: These rolls are improved as they bake by introducing steam into the oven. You may use a pan on the bottom of the oven and pour boiling water into it the moment the baking sheets are placed in the oven.

French Bread *(Clyde Brooks's version)*

1. Combine the water and yeast in a warm mixing bowl and stir to dissolve. Add the salt, sugar and 4 cups of the flour and stir and beat with the hands until well blended. Add more flour, about ½ cup at a time, mixing and stirring with the hands. The dough will be sticky.

2. Continue adding flour until the dough leaves the sides of the bowl almost clean. The dough at the proper point will be lumpy and sticky. Use only as much flour as necessary to achieve this.

3. Turn the dough out onto a well-floured board. Knead for about 10 minutes. Quickly fold the dough toward you. Quickly push it away with the heels of the hand and give the dough a quarter turn. As you knead, spoon a little more flour onto the board so the dough does not stick. Continue kneading, pushing the dough away and giving it a quarter turn and flouring the board lightly until the dough is smooth and pliable. Shape into a ball.

4. Place the ball of dough in a greased warm bowl and turn it in the bowl to cover lightly with the grease. Cover the bowl with a clean towel and set the bowl in a warm place. The temperature should be 85 to 90 degrees. Let stand until double in bulk. The rising time will take from 1 to 1½ hours (or longer if the temperature is too low).

5. If bread molds are to be used, grease enough molds for 2 or 3 loaves with oil or lard. Or grease a baking sheet with oil or lard and sprinkle lightly with cornmeal.

6. Punch the dough down when it is double in bulk and turn it onto an unfloured surface. Slice the dough into 2 or 3 equal parts.

7. Using the hands, shape one portion of dough at a time on a flat surface. Roll the dough into a long ropelike shape. Roll the dough back and forth under the palms until it is more or less uniform in diameter from one end to the other. Each

2½ cups water (105 to 115 degrees for granular yeast; 80 to 85 degrees for fresh yeast cake)
1 package granular yeast (or crumble 1 fresh yeast cake)
1 tablespoon salt
1 tablespoon sugar, optional
7 or more cups unbleached flour

"rope" should be about 1 inch shorter than the molds or the baking sheet.

8. Place the dough in the molds or on baking sheet. Place uncovered in a warm place (85 to 90 degrees) and let stand until double in bulk.

9. Preheat the oven to 450 degrees.

10. Holding a razor blade on the bias, slash each loaf 3 or 4 times lightly on the top. The slashes should be about ⅛ inch or slightly deeper. If desired, the dough may be brushed lightly with water, milk or lightly beaten egg or egg whites. This is to give color.

11. Place the loaves in the oven and bake for 15 minutes. Reduce the oven heat to 350 degrees and continue baking for 30 minutes or longer. If the loaves should expand and join each other at the sides, pull them apart and reverse their positions in the molds.

12. Remove the loaves from the oven and remove them from the molds or baking sheet. Place them on racks so that air can circulate freely.

Yield: 2 or 3 loaves.

Sourdough French Bread *(Sue Gross's version)*

1 cup sourdough starter (see recipe below)
2 cups warm water (the temperature should be about 80 degrees)
6 cups unbleached flour, plus flour for kneading
1 package granular yeast
1 tablespoon salt
Oil or lard

1. Combine in a warm bowl the sourdough starter, 1 cup of warm water and 2 cups of flour. Stir to blend and cover with plastic wrap. Let stand overnight in a warm but not hot place.

2. Dissolve the yeast in remaining cup of warm water. Add the yeast to the starter mixture. Add the salt and 4 cups of flour and stir to blend well.

3. Turn the mixture out onto a lightly floured board and knead patiently, adding more flour to the kneading surface as necessary. Knead for 10 to 15 minutes, or until the dough is smooth and elastic. Shape the dough into a ball.

4. Rub a mixing bowl lightly with oil or lard and add the ball of dough. Flop it around in the bowl until it is coated with grease.

5. Cover with a cloth and let stand in a warm place. The temperature should be 85 or 90 degrees. Let stand until double in bulk. The rising time will take from 1 to 1½ hours (or longer if the temperature is too low).

6. If bread molds are to be used, grease enough molds for 3

loaves with oil or lard. Or grease a baking sheet with oil or lard and sprinkle lightly with cornmeal.

7. Punch the dough down when it is double in bulk and turn it onto an unfloured surface. Slice the dough into 3 equal parts.

8. Using the hands, shape one portion of dough at a time on a flat surface. Roll the dough into a long ropelike shape. Roll the dough back and forth under the palms until it is more or less uniform in diameter from one end to the other. Each "rope" should be about 1 inch shorter than the molds or the baking sheet.

9. Place the dough in the molds or on baking sheet. Place the molds uncovered in a warm place (85 to 90 degrees) and let stand until double in bulk.

10. Preheat the oven to 450 degrees.

11. Holding a razor blade on the bias, slash each loaf 3 or 4 times lightly on the top. The slashes should be about ⅛ inch or slightly deeper. If desired, the dough may be brushed lightly with water, milk or lightly beaten egg or egg whites. This is to give color.

12. Place the loaves in the oven and bake for 15 minutes. Reduce the oven heat to 350 degrees and continue baking for 30 minutes or longer. If the loaves should expand and join each other at the sides, pull them apart and reverse their positions in the molds.

13. Remove the loaves from the oven and remove them from the molds or baking sheet. Place them on racks so that air can circulate freely.

Yield: 3 loaves.

Sourdough starter

1 package granular yeast
2 cups warm water (the temperature should be between 110 and 115 degrees)
2 cups unbleached flour

1. Empty the yeast into a warm mixing bowl and stir in the water. Stir until yeast is dissolved.

2. Add the flour and stir well until it is blended. Cover with plastic wrap and let stand at room temperature for about 48 hours. When ready, the starter will be bubbly with a somewhat yellowish liquid on top.

3. When part of the starter is removed to make bread, the remainder must be fed with more flour and water. Add 1 cup of flour and 1 cup of water to replace 1 cup removed. Stir and cover with more plastic wrap. Let stand in a warm place for 1 hour or more or until bubbling action is renewed. The starter may be used and replenished for years and it improves with age. Store starter in the refrigerator in a mixing bowl covered with plastic wrap or in a jar with a loose-fitting lid.

Yield: About 3 cups of starter.

Food Processor French Bread

1½ envelopes granular yeast
1 cup plus 4 tablespoons lukewarm water
2 tablespoons butter
3½ cups all-purpose flour, plus flour for rolling out the dough
1 teaspoon salt

1. In a mixing bowl, blend the yeast with 4 tablespoons of lukewarm water. Stir to dissolve the yeast.

2. In a saucepan, combine 1 cup of water with the butter. Heat slowly until the butter melts (a thermometer is not essential, but the best temperature for this is 95 to 110 degrees).

3. To the container of a food processor add 3½ cups unsifted flour and 1 teaspoon of salt. Blend the flour and salt by activating the motor on and off three times. Add the dissolved yeast mixture and the water and butter mixture. Process until the dough becomes a ball and clears the sides of the container, 5 to 10 seconds.

4. Lightly flour a clean surface and turn the dough out onto it. With floured fingers, knead the dough quickly and gently. This is primarily for shaping the dough. Do not add an excess of flour at any time. Shape the dough into a ball.

5. Put the ball of dough in a lightly buttered mixing bowl. Cover with a clean cloth and place the bowl in a warm place. Let stand until double in bulk, about 1 hour.

6. Turn the dough out onto a lightly floured surface and knead gently. Shape into a ball and return the dough to the bowl. Cover and let stand for about 1 hour, or until double in bulk. Turn the dough out and repeat the last step one more time, a total of two rising periods before the final shaping of the dough.

7. After the dough has risen in the bowl the second time, turn it out onto a lightly floured surface. Flatten with the fingers into a rough rectangle. Fold one-third of the dough toward the center of the rectangle. Roll like a jelly roll and transfer the loaf to a baking sheet with the seam on the bottom and the ends folded under. The dimensions of the loaf at this time are approximately 13½ inches long, 3½ inches wide and 2 inches high. Cover with a clean cloth and return to a warm place. Let stand until double in bulk, 30 minutes or longer.

8. As the dough rises, preheat the oven to 450 degrees.

9. Using a razor blade, make three parallel, diagonal gashes on top of the bread. Immediately place the pan in the oven. Put 4 ice cubes on the floor of the oven. Bake for 5 minutes and add 4 more ice cubes as before. Turn the pan on which the bread bakes so that the loaf bakes evenly.

10. Bake for 10 minutes (a total at this point of 15 minutes baking time) and reduce the oven heat to 400 degrees. Bake for 20 minutes longer. Transfer the bread to a rack and let cool.

Yield: 1 large loaf.

California Sourdough Whole Wheat Bread

Probably the best bread maker in America today is Bernard Clayton, Jr., a writer who has spent years traveling in France and the United States gathering the formulas and techniques of bread making. We visited him in his home in Bloomington, Indiana, where he indulges his passion for breads of all kinds, and where he shared his recipes and techniques with us. One of the great faults in bread making, Mr. Clayton maintains, is impatience. "Thirty minutes resting time for bread is a crime against nature. Two hours is much better and you have only to smell the dough to know the difference." We offer three of Mr. Clayton's excellent recipes here, and another, for kugelhopf, on page 561.

1	recipe for whole wheat sourdough sponge (see recipe below)
¼	cup all-natural dark molasses
1	tablespoon salt
3	tablespoons solid white shortening
2½ to	3 cups all-purpose flour

1. In a large bowl, combine the sponge, molasses and salt. Beat well with a wooden spoon. Add the shortening and beat vigorously, about 50 strokes.

2. Add 2½ to 2¾ cups of flour, kneading well inside the bowl. Turn the dough out onto a lightly floured board and continue kneading. If the dough feels moist, continue adding flour while kneading brusquely. Beat it and slam it down on the flat surface. Knead for about 6 minutes.

3. Let warm water run in a large bowl. When warm, drain and wipe dry. Lightly grease the bowl with shortening.

4. Shape the dough into a ball and put it in the bowl. Cover tightly with plastic wrap. Let stand in a warm place for about 1½ hours, or until more than double in bulk.

5. Lightly grease the insides of two loaf pans (pans that measure 8½- x4½- x2½-inches are suitable).

6. Turn the dough out onto a lightly floured board and knead briefly.

7. Divide the dough in half. Shape each half into a ball, then into an oval shape. Fold the dough in half over itself lengthwise and pinch the ends to seal. Place the dough, seam side down, in the pans and cover with wax paper. Let the dough rise for 30 minutes, or until it has risen about 2 inches above the rims of the pans.

8. Preheat the oven to 375 degrees.

9. Using a sharp blade, make a gash lengthwise down the center of each loaf. Make smaller, leaf-like gashes on either side of the lengthwise gash. Place in the oven and bake for about 40 minutes. As the loaves bake, turn the pans around at least once for even cooking.

Yield: 2 loaves.

Whole wheat sourdough
sponge

2 cups warm water
2 packages granular yeast
⅓ cup instant nonfat dry milk
3 cups whole wheat flour

1. This sponge must be made at least three days before using.

2. Combine all the ingredients in a large bowl. Stir well. Cover the bowl tightly with plastic wrap and let stand in a warm place.

3. Stir the mixture down once a day as it stands, always replacing the plastic wrap.

Yield: Enough sponge to produce 2 loaves of bread.

Old Milwaukee Rye Bread

1 recipe for sponge for rye
bread (see recipe below)
1 envelope granular yeast
1 cup warm water
¼ cup all-natural dark
molasses
2 tablespoons caraway seeds
2 eggs
1 tablespoon salt
1 cup medium rye flour
3 tablespoons solid white
shortening
5 to 5½ cups all-purpose flour
1 tablespoon milk

1. Stir down the sponge. Dissolve the yeast in the water. Add the yeast to the sponge, stirring. Add the molasses and 1 tablespoon caraway seeds. Stir to blend.

2. Add 1 lightly beaten egg and salt and blend once more. Add the rye flour and blend. Add the shortening and beat to blend. Add 2 cups of all-purpose flour and blend with a wooden spoon. Gradually add 2 more cups, kneading constantly. Add more flour, about 2 tablespoons at a time, until the dough has a proper pliable and workable consistency.

3. Turn the dough out onto a lightly floured board and knead for about 6 minutes or longer. Knead brusquely, not gently. Beat and slam the dough down on the board. Knead and beat the dough for about 10 minutes. When ready, the dough should weigh about 3½ pounds.

4. Let warm water flow into a large bowl until the bowl is heated. Drain and dry thoroughly. Grease the dough with shortening. Shape the dough into a ball and add it to the bowl. Cover lightly with plastic wrap. Set aside to let rise for 1 hour or longer, or until double in bulk.

5. There are several methods of shaping the bread before baking. If long bread tins or molds are to be used, grease them. Otherwise, use a Teflon baking sheet, ungreased.

6. Divide the dough into 4 portions of equal weight. Roll each piece into a long sausage shape on a flat surface, rolling with the palms of the hand. The shapes should be about 15 inches long. Cover loosely with wax paper and set aside to rise, about 1 hour, or until double in bulk.

7. Preheat the oven to 375 degrees.

8. Using a sharp blade, make several diagonal gashes on top of each loaf. Brush the tops with 1 egg beaten with milk. Sprinkle with the remaining 1 tablespoon caraway seeds.

9. Place in the oven and bake for about 40 minutes, or until crisp crusted and cooked through.

Yield: 4 loaves.

1. Combine the yeast and water in a large bowl. Stir to dissolve. Add the flour and caraway seeds and stir to blend. Cover lightly with plastic wrap.

2. Although this sponge is usable after 6 hours, it is best left to stand at room temperature from 1 to 3 days. Three days will give a more sour taste, which many people prefer.

Yield: Enough sponge for 2 to 4 loaves of rye bread.

Sponge for rye bread

1	package granular yeast
1½	cups warm water
2	cups medium rye flour
1	tablespoon caraway seeds

Cottage Cheese or Clabber Bread

1. Combine 2 cups of flour, the yeast and salt in a bowl and stir to blend. Make a well in the center. Add the 10 eggs and beat vigorously with a wooden spoon until well blended. Add the cottage cheese and beat to blend well.

2. Gradually beat in the pieces of butter and 2 more cups of flour. Beat to blend. Add 2 more cups of flour. Beat to blend.

3. Start adding more flour, about 2 tablespoons at a time, beating and kneading constantly. When a total of 7½ cups of flour have been added, turn the dough out onto a lightly floured surface and knead, adding as much flour to the surface as necessary to make a pliable, easily workable dough. Knead for about 10 minutes or longer, always dusting the board and dough with flour as necessary. Beat and slam the dough down as you work. This dough, when ready, should weigh about 5 pounds.

4. Let warm water flow into a large bowl until the bowl is heated. Drain and dry thoroughly. Grease the bowl with shortening.

5. Shape the dough into a ball and add it to the bowl. Cover tightly with plastic wrap and let stand for 1½ to 3 hours, or until double in bulk. Do not rush the rising. It may not quite achieve a double bulk. Lightly grease 3 9-inch cake pans with sides 1 inch high.

6. Turn the dough out onto a lightly floured surface and knead briefly. Divide the dough into three portions of equal weight. Make a ball of each piece and work the dough, folding it from the outer rim to the center. Press down the folded-in edges. Pat into a circle. Center them, folded-in side down, into the greased pans. Pat the dough to make it smooth to the

7½	to 8 cups all-purpose flour
1	envelope granular yeast
1	tablespoon salt
10	large eggs
2	cups cottage cheese
¼	pound sweet butter, cut into small pieces
1	egg, lightly beaten
1	tablespoon milk

edges of each pan. Cover loosely with wax paper and let stand for about 2 hours, until double in bulk.

7. Preheat the oven to 375 degrees.

8. Brush the tops of the bread with egg beaten with milk. Place in the oven and bake for 45 minutes. Pay particular attention to the bread as it bakes the last 10 minutes. Take care it does not burn.

Yield: 3 loaves.

Herb Bread

1 cup milk
3 tablespoons sugar or honey
3 tablespoons butter
1 teaspoon salt
1½ packages granular yeast
3½ cups flour, plus more flour as necessary for kneading
2 eggs
1 tablespoon chopped fresh ba .l, or 2 teaspoons dried

1. Combine the milk, sugar, butter and salt in a saucepan. Heat just until the butter melts. Let cool to lukewarm and stir in the yeast.

2. Spoon the flour into the container of a food processor (see note). Add the eggs.

3. Start blending the flour and eggs and add the yeast mixture. Process the dough until a ball forms and the dough pulls away from the sides of the container. It may be necessary to add another spoonful or so of flour to the dough to prevent it from sticking to the sides of the container.

4. Turn the dough out onto a lightly floured board and knead briefly, kneading in a little more flour if necessary but use as little flour as possible.

5. Shape the dough into a ball and put it in a lightly greased bowl. Cover with a damp towel and let stand until double in bulk, 45 minutes to 1 hour.

6. Punch the dough down. Knead briefly and shape it into an oval. Put this in a lightly buttered standard-size loaf pan. Cover and let rise for 45 minutes or longer.

7. Preheat the oven to 375 degrees.

8. Place the pan in the oven and bake. Check the bread after about 10 minutes and, if it is getting too brown, cover loosely with a sheet of aluminum foil. Reduce oven heat to 350 degrees and continue baking until done. Total baking time is 35 to 40 minutes. Turn out onto a rack to cool.

Yield: 1 loaf.

Note: This dough may, of course, be made in an electric mixer, in which case, put the milk and yeast mixture in the mixer bowl. Add the eggs and beat them to blend. Gradually add the flour, adding only enough so that the dough can be shaped into a ball without feeling sticky.

Herb and Cheese Bread

1. Blend the yeast with ¼ cup of lukewarm water. Stir to dissolve. Let stand briefly in a warm place.

2. Blend 2 tablespoons of butter and 1 cup of water and heat briefly until the butter melts. This must not be too hot.

3. Put the flour and salt in a food processor and blend. Remove cover and add yeast and butter mixtures. Add ½ cup of parsley. Blend until a ball forms.

4. Turn the dough out onto a lightly floured surface and knead briefly. Shape into a ball and place in a lightly buttered bowl. Cover with a clean towel and place in a warm place. Let stand until double in bulk, about 1 hour.

5. Turn the dough out once more onto a lightly floured board and knead briefly. Shape into a ball once more. Return the ball to the mixing bowl, cover and let stand until double in bulk.

6. Heat the remaining 2 tablespoons of butter in a saucepan and add the shallots. Cook until wilted. Add the remaining parsley, garlic, oregano, if desired, salt and pepper to taste and remove from the heat. Let cool slightly.

7. Turn the dough out once more onto a lightly floured board. Pat it flat with the fingers. Roll it out into a rectangle. Brush the top of the rectangle with a little beaten egg. Add the remaining egg to the parsley mixture.

8. Spoon the parsley and shallot mixture over the rolled out rectangle, leaving about a 2-inch border. Sprinkle with Parmesan cheese. Roll the rectangle jelly roll fashion and tuck in the ends.

9. Butter a standard loaf pan (9- x 5- x 2¾-inches) lightly. Add the dough, seam side down, and cover lightly with a clean cloth. Return to a warm, draft-free place and let stand until double in bulk, about 1 hour.

10. Preheat the oven to 425 degrees.

11. Place the pan in the oven and bake for 30 minutes. Reduce oven heat to 400 degrees and bake for 15 minutes longer.

12. Unmold onto a rack and let cool before slicing.

Yield: 1 loaf.

1½ packages granular yeast
¼ cup lukewarm water
4 tablespoons butter
1 cup water
3½ cups flour
Salt to taste
1¼ cups finely chopped parsley
1 tablespoon finely chopped shallots
1 teaspoon finely chopped garlic
½ teaspoon crushed, dried oregano, optional
Freshly ground pepper to taste
1 large egg, beaten but not frothy
2 tablespoons grated Parmesan cheese

Whole Wheat Orange Bread

2 cups water
4 tablespoons butter
4 cups all-purpose white flour
1 package granular yeast
2 teaspoons salt
½ cup brown sugar
½ cup honey
1 egg
Grated rind of 1 orange
2 cups whole wheat flour

1. Combine the water and butter in a saucepan and heat just until the butter melts, or to a temperature of 110 degrees. If the liquid becomes hotter, let it cool to that temperature.

2. Combine 2 cups of the white flour, yeast, salt and brown sugar in a mixing bowl. Add the water and butter mixture, honey, egg and orange rind. Blend briskly and thoroughly and work in the remaining white flour and the whole wheat flour.

3. Turn the mixture out onto a lightly floured board and knead until smooth and elastic. Shape into a ball.

4. Butter lightly a clean mixing bowl. Add the dough and turn it lightly to coat all sides. Cover the bowl with plastic wrap. Let stand in a warm place until double in bulk, about 2 hours.

5. Turn the dough out and knead it lightly. Cover and let rest 5 to 10 minutes.

6. Shape the dough into 2 loaves. Arrange each loaf in a greased 1½-quart loaf pan (see note). Let rise again in a warm place, about 1 hour. Preheat the oven to 375 degrees. Bake for 45 minutes.

Yield: 2 loaves.

Note: If glass loaf pans are used, lower temperature to 350 degrees.

Nut and Seed Bread

1 cup quick-cooking oatmeal
2¾ cups cold water
1 tablespoon salt
½ cup molasses
4 tablespoons melted butter
2 packages granular yeast
½ cup lukewarm water
⅛ teaspoon sugar
1 cup rye flour
1 cup whole wheat flour
½ cup wheat germ
⅓ cup bran flakes
1 cup plus 2 tablespoons broken walnuts or other nuts, or a combination of nuts and edible seeds such as hulled

1. Combine the oatmeal and 2 cups of cold water in a saucepan and bring to the boil. Remove from the heat.

2. Place the salt, molasses and butter in the bowl of an electric mixer and add the oatmeal mixture. Blend and let cool to lukewarm.

3. Blend the yeast with the ½ cup of lukewarm water and sugar and stir until dissolved. Let stand in a warm place until foamy. Add this mixture plus the remaining ¾ cup cold water to the dough, beating until smooth.

4. Stir on low speed and add the rye flour, whole wheat flour, wheat germ and bran flakes. Beat until smooth. Add the nuts and/or seeds and gradually add enough unbleached white flour to make a workable, soft dough. Turn the dough out onto a lightly floured board and knead for about 10 minutes.

5. Shape the dough into a ball and put it in a lightly greased

bowl. Cover with a damp cloth and let stand until double in bulk, 45 minutes to 1 hour.

6. Punch the dough down. Divide it in two and shape each half into an oval. Put each oval in a lightly buttered standard-size loaf pan. Cover and let rise.

7. Preheat the oven to 375 degrees.

8. Place the pans in the oven and bake for 35 to 40 minutes. Turn out onto a rack to cool.

Yield: 2 loaves.

sunflower seeds, sesame seeds, pumpkin seeds

4 to 5 cups unbleached white flour

Zucchini and Nut Bread

1. Preheat the oven to 350 degrees.

2. Grate the zucchini and set aside.

3. Beat the eggs with the sugar until pale yellow and thickened. Add the butter.

4. Sift together the flour, salt, baking powder, soda and cinnamon. Fold this into the egg mixture. Stir in the vanilla and walnuts.

5. Spoon and scrape the mixture into a buttered loaf pan (measuring about 9- x 5- x 2¾-inches). Bake for 1 hour, or until bread pulls away from the sides of the pan.

Yield: 1 loaf.

2 cups peeled, grated zucchini
3 eggs
1½ cups sugar
¾ cup melted butter
3 cups flour
1½ teaspoons salt
¼ teaspoon baking powder
1 teaspoon baking soda
1 teaspoon ground cinnamon
1 tablespoon pure vanilla extract
¾ cup chopped walnut meats

Banana Bread

1. Preheat the oven to 350 degrees.

2. Put the sugar and oil in the container of an electric mixer. Beat thoroughly to blend. Add eggs and beat well.

3. Sift together the flour, baking powder, soda, salt and nutmeg. Add this and beat well.

4. Mash the bananas to a pulp. Beat them into the batter. Fold in the walnuts.

5. Grease a standard loaf pan (9¼- × 5¼- × 2¾-inches) and pour in the batter. Bake for 1 hour.

Yield: 1 banana loaf.

Note: This bread does not slice well while warm. It is best to bake and let cool, then refrigerate before slicing. It freezes well wrapped closely in aluminum foil. It may then be heated in the foil and served.

⅔ cup sugar
⅓ cup peanut, vegetable or corn oil
2 eggs, lightly beaten
1¾ cups flour
2 teaspoons baking powder
¼ teaspoon baking soda
½ teaspoon salt
⅓ teaspoon grated nutmeg
3 ripe, not too firm, unblemished bananas
⅔ cup coarsely broken walnuts

Southern Corn Bread

⅓ cup sifted flour
1½ cups sifted cornmeal
1 teaspoon baking soda
½ teaspoon salt
2 eggs
1 cup buttermilk
1½ cups milk
1½ tablespoons butter

1. Preheat the oven to 350 degrees.
2. Sift the flour, cornmeal, baking soda and salt into a mixing bowl. Beat the eggs until foamy and stir them into the dry mixture. Stir in the buttermilk and 1 cup of milk.
3. Heat the butter in a 9- × 2-inch black skillet and, when it is very hot but not brown, pour in the batter. Carefully pour the remaining milk on top of the batter without stirring. Place the skillet in the oven and bake for 50 minutes, or until set and baked through.

Yield: 8 servings.

Note: If this is to be used for stuffing, it is best if it is a day or so old.

Salt Rising Bread

This is one of those regional American dishes for which some people have a passion and others something short of aversion. Salt-rising bread, a Southern specialty, is made by a natural fermentation and for a period of time it is a bit malodorous. The finished product is tangy and with a flavor best described as cheeselike.

2 medium-size potatoes, peeled and thinly sliced
2 tablespoons cornmeal
½ tablespoon sugar
1 teaspoon salt
2 cups boiling water
2 cups milk, scalded and cooled to lukewarm
⅛ teaspoon baking soda
8 cups sifted all-purpose flour, approximately
¼ cup soft shortening, or butter

1. Place the potatoes, cornmeal, sugar and salt in a 3-quart bowl. Add the boiling water and stir until the sugar and salt are dissolved. Cover with plastic wrap. Set the bowl in a pan of warm water over the pilot light of a stove, or where it will stay at about 120 degrees, until small bubbles show in the surface, for 24 hours or longer.
2. Put the potatoes in a sieve and press out excess moisture. Add this liquid to the potato water still in the bowl. Discard the potatoes.
3. Add the milk, baking soda and 4 cups of the flour to the bowl. Stir until smooth. Set the bowl again in the pan of warm water and let it stand for about 2 hours, until the dough is almost double in bulk.
4. Chop the shortening or butter into 1 cup of the remaining flour. Add this to the dough. Add enough additional flour,

about 3 cups, to make a moderately stiff dough. Knead on a floured surface quickly and lightly. Do not let the dough get cold.

5. Return the dough to the bowl, grease the surface of the dough, and let it rise for about 2 hours, until double in bulk.

6. Turn the dough out on a lightly floured surface and shape into 2 loaves. Place in greased loaf pans (9- × 5- × 3-inches) and grease the tops of the loaves. Let rise again for about 2 hours, until almost double in bulk, or slightly above the tops of the pans. Sprinkle the tops with cornmeal if desired.

7. About 15 minutes before the loaves have finished rising, preheat the oven to 400 degrees.

8. Bake the loaves for 15 minutes, then lower the oven temperature to 350 degrees and bake for about 35 minutes longer, or until the bread shrinks from the sides of the pans and is well browned. Cool on a rack.

Yield: 2 loaves.

Irish Soda Bread

1. Preheat the oven to 425 degrees.

2. Cut 1 tablespoon of butter bit by bit into the 4 cups of flour. Using the fingers, quickly rub the butter into the flour. Add the salt and soda and empty the mixture into a flour sifter. Sift it into another bowl. Empty any ingredients remaining in the sifter into this second bowl. Stir.

3. Rub a baking sheet with the remaining butter and sprinkle with flour. Shake off any excess flour and set aside.

4. Add the buttermilk to the flour and soda mixture gradually, stirring to blend. Use the hands and knead the mixture until it holds together and can be shaped into a ball. Turn it onto a lightly floured board and knead once more quickly, handling the dough as little as possible.

5. Shape the dough into a flat disc about 8 inches in diameter. Place the disc on the prepared baking sheet. Using a sharp knife, cut a fairly deep cross in the center. Place in the oven and bake for about 45 minutes.

Yield: 1 loaf.

4 cups white flour, plus a little flour for dusting the baking sheet and board
2 tablespoons very cold butter
1 teaspoon salt
1 teaspoon baking soda
1½ cups buttermilk

Beer Bread

1 envelope granular yeast
2 cups beer
Salt to taste
4½ cups flour, plus about ¾ cup additional flour for kneading
Oil or lard
1 egg white, lightly beaten
2 tablespoons sesame seeds

1. Put the yeast in a large, warm bowl. Heat the beer gently just until lukewarm. Do not overheat. Add the warm beer to the bowl and stir until the yeast is dissolved. Add salt and stir. Add 4½ cups of flour, kneading. Form into a ball.

2. Turn the ball of dough out onto a floured board and knead for about 10 minutes, until the dough is smooth, soft and elastic. Grease a large bowl with oil or lard and add the ball of dough. Turn the ball to coat all over with grease. Cover with a towel and let stand in a warm place until double in bulk, about 2 hours.

3. Turn the dough out and knead briefly once more. Shape into a ball and return to the bowl. Cover and let rise until double in bulk, about 45 minutes.

4. Turn the dough out and knead briefly. Divide the dough in half and roll each half out into a long sausage shape. Place the loaves in French bread molds or arrange them on a baking sheet sprinkled with cornmeal. Cover with a towel and let rise for 30 minutes.

5. Using a sharp razor blade, slash the tops of each loaf with three parallel slashes. Cover again and let rise for 30 minutes longer.

6. Preheat the oven to 400 degrees.

7. Uncover the loaves and brush the tops with egg white. Sprinkle with sesame seeds and place in the oven. Bake for 50 minutes, or until nicely browned and cooked.
Yield: 2 loaves.

Croissants

Morning croissants and café noir are as essential to the Parisian scene as the Rive Gauche and the Champs-Elysées. Most home cooks presume the making of croissants to be beyond their scope, but it involves only two things—patience and careful chilling of the dough. The dough must be rolled, folded and chilled several times so that the butter will not ooze out of the dough. It also helps if the surface on which the dough is rolled is cold. The ideal surface is marble, but Formica will do. Wood is not recommended.

1. Blend the lukewarm water with the yeast. Stir to dissolve and set aside briefly in a warm place.

2. Put the sugar in a small mixing bowl and add the salt. Add 2 tablespoons of milk. Blend and set aside.

3. In a saucepan, combine the remaining ¼ cup of milk with the 1 cup of water. Add 2 tablespoons of butter and heat gently, or just until butter is barely melted.

4. To the container of a food processor (or use the bowl of an electric mixer) add 4 cups of flour. Add the three various liquids to the flour and blend with the processor or mix thoroughly with the mixer.

5. Lightly butter a mixing bowl and add the ball of dough. Cover and let stand in a warm place for 45 minutes to 1 hour, or until double in bulk.

6. Turn the dough out onto a lightly floured board and pat with lightly floured fingers into a rectangle. Roll it with a rolling pin until the dough rectangle measures about 7½ by 11 inches. Transfer the rectangle of dough to a lightly floured baking sheet or jelly roll pan. Cover with a clean cloth and place in the refrigerator. Chill for 30 minutes.

7. Remove the dough to a lightly floured board, preferably chilled, and roll out with a pin to another rectangle measuring about 16 by 13 inches. Dot two-thirds of the rectangle of dough with the remaining 12 tablespoons of butter at room temperature (it must not be on the verge of melting). Smear the butter around but not to the margins of the dough. Do not cover the bottom third of dough with butter.

8. Fold the unbuttered third of dough toward the center. Fold the butter-smeared top third of dough over this. Gently roll it out into a rectangle about 14 by 16 inches.

9. Fold down the top third of dough toward the center. Fold the bottom third over this. Sprinkle somewhat liberally with flour and turn the dough. Sprinkle with flour. Put the dough on the baking sheet or jelly roll pan. Cover with a cloth and chill again for 30 minutes.

10. To facilitate rolling, cut the dough crosswise in half. Refrigerate once more for 1 hour.

11. Remove one-half of the dough and roll it out into a rectangle, about 9 x 16 inches, on a floured board. The dough should be about ¼ inch thick. Turn up the bottom third of the rectangle. Turn down the upper third of dough. Return to the baking sheet or jelly roll pan. Repeat with the other half of the dough and return to the refrigerator. Chill for 30 minutes.

12. Roll out the dough one more time to approximately the same 9- x 16-inch dimensions, using flour top and bottom but

2 tablespoons lukewarm water
2 teaspoons granular yeast
2 tablespoons sugar
1 teaspoon salt
2 tablespoons plus ¼ cup milk
1 cup plus 2 tablespoons water
14 tablespoons butter plus butter for greasing the mixing bowl and pan
4 cups flour plus flour for rolling out the dough
1 egg yolk, lightly beaten

sparingly. Cut the dough down the center. Cut each half into three or four triangles. Roll up the triangles from the base toward the top. Twist into crescents. Triangles may be large or small. Half the dough will make about 7 croissants of traditional size.

13. Brush a baking sheet or jelly roll pan with butter and arrange the croissants on it. Cover with a clean towel and let rest in a warm place until double in bulk, about 30 minutes. At this point you may roll out the other half of the dough, cut it and shape it into croissants. Or you may freeze it for future use.

14. As the dough rises, preheat the oven to 475 degrees.

15. Brush the croissants with the egg yolk beaten with 2 tablespoons water and place in the oven. Bake for 5 minutes and reduce the oven heat to 400 degrees and continue baking for about 10 minutes.

Yield: About 14 croissants.

Brioches

¾ cup plus 1 tablespoon milk
½ pound (2 sticks) butter
5 cups flour
2 packages granular yeast
¼ cup sugar
2 teaspoons salt
5 eggs
1 egg yolk

1. Combine the ¾ cup milk and the butter in a saucepan and heat just until the butter melts, about 110 degrees. If the liquid becomes hotter, let it cool to that temperature.

2. In a mixing bowl, combine 2 cups of flour, yeast, sugar and salt. Stir in the milk and butter mixture and 2 eggs.

3. Beat in 2 cups of flour and, when thoroughly blended, beat in the remaining eggs and flour. The dough will be soft and shiny. Shape into a ball.

4. Butter lightly a clean mixing bowl and add the dough. Cover with plastic wrap and let stand in a warm place until double in bulk, about 1½ hours. Punch the dough down. Cover and refrigerate overnight.

5. About 1½ hours before baking, punch the dough down once more and turn it onto a lightly floured surface. Divide the dough into approximately equal portions, each measuring about ¼ cup.

6. Nip off about ⅕ of each portion and set aside to be used as a topknot. Roll the larger portion into a ball, using the palms of the hands. Place the ball into a greased brioche tin. Use a razor blade and cut a cross on top of the ball. Roll the

nipped-off portion into a teardrop shape. Arrange the tear-drop, pointed side down, in the middle of the cross. Continue shaping the remaining dough in a similar manner until all the portions are used. Cover the shaped brioches and let rise until almost double in bulk.

7. Preheat the oven to 400 degrees.

8. When the brioches have risen, blend the egg yolk with the remaining 1 tablespoon of milk. Use a pastry brush and brush the top of each brioche with the mixture. Bake for 20 minutes.

Yield: 18 to 20 brioches.

Water Bagels

1. Place the yeast in a warm bowl and add the water, stirring to dissolve. Add the malted milk powder and sugar and stir until dissolved. Add the salt and flour all at once. Work the dough with the fingers and hands, kneading the mass into a stiff dough. Or use a mixer equipped with a dough hook.

2. Turn the dough out onto a lightly floured board and knead until smooth. Shape the dough into a ball and place it in an ungreased bowl. Cover with plastic wrap and let rise in a warm place until double in bulk.

3. Preheat the oven to 450 degrees.

4. Bring the ingredients for the water bath to the boil.

5. Punch the dough down and divide it into 16 equal portions. Roll each portion into a ball. Pierce the center of each dough ball with the index finger. Using the fingers, shape each portion of dough into a circle like a doughnut ring.

6. If the water bath is boiling, turn off the heat. When the bagels are dropped into it, the water should be just below the boiling point.

7. Drop the bagel rounds into the just-under-boiling water and let them "cook" for about 20 seconds on a side. Immediately lift the rounds from the water, using a slotted spoon.

8. Place the bagel rounds on an ungreased baking sheet and bake for about 20 minutes, or until golden brown.

Yield: 16 bagels.

The bagels:

1 package granular yeast
2 cups warm water
¼ cup natural-flavored instant malted milk powder
2 tablespoons sugar
1 tablespoon salt
5¾ cups unsifted white flour

The water bath:

2 quarts water
2 tablespoons natural-flavored instant malted milk powder
1 tablespoon sugar

Onion-topped bagels

½ cup dehydrated minced onion
(see note), soaked in water
and then squeezed dry
2 tablespoons oil
¼ teaspoon salt
½ egg white

1. There are two ways to prepare onion-topped bagels. The easiest is simply to sprinkle the bagels with dehydrated onions when they are removed from the water bath and are still wet. When using this method, the onions turn very brown, almost black when baked.

2. To produce a less dark onion topping, prepare the bagels in the basic recipe until they are ready for the oven. Combine the onion, oil, salt and egg white and brush the mixture onto the bagels. Bake as indicated until golden brown.

Note: Chopped fresh onions do not produce a product to taste like commercially prepared bagels.

Pita Bread

1 package granular yeast
2 tablespoons plus ⅓ cup
lukewarm water,
approximately
1 teaspoon sugar
1 egg, beaten
2 cups all-purpose flour
⅛ teaspoon salt
3 tablespoons oil

1. Dissolve the yeast in the 2 tablespoons of lukewarm water. Add the sugar and egg and stir well.

2. Sift together the flour and salt. Stir in the yeast mixture and 3 tablespoons oil. Add the remaining ⅓ cup lukewarm water and mix into a soft dough, adding a little more water if needed. Cover and let rise until double in bulk.

3. Punch the dough down and form into 16 flat cakes about 4 inches in diameter. Place the cakes on an oiled baking sheet and let rise until light, or almost double in bulk.

4. Preheat the oven to 375 degrees.

5. Prick the cakes with tines of a fork, brush with water or cooking oil and bake in the oven for 15 to 20 minutes, or until lightly browned. The pita should be puffed around the edges with a hollow in the center. Serve hot with appetizers.

Yield: 16 pita.

Baking Powder Biscuits

2 cups flour
Salt to taste
1 teaspoon baking powder
½ cup solid white vegetable
shortening at room
temperature
5 to 6 tablespoons cold water
¼ cup heavy cream, optional

1. Preheat the oven to 400 degrees.

2. Combine the flour, salt and baking powder in the container of a food processor. Add the shortening and cover. Blend while adding the water. Add 5 tablespoons and, if necessary, 1 additional tablespoon. Process until a ball forms and the dough comes away from the sides of the bowl.

3. Roll out the biscuit dough to ½-inch thickness. Using a 2½-inch round biscuit cutter, cut out the biscuits. Brush lightly with heavy cream, if desired.

4. Arrange on a greased baking sheet and bake for 20 minutes, or until lightly browned on top.
Yield: 16 biscuits.

Kugelhopf

1. Put the raisins in a bowl and add warm water to cover. Let stand for about 30 minutes.

2. Combine 3 cups of the whole wheat flour, brown sugar, yeast, salt and dry milk in a mixing bowl. Blend well. Make a well in the center and add the water. Beat the mixture for about 50 strokes. Add the egg and beat for about 10 strokes. Beat in the oil. Add the ground hazelnuts. Drain the raisins and squeeze to extract excess liquid. Add them, beating. Add the white flour and beat the mixture with a wooden spoon. Gradually add up to 1 more cup of whole wheat flour. Take care that you do not add an excess amount. The dough must remain pliable and easily workable when it is kneaded. Scrape out and use all the dough from the sides of the bowl.

3. Turn the dough out onto a lightly floured board. When the dough is easy to knead without adding any more flour, knead it brusquely, not gently, for at least 8 minutes. Beat and slam it against the board. Add more flour if, while kneading, the dough seems in any sense sticky.

4. Meanwhile, clean the bowl in which the dough was made. Add hot water and let stand until the dough is kneaded and ready to rest. Drain the water, wipe the bowl dry and grease it.

5. Shape the dough into a ball and add it to the bowl. Cover with plastic wrap stretched tightly across the top.

6. Brush the inside of a 10-cup kugelhopf mold with melted butter. You may have a little too much dough for the mold. If so, butter the inside of a smaller 3-cup tin with melted butter.

7. Arrange the whole almonds in a neat circle over the bottom of the kugelhopf mold. If the smaller mold is used, sprinkle the bottom with crushed almonds.

8. Punch the dough down and knead briefly. Cut off 2½ pounds of the dough and shape it into a ball. Press down to shape it into a circle. Make a hole in the center and shape the dough by hand to resemble a very large doughnut that will fit neatly into the kugelhopf mold around the funnel. Press down. Shape the remaining dough into the smaller tin. Cover

½ cup dark raisins
3 to 4 cups whole wheat flour, approximately
⅓ cup dark brown sugar, solidly packed
2 packages granular yeast
2 teaspoons salt
½ cup instant, nonfat dry milk
2 cups water
1 egg, lightly beaten
3 tablespoons vegetable oil
¼ cup roasted ground hazelnuts or almonds
1 cup all-purpose white flour
  Melted butter
15 whole blanched almonds and/or crushed hazelnuts or almonds

both with wax paper and set aside. Let stand for about 1 hour, or until double in bulk.

9. Preheat the oven to 375 degrees.

10. Place the molds in the oven. Bake the smaller bread for about 40 minutes, the larger for about 50 minutes.

Yield: 1 or 2 loaves.

Greek Easter Bread

¾ cup plus 1 tablespoon lukewarm milk
½ cup sugar
2 envelopes granular yeast
5½ to 6 cups flour
1 teaspoon salt
½ pound sweet butter, melted
5 eggs, lightly beaten
1 cooked red egg (see note)
1 egg yolk

1. In a bowl combine ¾ cup lukewarm milk, sugar and yeast and let stand in a warm place for 10 minutes.

2. In a large bowl, combine 5½ cups flour and salt. Make a well in the center and add cooled melted butter and eggs. Add yeast mixture and blend to form a soft sticky dough. Knead, adding a little more flour as necessary, for about 5 minutes, until dough is smooth and satiny. Place in a buttered bowl and stretch a sheet of plastic wrap over the bowl. Set in a warm, draft-free place to rise until double in bulk, about 1½ hours.

3. Punch down dough and knead for 5 minutes. Cut off 4 pieces, each piece about the size of a large egg. Place remaining dough into a round pan 10 inches in diameter and 2 inches high. Shape the small pieces of dough into twists about 5 inches long. Arrange the 4 twists from the center of the dough radiating to edge of dough. Put in a warm place to rise again until double in bulk, about 1 hour. Place the red egg in the center of the bread.

4. Preheat the oven to 375 degrees.

5. Brush entire surface of bread with a wash made from the egg yolk and remaining tablespoon milk. Bake for 30 minutes, until the bread is a deep golden brown and sounds hollow when tapped. Transfer to a rack and cool.

Yield: 12 or more servings.

Note: Color a hard-cooked egg with red Easter-egg dye according to package instructions.

Challah (*A sweet leavened bread*)

1. Place 6 cups of the flour in a large mixing bowl and make a well in the center. Blend the yeast with 1 cup of the water and stir to dissolve. Add this to the well in the flour. Using a fork, start stirring around the well, gradually incorporating ¼ of the flour—no more—into the yeast mixture. When approximately that amount of flour is blended into the yeast mixture, stop stirring. There is no need to remove the fork. It will be used for further stirring. Set the bowl in a warm, not too hot place, and let stand for 45 or 50 minutes.

2. Sprinkle the baking powder, cinnamon and salt over all. Add the vanilla, 3 of the eggs, the oil and ¾ cup of sugar. Add the remaining water and blend again, first using the fork and then the hands. Add 2 cups of flour, kneading and, if the mixture is still too sticky, add an additional cup of flour.

3. Work the mixture well with a wooden spoon to make a very stiff dough. If necessary, add more flour. Work with the hands for about 10 minutes. When the dough doesn't stick to the hands, it is ready. Shape the mixture into a rather coarse ball and cover. Let stand for about 20 minutes and turn it out onto a lightly floured board. Knead well, adding a little more flour to the board as necessary to prevent sticking. The kneading, which must be thorough and brisk, should take about 5 minutes. Flour a bowl well and add the ball, turning the dough to coat lightly with flour. Cover again and let stand for about 30 minutes.

4. Turn the dough out onto a flat surface once more and knead briefly. Using a knife, slash off about ⅛ of the dough at a time. As each portion is cut off, knead quickly and shape into a ball. Flour lightly. Return each piece as it is kneaded to a bowl to rest briefly. Continue until all 8 pieces are shaped and floured.

5. Take one piece of dough at a time and place it on a flat surface, rolling briskly with the hands to make a "rope" 12 to 15 inches in length. Continue until all the balls are shaped.

6. Align the ropes vertically side by side and touching. Start working at the top of the ropes. Gather the tops of the ropes together, one at a time, pinching down to seal well. Separate the rope down the center, 4 ropes to a side. Braid the ropes as follows: Bring the extreme outer right rope over toward the center next to the inside rope on the left. Bring the extreme outer left rope over toward the center next to the inside rope on the right. Continue with this procedure until the loaf is

8½ to 9 cups sifted, unbleached flour, plus additional flour for kneading
2 packages dry yeast
2½ cups lukewarm water
½ teaspoon baking powder
½ teaspoon cinnamon
1 tablespoon salt
1 teaspoon vanilla
4 large eggs
¾ cup corn oil
¾ cup plus ⅛ teaspoon sugar
1 tablespoon poppy seeds or sesame seeds

braided and each rope has been brought to the center. As the last ropes are brought over, it will be necessary to pull and stretch them a bit to get them to fit.

7. When the braiding is finished, gather the bottom ends of the ropes together and pinch them together just as at the top.

8. Meanwhile, generously oil the bottom and sides of a rectangular baking pan measuring about 15½- x 10½- x 2½-inches. Carefully gather up the braided loaf, using the hands and arms to help sustain the shape.

9. Cover with a towel and let stand in a warm spot for 1 hour or slightly longer, or until the loaf is well puffed and about twice the original volume.

10. Preheat the oven to 325 degrees.

11. Beat the remaining egg with the ⅛ teaspoon of sugar and, using a pastry brush, brush the loaf all over with the egg wash and sprinkle evenly with poppy or sesame seeds.

12. Place the loaf in the oven and bake for approximately 1 hour, or until well puffed, cooked through and golden.

Yield: 1 large loaf.

Torta de Masa   (A fine-grained, sweet Mexican corn loaf bread)

1	cup masa harina, a fine-grained cornmeal (see note)
	Salt to taste
1½	teaspoons baking powder
10	tablespoons sugar
10	tablespoons butter, cut into small pieces
¾	cup plus 1 tablespoon water
6	eggs, separated

1. Preheat the oven to 375 degrees. Butter a standard-size loaf pan measuring 9½- x 5¼- x 2-inches.

2. Sift together the masa harina, salt, baking powder and sugar into a mixing bowl.

3. Add the butter, blending with the fingers or a pastry blender until the mixture looks like coarse cornmeal. Scrape the mixture into the bowl of an electric mixer.

4. Add the ¾ cup water, beating on low speed. Add the yolks, beating on medium speed until well blended

5. Beat the whites until stiff and fold them in. Pour and scrape the mixture into the loaf pan. Brush with 1 tablespoon water. Place it in the oven and bake for about 45 minutes. Unmold the bread while it is still hot. Slice and serve hot or lukewarm.

Yield: 1 loaf.

Note: Masa harina is available in many supermarkets and in Spanish grocery stores.

Steamed Chinese Bread

1. Place the yeast, sugar, lard, ½ cup of flour and ½ cup of water in a mixing bowl. Blend. Let stand for 5 minutes.

2. Add 2½ cups more flour and remaining ½ cup of water. Stir to blend. Knead with floured fingers (use up to ¼ cup more for kneading but as little flour as possible). Knead until the dough does not stick to the board or fingers.

3. Shape the dough into a ball and place it in a mixing bowl. Cover with a damp cloth. Let stand in a warm place for about 3 hours, or until double in bulk.

4. Remove the cloth and punch the dough down. Add the baking powder and continue kneading, using up to ¼ cup of flour but as little as possible. Knead vigorously for about 10 minutes.

5. Line a steamer at least 11 inches in diameter with a damp cloth. Shape the dough into an oval loaf about 8½ inches long. Place this on the damp cloth in the steamer, cover with the steamer lid and let rise in a warm place for about 45 minutes. Place the steamer basket over boiling water in the steamer bottom and steam for 20 minutes. When cooked, the loaf will be pure white but firm to the touch. Let cool.

6. When cool, slice the loaf lengthwise down the center. Cut crosswise into about 22 slices, each about ¾ inch thick. Let stand in the steamer basket.

7. Five minutes before serving, cover and heat over boiling water for about 5 minutes. Serve with pork and duck dishes.

Yield: 8 servings.

1 envelope granular yeast
2 tablespoons sugar
1 tablespoon warm but not melted lard
3 cups flour plus additional flour for kneading
1 cup cold water
1 teaspoon baking powder

Pooris *(Puffed Indian bread)*

1. Combine the flour and salt in a mixing bowl. Stir to blend. Add the sesame oil and work with the fingers. Gradually add the water, kneading constantly. Add only enough to make a moderately firm dough. Cover loosely and set aside for 1 hour.

2. Uncover and knead the dough for about 1 minute. Break off about ½ cup of the dough at a time. Roll it between the palms into a sausage shape. Break off pieces of this "sausage" to make small marbles of dough, each about 1 inch thick. Con-

2 cups whole wheat flour
½ teaspoon salt
1 tablespoon sesame oil
⅔ cup water, approximately
Oil for deep frying

tinue until all the dough is shaped. There should be about 38 pieces in all.

3. Heat the oil until it is almost but not quite smoking.

4. Flatten each piece of dough into a small disc about 1½ inches in diameter. Roll each piece into a thin round pancake, about 3½ inches in diameter. When rolling, use an unfloured board.

5. Drop the pieces of dough, one at a time, into the oil. Cook, tapping down on the center of each puri. They should puff in the center like a balloon. When puffed, turn each puri in the oil and cook briefly until lightly browned. Drain on absorbent toweling.

Yield: About 38 pieces.

XIV. Desserts

Black Forest Cake

1. Prepare the spongecake and set aside.

2. Combine ½ cup of sugar and the water in a saucepan. Add the orange or lemon wedges and bring to the boil. Simmer about 3 minutes and let the syrup cool. Discard wedges.

3. Drain both cans of cherries separately and set cherries aside.

4. Combine the kirsch with ⅔ cup of the syrup. Set aside.

5. Place the chocolate in a saucepan and let it melt gradually in a warm place. When it is melted, gradually add 3 tablespoons of the remaining syrup, stirring.

6. Whip the cream and beat in the remaining tablespoon of sugar and the vanilla.

7. Fold 1½ cups of the whipped cream into the chocolate mixture. Set the remaining whipped cream aside.

8. Place the cake on a flat surface and, holding a long, sharp knife parallel to the bottom of the cake, slice the cake into thirds.

9. Place the bottom slice on a serving plate and brush with some of the syrup mixture. Add about half the chocolate mixture to the slice and smooth it over. Cover with the top slice but place it bottom side up. Brush the slice with syrup and add the remaining chocolate mixture, smoothing it over.

10. Using a pastry tube, pipe 3 rings of whipped cream around the cake. Pipe one ring in the center, another in the middle and the other around the rim. Arrange sour cherries in the center and between the middle and outer rings.

11. Top with the final slice of cake. Brush it with the remaining syrup. Add whipped cream to the top, but save enough cream to make rosettes on top of the cake. Smooth the whipped cream around the top and sides of the cake. Use a No. 4 star pastry tube and pipe 12 rosettes, equally spaced, around the upper rim of the cake. Make one rosette in dead center. Garnish each rosette with one dark sweet pitted cherry.

1   10-inch chocolate spongecake (see recipe below)
½   cup plus 1 tablespoon sugar
1   cup water
2   thin orange or lemon wedges
1   8-ounce can dark sweet pitted cherries (see note)
1   1-pound can sour cherries
⅓   cup kirsch
1   3-ounce (85-gram) bar of imported bittersweet chocolate
3   cups heavy cream
3   drops pure vanilla extract
    Scraped and/or grated chocolate for garnish

Garnish the top with scraped or grated chocolate. Refrigerate until ready to serve.

Yield: 10 servings.

Note: Fresh black Bing cherries may be poached in syrup, pitted and used in this recipe.

Chocolate spongecake

6 eggs
1 cup sugar
½ cup plus 3 tablespoons flour
4 tablespoons cornstarch
6 tablespoons cocoa
3 tablespoons melted butter

1. Preheat the oven to 375 degrees.

2. Butter a round cake tin (ours measured 10 by 2 inches). Sprinkle the inside with flour and shake the flour around until the bottom and sides are well coated. Shake out any excess flour.

3. Put the eggs into the bowl of an electric mixer. Bring about 2 quarts of water to the boil in a casserole to hold the mixing bowl. Set the bowl in the water and beat vigorously while adding the sugar. Beat constantly for about 5 minutes, or until the eggs are lukewarm.

4. Return the bowl to the electric mixer and continue beating on high speed until the mixture is thick, mousselike and at room temperature. To test, run a spatula through the mass. If it is ready, the spatula will leave a track.

5. Meanwhile, combine the flour, cornstarch and cocoa. Sift together two or three times. Fold the mixture into the batter, using a wooden spoon or spatula. Fold in the butter and pour the mixture into the prepared pan. Bake for 25 to 30 minutes, or until the cake pulls away from the pan. Turn the cake out onto a rack to cool.

Yield: 1 spongecake.

Honey-Chocolate Cake

11 tablespoons butter
1¾ cups honey
½ cup cocoa
2 eggs
1 teaspoon vanilla extract
2½ cups sifted cake flour
1½ teaspoons baking soda
½ teaspoon salt
1 cup milk
Honey frosting (see recipe below)

1. Preheat the oven to 325 degrees.

2. Grease and flour 3 round 9-inch cake tins.

3. Cream the butter until soft. Beat the honey in gradually. Add the cocoa and mix well. Beat in the eggs one at a time. Add the vanilla.

4. Sift together the dry ingredients. Add dry ingredients alternately with milk, beating constantly. Pour the batter into the prepared pans and bake for 50 minutes, or until the cakes test done.

5. Turn the cake rounds onto racks to cool. Spread a little frosting between each layer and stack them. Frost the top and sides of the cake and serve cut in wedges.

Yield: 16 to 24 servings.

1. Boil the honey over medium heat to the soft ball stage, 238 degrees on a candy thermometer.

2. Beat the egg whites and salt until stiff. Pour the hot honey into the egg whites in a thin stream, beating constantly. Add the vanilla and Cognac. Beat the frosting until it is thick enough to spread.

Yield: Enough for one 9-inch 3-layer cake.

Honey frosting

1½	cups honey
2	egg whites
⅛	teaspoon salt
½	teaspoon vanilla extract
1	tablespoon Cognac

Chocolate Cake

1. Preheat the oven to 350 degrees.

2. Beat the egg yolks and sugar until very thick and lemon-colored. Stir in the chocolate. Fold in the nuts.

3. Beat the egg whites until stiff but not dry and fold into the chocolate-nut mixture. Turn into a greased 10-inch spring form pan and bake for 1 hour, or until the center springs back when lightly touched with the fingertips. Cool in the pan. Serve, if desired, with whipped cream.

Yield: 8 to 12 servings.

10	eggs, separated and at room temperature or slightly warmer
14	tablespoons (about 1 cup) sugar
6	ounces bittersweet or semisweet chocolate, melted slowly over hot water and cooled
2	cups finely chopped (not ground) walnuts

Walnut and Almond Torte

1. Preheat the oven to 350 degrees.

2. Blend the nuts, zwieback, orange rind, cinnamon and cloves in a mixing bowl.

3. Beat the egg yolks with the 1½ cups sugar until light and lemon-colored, about 15 minutes. Add vanilla and fold into the nut mixture

4. Beat the egg whites until stiff but not dry and gently fold into the batter.

5. Butter a 12- x 15- x 3-inch pan and pour in the batter. Bake for exactly 1 hour without opening the oven door.

6. While the torte is baking, make the syrup. Combine the water, 3 cups sugar and lemon slice in a saucepan and simmer for about 20 minutes.

7. Pour the warm syrup over the torte immediately upon removing the torte from the oven. Let the torte stand for 24 hours. Cut into 3-inch squares and serve topped with whipped cream.

Yield: 20 pieces.

3	cups ground walnuts
3	cups ground almonds
16	pieces zwieback, ground Grated rind of 1 orange
½	teaspoon cinnamon
¼	teaspoon ground cloves
12	eggs, separated
1½	cups sugar
1	teaspoon vanilla
4	cups water
3	cups sugar
1	slice of lemon Whipped cream

Rosace à l'Orange *(Genoise with oranges)*

When Gaston Lenotre came to our kitchen to demonstrate his incredible skills, he talked of the pitfalls of pastrymaking. "Chefs de cuisine can cover up their mistakes because their cooking is imprecise," Mr. Lenotre told us. "You simply add more of this or more of that and the public never knows. Drop a platter of roast birds and they won't shatter. Drop a wedding cake and you start from scratch. In pastrymaking, everything must be precise or it's a failure. If the butter is too soft or not chilled enough in making puff pastry, if you overbeat or overheat your eggs, they cook or fall. If you overbeat your whites they start to weep."

Mr. Lenotre, generally considered to be the greatest pastry chef in France, prepared two classic French cakes for us, this rosace à l'orange and the following ambassadeur, both based on the genoise, one of the foundation cakes of French pastrymaking. He also made a very Gallic and delicious lemon meringue pie, which appears later in this chapter

1   genoise (see recipe below)
4   oranges
4   cups water
2¾   cups granulated sugar
⅔   cup dessert syrup (see recipe below), using Grand Marnier where indicated
Juice of ½ orange
1¼   cups crème patissière (see recipe below)
1¼   cups whipped cream
Butter for greasing the mold
Sugar to dust a mold

1. Prepare the genoise as much as a day in advance.

2. Trim off and discard the ends of the oranges. Cut the oranges into very thin slices.

3. Combine the water and sugar and bring to the boil. When the sugar dissolves, add the orange slices and simmer over very gentle heat for 2 hours. Pour the orange slices and syrup into a bowl and let stand overnight.

4. Prepare the dessert syrup and add the orange juice. Set aside.

5. Drain the orange slices. Set aside half of them for decorating. Cut the remaining slices into small pieces. The drained syrup may be used as a side dish for this dessert, flavored perhaps with a little rum. Fold the small pieces into the crème patissière. Fold this mixture into the whipped cream.

6. Select a round mold slightly larger and deeper than the genoise. Butter the bottom and sides and sprinkle with sugar. Line the bottom and sides of the mold with the reserved orange slices, edges overlapping so that both bottom and sides are completely covered.

7. Spoon half the crème patissière over the bottom layer of orange slices, smoothing it over.

8. Slice the genoise in half horizontally. Brush both halves with the orange-flavored dessert syrup. Place one layer on top of the crème patissière. Trim the sides of the genoise if neces-

sary to make it fit. Top with the remaining crème patissière. Add the second layer of genoise. Top with a small plate that fits snugly inside the mold. Cover with a weight. Refrigerate for 2 hours.

9. To unmold, remove the plate and weight. Dip the mold in hot water and invert it onto a serving dish. Keep refrigerated until ready to serve.

Yield: 8 or more servings.

1. It is almost as easy to prepare two cakes as one. This recipe is for two. Genoise keeps for a week in the refrigerator wrapped in aluminum foil. It freezes well.

2. Preheat the oven to 350 degrees.

3. Butter generously the bottom and sides of two 8-inch cake pans. Sprinkle with flour, shaking to coat evenly. Shake out excess. Refrigerate the pans.

4. Select a 2-quart metal mixing bowl that will fit snugly inside a slightly larger saucepan. Add enough water in the saucepan to almost touch the bottom of the bowl when it is added. Bring the water to the boil.

5. Put the eggs and sugar in the mixing bowl and beat vigorously using a heavy wire whisk. Set the bowl over the water, which should simmer constantly. The essential thing is to avoid overheating the egg mixture. At this point you may switch from the whisk to a portable electric beater. Use high speed initially.

6. Beat the mixture without stopping until it is thick and glossy and falls from the whisk or beater in a soft ribbon.

7. Transfer the bowl, beating constantly, to a flat surface. If an electric mixer is used, the total beating time on high speed is about 5 minutes. Then reduce to low speed for 10 minutes.

8. Using a rubber spatula or a large kitchen spoon, start folding in the flour, holding the flour sifter over the mixture and adding it fairly rapidly. It is best if you have an assistant as you fold.

9. After all the flour has been incorporated, start adding the butter, about a tablespoon or slightly less at a time, folding it in rapidly.

10. Split the vanilla bean in half lengthwise and scrape the seeds into the cake. Or use vanilla extract. Stir quickly. Pour the mixture into the two prepared pans.

11. Place in the oven and bake for 30 minutes, or until golden brown. Let the cake cool for about 10 minutes. Turn onto racks while still warm. Let cool completely before use.

Yield: 2 cakes.

Genoise

Butter for greasing cake pans
Flour for coating
5   large eggs, slightly less than 1¼ cups
1   cup granulated sugar
1¼   cups flour
4   tablespoons melted clarified butter
1   vanilla bean, or ½ teaspoon pure vanilla extract

Dessert syrup

Combine ⅔ cup water with ½ cup granulated sugar in a saucepan. Bring to the boil and simmer until the sugar dissolves. Let cool. Stir in 3 tablespoons of a liqueur such as Grand Marnier, kirsch or rum.

Yield: About 1 cup.

Crème patissière *(Pastry cream)*

1 cup milk
¼ vanilla bean, or ½ teaspoon pure vanilla extract
⅓ cup granulated sugar
3 egg yolks
2 tablespoons cornstarch
1 tablespoon soft butter, optional

1. Place the milk and split vanilla bean, if used, in a saucepan and bring to the boil. Cover and keep hot.

2. Put the sugar and egg yolks in a mixing bowl (this may be done in a mixer) and beat with a wire whisk until the mixture is golden yellow and forms a ribbon. Using the whisk, stir in the cornstarch.

3. Strain the hot milk into the egg and sugar mixture, beating constantly with the whisk. The vanilla bean may be rinsed off and stored in sugar.

4. Pour the mixture back into the saucepan and bring to the boil, stirring constantly with the whisk. Cook for 1 minute, stirring vigorously. Add the vanilla extract if used. If the pastry cream is not to be used immediately, rub the surface with butter to prevent a skin from forming as it cools.

Yield: About 1¼ cups.

Ambassadeur *(Genoise with candied fruit)*

1 genoise (see recipe above)
3½ tablespoons chopped candied fruit mix
3 tablespoons Grand Marnier
1¼ cups crème patissière (see recipe above)
1 cup dessert syrup (see recipe above)
1 cup almond paste, homemade (see recipe below), or purchased Confectioners' sugar Chocolate icing (see recipe below), optional

1. Prepare the genoise a day in advance. Similarly, soak the candied fruit in the Grand Marnier.

2. Prepare the crème patissière and let it cool. Divide it in half. Place one-half in the refrigerator. Drain the candied fruit and add it to the other half. Stir to blend.

3. Using a long, sharp knife, cut the genoise horizontally into three layers of equal thickness.

4. Brush the bottom layer generously with about one-third of the dessert syrup. Spread this neatly with half the blended crème patissière and candied fruit. Place the center cake layer on top. Brush with a third of the dessert syrup. Add the remaining crème patissière and candied fruit mixture, spreading it neatly. Top with the final cake layer and brush with the remainder of the dessert syrup.

5. Spread the entire cake with the refrigerated crème patissière. Chill in the refrigerator for 1 hour.

6. Roll out the almond paste to use as a covering for the cake. Roll out like dough, using confectioners' sugar rather than flour to roll it on and keep it from sticking. Cover a cold

surface with a light layer of confectioners' sugar. Shape the paste into a ball and flatten it. Cover the top lightly with confectioners' sugar and roll with a rolling pin. Add more sugar as necessary to prevent sticking. Roll the paste into a circle large enough to completely cover the top and sides of the cake. Pick up the dough like pastry. Cover the cake, pressing the dough and shaping it with the hands and fingers. Chill.

7. Using the chocolate icing and a pastry bag, squeeze out decorations on the surface of the cake. The traditional icing garnish is in script. The word Ambassadeur is piped out over the almond paste covering.

Yield: 8 or more servings.

	Almond paste
In a mixing bowl, combine the almond powder and confectioners' sugar. Add the egg white and blend quickly until smooth. **Yield:** About 1 cup.	⅔ cup plus 2 tablespoons powdered almonds 1¾ cups plus 2 tablespoons sifted confectioners' sugar 1 egg white from a small egg

	Chocolate icing
1. Melt the chocolate in the top of a double boiler over hot, not boiling, water. 2. Sift the sugar. Add the sugar and butter to the chocolate, stirring until smooth. Remove the saucepan from the heat and add the water, 1 tablespoon at a time. This cools the mixture a bit. 3. The mixture must be lukewarm when it is used or it will not spread or ooze from a tube properly. 4. Spread the icing on a cake or use it for decoration. **Yield:** About ¾ cup.	3½ ounces (3½ squares) semisweet chocolate ½ cup confectioners' sugar 2½ tablespoons butter, cut into pieces 2 tablespoons cold water

Marzapane (*An Italian almond cake*)

1. Preheat the oven to 350 degrees. 2. Beat the egg whites until they stand in very stiff peaks. 3. Beat in the sugar and fold in the almonds until thoroughly blended. Add the liqueur. 4. Pour the flour into a standard jelly roll pan measuring about 10 to 15 inches. Smooth it over with a spatula and cover the flour neatly with 4 overlapping sheets of rice paper. (The flour acts as insulation to keep the rice paper from burning.) Spoon the almond mixture on top and smooth it over with a	7 egg whites 3 cups superfine sugar 8 cups ground almonds 2 tablespoons Arum (an Italian orange liqueur available in liquor shops), or Grand Marnier 5 cups flour 6 sheets rice paper

spatula almost but not quite to the edge of the pan. Cover with 2 sheets of rice paper. Bake for 15 to 20 minutes. Remove the cake. Discard the flour and serve.

Yield: 12 or more servings.

Tourte Landaise *(An egg cake from the Landes region of France)*

½ pound sweet butter
4¼ cups cake flour
1 tablespoon baking powder
½ teaspoon salt
1 cup plus 2 tablespoons sugar
4 eggs, separated
1 cup milk
2 tablespoons lemon juice
3 tablespoons Pernod, Ricard or other anise-flavored liqueur
Crème patissière (see recipe page 572)

1. Place the butter in a heavy saucepan and let stand over gentle heat until melted. Let cool, but the butter should remain liquid.

2. Preheat the oven to 325 degrees.

3. Put the flour in a mixing bowl and add the baking powder and salt. Add the sugar and blend well. Make a well in the center of the flour and add the yolks, stirring and mixing. Add the milk alternately with the melted butter and, when blended, beat the batter with the hands. Combine the lemon juice and Pernod and add.

4. Beat the egg whites until stiff and fold them in.

5. Butter two 6-cup charlotte molds and add half the batter to each. Bake for 1 hour and increase the heat to 350 degrees. Bake for 10 minutes longer. Let stand briefly and then unmold the cakes. Let cool to room temperature. Serve sliced with crème patissière.

Yield: 8 to 12 servings.

Hazelnut Cheesecake

It is fascinating to discover the extent to which one ingredient can alter, even glorify, the nature of a dish. Some years ago we came into possession of a cheesecake recipe that seemed to be the essence of all great cheesecakes. It was delicate, rich and subtly flavored. Moreover, it was ultimately refined in texture. Sometime later we purchased a pound of toasted hazelnuts. These we ground and blended into the cake's batter. The result is to our minds a paradigm of cheesecakes. We hasten to add that hazelnuts are a luxury. Many supermarkets carry untoasted hazelnuts that may be roasted at home.

1. Because of the importance of oven temperature, the nuts must be toasted well in advance of proceeding with the recipe. If your hazelnuts are untoasted, preheat the oven to 400 degrees. Place the nuts on a baking sheet or in a skillet and bake them, stirring them often so that they brown evenly. When nicely browned, remove them and let cool.

2. When ready to make the cheesecake, preheat the oven to 300 degrees.

3. Place the nuts in the container of an electric blender or food processor and blend. If you want a crunchy texture, blend them until coarse-fine. If you want a smooth texture, blend them until they are almost pastelike.

4. Butter the inside of a metal cake pan 8 inches wide and 3 inches deep. Do not use a springform pan.

5. Sprinkle the inside with graham-cracker crumbs and shake the crumbs around the bottom and sides until coated. Shake out the excess crumbs and set the pan aside.

6. Place the cream cheese, cream, eggs, sugar and vanilla in the bowl of an electric mixer. Start beating at low speed and, as the ingredients blend, increase the speed to high. Continue beating until thoroughly blended and smooth. Add the nuts and continue beating until thoroughly blended.

7. Pour and scrape the batter into the prepared pan and shake gently to level the mixture.

8. Set the pan inside a slightly wider pan and pour boiling water into the large pan to a depth of about ½ inch. Do not let the edge of the cheesecake pan touch the other larger pan. Set the pans thus arranged inside the oven and bake for 2 hours. At the end of that time, turn off the oven heat and let the cake sit in the oven for 1 hour longer.

9. Lift the cake out of its water bath and place it on a rack. Let the cake stand for at least 2 hours.

10. Place a round cake plate over the cake and carefully turn both upside down to unmold the cake. Serve lukewarm or at room temperature.

Yield: 12 or more servings.

Note: The consistency of this cake is softer than most cheesecakes.

1½ cups shelled, toasted, hulled hazelnuts, or blanched, toasted almonds
Butter

⅓ cup graham-cracker crumbs, approximately

2 pounds cream cheese, at room temperature

½ cup heavy cream

4 eggs

1¾ cups sugar

1 teaspoon vanilla extract

Gingerbread

1 cup molasses (do not use blackstrap molasses)
½ pound butter
1 egg
1 cup sugar
2¼ cups flour
1½ teaspoons baking soda
1½ teaspoons ground ginger
1 teaspoon ground cinnamon
½ teaspoon ground cloves
¼ teaspoon grated nutmeg
Grated peel of 1 orange
Salt
½ cup boiling water
3 tablespoons sour cream

1. Preheat the oven to 350 degrees.
2. Combine the molasses and butter in a saucepan and bring just to the boil, stirring. Let cool.
3. Combine in the bowl of an electric mixer the egg and granulated sugar. Beat to blend.
4. Sift together the flour, baking soda, ginger, cinnamon, cloves and nutmeg. Add the orange peel and salt.
5. Gradually add the dry ingredients to the egg mixture. Spoon and scrape in the molasses mixture while beating. Add the boiling water and sour cream. Blend well.
6. Pour the mixture into a buttered 9- x 13-inch pan. Bake for 50 minutes. The center of the gingerbread will sink when it cools. Serve, if desired, with applesauce or sweetened whipped cream.

Yield: 8 to 12 servings.

Date-Nut Cake

8 tablespoons (1 stick) butter plus butter for greasing the pan
Flour
1 cup pitted diced dates
¾ cup dark seedless raisins
¼ cup golden seedless raisins
1 teaspoon baking soda
1 cup boiling water
1 cup sugar
1 teaspoon vanilla
1 egg
1⅓ cups sifted flour
¾ cup walnuts broken into small pieces

1. Preheat the oven to 350 degrees.
2. Butter a standard loaf pan (9½- x 5½- x 2¾-inches). Line the bottom with a rectangle of wax paper. Butter this rectangle and sprinkle with flour. Shake out the excess flour.
3. Put the dates and raisins in a mixing bowl. Dissolve the baking soda with the boiling water and pour it over the date mixture.
4. Cream together the sugar and 8 tablespoons butter. Beat in the vanilla and egg. Add the flour and mix well. Add the date mixture, including the liquid. Add the walnuts. Please note that this will be a quite liquid batter.
5. Pour the mixture into the prepared pan and smooth over the top. Place in the oven and bake from 1 hour to 1 hour and 10 minutes, or until the top of the cake is dark brown and a knife inserted in the center comes out clean.
6. Let cool for about 5 minutes. Unmold onto a rack. Remove the paper.

Yield: 1 loaf.

Bourbon-Pecan Cake

1. Preheat the oven to 350 degrees.
2. Put the butter into the bowl of an electric mixer. Start beating and gradually add the sugar, beating on high. Add the eggs, one at a time, beating well after each addition.
3. Sift together the baking powder, flour and salt. Beat the flour mixture, maple syrup and bourbon into the creamed butter, adding the ingredients alternately. Stir in the pecans.
4. Butter a small tube pan (one that measures 9½ inches in diameter, 6 cups, is suitable), loaf or Bundt pan and spoon in the mixture, smoothing it over on top.
5. Bake for 45 to 50 minutes. Let cool for 10 minutes. Remove from the pan and let cool. Serve sprinkled with confectioners' sugar.

Yield: 8 or more servings.

8 tablespoons butter at room temperature
½ cup dark brown sugar
2 large eggs
2½ teaspoons baking powder
2 cups flour
Salt to taste
½ cup maple syrup
½ cup bourbon, rum or Cognac
1½ cups coarsely chopped pecans
Confectioners' sugar for garnish

No-bake Fruitcake

1. Put the raisins, dates, figs, coconut and walnuts through a food chopper, using the medium knife. Or chop coarsely, using a food processor. Do not overblend, however.
2. Empty the mixture into a large mixing bowl and add the salt and vanilla and, if desired, the rum or Cognac. Blend well.
3. Spoon and pack the mixture into a mold. Two 6-cup loaf pans are suitable. Cover and place a weight on top. Refrigerate 3 days, or keep in a cold place to "age." Serve thinly sliced.

Yield: 5 pounds.

1 pound seedless raisins
1 pound pitted dates
1 pound dried figs or figlets
1 pound shredded coconut
1 pound shelled walnuts
¼ teaspoon salt
1 teaspoon vanilla extract
¼ cup rum or Cognac, optional

Mary Ann's Fruitcake

1. Preheat the oven to 250 degrees. Butter the inside of a 10-inch, 12-cup tube pan. Sprinkle liberally with flour and shake out the excess. Set the pan aside.
2. In a large mixing bowl, combine the raisins and pecan meats. Sprinkle the flour and salt over all and toss with the hands until thoroughly blended. Set aside.
3. Place the butter in the bowl of an electric beater. Start beating and gradually add the sugar. Cream the mixture well and add the egg yolks one at a time, beating constantly. Blend the soda and water and add it, beating. Beat in the Grand

1 pound golden seedless raisins
1 pound pecan meats, broken
3 cups sifted flour
1 teaspoon salt
1 pound butter at room temperature
2 cups sugar
6 eggs, separated
1 teaspoon baking soda
1 tablespoon warm water
¼ cup Grand Marnier

Marnier. Pour this mixture into the nut mixture and blend together with the hands.

4. Beat the whites until stiff and fold them in with the hands. Continue folding until the whites are not apparent.

5. Spoon and scrape the mixture into the prepared pan, smoothing the top with a spatula. Bake for 2 to 2¼ hours, or until the cake is puffed above the pan and nicely browned on top. If the cake starts to brown too soon, cover with aluminum foil. Remove the cake from the pan shortly after it is baked. Tapping the bottom of the cake pan with a heavy knife will help loosen it. Store the cake for at least 10 days. If desired, add an occasional touch of Cognac or rum to the cake as it stands. Keep it closely covered and refrigerated until ready to use.

Yield: 1 10-inch cake.

Creole Pralines

2 cups white sugar
1 cup dark brown sugar
¼ pound butter
1 cup milk
2 tablespoons corn syrup
4 cups pecan halves

1. Combine all the ingredients except the pecans in a heavy 3-quart saucepan. Cook for 20 minutes, stirring constantly, after the boil is reached.

2. Add the pecans and continue cooking until the mixture forms a soft ball when dropped into cold water.

3. Arrange several sheets of wax paper over layers of newspapers.

4. Stir the praline mixture well. Drop it by tablespoons onto the sheets of wax paper. Let cool. When cool, stack the pralines in an airtight container with wax paper between the layers.

Yield: 2 dozen.

Honey Brownies

4 tablespoons butter
4 squares (ounces) unsweetened chocolate
4 eggs
½ teaspoon salt
1 cup sugar
1 cup honey
1 teaspoon vanilla extract

1. Preheat the oven to 325 degrees.

2. Melt the butter and chocolate over low heat in a heavy saucepan.

3. Beat the eggs and salt in a mixing bowl until thick and pale yellow. Add the sugar and honey gradually, beating until the mixture is light in texture.

4. Add the melted chocolate and butter and vanilla. Stir in the flour. Add the nuts. Pour the mixture into a 9-inch square

pan and bake for 45 minutes, or until done. Cut in squares when cool.

Yield: About 16 brownies.

1 cup plus 2 tablespoons sifted flour
1 cup chopped pecans or walnuts

Chocolate Truffles

The only shameful thing about chocolate truffles is that they are like fresh roasted peanuts, insidiously good and, therefore, irresistible.

1. Preheat the oven to 200 degrees or lower.
2. Place the chocolate in a heatproof bowl and place the bowl in the oven. Watch carefully and remove the bowl just when the chocolate has softened.
3. Immediately beat in the butter, yolks and rum with a wire whisk. Beat with the whisk until the mixture becomes workable. Chill the chocolate mixture briefly until it can be shaped into balls between the palms of the hands. Shape the chocolate into round balls about 1 inch in diameter and roll them in powdered cocoa and/or confectioners' sugar. Arrange the "truffles" on a rack and let stand in a cool place for several hours.

Yield: 80 to 90 truffles.

1 pound semisweet chocolate
½ pound butter at room temperature
6 egg yolks
6 tablespoons dark rum
¾ cup powdered cocoa
¾ cup confectioners' sugar

Greek Easter Cookies

1. Preheat the oven to 350 degrees.
2. In a bowl, cream the butter and add the sugar. Beat until creamy. Add the egg, cream and orange liqueur and beat the mixture for 5 minutes.
3. In another bowl sift together the flour, salt and baking powder and blend into the butter mixture, ½ cup at a time, to form a soft dough.
4. Form the dough into 1½-inch balls and shape into twists. Brush the twists with egg yolk and sprinkle with sesame seeds. Place on cooky sheets and bake for 30 minutes, or until they turn a light golden color.

Yield: About 48 cookies.

½ cup sweet butter at room temperature
½ cup confectioners' sugar
1 egg
¼ cup heavy cream
2 tablespoons orange liqueur, or brandy
3 cups flour
½ teaspoon salt
1 teaspoon baking powder
1 egg yolk
Sesame seeds

Swiss Walnut Fingers

The cookies:

- **1 cup ground walnuts, about ¼ pound**
- **1 cup ground almonds, about ¼ pound**
- **½ cup flour**
- **3 tablespoons superfine sugar**
- **1 teaspoon grated orange rind**
- **¼ teaspoon ground allspice**
- **¼ teaspoon ground mace or nutmeg**
- **¼ teaspoon ground cinnamon**
- **½ cup chopped citron or other fruitcake mixture**
- **1 egg white, stiffly beaten**
- **1 tablespoon honey**
- **1 tablespoon Grand Marnier or Cognac**

The glaze:

- **2 tablespoons confectioners' sugar**
- **1 tablespoon water**
- **1 tablespoon Grand Marnier or Cognac**

1. Preheat the oven to 325 degrees.
2. Combine the ground nuts, flour, sugar, orange rind, spices, chopped citron and egg white. Heat the honey with the Grand Marnier and add it. Blend well with the hands.
3. Shape the batter into a rectangle about 3 inches by 12 inches. Cut into fingers about ¾ inch thick. Place the fingers on an oiled baking sheet and bake for ½ hour.
4. For the glaze, combine the sugar, water and Grand Marnier. Brush the mixture over the fingers and let stand until dry.

Yield: About 16 cookies.

Tuiles d'Amande *(Almond cookies)*

- **1 cup chopped almonds**
- **½ cup sugar**
- **3 tablespoons flour**
- **1 large egg**
- **1 teaspoon vanilla**

1. Preheat the oven to 375 degrees.
2. The texture of the almonds must not be too fine. The coarseness of the pieces should be like that of rice.
3. Place the almonds in a bowl and add the remaining ingredients. Blend well.
4. Grease a baking sheet with butter and sprinkle with flour. Shake off excess flour. Spoon about 1½ teaspoons of the mixture onto the prepared sheet. There should be about 32 mounds with about 2 inches of space between each. Flatten each spoonful with the tines of a dampened fork.
5. Place in the oven and bake for 8 to 10 minutes, or until golden brown. Do not let them become too dark.

6. Immediately remove them and place them top-side down in a small round ring mold. The purpose of this is to give each tile a slightly curved shape. Let cool briefly and turn out onto a flat surface. Let cool and serve.

Yield: 32 cookies.

Almond Macaroons

1. Preheat the oven to 325 degrees.

2. Cut the almond paste into ½-inch pieces and place in the container of a food processor fitted with a steel blade.

3. Add the sugar, 2 egg whites, almond extract and salt. Blend well until smooth and no lumps remain in the almond paste.

4. The mixture should be soft but not loose. If it seems too stiff, add the remaining egg white to a mixing bowl and beat lightly. Add it, a little at a time, to the almond mixture. Blend after each addition.

5. Spoon and scrape the mixture into a bowl and beat with a wooden spoon.

6. Cut a rectangle of brown paper (from a grocery bag) to fit a cooky sheet. Drop the dough by spoonfuls onto the paper, flattening the mounds lightly with the back of a spoon. Place them about 1½ inches apart. If desired, the paste may be squeezed from a pastry bag onto the sheet. Bake for 30 minutes, or until lightly browned.

7. Cool on a rack. To remove the macaroons, dampen the bottom of the baking paper. Continue dampening slowly and lightly until the macaroons loosen easily.

Yield: 18 or more macaroons, depending on size.

Note: Almond paste is available in cans in fancy food markets and many supermarkets. Do not use almond pastry filling for macaroons.

½ pound almond paste (see note)
1 cup granulated sugar
2 or 3 egg whites
¼ teaspoon pure almond extract
⅛ teaspoon salt

Tozzetti or Biscotti *(Hazelnut cookies)*

Whenever one travels for mostly gastronomic reasons, some dishes will be indelibly etched in the mind. Others will demand a few bites and then be forever lost to memory. On a recent trip through Italy, we sampled many desserts. In retrospect, one that remains entrenched in our memories is the fine hazelnut cookies we were served in the home of Jo and Roberto Bettoja in Rome. These cookies are prepared in many places throughout the world, including Little Italy in New York. Generally, they are made of almonds. Traditionally, they are dipped into a sweet wine before eating. They are also delicious when brushed with a little anise-flavored liqueur.

2	cups flour
1⅓	cups sugar
2	large eggs
1	tablespoon grated lemon rind
¼	cup anise-flavored liqueur such as Sambuca
¼	cup rum
1½	cups peeled, blanched hazelnuts, or whole or slivered almonds
2	teaspoons baking powder

1. Preheat the oven to 350 degres.

2. Lightly oil a large baking pan and dust with flour. Shake off excess flour.

3. Combine the flour, sugar, eggs, lemon rind, liqueur and rum in a mixing bowl and beat with a wooden spoon until thoroughly blended.

4. Beat in the hazelnuts and baking powder.

5. Using the hands, pick up half the dough and shape it into a long sausage shape. Arrange it on the prepared baking pan, off center and not too close to the edge of the pan. Arrange the other half alongside but not too close. Both masses will spread as they bake.

6. Place in the oven and bake for 1 hour. Remove the pan and let cool for about 20 minutes.

7. Carefully and gently run a spatula or pancake turner under the 2 pastries. Let stand until almost at room temperature. Using a serrated bread knife, cut each pastry into crosswise slices, each about 1-inch thick. Arrange these in one layer on a baking sheet and return to the oven to dry out, about 10 minutes. Let cool and store. These cookies are improved if a little anisette or other anise-flavored liqueur is poured or brushed over them in advance of serving.

Yield: About 36 cookies.

Polvorones *(Mexican butter cookies)*

½	pound butter at room temperature
⅓	cup confectioners' sugar
1	egg yolk
1	tablespoon Cognac, rum, kirsch or mirabelle
2	cups flour
1	cup granulated (not superfine) sugar
3	tablespoons cinnamon

1. Preheat the oven to 325 degrees.

2. Place the butter in the container of an electric mixer. Add the confectioners' sugar and start beating. Add the egg yolk and continue creaming with the beater. Add the Cognac and beat in the flour.

3. Shape the dough into 52 balls, each about 1 inch in diameter. Arrange the balls on an ungreased baking sheet and bake for 25 minutes, or until firm.

4. Let cool briefly and roll each ball in a blend of sugar and cinnamon.

Yield: 52 cookies.

Pine Nut Cookies

1. Preheat the oven to 300 degrees.
2. Cream together the butter and sugar.
3. Beat in the egg yolk, vanilla and flour. Mix in the nuts.
4. Drop the batter, a teaspoon or so at a time, onto a buttered, floured cooky sheet. Bake 20 to 25 minutes, or until pale golden. While still hot, remove with a spatula to a rack and let cool.

Yield: About 30 cookies.

¼	pound sweet butter
½	cup granulated sugar
1	egg yolk
1	teaspoon vanilla
1	cup sifted flour
½	cup toasted pine nuts

Mint Surprise Cookies

1. All of the ingredients should be at room temperature. Cream the butter and gradually add the granulated sugar, then the brown sugar. Beat in the egg, water and vanilla.
2. Sift together the flour, baking soda and salt. Blend into the butter mixture. Wrap in wax paper and chill for at least 2 hours.
3. Preheat the oven to 375 degrees.
4. Enclose each thin mint with about 1 tablespoon of the dough. The mints may be cut in half for a smaller cooky. Place on a cooky sheet that has been greased or lined with parchment paper. Top each cooky with a walnut half. Bake in the oven for 10 to 12 minutes, until lightly browned. Let stand a minute or so, then remove and cool on a cake rack.

Yield: About 24 cookies.

½	cup butter
½	cup granulated sugar
¼	cup firmly packed brown sugar
1	egg
1½	teaspoons water
½	teaspoon vanilla
1½	cups flour
½	teaspoon baking soda
½	teaspoon salt
24	thin, chocolate-covered mints, approximately
24	walnut halves, approximately

Baked Apples Pavillon

Years ago, when Le Pavillon was in its heyday as a restaurant of splendor and excellence, the pastry chef's baked apples occupied a place alongside the chilled oeufs à la neige, the mousses au chocolat and the gateaux St. Honoré on the cold dessert display. These were apple halves poached in syrup, filled with fruits and then topped with pastry cream and baked. Not the sort of baked apples likely to be found in a roadside diner.

5 medium-to-large-size
   apples, about 2 pounds
1 cup water
½ cup sugar
2 tablespoons honey
   Juice of ½ lemon
1½ cups bananas cut into ½-
   inch cubes, or crushed
   pineapple
¼ cup chopped ginger in syrup
   (sold in bottles), or
   crystallized ginger, or use an
   equal amount of kumquats
   in syrup
2 tablespoons syrup from the
   bottled ginger or kumquats
2 tablespoons dark rum
3 cups crème patissière (see
   recipe below)
3 tablespoons crumbs made
   from ladyfingers or
   spongecake

1. Peel the apples and split them in half. Using a melon ball cutter, scoop out the core of each apple. Trim away and discard the stem line leading from the core.

2. Combine the water, sugar, honey and lemon juice in a skillet large enough to hold the apple halves in one layer. Add the apple halves and cook, turning gently once or twice so that the apples cook evenly. Poach them for 5 to 8 minutes until just cooked. Do not overcook or they will become mushy.

3. Let the apple halves cool. Drain them upside down on a rack, but do not discard the cooking syrup.

4. Preheat the oven to 450 degrees.

5. Put the cubed bananas, chopped ginger and ginger syrup in a saucepan. Add ½ cup of the syrup in which the apples cooked. Bring to the boil and remove from the heat. Let cool. It will thicken slightly as it stands.

6. Arrange the apple halves cored side up on a baking dish large enough to hold them in one layer.

7. Spoon equal portions of the fruit mixture into and over the center of each apple half.

8. Blend the crème patissière with the rum and ½ cup of reserved syrup from the cooked apples.

9. Spoon the crème patissière over the filled apple halves. Sprinkle with the crumbs.

10. Place in the oven and bake for 15 to 20 minutes. Serve hot or lukewarm.

Yield: 10 servings.

Crème patissière (*Pastry cream*)

1½ cups milk
½ cup heavy cream
4 egg yolks
½ cup sugar
3 tablespoons cornstarch

1. Blend 1 cup of the milk and the cream in a saucepan and bring to the boil.

2. As the liquid is heated, put the egg yolks into a mixing bowl and beat until pale yellow. Add the cornstarch to the yolk mixture and beat well. Add the remaining ½ cup of milk and beat until blended.

3. When the milk and cream are at the boil, remove from the heat. Add the yolk mixture, beating rapidly with a wire whisk.

4. Return to the heat and bring to the boil, stirring constantly with the whisk. When thickened and at the boil, remove from the heat and let cool, stirring occasionally.

Yield: About 3 cups.

Apple Crisp

1. Preheat the oven to 375 degrees.

2. Combine the sugar, flour and butter in a mixing bowl and mix well with the fingers. Set aside.

3. Peel, quarter and core the apples. Cut the apple quarters into thin slices and place the slices in a bowl. Blend the cinnamon and nutmeg and sprinkle over the apples. Sprinkle with lemon rind. Add the lemon juice and toss with the hands to blend.

4. Arrange the slices in a not-too-shallow baking dish. Cover with the butter and sugar mixture, smoothing it over.

5. Place the dish in the oven. (If the ingredients are close to brimming over, place a pan under the dish to catch the overflow.) Bake for 1 hour.

Yield: 8 servings.

1½	cups brown sugar
1	cup flour
12	tablespoons butter
6 to	8 cooking apples, about 3 pounds
¼	teaspoon ground cinnamon
¼	teaspoon ground nutmeg
	Grated rind of 1 lemon
	Juice of ½ lemon

Soufflé aux Bananes

1. Generously butter the inside of 9- or 10-cup soufflé dish and put it in the freezer to chill.

2. In a mixing bowl, combine the 6 tablespoons of butter, flour and ½ cup of the sugar and work with the fingers to blend well. Shape into a ball.

3. Peel the bananas and cut into slices. Blend in a food processor or electric blender. There should be about 1½ cups. Pour the purée into a saucepan and add the milk, stirring to blend. Bring to the boil. Add the butter and flour ball, stirring constantly until thickened and smooth. Blend the cornstarch with the rum and stir it in.

4. Beat the yolks lightly, then beat them into the banana mixture. Cook, stirring rapidly, for about 30 seconds, then remove from the heat. Continue beating off heat for about 1 minute. Spoon the mixture into a mixing bowl, cover with a round of buttered wax paper and let cool.

5. Meanwhile, preheat the oven to 375 degrees.

6. Beat the egg whites until they start to stand in peaks and gradually beat in the remaining ¾ cup of sugar. Continue beating the whites to the stiff meringue stage. Using a wire whisk, beat about ⅓ of the whites into the soufflé mixture. Fold in the remaining whites with a rubber spatula.

6	tablespoons butter
½	cup flour
1¼	cups sugar
½	pound ripe, sweet but firm bananas (about 4)
3	cups milk
1	tablespoon cornstarch
3	tablespoons dark rum, kirsch or Cognac
8	eggs, separated

7. Remove the soufflé dish from the freezer and sprinkle the inside with sugar. Shake the sugar around to coat the bottom and sides. Shake out the excess sugar. Spoon the banana mixture into the soufflé dish. As a safeguard you may want to place a baking dish or sheet of aluminum foil on the bottom of the oven to catch any drippings. Place the soufflé in the oven and bake for 15 minutes. Reduce the oven heat to 350 degrees and bake for 30 minutes longer.

Yield: 6 to 8 servings.

Bing Cherries with Liqueurs

2½	quarts Bing cherries with stem
⅔	cup cassis syrup, available in wine and spirits shops
⅓	cup framboise, available in wine and spirits shops

Rinse the cherries and drain well. Place in a bowl and pour the liqueurs over them.

Yield: 8 or more servings.

Mango Slices with Champagne

3	very ripe but firm mangoes
½	cup confectioners' sugar
¼	cup framboise
	Chilled champagne

1. Peel the mangoes. Run a knife around the perimeter of the mangoes all the way to the pit. Use a large kitchen spoon and, starting at one end, carefully push the spoon's blade around the large pit of the fruit. Repeat on the other half of the mangoes. Discard the pit.

2. Cut the mango flesh into strips. Place the strips in a bowl and sprinkle with sugar. Add the framboise and chill. Spoon the fruit and liquid into 6 serving dishes and add champagne (or any good dry white wine) to taste.

Yield: 6 servings.

Oranges Mexicaine

2	cups orange wedges
¼	cup confectioners' sugar
2	tablespoons lime juice
1½	ounces tequila
1	ounce Cointreau

1. Put the orange wedges in a mixing bowl and sprinkle with the sugar and lime juice. Refrigerate.

2. When ready to serve, add the tequila and Cointreau.

Yield: 6 servings.

Southern Ambrosia

1. Peel and slice the oranges and put them into a crystal bowl.

2. Crack the coconut and remove the meat. Pare away the black skin and finely grate the pulp. Add this to the bowl. Sprinkle with confectioners' sugar and chill until ready to serve.

Yield: 6 servings.

Note: Some people add cubed bananas to this, others add pineapple cubes and some add a final garnish of whipped cream, but not in my mother's household.

4	large, sweet, seedless oranges
1	fresh coconut
⅓	cup confectioners' sugar

Pears à la Vigneronne

1. Peel and core the pears and cut each of them into eighths. Place the pears in a saucepan and add the wine and sugar.

2. Peel the lemon and cut the peel into very fine, julienne strips. Reserve the lemon for another use. Add the peel to the saucepan. Bring to the boil and simmer for 5 to 10 minutes, or until pears are tender. Transfer the pears and lemon peel to a serving dish.

3. Bring the liquid in the saucepan to the boil and add the remaining ingredients. Bring to the boil and cook for about 10 minutes. Pour the sauce over the pears. Let cool and chill.

Yield: 6 servings.

2½	pounds fresh, ripe, unblemished pears
2	cups dry white wine
½	cup sugar
1	lemon
1	2-inch length of cinnamon, or ¼ teaspoon ground
1	1-inch length vanilla, or 1 teaspoon vanilla extract
¼	cup orange marmalade
¼	cup apricot preserves

Pears Stuffed with Gorgonzola

1. Peel the pears but leave the stems intact.

2. Neatly slice off the stem end of the pears about one-third of the way down. Reserve both the base and top of the pears.

3. Using a melon ball scoop, scoop out the core, leaving a neat round cavity for stuffing.

4. Arrange the pear bottoms in a heavy casserole and replace the tops. Scatter the ginger around the pears and add the wine and water. Sprinkle with sugar and lemon juice. Cover with a tight-fitting lid and cook for about 10 minutes, or until tender but firm.

5. Mash the Gorgonzola with a fork until it is softened.

6	large pears, about ½ pound each
12	very thin slices fresh ginger
1	cup dry white wine
½	cup water
3	tablespoons sugar
	Juice of ½ lemon
½	pound Gorgonzola cheese at room temperature
⅔	cup pistachio nuts

Remove the pears from the casserole. Stuff the cavity of each pear with equal amounts of cheese. Replace the tops and set aside.

6. Cook down the liquid in the casserole until it is reduced to about ¼ cup.

7. Chop the pistachios. Dip the bottom of each pear in the syrup, then in pistachios. Return the pears, stem side up, to the casserole and spoon any remaining sauce over the pears. Add the remaining pistachios to the syrup and serve while still warm.

Yield: 6 servings.

Pears in Caramel Syrup

8 firm, unblemished, ripe Comice or Anjou pears
Juice of 1 lemon
2 cups sugar
⅓ cup coffee liqueur
Whipped cream, optional

1. Peel the pears, leaving the stem on. As each pear is peeled, drop it into water with lemon juice added to prevent discoloration.

2. Measure 3 cups of water into a saucepan and add 1 cup of sugar. Bring to the boil and add the pears. Cook the pears in the liquid, turning them gently on occasion, until they are tender but firm, about 20 minutes. Carefully remove the pears and reserve the syrup. Arrange the pears neatly on a serving dish.

3. Pour 1 cup of the reserved syrup into a saucepan and add the remaining 1 cup of sugar. Bring to the boil. Cook for 5 to 10 minutes until the syrup starts to caramelize, shaking the saucepan in a circular fashion. When quite brown but not burned, quickly remove the saucepan from the heat and add the remaining syrup. Bring to the boil again and add the coffee liqueur. Pour the sauce over the pears and chill. Serve cold with whipped cream if desired.

Yield: 8 servings.

Eugénie

1 pint red, ripe strawberries, plus 6 more for garnish

1. Pick over the berries and hull them. Rinse well and drain. Pat dry.

2. Cut 1 pint of berries into eighths and place in a bowl. Add 1 tablespoon of kirsch and set aside.

3. Lightly butter an 8-cup soufflé dish. Refrigerate.

4. Start beating the cream with a wire whisk or electric beater and, as it starts to stiffen, gradually beat in 3 tablespoons of sugar. Continue beating the cream until stiff.

5. Soften the gelatin and water in a small saucepan and heat, stirring, until the gelatin dissolves. Scrape this into a large mixing bowl and add remaining kirsch and 1 cup of the whipped cream, stirring rapidly with a whisk to blend well. Beat in 2 more tablespoons sugar and stir in the strawberries.

6. Add the remaining cream and fold it in with a rubber spatula. Spoon into the prepared mold. Refrigerate for several hours, or until set.

7. When ready to serve, dip the mold into a basin of hot water. Remove, dip again. Remove and dip a third time. Place a round serving dish over the mold, invert the dish and unmold the Eugénie. Garnish with the remaining strawberries, left whole or cut in half.

Yield: 10 to 12 servings.

4	tablespoons kirsch or framboise
3	cups heavy cream
5	tablespoons sugar
2	envelopes unflavored gelatin
¼	cup cold water

Macedoine de Fruits (A mixed fruit dessert)

1. Combine all the fruits in a mixing bowl and sprinkle with sugar. Blend well. Chill until ready to serve.

2. When ready to serve, add the Cognac, kirsch and Grand Marnier. Stir to blend and serve immediately.

Yield: About 6 servings.

1½	cups seedless grapes
1½	cups peeled, seeded peaches cut into wedges
1½	cups peeled, diced apples
1½	cups seedless orange sections
1½	cups peeled pears cut into wedges
5	tablespoons confectioners' sugar
3	tablespoons Cognac
3	tablespoons kirsch
3	tablespoons Grand Marnier

Miveh Makhlou (Persian fruit mélange)

Rosewater is a clear, highly aromatic flavoring that smells strongly of roses. It is much used in Middle Eastern cookery, particularly desserts, such as this Persian fruit mélange.

1 honeydew melon
1 cantaloupe
1 pint strawberries, stemmed
2 tablespoons slivered
  almonds
¼ cup chopped, skinless
  pistachios
1 cup seedless grapes
2 tablespoons rosewater
1½ cups orange juice, sweetened
  to taste
½ cup kirsch

1. Split the honeydew melon and the cantaloupe in half and scoop out the seeds. Using a melon baller, scoop out the flesh of both melons into a serving bowl.

2. Wash the berries under cold running water and pat dry. Add them to the bowl. Add the remaining ingredients and mix gently but thoroughly.

Yield: 8 servings.

Rote Grütze   *(A fruit and berry compote)*

1 1-pint-7-ounce bottle
  imported black currant
  beverage, available in
  specialty food shops
1 pint (2 cups) fresh or frozen
  raspberries
1 pint (2 cups) fresh or frozen
  blackberries
2 cups canned, undrained
  sour (tart) cherries
1 2-inch piece vanilla bean,
  or 1 teaspoon pure vanilla
  extract
  Peeled rind of ½ lemon
  Juice of 1 lemon
½ to 1 cup sugar
½ cup cornstarch
½ cup water
  Chilled heavy cream or
  whipped cream

1. Pour the black currant beverage into a large saucepan and add the raspberries, blackberries and cherries with their liquid. Split the vanilla bean in half and scrape the seeds into the mixture. Add the bean itself.

2. Add the lemon rind, lemon juice and sugar according to taste. Bring to the boil and stir until the sugar is thoroughly dissolved.

3. Blend the cornstarch and water and add it to the saucepan gradually, stirring constantly. Cook until thickened. Let cool. Remove the lemon rind and vanilla bean. Chill thoroughly. This compote should be served very cold. Serve with heavy cream or whipped cream.

Yield: 12 servings

Tapioca Pudding

I am not basically a dessert man. At least not in the passionate way of certain friends and acquaintances. I find most European pastries toothsome enough: a well-made roulade au chocolat; variations on a genoise; napoleons; éclairs; baked meringues. But these I can resist. Crêpes suzette have a certain appeal, but they do not interrupt my sleep with sweet anticipation.

No, it isn't these confections that make me salivate, that arouse the hounds of hunger at the conclusion of a meal. The dessert category that I find totally irresistible is purely and simply nursery desserts, those custards and mousses and glorious sensual puddings and sauces based on egg and cream. I am convinced that my craving for these desserts stems directly from the cradle and the years immediately following. First in a high chair, then sitting on a stack of Encyclopedia Brittanica (the telephone book in the town of my childhood was only a quarter-inch thick).

1. Combine the milk, tapioca and vanilla bean in a saucepan and bring to the boil, stirring constantly with a wooden spoon. Let cook for 6 to 7 minutes.

2. Combine the sugar and yolks in a mixing bowl and beat rapidly with a wire whisk until light and lemon-colored. Add a little of the hot tapioca mixture to the egg yolk mixture, stirring constantly. Return this mixture to the saucepan and, when it begins to boil, continue cooking, stirring constantly, for about 1 minute. Remove the vanilla bean. Pour the pudding into a serving dish and let cool. Chill until ready to serve.

Yield: 8 to 12 servings.

6 cups milk
½ cup minute tapioca
1 vanilla bean, or 1 teaspoon pure vanilla extract
½ cup sugar
3 egg yolks

Bread and Butter Pudding

1. Preheat the oven to 350 degrees.

2. Select a heatproof baking dish (ours was an oval one measuring 14- x 18- x 2-inches). Scatter the currants over the bottom.

3. Slice the bread. Preferably, the diameter of the bread should not exceed 3 inches. If much larger, cut the pieces in half. Cut off enough slices to cover the bottom of the dish neatly, the slices slightly overlapping top to bottom, arranging them in two or three rows as necessary. Butter each slice on one side only and arrange them buttered side up.

4. Beat the yolks, eggs and sugar until smooth. Stir in the milk until well blended. Strain this through a sieve over the bread.

5. Set the baking dish in a heatproof basin or larger baking dish. Add about 1 inch of water. Bring the water to the boil on top of the stove. Place in the oven and bake for 40 minutes to 1 hour, or until custard is set. Remove, place on a rack and cool. Serve sprinkled with confectioners' sugar.

Yield: 8 to 12 servings.

½ cup dried currants
18 slices untrimmed French bread, each slice about ½ inch thick
4 tablespoons melted butter
3 egg yolks
3 eggs
1 cup sugar
3 cups milk
Confectioners' sugar for garnish

Bread Pudding with Apples

1 pound firm but sweet cooking apples
2 tablespoons butter
1¼ cups sugar
¼ cup currants or raisins
¼ cup Calvados or applejack, optional
10 to 20 slices French bread, each slice about ½ inch thick
4 egg yolks
2 whole eggs
1 teaspoon pure vanilla extract
1 cup heavy cream
3 cups milk
Confectioners' sugar

1. Preheat the oven to 400 degrees.
2. Peel the apples then core, quarter and slice them thinly. There should be about 4 cups.
3. Heat the butter in a heavy skillet and add the apple slices. Sprinkle the apples with ¼ cup of sugar and add the currants. Sprinkle with Calvados and ignite it.
4. Arrange the bread slices, slightly overlapping, over the bottom of a baking dish. We used an 8- x 14-inch oval dish. Do not crowd the bread; use only enough to cover the bottom, slightly overlapping, in one layer. Spoon the apple mixture evenly over the bread.
5. Blend the yolks, whole eggs, the remaining cup of sugar, vanilla, cream and milk. Beat lightly and pour it over all. Set the baking dish in a larger baking dish and pour boiling water around it. Carefully place it in the oven and bake for 40 minutes. Carefully remove the pudding. When lukewarm, sprinkle the top evenly with confectioners' sugar put through a fine sieve. Run the pudding under the broiler until the top is nicely glazed.

Yield: 12 or more servings.

Riz à l'Impératrice   (*A molded rice dessert*)

1½ cups glacé fruitcake mix (candied citron, rind, cherries and so on, cut into small pieces)
1 tablespoon chopped candied ginger, optional
⅓ cup kirsch, mirabelle, framboise or other white liqueur
¾ cup rice
1 cup water
4 cups milk
1 vanilla bean, or 1 teaspoon pure vanilla extract
1¼ cups plus 1 tablespoon sugar
6 egg yolks
2 envelopes unflavored gelatin
1 cup heavy cream
Tangerine sections for garnish (see recipe below)

1. Place the candied fruit and ginger, if used, in a mixing bowl and add the liqueur. Let stand several hours or overnight.
2. Lightly oil an 8- or 9-cup decorative ring mold. Set aside.
3. Combine the rice with the water and bring to the boil. Drain.
4. Combine 3½ cups of milk and the rice in a small saucepan and bring to the boil. Add the vanilla bean, if it is to be used, and ¾ cup sugar. Stir and cover. Bring to the boil and simmer slowly for about 25 minutes, or until milk is absorbed. Remove the vanilla bean if used. The bean may be washed well, dried and stored in sugar for another use. If the vanilla bean is not used, add the vanilla extract at this point.
5. Combine the egg yolks and ½ cup of sugar in a mixing bowl and beat with a whisk or electric beater until light and lemon-colored. Beat in the gelatin.
6. Bring the remaining ½ cup of milk to the boil and gradually add it to the yolk mixture, beating. Bring to the boil, stir-

ring constantly. At the boil, remove the mixture from the heat and stir in the fruitcake mix plus the liqueur in which it soaked. Add the rice. Let cool.

7. Whip the cream, adding 1 tablespoon of sugar as it is beaten. When stiff, fold this into the rice mixture. Pour the mixture into the prepared mold and chill until firm.

8. Unmold onto a round platter and garnish with tangerine sections and whipped cream. Serve with apricot sauce.

Yield: 8 to 12 servings.

Whipped cream for garnish
Apricot sauce (see recipe below)

Divide 2 tangerines into sections. Remove and discard the threadlike membranes attached to the sections. Combine ¼ cup water and ¼ cup sugar in a saucepan and bring to the boil. Add the tangerine sections. Cover and simmer for about 5 minutes. Let cool in the syrup.

Tangerine sections for garnish

Combine the apricot jam and the water in a saucepan. Cook, stirring, until blended. Strain through a fine sieve. Let cool. Stir in the liqueur, if desired, and chill.

Yield: About 2¼ cups.

Apricot sauce

1	1-pound jar apricot jam or preserves
¼ to	½ cup water
¼	cup kirsch, mirabelle, framboise or other white liqueur, the same as used in the basic dessert, optional

Pouding au Liqueur

1. Preheat the oven to 400 degrees.

2. Melt the butter in a saucepan and add the sugar and flour, stirring with a whisk. Gradually add the milk, stirring rapidly with the whisk. When the mixture is thickened and smooth, remove it from the heat and add the yolks, one at a time, beating vigorously after each addition. Add the liqueur.

3. Beat the whites and fold them in.

4. Generously butter a 6-cup charlotte mold and pour in the mixture. Set the mold in a basin of water and bring the water to the boil on top of the stove. Set the dish in the oven and bake for 30 minutes. The pudding will rise like a soufflé and fall as it cools. Let stand until cool.

5. Run a knife around the inside rim of the mold. Unmold the pudding onto a serving dish. Serve with English custard flavored with the same liqueur as the pudding.

Yield: 6 to 10 servings.

4	tablespoons butter
½	cup sugar
½	cup flour
½	cup milk
5	eggs, separated
1	tablespoon Ricard, Pernod, framboise or other liqueur English custard (see recipe below)

English custard

5 egg yolks
⅔ cup sugar
2 cups milk
⅛ teaspoon salt

1. Place the yolks in a saucepan and add the sugar. Beat with a wire whisk until thick and lemon-colored.

2. Meanwhile, bring the milk almost, but not quite, to the boil.

3. Gradually add the milk to the yolk mixture, beating constantly. Use a wooden spoon and stir constantly, this way and that, making certain that the spoon touches all over the bottom of the saucepan. Cook, stirring, and add the salt. Cook until the mixture has a custardlike consistency and coats the sides of the spoon. Do not let the sauce boil, or it will curdle.

4. Immediately remove the sauce from the stove, but continue stirring. Set the saucepan in a basin of cold water to reduce the temperature. Let the sauce cool to room temperature. Add a tablespoon of liqueur. Chill for 1 hour or longer.

Yield: 8 to 12 servings.

Bavarois à la Vanille *(Vanilla-flavored Bavarian cream)*

4 cups milk
1 vanilla bean, split, or use 1½ teaspoons pure vanilla extract
8 egg yolks
1 cup sugar
3 envelopes unflavored gelatin
⅓ cup water
¼ cup mirabelle, kirsch or other liqueur, optional
2 cups heavy cream
English custard (see recipe above)
Whipped cream, optional

1. Bring the milk to the boil with the split vanilla bean. Do not boil further. If the bean is not to be used, add the vanilla extract later. Remove the vanilla bean, if used, rinse it off, dry it and reserve for later uses.

2. Place the yolks in a saucepan and add the sugar. Beat with a wire whisk until thick and lemon-colored.

3. Gradually add the milk to the yolk mixture, beating constantly. Use a wooden spoon and stir constantly, this way and that, making certain the spoon touches all over the bottom of the saucepan. Cook until the mixture has a custardlike consistency and coats the sides of the spoon. Do not let the sauce boil, or it will curdle. Add the vanilla extract, if used.

4. Soften the gelatin in the water and add it to the sauce, stirring to dissolve. Add the liqueur, if desired, and strain into a bowl. Let cool.

5. Whip the heavy cream until stiff and fold it into the sauce.

6. Rinse out a 10- to 12-cup ring mold without drying. Sprinkle the inside with sugar and shake out the excess. Add the custard mixture and place in the refrigerator. Chill several hours or overnight, until the custard is set.

7. When ready to serve, dip the mold into hot water and remove immediately. Wipe off and unmold. A damp, hot cloth could also be used on the mold. Serve with English custard

flavored with the same liqueur used in the Bavarian cream and, if desired, whipped cream.

Yield: 12 or more servings.

Pouding de Semoule *(Semolina pudding)*

1. Place the milk and ½ cup of the sugar in a saucepan and bring to the boil, stirring with a wire whisk.

2. Immediately start adding the cream of wheat, stirring vigorously with the whisk. Add the raisins and mint or vanilla extract. Cook, stirring frequently, for about 5 minutes.

3. Beat the yolks lightly. Turn off the heat beneath the cream of wheat mixture and immediately beat the yolks into the mixture. Reheat, while stirring, for about 5 seconds and remove the saucepan from the heat. Spoon the mixture into a mixing bowl. Let cool, but do not let the mixture chill or it will harden.

4. Whip the cream with the remaining sugar until stiff. Fold the whipped cream into the cream of wheat mixture. Pour the mixture into a lightly oiled 2½-quart mold and chill until firm. Unmold and serve with English custard flavored with Pernod and more sweetened whipped cream.

Yield: 10 to 12 servings.

4 cups milk
¾ cup sugar
1 cup quick-cooking cream of wheat
½ cup golden raisins
1 teaspoon mint extract, or pure vanilla extract
3 egg yolks
1 cup heavy cream
English custard (see recipe page 594)
Sweetened whipped cream

Rice Pudding

1. Pour the milk into a saucepan and add the vanilla bean or vanilla extract. Bring to the boil and add the rice and granulated sugar. Stir often from the bottom to prevent sticking. Cook until the rice is tender, about 40 minutes.

2. Add the raisins to a small bowl and pour boiling water over them. Let stand until rice is cooked.

3. Beat the eggs. Remove the rice from the heat and add the eggs, stirring rapidly.

4. Meanwhile, preheat the oven to 400 degrees.

5. Drain the raisins and add them to the cooked rice.

6. Grease a baking dish with the butter. We used an oval dish measuring 14- x 18- x 2-inches. Pour in the rice mixture. Sprinkle with cinnamon. Place the dish in a larger flameproof

7 cups milk
1 vanilla bean, or 1 teaspoon pure vanilla extract
1 cup rice
1½ cups granulated sugar
¾ cup raisins
2 large eggs
1 tablespoon butter
½ teaspoon ground cinnamon
2 tablespoons confectioners' sugar

dish and pour boiling water around it. Bring to the boil on top of the stove. Place the dish in the oven and bake for 30 minutes, or until custard is set. Remove from the oven and sprinkle with confectioners' sugar. Serve hot or cold.

Yield: 8 to 10 servings.

Charlotte Plombière

1½ cups glacé fruitcake mix (candied citron, rind, cherries and so on cut into small pieces)
¼ cup kirsch or other white liqueur
4 cups milk
1 vanilla bean, split, or use 1½ teaspoons pure vanilla extract
8 egg yolks
1 cup sugar
3 envelopes unflavored gelatin
⅓ cup water
16 to 18 "double" ladyfingers
2 cups heavy cream
Apricot sauce (see recipe page 593), or English custard (see recipe page 594)
Whipped cream, optional

1. Soak the fruitcake mix in the kirsch for 1 hour or longer, stirring occasionally.

2. Bring the milk to the boil with the split vanilla bean. Do not boil further. If the bean is not to be used, add the vanilla extract later. Remove the vanilla bean, if used, rinse and dry it and reserve for later uses.

3. Place the yolks in a saucepan and add the sugar. Beat with a wire whisk until thick and lemon-colored.

4. Gradually add the milk to the yolk mixture, beating constantly. Use a wooden spoon and stir constantly, this way and that, making certain the spoon touches all over the bottom of the sauce. Cook until the mixture has a custardlike consistency and coats the sides of the spoon. Do not let the sauce boil, or it will curdle.

5. Soften the gelatin in the water and add it to the sauce, stirring to dissolve. Add the vanilla extract, if used, and strain the custard into a bowl. Let cool. When the mixture is cool, add the fruitcake mixture and the marinating liquid. Fold it in.

6. Line a 10- to 12-cup mold with the ladyfingers. To do this, separate the "double" ladyfingers. Arrange enough of them in a petallike, symmetrical arrangement over the bottom, cutting them to fit. Remember to place them smooth-surface down so that when the charlotte is unmolded, this surface will appear on top. Line the sides of the mold with ladyfingers, smooth-surface against the side of the mold. Arrange the ladyfingers close together and trim each ladyfinger as necessary so that it fits neatly, top and bottom.

7. Add the custard mixture and place in the refrigerator. Chill several hours or overnight, until the custard is set.

8. When ready to serve, dip the mold in hot water and remove immediately. A damp, hot cloth could also be used on the mold to help loosen it. Serve with apricot sauce or English custard, and, if desired, whipped cream.

Yield: 12 or more servings.

Bananas with Maltaise Pudding

1. Pour the milk into a saucepan and start to heat.

2. Peel the orange, eliminating as much of the white pulp as possible. Cut the yellow skin into very fine julienne strips. Add this to the milk and continue heating just to the boil.

3. Add the farina gradually, stirring constantly. Cook for 5 minutes, stirring occasionally. Remove from the heat.

4. Immediately blend 5 tablespoons sugar with the egg yolks and add this to the hot farina, stirring rapidly with a whisk. Return briefly to the heat and, stirring constantly, bring just to the boil. Do not boil. Remove from the heat.

5. Spoon equal portions of the pudding mixture into 8 small, individual dessert bowls. Smooth over the top and let cool.

6. Meanwhile, place the raisins in a small bowl or cup and add boiling water to cover. Let stand until plumped.

7. Spoon the preserves into a saucepan and heat.

8. Peel the bananas and cut them first in half, then into quarters. Cut the pieces into cubes.

9. Heat the 3 tablespoons of butter in a skillet and add the cubed bananas. Sprinkle with remaining sugar and cook, stirring gently, for about 2 minutes. Add the Grand Marnier and spoon this over the pudding.

10. Drain the raisins and add them to the heated preserves. Spoon this over all and sprinkle with almonds.

Yield: 8 servings.

3½ cups milk
Peel from half an orange
½ cup quick-cooking farina (cream of wheat)
7 tablespoons sugar
3 egg yolks
½ cup raisins
1 10-ounce jar apricot preserves
3 firm, ripe, unblemished bananas
3 tablespoons butter
3 tablespoons Grand Marnier, rum or Cognac
¼ cup toasted, slivered, unsalted, blanched almonds

Indian Pudding

1. Bring the milk to the boil in a saucepan and add the cornmeal gradually, stirring constantly with a wire whisk. When the mixture is thickened and smooth, remove from the heat. Let cool.

2. Preheat the oven to 325 degrees.

3. Stir the mixture and add the eggs, stirring constantly. Add the suet, sugar, molasses, salt, ginger and cinnamon. Blend well.

4. Butter an 8- or 9-cup earthenware or other casserole. Pour in the mixture and smooth the top. Place in the oven and bake for 2 hours. If desired, serve with vanilla ice cream on top.

Yield: 10 to 12 servings.

5 cups milk
1 cup yellow cornmeal
2 eggs, lightly beaten
½ cup finely chopped suet
⅔ cup dark brown sugar
½ cup dark molasses
½ teaspoon salt
1 teaspoon ground ginger
½ teaspoon cinnamon
Butter

Budino al Cioccolato *(A chocolate crème caramel)*

The caramel base:

½ cup sugar
2 tablespoons water
Juice of ½ lemon

The chocolate custard:

2 cups milk
4 ounces (squares) semisweet chocolate
4 eggs
4 egg yolks
½ cup sugar

1. Preheat the oven to 350 degrees.
2. Select 8 ½-cup metal or oven-proof custard molds.
3. Combine the ½ cup of sugar, water and lemon juice in a saucepan and bring to the boil. Let cook, bubbling, until the syrup becomes a light amber color. Take care not to let the syrup burn or it will be bitter. The moment the syrup is ready, pour equal amounts of it quickly into the 8 molds. Swirl the syrup around so that it covers the bottom of each mold. Let cool at room temperature.
4. Heat the milk with the chocolate, stirring often until the chocolate is dissolved.
5. Beat the eggs, egg yolks and ½ cup sugar until thickened and smooth. Pour the milk mixture into the egg mixture and blend well. Strain the custard and skim off and discard surface foam.
6. Ladle the custard into the 8 prepared molds. Arrange the molds in a baking dish and pour boiling water around them. Place the dish in the oven and bake until the custard is set in the center, about 30 minutes.
7. Remove the custard molds and let cool. Unmold when ready to serve.
Yield: 8 servings.

Coeur à la Crème

1 cup cottage cheese
1 cup cream cheese
½ cup sour cream
½ cup heavy cream
Strawberries or fruit sauces for garnish (see recipes below)

1. The quantities listed here are for a 3-cup, heart-shaped mold. Coeur à la crème molds come in various sizes, starting with about a ½-cup volume. Quantities of ingredients for other molds will have to be adjusted accordingly.
2. In the bowl of an electric mixer combine the cottage cheese, cream cheese and sour cream. Beat until well blended.
3. Whip the heavy cream and fold it into the cheese mixture.
4. Line the mold completely with cheesecloth, letting the edges overlap the rim of the mold.
5. Spoon the cheese mixture into the mold, smoothing and packing it firmly into the mold. Fold the cheesecloth over the top. Cover with plastic wrap and refrigerate overnight.
6. Open up the cheesecloth and invert the mold onto the center of a platter. Carefully remove the cheesecloth.
7. Garnish with strawberry sauce or fruit sauce and serve with additional strawberry sauce and/or fruit sauce. Early rec-

ipes for this dessert call for eating the coeur à la crème with crème fraiche or heavy cream and a heavy sprinkling of sugar.

Yield: 10 or more servings.

Empty the defrosted strawberries into the container of a food processor or blender. If fresh strawberries are used, remove the stems and rinse the berries well. Drain and put in the container of a food processor or blender. Add the sugar and blend to a fine purée. Add the framboise. Serve chilled in a sauceboat.

Yield: 2½ cups.

1. Spoon and scrape the apricot and peach preserves into a saucepan. Add the water and bring to the boil, stirring. Cook for 5 minutes.

2. Pour the mixture into the container of a food processor and blend well. Let cool.

3. Peel the oranges, cutting away all the white pulp. Section the oranges by cutting between the fibrous segments. There should be about 1 cup of orange sections with juice.

4. Add the orange sections and their juice to the apricot mixture. Chill. Stir in the Grand Marnier and serve.

Yield: About 3 cups.

Strawberry sauce

2	10-ounce packages frozen strawberries, or use 2 pints of fresh strawberries
½	cup sugar or more to taste
2	tablespoons framboise, kirsch, mirabelle or other white liqueur made of berries

Fruit sauce with orange

1	cup apricot preserves
1	cup peach preserves
½	cup water
3	seedless navel oranges
2	tablespoons Grand Marnier

Trifle

1. Drop the peaches into boiling water for about 12 minutes. Drain immediately. Skin the peaches by pulling off the peel with a paring knife. Slice and pit the peaches. Add ½ cup of sugar and refrigerate.

2. Rinse, hull and drain the strawberries. Add ½ cup of sugar and refrigerate.

3. Bring the milk just to the boil. Put the whole eggs and egg yolks in a mixing bowl. Beat until light and lemon-colored. Add remaining ¼ cup of sugar. Pour half of the near-boiling milk over the eggs, beating vigorously. Return this mixture to the remaining milk and return the saucepan to the heat. Cook, stirring constantly this way and that over the bottom, using a wooden spoon. It may be best to use a heatproof pad under the saucepan. Cook the custard until it is slightly thickened, like thick cream, and coats the spoon. Strain the sauce into a mixing bowl. Add the vanilla, almond extract and sherry. Chill.

4. Cut the poundcake into ½-inch-thick slices. Spread

2	large, ripe, unblemished peaches
1¼	cups sugar
1	cup red, ripe strawberries
2	cups milk
2	whole eggs
2	egg yolks
1½	teaspoons pure vanilla extract
¼	teaspoon almond extract
2	tablespoons medium-dry sherry
1	frozen poundcake, defrosted
¾	cup apricot preserves, approximately
½	cup strawberry or currant preserves, approximately
1	cup sweetened whipped cream

enough slices with apricot preserves to arrange the slices spread-side up over the bottom and sides of a crystal bowl. Cut additional slices into convenient sizes as necessary to fill the empty spaces.

5. Add the peaches to the lined bowl and pour in the custard almost to the top. Spread any remaining poundcake slices with strawberry preserves and arrange spread-side up on top of the cake. Arrange the strawberries on top of this. Pipe sweetened whipped cream over the top.

Yield: 8 to 12 servings.

Tropical Flan

1⅓ cups sugar
4 cups light cream
Finely grated rind of 1 large lime
3 tablespoons lime juice
12 egg yolks
2 10-ounce packages frozen raspberries, optional

1. Adjust the rack to the center of the oven and preheat oven to 350 degrees.

2. Caramelize 1 cup of the sugar by placing it in a heavy skillet over moderately high heat. Stir occasionally with a wooden spatula until the sugar starts to melt, and then stir constantly until it has all melted to a smooth caramel. It should be a rich brown, but do not let it become too dark or it will have a bitter burned taste. If it is not cooked long enough, it will be tasteless.

3. Immediately pour the caramelized sugar into a 2-quart soufflé dish or other round ovenproof dish. Quickly tilt and turn the dish to coat the bottom and almost all the way up on the sides. Continue to tilt and turn the dish until the caramel stops running. Set aside.

4. Scald the cream, uncovered, in a heavy saucepan or in the top of a large double boiler over boiling water.

5. Meanwhile, mix the lime rind and juice together and set aside.

6. In a large mixing bowl, stir the yolks just to mix. When the cream forms tiny bubbles around the edge and a slight wrinkled skin on top, remove it from the heat. Add the remaining ⅓ cup of sugar and stir to dissolve. Very gradually, just a bit at a time at first, add it to the yolks, stirring constantly. Strain and then gradually stir in the lime rind and juice.

7. Pour into the caramelized dish. Place in a large pan; the pan must not touch the sides of the dish and must not be

deeper than the dish. Pour hot water into the large pan to about two-thirds of the way up the sides of the custard dish. Cover loosely with a cooky sheet or large piece of aluminum foil.

8. Bake for 1¼ hours, or until a knife inserted into the center comes out clean. Do not make any more knife tests than necessary. Do not insert the knife all the way to the bottom of the custard or it will spoil the appearance when inverted. Remove from hot water and place on a rack. Cool, uncovered, to room temperature. Refrigerate for 10 to 24 hours. Do not stint on the chilling time (see note).

9. If necessary, cut around the upper edge of the custard to release. Choose a dessert platter with a flat bottom and enough rim to hold the caramel, which will have melted to a sauce. Place the platter upside down over the custard. Carefully invert. Remove the dish. Refrigerate. Serve very cold with thawed and partly drained raspberries, if desired.

Yield: 6 to 8 portions.

Note: If flan is underbaked or if it is not refrigerated long enough, it will collapse when cut. It is best not to invert it too long before serving. The shiny coating will become dull as it stands.

To remove hardened caramel from utensils, place them in the sink and let hot water run over them until the caramel disappears.

Sheer Khorma (*A pistachio and almond dessert*)

1. Place the pistachios and almonds in a mixing bowl and add cold water to cover. Let stand overnight. Drain and rub off the skins.

2. Place the nuts in the container of a food processor or electric blender and blend. Do not blend to a purée. The texture should be coarse-fine. Set aside.

3. Break the vermicelli sticks in half. Heat the butter in a large saucepan and add the vermicelli. Cook, stirring, until vermicelli is nicely browned without burning. Add the milk and cream and bring to the boil. Add the pistachio mixture, saffron and sugar. Cook, stirring often, for about 15 minutes.

Yield: 12 or more servings.

1½ cups shelled pistachios
¾ cup almonds, shelled but with the skin on
⅛ pound Indian vermicelli
8 tablespoons butter
5 cups milk
¾ cup heavy cream
½ teaspoon saffron
5 tablespoons sugar

Quindin de Yá-yá (*An egg and coconut dessert*)

11   egg yolks
 1   whole egg
 2   tablespoons melted butter
 2   cups dessicated shredded
      unsweetened coconut,
      available in health food stores
 2   cups sugar

1. Preheat the oven to 375 degrees.

2. Combine the yolks and whole egg in the bowl of an electric mixer. Spoon in the butter. Add the coconut and sugar. Beat, gradually increasing speed, until the ingredients are thoroughly blended.

3. Lightly butter a 9- or 10-inch glass pie plate. Pour and scrape the mixture into the pie plate. Place the plate on a baking dish and pour boiling water around it. Bake for 2 hours, or until a needle comes out clean when inserted in the middle.

4. Invert the dish, while hot, onto a pie plate. It may be necessary to run a thin sharp knife around the rim of the pie to help it unmold. Serve immediately.

Yield: 12 to 16 servings.

Plum Pudding

The pudding:

½   pound beef suet taken from
     the kidney
 2   cups golden raisins
 2   cups black raisins
 2   cups dried currants
½   pound glacé fruits
½   pound candied citron
 2   cups fresh bread crumbs
½   cup flour
½   teaspoon ground allspice
½   teaspoon ground mace
½   teaspoon ground cinnamon
½   teaspoon ground nutmeg
½   teaspoon ground cloves
     Grated rind of 2 lemons
     Salt
¼   cup dark brown sugar
 8   eggs, separated
½   cup heavy cream
¼   cup Cognac or rum

The flour seal:

 2   cups flour
¼   cup water
 1   egg yolk, beaten

1. To steam these puddings, select a kettle or a steamer large enough to hold the sealed puddings. The pudding molds should be placed in the steamer baskets or on a rack above 1 inch of boiling water, which should be constantly replenished as it boils away. Puddings may also be baked. To do this, set the pudding molds in a basin of boiling water and place in an oven preheated to 375 degrees. Steam or bake the puddings for about 2 hours.

2. Remove the connecting and tough outer tissues from the suet. Place the suet in the freezer and let it stand until almost but not quite frozen. Remove it and place it on a flat surface. Chop it finely with a heavy knife or cleaver.

3. Combine the suet, raisins, currants, glacé fruits, citron and bread crumbs in a large mixing bowl and toss with the hands until blended. Sift together the flour and spices and sift this over the fruit mixture. Add the grated rind, salt to taste and brown sugar and toss to blend. Beat the yolks lightly and add the cream. Pour this over the fruit mixture. Add the Cognac and blend with the hands.

4. Beat the whites until stiff and add them. Fold them in with the hands.

5. Add equal portions of the batter to 4 greased 2-cup pudding molds (see note) with lids. Cover with the lids.

6. Combine the flour and water in a bowl, kneading to make a stiff dough. Divide it into four parts. Roll each part into a

rope large enough to encircle the lids. Flatten the rope slightly.

7. Brush around the top of the mold and the perimeter of the lids with egg yolk. Circle the rope around the top, pressing to seal the lid and the mold. Press the ends of the rope together to seal.

8. Arrange the molds in a steamer or in a water bath and steam or bake as outlined in step 1.

9. These puddings may now be served or they may be kept closely sealed for several weeks in the refrigerator. Cognac or rum may be added occasionally as they age. The puddings should be reheated in or over boiling water until piping hot before serving. Serve with hard sauce (see recipe below).

Yield: 4 1-pound puddings.

Note: Use ceramic or crockery heatproof molds.

Hard sauce

½   **pound butter**
4   **cups sifted confectioners' sugar**
1   **egg white**
1   **teaspoon pure vanilla extract**

1. Cream the butter and add 2 cups sugar and egg white alternately. Beat well after each addition.

2. Beat in remaining sugar and add the vanilla. Store in a screwtop jar. Serve at room temperature.

Yield: 4 cups.

Chocolate Mousse Cake

There are some desserts that become legends in their own time, and one of them is a chocolate mousse cake, a great specialty of the much-esteemed but now defunct Café Chauveron in New York. The Chauveron closed its doors in 1971 when the owner decided that the restaurant life could be more palmy in Miami Beach. A short while ago, at a gathering of French chefs, we greeted Raymond Richez, who had been the last chef of the Chauveron in Manhattan. We asked if he could recall the name of the pastry chef who had worked under him, the one who prepared the dessert in question. He smiled.

"I created that dessert," he said, "and it came about through an error. It was the regular pastry chef's day off and it was an especially busy day at work. It became obvious the kitchen was running out of chocolate mousse, and I decided to make one between a few hundred frantic orders. In my haste, I added about twice as much butter to the basic mousse as was usual. I was too busy to discard the mixture so I threw it in the refrigerator so as not the clutter the work area. It stayed there over night and when I removed the mousse I found it was stiff enough to cut with a knife. I had some leftover genoise, so I lined a loaf pan with slices of the cake, filled it with the mousse and served it with a sabayon sauce with rum. The customers loved it."

So would a few people we know, he was told. A few Sundays later he came to our kitchen to prepare the cake. It is a lasciviously rich, smooth, velvety confection served with an equally seductive rum-laden sabayon, otherwise known as zabaglione.

1 pound sweet chocolate
1 cup milk
½ cup sugar
6 egg yolks
1 pound butter at room temperature
2 cups heavy cream
1 genoise (see recipe page 571)
½ cup white rum
2 tablespoons confectioners' sugar
Sabayon sauce (see recipe below)

1. Put the chocolate, milk, sugar and egg yolks into a not-too-heavy metal bowl. Select a deep skillet in which the bowl will fit snugly. Bring about 2 inches of water to the simmer in the skillet. Set the bowl in the skillet. The bottom may touch the water, barely. Beat vigorously and constantly with a wire whisk. When the chocolate melts, remove the skillet from the heat. Continue beating the chocolate mixture, the bowl still resting inside the skillet.

2.. When the mixture is somewhat thickened and resembles a thin chocolate custard, remove the bowl from the skillet. Set the bowl on a cold surface such as marble or Formica. Continue beating vigorously until the mixture is warm.

3. Add the butter and beat until butter is melted and well blended. Continue beating until the mixture reaches room temperature.

4. Whip the cream until stiff and fold it into the mixture.

5. Place a baked genoise on a flat surface. Hold a long, sharp knife parallel to the surface and split the genoise through the center to make two layers. Select one or two loaf pans to fashion the mousse cake. Two loaf pans, each measuring 8½- x 4½- x 2½-inches are suitable. Cut each genoise layer into rectangles that will fit neatly inside the loaf pans and line the sides. This will make a "case" for molding the mousse. Set the remaining pieces and crumbs of the genoise aside for later use.

6. Sprinkle the lined pans with rum. Pour enough of the mousse mixture inside the lined molds to fill them. Set the remaining mixture aside for later use. Chill the filled molds in the refrigerator overnight.

7. To unmold, place the bottom of an empty loaf pan against the top of the mousse cake. Invert the cakes, one at a time, and let rest on the empty loaf pan.

8. Spread the top and sides of the cakes with the reserved mousse.

9. Make crumbs of the reserved genoise pieces using a food processor or electric blender. Sprinkle the crumbs over the top

and sides of the cakes. Tap lightly to make crumbs adhere. Sprinkle the top of each cake with 1 tablespoon of confectioners' sugar.

10. Slice the cake and serve with a dab of sabayon sauce.

Yield: 12 or more servings.

Sabayon

6 large egg yolks
1 cup sugar
½ cup light rum
2 cups heavy cream

1. Select a not-too-heavy metal bowl (one measuring about 4½ inches deep and 12 inches in diameter is good for this).

2. Select a deep skillet in which the bowl will fit snugly. Bring about 2 inches of water to the simmer in the skillet.

3. Put the yolks, sugar and rum in the bowl. Start beating, then set the bowl in the skillet containing the simmering water. The bottom may barely touch the water. Beat briskly and constantly with a whisk, making certain that the whisk covers all the bottom and sides of the bowl or the eggs will scramble.

4. When the mixture is thickened like a smooth custard, remove the bowl from the skillet and continue beating vigorously for 5 minutes or longer, until the bottom of the bowl is almost at room temperature.

5. Whip the cream until stiff and fold it into the sabayon mixture.

Yield: 12 or more servings.

Mousse au Chocolat *(Chocolate mousse)*

Once in a rare while, we discover a formula for a dish that seems the ultimate, the definitive, the ne plus ultra. Over the years we have printed recipes for a score or more desserts called mousse au chocolat. We are convinced that the finest chocolate mousse creation ever whipped up in our kitchen is the one printed here. As if you didn't know, mousse means foam in French. This mousse is the foamiest.

½ pound sweet chocolate
6 large eggs, separated
3 tablespoons water
¼ cup sweet liqueur such as chartreuse, amaretto, mandarine or Grand Marnier
2 cups heavy cream
6 tablespoons sugar
Whipped cream for garnish
Grated chocolate for garnish

1. Cut the chocolate into ½-inch pieces and place the chocolate in a saucepan. Set the saucepan in hot, almost boiling water and cover. Let melt over low heat.

2. Put the yolks in a heavy saucepan and add the water. Place the saucepan over very low heat while beating vigorously and constantly with a wire whisk. Experienced cooks may do this over direct heat. It may be preferable, however, to use a metal disc such as a Flame Tamer to control the heat. In any event, when the yolks start to thicken, add the

liqueur, beating constantly. Cook until the sauce achieves the consistency of a hollandaise or a sabayon, which it is. Remove from the heat.

3. Add the melted chocolate to the sauce and fold it in. Scrape the sauce into a mixing bowl.

4. Beat the cream until stiff, adding 2 tablespoons of the sugar toward the end of beating. Fold this into the chocolate mixture.

5. Beat the whites until soft peaks start to form. Beat in the remaining sugar and continue beating until stiff. Fold this into the mousse.

6. Spoon the mousse into a crystal bowl and chill until ready to serve. When ready to serve, garnish with whipped cream and grated chocolate.

Yield: 12 or more servings.

Mousse de Marrons   *(Mousse of brandied chestnuts)*

2　10-ounce jars imported brandied chestnuts in syrup
3　cups cold milk
2　envelopes gelatin
2　tablespoons cornstarch
2　tablespoons Cognac
4　eggs, separated
½　cup sugar
1　cup heavy cream

1. Remove and reserve 2 of the whole chestnuts to use as garnish.

2. Put the remaining chestnuts and their syrup in the container of a food processor or electric blender. Blend to a purée.

3. Spoon and scrape the purée into a mixing bowl. Add the milk and gelatin and stir until well blended. Spoon and scrape this into a saucepan and bring slowly to the boil, stirring constantly.

4. Blend the cornstarch with the Cognac and add it to the mixture, stirring. When thickened, add the yolks, stirring rapidly. Remove from the heat. Let cool.

5. Beat the whites and, when they stand in soft peaks, beat in ¼ cup of the sugar. Fold the whites into the chestnut mixture.

6. Whip the cream, gradually beating in the remaining sugar. Fold this into the mousse.

7. Pour the mixture into a crystal bowl. If desired, reserve a bit of the mixture to pipe on top as a garnish. To do this, let the mixture set only slightly. Using a star tube, pipe rosettes around the rim of the mousse and chill until set, preferably overnight.

8. As an added garnish, split the 2 reserved whole chestnuts in half. Arrange them symmetrically, cut side down, on top of the mousse. Serve cold.

Yield: 8 to 12 servings.

Mousse des Iles *(A ginger, rum and nutmeg mousse)*

1. Lightly grease the inside of an 8-cup mold with the oil, wiping off any excess oil.

2. Combine the milk, gelatin and ½ cup of sugar in a saucepan. Bring to the simmer and stir until gelatin dissolves. Stir in the nutmeg, crystallized ginger and fresh ginger.

3. Blend the cornstarch with the rum and add it, stirring. Cook, stirring, until the mixture thickens. Beat the yolks and add them to the mixture, stirring rapidly with a whisk. Remove from the heat. Let cool.

4. Beat the whites and, when almost stiff, beat in 4 tablespoons of sugar. Beat constantly until stiff. Fold this into the mixture.

5. Whip the cream and, when almost stiff, gradually add the remaining 2 tablespoons of sugar, beating constantly. Fold this into the mousse mixture.

6. Pour the mousse into the oiled mold and refrigerate for several hours or overnight until set. To unmold, wipe around the outside of the mold with a hot, damp sponge until the mousse loosens within.

Yield: 8 to 12 servings.

1	teaspoon peanut, vegetable or corn oil
3	cups cold milk
2	envelopes unflavored gelatin
½	cup plus 6 tablespoons sugar
1	teaspoon freshly grated nutmeg
¼	cup chopped crystallized ginger
1	tablespoon grated fresh ginger, or ½ teaspoon ground
4	teaspoons cornstarch
2	tablespoons dark rum
3	eggs, separated
⅔	cup heavy cream

Mousse de Citron Vert *(Lime mousse)*

1. Combine the ⅓ cup of sugar and water in a saucepan and bring to the boil, stirring until sugar dissolves.

2. Add the lime juice. Empty the gelatin into a small bowl and add enough water to moisten thoroughly. Stir this into the lime mixture. Bring to the boil, stirring, and remove from the heat. Let cool, but do not let the mixture set.

3. When the mixture is cool but still liquid, beat the cream until stiff with the remaining 2 teaspoons of sugar. Fold this into the lime mixture. Spoon into individual crystal glasses or molds. Chill until set. Serve with gelée de mandarines.

Yield: 6 to 12 servings.

⅓	cup plus 2 teaspoons sugar
¼	cup water
1	cup freshly squeezed, strained lime juice
1	envelope unflavored gelatin
1	cup heavy cream Gelée de mandarines (see recipe below)

1. Rub the tangerines all over with the sugar cubes, collecting as much skin oil on the cubes as possible.

2. Peel the tangerines. Cut the skin of 2 tangerines into very thin strips. Remove the sections. Carefully cut away and discard the membranous outer coating of each section. Remove and discard the seeds. Place the sections as they are prepared in a mixing bowl.

Gelée de mandarines *(Tangerine jelly)*

4	fresh tangerines or tangelos
30	pieces cubed sugar (called hostess cubes)
2	cups dry white wine
1	envelope unflavored gelatin

3. Pour the wine into a saucepan and add the sugar cubes and strips of tangerine peel. Add the gelatin and bring to the boil slowly, stirring constantly with a wooden spoon. Strain. Let cool.

4. Pour about 1½ cups of the liquid into the bottom of a crystal bowl. Chill until almost set. Arrange a circular pattern of tangerine sections in the center. Chill once more until set. Continue adding layers of the liquid and patterns of tangerine sections until all the ingredients are used. Chill until ready to serve.

Yield: 8 or more servings.

Pie Pastry

2¼ cups flour
Salt to taste
1 cup solid white shortening
4 to 6 tablespoons ice water

1. Put the flour and salt into the container of a food processor. Add the shortening cut into small pieces and blend briefly. Add the ice water and blend briefly until the pastry pulls away from the sides of the container.

2. If a food processor is not used, put the flour and salt in a mixing bowl. Add the shortening and cut it in with two knives or a pastry blender until the mixture looks like coarse cornmeal. Using a fork, start tossing the mixture while adding the water. Add just enough water so that the dough holds together.

3. Shape the dough into a ball. Roll it out on a lightly floured board and use to line a 9- or 10-inch pie plate.

Yield: Pastry for a 1- or 2-crust pie.

How to bake a pie shell

Prick the bottom and sides of a pastry shell with the tines of a fork. If there is time, freeze the pastry for 15 minutes or longer before baking. This is not essential but it will help prevent shrinkage.

Preheat the oven to 425 degrees. Place the pie shell on a baking sheet and bake for 12 to 15 minutes, turning as necessary so that it browns evenly. Let cool before filling.

Tart Pastry

2 cups flour
¼ teaspoon salt
2 tablespoons sugar
12 tablespoons very cold butter

1. Place the flour, salt and sugar in the container of a food processor. Cut the butter into small pieces and add it. Add the yolks. Blend briefly and add the water. Blend just until the pastry pulls away from the sides of the container.

2. If a food processor is not used, place the flour, salt and sugar in a mixing bowl. Cut the butter into small bits and add it. Using the fingers or a pastry blender, cut in the butter until it has the texture of coarse cornmeal. Beat the yolks and water together and add, stirring quickly with a fork.

3. Gather the dough into a ball, wrap in wax paper and chill for at least 1 hour. This dough may also be frozen for later use.

Yield: Pastry for a 10-inch tart.

2 egg yolks
2 tablespoons ice water

Preheat the oven to 425 degrees. Line the shell with a sheet of wax paper and add enough dried beans to cover the bottom of the shell. Or use aluminum nugget weights. This will prevent the shell from buckling during the initial baking.

Place the tart tin on a baking sheet and bake for 10 minutes. Remove the wax paper and dried beans. Return to the oven and bake for 2 minutes longer. It is now ready to be filled and baked.

How to bake a tart shell

Mississippi Pecan Pie

1. Preheat the oven to 350 degrees.

2. Roll out the pastry and line a 10-inch pie tin.

3. Combine the corn syrup and sugar in a saucepan and bring to the boil. Cook, stirring, just until the sugar is dissolved.

4. Beat the eggs in a mixing bowl and gradually add the sugar mixture, beating. Add the remaining ingredients and pour the mixture into the pie shell. Bake for 50 minutes to 1 hour, or until the pie is set.

Yield: 8 servings.

Pastry for a 10-inch pie
1¼ cups dark corn syrup
1 cup sugar
4 whole eggs
4 tablespoons melted butter
1½ cups chopped pecan meats
1 teaspoon pure vanilla extract
2 tablespoons dark rum

Pumpkin Cream Pie

One of the curious things about holiday customs in America is the general inability to relate holiday ornaments to the stove. The vast majority of Easter eggs go for naught once the day is done. And so with pumpkins. Hundreds of thousands of pounds of these joyous delights never see the inside of a saucepan. Whereas most recipes for pumpkin pie call for canned pumpkin, a pie made with the fresh pulp is infinitely more delicate and delicious. Please note that we are not recommending the use of a carved pumpkin with a funny face several days old. But the use of a fresh pumpkin and, preferably, a small, young one newly picked.

Pastry for a 9-inch pie
3 cups fresh pumpkin purée (see recipe below), or use canned pumpkin
¾ cup sugar
½ teaspoon salt
½ teaspoon grated nutmeg
¼ teaspoon grated cinnamon
1 teaspoon grated fresh ginger root, or ½ teaspoon powdered ginger
3 large eggs, lightly beaten
1 cup heavy cream

1. Preheat the oven to 425 degrees.
2. Line a pie dish with the pastry and build up a fluted edge. Chill.
3. Combine the remaining ingredients in a mixing bowl. Blend well. Pour the mixture into the prepared shell and place in the oven.
4. Bake for 15 minutes. Reduce the heat to 350 degrees. Bake for 30 to 40 minutes longer, or until the filling is set. Serve, if desired, with sweetened and/or rum-flavored whipped cream.
Yield: 6 to 8 servings.

Fresh pumpkin purée

---

1 3- to 4-pound pumpkin

1. Cut around and discard the stem of the pumpkin.
2. Cut the pumpkin into eighths. Scoop away and discard the seeds and fibers from the pumpkin pieces. Place the unpeeled pumpkin pieces in the top of a steamer large enough to hold them. Cover and steam over boiling water for about 15 minutes, or until the pumpkin flesh is tender.
3. Remove and let cool. When cool enough to handle, scrape the flesh from the outer peel. Discard the peel. Blend the flesh, using a food processor or blender, or put it through a ricer.
Yield: About 3½ cups.
Note: This purée can be kept indefinitely in the freezer.

Mincemeat Pie

½ pound cooked beef
½ pound cooked beef tongue
1 pound black currants
1½ pound black raisins
2 ounces chopped candied lemon peel
2 ounces chopped candied orange peel
½ cup chopped diced candied citron
½ cup chopped glacéed cherries

1. The texture of mincemeat is a question of personal taste. Some like it fine, some medium and some coarse. If you want it coarse, the various fruits and meats should be chopped or cubed by hand. If you want it medium or fine, use a food processor or, more tediously, an electric blender and process or blend to the desired texture. Some sources recommend grinding the mince meat; others recommend grinding half the ingredients and chopping the rest. Take your choice.
2. Cube or chop the beef, tongue, currants, raisins, lemon peel, orange peel, candied citron, cherries, pineapple and suet. Pour this mixture into a bowl.

3. Add the remaining ingredients and mix well with the hands. There should be about 12 cups. Spoon the mixture into fruit jars and seal tightly. Let it age for at least 3 weeks, and preferably a month, before using. Store in a cool place to age.

4. When ready to bake, preheat oven to 450 degrees.

5. Roll out pie pastry and line a 9-inch pie plate. Fill with 3 to 4 cups mincemeat. Cover the pie with upper crust. Bake for about 30 minutes.

Yield: 3 to 4 pies.

½	cup chopped glacéed pineapple
¾	pound finely chopped or ground suet
2	cups brown sugar
2	cups peeled, cored, finely diced apple
	Grated rind of 1 lemon
	Grated rind of 1 orange
¼	cup lemon juice
1	teaspoon ground nutmeg
½	teaspoon ground cloves
½	teaspoon ground allspice
1	teaspoon ground cinnamon
2	cups Cognac or other brandy
½	cup dry sherry
½	teaspoon salt, or to taste
	Pastry for a 9-inch pie

Chocolate Sabayon Pie

1. Bake the pastry shell and let it cool.

2. Combine the chocolate and water in a saucepan. Place the pan in a basin of barely simmering water and let stand, stirring as necessary, until the chocolate melts.

3. As the chocolate melts, put the egg yolks and sugar in the bowl of an electric mixer. Add the crème de cacao and set the bowl in a basin of barely simmering water. Beat vigorously with a wire whisk until the sauce becomes rich and thick, like a stiff custard.

4. Let the melted chocolate cool slightly (if it is too hot when added to the sauce, it will tend to cook the eggs). Add the chocolate to the sauce and fold it in with a plastic spatula. Beat in the rum.

5. Whip the 1½ cups of cream until stiff. Fold this into the chocolate mixture. Spoon into the baked pastry shell and chill. Serve cold. Garnish with additional whipped cream, if desired.

Yield: 8 or more servings.

	Pastry for a 10-inch pie
10	ounces sweet or bittersweet chocolate squares
¼	cup plus 2 tablespoons water
2	egg yolks
1	tablespoon sugar
3	tablespoons crème de cacao, or any other chocolate-flavored liqueur
2	tablespoons dark rum
1½	cups heavy cream
	Whipped cream for garnish, optional

Lemon Meringue Pie

Sweet short pastry dough
(see recipe below)
1 cup milk
¼ vanilla bean split
lengthwise, or ½ teaspoon
pure vanilla extract
2 tablespoons granulated
sugar
3 egg yolks
3 tablespoons cornstarch
Juice of ½ lemon, or more if
a stronger lemon flavor is
desired
Finely grated rind of ½
lemon
French meringue (see recipe
below)
1 or 2 tablespoons confectioners'
sugar

1. Preheat the oven to 425 degrees.
2. Line a quiche tin with a removable bottom with the rolled out dough.
3. Cover the bottom of the pan with wax paper and add dried beans to weight the dough down. This will prevent the dough from buckling. Bake the pastry for 25 minutes, or until nicely golden and cooked. Remove the pastry and allow to cool. Remove the beans and waxed paper.
4. Place the milk and split vanilla bean, if used, in a saucepan and bring to the boil. Cover and keep hot.
5. Put the sugar and egg yolks in a mixing bowl (this may be done in a mixer) and beat with a wire whisk until the mixture is golden yellow and forms a ribbon. Using the whisk, beat in the cornstarch.
6. Strain the hot milk into the egg and sugar mixture, beating constantly with the whisk. The vanilla bean may be rinsed off and stored in sugar.
7. Pour the mixture back into the saucepan and bring to the boil, stirring constantly with the whisk. Cook for 1 minute, stirring vigorously. If vanilla extract is used, add it. Add the lemon juice and grated rind. Pour the mixture into the baked pastry shell.
8. Spoon half the meringue onto the filling and smooth it over with a spatula. Fit a pastry bag with a star tube and spoon in the remaining meringue. Pipe the meringue out in star-shaped peaks to cover the tart.
9. Return the pie to the oven and bake for about 5 minutes, or until the meringue is lightly browned. Watch carefully that the meringue does not burn.
10. Sift confectioners' sugar over the top and run the pie briefly under the broiler to give it a further light glaze.
Yield: 6 or more servings.

Sweet pastry with almonds

3 tablespoons confectioners'
sugar
¼ teaspoon salt
1 cup flour
3 tablespoons powdered
almonds
6 tablespoons cold butter
1 large beaten egg
¼ teaspoon pure vanilla extract

1. Put the sugar, salt, flour and almonds in the bowl of an electric mixer or food processor. Add the butter cut into small pieces.
2. Stir or process the ingredients and beat in the egg and vanilla. Mix rapidly. The dough should not be worked for a long period of time. Wrap in foil or plastic wrap and let stand overnight before rolling.
Yield: Pastry for a 9- or 10-inch pie.

1. Do not make this meringue until you are ready to use it. Beat the egg whites in the bowl of an electric mixer or by hand, using a wire whisk. When they stand in peaks, beat in the 2 teaspoons of granulated sugar.

2. Continue beating the meringue until quite stiff. Blend remaining ⅓ cup of granulated sugar with the confectioners' sugar and sift this over the whites, folding the mixture in with a rubber spatula.

Yield: Meringue for a 9- or 10-inch pie.

French meringue

3   egg whites
⅓   cup plus 2 teaspoons granulated sugar
½   cup confectioners' sugar

Sour Cream Lime Pie

Ann Seranne, who brought us into the "food world" more than two decades ago as a receptionist and sometime writer for *Gourmet* magazine, makes some of the best pies in the world, kneading the dough and rolling it out with a speed and dexterity that is a marvel to behold. This is one of her best.

1. Bake the pie shell and let it cool.

2. Combine the sugar, cornstarch, butter, lime rind, lime juice and light cream in a saucepan. Bring slowly to the boil, stirring constantly. Cook until thickened and smooth.

3. Remove from the heat and let cool. Fold in the sour cream.

4. Pour the mixture into the baked pie shell. Spoon and smooth over the sour cream topping or sweetened whipped cream. Sprinkle with grated rind, if desired.

Yield: 6 to 8 servings.

Pastry for a 9-inch pie
1   cup sugar
3   tablespoons cornstarch
¼   cup butter
1   tablespoon grated lime rind
⅓   cup lime juice
1   cup light cream
1   cup sour cream
   Whipped sour cream for topping (see recipe below), or sweetened whipped cream
   Grated lime rind for garnish, optional

Whip the heavy cream and fold in the sugar. Fold in the sour cream and use as a topping for sweet custard pies.

Yield: 2 cups.

Whipped sour cream topping

1   cup heavy cream
1   tablespoon confectioners' sugar
1   cup sour cream

Blueberry Pie

Pastry for a 9-inch pie
¾ cup sugar
3 tablespoons quick-cooking tapioca
¼ teaspoon salt
Dash of ground cinnamon
4 cups blueberries
1 tablespoon lemon juice
1 tablespoon butter

1. Preheat the oven to 425 degrees.
2. Line a 9-inch pie plate with half the pastry.
3. Mix the sugar, tapioca, salt and cinnamon. Sprinkle the mixture over the berries. Add lemon juice. Spoon the berries into the prepared pie plate and dot with the butter.
4. Cut the remaining pastry into strips and make a lattice top for the pie. Trim edges, moisten and border with a strip of pastry.
5. Bake for about 50 minutes.
Yield: 6 to 8 servings.

Papaya Coconut Pie

Pastry for a 9-inch pie
1½ cups cubed papaya or mango out of the shell
1 cup sugar
Salt to taste
½ teaspoon cinnamon
¼ teaspoon ground cloves
2 large eggs, lightly beaten
1 cup milk
¾ cup finely grated fresh coconut (see instructions below)
2 tablespoons honey, warmed

1. Preheat the oven to 425 degrees.
2. Line a 9-inch pie plate with pastry. Refrigerate.
3. Combine the papaya and ½ cup sugar in a saucepan and cook over moderate heat, stirring often, until the sugar is dissolved. Cover and cook for about 5 minutes.
4. Put the remaining ½ cup sugar in a mixing bowl. Add the salt, cinnamon, cloves, eggs and milk. Stir in ¼ cup coconut. Pour the mixture into the unbaked pie shell.
5. Place in the oven and bake for 15 minutes. Reduce oven heat to 350 degrees and continue baking for 30 minutes longer. During the last 15 minutes of baking, remove the pie and sprinkle the top with the remaining coconut. Drizzle warmed honey over the top and return to the oven to complete baking.
Yield: 6 to 8 servings.

Grated fresh coconut

Using a hammer over a sink, crack 1 small coconut at 4 or 5 points. This should produce 4 or 5 large pieces. Discard the inner coconut liquid. Rest one piece at a time, shell side down, over a gas or electric burner. Let stand over moderately low heat for about 1 minute. Using a towel to protect the fingers, lift the coconut and lift the flesh part from the shell. It should come off easily. Using a swivel-bladed vegetable scraper, scrape away the dark exterior, leaving only the white meat. Cut the meat into small cubes. There should be about 3 cups of cubes. Put the cubes into the container of a food processor or electric blender and blend.

Tarte aux Pommes *(French apple tart)*

1. Preheat the oven to 400 degrees.

2. Line a 10-inch pie tin, preferably a quiche pan with a removable bottom, with pastry. Refrigerate or place in the freezer.

3. Core and peel 3 of the apples. Cut them into eighths. Cut these pieces into thin slices. There should be about 2 cups.

4. Heat 1 tablespoon of butter in a small skillet and add the apple slices. Sprinkle with lemon rind and ¼ cup of sugar. Cook, shaking the skillet and stirring, for about 10 minutes. Add the Calvados, if desired. Mash the apples lightly with a fork. Chill.

5. Core, peel and neatly slice the remaining apples.

6. Spoon the cooked apples over the bottom of the prepared pie tin. Arrange the fresh apple slices in a circular pattern over the cooked pulp. Sprinkle with remaining sugar and dot with remaining butter.

7. Bake for 40 to 45 minutes, or until apples are done and pastry is browned.

8. Heat the preserves and put through a sieve. Brush this over the tart. Cool and serve.

Yield: 6 to 8 servings.

Pastry for a 10-inch tart
6 or 7 firm, unblemished apples, about 2½ pounds
2 tablespoons butter
Grated rind of 1 lemon
½ cup sugar
1 tablespoon Calvados, rum or brandy, optional
½ cup apricot preserves

Strawberry Tart

1. Bake the tart shell and let it cool.

2. Spoon the crème patissière into the pie shell and smooth it over. Arrange the strawberries bottom side down, close together and symmetrically over the crème patissière.

3. Spoon the marmalade into a saucepan and add the water. Cook, stirring, until the marmalade is thinned. Put it through a strainer.

4. When the marmalade is cooled but still liquid brush the berries with it. Sprinkle the almonds over all. Cut into wedges to serve.

Yield: 8 to 10 servings.

Note: To toast the almond slivers, put them in one layer in a heatproof dish and bake at 350 degrees, stirring occasionally, until nicely browned.

Pastry for a 10-inch tart
Creme patissière (see recipe page 572)
3 pints firm, fresh, red, ripe strawberries, hulled, rinsed and drained.
1 cup orange marmalade
1 tablespoon water
⅓ cup toasted almond slivers (see note)

Orange Tart

Pastry for a 10-inch tart
2 large seedless oranges
5 thin lemon slices
¼ cup sugar
¼ cup Grand Marnier
½ cup orange marmalade

1. Preheat the oven to 500 degrees.
2. Prepare the tart pastry, adding the grated rind of ½ lemon with the sugar. Lightly butter a 10-inch pie tin. Sprinkle with flour to coat lightly and shake out the excess flour. Line the pie tin with pastry and refrigerate.
3. Trim off and discard the ends of the oranges. Slice the oranges as thinly as possible. Arrange the orange and lemon slices in one layer in one or two baking dishes with rims. Sprinkle lightly with the sugar, then with the Grand Marnier.
4. Bake the slices for 10 to 15 minutes, taking care that they do not burn. Turn the slices and continue baking for about 5 minutes, or until sticky and a bit crisp. Remove from the oven.
5. Reduce the oven heat to 400 degrees.
6. Arrange the orange and lemon slices neatly in overlapping circles over the center of the pastry.
7. Melt the marmalade and brush it over the filling. Bake for 5 minutes and reduce the oven heat to 350 degrees. Bake for 30 to 35 minutes longer. Let cool.
   Yield: 6 to 8 servings.

Crostata di Marmellata   (Italian marmalade pie)

Pastry for a 10-inch tart
1 pound marmalade
1 egg yolk
1 tablespoon cold water
1 tablespoon granulated sugar

1. Preheat the oven to 400 degrees.
2. Prepare the tart pastry, adding grated rind of ½ lemon with the sugar. Chill the dough. Divide it in half. With a rolling pin roll out half the dough into a circle large enough to fit a 10-inch pie dish with a fluted edge. Fit the pastry in the pie dish, prick the bottom with a fork and bake for 10 minutes.
3. Remove the pastry from the oven and spread the marmalade evenly with a spatula over the pastry.
4. Roll out the second batch of dough and cut it into strips ¾ inch wide, using a pastry wheel. Arrange half the strips 1 inch apart over the pie. Repeat with remaining strips going in the opposite direction to make a diamond or square pattern.
5. Beat the yolk with the water and brush the strips with the mixture. Sprinkle with sugar and bake for 15 to 20 minutes, or until the pie strips are nicely golden.
   Yield: 6 to 8 servings.

Pear and Ginger Tart

1. Bake the tart shell and let it cool.

2. Preheat the oven to 425 degrees.

3. Peel 6 of the pears and cut each of them into eighths. Cut away and discard the cores.

4. Place the pear wedges in a saucepan and add the sugar, ginger and water. Cover and cook until tender but still firm, 8 to 10 minutes. They must not be mushy. Turn the pear wedges as they cook so that the pieces cook evenly. Chill throughly. Drain but reserve 4 tablespoons of the pear liquid.

5. Arrange the pear wedges close together in the pastry shell.

6. Peel and quarter the remaining 2 pears. Scoop out and discard the cores. Cut the quarters into thin slices. Arrange the slices symmetrically over the cooked pears.

7. Combine the apricot preserves with the reserved pear liquid. Bring to the boil and strain. Brush tart with half of the apricot mixture. Bake for 30 minutes.

8. Remove from the oven and brush with remaining sauce. Let stand until warm. Serve with whipped cream, if desired.

Yield: 8 to 10 servings.

	Pastry for a 10-inch tart
8	ripe but firm Comice or Anjou pears, about 3 pounds
⅔	cup sugar
¾	teaspoon powdered ginger
½	cup water
6	tablespoons apricot preserves Whipped cream, optional

Clafoutis (*A cherry custard tart*)

1. Bake the tart shell and let it cool.

2. Pit the cherries, using a small cherry or olive pitter, or a small knife or the curved end of a small, ordinary hair pin (insert the pointed ends in a cork to make a permanent pit extractor).

3. Preheat the oven to 375 degrees.

4. Combine the sugar and eggs and beat well with a whisk. Stir in the cherries, milk, cream, almond extract and vanilla extract. Pour the mixture into the pie shell.

5. Place the pie in the oven and bake for 40 minutes, or until set in the center. Remove and sprinkle with confectioners' sugar, using a small sieve.

Yield: 6 to 8 servings.

	Pastry for a 10-inch tart
1½	pounds black Bing cherries
½	cup sugar
2	eggs
⅓	cup milk
⅓	cup heavy cream
½	teaspoon almond extract
½	teasoon vanilla extract
3	tablespoons confectioners' sugar for garnish

Midsummer Tart with Fruits and Berries

Murmurs of approval at the end of a meal or the sound of clapping hands across footlights, it all adds up to the same thing: the sound that says love, to borrow a phrase from a Broadway musical of a few years back. Applause, says Uta Hagen, is why she cooks. If there were no one there to say "Thank you very much, that was delicious," she'd stand up and eat from the refrigerator. The actress and neighbor is an excellent and enthusiastic cook who has an immaculate garden that she tends herself. This is her splendid fruit tart, taking advantage of seasonal berries, which, of course, she picks herself while the dew is still on the vine.

Pastry for a 9-inch tart
1 quart fresh strawberries, blueberries, blackberries or raspberries
1 cup fruit jelly such as crab apple, currant, beach plum or apple
2 tablepoons Grand Marnier, kirsch or framboise
¼ cup toasted almonds
Whipped cream

1. Bake the tart shell and let it cool.
2. Place the tart on a serving dish and fill with the berries. Place the largest and best berries in the center with the other berries piled around.
3. Heat the jelly over low heat and stir in the liqueur. Let cool slightly and spoon this over the fruit. Garnish with toasted almonds, sprinkling them in a ring around the berries. Chill for at least 1 hour before serving. Serve with whipped cream on the side.
   Yield: 6 to 10 servings.

Visidantine (*An almond tart*)

Pastry for a 9-inch tart
¼ pound butter at room temperature
⅔ cup sugar
1⅓ cups ground, blanched almonds
3 large eggs
1 tablespoon dark rum
1 cup thinly sliced blanched almonds
¼ cup apricot preserves

1. Roll the dough in a circle on a lightly floured board. Line a 9-inch quiche tin with a removable bottom with the mixture. Build up the sides slightly. Prick the bottom. Refrigerate. There will be leftover dough, which may be used to make an assortment of cookies.
2. Preheat the oven to 400 degrees.
3. To prepare the filling, cream the butter in the bowl of an electric mixer.
4. Separately, blend the sugar and ground almonds. Add about ⅓ of the mixture and 1 egg to the butter. Beat well. Add another ⅓ of the mixture and 1 more egg and beat well. Add the final ⅓ of almond mixture and the last egg and blend well. Beat in the rum.
5. Spoon and scrape this mixture into the prepared pan and

sprinkle with the almonds. Place in the oven and bake for 35 minutes. Remove the tart from the ring.

6. Melt the apricot preserves with a little water over low heat, stirring. Spread this over the top of the tart.

Yield: 6 to 8 servings.

French Nut Pie

1. Bake the tart shell for 15 minutes and let it cool.

2. Put the nuts into the container of a food processor and chop them coarsely by blending for only a few seconds. Do not overblend or the nuts will become too fine. Set aside.

3. Combine the honey, brown sugar, granulated sugar and butter in a saucepan. Boil for exactly 33 minutes. Add the nuts and cream and remove from the heat. Let cool.

4. Add the cooled nut filling to the tart shell and smooth it over. Let stand in a cool place until the filling sets (it will not become hard). If desired, spread with lightly sweetened whipped cream, flavored with rum or Cognac, and serve.

Yield: 8 to 12 servings.

Pastry for a 10-inch tart
2 cups whole pecans and/or walnuts
¼ cup honey
¾ cup light brown sugar
½ cup granulated sugar
2 tablespoons butter
½ cup heavy cream

Tarte au Sucre *(Sugar pie)*

1. In a mixing bowl, cream together 1 cup of butter and the flour.

2. Dissolve the yeast in the water and stir it into the butter-flour paste. Beat in the egg yolks, one at a time, using a wooden spoon.

3. Butter a 10-inch quiche pan with a removable bottom. Spread the mixture all over the bottom, smoothing it over with a spatula. Place in a warm place and let rise for 1 hour.

4. After the pie has been resting for 45 minutes, preheat the oven to 350 degrees. Place the pie in the oven and bake for about 7 minutes.

5. Remove the pie. Coarsely crush the sugar cubes (using a towel and mallet or hammer). Sprinkle this evenly over the top of the pie. Dot evenly with the remaining 3 tablespoons of butter. Continue baking for 20 to 25 minutes longer. Serve at room temperature.

Yield: 8 or more servings.

1 cup plus 3 tablespoons butter
1 cup plus 3 tablespoons flour
1¾ envelopes granular yeast
⅓ cup water
5 egg yolks
10 sugar cubes (called hostess cubes)

Profiteroles *(Cream puffs)*

There are numerous desserts in a pastrymaker's art that border on the miraculous—things that puff in the oven out of all proportion to what they were when they went in. One of the most impressive of these—and one easily within the scope of any talented amateur cook—is a dessert whose base is called pâte à choux in French, cream-puff paste in English. It is best known as the base for éclairs and profiteroles, or cream puffs. The pastry is piped onto a greased, floured baking sheet and baked briefly until puffed and golden brown.

More difficult, if not the most difficult of all pastries to make, is the glory known as puff pastry, which is used for napoleons and vols au vents. If the technique can be mastered, it is one of the most gratifying.

1 recipe for pâte à choux (see recipe below)
1 recipe for crème patissière (see recipe page 572)
1 recipe for mocha or cocoa frosting (see recipe below)

1. Preheat the oven to 425 degrees.
2. Rub a baking sheet all over with butter and sprinkle with flour. Shake the baking sheet this way and that until the surface is coated with flour. Shake off excess.
3. Fit a pastry bag with a round tipped, number 6 pastry tube. Spoon the pâte à choux into the bag. Holding the pastry bag straight up with the tip close to the floured surface of the pan, squeeze the bag to make mounds of pastry at intervals all over the pan. There should be about 36 mounds.
4. The mounds may have pointed tips on top. To flatten these, wet a clean tea towel and squeeze it well. Open it up, fold it over in thirds. Hold it stretched directly over the mounds, quickly patting down just enough to rid the mounds of the pointed tips. Do not squash the mounds.
5. Place the pan in the oven and bake for 30 minutes, or until the cream puffs are golden brown and cooked through. Remove and let cool.
6. Outfit another pastry bag with the same number 6 pastry tube. Spoon the crème patissière into the bag. Slit a small hole in the side of each cream puff and insert the tip of the bag. Squeeze enough crème patissière into the hole to partly fill the cream puff. Decorate the top of each cream puff with frosting, using a palette knife or a pastry bag outfitted with a star tube. Chill until frosting sets.

Yield: About 36 cream puffs.

1. Put the water in a saucepan and add the butter, salt to taste and sugar. Bring to the boil.

2. Add the flour all at once, stirring vigorously and thoroughly in a circular fashion with a wooden spoon until a ball is formed and the mixture cleans the sides of the saucepan.

3. Add the eggs, one at a time, beating vigorously and rapidly with the spoon until the egg is well blended with the mixture. Add another egg, beat and so on until all 4 eggs are beaten in.

Yield: Enough cream puff paste for 36 cream puffs or 20 éclairs.

Pâte à choux *(Cream puff paste)*

1	cup cold water
8	tablespoons butter
	Salt
½	teaspoon sugar
1	cup flour
4	large eggs

1. Place the butter in a small mixing bowl. Using a whisk or electric beater, start creaming the butter.

2. Add the powdered cocoa. Separately, blend the freeze-dried coffee with the boiling water.

3. Start blending the butter and cocoa and add the liquid coffee. Beat in a small pinch of salt.

4. Use as a frosting on cookies, cream puffs and so on.

Yield: About ¾ cup.

Mocha frosting

2½	tablespoons butter at room temperature
1	tablespoon powdered cocoa
1	tablespoon freeze-dried coffee or espresso
1	tablespoon boiling water
1	cup confectioners' sugar
	Pinch of salt

Profiteroles au Chocolat

Bake the profiteroles but do not fill with pastry cream. Split them in half and scoop a small portion of ice cream onto the bottom of each cream puff. Cover with the cream puff top. Spoon the chocolate sauce over and serve immediately.

Yield: 12 or more servings

36	profiteroles (see recipe above)
36	small scoops vanilla ice cream
	Chocolate sauce (see recipe below)

1. Break up the chocolate and put it in a saucepan. Add the water and sugar and cook, stirring as necessary, until chocolate melts.

2. Off heat, add the cream and butter. Keep warm without boiling.

Yield: 3½ cups.

Chocolate sauce

1	pound dark, sweet chocolate
⅔	cup water
3	tablespoons sugar
1	cup heavy cream
4	tablespoons butter

Éclairs

Follow the recipe for profiteroles (cream puffs), but rather than make mounds of pastry as indicated, pipe the pâte à choux mixture out at intervals into straight ribbons, each about 4 inches long. There should be about 20 ribbons of paste in all. Smooth over the ends of the ribbons with a spatula. Place the pan in the oven and bake for 20 minutes, or until the éclairs are golden brown and cooked through. Remove and let cool. Decorate the top of each éclair with frosting, using a palette knife or pastry bag outfitted with a star tube. Chill until frosting sets.

Yield: About 20 éclairs.

Puff Pastry

5 cups flour plus additional as necessary
1½ pounds sweet butter
⅓ teaspoon salt
1½ cups water

1. Place the flour and butter in the freezer and let stand until very, very, cold.

2. Spoon ¾ cup of flour onto a flat, cold surface, preferably marble. Make a well in the center and add 1¼ pounds of butter. Using a pastry cutter or knife, chop the butter until it is coarse-fine. Knead it, incorporating the flour a little at at time. Knead the mixture well and shape it into a square measuring about 4½ by 2 inches. Wrap the square in a length of wax paper and place in the refrigerator to chill, 10 minutes or longer.

3. Clean the work surface and add remaining flour. Make a well in the center and add salt and the remaining ¼ pound of butter. Cut the butter into coarse-fine pieces. Pour 1 cup of cold water into the well. Add flour if necessary to keep the water from overflowing. Start working the three elements together, gradually incorporating the flour and adding more water as necessary. The total amount of water used in preparing this recipe was 1 cup plus 6 tablespoons. Knead the mixture well, scraping the work surface as necessary with a spatula or pastry scraper. Push the dough out with the heel of the hand as you work. Have ready additional flour (other than the 5 cups) for flouring the board as you knead to keep the dough from sticking. The additional flour added in this step should be about 6 tablespoons.

4. Gather the dough into a ball and place it on a lightly floured board. Flatten it slightly. Using a knife or pastry cutter, make slashes about ½ inch deep in the top of the dough to make a cross.

5. Using the fingers, open up the four edges of the dough formed by the slashes. Roll out the four edges, cloverleaf fashion. The center of the cloverleaf should be slightly padded and large enough to hold the square of dough that is being chilled. The four "clovers" should be large enough to completely envelop the square of dough when it is added. Always sprinkle the dough with as little flour as necessary to prevent sticking.

6. Add the square of chilled dough and fold one "clover" over it, stretching the edges down and almost under the dough. Fold over another "clover," stretching the edges down and almost under the dough. Fold over the third and finally the fourth "clover." When the fourth "clover" is folded over, stretch the edges under the dough without tearing. Press the dough with the fingers to make a 10-inch square.

7. Roll out the dough into a 10- x 15-inch rectangle. Line a jelly roll pan with wax paper and place the rectangle of dough on it. Cover with a slightly damp cloth and refrigerate for 20 minutes or longer.

8. Lightly flour a flat surface. Remove the damp cloth and tip the puff pastry out onto the surface.

9. Roll out the pastry. Sprinkle both the work surface and the dough lightly with flour as necessary to prevent sticking. Roll the dough into a rectangle measuring about 16 by 30 inches (about ¼ inch thick).

10. Fold the dough into thirds. Fold the right side over and brush the flour from the surface of the dough.

11. Neatly fold over the left side of the dough, brush off the surface and make a slight indentation with one finger to indicate the first folding step is concluded. Repeat the step lining a jelly roll pan with wax paper, covering the dough with a damp cloth, and chilling for 20 minutes.

12. Repeat steps 7 through 11. When the dough has been rolled out and properly folded, make two indentations in the center of the dough. Refrigerate at least 20 minutes and preferably overnight. (Note: In this step the dough may be made even flakier if it is rolled into a rectangle measuring about 15 by 29 inches. The dough may then be folded into quarters instead of thirds by folding both ends toward the center and folding both halves over each.)

13. Repeat the rolling and folding through a total of five procedures (and five finger indentations). The dough is now ready to be used for any desired purpose.

Yield: About 3½ pounds of puff pastry. One portion at a time can be used and the remainder frozen.

Napoleons

1½ pounds puff pastry (see recipe page 422)
1 egg, lightly beaten
1¾ cups crème patissière (see recipe page 572)
Whipped cream
Confectioners' sugar

1. Preheat the oven to 375 degrees.

2. Roll out the puff pastry into a ¼-inch-thick rectangle. It may measure about 18 by 25 inches. Prick it liberally with a fork. Arrange it on a large baking sheet and brush with beaten egg. Let rest in the refrigerator for 1 hour.

3. Bake the pastry sheet for 30 minutes, or until puffed and golden brown. Let cool.

4. Cut the pastry lengthwise into strips about 5 inches wide. Spread one strip with crème patissière. Cover with another strip, more pastry cream, and so on. Chop any scraps of baked pastry. Spread the top and sides of the napoleon with whipped cream and garnish the top and sides with chopped pastry. Sprinkle with confectioners' sugar and serve.

Yield: 20 or more napoleons.

Vol-au-Vents *(Patty shells)*

Puff pastry (see recipe page 422)
1 whole egg, beaten

1. Prepare the puff pastry. There is sufficient pastry for 20 3-inch patty shells. Divide it in half to prepare 10. The remaining pastry may be closely wrapped in foil or plastic wrap and frozen.

2. To prepare patty shells for 10, roll out half the puff pastry into a rectangle measuring about 13 by 17 inches. With the fingers flick a little water over a cooky sheet.

3. Use a 3-inch biscuit cutter and cut out circles of puff pastry. Arrange half the circles uniformly over the cooky sheet. All scraps of leftover dough may be pressed together and used for dishes like napoleons.

4. Brush the tops of each circle with a little beaten egg.

5. Using a 1-inch biscuit cutter, cut out the centers of the remaining 10 rounds of pastry. Arrange these neatly placed on top of the rounds on the baking sheet.

6. Brush the tops of the circles with a little beaten egg. Refrigerate for several hours.

7. Preheat the oven to 425 degrees.

8. Bake the shells 30 to 40 minutes. In the course of baking, note carefully that the shells do not tend to become lopsided. If they seem to go in that direction, cover lightly with a piece of cardboard.

9. When cooked, use a small paring knife and carefully lift out and reserve the centers of each patty shell. Serve the shells

filled with creamed dishes such as chicken, shrimp, ham or sweetbreads. Garnish each serving with the reserved small center removed from the baked patty shell.

Yield: 10 to 12 patty shells.

Vanilla Ice Cream

1. Put the yolks and sugar in a heavy casserole. Beat with a wire whisk until pale yellow.

2. In another saucepan, combine the milk and cream. If the vanilla bean is used, split it down one side and add it. Bring just to the boil.

3. Add about ½ cup of the hot mixture to the egg yolk mixture and beat rapidly. Add the remaining hot mixture, stirring rapidly. Scrape the tiny black seeds from the center of the vanilla bean into the custard. Heat slowly, stirring and scraping all around the bottom with a wooden spoon. Bring the mixture almost, but not quite, to the boil. The correct temperature is 180 degrees. This cooking will rid the custard of the raw taste of the yolks.

4. Pour the mixture into a cold mixing bowl. This will prevent the mixture from cooking further. Let stand until cool or at room temperature. If the vanilla bean is not used, add the vanilla extract at this point.

5. Pour the mixture into the container of an electric or hand-cranked ice cream freezer. Freeze according to the manufacturer's instructions.

Yield: 8 to 12 servings.

6 egg yolks
1 cup sugar
4 cups milk
1 cup heavy cream
1 vanilla bean, or 2 teaspoons pure vanilla extract

Chocolate Ice Cream

Prepare the recipe for vanilla ice cream but use only ¾ cup of sugar.

Put 8 ounces (8 squares) of chocolate in a small, heavy saucepan. You can vary the chocolate to your own taste, using sweet, semisweet or bitter. Or you can use a combination of two. Set the saucepan in a larger pan containing boiling water. Let the chocolate stand over its hot water bath until softened. Stir with a rubber spatula until smooth.

Add the melted chocolate to the hot vanilla custard. Pour a little of the custard into the saucepan to retrieve the chocolate that clings to the bottom and sides of the saucepan. Scrape this into the custard.

Proceed to freeze the custard as for vanilla ice cream.

Coconut Ice Cream

Prepare the recipe for vanilla ice cream but eliminate the vanilla bean or extract. In its place, add ½ cup of sweetened coconut cream (available in cans) and 2 cups of sweetened, flaked or shredded coconut. Proceed as directed for vanilla ice cream.

Fresh Strawberry Ice Cream

4 pints (8 cups) strawberries
1½ cups sugar
5 egg yolks
1 cup heavy cream

1. Pick over the strawberries. Pluck away the stems, cut away the bruised and unripe spots. Rinse the strawberries well and drain. Pour them into a mixing bowl and sprinkle with sugar. Stir. Cover and refrigerate overnight.

2. Drain the strawberries and reserve the syrup. There should be about 1½ cups of syrup.

3. Put the yolks in a mixing bowl and beat well. Add the syrup and cream and stir to blend.

4. Pour the mixture into a heavy saucepan and heat. Use a wooden spoon and stir constantly, this way and that, making certain that the spoon touches all over the bottom of the saucepan. Cook until the mixture has a custardlike consistency and coats the sides of the spoon (180 degrees). Do not let the sauce boil or it will curdle.

5. Immediately remove the saucepan from the heat but continue stirring. Set the saucepan in a basin of cold water to reduce the temperature. Let the sauce cool to room temperature.

6. Pour the custard into the container of an electric ice cream freezer. Freeze according to the manufacturer's instructions. When partly frozen, add the strawberries. Continue freezing until solid.

Yield: 12 servings.

Lemon Lotus Ice Cream

4 lemons
2 cups sugar
4 cups (two pints) half-and-half
2 cups milk

1. Trim off and discard the ends of 1 lemon. Cut the lemon into thin slices. Remove the seeds from the slices and cut the slices in half.

2. Squeeze the remaining 3 lemons and combine the juice with the sugar in a mixing bowl. Add the lemon slices and re-

frigerate, preferably overnight. Stir until all the sugar is dissolved.

3. Combine the half-and-half and milk in the canister of an ice cream freezer. Chill thoroughly, preferably in the freezer, for 10 to 25 minutes. Do not allow the mixture to freeze.

4. Add the lemon and sugar mixture to the cream mixture and install the canister in the ice cream freezer. Freeze according to the manufacturer's directions. Keep frozen until ready to serve.

Yield: 6 servings.

Fresh Mango Ice Cream

1	cup heavy cream
2	cups milk
5	egg yolks
1	cup sugar
	Salt to taste
1	teaspoon pure vanilla extract
2	fresh, ripe, unblemished mangoes
¼	cup dark rum

1. In a saucepan with a heavy bottom, combine the cream, milk, egg yolks, ½ cup sugar, salt and vanilla extract. Cook over low heat or in a double boiler, stirring constantly with a wooden spoon all around the bottom to make sure the custard does not stick.

2. Continue cooking and stirring until the custard is as thick as heavy cream (180 degrees). Remove the custard from the heat immediately, stirring constantly for a minute or so. Let cool.

3. Run a knife around the circumference of each mango, cutting through to the large seed in the center. Using a heavy kitchen spoon, run it inside each mango and around the seed. Scrape the flesh from the seed into a mixing bowl. Scoop out the flesh in each half. Chop the flesh and add the remaining ½ cup of sugar. Stir to dissolve. Add this to the custard and add the rum.

4. Pour the mixture into the container of an electric ice cream freezer and freeze according to the manufacturer's instructions.

Yield: 8 to 10 servings.

Coupe Normande *(Vanilla ice cream with apples and Calvados)*

4	firm cooking apples
4	tablespoons butter
½	cup sugar
¼	cup Calvados or applejack
6	servings vanilla ice cream

1. Core and peel the apples. Cut them into quarters and cut the quarters into slices. There should be about 4 cups.

2. Heat the butter in a heavy skillet and add the apples. Cook, stirring gently and tossing, for 6 to 10 minutes. The slices should remain firm and not become mushy. Add the

sugar and cook for 2 minutes, stirring and tossing gently. Sprinkle with the Calvados and ignite it. Serve hot or warm over ice cream.

Yield: 6 servings.

Granité au Citron Vert *(Lime ice)*

One of our earliest associations of food and rhyme is, of course, the four lines of nonsense: I scream, you scream, we all scream for ice cream. But if we go wild for ice cream, we go absolutely bananas for any pure fruit ice, the kind known in French as a granité and in Italian as a granita.

2 cups sugar
2 cups water
2 tablespoons grated lime rind
2 cups freshly squeezed lime juice

1. Combine the sugar and water in a saucepan and bring to the boil. Simmer for 5 minutes. Let cool.

2. Add the lime rind and juice. Pour the mixture into the container of an electric ice cream freezer and freeze according to the manufacturer's instructions. Serve individual portions, if desired, with cold vodka poured over.

Yield: 12 or more servings.

Note: This is a delicious but somewhat tart ice. If you prefer it less tart, simply increase the water to 3 cups and do not alter the other quantities.

Granité de Pamplemousse *(Grapefruit ice)*

Follow the recipe for lime ice, but substitute grated rind of 1 grapefruit for the lime rind. Substitute 4 cups of fresh grapefruit juice and ⅓ cup of lemon juice in place of 2 cups of lime juice.

Granité de Fruits au Cassis *(Fruit ice with cassis)*

4 cups fresh strawberries or raspberries
2 cups water
1¼ cups sugar
2 tablespoons lemon juice
1½ cups syrop de cassis, available in wine and spirit shops

1. Pick over the berries and remove the stems. Rinse in cold water and drain. Put the berries in the container of a food processor or electric blender and blend, stirring down as necessary. There should be about 2 cups of purée.

2. Combine the water and sugar in a saucepan and bring to the boil. Simmer for 5 minutes. Cool, then chill thoroughly. Add the fruit purée, lemon juice and cassis.

3. Pour the mixture into the container of an electric or hand-cranked ice cream freezer and freeze according to the manufacturer's instructions. This may be served with more cassis poured over.

Yield: 2 quarts, or 12 to 14 servings.

Granita di Caffe con Panna *(Coffee ice with whipped cream)*

1. Prepare the coffee and stir in the freeze-dried or instant coffee.

2. Combine the sugar and water in a saucepan and bring to the boil. Cook for 5 minutes. Cool and add to the coffee mixture. Chill.

3. Add the cream. Pour the mixture into the container of a hand-cranked or electric ice cream machine and freeze according to the manufacturer's instructions. Serve in individual portions with a little Kahlua and/or whipped cream on top.

Yield: 12 or more servings.

Note: To make relatively strong espresso coffee, brew 1 cup of ground espresso or dark roast coffee with 4 cups of water. Or increase the coffee to 1½ cups for very strong coffee.

3½	cups very strong espresso coffee (see note)
2	tablespoons freeze-dried or instant espresso
2½	cups sugar
2	cups water
1	cup heavy cream
	Kahlua and/or sweetened whipped cream, optional

Sabayon Glacé *(Frozen zabaglione)*

1. Use a heavy, deep saucepan or the eggs will scramble. Or if you want to be extra cautious, cook this dessert in the top of a double boiler over boiling water. The latter is clumsy, however.

2. Place the yolks in the saucepan and add the sugar and water. Use a wire whisk and beat vigorously over a Flame Tamer or asbestos pad if the saucepan is used, or over boiling water if the double boiler is used. Beat thoroughly until the mixture is quite foamy and thickened.

3. Gradually beat in the Strega. Immediately place the saucepan into a basin of cold water containing ice and continue beating until cool.

4. Beat the heavy cream until stiff. Add a third of the cream to the sauce and beat it in. Fold in the remainder. Spoon the mixture into 8 or 10 small parfait glasses and place in the freezer. Let stand for about 1 hour and serve.

Yield: 8 to 10 servings.

7	egg yolks
½	cup sugar
2	tablespoons water
⅓	cup Strega, the Italian liqueur
1	cup heavy cream

Strawberry Sherbet

2½ quarts red, ripe,
   unblemished strawberries
2 tablespoons lemon juice
1¾ cups plus 2 tablespoons
   sugar
1½ cups water
   A few drops of red food
   coloring, optional
2 egg whites

1. Pick over the strawberries and remove the stems. Rinse and drain well. Put the strawberries in the container of a food processor or electric blender and process to a fine purée. There should be about 4 cups of purée. Add the lemon juice.

2. Combine 1¾ cups of sugar and the water in a saucepan and bring to the boil. Cook for 10 minutes over moderately high heat. Pour into a mixing bowl to cool. Add the purée. If the mixture is quite pale, you may want to add a few drops of red food coloring.

3. Pour the mixture into the container of an electric or hand-cranked ice cream freezer. Freeze according to the manufacturer's instructions.

4. Meanwhile, put the egg whites in a mixing bowl and start beating. When they are light and frothy, add the remaining 2 tablespoons of sugar. Add the sugar gradually and continue beating until stiff.

5. When the strawberry mixture is frozen, add the beaten egg white to it. Continue freezing to a sherbet consistency.

Yield: 12 to 18 servings.

Frozen Strawberry Soufflé

3 cups sliced strawberries
1¼ cups plus 3 tablespoons
   sugar
3 egg yolks
2 tablespoons framboise,
   mirabelle, kirsch or other
   white spirit, optional
1½ cups heavy cream
3 or 4 whole and/or sliced
   strawberries for garnish

1. Blend the strawberries and ½ cup of sugar in a skillet. Cook, stirring occasionally, until sugar and the liquid from the berries thicken, about 10 minutes. Remove and let cool thoroughly.

2. Select a 2-quart mixing bowl that will fit snugly inside a larger saucepan. Add about 2 inches of water to the saucepan and bring to the simmer.

3. To the mixing bowl add the egg yolks and ¾ cup sugar and beat vigorously and thoroughly with a wire whisk or portable electric mixer, making certain to scrape around the inside bottom of the bowl with the beater.

4. Fit the mixing bowl inside the saucepan (over but not in the water), and continue beating. Beat for about 10 minutes or less, until yolks are quite thick and pale yellow. Beat in the framboise. Add the berry mixture and fold it in. Chill thoroughly.

5. Whip 1 cup of the cream until stiff and fold in 2 tablespoons of sugar. Fold this into the strawberry mixture.

6. Chill a 6- to 7-cup soufflé dish in the freezer.

7. Neatly tie a "collar" made of wax paper or aluminum foil around the soufflé dish. The top of the paper or foil should extend about 2 inches above the top of the dish.

8. Pour the soufflé mixture into the dish. Place in the freezer and let stand overnight.

9. Whip the ½ cup of cream. Beat in the remaining 1 tablespoon of sugar. If desired, outfit a pastry bag with a star tube and pipe the cream around the top in a fancy pattern. Decorate with whole and/or sliced strawberries.

Yield: 8 or more servings.

Frozen Lemon Soufflé

1. Select a skillet with deep sides into which a 2-quart bowl will fit comfortably. Add enough water to come up around the sides of the bowl without overflowing. Start to heat water.

2. Drop yolks and 1½ cups of the sugar into the bowl and beat with a whisk or portable electric mixer until light and lemon-colored. Add the lemon juice and, when the water is boiling, set the bowl in the skillet and continue beating for about 10 minutes, or until the egg mixture is like a very thick, smooth and creamy custard. The temperature of the egg mixture at this point should be 120 to 140 degrees.

3. Scrape the mixture into another mixing bowl and stir in the lemon rind. Let cool and chill thoroughly.

4. Tear off a length of wax paper that will fit around the outside of a 5-cup soufflé dish, adding 1 or 2 inches for overlap.

5. Fold the wax paper lengthwise into thirds. Wrap it around the outside of the soufflé dish about 2 inches above the rim, making sure that it overlaps itself at the ends by at least 1 inch. Secure it with string or paper clips.

6. Beat the heavy cream and, when it starts to thicken, add 2 teaspoons of sugar. Continue beating until stiff. Fold this into the egg mixture.

7. In a separate bowl beat the whites. When they start to mound, add the remaining ¼ cup of sugar, beating constantly. Continue beating until whites are stiff. Fold them into the soufflé mixture.

8. Pour the mixture into the prepared dish and place in the freezer. Let stand for several hours—or overnight—until frozen.

9. Remove the wax paper. Decorate if desired with whipped cream, piped out of a pastry tube, and candied flowers.

Yield: 8 servings.

12 egg yolks
1¾ cups plus 2 teaspoons sugar
¾ cup lemon juice (from approximately 4 lemons)
Grated rind of 1 lemon
½ cup heavy cream
6 egg whites
Whipped cream for garnish, optional
Candied flowers for garnish, optional

Mango Kulfi

1 cup canned mango slices in syrup
1 cup canned mango pulp
1 14-ounce can sweetened condensed milk
1 cup heavy cream
2 cups milk
⅛ teaspoon grated nutmeg
¼ teaspoon pure vanilla extract

1. Put the mangoes with syrup and mango pulp into the container of a food processor or electric blender. Blend to a fine purée. Add the condensed milk, cream and milk and blend well. Add the nutmeg and vanilla extract.

3. Pour the mixture into small molds and freeze. Unmold and serve.

Yield: 8 or more servings.

Note: The mango slices and pulp may be omitted and the contents of a 3-ounce package of ground almonds substituted.

Oeufs à la Neige *(Meringues in custard)*

4 cups milk
1¼ cups granulated sugar
1 vanilla bean, or 1 teaspoon vanilla extract
6 eggs, separated
½ teaspoon cornstarch
Pinch of salt
Kirsch or rum (optional)
¼ cup water

1. Bring the milk to the boil in a skillet. Add 6 tablespoons of the sugar and the vanilla bean or vanilla extract. Stir to dissolve the sugar.

2. Beat the egg whites until stiff. While beating, gradually add 6 tablespoons sugar, the cornstarch and the salt.

3. When the meringue is stiff, outfit a pastry bag with a star tube, number 4. Fill it with the meringue and pipe it out in a 2-inch circle onto a baking sheet. Pipe out the meringue to make layer upon layer on the bottom circle. This will produce a small, roundish "beehive" pattern or, if you prefer, a kind of rosette about 2 inches high. Continue making rosettes until all the meringue is used. The meringue is sufficient to produce 16 to 18 rosettes or "eggs."

4. Using a metal spatula, transfer the rosettes, as many as the skillet will hold, into the milk.

5. Simmer for about 30 seconds on one side, then, using a slotted spoon, gently turn the "eggs" over. Poach the other side for 30 seconds.

6. Drain the "eggs," which should be quite firm by now, on paper toweling. Let cool while preparing the remainder of the recipe.

7. Strain the milk in which the "eggs" cooked. If a vanilla bean was used, remove it, rinse and wipe dry, then store in sugar for another use.

8. Beat the egg yolks until light and lemon-colored. Gradually pour into the strained milk. Stir over low heat just until the custard coats the spoon.

9. The custard may be flavored with kirsch or rum. In any event, strain the custard into a wide, shallow serving dish and cover with the "eggs." Chill.

10. Combine the remaining sugar with the ¼ cup of water in a saucepan. Cook until the caramel is dark amber in color, but do not let it burn.

11. Before the caramel has a chance to set, pour it in a thin thread all over the tops of the "eggs."

Yield: 10 or more servings.

Dacquoise

Dacquoise is, without question, one of the finest and most sought-after desserts in fine restaurants. One of the first places we ever encountered it was at the distinguished Coach House. One of the restaurants where we've most recently sampled it is the Windows on the World at the World Trade Center. A dacquoise is a layered meringue dessert made with hazel or other nuts, the layers put together with a rich butter cream. One of the finest dacquoises we've ever sampled was prepared in our kitchen by our good friend and master pastry chef, Albert Kumin, now the White House pastry chef.

1. Preheat the oven to 250 degrees.

2. Select one or two baking sheets of sufficient size so that three 9-inch circles can be traced on them without overlapping. Butter the baking sheet or sheets evenly. Sprinkle with flour and shake it around to coat the surface evenly. Shake off excess flour. Using a round-bottom 9-inch cake tin or false bottom and a pointed knife, outline three 9-inch circles over the flour-coated baking sheet.

3. Place the egg whites in the bowl of an electric beater. Beat until they stand in peaks. Gradually beat in half of the granulated sugar. Continue beating until stiff. Blend 1 cup of the nuts and remaining granulated sugar. Fold this into the meringue.

4. Outfit a pastry bag with a number 4 star pastry tube. Add the meringue to the bag and squeeze out the meringue in a neat spiral to completely fill the 3 circles. Squeeze from the pe-

5 egg whites, about ¾ cup
9 tablespoons granulated sugar
1⅓ cups ground hazelnuts, almonds or walnuts
Butter cream (see recipe below)
¼ cup confectioners' sugar, approximately

rimeter of each circle going toward the center or vice versa. Fill in any empty spots. Smooth over the meringue with a spatula. Do not discard any unused meringue, but squirt it out onto the baking sheet apart from the circles. This will be used later for garnish.

5. Place the baking sheet in the oven and bake for 45 minutes, or until firm and set. Remove from the oven and gently run a metal spatula beneath the meringues to loosen them while still warm. Let cool.

6. Select the nicest of the 3 meringue circles for the top layer. Use a metal spatula and smoothly spread one of the circles with butter cream. Add a second circle and spread it similarly. Add the top circle. Spread a light layer of butter cream over the top. Smoothly spread the sides of the dacquoise with butter cream.

7. Blend any leftover pieces of meringue to make fine crumbs. Blend these with the remaining ⅓ cup ground nuts. Coat the sides of the cake with this and sprinkle any leftover mixture on top of the dacquoise. Sprinkle the top with confectioners' sugar.

8. Chill the dacquoise for an hour or longer to facilitate slicing. The dacquoise or leftover portions of it may be wrapped closely and frozen.

Yield: 12 or more servings.

Butter cream

6 egg whites, slightly more than ¾ cup
1¾ cups superfine sugar
1 pound sweet butter at room temperature

1. Combine the egg whites in the bowl of an electric mixer. Set the bowl in a basin of boiling water and start beating with a wire whisk. Gradually add the sugar, beating rapidly with the whisk. Continue beating until the mixture is somewhat thickened. Ideally, the temperature for the mixture should be about 105 degrees. In any event, a "ribbon" should form when the whisk is lifted.

2. Transfer the bowl to the electric beater and start beating on high speed. Continue beating for about 20 minutes, or until the mixture is at room temperature. Gradually add the butter, beating constantly. This butter cream may be flavored variously (see flavored butter cream below).

Yield: 5 to 6 cups.

Flavored butter cream

Mocha butter cream: Blend 1 tablespoon or more of instant or freeze-dried coffee with 1½ tablespoons Cognac or rum. Blend this into the butter cream.

Chocolate butter cream: Melt 3 ounces of sweet chocolate with 1 tablespoon of water and blend it into the butter cream.

Mont Blanc (*A classic chestnut dessert*)

1. Preheat the oven to 150 degrees.

2. Put the egg whites into the bowl of an electric mixer and start beating on low speed. Gradually increase the speed to high while adding 7 tablespoons of sugar, 1 tablespoon at a time. Remove the bowl and, using a plastic spatula, fold in the remaining 7 tablespoons of sugar.

3. Butter a baking sheet and sprinkle with flour. Shake it around to coat the surface evenly. Shake off excess flour. Using a round 9-inch cake tin or false bottom and a pointed knife, outline a perfect circle over the flour-coated baking sheet.

4. Outfit a pastry bag with a number 4 star pastry tube. Add the meringue to the bag and squeeze out the meringue in a neat spiral to completely fill the circle. Cover this layer with another layer of meringue, squeezing out the meringue in the same pattern.

5. Transfer the point of the pastry tube to the center and make a small, piled up beehive pattern, circling around and around with the tip while pushing out the meringue. The "beehive" should measure about 3½ inches wide and 2½ inches high.

6. Place the baking sheet in the oven and bake for about 2 hours, turning the sheet in the oven so that the meringue bakes evenly. When ready, the meringue should be dried out and crisp. Remove and let cool.

7. Meanwhile, as the meringue bakes, peel the chestnuts.

8. Combine the chestnuts, water, sugar and vanilla bean, if used. If not used, add the vanilla extract later. Bring to the boil and simmer for about 2 hours, or until the chestnuts are thoroughly tender. Do not drain. If the vanilla extract is used, add it. Cool.

9. Put the chestnuts through a food mill and blend well with a spoon. Refrigerate until the mixture is quite cold.

10. Outfit a meat grinder with a large blade. Hold a 6-cup ring mold under the blade where the chestnut purée will come out. Add the chestnut purée to the grinder and grind, turning the mold gradually to catch the strands of chestnuts as they emerge. It should look like strands of macaroni.

11. Carefully invert the meringue over the mold, fitting the center of the meringue into the center of the mold. Invert both, letting the chestnut ring fall onto the meringue border.

12. Whip the cream and flavor it with the sugar and vanilla extract. Pipe it onto the center of the meringue, using a pastry

The meringue:

⅔ cup egg whites
14 tablespoons superfine granulated sugar
Flour

The chestnuts:

2 pounds chestnuts, peeled (see instructions below)
3 cups water
3 cups sugar
1 vanilla bean, or 2 teaspoons pure vanilla extract

The garnish:

1½ cups heavy cream
2 tablespoons superfine granulated sugar
1 teaspoon pure vanilla extract
¼ cup confectioners' sugar

bag outfitted with a star tube. Sprinkle with confectioners' sugar through a sieve onto the chestnut ring and serve cold.
Yield: 12 servings.

How to peel chestnuts

Use a sharp paring knife and insert the tip to one side of the thick, oval "crown" of a chestnut. Bring the tip around the chestnut, circular fashion, to the other side of the crown. Continue until all the chestnuts are thus carved.

Put the chestnuts in a skillet with water to cover and salt to taste. Bring to the boil and simmer for 15 to 20 minutes, or until the shells can easily be removed with the fingers. Drain. When cool enough to handle, peel the chestnuts. Remove both the outer shell and the inner peel.

"Forget-it" Meringue Torte

Butter
9 to 11 egg whites
¼ teaspoon cream of tartar
2½ cups sugar
1 teaspoon pure vanilla extract
½ teaspoon almond extract
1 cup heavy cream, whipped and sweetened to taste
Sliced sweetened fruit such as peaches, or berries such as strawberries or raspberries

1. Preheat the oven to 450 degrees.

2. Butter the bottom and sides of an angel food cake pan with removable bottom.

3. Use enough egg whites to make 1½ cups. Empty them into the container of an electric mixer. Beat them until they become frothy and add the cream of tartar. Gradually add the sugar, beating constantly. After all the sugar has been added, beat in the vanilla and almond extracts. Continue beating until the meringue is quite stiff and has a high, glossy sheen.

4. Spoon the meringue into the prepared pan. Smooth over the top.

5. Place the pan in the oven and immediately turn off the oven heat. Do not open the oven door for several hours, preferably overnight.

6. Remove the meringue from the oven. Remember that the meringue will have a ragged look at this point. A crisp, browned crust may have formed that clings to the rim of the pan. Do not bother. Break it off and discard, or crumble it for decoration. In any event, remove the center section of the pan. Using a spatula or pancake turner, loosen the bottom of the meringue. Unmold the meringue ring onto a round plate.

7. Garnish the bottom and sides of the meringue ring with sweetened whipped cream and decorate with the crumbled meringue topping and the sliced sweetened fruit or berries. A good sauce is 3 packages of frozen raspberries, defrosted, sweetened with ½ cup of sugar and framboise or kirsch to taste.
Yield: 12 or more servings.

Galaktoboureko (*A rich milk and egg pastry*)

1. In a saucepan scald the 2 quarts of milk and set aside to cool.

2. In a bowl, beat the eggs until they are frothy. Gradually beat in the sugar and semolina and beat for about 2 minutes more. Add vanilla and remaining cup of cold milk and add the mixture to the warm milk.

3. Cook over low heat, stirring constantly, until mixture thickens and coats the spoon. Do not allow mixture to boil. Remove from heat and add 4 tablespoons butter, cut into pieces, and continue stirring until butter melts. Cool the custard, cover with wax paper and chill for 3 hours.

4. Preheat the oven to 400 degrees.

5. Melt the remaining butter. Butter a 16- x 11- x 12-inch pan and add half the phyllo pastry, one leaf at a time, and brush each leaf with butter as it is added. Have the pastry overlap the edges of the pan. Keep the remaining leaves covered with plastic wrap.

6. After half the leaves have been placed in the pan, pour in the custard, spreading it evenly, and fold the edges of the leaves over the custard. Arrange remaining phyllo leaves over the custard in the same manner and brush each leaf with melted butter. Trim the edges to 1 inch and fold them inward and under.

7. Cut the top layers of leaves, down to the custard, into strips about 2 inches wide and then cut strips diagonally to form diamond patterned pieces. Bake for 15 minutes and then reduce the oven heat to 350 degrees. Bake for 45 minutes longer, or until top of pastry is golden brown and flaky.

8. While pastry is baking prepare the syrup. In a saucepan combine the sugar, water, cinnamon and lemon juice. Bring to the boil over low heat, stirring constantly until syrup thickens and coats the spoon. Cool the syrup and pour over warm pastry.

Yield: About 40 pieces.

The filling and pastry:

2 quarts plus 1 cup milk
10 large eggs
1 cup sugar
⅔ cup fine semolina, or cream of wheat
2 teaspoons vanilla
1 pound sweet butter
1 pound phyllo pastry

The syrup:

18 ounces sugar
12 ounces water
1 stick cinnamon
Few drops of lemon juice

Crêpes Suzette

Crêpes suzette, as served traditionally in a restaurant, are demanding of space and time. The maître d'hôtel carefully adds the crêpes to the crêpe butter, turning and folding with fork and spoon. The version here is much simplified. The crêpes are smeared with crêpe butter, arranged in quantity in a crêpe pan or other dish and heated in the oven. They are then ready to be finished and served without fuss to numerous guests.

The crêpes:

- 2 cups flour
- 3 eggs
- 2½ to 3 cups milk
- 1 tablespoon sugar
- 4 tablespoons melted butter
- 1 tablespoon vanilla
- 1 teaspoon salt

The crêpe butter:

- 24 lumps of sugar (called hostess cubes)
- 2 oranges
- ¾ pound sweet butter at room temperature
- ¼ cup sugar
- 1 tablespoon lemon juice
- ¾ cup orange juice
- 2 tablespoons Grand Marnier

For flaming:

- 1 tablespoon sugar
- ½ to ¾ cup Cognac

1. Place the flour in a mixing bowl and make a well in the center. Add the eggs and, while stirring with a wire whisk, add ½ cup of the milk. Beat to make as smooth as possible. Add more milk to make the batter the consistency of heavy cream. Put the mixture through a fine sieve. Or it may be blended. If it is blended, it must be left to stand for 2 hours or longer. In any event, stir in the sugar, butter, vanilla and salt.

2. Rub the bottom of a crêpe pan with a piece of paper toweling that has been dipped in butter. This is necessary for the first crêpe, but probably unnecessary afterward if the crêpe pan has been properly cured.

3. Spoon 2 to 4 tablespoons of the crêpe batter into the pan and quickly swirl the pan around this way and that until the bottom is evenly coated. The crêpes should be quite thin. Cook briefly until the crêpe sets and starts to brown lightly on the bottom. Using a spatula, turn the crêpe in the skillet and cook briefly on the other side without browning. Turn out onto wax paper. A properly made crêpe, held up to the light, looks like lace. Continue cooking until all the batter is used.

4. Preheat the oven to 400 degrees.

5. When all the crêpes are made, prepare the crêpe butter. Rub the lumps of sugar all over the skin of the oranges, then squeeze the oranges and save the juice. Place the lumps between sheets of wax paper and crush them with a rolling pin. Pour the crushed sugar into a bowl and add the butter, sugar, lemon juice, ¾ cup of orange juice and Grand Marnier. Beat to blend well, preferably with an electric mixer.

6. Smear the top (the unbrowned side) of each crêpe with 1 teaspoon or so of crêpe butter and fold once, then twice to make a triangle. Rub the bottom of a large skillet (there are special crêpe skillets that are convenient but not essential) with the remaining melted crêpe butter.

7. Arrange the crêpes over the butter and sprinkle 1 tablespoon of sugar over all.

8. Heat to bubbling on top of the stove and place in the oven for 5 minutes. Sprinkle the Cognac over the crêpes. Ignite it and ladle the sauce over the crêpes until the flame dies.

Yield: 24 to 36 crêpes.

Crêpes Soufflé

1. Preheat the oven to 400 degrees.

2. Melt 2 tablespoons of butter in a saucepan. Blend the flour and cornstarch and add it, stirring with a wire whisk. When blended, add the milk, stirring constantly with a wire whisk. When the mixture is thickened and smooth, lower the heat. Add the vanilla.

3. Beat the egg yolks and add them to the sauce, beating constantly and rapidly with the whisk. Do not boil or the sauce will curdle. When thickened, remove immediately from the heat. Spoon the custard into a mixing bowl. Cool slightly. Fold in the praline.

4. Beat the egg whites until stiff and add about ⅓ of them to the custard mixture. Beat them in quickly with the whisk. Add the remaining whites and fold them in with a rubber spatula.

5. Butter a baking and serving dish large enough to hold 12 filled, rolled crêpes. If necessary, use two baking dishes.

6. Arrange the crêpes on a flat surface and fill the centers with equal portions of the custard mixture. Roll the crêpes to enclose the filling.

7. Arrange the filled crêpes on the baking dish. Brush with melted butter and sprinkle with slivered almonds. Sprinkle half the confectioners' sugar over all.

8. Place in the oven and bake for 10 minutes, or until nicely puffed and slightly brown on top. Remove from the oven and sprinkle with remaining confectioners' sugar. Serve with sauce anglaise pralinée on the side.

Yield: 6 servings.

12 crêpes (see recipe below)
2 tablespoons butter
2 tablespoons flour
1 teaspoon cornstarch
2 cups milk
¼ teaspoon pure vanilla extract
4 large eggs, separated
½ cup pulverized praline (see recipe below)
2 tablespoons melted butter
¼ cup toasted, blanched, slivered almonds
2 tablespoons confectioners' sugar
Sauce anglaise pralinée (see recipe below)

1. Blend the flour, egg, sugar and salt in a mixing bowl. Gradually add the milk, stirring constantly.

2. Select a small crêpe pan (5 or 6 inches in bottom diameter) and melt the butter. Pour the butter into the crêpe batter, stirring constantly. Strain through a fine sieve. Add the vanilla.

3. Add about 2 tablespoons or slightly less of the batter to the crêpe pan. Cook for 45 seconds to 1 minute to a side (the crêpe should be lightly browned) and turn the crêpe. Cook for about 30 seconds on the second side and transfer to a flat surface. Add more batter and cook as before. Continue until all the batter is used.

Yield: 12 to 14 crêpes.

Crêpes

½ cup flour
1 large egg
1 teaspoon sugar
⅛ teaspoon salt
¾ cup milk
3 tablespoons butter
½ teaspoon vanilla extract

Sauce anglaise pralinée
(English custard with praline)

⅓ cup sugar
2 large egg yolks
1 cup milk
¼ teaspoon pure vanilla extract
1 tablespoon dark rum
½ cup ground praline (see recipe below)

1. Combine the sugar and yolks in a saucepan and beat with a wire whisk until thickened and pale yellow. Place the saucepan over low heat.

2. Heat the milk almost but not quite to the boiling point. Add the milk to the yolk mixture, stirring rapidly with the whisk. Cook, stirring constantly, until the custard coats the back of wooden spoon. Do not boil.

3. Remove immediately from the heat and add the vanilla. Cool. Add the rum and ground praline.

Yield: About 1¼ cups.

Hazelnut or almond praline

1 cup sugar
¼ cup water
1¼ cups whole hazelnuts or almonds
   Vegetable oil

1. You must use a very heavy saucepan for this. Blend the sugar and water in the saucepan and stir well. Cook the mixture over moderate heat for about 5 minutes (to a temperature of about 248 degrees).

2. Remove the syrup from the heat and add the nuts. Stir, off heat, until the syrup starts to become grainy. Return the mixture to the heat, stirring. The syrup will become white and hardened. Cook, stirring constantly, until the crystallized syrup becomes liquid again.

3. Meanwhile, rub a marble or Formica surface with a light coating of vegetable oil.

4. Cook the nuts in syrup for 10 to 15 minutes, until the syrup becomes dark caramel-colored. Cooking time will depend on the intensity of the heat. Take care that the caramel coating does not burn or it will be bitter. As soon as the proper color is achieved, spoon and scrape the mixture onto the oil-coated marble. Let stand until cool and totally hardened like peanut brittle.

5. Break up the candy and put it in the container of a food processor or electric blender. Blend until the texture is like ground nuts, but not too fine.

Yield: 2 cups.

Note: Ground or pulverized praline is delicious on top of ice cream, as a garnish for frozen soufflés and so on. Leftover praline should be kept in a tightly sealed jar in a cool place.

Soufflé aux Ananas   *(Pineapple soufflé)*

6 tablespoons butter
1¼ cups sugar
½ cup flour

1. Butter a 2½-quart soufflé dish and place it in the refrigerator or freezer.

2. Place the 6 tablespoons of butter, ½ cup sugar and flour

in a mixing bowl and knead with the fingers until well blended. Shape into a ball and set aside.

3. Heat the milk to boiling and add the butter mixture, stirring constantly with a wire whisk until blended and smooth.

4. Drain the pineapple but reserve both the pulp and juice. Put 1½ cups of pulp into the container of a food processor or blender and blend to a purée. Reserve the remaining pineapple for the sauce. Add the purée to the milk and butter mixture.

5. Blend the cornstarch with the rum and add it, stirring rapidly. Add the yolks and cook, stirring, for about 1 minute. Remove from the heat and spoon the sauce into a large mixing bowl. Cover with a round of buttered wax paper and let cool.

6. Preheat the oven to 400 degrees.

7. Beat the egg whites gradually, adding the remaining ¾ cup sugar. Beat to a stiff meringue stage. Beat half the egg whites into the soufflé mixture. Fold in the remaining whites. Pour the mixture into the prepared soufflé dish. Bake for 30 minutes, or until puffed high and nicely browned on top. Serve with apricot and pineapple sauce, if desired.

Yield: 6 to 8 servings.

Note: If we lived in a region where fresh pineapple grows, we would use fresh pineapple in this recipe. Most pineapples bought here, however, have little flavor and are not sweet enough. Thus, for this recipe we prefer canned pineapple.

3 cups milk
1 20-ounce can crushed pineapple
1 tablespoon cornstarch
3 tablespoons dark rum
8 eggs, separated
Apricot and pineapple sauce (see recipe below), optional

Spoon the preserves into a saucepan and add the pineapple juice. Stir to blend and add the pineapple and rum. Bring to the boil and serve hot.

Yield: About 2 cups.

Apricot and pineapple sauce

1 12-ounce jar apricot preserves
½ cup liquid from canned pineapple
½ cup crushed pineapple
¼ cup rum

XV. Sauces, Stocks and Accompaniments

Mayonnaise

1 egg yolk
 Salt and freshly ground pepper
1 teaspoon imported mustard,
 such as Dijon or Düsseldorf
1 teaspoon vinegar or lemon
 juice
1 cup peanut, vegetable or olive
 oil

1. Place the yolk in a mixing bowl and add salt and pepper to taste, mustard and vinegar. Beat vigorously for a second or two with a wire whisk or electric beater.

2. Start adding the oil gradually, beating continuously with the whisk or electric beater. Continue beating and adding oil until all of it is used. If the mayonnaise is not to be used immediately, beat in a tablespoon of water. This will help stabilize the mayonnaise and retard its turning when stored in the refrigerator.

Yield: About 1 cup.

Food Processor Mayonnaise

2 egg yolks
 Salt to taste
2 teaspoons imported mustard,
 such as Dijon or Düsseldorf
1¼ cups peanut, vegetable or
 olive oil
 Freshly ground pepper to
 taste
2 teaspoons or more vinegar or
 lemon juice

1. Place the yolks in the container of the food processor equipped with the steel or plastic blade.

2. Add the salt and mustard and activate the food processor for a split second only. If the yolks are overhomogenized, they may break down. Have the oil in a measuring cup with a pouring spout. Start the motor while simultaneously adding the oil in a thin stream. After half the oil has been added, it can be added more rapidly. Add the remaining ingredients, processing just enough to blend. Spoon into a jar and refrigerate.

Yield: About 1½ cups.

Anchovy mayonnaise

For each cup of mayonnaise, add 1 tablespoon of anchovy paste or chopped anchovies.

For each cup of mayonnaise, use ½ cup of diced, seeded cucumbers. Sprinkle the cucumber with salt and refrigerate 30 minutes. Drain, add the cucumber to the mayonnaise and blend well.

Cucumber mayonnaise

To each cup of mayonnaise, add ¼ cup of chopped cornichons or sour pickles, 1 tablespoon chopped, drained capers, 1 teaspoon mustard, 1 chopped anchovy, 1 teaspoon chopped parsley, ½ teaspoon chopped tarragon.

Sauce rémoulade

For each cup of mayonnaise, add ¼ cup chopped fresh dill and the juice of ½ orange.

Orange and dill mayonnaise

For each cup of mayonnaise, blend in the food processor or electric blender ½ cup chopped watercress, 1 teaspoon chopped parsley, 1 teaspoon fresh tarragon leaves and 1 teaspoon chopped chives. Add to the mayonnaise.

Sauce verte (*Mayonnaise with green herbs*)

Place 2 tablespoons finely chopped shallots in cheesecloth and run under cold water. Squeeze to extract most of the moisture. Add the shallots to 1 cup of mayonnaise.

Shallot mayonnaise

Tartar Sauce

1. Place the yolk in a mixing bowl and add the vinegar, mustard, Tabasco, salt and pepper to taste. Beat vigorously for a second or two with a wire whisk or electric beater.

2. Start adding the oil gradually, beating continuously with the whisk or electric beater. Continue beating and adding oil until all of it is used. Add more salt to taste if necessary, and the lemon juice.

3. Add the remaining ingredients and blend well.

Yield: About 1½ cups.

1 egg yolk
1 teaspoon wine vinegar
2 tablespoons prepared mustard, such as Dijon or Düsseldorf
  A few drops of Tabasco sauce
  Salt and freshly ground pepper
1 cup light olive oil or a combination of olive oil and peanut, vegetable or corn oil
  Lemon juice to taste
¼ cup finely chopped parsley
3 tablespoons finely chopped onion
¼ cup finely chopped cornichons or sour pickles
3 tablespoons chopped drained capers

Hollandaise Sauce

12 tablespoons butter
3 egg yolks
2 tablespoons cold water
Salt to taste
2 teaspoons lemon juice
⅛ teaspoon cayenne pepper

1. Place a skillet on the stove and add about ½ inch of water. Bring the water to the simmer. Have ready a 1½-quart saucepan.

2. Place the butter in another saucepan and place it over very low heat (perhaps using an asbestos pad or a Flame Tamer).

3. Set 1½-quart saucepan in the simmering water in the skillet. Place the egg yolks in the saucepan. Add the cold water, salt and 1 teaspoon lemon juice. Start beating the egg yolks with a wire whisk, stirring in a back-and-forth and circular fashion, making certain that the whisk covers the bottom of the saucepan so that the yolks do not stick. It is important that the heat beneath the saucepan be moderate.

4. When the egg yolks become custardlike and thickened, start adding the melted butter.

5. Continue beating, stirring constantly and vigorously, until all the butter is added. Add the remaining lemon juice and cayenne.

Yield: About 1 cup.

Blender Hollandaise Sauce

½ cup butter
3 egg yolks
Juice of ½ lemon
Salt to taste
Pinch of cayenne pepper

1. Melt the butter and keep it hot, but do not brown.

2. Put the yolks, lemon juice, salt and cayenne in the container of an electric blender. Blend on low speed, gradually adding the hot butter until the sauce is thickened and smooth.

Yield: About ¾ cup.

Béarnaise Sauce

½ pound butter
2 tablespoons red wine vinegar
½ teaspoon freshly ground pepper
1 tablespoon finely chopped shallots
3 teaspoons chopped fresh tarragon, or 1½ teaspoons dried

1. Place the butter in a saucepan and let it melt gradually over low heat.

2. Meanwhile, combine in a saucepan the vinegar, pepper, shallots and 2 teaspoons chopped fresh tarragon (or 1 teaspoon dried). Cook over low heat until the vinegar has evaporated. Let the saucepan cool briefly.

3. Add the egg yolks and water to the shallot mixture and start beating vigorously with a wire whisk. Place over low heat

and continue beating rapidly until the yolks start to thicken. Take care that they do not overheat or they will scramble. Beat in the 1 tablespoon of cold butter and remove from the heat.

4. Tilt the pan with the hot melted butter and add the golden, clear liquid, spoonful by spoonful, to the egg yolk mixture, beating rapidly with the whisk. Continue beating until all the golden liquid is added. Discard the thin milky liquid that settles on the bottom.

5. Line another saucepan with cheesecloth and scrape the sauce into it. Squeeze the sauce through the cheesecloth and into the pan. Beat in the remaining chopped tarragon and salt and pepper to taste.

Yield: About ¾ cup.

2	egg yolks
1	tablespoon water
1	tablespoon cold butter
	Salt

Mornay Sauce

1. Melt the butter in a saucepan and add the flour, stirring with a wire whisk. When blended, add the milk, stirring rapidly with the whisk. When thickened and smooth, add the cream, stirring.

2. Remove from the heat and add the cheese, salt, pepper and cayenne. Add the yolks, stirring rapidly. Heat, stirring, without boiling.

Yield: About 3½ cups.

3	tablespoons butter
4	tablespoons flour
2½	cups milk
½	cup heavy cream
¼	cup grated Gruyère or Cheddar cheese
	Salt and freshly ground pepper to taste
	Pinch of cayenne pepper
2	egg yolks, lightly beaten

Sauce Ravigote

Combine the onion, capers, parsley, tarragon, chives and vinegar in a mixing bowl. Gradually add the oil, stirring vigorously with a wire whisk. Add salt and pepper to taste. Serve with boiled beef or poached fish.

Yield: About 1½ cups.

3	tablespoons finely chopped onion
2	tablespoons drained capers, chopped
¼	cup finely chopped parsley
2	tablespoons finely chopped tarragon
2	tablespoons finely chopped chives
¼	cup wine vinegar
1	cup olive oil
	Salt and freshly ground pepper

Sauce Vinaigrette

2 tablespoons prepared
mustard, such as Dijon or
Düsseldorf
1 tablespoon red wine vinegar
¼ cup olive oil
¼ cup peanut, vegetable or corn
oil

Blend the mustard and vinegar in a mixing bowl. Gradually beat in the oils with a wire whisk.
Yield: About ½ cup.

Sauce Raifort (Horseradish sauce)

¼ to ⅓ cup grated horseradish,
preferably fresh, although
bottled may be used
1½ tablespoons butter
2 tablespoons flour
½ cup beef broth
½ cup milk
½ cup heavy cream
Salt and freshly ground
pepper
A few drops Tabasco sauce
¼ teaspoon grated nutmeg

1. Grate the horseradish and set aside.
2. Melt the butter in a saucepan and add the flour, stirring with a wire whisk. When blended, add the beef broth and milk, stirring rapidly with the whisk.
3. When thickened and smooth, add the cream, stirring constantly. Add the remaining ingredients to taste. Stir in the horseradish just before serving. If bottled horseradish is used, it may be drained well before adding to eliminate some of the vinegar, although some may find that flavor desirable.
Yield: About 2 cups.

Caper sauce

Follow the recipe for horseradish sauce, but substitute 2 or 3 tablespoons of drained capers for the horseradish.

Mustard Cream Sauce

⅓ cup dry mustard
2 tablespoons water
⅓ cup dry white wine
1 tablespoon white wine
vinegar
¼ cup finely chopped shallots
1 teaspoon freshly ground
pepper
1 bay leaf
¼ teaspoon dried thyme
2 cups heavy cream

1. Combine the mustard and water and stir until smooth. Let stand for at least 20 minutes before using.
2. Combine the wine, vinegar, shallots, pepper, bay leaf and thyme in a small saucepan and cook over high heat until most of the liquid evaporates. Add the cream and stir. Cook, stirring often, for about 10 minutes.
3. Add the mustard according to taste and put the sauce through a sieve. Reheat before serving.
Yield: About 2 cups.

Hot Mustard

Blend the ingredients. Let stand for at least 15 minutes to develop flavor.
Yield: ¼ cup.

⅓ cup powdered mustard
2 tablespoons cold water, white wine, milk or beer
A touch of salt

Sauce Piquante (A mustard and pickle sauce)

Melt half the butter in a saucepan and add the onion and garlic. Cook until wilted and add the vinegar. Cook for about 2 minutes and add the bay leaf, brown sauce, beef broth and pickles. Simmer for 10 minutes and stir in the mustard. Swirl in the remaining tablespoon of butter. Serve hot with tongue or pork.
Yield: About 2¼ cups.

2 tablespoons butter
⅓ cup finely chopped onion
1 clove garlic, finely minced
1 tablespoon wine vinegar
½ bay leaf
1⅓ cups brown sauce, or canned beef gravy
½ cup fresh or canned beef broth
⅓ cup thinly sliced sour pickles, preferably imported cornichons
1 teaspoon prepared mustard, such as Dijon or Düsseldorf

Mushroom Sauce

1. Melt the butter in a saucepan and add the onion. When wilted, add the mushrooms and cook until they give up their liquid. Cook until the liquid evaporates and sprinkle with salt and pepper to taste.
2. Sprinkle with flour, stirring with a wire whisk. When blended, add the broth, stirring rapidly with the whisk. When blended and smooth, continue cooking, stirring occasionally, for about 15 minutes. Add the cream and simmer for about 5 minutes longer.
Yield: About 2 cups.

1 tablespoon butter
2 tablespoons finely minced onion
4 medium-size mushrooms, about ¼ pound, cut into small cubes
Salt and freshly ground pepper
2 tablespoons flour
1 cup fresh or canned chicken broth
½ cup heavy cream

Watercress Cream Sauce

6 tablespoons butter
6 tablespoons flour
3 cups fresh or canned chick broth
1 bunch watercress
1 cup heavy cream
Salt and freshly ground pepper
¼ teaspoon grated nutmeg

1. Melt 4 tablespoons of butter in a saucepan and add the flour, stirring with a wire whisk. When blended, add the broth, stirring rapidly with the whisk. Cook for about 20 minutes, stirring often.

2. Meanwhile, cut off and discard the tough bottom stems of the watercress. Drop the cress into a small saucepan of boiling water and simmer for about 30 seconds. Drain, squeeze to extract most of the liquid and chop. There should be about ⅓ cup. Set aside.

3. Add the cream to the sauce. Add the salt and pepper to taste and nutmeg. Simmer for about 15 minutes. Strain the sauce through a very fine sieve. Return it to a saucepan and stir in the watercress. Swirl in the remaining 2 tablespoons of butter and serve piping hot.

Yield: About 3½ cups.

Watercress Mayonnaise Sauce

1 tablespoon prepared mustard, such as Dijon or Düsseldorf
1 tablespoon red wine vinegar
Salt to taste
3 drops Tabasco sauce
1 egg yolk
1 cup peanut or olive oil, or a mixture of both
Lemon juice to taste
2 tablespoons heavy cream
½ cup chopped fresh watercress

1. Combine the mustard, vinegar, salt and Tabasco in a mixing bowl. Add the yolk and stir rapidly with a wire whisk. When blended, start adding the oil, stirring rapidly with the whisk.

2. Add more salt and lemon juice to taste. Beat in the cream. Stir in the watercress and serve.

Yield: About 1½ cups.

Beurre Nantais   *(Herb butter sauce)*

¼ cup finely chopped shallots
3 tablespoons wine vinegar
¼ teaspoon freshly ground pepper, preferably white
2 to 4 tablespoons cold water
¾ pound (3 sticks) cold butter
1½ teaspoons finely chopped tarragon

1. Combine the shallots, vinegar, pepper and water in a 4-cup saucepan. Bring to the boil and simmer until the liquid is reduced to about half. If the mixture becomes too dry, add a little more water.

2. Cut the butter into 1-inch cubes. Add about one-third of it to the sauce, stirring vigorously and cook over low heat. Do not let this sauce boil at any point or it will curdle. Continue adding the butter, about one-third at a time. Continue stirring

until butter is heated through and melted. Beat constantly until the butter sauce is piping hot.

3. Remove from the heat and stir in the tarragon, chervil, if desired, parsley and lime juice, beating. Add salt and pepper to taste and serve immediately.

Yield: About 1¾ cups.

1½ teaspoons finely chopped fresh chervil, optional
1½ teaspoons finely chopped parsley
Juice of 1 lime, or the juice of ½ lemon
Salt and freshly ground pepper

Sauce Joinville   *(Cream sauce with shrimp and mushrooms)*

1. Melt 3 tablespoons of the butter in a saucepan and add the flour, stirring with a wire whisk. When blended, add the fish stock, stirring rapidly with the whisk. When blended and smooth, continue to cook, stirring frequently, for about 20 minutes. Add the cream, stirring. Add salt and pepper.

2. Bring to the boil and add the yolk, stirring rapidly with the whisk. Swirl in 4 tablespoons of butter. Remove from the heat.

3. Meanwhile, as the sauce is being made, thinly slice the mushrooms and cut the shrimp into ½-inch cubes.

4. Heat 1 tablespoon of butter in a saucepan and add the shallots. Stir briefly and add the mushrooms. Cook for about 5 minutes, until wilted and limp. Add the shrimp, salt and pepper. Cook, stirring occasionally, for about 1 minute and add the wine. Cook, stirring occasionally, for about 5 minutes. Add the sauce, stirring. Add salt to taste and bring just to the boil. Add the lemon juice and serve.

Yield: About 3 cups.

8 tablespoons butter
4 tablespoons flour
2 cups fish stock
1 cup heavy cream
Salt and freshly ground pepper
1 egg yolk
½ pound fresh mushrooms
½ pound shrimp, shelled and deveined
3 tablespoons finely chopped shallots
¼ cup dry white wine
Juice of ½ lemon

Shrimp Sauce

1. Cook the shrimp in the shell for about 5 minutes in water to cover. Drain and let cool. Shell and devein the shrimp and cut them into small, bite-size pieces.

2. Melt the butter in a saucepan and add the flour, stirring with a wire whisk. Blend the clam juice and cream and add it to the saucepan, stirring rapidly with the whisk. When thickened and smooth, add the sherry, bay leaf, nutmeg and celery seed. Add the salt and pepper to taste. Let simmer for about 5 minutes. Serve hot.

Yield: About 1½ cups.

½ pound shrimp in the shell
2 tablespoons butter
2 tablespoons flour
¾ cup clam juice
¾ cup cream
1 tablespoon dry sherry
1 bay leaf
⅛ teaspoon ground nutmeg
½ teaspoon celery seed
Salt and freshly ground pepper

Sauce Danoise *(Cream sauce with anchovy butter)*

6 tablespoons butter at room
  temperature
8 anchovies, chopped
2½ tablespoons flour
1 cup water
½ cup heavy cream
  Salt to taste (use very little as
  anchovy butter, which is
  salty, will be added later)
  Freshly ground pepper to
  taste
⅛ teaspoon cayenne pepper
  Juice of half a lemon
1 egg yolk

1. Combine 4 tablespoons of the butter with the chopped anchovies and blend well. Put through a sieve and set aside.

2. Melt remaining 2 tablespoons of butter in a saucepan and add the flour, stirring with a wire whisk. Add the water and cream, stirring vigorously with the whisk, until thickened and smooth. Add salt, pepper and cayenne. This may be made in advance.

3. When ready to serve, bring the sauce to the boil and add the lemon juice and egg yolk, stirring rapidly with the whisk. Bring the sauce just to the boil, but do not boil, or the egg may curdle. Remove the saucepan from the heat and immediately stir in the anchovy and butter mixture. Do not reheat, or the sauce may separate. Serve with hot poached salmon and other fish.

Yield: About 2 cups.

Fresh Tomato Sauce

3 red, ripe, unblemished, fresh
  tomatoes, about ¾ pound
2 tablespoons butter
2 tablespoons finely chopped
  onion
¼ bay leaf
1 teaspoon chopped fresh or
  dried thyme
  Salt and freshly ground
  pepper to taste
1 tablespoon chopped fresh
  basil leaves

1. Peel the tomatoes and cut away the cores. Chop the tomatoes. There should be about 2 cups.

2. Heat 1 tablespoon of butter in a small wide skillet and add the onion. When wilted, add the tomatoes, bay leaf, thyme, salt and pepper. Cook for about 15 minutes.

3. Pour the sauce into the container of a food processor or blender and blend. Return to the skillet. Reheat and swirl in the remaining butter. Put through a fine sieve, if desired. Stir in the basil leaves.

Yield: About 1¾ cups.

Tomato Sauce

2 tablespoons butter
1½ tablespoons finely chopped
  onion

Melt 1 tablespoon butter in a saucepan and add the onion and garlic, stirring. When wilted, add the tomatoes, bay leaf, salt and pepper to taste and cook, stirring occasionally, for about 30 minutes. Swirl in the remaining butter and serve hot.

Yield: About 2 cups.

½ teaspoon finely minced garlic

2 cups canned tomatoes that have been blended or sieved

¼ bay leaf

Salt and freshly ground pepper

Sauce Dugléré

1. Core, peel and chop the tomatoes. There should be about 3 cups.

2. Heat the butter in a saucepan and add the shallots and onion. Cook until wilted and sprinkle with flour. Add the tomatoes, salt and pepper to taste. Cook, uncovered, for about 15 minutes. Add the wine and fish stock and continue cooking for about 10 minutes.

3. Add the cream and bring to the boil. Serve piping hot. Serve with fish and fish mousses.

Yield: About 3½ cups.

1½ pounds fresh, red, ripe tomatoes, or use 3 cups imported canned tomatoes

2 tablespoons butter

2 tablespoons finely diced shallots

¼ cup finely diced onion

1 tablespoon flour

Salt and freshly ground pepper

¼ cup dry white wine

½ cup fresh fish broth, or use bottled clam juice

1 cup heavy cream

To the sauce Dugléré, add 1 tablespoon Pernod, Ricard or other anise-flavored liqueur.

Tomato and cream sauce with Pernod

Salsa Cruda *(Raw tomato and chili sauce)*

Chop the tomatoes and combine with the remaining ingredients. Stir until the ice melts. Serve with grilled meats, chicken and chili con carne.

Yield: About 2 cups.

2 cups drained, canned tomatoes or fresh cubed tomatoes

2 tablespoons red wine vinegar

½ cup finely chopped onion

Salt and freshly ground pepper

1 or 2 fresh or canned serrano chilies, finely chopped

1 ice cube

1 tablespoon or more chopped fresh coriander, optional

Brown Chili Sauce

2 pounds chicken necks and wings chopped into 1-inch lengths
2 tablespoons flour
2 teaspoons ground cumin
1 tablespoon chopped garlic
3 or more tablespoons chili powder
1 tablespoon dried oregano
2 tablespoons tomato paste
1 cup fresh or canned beef broth
2 cups water

1. Put the chicken pieces in a heavy saucepan and cook, stirring often, until browned. It is not necessary to add fat, but the pieces must be stirred to prevent sticking.

2. Pour off the fat from the saucepan and sprinkle the chicken pieces with flour, cumin, garlic, chili powder and oregano. Stir and add the tomato paste. Stir once more and add the broth and water. Stir constantly until the sauce boils. Cook for about 40 minutes, stirring often from the bottom to prevent sticking.

3. Strain the sauce, discarding the solids, and serve hot. This sauce is good with tacos, enchiladas, hamburgers and so on.

Yield: About 2 cups.

Sauce Madère

2 tablespoons thinly sliced shallots
½ cup Madeira
3 cups demi-glace (see recipe page 658)
Salt to taste
2 tablespoons butter

1. Combine the shallots and wine in a saucepan. Bring to the boil and cook until most of the wine is reduced.

2. Add the demi-glace and cook for about 15 minutes, or until reduced to 2 cups. Add salt to taste.

3. Strain the sauce through a fine sieve. Swirl in the butter. If desired, add another tablespoon of Madeira to the sauce before serving.

Yield: About 2 cups.

Sauce au Moules Safranée *(A saffron and mussel sauce)*

1 quart mussels, the smaller the better
5 tablespoons chopped shallots
3 cups heavy cream
1 teaspoon finely chopped saffron
Salt (use very little because the mussels are salty)
Freshly ground pepper

1. Scrub the mussels well and rinse in several changes of cold water. Drain.

2. Combine the shallots, cream, saffron, salt and pepper to taste in a kettle large enough to hold the mussels. Cook for about 10 minutes and add the mussels. Cover and cook until the mussels open, about 5 minutes.

3. Spoon out the mussels, using a slotted spoon. Remove the mussels from the shells. Pull off and discard the rubberlike

band around each mussel. Put the shucked mussels into a saucepan.

4. If the cream sauce is not thick enough to coat a spoon, boil it down until it is. Strain the sauce, preferably using a French sieve called a chinois. Add the sauce to the mussels and bring just to the boil. Serve immediately over poached fish.

Yield: About 3 cups.

Crème Fraîche *(A thickened fresh cream)*

Pour the cream into a jar or mixing bowl. Add the buttermilk and stir. Cover tightly with plastic wrap and let stand in a slightly warm place for 12 hours or longer, or until the cream is about twice as thick as ordinary heavy cream. Refrigerate and use as desired on fresh fruits, fruit pies and so on. Keep closely covered.

Yield: About 1 cup.

1 cup heavy cream
1 teaspoon buttermilk

Southern Barbecue Sauce

Combine all the ingredients except the lemon in a saucepan. Add the juice of the lemon. Cut the lemon into quarters and add it. Heat thoroughly without boiling. Use to baste chicken, fish, spareribs and so on as they are grilled. This sauce will keep for days, tightly sealed, in the refrigerator.

Yield: About 2¾ cups.

2 tablespoons butter
6 tablespoons cider vinegar
¼ cup water
1½ cups ketchup
2 tablespoons Worcestershire sauce
¼ teaspoon Tabasco sauce, or more to taste
1 teaspoon finely chopped garlic
3 tablespoons peanut, vegetable or corn oil
Salt and freshly ground pepper to taste
¼ teaspoon red pepper flakes
½ bay leaf
2 tablespoons sugar
1 teaspoon paprika
1 lemon

Country Barbecue Sauce

3 tablespoons peanut oil
2 cups finely chopped onion
1 1-pound can imported plum tomatoes
1 cup ketchup or chili sauce
¼ cup white vinegar
¼ cup Worcestershire sauce
   Salt to taste
1 teaspoon ground black pepper
1 or 2 tablespoons chili powder
½ teaspoon cayenne pepper
1½ cups water
1 teaspoon dried oregano
1 teaspoon cumin powder
2 to 4 tablespoons honey

Heat the oil in a large, deep skillet or casserole and add the onion. Cook, stirring often, until golden. Add the remaining ingredients and bring to the boil. Simmer, stirring frequently, for about 45 minutes. Let stand overnight before using. Use for basting meats when they are barbecued.

Yield: 3 to 3½ cups.

Sanbaizu Sauce   (*A Japanese soy and vinegar sauce*)

½ cup rice vinegar
1½ tablespoons sugar
1 teaspoon salt
1 teaspoon soy sauce
¼ teaspoon monosodium glutamate, optional

Blend the vinegar, sugar, salt, soy sauce and monosodium glutamate, if used. Add more sugar, salt or soy sauce according to individual taste.
Yield: About 9 tablespoons.

Nuoc Mam Sauce

1 cup fish sauce, available in bottles where Oriental foods are sold
1 tablespoon finely chopped fresh ginger
2 cloves garlic, finely chopped
1 teaspoon hot red pepper flakes (or use a little cayenne to taste)
3 tablespoons lemon juice
2 tablespoons sugar
¼ cup water

Combine all the ingredients and stir to blend. Place equal portions into individual bowls and serve with Vietnamese dishes. Leftover sauce may be kept refrigerated for a week or longer.
Yield: About 1½ cups.

Ketjap Manis *(Indonesian sweet soy sauce)*

1. Put the sugar in a heavy saucepan and cook over moderate to low heat, stirring, until the sugar melts and starts to turn brown. Continue cooking, stirring constantly, until the sugar takes on a deep amber color. Take care that the sugar does not burn or it will be bitter.

2. When the sugar is properly caramelized, add the soy sauce and remaining ingredients. Bring to the boil, stirring constantly, and let simmer slowly for about 15 minutes.

3. Let cool. Pour the syrup into one or more bottles. This will keep for months if properly refrigerated.

Yield: About 3 cups.

2½ cups sugar
1 bottle (1 pint, 6 ounces) dark soy sauce
3 cloves garlic, peeled and crushed
1 piece star anise
2 salam leaves
2 slices laos
½ cup water

Mango Chutney

Put the garlic, mangoes, onion, sugar, vinegar and lime juice in a saucepan and simmer for 10 minutes. Add the remaining ingredients and cook until the fruit is soft, about 20 minutes. The chutney can be kept in the refrigerator for about 6 months without sterilization.

Yield: 8 pints.

4 cloves garlic, crushed
10 cups cubed mangoes or apples
2 cups chopped onion
2 pounds brown sugar
3 cups vinegar
1 cup lime juice
2 lemons, chopped, peel and all
Peel of 2 oranges
Peel of 1 grapefruit
10 slices pineapple, drained
1 tablespoon ground nutmeg
1 tablespoon cinnamon
1 tablespoon ground ginger
1 tablespoon cloves
1 tablespoon salt
1 teaspoon freshly ground pepper
1 drop Tabasco sauce
1 cup pitted prunes or dates

Fresh Green Chutney

1 cup loosely packed, chopped
  fresh coriander leaves
1 fresh hot green chili, trimmed
  and sliced
3 tablespoons water
1 cup unflavored yogurt
  Salt and freshly ground
  pepper to taste
½ teaspoon ground cumin
  (preferably made from roasted
  cumin seeds)
1 tablespoon lemon juice

Combine the coriander and chili in the container of a food processor or blender. Add the water and blend to a smooth paste. As the mixture is blended, stir down as necessary with a plastic spatula. Spoon and scrape the mixture into a mixing bowl. Add the remaining ingredients and blend well.

Yield: About 1½ cups.

Ginger and Green Chili Sauce

½ cup fish sauce, available in
  bottles where Oriental foods
  are sold
⅓ cup freshly squeezed lime
  juice
1 tablespoon finely minced
  garlic
1 tablespoon finely minced
  ginger
1 or 2 hot, fresh, red or green
  chilies, or use ½ teaspoon
  or more ground red pepper
  flakes
1 scallion, trimmed and
  chopped
½ cup loosely packed chopped
  fresh coriander leaves
1 tablespoon chopped fresh
  basil leaves, optional

Combine the fish sauce, lime juice, garlic and ginger in a mixing bowl. Blend. Cut the chili on the diagonal into very thin slices. Add it to the sauce. Add the remaining ingredients and serve at room temperature with hot meats.

Yield: About 1¼ cups.

Chicken Broth

1. Place the chicken pieces in a large saucepan or kettle. Add the remaining ingredients and bring to the boil over moderate heat. Simmer, uncovered, for 2 hours. Using a large kitchen spoon, skim from time to time all the scum and foam that rises to the top of the soup as it boils.

2. Place a sieve over a large mixing bowl and line it with a piece of cheesecloth that has been rinsed in cold water and wrung out. Very carefully pour the soup into the sieve so that it is strained into the bowl. Discard all the solid matter.

Yield: 4 to 6 cups.

Note: Leftover chicken broth can be frozen.

3 pounds bony chicken parts, such as wings, necks and backs
1 bay leaf
1/2 teaspoon thyme
12 peppercorns
2 ribs celery with leaves
1 large onion, peeled and stuck with 2 cloves
1 carrot, scraped and coarsely chopped
6 sprigs parsley
10 cups water
1 tablespoon salt

Beef Broth

1. Place the bones in a kettle and add cold water to cover. Bring to the boil and simmer for about 2 minutes. Rinse well under cold water.

2. Return the bones to a clean kettle and add the 4 quarts of water and remaining ingredients. Simmer for 3 hours. Strain. Discard the solids.

Yield: 3 or more quarts.

Note: Leftover beef broth can be frozen.

5 pounds meaty neckbones of beef
32 cups (4 quarts) water
1 large carrot, trimmed and scraped
1 turnip, trimmed and peeled
1 large onion, peeled and stuck with 2 cloves
1 large rib celery, cut in half
1 clove garlic, left whole
1 bay leaf
2 sprigs fresh thyme, or 1/2 teaspoon dried
Salt to taste
24 peppercorns, crushed

Fond Brun or Demi-Glace *(Brown sauce)*

3 pounds veal bones, cracked
1 cup coarsely chopped celery
  with a few leaves
½ teaspoon thyme
1 cup thinly sliced carrots
1½ cups coarsely chopped onion
16 cups water
16 parsley stems tied in a
   bundle with 1 bay leaf
16 peppercorns, crushed

1. Preheat the oven to 400 degrees.

2. Arrange the bones in one layer over a baking dish (a dish that measures about 18- x 12- x 2½-inches is suitable). Place the bones on the floor of the oven and bake for about 20 minutes, or until bones start to take on color. Stir to redistribute them.

3. Bake for 10 minutes longer and scatter the celery, thyme, carrots and onion over the bones. Continue baking for 15 minutes, or until the bones are nicely browned.

4. Remove the pan and spoon and scrape the bones and vegetables into a kettle. Pour off any fat that may have accumulated in the pan, but do not wash it.

5. Add to the pan 2 cups of the water and stir to dissolve the brown particles that cling to the bottom and sides of the pan. Add this to the bones. Add the remaining 14 cups of water and the parsley bundle with bay leaf and peppercorns. Bring to the boil and simmer for about 5 hours. Skim the surface of scum and fat as it accumulates.

6. Strain the sauce. There should be about 5 cups. Chill. Scrape off the surface fat. Return the sauce to a saucepan and bring to the boil. Cook for about 45 minutes or until reduced to about 3 cups.

Yield: About 3 cups.

Note: Left over brown sauce can be frozen.

Brown Chicken Base

4 pounds bony chicken parts
  such as wings, backs, necks
  Salt and freshly ground
  pepper to taste
¾ cup coarsely chopped carrots
¾ cup coarsely chopped celery
1 cup coarsely chopped onion
1 clove garlic, finely minced
1 cup dry white wine
4 cups fresh or canned chicken
  broth
6 sprigs parsley
1 bay leaf
1 teaspoon thyme
½ cup chopped tomato

1. Cut the chicken pieces into 2-inch lengths. Place them in a kettle and cook, stirring frequently, for about 10 minutes. It is not necessary to add fat. The chicken will cook in its natural fat. Sprinkle the chicken with salt and pepper.

2. Add the carrots, celery, onion and garlic. Cook, stirring frequently, for 10 to 15 minutes longer or until chicken parts are nicely browned. Add the wine, broth, salt and pepper to taste, parsley, bay leaf, thyme and tomato. Cook, uncovered, for about 1 hour, stirring frequently. Strain, using a wooden spoon to extract as much liquid from the solids as possible. Discard the solids.

Yield: About 3 cups.

Note: Leftover chicken base can be frozen.

Fish Stock

If the fish heads are used, the gills must be removed. Run the bones under cold running water. Place the bones in a kettle or deep saucepan and add the remaining ingredients. Bring to the boil and simmer for 20 minutes. Strain.

Yield: About 6 cups.

Note: Leftover stock can be frozen.

2 pounds bones from a white-fleshed, nonoily fish, including heads if possible but with gills removed
6 cups water
1 cup dry white wine
1 cup coarsely chopped celery
1 cup coarsely chopped onion
3 sprigs fresh thyme, or 1 teaspoon dried
1 bay leaf
10 peppercorns
  Salt to taste
1 medium-size tomato, cored, optional

Dashi (*Japanese soup stock*)

1. Place the water in a saucepan and add the kombu. Bring to the boil and immediately remove the kombu. Do not let the kombu cook.

2. Add the katsuobushi and stir. Remove from the heat immediately. Strain through flannel.

Yield: About 5 cups.

Note: Both kombu and katsuobushi are available in Japanese markets.

5 cups cold water
1 large square kombu (kelp), measuring about 7 by 7 inches (see note)
3 cups loosely packed packaged katsuobushi or dried bonito shavings (see note)

XVI. Equipment

We have long been amused by that segment of the public that will spend prodigal sums of money on their hobbies—golf, tennis, travel—and yet let their kitchens go begging. Furnishing a kitchen properly, which is to say comfortably, seems to inspire a certain guilt in some misguided souls. Not ours. Cooking is a chief hobby and an endless pleasure, and we gleefully accommodate our purse to the kitchen rather than the other way around. Attempting to cook with a poor stove and a tin skillet is no more fun than trying to climb a greased pole or play tennis with a loosely strung racket.

When it comes to gadgets, I am an unabashed fanatic. I can number among my acquisitions assorted Japanese rice cookers, tempura pots, half a dozen can openers and one of the most elaborate collections of cork extractors known to man. Other enthusiastic purchases that I have forfeited to charity are two crock pots, four electric sandwich machines, a glorious looking cheese and sausage slicer, electric woks and assorted ice cream makers.

Assuming you have a stove (we still prefer the Garland although there are many other good brands on the market) and other large equipment for your kitchen, we offer herewith a check list of utensils we consider basic to any kitchen, as well as a few of our favorite things—some essential and some unquestionably in the luxury class. Speaking of stoves, the only thing we have found a microwave oven good for is cooking bacon. But it's the most expensive bacon we've ever eaten.

Basic Equipment:

A 10-inch black iron skillet

Stainless steel or enamel-on-cast-iron saucepans with 1, 2 and 3-quart capacities

Three sturdy stainless steel chopping knives with 8-, 10- and 12-inch lengths (a lot of old-timers out there swear by carbon steel, but they're living in the Dark Ages)

A stainless steel paring knife

A swivel-bladed paring knife

A serrated-edge bread knife

Metal spatula

Plastic spatula

Long, two-pronged fork

Two long metal kitchen spoons, one slotted

Graduated metal measuring cups and glass measuring cups

Metal measuring spoons

Nest of mixing bowls

Can opener and beer can opener

Flour sifter

Grater with assorted grating surfaces

Nest of metal funnels

Medium-size sieve or strainer

Colander

Pie plate

Kitchen tongs for turning foods as they cook

Rotary beater

Two wooden spoons

Wire whisk

Pair of sturdy kitchen scissors

Tea kettle

Tea pot

Coffeemaker

Toaster

Pastry brush

Pepper mill

Kitchen timer (the choicest can be set for minutes and hours)

Dish draining rack

Polyethylene chopping block of good size

Three-quart heavy, ovenproof casserole (Dutch oven)

Spice rack outfitted with bay leaves, thyme, peppercorns, tarragon, cayenne pepper, nutmeg, oregano, dry mustard, basil and paprika

Corkscrew (we are convinced that the best is the old-fashioned design with wings that open as the screw is inserted and pulls up the cork when the wings are pushed down)

Canister set for flour, salt and sugar

Rolling pin and pastry blender

Dispenser for wax paper, aluminum foil, paper towels and plastic wrap

Electric mixer

Electric blender

Spaghetti kettle

Loaf pan

Two-quart soufflé dish

Trussing needle and ball of trussing twine

Roasting pan
Ladle
Aprons and sponges for washing the dishes
Meat grinder (the kind that clamps onto a work surface)
Wok (not electric)
Nutmeg grater

Some of My Favorite Things:

Rotary cheese grater for hard cheeses such as Parmesan and Romano

Food mill, which is ideal for purée of vegetables as well as for some soups and sauces

Meat mallet for lightly pounding the likes of veal scaloppine. It is also good for crushing garlic, cloves and whole spices. Make certain that the bottom surface is flat and not with a "claw" pattern

Salad drier (we prefer the Swiss import called a Rotor)

Metal heat controller for creating a gentle heat and spreading it over the bottom surface of a saucepan (we prefer the one called Flame Tamer)

Metric scale

Pastry scraper, primarily for scooping up doughs, but it is convenient for lifting quantities of food and for scraping surfaces to clean them

Knife sharpener (one of the best is a small, easily stored gadget called Zip-Zap that costs only about $3)

Oven thermometer

Chinois, a fine-meshed strainer to remove lumps in custards, batters and sauces

Lemon zester for carving "twists" for martinis or giving a neat pattern to slices for garnishing dishes

Juice extractor, preferably with two squeezer heads—one for limes and lemons, the other for oranges and grapefruit

Coffee mill, which we use for grinding such things as coriander seeds, cumin, allspice, even peppercorns

Scrubbing brush (the best all-purpose one we've found is called Lola, which has a long-lasting and replaceable head)

Ice cream maker, any sturdy model with a revolving canister

Luxury Items (but so is a fine set of golf clubs):

First and foremost is the Cuisinart food processor, that paragon of imports that blends, chops, slices and prepares pastries and mousses in seconds, plus grinds meats to perfection

A sturdy rotary manual can opener that can be screwed onto work surfaces (we prefer the one made by Edlund, which opens cans of almost any shape and size from large tomato cans to odd-shaped matjes herring cans)

For someone with an absolute passion for homemade sausages, the Tre Spade import is a veritable Rolls-Royce among sausage stuffers. It comes with an assortment of stuffing horns in various diameters to fit any size casing and is manually operated.

For pasta lovers, an Italian import that kneads dough and produces several varieties of pasta: flat sheets for ravioli plus strands of spaghetti in thin or slightly broader sizes. It is made by Bialetti and is equipped with two "heads" or rollers: one for rolling out and the other for cutting the dough.

XVII. Questions and Answers

Cooking well does not mean cooking by inviolable rules or those sacrosanct principles set down a century ago in French kitchens. It is, or should be, a pleasurable occupation enhanced by your own taste and experience. If there are no set rules, there are, however, certain techniques and preferences that one learns through long practice. I have included here my answers to the most asked questions from readers of the food columns of *The New York Times*.

Baking Is it necessary to chill dough before rolling?

It is not imperative, but it helps. Chilling and "resting" the dough facilitates handling when it is rolled out. Theoretically, the chilling also tends to retard shrinking once the dough is baked. After the dough is chilled, it should stand for an hour or so before rolling. There is no reason, however, if pressed for time, the dough cannot be prepared and rolled out immediately. If the dough has a high fat content, it is best to roll it out—particularly in warm weather—on a chilled surface.

When a recipe says "Bake at 425 degrees for 10 minutes, then reduce the heat to 350 degrees," does one simply turn the setting to 350 or is it necessary to keep the oven door open until the thermometer reads 350?

Unless the recipe specifies leaving the oven door open, don't do it. Simply turn the setting to the desired lower temperature.

If a recipe says to bake a casserole covered, can it be cooked on top of the stove?

Yes. There is a difference in results, but it is minimal in most cases.

664

On several occasions I have seen recipes that call for adding *Eggs*
two or more eggs, one at a time. Can you please tell me if this
isn't a waste of time?

No, and if you want to waste your time, try adding them all
at once in those recipes. One of the most obvious recipes that
calls for this technique is a basic cream puff paste. You blend
flour and water and cook, stirring rapidly, until the mixture
comes away neatly from the sides of the saucepan. Then you
beat in the eggs, one at a time, generally with a wooden
spoon. If you add them in this fashion, the mixture homoge-
nizes or comes together quite nicely. Gradually, logically, and
step by step. If, on the other hand, you tried to add the eggs
all at once, it would require considerable expertise, beating
and time to get them to homogenize using either a spoon or
machine.

From the standpoint of nutrition, are brown eggs superior to
white eggs as one of my neighbors insists?

According to poultry experts, the nutritional value is identical. We asked Sal Iacono, our knowledgeable poultry grower
in East Hampton, and he states that many people come to his
farm asking for brown eggs. It is his opinion that many of his
local customers grew up on farms where they produced Rhode
Island reds, which lay brown eggs. For them, the preference is
a matter of what they're accustomed to. Summer and weekend
residents and other city folk seem to prefer brown eggs on the
ground that most of the eggs sold them in town are white.
Therefore, a brown egg seems more "countrified."
We heard the following from a reader:
"In England one always buys brown eggs for boiling at
breakfast, in that their shells are much thicker than white ones
and less apt to crack. Try it."
We did. You're right.

You printed a recipe for a dessert mousse and it called for
three egg yolks to be added to a sauce before cooling. I added
them to the hot sauce, and they actually cooked before they
could be blended in. Could you let me know what I did
wrong?

Sauces thickened with egg yolks are among the trickiest to

prepare. Skilled cooks can add egg yolks directly to a hot, even boiling sauce, but this is certainly not recommended for novices or those who are unsteady of hand or faint of heart. The moment the yolks are added, you must stir the sauce as rapidly as possible and withdraw the sauce from the heat. A more certain method of adding the yolks is to beat them in a mixing bowl. Add a little of the hot sauce and blend quickly. Then add this mixture to the saucepan, stirring as rapidly as possible with a whisk.

Can you tell me why the shells of some hard-cooked eggs can be removed with a minimum of fuss while others, sometimes from the same cooking water, are almost impossible to remove without ruining the smooth white surface of the eggs?

The reason most often volunteered by poultry and egg experts is that very fresh eggs are difficult to peel, while the shells of eggs that are several days old can be removed with ease. Theorists claim that the eggs of a certain age develop a very thin air pocket between the whites and the shell, thus facilitating the shells' removal once cooked. To my knowledge there is no infallible solution to the problem, but I find that the addition of salt to the water in which eggs are to be cooked seems to contribute a positive factor in the shell removal when the eggs are ready.

Here are a few suggestions from readers:

Available in any good kitchen supply store is a little gadget that pierces eggshells. Simply pierce the shell of the raw egg, submerge in a pan of water, cook the required length of time and, presto, the shell comes right off.

Another trick: When the egg has been cooked, remove a little of the shell. Slip a teaspoon between the shell and the egg and rotate the spoon. In seconds the chore is accomplished.

Boil water with lots of salt. Make a hole in the raw egg by sticking a pin or needle in the shell. Do it to either end of the egg. Carefully drop eggs into the boiling water. Time them for 10 minutes. Run under cold water, cracking eggshells a bit so the cold water can get to the egg itself. Let eggs sit in cold water for a while, then remove.

Poke a needle hole in the large end before boiling. Drain immediately after boiling. Fill a pan with ice cubes and then with cold water. Gently crack each shell on all sides and return to water for five minutes. Peel, starting from the large end.

For beautiful shelled hard-boiled eggs, put a little butter in the water.

One of your recipes called for a dozen egg whites. What am I supposed to do with the egg yolks?

It is best to freeze the yolks. This can be done by putting them all in a plastic container, covering closely with the lid and freezing. Or put the yolks in ice trays and freeze. Unmold the frozen yolks and refreeze tightly wrapped in plastic. The same can be done for egg whites. Both freeze exceedingly well.

You seem to prefer egg yolk for mayonnaise. Since I make a small, one-egg quantity, I don't want to bother with having a white of one egg so I use the whole thing. Can you tell me why you prefer the yolk?

The difference between a mayonnaise made with an entire egg and that made with the yolk is relatively minor. Logically, of course, an all-yolk mayonnaise is "richer" to the taste than one made with the whole egg. If mayonnaise is to be prepared in very large batches, for a party or benefit, for example, the whole egg product would be preferable. On the other hand, mayonnaise in most home kitchens is generally made with one cup of oil and this is sufficient for one yolk. If the whole egg is used, the oil should be increased accordingly.

Can you tell me precisely what a bain marie is and how the name came about?

Equipment

A bain marie is a device widely used in professional kitchens throughout the world. It consists of a tray or container for water that is kept hot but below the boiling point. Saucepans containing sauces are placed in this water to be kept anywhere from warm to hot. These are sauces that, if subjected to a more intense heat, would risk curdling. A double boiler is a variation of the bain marie.

The name bain marie is often associated in a farfetched manner to the Virgin Mary. One speaks of "the gentle voice of Mary," and thus some learned tomes relate the gentle heat of the water to the gentle quality of her voice. On the other hand, the *Dictionnaire de la Langue Française* by Bloch and von Wartburg (published in France) states that the name bain marie originated in the fourteenth century. The utensil was for centuries employed by alchemists. Moses' sister, it seems, was an early alchemist and thus the utensil was named for her.

I have a beautiful old wooden salad bowl that has recently taken on a rancid smell, probably from the continuous use of oil in the salad. I fear it would be unhealthy to use it in its present state. Is there any way to clean the bowl and remove the odor?

You should try scrubbing it often with any of several things and, perhaps, try them all at intervals. Scrub with lemon and coarse salt, rubbing thoroughly and for a prolonged period inside the bowl. Rinse well and let stand in the open air (one trusts it is a good solid wood and will not warp). Or use a strong scouring powder. At some point you might try soaking the inside of the bowl with a strong hot vinegar solution, letting it stand overnight. Then rinse and scrub once more and let stand in the open air. You may have to soak the bowl several times, drying well after each soaking. If after a reasonable period the odor has not dissipated sufficiently, you might use the bowl as a planter.

Why should an omelet pan be used only for making omelets? I have always heard that they should never be used for anything else and have not permitted anyone in my family to use it for other than this purpose. However, I have been challenged to explain why this is so and trust that you can supply me with an answer.

There is no absolute reason why an omelet pan could not be put to other uses, provided extreme care is used. The only reason it is not recommended is the off-chance that the pan will be scratched in washing. Amateurs have an unfortunate habit at times of removing their dirty work by scrubbing the surfaces of cooking utensils with steel wool or other abrasives. A surface thus marred will more than likely produce an omelet that sticks.

We are not of the thought that an omelet pan should never

be washed. If it isn't used at reasonable intervals, the oil, butter or other fat used in making an omelet will become rancid and produce a foul-tasting product. The pan should be washed in warm or hot water with detergent or soap while using a soft sponge or cloth. It should be dried immediately, particularly if it is an iron pan, and preferably over heat to prevent rust from forming.

You recently stated that glass measuring cups should be used for liquids and metal measuring cups for solids. Why the distinction?

For the sake of accuracy. Most glass cups are designed so that they may be held up to eye level to permit the cook to determine with great accuracy the exact volume of liquid. On the other hand, you can be assured of far greater accuracy in measuring solids such as sugar and flour if they are added to the brim of metal measuring cups (or metal measuring spoons) and then leveled off smoothly, using a spatula or knife.

Could you please explain how to clean a flour sifter? Wiping and shaking it clean never seems to be adequate.

I shake out the flour from my flour sifter after each use. When, on those rare occasions, I find it necessary to give the sifter a thorough cleaning, I entrust that job to my handy electric dishwasher. On the other hand, my sifter is an all-metal utensil (specifically, a Foley five-cup sifter) purchased several years ago. It has had many a bath without damage. Some sifters, particularly those with wooden parts, may not take kindly to the dishwasher treatment.

I have purchased a new skillet and the manufacturer's instructions say to "season" the skillet before using. They do not give the method for seasoning, however. Do you know?

The usual method is to add a hefty quantity of cooking or salad oil to the skillet. Place it on the stove and heat the oil almost, but not quite, to the smoking point. Turn off the heat and let the skillet stand until the oil is cool. Pour out the oil and the skillet, when cleaned, is ready for use.

le 4 Septembre 1965
Aux Sources

les œufs du Perigord en Gelés

les delices de "Gardiner Island" Poulette

Rognonnade de Veau Poêlee dans son jus.

Gratin de Courgettes Dauphinois.

Aubergines Sautees Milanaise

Cœur de laitue Vinaigrette

Plateau de fromages du Continent.

Sorbet Citron à la "Craig"

Créme brulée Moka

Gateau Surprise.

Chateau Beausejour 1953

Cramant Blanc de Blanc Brut 1959

30 August 1971

Curried tomato bisque

Escalope de veau Viennoise
pommes natures

Salade panachée
Brie

Celestine de chocolat au Grand Marnier

Château Pichet Caillou
1964

Chassagne- Montrachet

Nora Ephron loved every bit of it

```
      H  H
     OHOFF
    HF OF
   HOFF
  HOFF F
   HOFF
```

Dan Greenburg, husband of the above-mentioned,
former Managing Editor of Eros Magazine, feels
that the bisque, veau, pommes, salade, brie, et al,
were uniformly and obscenely delicious.

Eleanor Hempstead thinks everything
was simply wonderful — as usual!

A friend of mine, a fabulous cook, states flatly that you should never wash a skillet. Do you agree?

It depends on the skillet. An iron skillet, particularly one that is used frequently, should not be washed except when it becomes essential. Such an iron skillet would include those used for making crêpes, omelets, and for sautéeing potatoes. In other words, those dishes where a well-used or cured but smooth surface is necessary for best results.

As skillets are used—and the more the better—they develop a natural surface coating that prevents sticking. These skillets should be cleaned with salt and paper toweling. Simply sprinkle the bottom and sides after each use with salt, preferably coarse salt such as kosher salt, and rub briskly with dry paper toweling. If no particles have stuck to the bottom after using, it is not even necessary to use salt. If the skillet has been subjected to foods that cling relentlessly to the bottom, it may be necessary to use an abrasive such as a plastic or steel wool scrubber. At any time water is used to clean an iron skillet, the surface must be wiped dry immediately or it will rust.

Flour Can you tell me the difference between cake flour and "regular" or all-purpose flour? Is semolina a kind of flour?

Although there are many kinds of flour in this world—including cornstarch, which is made from corn and also known as corn flour, and rice flour made from rice—the most common flours are those made with wheat. The characteristics of wheat vary. All-purpose flour is a blend of hard and soft wheat. Cake flour is, by and large, made from soft wheat. Some sources state that you may substitute all-purpose flour in recipes calling for cake flour. To do this, sift the flour two or more times and use one cup of this—removing two tablespoons of the flour—for each cup of cake flour called for.

Semolina is, indeed, a form of flour and, to professionals, absolutely essential for pasta-making. It gives a firmer texture to noodles because it has a higher gluten content. Semolina is a bit more grainy than all-purpose flour, and it has a pale golden color as opposed to the white cast of all-purpose flour.

Is it essential to sift flour?

Generally speaking, no. It is my belief that years ago it was the better part of wisdom to sift flour before using for the simple reason that small insects were fairly common in most flour barrels. That is in the days when most of the flour consumed in America was sold in bulk form. On the other hand, if you have a reliable recipe that specifies sifting the flour, by all means do it. That would indicate, probably, that the recipe had been tested with the sifted flour and, therefore, it should be sifted. Quite logically, sifted flour is lighter than that which is taken directly from the bag. And it is the weight of the flour rather than the volume that has a direct bearing on the end results of a dish.

Food Processor

Do you use a food processor for chopping onions and garlic?

Rarely do we chop onions in a food processor because the onions tend to become too wet and the pieces of onion lack the precise cubed effect we generally desire. If, on the other hand, we were to prepare a dish to serve a vast number of people—chili con carne, for example—when the texture of the onions was unimportant, we would undoubtedly use the machine. A food processor does an excellent job of chopping large quantities of garlic, say ten or twelve cloves. It is also excellent for chopping fresh, peeled ginger root. It is an enormous help in preparing a menu that includes several Chinese dishes that include chopped ginger and garlic in the list of ingredients.

Quite often you print recipes for homemade mayonnaise, always recommending a wire whisk to prepare it. I use a food processor and it works like a charm. Why don't you?

Probably because if you know how to go about it, you can make mayonnaise in only a minute or so with a whisk. Also, for someone not accustomed to using a food processor for making mayonnaise, there is, I believe, a greater risk that the sauce may curdle or separate. If, for example, the machine beats the yolks for a few seconds too long before the sauce is made, the yolks become overhomogenized and will not thicken properly. On the other hand, a food processor, properly used, is cordially recommended.

Freezing

Can you give me some specific and general advice on freezing cooked dishes?

After foods are cooked (and I can think of no examples where I would partly cook a dish and then freeze it), I let them cool to room temperature. I pack the foods into plastic freezer containers and seal them tightly. The containers I use are standard pieces to be found in most hardware stores and supermarkets. I freeze foods in a home freezer set at the lowest temperature. This is important, for the foods should be frozen as quickly as possible.

To reconstitute foods, I simply empty them into a saucepan or other suitable utensil and let them heat gently, generally with the aid of a heat control device such as a metal pad or Flame Tamer. I defrost them slowly (but within minutes) and bring to the boil. Alternatively, I would defrost the foods overnight in the refrigerator. When dishes are reheated, I taste them and revise the flavors and seasonings, herbs, spices, salt, pepper and so forth, according to my own palate. Much has been made of the fact that the flavors and sharpness of spices in foods are diminished in freezing. I find this to be relatively slight.

Frying   Quite often, when I fry foods like scallops or fish, the pieces do not brown well. If the pieces are coated with flour, they stick together or stick to the bottom of the pan. Can you tell me what I'm doing wrong?

There could be several reasons and possibly a combination of things. One of the things to avoid is crowding the pieces of scallop, fish or whatever in the skillet. When browning most foods it is best if a little room is left between each piece as it cooks. Particularly in the case of cubed meat, if the pieces touch they start to give up their juices and this prevents browning. You should use a very heavy skillet for browning foods, and you should also let the fat become very, very hot before the foods are added.

Measurements   People who write recipes try my soul when they tell me to add a "dash" of something. Tabasco, for example, or Cognac. How much is a dash?

A dash is a judicious amount and it is, in my mind, a perfectly reasonable measure of volume for certain recipes. Tastes vary greatly, but in this case the taste is left up to the individual cook. I, for example, like very spicy foods and would probably add a touch more of a peppery spice. A dash of Tabasco would, in most cases, imply from one to three drops; of Cognac, from a teaspoonful to a tablespoon. If it is a genuine problem for you, I would propose that you start with a very small, if not to say tiny, amount and keep adding until the flavor of the dish suits your sensibility or palate.

Molds

I frequently have trouble unmolding foods that have either been baked or chilled in molds. Are there any rules of thumb about how to facilitate unmolding such foods?

For foods baked in molds, it is presumed that the mold in which the food was cooked was generously buttered or oiled, or lined with buttered paper before the food was baked. Generally speaking, it is best to let the dish stand briefly, although this is not absolutely essential. Using a small, sharp knife such as a paring knife, carefully and quickly run the knife around the perimeter of the food, holding the knife close to the sides of the mold. Invert a plate over the mold, then quickly turn the plate over to its upright position, inverting the mold at the same time. If the food does not immediately loosen itself from the mold, tap the bottom of the mold (now inverted) in several places with the back of a heavy knife.

For cold gelatin molds taken from the refrigerator, it is presumed that the mold was rinsed out with cold water or was lightly oiled to prevent the foods from sticking. When the food has set, use a small, sharp knife such as a paring knife and carefully and quickly run the knife around the perimeter of the food, holding the knife close to the side of the mold. There are two ways to proceed from here. If you are dexterous enough and the dessert is firm enough, you may run the inverted mold under running hot water, turning the mold quickly right side up when you feel the gelatin mixture start to loosen. Wipe off the bottom of the mold, then invert onto a plate as usual. Or, invert the mold onto a plate and cover the mold all over with towels that have been soaked in very hot water and wrung out. Continue adding hot towels until the gelatin mixture loosens. If the mixture does not loosen, try tapping the mold with the back of a knife. That failing, turn the mold right side up, serve directly from the mold and pretend it's the thing to do.

Pasta

I need help in cooking spaghetti. I've tried all the tricks but no matter what I do, the strands of spaghetti always stick together. I use lots of water (for each pound of spaghetti, as the package directions say, I use a gallon of water) and I have added oil to the kettle but invariably some of it sticks. What do you recommend?

It is important that you use lots of water, but I have always thought the addition of oil a needless waste. The solution is actually quite simple. Do not add the pasta until the water is at a top, rolling boil. Add it all at once and, immediately, using a long fork, start stirring the pasta, making certain that for the first minute or so the strands are almost constantly moving so that they have no chance to become glued together. Stir at least until the water returns to a vigorous boil. Once the spaghetti (or any other kind of pasta) is moving about freely in the water because of the intense boiling action there is small likelihood that the strands or pieces will stick.

Quantities   I am frequently in a quandary to know how much fish, chicken or beef to buy to serve any number of guests who may be coming for dinner. Is there any rule of thumb about this?

A very broad rule of thumb. One pound of boneless meat will serve approximately four people with average appetites. One pound of meat with a sizable amount of bone will serve one person. One whole fish weighing one pound will serve one person, but a pound of fish fillets will serve two or three people. Each pound of ready-to-cook chicken or duck with bone in will serve two people.

On occasion I see recipes that yield, to choose an arbitrary figure, 12 servings. Quite often these recipes might interest me, but I rarely cook for more than four or, on occasion, six. Can I simply divide the ingredients by two or three and proceed from there with the same baking time or whatever?

Dividing recipes is easy and generally recommended, but you must exercise your own judgment on some points of cooking. For example, if you have a cake batter made with a dozen eggs and the recipe specifies baking the cake for an hour, it is quite obvious that a cake batter made with half the eggs plus half the other ingredients must bake a shorter while. On the other hand, if your recipe is for a sauté of chicken, the cooking time should remain more or less the same. You would, of course, have to select a smaller skillet or casserole to cook the chicken in.

Is there a great difference between long-grain rice and short- *Rice*
grain rice? Should rice be salted when cooking?

There are differences in taste, but they are subtle enough in most instances as to be inconsequential. In Western kitchens, long-grain rice is usually preferred when you want to serve rice as a separate dish. When cooked, long-grain rice (and the name means specifically that—the grains are longer than in short- or medium-grain rice) tends to be fluffier and lighter than short-grain. Thus it is often recommended for rice salads and so on. Short- and medium-grain rice cooks to a moister state and is preferred for custards, rice puddings and dishes that are destined to be unmolded. The grains stick together. Short-grain rice is often used by Chinese and Japanese cooks because of this characteristic. It is easier to handle with chopsticks.

As to whether you should salt rice or not, use salt for Western cookery, no salt for Oriental cookery. No-salt rice offers a greater contrast to flavors like soy sauce, ginger, curries and so on.

Some time ago you printed a recipe calling for a beurre *Sauces*
manié. (This is a blend of flour and butter that is added to soups or sauces.) I use very little butter in my cooking. Can I substitute flour and water to thicken the soup or sauce?

Of course you can. The flour and water mixture will thicken the soup or whatever, but the results won't be the same. For one chemical reason or another, when a beurre manié is added to a soup or sauce, the raw taste of the flour is not apparent. If you add flour blended with water, the raw taste of the flour is going to be apparent in whatever you are cooking. Also, a beurre manié will give you a smoother or silkier result.

You have stated that you do not approve of preparing salad dressing containing chopped garlic in advance because in a short while, a day or so later, the garlic does not taste fresh. Would you sanction keeping chopped garlic in the refrigerator for a day or longer?

Nouvel An 1977-78

Insalata di Rigatoni
Huitres à la Chipolata
Brandade de Morue
Cervelas aux Lentilles
L'oie Farcie
Jambon Belle Aurore
Boudins Blancs Noirs
Paté en Croute de Faisan
Paté en Croute au Foie Gras
Salade à l'orange Marocaine
Salade de tomates
Fromage de Brie

Bûche Lenôtre
Strawberry Cake Lenôtre
Bagatelles aux Fraises
Fruit cake
Mince Pie
Cheese cake   Chaun Giolobi
Pain Forte

· January ·1978

Mousse de Pigeon Joseph Baum.
P'Cha
Kippered Salmon
Nova Scotia Salmon
Smoked Brook Trout
Schmaltz Herring
Matjas Herring
Smoked Sturgeon
Brandade de Morue
Ed Giobbi's Sicilian olives
Bagels and Bialys
Mincemeat Tarts
Panforte
Fruit Cake

Glögg
Bloody Marys
Krug Champagne
Boyer Brut

(SAM AARON)

Edward Roth
Janis Saugman · Beverly Best yet. ☺ 1978 ·
Joe Baum.
Budd Jervison

"Candy is dandy, but likker is quicker". - O. Nash
thank you.
Judy Levinson

All things are best when freshly chopped, garlic, onions and so on. On the other hand, freshly chopped garlic properly stored will keep for a day or longer in the refrigerator. Spoon it into a small container (a small, deep saucer, for example) and pack it down with a rubber spatula to prevent air bubbles. Cover with a light layer of oil such as olive oil and smooth it over. Cover closely with plastic wrap and chill. It will stay relatively fresh.

In one of your recipes you specified adding heavy cream to a sauce and cooking it down for eight to ten minutes. I have never boiled heavy cream before. I always felt that boiling it destroyed its silken quality. I would like further convincing that you really intended that the cream be boiled and reduced.

Be convinced. Cooking down heavy cream to give a finer, more silken consistency to a sauce is as old as the history of modern French cookery. It is generally cooked down over high heat.

Most recipes that call for a roux specify cooking butter and flour together briefly before adding a liquid like milk or chicken broth. I have a friend from Louisiana who insists that a proper roux should always be browned before it is used. Is this true?

A brown roux in Louisiana is a staple of Cajun and other Louisiana cookery. In those kitchens it is usually made with oil or bacon fat, the flour added and stirred for a long period until the flour takes on a brown amber color. This is the basis for many soups, stews and other dishes. In traditional French cooking, however, a roux is simply butter cooked with flour and generally without browning. There are certain chefs who contend that a roux should be cooked for several minutes without browning to get rid of any trace of a raw taste in the flour. Generally speaking, however, this is a tedious refinement.

In most Chinese cookbooks, recipes call for light and/or dark soy sauce. I do not know how to differentiate between the two. Can you give me a clue?

In Chinatown and in groceries where Oriental foods are sold, there are some bottled soy sauces labeled "thin," which is the same as "light," and "black," which is the same as "dark." You can determine the difference by holding the top of the bottle of soy up to the light and holding the bottle at an angle. The "dark" soy sauce will have a greater viscosity. It is somewhat thicker and more opaque than the "light." Dark soy gives both color and depth of flavor to foods.

A more comprehensive answer was received from a lecturer in home economics: "Light soy sauce," she elaborated, "is saltier than dark. It is made from soy bean extract, salt wheat and yeast. Some of these have sugar added, but good ones don't. Dark soy sauce, also called thick, black or heavy, always has molasses and caramel and soy extract, salt wheat and yeast.

"Therefore, now that ingredients must be listed on the label, the key word is molasses and/or caramel. This you will recognize as dark soy sauce, as light soy will never have these ingredients. Also, if the bottle is tipped to one side, the dark soy clings to the glass longer and, therefore, the glass clears more slowly. Light soy sauce clears instantly."

I do a great deal of Chinese cooking and many of the recipes call for oyster sauce. One, can you tell me the ingredients? Two, can you tell me how long bottled, commercially made oyster sauce can be kept after it has been opened?

The primary ingredients of oyster sauce are shucked oysters, soy sauce, salt and seasonings such as garlic, ginger, sugar and leeks. The sauce is simmered a long time and is generally thickened with cornstarch. Tightly capped, it will keep several days in a cool place. It will keep indefinitely refrigerated.

I know that tomato purée, tomato paste and tomato sauce cannot be substituted one for the other in recipes. But I am curious to know the differences in each.

Tomato purée consists of tomatoes that have been blended or otherwise converted into a smooth mixture. The tomatoes are always cored before they are blended. They may or may not have the skins and seeds removed before preparing. Tomato paste consists of tomatoes or a tomato purée that has been cooked down to a pastelike consistency. A tomato sauce is simply a sauce made with tomatoes. The seasonings will vary, but onions and celery are frequently used.

In a recent recipe for veal scaloppine the cook was instructed to "reduce the wine slightly." I assume that this means to add a little cold water. Right?

Wrong. Adding a little cold water would not produce anything; it would only dilute the sauce in a most abominable fashion. You reduce the wine by cooking it down over moderately high or high heat.

Shrimp Is it really necessary to remove the black vein down the back of shrimp or is this done for cosmetic reasons?

The removal of the dark vein or intestinal tract of the shrimp is more than anything else a gastronomic refinement, cosmetic or otherwise. If the shrimp themselves are not spoiled, there is certainly nothing deleterious about that vein. In many cultures shrimp cooked in the shell are served in the shell and they are plopped into the mouth with gluttonous abandon the moment the shells are removed, vein and all. If shrimp are to be served in a less regional fashion, and particularly if they are to be served cold, they should be deveined before serving. On rare occasions that dark vein can be a bit gritty.

Snails How do you wash snail shells?

I rinse them in a basin of warm water containing a detergent to rid them of their initial crumbs, butter and so on. I then place them in a kettle or saucepan with water to cover and a capful of ammonia. I bring them to the boil for a few seconds and drain. They are then given a second go-around with warm water with detergent. Drain and add hot water and then a final draining, this time opening-side down.

Soup A recipe for a Chinese soup lists two tablespoons of cornstarch dissolved in three tablespoons of water among the ingredients. This is to be added to the soup at the very end. My question is, should the soup be boiling when the mixture is added and how long should it take for the soup to thicken?

The soup should be boiling or at least simmering when the cornstarch mixture is added. The soup will thicken within seconds and be ready to serve. Unlike flour, the cornstarch will not impart the raw taste of the starch to the soup. In most cases, soups thickened with flour should be cooked for a while after the flour is added to rid the soup of the floury taste.

Can you tell me what a bouquet garni is? Is it a combination of vegetables or is it a kind of spice?

Spices and Herbs

In its broadest sense, a bouquet garni is any small bunch of herbs and seasonings tied together and added to a soup, stew, liquid for cooking fish (a court bouillon), and so on. The most basic and traditional bouquet garni consists of parsley, thyme sprigs and bay leaf tied with string into a small bundle. When fresh thyme sprigs are not available, a little dried thyme is substituted for the fresh. The bouquet garni is removed, of course, once a dish is cooked.

Many recipes call for capers. I use them, enjoy them but don't actually know what they are. Would you be good enough to unfuddle me?

Capers are the buds of the caper plant, which is a bush or shrub that flourishes in Mediterranean regions. There are caper plants grown to a limited extent both in America and Britain. The tiny buds have a slightly greenish cast and, if allowed to develop, produce tulip-shaped flowers.

A reader recently wrote to state that she had difficulty finding cayenne pepper on her grocery shelves. She asked if white pepper might be substituted and we answered no. To get down to basics, why is it becoming more difficult to find cayenne pepper, which was plentiful in my childhood?

The question was put to Marshall Neale, a spokesman for the American Spice Trade Association, and he replied as follows:

"The spice industry is phasing out 'cayenne' as a labeling term, and using the simpler designation 'red pepper' to signify all hot, ground red (capsicum) pepper. You are right that tradition years ago dictated that the hottest ground red pepper product was called 'cayenne.' But, in trade practice, this did not refer to any particular variety and there never was a heat standard for it. So, the new move becomes more realistic labeling from the consumer's standpoint. It's all simply 'red pepper' and that means very hot (as a frame of reference, this is the ground version of 'crushed red pepper'—the fiery product which is frequently seen on the tables of pizzerias and other Italian-style restaurants)."

I do not have a great deal of storage space for dried herbs and spices. Could you name the five herbs and spices that you consider indispensable for a spice shelf, besides salt, pepper, onion, garlic and paprika?

I personally dislike powdered onion and garlic and would not have any of it in my kitchen. Also, I use only fresh parsley and, therefore, would not include that. The two most essential spices seem to be bay leaves and thyme. After that, cloves, nutmeg and oregano. I would use only whole nutmeg to be grated when ready to use. The following are also important: dried basil when fresh basil is not available; cayenne pepper; chili powder; rosemary; coriander; cinnamon, and tarragon. The number of spices in my pantry exceeds fifty.

You have printed a recipe that calls for cutting a bud of garlic in half to remove and dispose of the center sprout that occurs in some heads of garlic at a certain age and in certain seasons. Is that center part not the most tender?

The removal of that center sprout is a conceit of certain chefs we have known. These chefs contend that the small piece is bitter. In theory, they are undoubtedly right, but we do not make a practice of removing it.

When I cook fresh garlic cloves (fry or sauté), the results are often bitter and acrid. How does one properly cook garlic in a frying pan?

The problem may lie in the overcooking of the clove. Garlic, when browned, tends to be bitter to the taste. Whether chopped or left whole, it should not be cooked until brown if it is to be included in the finished dish. Numerous fine Italian cooks (and others) will brown a clove in oil before finishing a dish. The garlic clove is removed before the other ingredients are added. It is used then simply to "perfume" the oil prior to further cooking.

Would you kindly advise where white peppercorns may be purchased? I have looked in numerous supermarkets and can only find black pepper. Incidentally is there a difference in flavor between the white and black peppercorns?

White peppercorns are available in many specialty shops where fine foods are sold. Both black and white peppercorns are the fruit of the plant known as *Piper nigrum*. Black pepper is processed from dried unripe fruit of the plant; white pepper is processed from dried fruit that is almost, but not quite, ripe. The flavors of the two are almost undistinguishable to the average palate, and the principal recommendation of the white pepper as opposed to the black is in its use in sauces and soup. The reason being that ground black pepper shows up as tiny black specks and white is almost indiscernible. This is a very tiny matter, however, For all practical purposes the two are interchangeable.

You have stated that you use only kosher salt in your kitchen. Is this true and why? Does it make foods saltier or less salty?

Actually, the reason has more to do with the tactile nature of the product than any other. I happen to like the feel of the salt when it is picked up in the fingers. Salt manufacturers state that "salt is salt" and a pound of one pure salt is no saltier than a pound of any other pure salt. Take note, however, that this has to do with weight, which is one reason recipes specify "salt to taste." A teaspoon of kosher salt, which is somewhat coarse, will weigh less than an equal quantity of a salt of fine grain.

When one buys vanilla beans, how often can they be used? How should they be stored after use?

Vanilla beans are an expensive flavoring agent, available in shops that specialize in food delicacies. One vanilla bean can be re-used honorably a number of times, as often, in fact, as it still maintains a reasonable aroma and continues to impart flavor. Some recipes call for splitting vanilla beans before adding them to milk and so on before cooking. When split, the tiny, dark center beans are released into the liquid and those contain flavor also.

After a vanilla bean has been used—to prepare ice cream or a custard, for example—the bean should be washed well in cold water. It is then best stored in a container of sugar, which serves a double purpose. It prevents the bean from drying out and also flavors the sugar. The flavored sugar may then be used for any desserts that benefit from a vanilla flavor.

Stocks   What is the difference between chicken broth and chicken stock?

The two terms are used interchangeably. They are the liquid that results by cooking chicken in a liquid, generally water, and frequently with seasonings added such as herbs and spices or vegetables. The same, of course, applies to beef broth and beef stock, veal broth and veal stock and so on. Most canned versions are labeled broth rather than stock.

Can a court bouillon—the poaching liquid for fish—be used over and over again? And can it be frozen after use?

You will probably not find a dictum in the writing of Escoffier and other authorities against using a court bouillon a second or even a third time around. On the other hand, the chef would be rare who would make a practice of re-using the liquid. The fresher and purer a court bouillon in which a fish is cooked, the better the fish will taste. And if you were to freeze a once-used court bouillon, think of the space you'd waste.

Storage   How do you keep coffee fresh? There have been times when, after a long vacation, my ground, roasted coffee tastes stale when brewed.

Keep opened tins of coffee in the refrigerator, where it keeps quite nicely for long periods. Coffee beans can be kept for months in the freezer.

Is it safe to wrap fruitcakes in aluminum foil if Cognac or other alcohol is sprinkled on the cake? Also, can foods with a high acid content be stored safely in aluminum foil?

Our friendly informant from the Reynolds Wrap people in Richmond, Virginia, strongly recommends that you first enclose your fruitcake in cheesecloth after adding the Cognac. Then wrap the cake in foil to prevent its drying out.

Alcohol, acids and salt can cause foil to "pit," because of chemical or electrolytic action. We are told that this pitting is not toxic or harmful and that foods wrapped in foil that has pitted are perfectly safe to eat if the pitting is scraped away. The most adverse thing about the pitting is esthetic.

In many Chinese recipes, fresh ginger is called for. I have bought it by the pound often and often have a large amount left. What is the recommended way to keep fresh ginger so that it does not dry up or rot? I keep mine briefly in the vegetable bin of the refrigerator.

I keep fresh ginger in a plastic bag in the refrigerator. On the other hand, I use it in such quantities it rarely remains there for more than a week or two.

Some Chinese cooks recommend peeling it and pouring dry sherry or the Chinese wine called hsao-hsing over it. Within recent weeks, an acquaintance from India showed me a bottle of her "freshly grated" ginger, which she keeps in a storage bottle in her refrigerator. She adds a blend of equal parts of white vinegar and water, just enough to moisten well, and it will keep fresh for months. She cautioned that the grated ginger should not be overly wet or the preserving liquid (vinegar and water) will extract too much flavor from the ginger.

Readers came up with the following methods for keeping ginger fresh:

Wrap it in plastic and put it in the freezer. When it is to be used, a wash in hot water will enable you to peel the skin off easily and the ginger is ready to be sliced or chopped.

Keep it in a plastic bag, freeze and grate as needed.

You can have a supply of really fresh ginger on hand by simply planting a piece in a flower pot in ordinary potting

27 Juin. 1970.

Clams en Coquille.
Sauce Mississipi

Poulet Froid au Vinaigre _Jean Jacques_

Almaden sans Année
château La Laguna 1962 Lapin Pierre. Moulles au Beurre
Chambertin Clos de Bèze 1962
Stingers

Jean Whitman
Jean Jacques Painblanc   Salade "Dure" du Jardin
Arlette Painblanc   Quel Jardin ?.....

Alden Whitman

Pierre Franey
Jeannette Rattray   Fromages.

Tarte au Pommes _Jean Jacques_

Dernier Gougé

689

soil. I had originally expected the root to send up green shoots. Instead, the ginger grew downward. And when I dug up the root after a few weeks, I had a whole cluster of tender, fresh roots! The new growth is much more tender than the old root and very flavorful.

How long can mayonnaise safely be kept in the refrigerator?

Commercially prepared mayonnaise has an indefinite storage life if properly refrigerated. Homemade mayonnaise should be kept only a few days and no longer than a week to guard against spoilage.

When I bring onions home from the market, I leave them in the plastic bag in which they are sold and place them in a vegetable drawer in my pantry. They keep fairly well for a while and then start to sprout. Is there any way to foil this?

Yes. By all means remove them from the bag, be it plastic or otherwise, to permit air to circulate around them. Place them in a ventilated and not-too-warm spot—if the vegetable drawer is well perforated with fairly large holes, it should be satisfactory—and they should keep for weeks.

How do I store green or red peppers—specifically the hot chilies that I use for Mexican cookery?

We learned from our friend Diana Kennedy some years ago that the best way to keep these chilies is to place them in a porous, brown paper bag and seal them loosely. Place in the refrigerator and they will keep for days.

Is there any secret to keeping parsley crisp and fresh for several days after purchase? I keep mine refrigerated in a plastic container with a tight-fitting lid, but it still gets moist and limp after two or three days. Any solution?

When the parsley is purchased or cut, do not wash it immediately. Stick the cut ends in a jar just large enough to hold the bottoms and add cold water to the jar. Cover loosely with a plastic bag and place in the refrigerator.

This is also an excellent method for keeping coriander fresh and crisp. The coriander generally comes with roots and all. Do not cut them off, but place them in a jar, add the water, cover loosely with plastic and refrigerate. It keeps well for several days.

My collection of spices has been growing over the years, many of them seldom used. I keep them in glass jars or their original containers. How long do they keep?

It is impossible to predict precisely how long any spice will keep. Under ideal conditions some spices will retain their character and flavor over a period of years. Ideally, the spices should be kept in a tightly closed container in a cool, dark place. Some indication of the strength of spices can be gained from the color. As spices age and lose strength, the color tends to dissipate. Green spices (or dried herbs) tend to lose the bright green color and turn brown. Red spices such as hot chilies also lose their bright aspect. The only sure test for strength is through the senses of taste and smell.

What do you do with the can of tomato paste after you've removed the tablespoon needed for the recipe? I put the can in the refrigerator where it develops a white, fuzzy film, and I promptly throw it out.

This condition and occasionally a dark surface on the paste are caused by exposure of the surface to air and bacteria. You might transfer the tomato paste to a smaller container with a screw top and make it airtight until ready to use again. You might also freeze the tomato paste until ready for another use.

This question brought forth a host of interesting ideas from readers for preserving the unused tomato paste.

Smooth out the paste remaining in the can with the back of the spoon, then overlay its surface with a small amount of vegetable oil. This keeps the air away. To use, just tip the can, exposing fresh tomato paste and spoon out.

You clean the rim of the can carefully, seal it with plastic wrap (or collect a plastic cap that just fits, a quest in itself) and freeze it. When next you need a tablespoon, you remove from freezer and open the bottom of the can with can opener (the around-the-rim type). Within a few minutes you will be able to push the bottom up, forcing the frozen paste over the top.

About three-quarters inch or so equals a tablespoon, which you slice off. Refreeze immediately and use in that manner until done.

Lay a sheet of wax paper on a baking sheet and measure out the tomato paste in teaspoon and tablespoon quantities, in whatever proportion the cook feels is most useful, leaving about two inches between dollops. Freeze the paste on the wax paper on the baking sheet. Once it's frozen, roll up the paper, with the paste blobs on it, as closely as possible. Fold it in half and store in a tightly closed plastic bag in the freezer.

I recently received a birthday present, a jar containing five black truffles from France. I have always bought small cans of truffles, just enough for one use. I'm afraid to open these for fear that unused truffles will spoil. How do I preserve them once opened?

Place them in a jar and cover with a fortified wine such as Madeira, marsala or sherry. We prefer Madeira. Close the jar tightly and refrigerate. Use as desired.

Substitutions   Can dried bread crumbs and fresh bread crumbs be used interchangeably?

The occasions on which we have used dried bread crumbs are exceedingly rare. Dried bread crumbs refer to commercially sold bread crumbs. Fresh bread crumbs are those prepared by putting bread slices in a blender or food processor and blending until the crumbs come out fine. Freshly made bread crumbs, by the way, can be spooned into glass jars with a tight seal and stored for a week or longer in the refrigerator. Fresh bread crumbs give a better texture to breaded dishes and to such things as meat loaf.

If light cream is called for in a recipe, will a blend of half heavy cream and half milk suffice?

Yes. It is difficult to specify precisely what proportion of cream to milk would be the equivalent of commercial light cream, but the blend could be substituted.

Can lemon or orange extract be substituted for grated lemon or orange peel? I sure get tired of scraping my skin as well as the fruit on the grater.

It is possible to substitute the one for the other, but the results will not be the same. The flavor of grated orange or lemon rind is piercingly alive; the flavor of lemon or orange extract is dull and artificial. Like so many things, this is a question of personal taste.

Where we live there is a constant problem in not finding juniper berries. We have a larder full of frozen game and many game recipes call for juniper berries. Is there a substitute?

You might try a dash—a tablespoon, perhaps—of any good grade of highly perfumed gin. The principal flavoring agent for top quality gin is juniper berry.

If a recipe calls for currants and you already have raisins in the house, must you run out and try to locate hard-to-find and more expensive currants? Is it possible to make obvious substitutions in recipes?

Not only possible but highly recommended as long as the substitutions are intelligent. Currants could be substituted for raisins and vice versa, although the texture of currants is less moist and firmer. Currants are at times preferred to raisins in cakes and cookies for esthetic reasons. In the same sense, pecans can generally be substituted for walnuts; a cup of candied citrus for an equal amount of candied pineapple and so on. The results will not be identical, of course. Make substitutions, but don't be indiscriminate and bizarre unless that, too, is your intent.

Are all cooking oils interchangeable? Can a good salad oil be used for all dishes?

Although one oil may be substituted for another in the preparation of salads, in frying, sautéeing, and so on, such indiscriminate, ill-considered use is by no means recommended. Almost every category of oil has its own particular qualities. Olive oils alone come in many strengths and should be used according to taste. Among the three most popular "cooking" oils—corn, vegetable and peanut—corn and peanut are a personal preference. They seem to give off less odor for frying. If you wish to experiment with such flavors, you might also consider the less well-known safflower and sesame oils, these available in health food stores. The flavor of sesame is much more pronounced when purchased from Chinese sources and is not generally recommended for frying. It is best used as a flavoring agent.

Would you please suggest a suitable substitute for wine in recipes?

Generally speaking, a broth such as fish, chicken or beef can be substituted, substituting it volume for volume. You should, of course, use a fish broth for fish dishes, chicken broth for chicken or other poultry, beef broth for beef and so on.

When baking with yeast, some recipes call for "cakes" of fresh yeast or packages of dried, granular yeast. Are these two interchangeable and how much fresh yeast could be substituted for the granular kind?

A package of granular yeast contains approximately two and one-half teaspoons of yeast. Yeast cakes come in two sizes, six-tenths of an ounce and two ounces. You should substitute a six-tenth of an ounce cake for one package of granular yeast. Or use slightly more than one-quarter of a two-ounce cake.

Terminology   I have a collection of French cookbooks and many of them use the phrase monter au beurre when finishing a sauce. Precisely what is this technique?

When you monter au beurre, you add any given quantity of butter to a sauce at the very end. Actually, when the butter is added, it is not stirred in. It is swirled in by maneuvering the skillet or saucepan in a circular fashion until the butter is gradually incorporated into the sauce. In theory, the butter added this way tends to bind the sauce and make it a trifle thicker. It also gives the sauce a silken quality.

Someone has recently sent me a recipe from Australia that calls for corn flour. I can't find corn flour in any grocery stores or supermarkets. Can I substitute cornstarch?

Corn flour is the common British word for cornstarch. The two are identical.

I recently saw reference in a French cookbook to a blanc legume, which sounds like a white vegetable. Can you tell me what it is?

It is not a vegetable but rather a "whitener" made of flour and water, which is added to the liquid in which vegetables are cooked to keep them white. A blanc legume is used chiefly for cooking artichokes, which darken rapidly on oxidation. It is sometimes used in cooking cauliflower. The technique for adding it is to place a sieve over the cooking utensil containing the vegetable, which is covered by cold water. Flour is added to the sieve and water is poured over it so that it is added slowly and evenly to prevent lumping.

Can you please explain the meaning of the term "drawn" butter, which is frequently listed on the menus of seafood restaurants?

Drawn butter is synonymous with clarified butter. We prefer the latter term. The term drawn butter originated with the idea of "drawing off" the golden liquid of melted butter, discarding the milky solids. Clarified butter has many uses in cooking. It is preferable for making butter sauces such as hollandaise and béarnaise. It is preferable for sautéeing or frying foods because the burning point is higher than that of regular butter. Clarified butter will keep quite a while in the refrigerator.

Whenever I read French menus I become confused by some of the nomenclature. In my French class I was taught that adjectives should have the same gender as the nouns they modify. And yet this doesn't happen on French menus. Take beef in burgundy wine sauce. Beef is masculine, yet the dish is listed as boeuf bourguignonne; snails is masculine, but are listed as escargots bourguignonne. Why do they not have the masculine ending, bourguignon?

Because there is an elision involved in most French menu terminology. Spelled out in toto these dishes would be listed as boeuf à la mode bourguignonne and escargots à la mode bourguignonne and so on. The à la mode is dropped for the simple reason that it would be unnecessary clutter and boringly repetitive if spelled out for each dish.

13 June 1965

Assiette de crudités du jardin

Bouillabaisse Gardiniés Bay

Bavaroise/Sauce secrète au Jacques Pépin

Moka Express

Almaden Mountain White Chablis

Remy Martin

Green Things

Chartreuse Verte

Jeannette Rattray

Betty Mary

Jacques Pépin

What is the difference between a pâté and a terrine?

There isn't any. Originally, a terrine was a ground meat mixture baked in an earthenware utensil. The name derives from the word terra meaning earth. Baked meat creations cooked in such molds are often referred to as terrines. The word pâté stems from "paste" and is related to such words as pastry and pasta. It is an educated guess that meat creations baked in pastry were dubbed pâté as a result. Today, pâtés are often cooked in and served from "terrines" or earthenware molds. And terrines are often pastry-covered before baking.

What is the best quick-reference work or "translator" of terms used in French cookery?

By far the most concise and practical work of this nature is *Le Répertoire de la Cuisine,* the original of which, in French, is an aide-memoire on many chefs' bookshelves. The English translation of the book has recently been reprinted in this country by Barron's publishing house, and the standard edition costs $6.95; the larger, deluxe and expanded edition, $10.95. It is an impressive work and the translation is generally good. A typical entry is as follows: Normande sauce: "Fish velouté with mushroom essence and oyster juice, cohered with yolk of eggs and cream. Reduced and finished with butter and cream."

I have a thirty-year-old cookbook that instructs the reader to "try out" salt pork. How do you try it out? Soaking it, smelling it or cooking it?

Cooking it. The term "trying out" fat is more old-fashioned than your cookbook. Although it is still in common usage in some regions of this country, it simply means to cook the salt pork—and the technique is hastened if the salt pork is cut into small cubes—until it is rendered of its fat. This is a common technique for such regional dishes as chowders. Both the liquid fat and the rendered solids may be used in preparing the soup.

Toasting

I am never happy with the toast that pops out of my toaster. What do you recommend?

The best of all possible toast is made in the oven. This takes a bit more time and effort, however, than making it in a toaster. To bake toast, preheat the oven to 400 degrees and trim off the crusts of the bread slices. Butter one side of each slice and arrange the slices, buttered side up, on a baking sheet. Place in the oven and bake for five minutes or so, or until the slices are golden brown on one side. Turn and continue baking until golden brown all over.

Quite often these days one finds reference to a chinois, often described as "a sieve used in French kitchens." Can you describe this utensil in greater detail?

Utensils

A typical chinois is made with closely woven, fine metal strands. It is probably the most finely meshed sieve used in the home. Its purpose is in straining sauces. When the sauce is emptied into the chinois, the liquid passes through as in most sieves. With a chinois, however, the solids are pressed firmly inside the utensil, so that as much of the liquid essence of the solids can be extracted, usually using a heavy metal spoon to press them. If the same sauce is prepared using a regular sieve, the sauce will not be as fine in texture. The name, incidentally, derives from the fact that the shape of the sieve resembles, to some chefs' minds, a coolie hat turned upside down.

In your column, when a recipe calls for cut up or chopped garlic, the use of a garlic press is never suggested. Does the use of a garlic press alter the flavor of the garlic in any way?

To my taste, garlic put through a press takes on a smell and taste reminiscent of acetylene gas. There are also some schools of cookery where the texture of not-too-finely chopped garlic is a desirable characteristic in certain dishes. The spicy dishes of the Chinese kitchen are complemented by coarsely chopped garlic. An honest answer is that cooks who use a garlic press are lazy.

Do you put silver knives in your dishwasher?

Most of them. I have a very few antique knives that belonged to my family made long before dishwashers were invented. It is taking a chance to wash them in a dishwasher. A member of a silverware manufacturer's association told me some years ago that the vast majority of silver knives manufactured today are dishwasher-proof. In an earlier age, the blades and handles of knives were not permanently anchored and the old-fashioned fixatives stood a good chance of giving way when subjected to very hot water and suds.

Sometimes when I slice onions, the knife leaves a dark stain on the surface. This doesn't happen invariably. Can you explain?

It will never happen if you use a stainless steel knife. A carbon steel blade tends to discolor the cut surface of foods that contain acids and I presume there is some acid content in onions. If you cut a lemon with a carbon steel blade (non-stainless) the rind will discolor. If the knife is left to stand you will notice that the blade itself becomes quite dark and almost blackened. I strongly recommend stainless steel blades for foods such as lemons, oranges, onions and apples.

Is there a kitchen "rule of thumb" as to when to use a wooden spoon or a wire whisk to stir sauces?

A wooden spoon is generally used to stir sauces that contain ingredients such as tomato pieces, vegetables and so on. The spoon can reach to the bottom of a saucepan for stirring to prevent the sauces and ingredients from sticking on the bottom. A wire whisk is generally used for smooth sauces in which the wires of the whisk can flow freely without having the center of the whisk clogged with the bulky ingredients, which could be difficult to shake off. A wire whisk's greatest use is in the preparation of cream sauces and mayonnaise.

How do you recommend cleaning wooden cooking utensils to remove harmful bacteria?

By washing them well with warm or hot water containing a detergent. I have very few cooking utensils that will not fit into the automatic dishwasher.

Vegetables   How do you go about preventing the flesh of avocados from darkening once they are peeled?

A little lemon juice sprinkled on the avocado will prevent discoloration. You should make certain that the avocado, if cubed, is lightly tossed in the lemon juice so that all pieces are coated or, if the avocado is halved, that the cut surfaces are brushed with lemon juice. Many people who make guacamole—the avocado mix with onion, fresh coriander, chilies and so on—add the avocado seed to the mixture. They say this prevents discoloration.

What is hummus?

Hummus is the Middle Eastern name for chick-peas. Most Americans who dine in Middle Eastern restaurants know it best in the preparation known as hummus bi tahini, or chick-peas blended with lemon juice, garlic, salt, olive oil and tahini, which is a paste of sesame seeds.

I have several questions relative to fresh mushrooms. Must they be refrigerated after purchase? Should they be washed prior to using? Approximately how long do they stay fresh and should the stems be cut off before using?

Mushrooms, by all means, should be refrigerated after purchase to prevent their turning dark when left standing at room temperature. Although the soil or other material in which mushrooms are cultivated is pure, it is best to rinse the mushrooms in cold water and drain them well before cooking. This will remove the foreign particles that cling to them and will help keep them white.

There is no way to state definitely how long mushrooms will keep after purchase. If they are in excellent, newly harvested condition, they should keep in the refrigerator, in peak condition, for one and perhaps two days. They will still be good for cooking after five days and even up to a week. They may also be frozen and used for cooking, but not for serving fresh.

Are green onions and scallions one and the same?

Yes. In some sections of the United States, however, notably the South, some regional cookbooks specify shallots when they actually mean scallions or green onions. Shallots are similar to scallions only in that they both have an onion flavor and belong to the onion family.

When cooking with tomatoes, is it necessary to remove the seeds? Many cookbook authors state that the seeds will make a sauce bitter.

We know excellent cooks who declare that seeds do contribute a certain bitterness to sauces, but I believe this contribution is minimal and, quite honestly, I do not strain most tomato sauces that are to be used for pasta. On the other hand, a tomato sauce made with cream is more refined if the sauce is strained and the seeds removed. It is my own opinion that seeds should be removed from tomatoes (those to be broiled or stuffed, for example) more for esthetic reasons than because of taste.

Many recipes call for a tomato to be "peeled and seeded." I know how to peel a tomato but I cannot figure out how to seed one. Can you help?

The standard technique is as follows: Cut the tomato in half crosswise. Take up one half at a time and hold it over a bowl or basin. Slowly, gently, but firmly squeeze the tomato half, turning the tomato around as necessary to extract the seeds. There will probably be a few seeds left, but ignore them.

What is the difference between a sweet potato and a yam?

According to a spokesperson for the United Fresh Fruit and Vegetable Association: "Botanically, all sweet potatoes and yams sold in the United States today are basically sweet potatoes. One variety is copper-skinned and a deep orange color inside. It is moist, sweet and juicy and this variety is marketed as yams, when in fact they are botanically a variety of the sweet potato.

"The other variety is tan in color on the outside and light, creamy yellow on the inside. This variety is very dry, as compared to the moist variety that is usually purchased in preference. The true yam is not grown in continental United States, but may be found in tropical areas to a limited extent."

Vinegar   What is rice vinegar and where may I purchase it?

Rice vinegar is an excellent vinegar most commonly used in

the preparation of Japanese dishes such as the cold rice for sushi and the salads known as sunomo. The vinegar, almost colorless but sometimes with a pale yellowish cast, is made from sake mash. Sake, of course, is the traditional rice wine of Japan, and the mash is the soft pulp that remains after the clear beverage has been drawn off. Rice vinegar is wholly adaptable to almost any salad dressing that calls for vinegar. It is commonly available in supermarkets and grocery stores in metropolitan areas.

Are some wines better for cooking than others?

Wine and Spirits

The finer the wine you use in a sauce, the finer the sauce will be. Ideally, you should use the same wine to make your sauce as that which you will drink with the dish. This is not always feasible, however. If you have one single bottle of a rare vintage burgundy, for example, you probably wouldn't want to use it in your red wine sauce. Thus, you should use some good, substantial bottle within your means. In many instances the wine must be matched to the sauce. For example, you should use a burgundy for beef bourguignonne, a bordeaux for a sauce bordelaise, madeira for a sauce madère and so on. Any decent dry white wine or dry red wine suitable for drinking is certainly suitable for cooking. And if it isn't suitable for drinking, throw it out. Or throw it in the vinegar bottle unless it tastes "corky," a condition that is irremediable.

I tried one of your recipes that called for flaming a dish with Cognac. When I added the spirit, no amount of coaxing could make it flame. Do you have any suggestions?

Spirits and Liqueurs

The flaming is, as stated often before, more or less irrelevant. The alcohol dissipates naturally when subjected to the heat of cooking. In all probability, the reason the Cognac would not take fire, however, is that it was poured from a cold bottle, or perhaps you delayed too long in igniting it with a match or other flame. You can aid the process by warming the Cognac gently in a saucepan before flaming it.

When making desserts and other things like duck à l'orange, are Grand Marnier, Triple Sec and Cointreau interchangeable?

Triple Sec and Cointreau are excellent products for specific purposes but they are definitely second choice when it comes to dishes like soufflé à l'orange, crêpes Suzette and duck à l'orange. They simply do not have the body and elegant assertiveness of Grand Marnier. Triple Sec and Cointreau are made, generally, from dried orange peel plus sugar and white alcohol. Grand Marnier is a blend of orange essence and Cognac. On the other hand, in a drink such as a margarita, Triple Sec and its ilk are essential and Grand Marnier cannot be successfully substituted. In that case it is too overpowering and the Cognac in the drink combats the tequila.

Is it acceptable to use dry white vermouth in recipes calling for a little dry white wine to deglaze a pan?

Definitely, and we have used it often when the vermouth was handy and the dry white wine was not. But only in recipes that call for half a cup or less. I would think twice about using more than half a cup of dry vermouth. Vermouth, of course, has a base of wine to which various flavors such as spices and the roots and bark of plants are added.

Metric Conversions

General Conversions

Weight	AMERICAN	BRITISH	METRIC
	1 ounce	1 ounce	28.4 grams
	1 pound	1 pound	454 grams

Volume	AMERICAN	BRITISH	METRIC
	1 U.S. teaspoon	1 U.K. level teaspoon	5 milliliters
	1 U.S. tablespoon (3 teaspoons)	1 U.K. dessertspoon	15 milliliters
	1 U.S. cup (16 tablespoons)	⅚ breakfast cup (8 fluid ounces)	236 milliliters (about ¼ liter)
	1 U.S. quart (4 cups)	⅚ Imperial quart	1 scant liter
	1 U.S. gallon (4 quarts)	⅚ Imperial gallon	3¾ liters

Length	AMERICAN	BRITISH	METRIC
	1 inch	1 inch	2½ centimeters (25 millimeters)
	12 inches (1 foot)	12 inches (1 foot)	30 centimeters

Note: All conversions are approximate. They have been rounded off to the nearest convenient measure.

Oven Temperatures

FAHRENHEIT	CENTIGRADE	BRITISH REGULO SETTING	FRENCH SETTING
212°F	100°C		1
225°F	107°C	¼	2
250°F	121°C	½	3
275°F	135°C	1	3
300°F	149°C	2	4
325°F	163°C	3	4
350°F	177°C	4	4
375°F	191°C	5	5
400°F	204°C	6	5
425°F	218°C	7	6
450°F	232°C	8	6
475°F	246°C	8	6
500°F	260°C	9	7
525°F	274°C	9	8
550°F	288°C	9	9

Selected Measurements

	AMERICAN (SPOONS AND CUPS)	BRITISH (OUNCES AND POUNDS)	METRIC
Bread Crumbs	1 cup	2 ounces	60 grams
Butter	1 teaspoon	⅙ ounce	5 grams
	1 tablespoon	½ ounce	15 grams
	½ cup (1 stick)	4 ounces	115 grams
	1 cup (2 sticks)	8 ounces	230 grams
	2 cups (4 sticks)	1 pound	454 grams
Cheese (Grated)	1 cup	3½ ounces	100 grams
Flour (All-purpose, unsifted)	1 teaspoon	⅛ ounce	3 grams
	1 tablespoon	⅓ ounce	9 grams
	1 cup	4¼ ounces	120 grams
	3⅔ cups	1 pound	454 grams

	AMERICAN (SPOONS AND CUPS)	BRITISH (OUNCES AND POUNDS)	METRIC
Herbs *(Fresh, chopped)*	1 tablespoon	½ ounce	15 grams
Meats *(Cooked and finely chopped)*	1 cup	8 ounces	225 grams
Nuts *(Chopped)*	1 cup	5½ ounces	155 grams
Onions *(Raw—chopped, sliced, or minced)*	1 tablespoon 1 cup	⅓ ounce 5 ounces	9 grams 140 grams
Peas *(Fresh)*	1 pound unshelled = 1 cup shelled	1 pound, unshelled	454 grams, unshelled
Rice *(Raw)*	1 cup	7½ ounces	215 grams
Spinach *(Fresh, cooked)*	1¼ pounds, raw = 1 cup, cooked (squeezed dry, chopped)	1¼ pounds, raw	550 grams, raw
Sugar *(Regular granulated or superfine granulated)*	1 teaspoon 1 tablespoon 1 cup	⅙ ounce ½ ounce 6½ ounces	5 grams 15 grams 185 grams
Confectioners' (Powdered, unsifted)	1 teaspoon 1 tablespoon 1 cup	⅛ ounce icing sugar ⅓ ounce icing sugar ¾ ounce icing sugar	4 grams 9 grams 100 grams
Tomatoes *(Fresh)*	¾–1 pound, whole = 1 cup, peeled and seeded	¾–1 pound, whole	340 grams
Vegetables *(Raw—chopped fine, such as carrots or celery)*	1 cup	8 ounces	225 grams

A Note to the User: All conversions are approximate. The weights have been rounded off to the nearest useful measure for the purposes of the recipes in this volume. Weights and measures of specific ingredients may vary with altitude, humidity, variations in method of preparation, etc.

Acknowledgments

Many amateur cooks and professional chefs have been generous with their time and in sharing techniques and recipes that are included in this book. To all we are grateful.

Rita Alexander
  Date-nut cake
  Pine nut cookies

Tehmina Alphonse
  Mango kulfi

Manina Anagnostou
  Spanakopetes

Jean Banchet of Le Francais restaurant
  Quiche of sweetbreads and mushrooms
  Saumon à l'oseille
  Coupe Normande

Barefoot Caterers of Malibu (Heidi Hagman and Jonine Bernstein)
  Gravlax
  Spanakopitta (attributed to Eva Zane)
  Mushroom and cheese-stuffed zucchini

Jo Bastis
  Meat-filled phyllo rolls

Laura Benson
  She-crab soup
  Steamed rutabaga
  Gingerbread
  Trifle

Jo and Angelo Bettoja
  Caponata
  Palle de pasta
  Tozzetti

708

Stephen Bierman
>Chicken au poivre
>Stuffed chicken breasts with tomato sauce

Cleopatra Birrenbach
>Abgushteh limon
>Fosenjohn

Paul Bocuse
>Poulet sauté au vinaigre
>Navarin de homards

Ann Bolderson
>Gazpacho
>Chicken Parmesan
>Banana bread
>Mango chutney

Clyde Brooks
>French bread

Bart Campbell
>Barbecued country spareribs

Paschall Campbell
>Lemon lotus ice cream

Teresa Candler
>Bagna caôda
>Crostata di marmellata

Alain Chapel
>Gâteau de foies blonds
>Mousse de citron vert
>Tarte au sucre

Alexa, Lygia and Molly Chappellet
>Nut and seed bread
>Herb bread
>Forget-it meringue torte

Pramoda Chitrabhanu
>Zucchini and tomatoes Gujarati-style
>Vegetable koorma
>Suki bhaji
>Pooris

Bernard Clayton
California sourdough whole wheat bread
Old Milwaukee rye bread
Cottage cheese or clabber bread
Kugelhopf

Christine Cotsibos
Hamburger and nut stuffing à la grecque

Paul Damaz
Caldo verde

Christine Drechsler
Rouladen
Rote grütze

Sarah Elmaleh
Spicy tomato salad Moroccan-style
Spicy orange salad

Dorotea Elman
Xin xin
Vatapa joda
Quindin de ya-ya

Neset Eren
Turkish-style grilled lamb on skewers

Ann and Edward Faicco
Breaded pork cutlets
Pork cutlets parmigiana
Pork and potato stew
Pasta with sausages and pork

Joseph Famularo
Braccioli
Pasta with ginger and garlic
Artichokes stuffed with sausage
Manicotti with creamed chicken and almonds

Margaret Field
Chili con carne with cubed meat

Blanche Finley
Oven-baked chicken wings with honey

Gail Garraty
Broiled snappers with herbs
Marinated snappers
Beet and yogurt soup

Ed Giobbi
Pasta con asparagi
Pasta with broccoli
Penne or rigatoni modo mio
Cold pasta and broccoli with pesto
Spaghetti carbonara

Freddy Girardet
Brie and roquefort loaf
Escalopes de bar rayé aux huitres
Ragout de homard aux primeurs

Ed Gorman
Wash-boiler clambake

Jacques Grimaud
Poulets rotis à la piperade
Haricots verts à la paysanne landaise
Tourte landaise

Sue Gross
Sourdough French bread
Water bagels
Honey-chocolate cake
Honey brownies

Michel Guerard
Sea bass with tomato sauce

Dorothy Guth
Bourbon pecan cake
Creole pralines

Uta Hagen
Midsummer tart with fruits and berries

Ken Hansen of Scandia restaurant
Scandinavian fish stuffed with sauerkraut
Scandinavian stuffed cabbage

Kathleen Haven and Marie Zazzi
Pescado veracruzano
Frijoles de olla

Marcella Hazan
Pesce al salmoriglio
Homemade pasta
Sugo di canestrelli
Sugo alla suffi
Pesto genovese
Fried fennel
Funghi trifolati

Maida Heatter
Tropical flan

Eleanor Hempstead
Mint surprise cookies

Eleanor Hutflas
Clam fritters

Madhur Jaffrey
Grilled boneless leg of lam
Bengalese cabbage with mustard seeds and coconut
Fresh green chutney

Steve Johnides
Moussaka à la grecque

Danny Kaye
Stir-fry oysters and shrimp
Batter-fried scallops
Lion's head

Diana Kennedy
Mushroom tacos
Green chili gordas
Swiss walnut fingers

Chieko Kobashi
Kushiyaki
Kani kiyuri ikomi

Gunter Kraftner of the Swedish Embassy

Matjes herring with dill and sour cream
Herring tidbits with leeks and onion
Mousseline of chicken with mushroom sauce

Albert Kumin

Black forest cake
Puff pastry
Vol-au-vents
Napoleons
Dacquoise

Aline Landais

Blanquette de veau

Pierre Larré

Pan-fried trout

Pierre Laverne of La Côte Basque

Striped bass fermière

Virginia Lee

Pine nut meatballs with dark sauce
Spicy jellied chicken
Sesame seed fish
Bean sauce hot fish
Crystal fish
Yuan Pao
Cold shrimp, cucumber and tree ears
Steamed Chinese bread
Snow peas and abalone mushrooms
Chinese vegetable casserole
Chinese New Year bean sprouts

Calvin Lee

Chicken wings with oyster sauce

Gaston Lenotre

Rosace à l'orange
Ambassadeur
Lemon meringue pie

Leon and Aphrodite Lianides
  Bourekakia
  Mayeritsa avgolemono
  Roast baby lamb with artichokes
  Greek salad
  Greek Easter bread
  Walnut and almond torte
  Greek Easter cookies
  Galaktoboureko

David Liederman
  Duck with green peppercorn sauce
  Baked lobster with herbed butter (attributed to Paul Bocuse)

Joseph Macaluso
  Chicken and sausage with olive and anchovy sauce
  Broccoli di rape

Egi Maccioni
  Pizza with anchovies and cheese
  Pizza with mushrooms and cheese
  Piccioni alla contadina
  Spinach ravioli
  Orange tart

Rosemary Manell
  Salmon pâté
  Food processor mayonnaise
  Almond macaroons

Jennifer Manocherian
  Leg of lamb Persian-style
  Rice with dill Persian-style

Isabelle Marique
  Carbonnade flamande

Barbara McGinnis
  Leg of lamb with flageolets

Ismail Merchant
  Dahi shrimp
  Bhuna ghost
  Green beans with mustard
  Sheer khorma

Migliucci family of Mario's restaurant
  Beef scaloppine casalinga
  Striped bass marechiare
  Zucchini fritti
  Melanzane ripieni
  Gnocci di patate

Jean Mincielli of Le Duc restaurant
  Raw fish with green peppercorns
  Lobster cooked on seaweed
  Cold shrimp salad à la grecque

Dorothy Moore
  High-temperature roast leg of lamb

Pat Moore of Charles Dickens Pub
  Roast ribs of beef
  Fish and chips

Luigi Nanni of Nanni's restaurant
  Baked stuffed clams
  Fish soup with pasta
  Clam soup
  Pollo alla campagnola
  Anguilla scarpione
  Calamari alla Nanni
  Ragu abruzzese
  Marzapane

Marco Nesi of La Pace
  Crostini La Pace
  Confit de porc

Guy Pascal of La Côte Basque
  Tuiles d'amande
  Eugénie
  Visidantine

Paula Peck
  Chicken breasts Mexican-style

Jacques Pépin
  Cold zucchini soup

George Perrier
Chicken albufera

Josephine Premice
Chicken Haitian-style
Okra Guadeloupe-style

Joseph Renggli of the Four Seasons
Steak au poivre
Sauté of veal with mushrooms and crabmeat
Striped bass in phyllo pastry
Paupiettes of trout mousse with leeks
Calf's brains and winter greens
Mushrooms with herbs
Sautéed sweet peppers
Pears stuffed with gorgonzola

Irma Rhode
Sweet potato salad

Raymond Richez
Macquereau au vin blanc
Fillets de sole Therese
India House lamb curry
Chocolate mousse cake

Cecile Rivel
Chicken Indonesian-style
Whole wheat orange bread

Maria Robbins
Shchi
Piroshki
Fau

Petita Robles
Paella

Margarita de Rosenzweig-Dias
Pozole
Carne en salsa verde
Carne en salsa roja
Torta de mesa
Polvorones

Rita Rosner

No-bake fruitcake

Paul Sandblom

Herring salad
Herring rolls
Spicken herring
Mustard herring
Marinated sprats

Sarah Schecht

Challah

Jeannette Seaver

Gigot au pastis

Ann Seranne

Mexican quiche with chilies and cheese
High-temperature rib roast of beef
Deep-dish curried chicken pie

Pita bread

Sour cream lime pie

Daulat Ram Sharma of Gaylord's restaurant

Murghi massala
Murghi tikka
Jingha tarhi
Bangan bartha

Dinah Shore

Sunday omelet crêpe
Cream of fresh tomato soup
Cioppino
Stuffed red snapper

Ayesha Singh

Chicken korma
Shahi biryani

Jeri Sipe

Sesame chicken wing appetizers
Chinese-style barbecued pork
Lemon chicken
Sesame chicken with garlic sauce
Hot spicy cucumber salad

Alain Sinturel and Jean Pierre Pradie of Les Trois Petits Cochons

 Crème d'avocats
 Crêpes aux fruits de mer Nantua

Metita Soeharjo (and Copeland H. Marks)

 Satay bumbu
 Sambal goreng udang
 Acar

Karen Sriuttamayotin

 Tom yam kung
 Nua pad kanha
 Grilled beef and romaine salad Thai-style

Paul Stiendler

 Fish chowder à la caraja
 Veal scaloppine with avocado and tomato
 Lobster salad à l'aja

Wen dah Tai, formerly of Uncle Tai's Hunan Yuan restaurant

 Hot and sour fish soup
 Hunan beef
 Lamb with scallions
 Shredded chicken with bean sprouts
 Hunan shrimp
 Sliced duck with young ginger shoots

John Tovey of Miller Howe Hotel

 Pork chops in mustard cream sauce

May Wong Trent

 Chinese beef balls with two kinds of mushrooms
 Vietnamese grilled pork patties
 Sesame chicken with asparagus ring
 Vietnamese grilled lemon duck

Jean Troisgros

 Escalopes de veau Troisgros
 Panaché de poisson
 Salade de poulet

Jean Vergnes

> Trout meunière with pecans
> Spaghetti primavera (with Sirio Maccioni of Le Cirque restaurant)

Alfredo Viazzi of Alfredo's restaurants

> Mozzarella fresca con pomodoro e acciughe
> Fettucelle Alfredo
> Tagliarini verdi ghiottona
> Tagliarini verdi ai quattro formaggio

Jesus Villalba

> Cold avocado soup
> Stuffed roast suckling pig
> Frituras de bacalao

Tsung Ting Wang of the Shun Lee Palace and Shun Lee Dynasty

> Hunan lamb
> Pon pon chicken
> Chicken soong
> Shrimp and crabmeat Szechwan-style

Paula Wolfert

> Moroccan chicken with lemon and olives
> Couscous
> Moroccan brains salad
> Cooked tomato and green pepper salad Moroccan-style
> Stuffed tomatoes and zucchini Moroccan-style

Shirley and Peter Wood

> Fish soup with aioli
> Grilled fish in foil
> Zucchini and nut bread

Cynthia Zeger

> Gefilte fish
> Chocolate cake

We are indebted to a number of photographers whose work is reproduced in this book:

Bill Aller/NYT, first, sixth and ninth (upper right and lower left) pages of the picture section.

James Hamilton, second (middle left, lower left and upper right), fourth (upper), ninth (upper left and lower right), eighth, tenth, eleventh, twelfth, thirteenth, fourteenth, fifteenth and sixteenth pages of the picture section.

Mark Kaufman, frontispiece, second (upper left) and fifth (lower left) pages of the picture section.

Gene Maggio/NYT, seventh page of the picture section.

Jack Manning/NYT, page 31.

Irving Newman, fourth (lower) page of the picture section.

Arthur Schatz, page 2 and the third page of the picture section; copyright © 1975 by Arthur Schatz, *People Weekly*.

John Vachon, fifth (lower right) page of the picture section.

Index